GENERAL LABOUR HISTORY OF AFRICA

Workers, Employers and Governments, 20th–21st Centuries

Edited by
Stefano Bellucci and Andreas Eckert

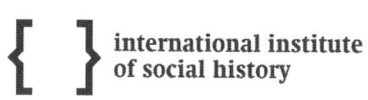 JAMES CURREY

In association with the ILO Regional Office for Africa, IISH, and re:work

 { } international institute of social history  re: work

© International Labour Organization 2019
First published 2019

Published by
James Currey
an imprint of
Boydell & Brewer Ltd
PO Box 9, Woodbridge
Suffolk IP12 3DF (GB)
www.jamescurrey.com

and of
Boydell & Brewer Inc.
668 Mt Hope Avenue
Rochester, NY 14620–2731 (US)
www.boydellandbrewer.com

in association with
ILO Regional Office for Africa
Avenue Jean Paul II
Abidjan (Côte d'Ivoire)
www. ilo.org

The designations employed in ILO publications, which are in conformity with United
Nations practice, and the presentation of material therein do not imply the expression of
any opinion whatsoever on the part of the International Labour Office concerning the legal
status of any country, area or territory or of its authorities, or concerning the delimitation
of its frontiers.

The responsibility for opinions expressed in signed articles, studies and other contributions
rests solely with their authors, and publication does not constitute an endorsement by the
International Labour Office of the opinions expressed in them.

Reference to names of firms and commercial products and processes does not imply their
endorsement by the International Labour Office, and any failure to mention a particular
firm, commercial product or process is not a sign of disapproval.

British Library Cataloguing in Publication Data
A catalogue record for this book is available on request from the British Library

ISBN 978-1-84701-218-0 (James Currey cloth)
ISBN 978-1-84701-210-4 (paperback edition)

ISBN 978-92-2-133111-7 (ILO paperback edition)

This publication is printed on acid-free paper

Printed and bound in Great Britain by TJ International Ltd, Padstow, Cornwall

CONTENTS

Part VI: The State, Unions and Welfare

Part VII: Conclusions

MAPS AND FIGURES

Maps

Figures

The editors, contributors and publisher are grateful to all the institutions and persons listed for permission to reproduce the materials in which they hold copyright. Every effort has been made to trace the copyright holders; apologies are offered for any omission, and the publisher will be pleased to add any necessary acknowledgement in subsequent editions.

TABLES

NOTES ON CONTRIBUTORS

Gareth Austin is Professor of Economic History at the University of Cambridge, specializing in African and comparative economic development. A former editor of the *Journal of African History*, his publications include *Labour, Land and Capital in Ghana: From Slavery to Free Labour in Asante, 1807–1956* (Rochester, NY: University of Rochester Press, 2005) and, as co-editor, *Economic Development and Environmental History in the Anthropocene: Perspectives on Asia and Africa* (London: Bloomsbury Academic, 2017).

Franco Barchiesi is an Associate Professor in the Department of African American and African Studies and the Department of Comparative Studies at Ohio State University, and a senior editor of *International Labor and Working Class History*. He is the author of *Precarious Liberation: Workers, the State, and Contested Social Citizenship in Postapartheid South Africa* (Albany, NY: SUNY Press, 2011).

Stefano Bellucci is Senior Researcher at the International Institute of Social History, Amsterdam; he is also Lecturer at the Institute for History of Leiden University. He co-edited 'African Labor Histories', in *International Labor and Working-Class History* (Cambridge: Cambridge University Press, 2014) and 'Labour in Transport: Histories from the Global South (Africa, Asia, and Latin America), *c.*1750 to 1950', *International Review of Social History* (Cambridge: Cambridge University Press, 2014).

Sara S. Berry is Professor Emerita in the History Department at Johns Hopkins University. Her major publications include *No Condition is Permanent: The Social Dynamics of Agrarian Change in Sub Saharan Africa* (Madison, WI: University of Wisconsin Press, 1993) and *Chiefs Know their Boundaries: Essays on Property, Power and the Past* (Portsmouth: NH: Heinemann, 2001).

Akua O. Britwum is an Associate Professor of Gender and Labour Studies in the Department of Labour and Human Resource Studies at the University of Cape Coast, Ghana. Her publications include, as co-editor, *Crossing the Divide: Precarious Work and the Future of Labour* (Durban: KZN Press, 2017).

Carolyn A. Brown is Professor of History at Rutgers University. Her book, *We Are All Slaves: African Miners, Culture, and Resistance at the Enugu Government Colliery, Nigeria, 1914–1950* (Portsmouth, NH: Heinemann, 2003) was voted 'Best Book of 2003' by the International Labor History Association. She is co-editor of *Africa and World War II* (Cambridge: Cambridge University Press, 2015).

Deborah Bryceson is Honorary Fellow and Professor in the Centre of African Studies at the University of Edinburgh, and Senior Research Associate in the International Gender Studies Centre at the University of Oxford. Her publications include *How Africa Works: Occupational Change, Identity and Morality in Africa* (Rugby: Practical Action Publishing, 2010) and *Farewell to Farms: De-Agrarianization and Employment in Africa* (Farnham: Ashgate, 1997).

Frederick Cooper is Professor of History at New York University. His recent publications include *Citizenship between Empire and Nation: Remaking France and French Africa, 1945–1960* (Princeton, NJ: Princeton University Press, 2014) and *Africa in the World: Capitalism, Empire, Nation-State* (Cambridge, MA: Harvard University Press, 2014).

Leyla Dakhli is a Researcher in the French Center for National Research (CNRS) at the Marc Bloch Centre, Berlin. Her publications include *Histoire du Proche-Orient contemporain* (Paris: La Découverte, 2015) and *Le Moyen-Orient (fin XIXe–XXe siècle)* (Paris: Éditions du Seuil, 2016).

Andreas Eckert is Professor of African History at Humboldt University in Berlin, Germany. Since 2009 he has also been director of the International Research Center for Work and Human Lifecycle in Global History. A former editor of the *Journal of African History*, his works include editing *Global Histories of Work* (Berlin: De Gruyter Oldenbourg, 2016), and he is a regular contributor to the German newspapers *Frankfurter Allgemeine Zeitung* and *Die Zeit*.

Babacar Fall is Professor of History and Education at Université Cheikh Anta Diop of Dakar Senegal. As a former Fellow, he is also affiliated to the Freeman Spogli Institute for International Studies at Stanford University. He is the founding director of the Institute of Advanced Study in Saint-Louis, Senegal. His publications include *Le travail forcé en Afrique Occidentale Française: 1900–1945* (Paris: Karthala, 1993) and *Social History in French West Africa: Forced Labor, Labor Market, Women and Politics* (Amsterdam: SEPHIS-CSSSC, 2002).

Laurent Fourchard is Research Professor at Sciences Po Paris in the Centre for International Relations (CERI). His publications include *Trier, exclure et policer. Vies urbaines en Afrique du Sud et au Nigeria* (Paris: Presses de Sciences Po, 2018), and he is co-editor of *Governing Cities in Africa* (Cape Town: HSRC Press, 2013).

Bill Freund is Professor Emeritus of Economic History at the University of KwaZulu-Natal, South Africa. His books include *The African Worker* (Cambridge: Cambridge University Press, 1988) and *The Making of Contemporary Africa* (3rd edn, Basingstoke/Boulder, CO: Palgrave Macmillan/Lynne Rienner Publishers, 2016).

Joël Glasman is a Professor of African History at the University of Bayreuth, Germany. His publications include *Les Corps Habillés au Togo* (Paris: Karthala, 2015).

Rana Jawad is Senior Lecturer in Social Policy at the University of Bath. She is founder and convenor of the Middle East and North Africa Social Policy Network and has extensive research and consultancy experience of social policy issues in this region.

Daniel Roger Maul is Associate Professor of Contemporary History at the University of Oslo, Norway. His publications include *Human Rights, Development and Decolonization – The International Labour Organization 1940–1970* (Basingstoke: Palgrave, 2012) and *The ILO: 100 years of Global Social Policy* (Berlin: DeGruyter, 2019).

Michelle R. Moyd is Associate Professor of History at Indiana University, Bloomington. Her publications include *Violent Intermediaries: African Soldiers, Conquest, and Everyday Colonialism in German East Africa* (Athens, OH: Ohio University Press, 2014).

Patrick Neveling is Senior Researcher in the Historical Institute at the University of Bern, and Associate in the Department of Anthropology at the University of Bergen. He is the co-editor of 'The Making of Neoliberal India', *Contributions to Indian Sociology* (Thousand Oaks, CA: Sage Journals, 2014) and 'Capitalism and global anthropology: Marxism resurgent', *Focaal: Journal of Global and Historical Anthropology* (New York: Berghahn, 2018).

Samuel A. Nyanchoga is a Professor of History and the current Dean of the Faculty of Arts and Social Sciences at the Catholic University of Eastern Africa; coordinator of security studies at the Tangaza University College; a

Senior Research Fellow at the Nantes Institute of Advanced Studies, France; Fulbright Scholar at Boston College; and Research and Academic Associate at the University of Birmingham and Bath Spa University. His publications include *Consequences of Slavery Heritage at the Kenya Coast* (Nairobi: CUEA Press, 2014) and *Contemporary Issues in Kenyan History and Challenges of Nationhood* (Nairobi: Kolbe Press, 2016).

Helena Pérez Niño is Lecturer in Political Economy of Development in the Centre of Development Studies at the University of Cambridge. She has conducted research on migrant labour, export logistics, natural resources and foreign aid especially in Southern Africa.

Rory Pilossof is a Senior Lecturer in the International Studies Group at the University of the Free State, Bloemfontein. He is also a visiting Research Fellow in the School of History at the University of Kent and the Principal Investigator on a British Academy/Newton Advanced Fellowship exploring labour relations in southern Africa. He is the author of *The Unbearable Whiteness of Being: Farmers' Voices from Zimbabwe* (Harare: Weaver Press, 2012).

Luca Puddu is a Lecturer in African History and Institutions at Sapienza University of Rome and a researcher at the Department of History, Cultures and Civilizations at the University of Bologna.

Richard L. Roberts is the Frances and Charles Field Professor of History at Stanford University. He is the author of eleven books and volumes on the social and economic history of Africa including *Litigants and Households: African Disputes and Colonial Courts in the French Soudan, 1895–1912* (Portsmouth, NH: Heinemann, 2005) and most recently editor, with Annie Bunting and Benjamin N. Lawrance, of *Marriage by Force? Contestation over Consent and Coercion in Africa* (Athens, OH: Ohio University Press, 2016).

Samuel Andreas Admasie is Regional Representative of the International Institute of Social History in Africa and a Senior Lecturer at the Institute of Peace and Conflict Studies at the University of Hargeisa.

Ben Scully is a Senior Lecturer in the Department of Sociology at the University of the Witwatersrand in Johannesburg, South Africa. His research focuses on labour, social welfare and economic development in Africa.

Julia Tischler is Assistant Professor of African History at Basel University, Switzerland. Her publications include *Light and Power for a Multiracial Nation:*

The Kariba Dam Scheme in the Central African Federation (Basingstoke: Palgrave, 2013) investigated late colonial developmentalism.

Hakeem Ibikunle Tijani is a Professor of History at the National Open University of Nigeria. A Distinguished Asante Research Award recipient at the University of Georgia, Athens, he is the author of *Britain, Leftist Nationalists and the Transfer of Power in Nigeria, 1945–1965* (London: Routledge, 2006) and *Union Education in Nigeria: Labor, Empire and Decolonization since 1945* (Basingstoke: Palgrave, 2012). He is a Fellow of the Royal Historical Society and a Member of the Nigeria Academy of Letters.

Dmitri van den Bersselaar is Professor of African History at the University of Leipzig. His research interests include the impact of multinational business on local African cultures of work and labour. His works include *The King of Drinks: Schnapps Gin from Modernity to Tradition* (Leiden: Brill, 2007).

FOREWORD

The *General Labour History of Africa* tells the story of African labour. It is an exposition of how African labour has evolved in different phases of contemporary history. At the time of the Treaty of Versailles, which spurred the creation of the International Labour Organization in 1919, the general motivation of a number of players was the stern belief that 'Universal and lasting peace can be accomplished only if it is based on social justice.' Since 1919 the ILO has continued to work to promote social justice, and has improved working conditions, workers' rights and employment creation.

The journey has been turbulent at times. The twentieth century witnessed not only the wrath of two world wars, but also the Great Depression and its associated soaring unemployment and impoverished work conditions. But the complete history of labour needs to be told. While attempts have been made to create a truly global history of labour, the African component has largely been missed. This volume is an immense contribution to filling this gap. It surveys the historical development of African labour, giving the relevant timelines and charting the salient themes. It could not have come at a better time, for the ILO celebrates its centenary in 2019. The volume is a unique contribution to this celebration from an African perspective, as it presents the continent's history and gives it a significantly African voice. This is the first such volume to bring together critical inputs from world-renowned historians and labour experts discussing the evolution of African labour in a focused approach that analyses the issues in a simple but assertive manner.

The volume comes at a crucial time indeed. More than ever before, the significance of labour dynamics has been highlighted and labour issues recognized as the glue of development policy. African economic growth, which has recently been largely jobless, has sparked ever more thoughtful discourse on the social fabric, which is necessary to cushion the effects of growth that does not trickle down to the masses. This is also the time when, led by the United Nations, the world is devoting its resources to support the 2030 Agenda for Sustainable Development. The lessons learned in labour history can spur the implementation of Sustainable Development Goals. But it is also a time when Africa has expressed aspirations for its people through the African Union Agenda 2063 and other frameworks. As Africa looks forward to what needs to be done, we need thorough reflection on where we are coming from. This volume supports this forward-looking process. It looks at various types of labour, and the challenges faced, as they evolved in the period covered.

The ongoing discourse on the future of work, at the ILO and elsewhere, provides even more of a platform to understand our labour history. Africa has and continues to engage with all the future-of-work themes, including work and society, decent jobs for all, the organization of work and production, and the governance of work. The dynamics of labour and how different forces affect labour outcomes are crucial to providing information on how to engage better as the world becomes more technological and more urbanized, and the labour force continues to grow.

As is to be expected, the critical issues that underlie African labour are discussed in this book. The starting point is wage labour, including the precarious and informal labour that characterized Africa in the past and still defines the continent today. With informality a norm rather than an exception in Africa, the informal economy contributes hugely to its GDP and forms a significant source of employment. Informality, unfortunately, is synonymous with decent work deficits.

The volume also traces the evolution of African labour in key economic sectors in African development: agriculture, mining, industry and transport. Agriculture is still Africa's largest employer, but without the development of the other sectors, agriculture will remain static. The volume exposes the need to understand each of the sectoral labour histories, not in isolation but in parallel, to appreciate the linked historical developments in all the economic sectors. It provides an important benchmark of what was possible in the sectors and provides the necessary background for future development and what we should do better going forward.

Additionally, the volume presents the international dimension and mobility of labour as well as the critical attributes of African labour history. A focus is on the development of the ILO and how Africa was embedded into the organization over the years in the midst of such vices as colonialism. The dynamics regarding the formation of the first-ever ILO office in Africa are spelled out, as is the contribution of African discourse to the ILO's agenda. Issues of migrant labour are at the core in the book.

Authors also analyse the varieties of work in African labour history. There is vital elucidation of not only domestic labour, but also military labour, illicit labour, white-collar labour and entertainment labour. The relevance of these types of work cannot be overemphasized. The importance of domestic work has been demonstrated by the adoption of the ILO Domestic Workers' Convention, 2011 (No. 189), which offers specific protection to domestic workers and lays down basic rights and principles requiring member states to take measures favourable to supporting decent work for domestic workers. The histories of the various types of work herein, taken together, form an account of a continuous series of measures undertaken to achieve decent work.

An important category that is also relevant today and has been given space in the book is entrepreneurial labour. In fact, policies to support entrepreneurship, particularly for youth, tend to dominate government objectives and direct industrial policy. The book offers a vital treatise regarding capitalists, entrepreneurship and professional labour.

Furthermore, the role of the state and welfare, presented in the framework of labour and the state, forms a critical part of the book. Discussion revolves around trade unions, social welfare, and mutualistic and cooperative labour. Even today, these institutions play vital roles in the promotion of decent work, which is a collective effort to support social and economic development.

This work, the first of its kind, successfully underscores the importance of African labour. It has collected historical information that was otherwise scattered into one volume, giving significant content for possible future use. The volume shows Africa's resolve to be part of the global initiative to improve its labour, to act decisively and take destiny into its hands.

Cynthia Samuel-Olonjuwon
ILO Assistant Director-General and Regional Director for Africa

ACKNOWLEDGEMENTS

This book was possible thanks to a generous grant provided by the ILO Regional Office for Africa. Further support was provided by the International Research Center Work and the Human Life Cycle in Global History (re:work) of Humboldt-Universität of Berlin and by the International Institute of Social History of Amsterdam. The ILO Regional Office for Africa made many significant contributions to this publication. Regional Director Cynthia Samuel-Olonjuwan enthusiastically embraced the project from the beginning and provided vital support throughout the process. Senior Economist Ken Chamuva Shawa reviewed the manuscript and coordinated the peer review process. Deputy Director Peter Van Rooij played a key role in finalizing the volume. Guebray Berhane Guebray, Joseph Jean Marie Momo and Mary Mugambi provided key communications and administrative support. Chris Edgar and Alison Irvine of ILO Publishing in Geneva also made important contributions at different stages. Beate Andrees, Samuel Asfaha, Mohammed Mwamadzingo and Simon Steyne of ILO Geneva and Sophie de Coninck of ILO Abidjan provided comments on the draft manuscript. Regina Monticone, formerly of ILO Geneva, was pivotal at the very beginning of this project as she helped develop the idea as part of the ILO Century Project. Kidest Getahun of the ILO Office in Addis Ababa offered invaluable administrative support. Many more ILO local staff participated in the organisation of two authors' conferences, on 11–12 December 2013 in Addis Ababa, Ethiopia, and on 10–11 December 2015 in Dar es Salaam, Tanzania. We are very grateful to them.

The publisher, James Currey (Boydell & Brewer), was crucial in bringing the project into fruition. In particular, we would like to thank Jaqueline Mitchell, James Currey's Commissioning Editor, but also Head of Pre-Press Rohais Landon. Manfred Boemeke has been a brilliant, professional and efficient language editor, who did much more than just standardizing and ameliorating the text. At its start, in 2013, the project benefitted enormously from the support of Anshu Padayachee, then Chief Executive Officer of South Africa-Netherlands Research Programme on Alternatives in Development (SANPAD), Firmin Matoko, then Director of the UNESCO Liaison Office with the African Union and the United Nations Economic

Commission for Africa (UNECA), Muna Abdalla then Director of International IDEA Liaison Office to the African Union, and Andreas Eshetè, former President of Addis Ababa University. Above all, our thanks go to Hanan Sabea of the American University in Cairo and G. Ugo Nwokeji of the University of California, Berkeley. Hanan's and Ugo's editorial work was invaluable during the first steps of the project; their companionship is and will always be very important to us. Several other people in different institutions have contributed directly and indirectly to the development of the book. At the African Studies Centre Leiden, Jan-Bart Gewald, now the Director, has been not only a supporter and promoter of the project since its start but enabled the organisation of the 'International workshop on wage labour, capital and precarity in African and global history' on 13–14 March 2015 in Leiden. At re:work, Felicitas Hentschke made sure that things went smoothly. Many colleagues discussed and suggested improvements to the content as well as the structure of the project. Marcel van der Linden, the towering figure in global labour history, gave valuable insights. In this respect, we are grateful also to Leo Lucassen, Marien van der Heijden, and especially Ineke Kelly of the International Institute of Social History of Amsterdam. At Leiden University, Mirjam de Bruijn and Meike de Goede provided support with comments and suggestions. Of the many other colleagues who gave feedback, we would particularly like to mention Pierluigi Valsecchi of the University of Pavia, Mahua Sarkar of the University of Binghamton, Mohamed Salih of the International Institute of Social Studies in The Hague, Mark McQuinn of SOAS University of London, and Peter Waterman with whom the project was discussed just before he very sadly passed away.

The friendship and solidarity expressed by African unionists was very precious indeed and encouraged us to continue throughout the years of bringing this book to completion; especially the two main regional workers' organisations, the African Regional Organisation of the International Trade Union Confederation (ITUC-Africa) and the Organisation of African Trade Union Unity (OATUU) and their respective Secretary Generals, Kwasi Adu-Amankwah and Mezhoud Arezki. Other unionists who contributed with reviews and comments at different stages of the project were Hilma Mote and Rhoda Boateng, who are both researchers and unionists. Craig Phelan of the Solidarity Centre (AFL-CIO) in Abuja has always been a friend to count on for discussions and support.

Finally, we are grateful to the many authors who participated in this project and who patiently bore with us through the project's seven long years. They not only provided excellent chapters but also served as peer reviewers for each other's contributions during the internal cross-peer-reviewing process. We are grateful for the thorough and serious approach they took to this task, which resulted in sometimes painful decisions. Amongst the authors, we owe particular thanks to Frederick Cooper who wrote the postscript to the book and commented on all the chapters.

Above all, we wish to thank Jacqueline Rutte at the International Institute of Social History: without Jacqueline's excellent managerial skills and personal qualities on many fronts, from the organisation of conferences to communications, this book would not have been possible.

STEFANO BELLUCCI AND ANDREAS ECKERT
Amsterdam and Berlin, January 2019

The 'Labour Question' in Africanist Historiography

STEFANO BELLUCCI AND ANDREAS ECKERT

The year 2019 marks the centenary of the International Labour Organization (ILO).[1] The *General Labour History of Africa* (*GLHA*) is the result of cooperation between the ILO and a group of Africanist labour historians who came together to write a history of African workers and work in Africa since the beginning of the twentieth century.[2] The *GLHA* is intended, first, to contribute to a substantial understanding of labour in Africa throughout history and, secondly, to advance African labour studies by incorporating insights from the emerging field of global history and its variant, global labour history.[3] Following the insights of global history, the *GLHA* is not the history of the making of the working class in Africa, but rather the history of the complex world of labouring people, which includes the industrial working class as well as many other categories. Indeed, the *GLHA* is the history of all working people, including affluent entrepreneurs, household labourers, careworkers, 'informal' workers and unfree workers.

---

[1] More information is available at: https://www.ilo.org/100

[2] Two GLHA authors' workshops were organized by the editors of this volume, with the collaboration and generous support of the ILO Regional Office for Africa (then based in Addis Ababa); they took place in Addis Ababa on 11–12 December 2013 and in Dar es Salaam on 10–12 December 2015. These gatherings served as fora for discussion and exchange among authors, editors and the ILO itself.

[3] Marcel van der Linden, *Workers of the World: Essays toward a Global Labor History* (Leiden: Brill, 2008); Andreas Eckert, ed., *Global Histories of Work* (Berlin: De Gruyter, 2016); Karin Hofmeester and Marcel van der Linden, eds, *Handbook Global History of Work* (Berlin: De Gruyter, 2018).

In this introduction, we will provide a brief reflection and survey on African labour historiography in the last century.[4] Our intention is to sketch the wider academic background to this volume, its main concerns, and its place within current intellectual debates. A comprehensive discussion of African labour history in relation to the *GLHA* project, based on the individual chapters, is provided in the conclusions to this volume by Frederick Cooper.

LABOUR HISTORIOGRAPHIES

In the first decades of the twentieth century, scholarly production on labour in Africa was closely linked to the agenda of colonial administrations. Studies on labour were preoccupied with the understanding of African social patterns and movements of people, and they were conducted under the auspices of colonial interests eager to control the African labour force. African labour was scarce and very much in demand for the *mise en valeur* and development of the colonies. It must be emphasized, however, that, until the 1930s, colonial officials and scholars alike conceptualized Africans usually as 'natural peasants' and were uncertain about whether Africans, even after decades of the 'civilizing mission', would work without direct coercion. Thus, hardly any effort was made to consider labour as a social issue. Typically, in the British colonial administrative apparatus, a 'labour department' did not exist, labour problems being usually handled by Native Affairs Departments. This situation remained substantially unchanged until the Second World War, which marked the beginning of decolonization.

Decolonization marked a historical passage in the study of African labour as well. Scholarly production on African labour activism and trade unionism, often starting from the very few workplaces where workers' organizations were allowed, slowly increased after 1945. In some instances, trade unions played an important role in supporting the struggle for independence of African colonies, and it is not by coincidence that they were the main research

---

[4]   For some recent reflections, see Frederick Cooper, 'From Enslavement to Precarity? The Labour Question in African History', in *The Political Economy of Everyday Life in Africa: Beyond the Margins*, ed. Wale Adebanwi (Woodbridge: James Currey, 2017), 135–56; Bill Freund, 'Sub-saharan Africa', in *Handbook Global History of Work*, ed. Karin Hofmeester and Marcel van der Linden (Berlin: De Gruyter, 2018), 63–81; Stephen Rockel, 'New Labor History in Sub-Saharan Africa: Colonial Enslavement and Forced Labor', *International Labor and Working Class History*, 86.2 (2014), 159–72.

topic of African labour studies during that period.[5] Furthermore, trade unions' claims against foreign capitalists fit well into the anti-colonial agenda. The post-independence reality, though, was one in which nationalist and labour interests were not always congruent, despite the fact that the political elites of young independent African nations often grew out of the labour movement.[6]

Largely influenced by Marxist theories, studies now also emerged on proletarianization.[7] There was a widespread idea that African workers employed in modern sectors such as mining, transport, industry or building could eventually form an African working class. Trade unions were sometimes identified as the uncontested representatives of the African proletariat.[8] This view of history proved to be for a good part teleological. In fact, while the twentieth century did indeed see the making of a working class in Africa, trade unions only represented a tiny proportion of it. At times, different unions and professional associations worked together, for example

---

[5]   Cf. W. S. Mare, *African Trade Unions* (London: Longmans Green, 1949); Walter Bowen, *Colonial Trade Unions* (London: Fabian Society, 1954); W. A. Warmington, *A West African Trade Union: A Case Study of the Cameroons Development Corporation Workers' Union and its Relations with the Employers* (London: Oxford University Press, 1960); R. W. Williams, 'Trade Unions in Africa', *African Affairs*, 54.217 (1955), 267–79; G. Fischer, 'Syndicats et décolonisation', *Présence Africaine*, 34/35 (1960/61), 17–60.

[6]   Sekou Touré from Guinee-Conakry is one example for this connection. See Frederick Cooper, *Decolonization and African Society: The Labor Question in French and British Africa* (Cambridge: Cambridge University Press, 1996).

[7]   Cf. David Webster, 'From Peasant to Proletarian: The Development/ Underdevelopment Debate in South Africa', *Africa Perspective*, 13 (1980) 1–15; Walter Elkan, *Migrants and Proletarians: Urban Labour in the Economic Development of Uganda* (Oxford: Oxford University Press, 1960); Richard Sandbrook, *Proletarians and African Capitalism: The Kenyan Case, 1960–1972* (Cambridge: Cambridge University Press, 1975); Charles van Onselen, 'Worker Consciousness in Black Miners: Southern Rhodesia, 1900–1920', *Journal of African History*, 14.2 (1973), 237–55; A. G. Hopkins, 'The Lagos Strike of 1897: An Exploration in Nigerian Labor History', in *Peasants and Proletarians: The Struggles of Third World Workers*, ed. R. Cohen, P. C. W. Gutkind and P. Brazier (New York: Monthly Review Press, 1979), 87–106.

[8]   This happened especially in the case of South Africa; see Gay W. Seidman, 'From Trade Union to Working-Class Mobilization: The Politicization of South Africa's Non-Racial Labor Unions', in *Breaking the Links: Development Theory and Practice in Southern Africa*, ed. Robert E. Mazur (Trenton, NJ: Africa World Press, 1990), 223–55; Rob Lambert, 'Political Unionism and Working Class Hegemony: Perspectives on the South African Congress of Trade Unions, 1955–1965', *Labour, Capital and Society*, 18.2 (1985), 244–77; Anthony W. Marx, 'South African Black Trade Unions as an Emerging Working-class Movement', *The Journal of Modern African Studies*, 27.3 (1989), 383–400.

in fighting against European colonialism; at other times, these organizations clashed with one another.

Differences between political and workers' organizations widened after independence. Political leaders of independent countries, former trade unionists among them, were acutely aware that they lacked the resources to ensure that the demands of a citizenry would be met. Many of them built up relations of patronage with power brokers inside the nation, but also clientelistic networks with former colonizers. By this, they undermined democratic processes and the kind of social movements, such as labour movements, that had helped them get into power.[9] Desperate as they were to modernize and industrialize, most African governments sacrificed the needs and interests of rural people.[10]

African labour studies, during the postcolonial years in the 1960s and 1970s, were deeply entwined with the debates on labour and economic policies taking place at the time in newly independent African nations. Labour research was also very much influenced by the then contemporary political debate.[11] A major effect of labour scholars' activism was that academic production remained somehow static or ahistorical. Although of high quality, labour studies were very much confined to national experiences; they were somehow 'Thompsonian', that is, centred on the analysis of the making of *national* working classes.[12] Nonetheless, these studies represent a respectable literature which informed the following wave of labour studies

[9]   Frederick Cooper, *Africa since 1940: The Past of the Present* (Cambridge: Cambridge University Press, 2002); Paul Nugent, *Africa since Independence: A Comparative History* (Basingstoke: Palgrave Macmillan, 2004).

[10]   Some regimes, however, very much emphasized the crucial role of rural labour and rural workers, both in theory *and* practice. The most notable (and highly ambivalent) case has arguably been Tanzania. See, for example, Leander Schneider, *Government of Development: Peasants and Politicians in Postcolonial Tanzania* (Bloomington, IN: Indiana University Press, 2014).

[11]   Cf. Sheila T. van der Horst, *African Workers in Town: A Study of Labour in Cape Town* (Cape Town: Oxford University Press, 1964); Willard A. Beling, *Modernization and African Labor: A Tunisian Case Study* (New York: Praeger, 1965); Willard A. Beling and Michael F. Lofchie, *The Role of Labor in African Nation Building* (New York: Praeger, 1968); Peter Harries-Jones, *Freedom and Labour: Mobilization and Political Control on the Zambian Copperbelt* (Oxford: Blackwell, 1975).

[12]   Francis Wilson, *Labour in the South African Gold Mines 1911–1969* (Cambridge: Cambridge University Press, 1972); Anthony Clayton and Donald Cockfield Savage, *Government and Labour in Kenya, 1895–1963* (London: Cass, 1975); Robin Cohen, *Labour and Politics in Nigeria, 1945–71* (London: Heinemann, 1974); Elena L. Berger, *Labour, Race, and Colonial Rule: The Copperbelt from 1924 to Independence* (Oxford: Oxford University Press, 1974).

in the 1980s, but they somehow overemphasized the proletarianization thesis: that the rise in numbers of wage workers is directly linked to a process of alienation and proletarianization, which includes the beginning of the development of class consciousness in Africa.[13]

With the end of the Cold War, and on the eve of what is now called the neoliberal era, it became increasingly evident that the African working classes did not evolve into a revolutionary proletariat. In the 1980s and 1990s labour studies suffered a decline[14] – with perhaps the notable exception of South Africa, where numerous books and articles continued to be published on that topic.[15] Scholars turned their attention to political issues such as democratization, good governance, civil society, or socio-economic issues such as development, growth, gender, environment, childhood and so on. Labour, although crucial to understanding the political and socio-economic advancement of a society, almost disappeared from the academic research agenda. Social phenomena were increasingly explained through regression analyses and other statistical or economic models. Social sciences came to suffer an inferiority complex vis-à-vis economics and econometrics. For economists, what matters is for African economies to attract foreign direct investment. In this context, labour came to be a cost to be reduced and an ordinary variable for market analysis at best.[16]

The exception that, as it were, proved the rule in this trend towards a *baisse* of labour studies in Africa was Frederick Cooper's monograph *Decolonization and African Society*, published in 1996. With such a dearth of scholarship on the question of labour of Africa, this book provided much-needed intellectual nourishment and soon became one of the most cited studies in African history (and beyond). Interestingly enough, Cooper's work

---

[13] On this literature, see Bill Freund, 'Labor and Labor History in Africa: A Review of the Literature', *African Studies Review*, 27.2 (1984), 1–58.

[14] On this 'eclipse', see, for example, Jean Copans, 'Pourquoi travail et travailleurs africains ne sont plus à la mode en 2014 dans les sciences sociales. Retour sur l'actualité d'une problématique du XXe siècle', *Politique Africaine*, 133 (2014), 25–44.

[15] For a critique of the often very parochial feature of this literature, see Philip Bonner, Jonathan Hyslop and Lucien Van Der Walt, 'Rethinking Worlds of Labour: Southern African Labour History in International Context', *African Studies*, 66.2–3 (2007), 137–57.

[16] See, for example, David Canning, Sangeeta Raja and Abdo S. Yazbeck, *Africa's Demographic Transition: Dividend or Disaster?* (Washington, DC: World Bank, 2015); for the North African case, see Merih Celasun, *State-owned Enterprises in the Middle East and North Africa: Privatization, Performance and Reform* (London: Routledge, 2001); for the South African case, see J. D. Lewis, 'Promoting Growth and Employment in South Africa', *South African Journal of Economics*, 70.4 (2002), 725–76.

was not read so much as a contribution to labour history but as an argument about decolonization and the complex interplay between the European metropoles, international organizations, the local colonial administrations and African activists that shaped this period.

In the past two or three decades, so-called neoliberal reforms have meant the establishing of representative democracy and privatization in one African country after another. This process has brought an increase in both multi-party elections in Africa and, generally, economic growth. The problem is that growth and democracy went hand in hand with a dramatic increase in social and economic inequalities. Many scholars, especially Keynesians, attribute the increase of inequality to a weakening of the state as the arbiter in economic and social affairs. Others see the surge of inequalities as the result of a generalized neglect of the labour question in politics, academia and the media. Democratic transformations – of course, a positive development – seem not to have positively contributed to the improvement of the living and labour conditions of African workers, who largely remain 'working poor'.[17] For this reason, at the turn of the millennium, the labour question appears slowly to have re-emerged from the limbo in which academic research had contributed to putting it.[18] This is not only true for Africa but applies to most regions of the world and is closely linked to new approaches that emphasize the importance of international and global perspectives.

INTERNATIONAL AND GLOBAL PERSPECTIVES

Within the small circles of labour historians, some scholars came to develop, in the 1980s, the so-called new international labour studies (NILS) approach. Methodologically, the NILS was seen to stand in opposition to previously established approaches to labour studies in Africa, which Robin Cohen, for example, called 'technicist'.[19] The NILS approach has international unionism and industrial relations at its core, and although it could be seen as a precursor of global labour history, at the centre of the NILS labour predicament there are national working classes. Gay Seidman, for example,

---

[17] The notion of 'working poor' was initially elaborated by Sabyasachi Bhattachariya in *The Labouring Poor and their Notion of Poverty: Late 19th and Early 20th Century Bengal* (Noida: V.V. Giri National Labour Institute, 1998). For a thorough discussion, developed from the example of India, see Jan Breman, *Footloose Labour: Working in India's Informal Economy* (Cambridge: Cambridge University Press, 1996).

[18] For an overview, see the final part of this introduction.

[19] Robin Cohen, *Contested Domains: Debates in International Labour Studies* (London: Zed Books, 1991).

compared labour politics in Brazil and South Africa within the paradigm of the NILS, and he took an important step by moving away from the study of North–South interactions and focusing instead on a South–South comparison.[20] However, by the mid-1990s interest in the NILS as a field of research had declined, in tandem with the end of the socialist experiment.

While the NILS represented a valid initiative towards a transnational and transcontinental study of labour relations and workers' movements, it failed to live up to expectations. In particular, the NILS followed the fate of labour internationalism. The prediction that the 'objective' development of transnational capitalism (through multinational corporations) would create the conditions for 'subjective' transnational labour solidarity (transnational class consciousness) did not materialize.

As appropriately noted by Schler, Bethlehem and Sabar, since the 1990s postcolonial critiques have gained prominence, and labour studies have also come to 'incorporate a conscious rejection of essentialist categories'.[21] Studies of labourers have shifted from their former rigorously materialist orientation to reflect a growing preoccupation with representation, imagery and ideology as the means through which the African working classes negotiate their place in global markets.[22] Concerned with the ethereal spread of postmodernist ideas to labour studies, Frederick Cooper rightly warned against an overemphasis on representations and called for a stronger focus on 'the nitty-gritty of labour'.[23] Many chapters of the *GLHA* take up this approach and attempt to take into considerations the practices of work.

At the forefront of recent developments in history as a discipline is the idea of global history – an approach that has been transforming the study of history over the past few decades.[24] Within this broader context, global labour history has served to open history up to wider reflections that are not limited to the 'traditional' analysis of the industrial working classes, defined

[20] Gay W. Seidman, *Manufacturing Militance: Workers' Movements in Brazil and South Africa, 1970–1985* (Berkeley, CA: University of California Press, 1994).

[21] Lynn Schler, Louise Bethlehem and Galia Sabar, 'Rethinking Labour in Africa, Past and Present', *African Identities*, 7.3 (2009), 288.

[22] *Ibid.*, 288–9.

[23] Frederick Cooper, 'Back to Work: Categories, Boundaries and Connections in the Study of Labour,' in Racializing Class, Classifying Race: Labour and Difference in Britain, the USA, and Africa, ed. P. Alexander and R. Halpern (London: Macmillan, 2000), 213.

[24] Sebastian Conrad, *What Is Global History?* (Princeton, NJ: Princeton University Press, 2016).

by reference to national borders.[25] By going beyond an analysis of the industrial working class and trade unions, the global labour history approach helps us to see the bigger picture of labour and to identify patterns and trends of labour transformations in Africa over an extended period. In fact, the history of labour in Africa cannot limit itself to the study of industrial sectors or trade unions but must take into consideration labour outside this realm – for example labour in the family, rural worlds, kinship, the informal sector and so on.

One of the main insights of global labour history has been that the male proletarian does not represent the quintessential worker but is rather one among a number of categories of workers whose histories are connected.[26] Analysing work beyond free wage labour and proletarianism became increasingly important, as it allowed for marginalized groups and their activities to form part of labour history. This approach also re-evaluated African labour history, which – as a result of the rather small number of wage workers in all phases of African history – seemed for a long time to be a sideshow, a clear instance of a region that simply does not fit the patterns familiar to a dominant North Atlantic framework.

Global labour history emphasized interaction and entanglements between different world regions, while taking for granted that the growing circulation of goods, people and ideas not only produced common ground, but also disassociations, differences and the search for particularities.[27] There is a certain general tendency within global history of 'doing history backwards' and to limit research to identifying the flows and nodal points of globalization.[28] In labour history, this trend finds its expression in the focus on seamen and other mobile sectors of the African labour force, which contributed to the emergence of global commodity and labour markets. While there is nothing wrong with this, it is crucial not to overlook other parts of the workforce – non-plantation rural labour, for instance – as the globalization of labour not only means unbounded mobility, but spatial

---

[25] For a recent overview, see Andreas Eckert and Marcel van der Linden, 'New Perspectives on Workers and the History of Work: Global Labor History', in *Global History, Globally: Research and Practice around the World*, ed. Sven Beckert and Dominic Sachsenmaier (London: Bloomsbury, 2018), 145–61.

[26] This is one of the major points made by Van der Linden, *Workers of the World*.

[27] See as an example the special issue 'Labour in Transport: Histories from the Global South (Africa, Asia, and Latin America), c.1750 to 1950', *International Review of Social History*, 59.22 (2014), ed. Stefano Bellucci, Larissa Rosa Corrêa, Jan-Georg Deutsch and Chitra Joshi.

[28] Frederick Cooper, *Colonialism in Question: Theory, Knowledge, History* (Berkeley, CA: University of California Press, 2005), ch. 4.

immobility as well, and we need to see the contradictions and unevenness of global processes of incorporation.

Moreover, one could cast doubt on the perception of 'the global' manifesting itself in Africa in the form of connections, and instead emphasize disconnection, segmentation and segregation. In general, Africanist labour scholars specifically criticize the idea of workers' 'teleconnections' in global commodity chains put forward by van der Linden.[29] As Franco Barchiesi has pointed out, colonial and postcolonial Africa shows, after all, 'that the globalization of capital did not only provide a minority of unionized workers with new opportunities to converse with the global working class. It has also, and more importantly, excluded and marginalized multitudes of producers, households, and communities.'[30]

The *GLHA* is not only part of an ongoing effort to bring labour history back into Africanist historiography and, at the same time, to imbue labour history with an Africanist perspective, it also seeks to be a pivot for studying labour in Africa from the global perspective. This is why the different topics in these chapters are largely based on five methodological assumptions: 1) labour history is the history of labour movements and trade unions, but also that of non-unionized working people as well as that of employers, entrepreneurs and capitalists; 2) labour history must not overlook the categories of unpaid and unfree workers; 3) comparative studies should be freed from what Marcel van der Linden calls the 'error of contamination',[31] that is, measuring everything happening in one place in complete isolation from processes occurring in other distinct areas; 4) history cannot be seen solely as originating mainly in the North Atlantic world, and then spreading to other societies and continents, given that historical processes can equally find their source in the global South, including Africa of course; and 5) labour history transcends national borders as the perimeter of analysis and gives way to local as well as global connections, between workers, companies (employers or workers) and commodities (the products of labour).

---

[29] Van der Linden, *Workers of the World*, 372–8.

[30] Franco Barchiesi, 'How Far from Africa's Shore? A Response to Marcel van der Linden's Map for Global Labor History', *International Labor and Working-Class History*, 82 (2012), 77.

[31] See Marcel van der Linden, *Globalizing Labour Historiography: The IISH Approach*, 2002, http://www.hartford-hwp.com/archives/10/142.html (accessed 10 January 2018).

A CENTURY OF THE FREE AND UNFREE

'Freedom' and 'free labour' stand as central concepts through which the world of labour has been reflected and interpreted at least for the past two centuries. Considering the world of work relations and labour policies, the binomial 'free' and 'unfree' is of particular importance – especially in view of the centrality of the ideology of 'free labour' from the nineteenth century onwards – in slave, post-emancipation and colonial contexts. Indeed, the idea of modern 'freedom' helped to shape contemporary political language and provided a set of standards through which social experience is read. First, it created a master narrative that constructed the history of Western societies as a progressive path towards 'freedom' and 'emancipation', embedded in particular forms of social relations, institutions and values. Secondly, it set this narrative as the model towards which institutions and values developing in different cultural and social contexts should progress, and against which they ought therefore to be evaluated.[32]

In societies where slavery was an objective reality – as in Africa – the distinction between 'free' and 'unfree' became essential, especially once slavery as an 'institution' became a public abomination. In these contexts, the clear divide between 'slavery' and 'freedom' became the source of all kinds of social and political anxieties and fostered various logics of continuity and discontinuity. And even if there seems to be a long-term trend towards 'free wage labour', so-called free labour 'cannot be seen as the only form of exploitation suitable for modern capitalism, but rather as one alternative among several'.[33]

In Africa, slavery died slowly and, as many chapters in this volume show, gave way to a mix of different forms of labour relations. Desperate to make their overseas territories economically viable, colonial administrations,

---

[32] See Robert J. Steinfeld, *The Invention of Free Labour: The Employment Relation in English and American Law and Culture, 1350–1870* (Chapel Hill, NC: University of North Carolina Press, 1991); Robert J. Steinfeld, *Coercion, Contract and Free Labor in the Nineteenth Century* (Cambridge: Cambridge University Press, 2001); Tom Brass and Marcel van der Linden, eds, *Free and Unfree Labour: The Debate Continues* (Berne: Peter Lang, 1997). See also the articles in the thematic issue 'Shifting Boundaries between Free and Unfree Labor', *International Labor and Working-Class History*, 78.1 (2010), ed. Carolyn A. Brown and Marcel van der Linden.

[33] See Marcel van der Linden, 'Labour History beyond Borders', in *Histories of Labour: National and International Perspectives*, ed. Joan Allen, Alain Campbell and John McIlroy (Pontypool: Merlin Press, 2010), 368. However, the view that different modes of production coexist within global capitalism and constitute the very nature of its historical development had already been put forward by scholars such as Paul Sweezy, Immanuel Wallerstein and Samir Amin.

although praising the gospel of free labour, resorted to various devices for mobilizing unfree labour. These included forced labour, conscription into the army or police forces, and the recruitment of contract labour by all kinds of dubious means.

The colonial discourse of development that began in the 1930s re-labelled work that otherwise could have been classified as forced labour as 'voluntary work', 'self-help' or 'human investment'. In this process, certain sections of African labour were rendered invisible as workers, and instead constructed as 'beneficiaries', 'participants' and 'volunteers'.[34] The issue of forced labour continued to be debated after independence. In 1962 the ILO Committee of Experts on the Application of Conventions and Recommendations criticized a number of recently independent African countries, such as Guinea and the Ivory Coast, for having set up new forms of forced labour in the form of compulsory labour services for young people. As Daniel Maul points out: 'To be accused of a "classically colonial crime" such as forced labour was particularly hard for the postcolonial nations to stomach', and they reacted very bitterly.[35] As many chapters in this volume suggest, the problem of 'unfreedom' never went away: it is diffused and can be found in many sectors or embedded in various labour relations. In this regard, one widely discussed and highly controversial aspect is child labour. According to the ILO, in 2016 Africa had the largest number of child labourers worldwide: 72.1 million African children were estimated to be labouring, 31.5 million in hazardous work.[36] This is without any doubt a real issue, but there is a danger of thinking of it as just another peculiar feature of African culture.[37]

[34] Benedetta Rossi, 'What "Development" Does to Work', *International Labor and Working-Class History*, 92 (2017), 7.

[35] Daniel Maul, *Human Rights, Development and Decolonization: The International Labour Organization, 1940–70* (Basingstoke and Geneva: Palgrave Macmillan and ILO, 2012), 265. For a detailed long-term view on continuities of forced labour, see Alexander Keese, 'Hunting "Wrongdoers" and "Vagrants": The Long-term Perspective of Flights, Evasion, and Persecution in Colonial and Postcolonial Congo-Brazzaville, 1920–1980', *African Economic History*, 44 (2016), 152–80.

[36] International Labour Office, *Global Estimates of Child Labour: Results and Trends, 2012–2016* (Geneva: ILO, 2017).

[37] For a complex and differentiated view, see Gerd Spittler and Michael Bourdillon, eds, *African Children at Work: Working and Learning in Growing Up for Life* (Münster: LIT, 2012). For a historical perspective, see Beverly Grier, *Invisible Hands: Child Labor and the State in Colonial Zimbabwe, 1890–1965* (Portsmouth, NH: Heinemann, 2005). Regrettably, a chapter on child labour for this volume could not be finalised, due to the complexity of the issue and differing views.

In 2016 the ILO also estimated that 'there were a total of over 9.2 million victims of modern slavery in Africa'.[38] Immigrant workers from Africa are part of this number. The question is how to label all those Africans who by their own initiative cross the Mediterranean Sea to Italy or Spain, or the Atlantic to the Canary Islands, to seek wage labour. Those Africans who, between the sixteenth and nineteenth centuries, were sent across the Atlantic to work on slave plantations in the Americas were coerced, and they were called 'slaves'. Today's migrants, however, are in some ways the freest of the free: 'they not only agree to leave Africa for Europe, but they go to great effort and great risk to do so'.[39] This is certainly an issue that will require further analysis.

To conclude, labour always was, and remains, a profoundly political, fundamentally social, and economically crucial question. The chapters in this volume attempt to contribute to the understanding of Africa by offering analyses and insights on many different aspects of the history of African working people over the past hundred years. The *General Labour History of Africa* is both a comprehensive reference book and a catalyst for advancing the study of African labour history, understood here as the history of those who produce wealth and well-being often in silence and often in poor conditions and to whom this book is dedicated.

STRUCTURE OF THE VOLUME

This volume comprises six parts plus a conclusive section. These subdivisions are concomitant with various aspects connected to the study of African labour history. As stated by various authors, the twentieth century is the century of the expansion in Africa of one particular form of labour relation: free wage labour. However, this does not mean that, between 1900 and today, free wage workers were the overwhelming majority of the African labour force. On the contrary, for most of the twentieth-century wage workers remained a minority in comparison with tributary, household and unfree workers. But the century of wage labour means that since 1900, free wage workers have progressively increased in proportion to all others, and today free salaried workers constitute certainly a substantial portion of workers in Africa, especially in relation to unfree forms of labour relations. For these reasons, the first section of this book deals with free and unfree labour,

---

[38] International Labour Organization, *Regional Brief for Africa. 2017. Global Estimates of Modern Slavery and Child Labour*, https://goo.gl/9MEqM7 (accessed 30 January 2018).

[39] Cooper, 'From Enslavement to Precarity?', 140.

containing an historical overview of wage labour in Africa (Chapter 1), the history of precarious and informal labour (Chapter 2) as well as the history of unfree forms of labour (Chapter 3). Part 2 focuses on sectors representing the emergence and development of wage labour in Africa: agriculture and plantations (Chapter 4), mining (Chapter 5), industry (Chapter 6) and transport (Chapter 7). An important aspect of African labour history of the period under consideration is the internationalization of the labour question, which occurred also with the creation of international organizations such as the ILO (Chapter 8) and labour mobility or international migration (Chapter 9). These histories are dealt with in the third part of this volume. Part IV, on varieties of work, contains essays dealing with labour sectors or situations where 'classic' labour categories do not hold. These include African domestic work (Chapter 10) and work in semi-legal or criminal activities (Chapter 12). In both sectors, the borders between free and unfree as well as between various forms of labour relations are blurred. The chapters on labour in the security sector (Chapter 11), on white-collar labour (Chapter 13) and on sport, tourism and entertainment (Chapter 14) are also part of the fourth section. In these cases, complexities of definition arise from the fact that in these sectors it is possible to find destitute workers next to extremely rich ones, managers or 'stars' who are self-employed. A comprehensive labour history of Africa cannot do without the history of employers. Thus, the fifth section of this book presents a history of capitalists (Chapter 15) and entrepreneurs more generally (Chapters 16 and 17). Finally, an important aspect of contemporary African labour history is the existing relationship between labour and the state and public structures. Part VI includes chapters on labour legislation (Chapter 18) and cooperativism and mutualism (Chapter 21). The histories of African trade unions (Chapter 19) and the welfare state (Chapter 20) are also part of this section. The concluding section (Chapter 22) contextualizes the contributions to this volume within broader debates on the place of African labour in world history.

PART I
FREE AND UNFREE LABOUR

ONE
Wage Labour

ANDREAS ECKERT

Department of Asian & African Studies and International
Research Collegium 'Work and Human Lifecycle in Global
History' (re:work), Humboldt University Berlin

WAGE LABOUR, AFRICAN LABOUR HISTORIOGRAPHY AND GLOBAL LABOUR HISTORY

Karl Marx defined the worker as a category that does not apply to all times and places. According to Marxist theory, the worker becomes a meaningful social category only when labour power becomes a commodity, that is, when a class of people without access to the means of production is created. In this context Marx famously assumed that labour power in capitalism can become a commodity in only one way, namely through free wage labour in which the worker 'as a free individual can dispose of his labor power as his own commodity' and 'has no other commodity for sale'.[2] This powerful idea led to a rather narrow concept of the working class. As Marcel van der Linden put it: 'If only the labor power of *free* wage laborers is commodified, it implies the "real" working class in capitalism can only consist of such workers.'[3]

As questionable as Marx's hypothesis may be, for a long time it appeared self-evident, as it seemed to correspond to the process by which

---

[1] For some of the points developed in this chapter, see Andreas Eckert, 'Capitalism and Labor in Sub-Saharan Africa', in *Capitalism: The Reemergence of a Historical Concept*, ed. Jürgen Kocka and Marcel van der Linden (London: Bloomsbury, 2016), 165–85.

[2] Karl Marx, *Capital: A Critique of Political Economy*, vol. I, trans. Ben Fowkes (Harmondsworth: Penguin, 1976), 272.

[3] Marcel van der Linden, *Workers of the World: Essays toward a Global Labor History* (Leiden: Brill, 2008), 19.

a proletariat was formed in the North Atlantic region.[4] In this context, two assumptions seem to be important. First, there was a fundamental change in the mid-nineteenth century linked with industrialization, when new ideas and work practices emerged. Work was legally codified, and from then on established the link between the individual and broader social groups, and especially the nation state: labour became the basis of the social and political order.[5] In the context of the nation state and the emerging welfare state, the difference between work or labour (in the sense of gainful employment, largely performed by men) and non-work (including other activities, for example at the household level, and largely performed by women) developed. Moreover, the difference between having work in the sense of gainful employment and being unemployed was reflected in the language and the statistics of the time and also became part of social policy.[6] Until this period, *Arbeit, travail,* 'work' and 'labour' had been defined in different ways but had never been limited to marketable work.[7] But from the nineteenth century onwards, in the industrialized world, work came to be defined more or less exclusively as gainful occupation, with wage labour as its most important and most widespread form.[8]

Studies on the British Empire have argued that anti-slavery played a crucial role in the process of privileging wage labour within the Atlantic-centred capitalist economy. Within the anti-slavery movement, the question of whether slavery would be clearly separated and rendered excisable from other forms of labour remained an open question for a while. In the end a narrowing definition of wage labour emerged that was clearly distinguished from slavery, and workers' organizations used assertions of maleness,

---

[4]   *Ibid.*

[5]   See, for instance, Bénédicte Zimmermann et al., eds, *Le travail et la nation: histoire croisée de la France et de l'Allemagne* (Paris: Éditions de la MSH, 1999); Jürgen Kocka, 'Work as a Problem in European History', in *Work in a Modern Society : The German Historical Experience in Comparative Perspective*, ed. J. Kocka (Oxford: Berghahn Books, 2010), 1–16.

[6]   Christian Topalov, *Naissance du chômeur* (Paris: Belin, 1984); Bénédicte Zimmermann, *La constitution du chômage en Allemagne: entre profession et territoire* (Paris: Éditions de la MSH, 2000). The emergence of the welfare state is a good example of the fact that capital has been engaged with taming the excesses of some of its constituents, including wage workers, in the interests of stability. See Peter Baldwin, *The Politics of Social Solidarity: Class Bases of the European Welfare State 1875–1975* (Cambridge: Cambridge University Press, 1990).

[7]   Keith Thomas, *The Oxford Book of Work* (New York: Oxford University Press, 1999).

[8]   Robert Castel, *Les métamorphoses de la question sociale: chronique du salariat* (Paris: Gallimard, 1999).

whiteness and Englishness to make claims.[9] This development had significant consequences for the ways in which African labour would be conceptualized: 'At a time when European elites were learning to think about workers as a class, they were confronting Africans as a race.'[10]

Consequently, much of the labour historiography on the North Atlantic realm (and beyond) focused on wage labour.[11] African labour history did not make a difference. Especially in its heyday between the late 1960s and early 1980s, the history of work in Africa was often treated as the history of wage labour. This chapter attempts to clear some paths in entering a vast subject by linking major related historiographical debates with the presentation of some crucial transformations in the ambivalent history of wage labour in twentieth-century Africa. It mainly looks at four broad thematic fields in which wage labour features prominently: first, labour mobilization in agrarian contexts that do not easily fit into the categories of 'peasant' or 'capitalist' agriculture; second, South Africa, probably the only region south of the Sahara where something like Marx's vision of original accumulation – the forceful removal of most cultivators from the land and the legal and administrative structure that enforced this process – took place; third, colonial imaginings of a working class, the role of labour struggles and the complexities of the proletarianization process during the decolonization period; and fourth and finally, the stagnation and often relative decline of formal wage employment, and the rise of 'informality' and 'precarity' in independent Africa.[12]

During the 1970s and early 1980s labour history was regarded as one of the most vibrant subfields of Africanist historiography. 'No subject has in recent years', Bill Freund proudly announced in 1984,

> so intruded into the scholarly literature on Africa as the African worker. Labor has become a fundamental issue to those who seek to develop African economies or to revolutionize African polities. The elucidation and debate

---

[9]   Thomas C. Holt, 'The Essence of the Contract: The Articulation of Race, Gender, and Political Economy in British Emancipation Policy, 1838–1866', in *Beyond Slavery: Explorations of Race, Labor, and Citizenship in Postemancipation Societies*, Frederick Cooper, Thomas C. Holt and Rebecca J. Scott (Chapel Hill, NC: University of North Carolina Press, 2000), 33–60.

[10]   Frederick Cooper, 'African Labor History', in *Global Labour History: A State of the Art*, ed. Jan Lucassen (Berne: Peter Lang, 2006), 100.

[11]   Joan Allen et al., eds, *Histories of Labour: National and International Perspectives* (Pontypool: Merlin Press, 2010).

[12]   It should be added that this chapter almost exclusively deals with developments in sub-Saharan Africa, while a few references are made to developments in North Africa, mainly Egypt.

about the relationship of labor to historical and social issues is currently under way over an impressive range of places and a number of languages.[13]

The historians whose work Freund presented and discussed reinterpreted the colonial period as a period when capitalist modes of production were introduced to Africa. Most authors stressed the autonomy of the working class, whose situation was rarely connected with the colonial situation. Much emphasis was laid instead upon the specific needs of capital in Africa at different times and different places. Many studies also emphasized what Robin Cohen called 'hidden forms of consciousness among African workers', which were placed into contrast with more conventional forms of labour resistance such as strikes.[14] A number of comprehensive collected volumes were published, each representing a specific pattern of African labour history.[15] The most vibrant historiography on labour could be found, not surprisingly, in South Africa, where wage labour played a comparatively important role.[16] From the 1970s to the 1990s the historiography on labour in North Africa, especially in the case of Egypt, also strongly focused on working-class and labour movements, and, as in the case of their sub-Saharan counterparts, with strong reference to E. P. Thompson.[17]

In the late 1980s African labour history – as labour histories of other world regions – ceased to generate the kind of intellectual excitement that it had before. There are numerous reasons for this. One was probably the fact that labour history was too embedded in the metanarrative of

[13]   Bill Freund, 'Labor and Labor History in Africa: A Review of the Literature', *African Studies Review*, 27.2 (1984), 1. This article offers an excellent historiographical overview on African labour history in its heyday.

[14]   Robin Cohen, 'Resistance and Hidden Forms of Consciousness among African Workers', *Review of African Political Economy*, 19 (1980), 8–22.

[15]   Cf. Richard Sandbrook and Robin Cohen, eds, *The Development of an African Working Class: Studies in Class Formation and Action* (London: Longman, 1975); Peter C. W. Gutkind et al., eds, *African Labor History* (Beverly Hills, CA: Sage, 1978); Michel Agier et al., eds, *Classes d'ouvrières d'Afrique Noire* (Paris: Karthala, 1987).

[16]   Bill Freund, 'Labour Studies and Labour History in South Africa: Perspectives from the Apartheid Era and After', *International Review of Social History*, 58.3 (2013), 493–519.

[17]   Zachary Lockman, 'Reflections on Labor and Working-Class History in the Middle East and North Africa', in *Global Labour History: A State of the Art*, ed. Jan Lucassen (Berne: Peter Lang, 2006), 117–46. Related studies include Joel Beinin and Zachary Lockman, *Workers on the Nile: Nationalism, Communism, Islam, and the Egyptian Working Class, 1882–1954* (Princeton, NJ: Princeton University Press, 1987); Ellis Goldberg, *Tinker, Tailor and Textile Worker: Class and Politics in Egypt, 1930–1952* (Berkeley, CA: University of California Press, 1986).

proletarianization.[18] This thesis brings together a number of processes, and while historians have never been so naive as to assume that the story of proletarianization is everywhere the same, they treat the overall trend as universal: cultivators and artisans are deprived of access to the means of production, they move to cities or are forced into insecure wage labour jobs in the agrarian sector, their skills are devalued; in the process, workers develop a sense of their collective identity as the sellers of labour power and a class identity, they form trade unions and other labour organizations, they go on strike and they collectively challenge capital. Accordingly, most Africanist labour historians of the 1970s and 1980s assumed that Africa was becoming 'proletarianized', that its working class was growing and was becoming more self-conscious. However, fundamental questions remained. How did so many Africans come to depend at least partly on wages for their livelihood? And how did Africans try to redefine categories and practices imposed on them, such as private property, time and discipline? How did they attempt to seek alternatives to wage labour in responding to their growing interest in purchased commodities?[19]

The decreasing interest in labour history since the 1980s also reflected the fact that organized labour was on the decline in Africa, as elsewhere in the world. Unionization and worker solidarity had not brought about radical political transformation, as many labour historians, among others, had hoped. In industrial regions such as the Zambian Copperbelt, global trade arrangements and economic policies had changed employment patterns, reduced union membership and denuded sectors that used to offer employees regularized wages and benefits.[20] Moreover, political changes altered the landscape of workers' rights and representation, as the push towards multi-party democracies often fractured and weakened the political clout of unions and workers' organizations.[21] In Africa, job insecurity is the norm, not the exception. Not only in Africa, but in many parts of the world, masses of poor people who had left the countryside in search of a better life were not turned into proletarians. Instead, they were often 'recruited into informal slums where they eke out a living via a complex range of livelihood

[18]   The following paragraph is based on Frederick Cooper, *Decolonization and African Society: The Labor Question in French and British Africa* (Cambridge: Cambridge University Press, 1996), 12f.

[19]   Cooper, 'African Labor History', 115f.

[20]   James Ferguson, *Expectations of Modernity: Myths and Meanings of Urban Life on the Zambian Copperbelt* (Berkeley, CA: University of California Press, 1999); Miles Larmer, *Mineworkers in Zambia: Labour and Political Change* (London: I.B.Tauris, 2007).

[21]   Emily Lynn Osborn, 'Work and Migration', in *The Oxford Handbook of Modern African History*, ed. John Parker and Richard Reid (Oxford: Oxford University Press, 2013), 203.

strategies to which agriculture and formal sector wage labour alike are often marginal'.[22] The relative decline of wage labour also produced what has been called a crisis of masculinity. Young men whose social power long rested on their ability to earn wages increasingly found themselves in a more precarious position. In turn, others, notably women and pensioners, acquired new powers and possibilities. This transformation is partly due to the relative expansion of work in service industries that are more open to women than the 'blue-collar' industrial jobs of the past.[23]

In short, the narrative of proletarianization did not work in Africa. The penetration of wage labour was comparatively late, uneven and contested, and wage labour coexisted with complex non-capitalist relations. During the twentieth century, even in South Africa, few people had an entire 'working life' that was devoted to wage labour. However, it would be wrong to replace the older exclusive focus on wage labour simply with a new priority on informal and precarious work.[24] As important as it is to carefully identify structure and history where many observers only see 'informality', and to pay heed to the ways in which people make their living beyond wage labour – on the margins, in circumstances that are both precarious and unpredictable – it remains a crucial task for African labour historiography to bring out 'the variety of ways in which wage labour became part of people's lives in particular locations'.[25] This effort echoes one of the aims of 'global labour history', namely to locate the extensive and complicated 'grey areas' replete with transitional locations between the 'free' wage labourers and other forms of labour, to take into consideration that households often combine several modes of labour and to have an eye for the possibility that individual

[22] James Ferguson, *Give a Man a Fish: Reflections on the New Politics of Distribution* (Durham, NC: Duke University Press, 2015), 23.

[23] For the South African context, see Franco Barchiesi, *Precarious Liberation: Workers, the State, and Contested Social Citizenship in Postapartheid South Africa* (Albany, NY: SUNY Press, 2011). Among the fast-growing literature on other parts of Africa, see Aili Mari Tripp, *Changing the Rules: The Politics of Liberalization and the Urban Informal Economy in Tanzania* (Berkeley, CA: University of California Press, 1997); Dmitri van den Bersselaar, 'Old Timers Who Still Keep Going: Retirement in Ghana', *Österreichische Zeitschrift für Geschichtswissenschaften*, 22.3 (2011), 136–52. The central role of working women in urban Egypt in keeping their families afloat is highlighted by Diane Singerman, *Avenues of Participation: Family, Politics, and Networks in Urban Quarters of Cairo* (Princeton, NJ: Princeton University Press, 1995).

[24] See the chapter by Barchiesi in this volume.

[25] Cooper, 'African Labor History', 103; Osborn, 'Work and Migration', 203.

labourers can combine different modes of labour, both synchronically and diachronically.[26]

The observation that full-time wage labour over the course of an entire career was not a global norm, but rather the exception in many parts of the world, led to the insight that the male proletarian does not represent the quintessential worker but is rather one among a number of categories of workers whose histories are connected. Analysing work 'beyond wage labour' becomes increasingly important as it allows for marginalized groups and their activities to form part of labour history. 'Free' wage labour is more and more regarded not as *the* capitalist norm, but as one (important) alternative among several forms of exploitation suitable for modern capitalism.[27]

LABOUR MOBILIZATION AND LABOUR ARRANGEMENTS IN AGRARIAN CONTEXTS

The arguments of both modernization theorists and Marxists often rested on assumptions about the 'backwardness' of Africa's rural economies. Again, in the 1970s one important historiographical branch highlighted rural proletarianization (especially in the context of southern Africa) and employed a rather linear view of agrarian change, which interpreted proletarianization as the last stage of a direct sequence leading from the independent to the impoverished peasant, and finally to the (migrant) worker.[28] On the other hand, social histories of rural labour highlighted the complexities and shifts in labour arrangements, especially in the context of cash-crop production.

---

[26] Van der Linden, *Workers of the World*, 32.

[27] Andreas Eckert, ed., *Global Histories of Work* (Berlin: De Gruyter, 2016).

[28] Giovanni Arrighi, 'Labour Supplies in Historical Perspective: A Study on Proletarianization of the African Peasantry in Rhodesia', in *Essays on the Political Economy of Africa*, ed. Giovanni Arrighi and John S. Saul (New York: Monthly Review Press, 1973), 180–234. Critical of this approach are Terence Ranger, 'Growing from the Roots. Reflections on Peasant Research in Central and Southern Africa', *Journal of Southern African Studies*, 5.1 (1978), 101–7; Frederick Cooper, 'Peasants, Capitalists, and Historians', *Journal of Southern African Studies*, 7.2 (1981), 284–314. The interest in African peasants (and their role in capitalist development in Africa) in the 1970s is reflected in numerous collected volumes and monographs. See Martin A. Klein, ed., *Peasants in Africa: Historical and Contemporary Perspectives* (Beverly Hills, CA: Sage, 1980); Robin H. Palmer and Neil Parsons, eds, *The Roots of Rural Poverty in Central and Southern Africa* (Berkeley, CA: University of California Press, 1979); Colin Bundy, *The Rise and Fall of the South African Peasantry* (Berkeley, CA: University of California Press, 1979). See the chapter by Tischler in this volume.

Colonial governments (and their predecessors) generally showed little interest in the conditions under which Africans worked for each other in small-scale farming. Crop production was often based on flexible relations of production, neither 'peasant' nor 'capitalist'. In general, the commercialization of agricultural production led to an increase in the use of hired labour in African rural economies, although in most African rural areas hired workers never provided a significant part of the total labour devoted to agricultural production. During the twentieth century, agricultural labour remained to a large extent 'family labour'.

The extent of wage employment varied considerably. It was most common in the cocoa economies of Ghana and Nigeria.[29] In her classic study on Ghana, Polly Hill, in 1963, noted: 'During the first stage of the migration the farmer depended on family labour and his cash outlay on day-to-day operations was possibly negligible … The second stage … was reached when the farmer had successfully established a sufficient area of bearing cocoa to support a labourer from its proceeds.'[30] In essence, Hill argued that, from the 1890s, Ghanaian cocoa farmers acted according to capitalist principles of profit motive and market forces, but they drew upon local resources such as established patron–client networks and kinship ties to meet labour demands.[31]

Later work on cocoa production in Ghana further stressed regional differences in the recruitment of paid workers.[32] The period after the Second World War, with booming world markets for crops, saw a significant increase in the demand for agricultural labour. According to the report of the Gold Coast Labour Department, in 1951–53 3,391 cocoa farmers in

---

[29] The best study on this development is Sara Berry, *No Condition is Permanent: The Social Dynamics of Agrarian Change in Sub-Saharan Africa* (Madison, WI: University of Wisconsin Press, 1993). The following paragraphs draw heavily from this insightful study.

[30] Polly Hill, *The Migrant Cocoa-Farmers of Southern Ghana: A Study in Rural Capitalism* (Cambridge: Cambridge University Press, 1963), 188. For a careful evaluation of this book and its implications for consequent research, see Gareth Austin's introduction to a reprint of Hill's *Migrant Cocoa-Farmers* (Hamburg: LIT, 1997), ix–xxviii.

[31] For an example from Cameroon on the integration of commercial farming into the local economy and the importance of pre-colonial commercial networks and labour recruitment patterns, see Andreas Eckert, 'African Rural Entrepreneurs and Labor in the Cameroon Littoral', *Journal of African History*, 40.1 (1999), 109–26.

[32] Inez Sutton, 'Labour and Commercial Agriculture in Ghana in the Late Nineteenth and Early Twentieth Centuries', *Journal of African History*, 24.4 (1983), 461–83; Gareth Austin, *Labour, Land and Capital in Ghana: From Slavery to Free Labour in Asante, 1807–1956* (Rochester, NY: University of Rochester Press, 2005).

Ashanti employed over 30,000 labourers, exclusive of 'family workers'.[33] More important than this trend is Sara Berry's insight into the importance of 'exploitation without dispossession' for the mobilization of rural labour. Those who controlled land well suited to cocoa production often leased it to entrepreneurial strangers who in turn obtained labour through a variety of arrangements, from using kinsmen to casual labour by strangers, until the trees were bearing. More labour came from casual labour migrants and hired labourers. In West African areas of cocoa production, African farmers were often able to attract seasonal migrant labour, especially from less favourably endowed regions. These migrants tended to replace slaves who had left to become free peasants or free labourers themselves.[34]

The possibilities of exploitation in such a system were limited. Planters could not exploit workers too intensely or prevent others from gaining access to land and labour, because their own security of tenure and ability to recruit labour depended on connections of community and clientage. In the course of time, new planters faced increasing difficulties in getting started, and land disputes became more widespread, but this did not (yet) lead to what Marx has called 'original accumulation'.[35] In fact, at least partly in order to avoid proletarianization, colonial administrations often tended to discourage the sale of land among the local population. This went hand in hand with the decision not to introduce compulsory land registration and an ongoing interpretation of 'customary law' as opposed to private and collective land alienation. The hope of preventing the appearance of a landless class that would be difficult to control very much fuelled this policy.[36]

In essence, in those parts of Africa that had not been deeply affected by the slave trade or by slavery, African cultivators were faced with a colonial state whose presence was highly uneven and with local elites whose capacity to manipulate the system in their own favour was rather varied. This resulted in a patchwork of economic conditions across the continent, ranging from islands of European-controlled plantations and mines surrounded by larger labour catchment areas, to regions where African farmers developed,

---

[33] Berry, *No Condition is Permanent*, 139.

[34] Gareth Austin, 'Cash Crops and Freedom: Export Agriculture and the Decline of Slavery in Colonial West Africa', *International Review of Social History*, 54.1 (2009), 1–37.

[35] Carola Lentz, *Land, Mobility, and Belonging in West Africa* (Bloomington, IN: Indiana University Press, 2013); Catherine Boone, *Property and Political Order: Land Rights and the Structure of Conflict in Africa* (New York: Cambridge University Press, 2014).

[36] Gareth Austin, 'Capitalism in the Colonies', in *The Cambridge History of Capitalism*, vol. II, ed. Jeffrey G. Williamson and Larry Neal (Cambridge: Cambridge University Press, 2014), 327.

as described above, sophisticated systems of labour mobilization in the production of cash crops and partly accumulated considerable wealth and influence. In other zones, outlets for produce were limited, and the seasonal export of male labour power to plantation and mining areas represented the only possibility for buying important commodities and paying taxes. Finally, in many areas, Africans could simply evade efforts to exploit them but could generate little economic surplus.

During the colonial period and afterwards, women remained the bedrock of food production. In some areas, women managed to extend their role in agriculture into producing cash crops and thus played a bigger role in agricultural labour than the colonial regimes intended. In the Lower Tchiri Valley in Malawi, cotton cultivation enabled women to acquire a stake in production, but, in the context of labour migration and increasing constraints on the rural economy, they again became more dependent on remittances from male wage earners working elsewhere.[37] Women's centrality in both agricultural production and household reproduction thus led to increasing pressures, especially from male elders, to leave out-migration to the more dispensable young males. Moreover, especially in southern Africa but also in Kenya, colonial administrations enforced rigorous laws to prevent women from moving to cities, although even in the face of such harsh policing, women asserted their own space in urban life and occupied occupational niches such as cooking, brewing and prostitution.[38]

SOUTH AFRICA

It is not at all evident that, during the colonial period, many Africans wanted to commit themselves to a life of wage labour. On the other hand, Africans did not simply resist wage labour in all its forms. For instance, a period of wage labour could enable a young man to improve a farm or

[37]   Erez Mandala, *Work and Control in a Peasant Economy: A History of the Lower Tchiri Valley in Malawi, 1859–1960* (Madison, WI: University of Wisconsin Press, 1990). For an incisive study on cotton production in Mozambique, see Allen Isaacman, *Cotton is the Mother of Poverty: Peasants, Work, and Rural Struggle in Colonial Mozambique, 1938–1961* (London: James Currey, 1996). The author emphasizes that, in many regions of Mozambique, cotton production was imposed on women because men were away working in mines.

[38]   Frederick Cooper, *Africa since 1940: The Past of the Present* (New York: Cambridge University Press, 2002), 33, 125; Iris Berger, *Threads of Solidarity: Women in the South African Industry, 1900–1980* (London: James Currey, 1992); Luise White, *The Comforts of Home: Prostitution in Colonial Nairobi* (Chicago: University of Chicago Press, 1992).

plant trees, so that wage labour became a particular moment in a life cycle that embraced different economic activities. South Africa might be regarded as an exceptional case, where the systematic alienation of land since the late nineteenth century produced a workforce resembling the proletariat of industrial Europe. But even here, some people managed to work 'for no man – black or white', such as the sharecropper Kas Maine as portrayed by Charles van Onselen.[39] Nevertheless, the mineral discoveries in the second half of the nineteenth century and the subsequent expansion of the industrial sector of the economy led to the emergence of an industrial workforce that included thousands of European immigrants and a large number of Africans. The workforce in the South African mines was divided along racial lines, whereby Europeans were assigned to supervisory positions while Africans were relegated to unskilled and menial tasks. The Land Act of 1913 consolidated a policy of depriving the vast majority of black South Africans of land ownership. This Act was crucial in driving down black real wages for two reasons. It not only reserved 93 per cent of the land to whites but also prohibited African tenancy on white-owned land. Before 1913, sharecrop tenancy had probably been the most important way by which black farmers could sell produce to the market, rather than selling their labour power.

The key to the capitalist character of South African development can be located in agriculture. Since the seventeenth century a culturally and socially distinct landowning class had been emerging, one that tightened its grip on land in the context of industrialization, forcing tenants to become wage labourers and bringing about a landless African proletariat in the process. 'Reserves' introduced by the South African state increasingly became dumping grounds for Africans who were no longer 'useful' to the capitalist economy. The attempts of mine owners to reduce labour costs sparked off confrontation with European workers and culminated in a large-scale strike in 1922.[40] Although the strike was defeated, white workers were able to use their voting power and helped to elect a new government in 1924 that introduced a number of reforms that were intended to co-opt white workers and set them apart from black workers. Despite their lack of legal rights, black workers began to organize themselves and launched numerous strikes. Black workers continued to protest against their harsh working conditions and low wages under the apartheid regime. It is a commonplace that the

[39] Charles van Onselen, *The Seed is Mine: The Life of Kas Maine, a South African Sharecropper, 1894–1985* (New York: Hill and Wang, 1997), 3.

[40] Jeremy Krikler, *White Rising: The 1922 Insurrection and Racial Killing in South Africa* (Manchester: Manchester University Press, 2005).

South African trade union movement played a pivotal role in the anti-apartheid struggle and remained a powerful force following the transition to black majority rule in 1994.[41]

Much of the older literature on South African labour employed a 'from kraal to compound' approach. Related interpretations emphasized the linearity of the process of migrant labour, the power of the capitalist colonial state and the settlers, the complicity of African elites and the irreversibility of labour migration as incomplete but inevitable proletarianization.[42] The literature on South African labour history has undergone a remarkable transformation during the past four decades, which, given the significant influence it has exerted upon labour historiography on Africa in general, is instructive for the changing perspectives on the history of wage labour south of the Sahara. What remains a telling lacuna in much of the literature on wage labour is an analysis of 'what people do when they work, why they do it, and how workers and managers alike try to shape the pace, intensity, and quality of what gets done'.[43]

In the late 1970s a number of South African social historians became aware of the considerable distance between the analytical concept of 'class' and the concrete local experiences of 'real' classes with their overlapping ideologies and practices. A crucial study in this context was Charles van

---

[41] For a good introduction to the complex history of twentieth-century South Africa in which the aspect of labour plays a crucial role, see Robert Ross et al., eds, *The Cambridge History of South Africa, Volume 2, 1885–1994* (New York: Cambridge University Press, 2011); Peter Alexander, *Workers, War and the Origins of Apartheid: Labour and Politics in South Africa, 1939–1948* (Oxford: James Currey, 2000).

[42] Frederick Johnstone, *Class, Race and Gold: A Study of Class Relations and Racial Discrimination in South Africa* (London: Routledge and Kegan Paul, 1976).

[43] Frederick Cooper, *On the African Waterfront: Urban Disorder and the Transformation of Work in Colonial Mombasa* (New Haven, CT: Yale University Press, 1987), 5, already noted this thirty years ago. Elsewhere, Cooper emphasized in his critique of poststructuralist and postcolonial approaches the importance of the 'nitty-gritty of labour', and noted that we should not assume that 'people spent all day thinking about who they are; they had other things to do'. Frederick Cooper, 'Back to Work: Categories, Boundaries and Connections in the Study of Labour', in *Racializing Class, Classifying Race: Labour and Difference in Britain, the USA and Africa*, ed. Peter Alexander and Rick Halpern (Basingstoke: Palgrave Macmillan, 2000), 213. There are, of course, exceptions confirming that rule, and recent research on the 'informal' or 'non-wage sector' provides very careful descriptions on work practices. See Trevor H. J. Marchand, *The Masons of Djenné* (Bloomington, IN: Indiana University Press, 2009). A few anthropologists also offered impressive ethnographies of the nitty-gritty of work of herders and hunters in West Africa. See Gerd Spittler, *Hirtenarbeit. Die Welt der Kamelhirten und Ziegenhirtinnen von Timia* (Cologne: Köppe, 1998).

Onselen's *Chibaro*, in which the author presented a rich and varied history 'from below'. Capital accumulation and social control are dominant themes in *Chibaro*, almost organizing principles of the narrative, and black wage workers are frequently portrayed as victims of an omnipotent capitalist class. 'The compound', van Onselen emphasized, was 'the college of colonialism, that did much to rob Africans of their dignity and help mould servile black personalities'.[44] He describes a vibrant workers' culture, but this culture was largely either the product of drawn-out struggles with capital or the result of the capitalists' strategy of social control. Drunkenness, loafing, theft, desertion, witchcraft and the Watchtower movement were the 'hidden struggles' with capital through which workers constructed a class consciousness; at the same time, employers saw mine dancing and sport as a means of defusing class consciousness. Liquor drew men to the mines and held them there by raising their consumer needs; education and religion produced a disciplined and acquiescent workforce; and even sex serviced the needs of the industry.[45] Van Onselen's work definitely opened new and important horizons for the history of wage labour in Africa, but he underestimated the range of experiences and cultural resources that shaped the world view of migrating mineworkers. As he saw resistance as the black miner's natural response to his environment, he inverted into working-class values the vices – such as drunkenness, theft and laziness – through which Europeans had given visibility to Africans. At the same time, by portraying culture in terms of response rather than initiative, or in terms of employers' strategies, he ultimately subordinated the workers' lived experience to the rhythms of capital accumulation.[46]

Although more and more historians of labour in South Africa developed an interest in culture, the result was a largely administrative history, according to which Europeans built institutions and took decisions that shaped the outlines of workers' lives; the compound remained a prison, drinking purely a problem, leisure and Christianity functioned to assist the accumulation of

[44] Charles van Onselen, *Chibaro: African Mine Labour in Southern Rhodesia 1900–1933* (London: Pluto Press, 1976), 157. For the following sketch, see Patrick Harries, *Work Culture, and Identity: Migrant Laborers in Mozambique and South Africa, c.1860–1910* (Portsmouth, NH: Heinemann, 1994), xi–xix.

[45] Jonathan Crush and Charles Ambler, eds, *Liquor and Labor in Southern Africa* (Athens, OH: Ohio University Press, 1992).

[46] In his following book, van Onselen took the argument beyond the compound and conceptualized the world of mines as the product of complex interactions and strategies of numerous actors. See *Studies in the Social and Economic History of the Witwatersrand, 1886–1914, Vol. 1: New Babylon; Vol. 2: New Nineveh* (Johannesburg: Ravan Press, 1982).

capital, and coercion was the most visible aspect of everyday labour relations. Migrant labour was viewed at best as an appendage rather than an integral, if not dominant, part of workers' lives in the fields, and the systems of signification brought from the rural areas and developed by miners in and around their places of work were subsumed in an anonymous, industrial homogeneity.[47] Thus, radical historians initially viewed culture as a source of raw data that would provide the narrative with 'nuance and texture', allowing history to 'resonate' with the lives of ordinary people. Oral testimony became a crucial part of this enterprise, partly so as to 'reconstruct and record' the lives of 'obscure, ill-educated people', but also to examine consciousness as a product of everyday experience.[48] Dunbar Moodie provided a series of remarkable studies on the social networks, forms of identity and moral economy constructed by black workers in the gold mines. He conceptualized mines not only as sites of harsh exploitation, but also as locations where workers developed alternative life forms.[49]

Finally, it has been shown that capitalism did not necessarily generate altogether new migratory patterns in southern Africa. By the nineteenth century, Mozambican men were frequently travelling great distances to access new markets and opportunities for hunting and trading. When the mines first opened in South Africa, these footloose men needed little encouragement to go and work in them.[50] After the end of apartheid, labour history on and in South Africa lost much of its dynamic, but there is some recent work that examines current labour struggles in a historical perspective, analyses the connections between wage labour and social citizenship in the democratic transition, or explores the dynamic transformations of trade union activities and shop floor conflict during the apartheid era.[51]

---

[47]   This applies to two otherwise excellent studies on the early history of Kimberley. See William Worgner, *South Africa's City of Diamonds: Mine Workers and Monopoly Capitalism in Kimberley, 1867–1895* (New Haven, CT: Yale University Press, 1987); Robert Turrell, *Capital and Labour on the Kimberley Diamond Fields, 1871–1890* (Cambridge: Cambridge University Press, 1987).

[48]   For this literature, see Tim Keegan, *Facing the Storm: Portraits of Black Lives in Rural South Africa* (London: Zed Books, 1988); Belinda Bozzoli (with Mmantho Nkotsoe), *Women of Phokeng: Consciousness, Life Strategy, and Migrancy in South Africa, 1900–1983* (London: James Currey, 1991).

[49]   T. Dunbar Moodie (with Vivienne Ndatshe), *Going for Gold: Men, Mines and Migration* (Berkeley, CA: University of California Press, 1994).

[50]   Harries, *Work Culture.*

[51]   Peter Alexander et al., *Marikana: A View from the Mountain and a Case to Answer* (Johannesburg: Jacana, 2012); Franco Barchiesi, 'Wage Labor and Social Citizenship in the Making of Post-Apartheid South Africa', *Journal of Asian and African Studies,*

IMAGINING A WORKING CLASS

'Free labour' was a central category of colonial thinking, although the gap between ideology and practice remained conspicuous.[52] Colonial rulers, confronted with a wide array of constellations on the ground, emphasized their task of turning Africans into reliable commodity producers. However, African rulers and slave holders, as much as peasants and slaves, redefined their relationship into something other than that of employer and worker, working out with each other relationships of long-term dependency not linked to specific labour services. Colonial rulers soon found that they could maintain order only by forging alliances with the very elites whose tyranny they had previously agitated against. Colonialism in most of the continent soon settled for living off the surplus production of peasants or extracting surplus value from labourers who retained a strong foothold in their villages. Many Africans were moving back and forth between wage labour, cash-crop production, small-scale marketing and food growing. Colonial rule produced a huge new demand for labour for the construction of roads, railways, dockyards and building, for work on European plantations, mines and other projects, as well as for increased food production. Colonial officials found it convenient to leave agricultural production to (former) slave owners and chiefs, or enlist their aid to supply the labour required for public, and even private, purposes. Moreover, desperate to make their territories economically viable, they resorted to various devices for mobilizing unfree labour themselves. These included forced labour, conscription into the army or police forces, and the recruitment of contract labour by all kinds of dubious means.[53] The Portuguese colonies were particularly notorious for relying

---

42.1 (2007), 39–72; Alex Lichtenstein, 'Making Apartheid Work: African Trade Unions and the 1953 Native Labour (Settlement of Disputes) Act in South Africa', *Journal of African History*, 46.2 (2005), 293–314.

[52] Frederick Cooper, 'Conditions Analogous to Slavery: Imperialism and Free Labor Ideology in Africa', in *Beyond Slavery*, F. Cooper et al. (Chapel Hill, NC: University of North Carolina Press, 2000), 107–49.

[53] There is a rich literature on the slow death of slavery and on the complex transition from slave labour to other forms of labour, including forced labour. See Martin A. Klein, *Slavery and Colonial Rule in French West Africa* (New York: Cambridge University Press, 1998); Suzanne Miers and Martin A. Klein, eds, *Slavery and Colonial Rule in Africa* (London: Frank Cass, 1999); Suzanne Miers and Richard Roberts, eds, *The End of Slavery in Africa* (Madison, WI: University of Wisconsin Press, 1988); Jan-Georg Deutsch, *Emancipation Without Abolition in German East Africa, c.1884–1914* (Oxford: James Currey, 2006); Kevin A. Grant, *A Civilised Savagery: Britain and the New Slaveries in Africa, 1884–1926* (New York: Routledge, 2005); Frederick Cooper, *From Slaves to Squatters: Plantation Labor and Agriculture in Zanzibar and Coastal Kenya, 189–1925* (New

on forced labour, and parts of Portuguese-ruled Africa fell at the far end of the spectrum of brutality of labour practices. However, at least until the 1940s, institutionalized violence to extract African labour was by no means a peculiarly Portuguese approach.[54]

After the First World War, during which Africans experienced a massive increase in forced labour, the debates of the day were about the necessity for forced labour and the extent to which Africa was becoming diseased and depopulated due to the colonial demand for labour. The newly founded League of Nations took up this issue. The debates culminated in the Forced Labour Convention of the International Labour Organization of 1930.[55] The realities on the ground in Africa were much more complex, and hierarchies and forms of exploitation much more subtle, than the discussions about forced labour in Geneva recognized. Moreover, neither the missionary critics who asked 'Africa: Slave or Free?' nor League of Nations investigators questioned the premise of colonial rule itself; consequently, the resulting

---

Haven, CT: Yale University Press, 1980); Ahmad Alawad Sikainga, *Slaves into Workers: Emancipation and Labor in the Colonial Sudan* (Austin, TX: University of Texas Press, 1996); Thaddeus Sunseri, *Vilimani: Labor Migration and Rural Change in Early Colonial Tanzania, 1884–1915* (Portsmouth, NH: Heinemann, 2002); Opolot Okia, *Communal Labor in Colonial Kenya: The Legitimization of Coercion, 1912–1930* (Basingstoke: Palgrave Macmillan, 2012). In the British colonies, the Master and Servant law provided a legal framework for administrators to recruit and control labour, while in French Africa, the *indigénat* became a wide-ranging instrument in the hands of local colonial officials to use as they saw fit, for instance in conscripting Africans for public works. See David Anderson, 'Kenya, 1895–1939: Registration and Rough Justice', in *Masters, Servants, and Magistrates in Britain and the Empire, 1562–1955*, ed. Douglas Hay and Paul Craven (Chapel Hill, NC: University of North Carolina Press, 2004), 498–528; Gregory Mann, 'What was the Indigénat? The Empire of Law in French West Africa', *Journal of African History*, 50.3 (2009), 331–53. See the chapter by Fall and Roberts in this volume.

[54] Eric Allina, *Slavery by Any Other Name: African Life under Company Rule in Colonial Mozambique* (Charlottesville, VA: University of Virginia Press, 2012); Alexander Keese, 'Searching for the Reluctant Hands: Obsession, Ambivalence, and the Practice of Organising Involuntary Labour in Colonial Cuanza-Sul and Malange Districts, Angola, 1926–1945', *Journal of Imperial and Commonwealth History*, 41.2 (2013), 238–58; Jelmer Voss, 'Work in Times of Slavery, Colonialism, and Civil War: Labor Relations in Angola from 1800 to 2000', *History in Africa*, 41 (2014), 363–85.

[55] J. P. Daughton, 'ILO Expertise and Colonial Violence in the Interwar Years', in *Globalizing Social Rights: The International Labour Organization and Beyond*, ed. Sandrine Kott and Joëlle Droux (Basingstoke and Geneva: Palgrave Macmillan and ILO, 2013), 85–97; Cooper, 'Conditions Analogous to Slavery', 132–4. One important text voicing contemporary concerns about abuses in labour recruitment was Raymond Leslie Buell, *The Native Problem in Africa*, 2 vols (New York: Macmillan, 1928).

debate sought only to draw distinctions between labour policies considered acceptable and not acceptable in a European-dominated Africa.

Officials in the colonies wanted to use the labour of Africans as much as they could, but, at the same time, firmly believed in the necessity of stable African communities under the control of male elders. European administrators saw mining towns or cities as sites of labour, but not of the reproduction of the labour force. Those Africans who had left this imagined traditional village life and permanently settled in the cities were labelled 'detribalized'.[56] Until the 1930s European colonizers perceived Africans essentially as 'primitive tribesmen', whose unskilled or casual labour could be extracted when needed. These assumptions slowly began to be challenged in the decade before the Second World War. The capacity of African workers for industrial action that suddenly manifested itself was of fundamental importance here. From the mid-1930s a wave of strikes in cities and mining towns shook various colonies in British and French Africa; the strikes continued in the period after 1945.[57] It is important to note that these strikes were rarely confined to workplaces; in many of these struggles trade unions only played a minor role at best. Often urban social networks were crucial in organizing and running strikes. In many ways, the composition of the strikers reflected the complex mix of the urban populations, consisting of wage labourers, casual labourers, artisans, those who worked outside the wage sector and those who were called by official sources the 'floating population'.[58]

[56] Cooper, 'Conditions Analogous to Slavery', 129. Note that, in this context, women also participated in migratory initiatives in order to get away from patriarchal authority. See Marie Rodet, 'Forced Labor, Resistance, and Masculinities in Kayes, French Sudan, 1919–1946', *International Labor and Working Class History*, 86 (2014), 107–23.

[57] Cooper, *Decolonization*. The Second World War was crucial to this story, as it brought for African workers 'contradictory experiences of "progressive" reform within authoritarian labor systems and the preservation of archaic oppressive systems of labor mobilization and control'. See Carolyn A. Brown, 'African Labor in the Making of World War II', in *Africa and World War II*, ed. Judith A. Byfield et al. (New York: Cambridge University Press, 2015), 43.

[58] Since the 1970s strikes have constituted a centrepiece of empirical research in Africanist labour historiography. See, among many others, Wale Oyemakinde, 'The Nigerian General Strike of 1945', *Journal of the Historical Society of Nigeria*, 7.4 (1975), 693–710; Richard A. Joseph, 'Settlers, Strikers and Sans-Travail: The Douala Riots of 1945', *Journal of African History*, 15.4 (1974), 669–87; Frederick Cooper, '"Our Strike": Equality, Anticolonial Politics and the 1947–48 Railway Strike in French West Africa', *Journal of African History*, 37.1 (1996), 81–118.

A desire to mould 'more productive and orderly' colonies after the war, alongside an increasingly demanding African workforce and urban centres growing beyond colonial control, induced a shift in labour policy that emphasized 'stabilization'. The colonial state tried to conceptualize structures that would allow for a stable, 'detribalized' urban working class in towns focused on the European family model.[59] Colonial authorities thus initiated a set of projects, including the creation of living spaces, the approval of moderate trade unions and the establishment of social security systems. Such change, however, was not affordable nor politically manageable. Dualist policies that tried to draw a ring around a section of modernizable Africans broke down rapidly. To some extent, African labour organizers turned the new discourse to their own advantage by making claims desired by their followers, while African politicians found the resulting impotence of colonial administrators opportune. Major shifts in approach were especially dramatic and distinct in French West Africa, where elements of destructive compulsion were still firmly in place in the 1930s, but where the impulse towards modernization and assimilation quickly became much stronger.[60]

The fields of social security and unemployment refer to the contradictions and half-heartedness in the colonial efforts to create a new 'wage labourer' in Africa who should cease to be an African. According to dominant post-war colonial conceptions, African workers, in order to become 'proper workers', ought to be civilized, live in proper families and learn the dignity of labour. In this context, in a number of colonies, a set of social institutions was created for relatively small groups of formal sector workers.[61] Probably the most ambitious of these was the system of family allowances for the French colonies during the 1950s, which provided cash allowances to workers' families for the support of children. There are other examples as well. The major mining companies in the Zambian Copperbelt provided modest pensions to mineworkers, while Union Minière in Katanga went further by providing a broad package of social support meant to encourage

---

[59] At this point it is important to mention that, at least for some parts of West Africa, several authors argue that working-class experiences go back to nineteenth-century artisans. See Ibrahim Abdullah, 'Rethinking African Labour and Working-Class History: The Artisan Origins of the Sierra Leonean Working Class', *Social History*, 23.1 (1998), 80–96.

[60] Cooper, *Decolonization*.

[61] For the following, see Ferguson, *Give a Man a Fish*, 72–4; on family allowances in French West Africa, see Cooper, *Decolonization*, 305–20; on pensions in the copper field, see Ferguson, *Expectations*; on social support in the Congo, see John Higginson, *A Working Class in the Making: Belgian Colonial Labor Policy, Private Enterprise and the African Mineworkers, 1907–1951* (Madison, WI: University of Wisconsin Press, 1989).

the 'stabilization' of the workforce. An ideology of familism was central to all these schemes, which were meant to support not only the worker but also his recognized dependants. However, administrations had the utmost difficulty in putting these schemes into practice. Necessary information, such as documentation of births, and reliable ways of assigning particular children to particular families and a single, bona fide wife to each wage earner were difficult to obtain, even in the case of 'advanced' formal sector workers. In this context, much 'social welfare' was restricted to recreational activities and adult education classes for formal sector workers in privileged industries and occupations.[62]

At this time, the idea that Africans could be unemployed still seemed to be rather strange to most European colonial officials. However, in the context of rapid urbanization, the problem of a reserve army of unemployed or jobless young men observable in towns caused increasing attention. In 1958 the French ethnographer and film-maker Jean Rouch produced the ethnofiction *Moi, un noir*, featuring three young men from Niger who had left their country to find work in the Treichville quarter of Abidjan, the capital of Ivory Coast. In the opening sequences providing impressions of Treichville and the plateau area (the business quarter of Abidjan), an off-camera voice tells us: '*Chaque jour des jeunes gens arrivent dans les villes d'Afrique. Ils ont abandonné l'école ou le champ familial pour essayer d'entrer dans le monde moderne. Ils ne savent rien faire et tout faire. Ils sont l'une des maladies des nouvelles villes africaines: la jeunesse sans emploi.*'[63] These words echoed a growing anxiety among colonial administrators, social scientists and African nationalist politicians in late colonial Africa: urban unemployment, conceived as a problem of the male youth.

However, in the very same year, 1958, the International Labour Office published its *African Labour Survey* and observed 'considerable underemployment' on the continent; it also concluded that 'unemployment, except in a few towns in the form known in highly industrialised countries, exists only to a limited extent; there are usually more offers of employment than applications for jobs'.[64] In general, colonial officials downplayed the issue of unemployment. For instance, in order to challenge the protests

---

[62] Andreas Eckert, 'Regulating the Social: Social Security, Social Welfare and the State in Late Colonial Tanzania', *Journal of African History*, 45.3 (2004), 467–89.

[63] This sequence can be found at https://www.youtube.com/watch?v=_jJspPtRmkQ (accessed 10 August 2016). On Rouch's oeuvre, see Paul Henley, *The Architecture of the Real: Jean Rouch and the Craft of Ethnographic Cinema* (Chicago: University of Chicago Press, 2009).

[64] International Labour Office, *African Labour Survey* (Geneva: ILO, 1958), 404.

of African trade unionists about the rising unemployment in the cities, a representative of the Labour Department in Tanganyika suggested: 'I can't help feeling it's a problem on which we ought to be better informed, if only we show that we know what we are talking about if we say the problem is not serious.'[65] In most late colonial labour laws, unemployment compensation was held to be particularly undesirable, because most officials would not acknowledge that the African wage worker who was not working was in fact a worker.

One also has to emphasize the gendered way in which the 'unemployment problem' was interpreted. Throughout the colonial period, employment and unemployment were overwhelmingly associated with men. Women had for long entered urban centres and, facing restrictions on the kind of waged employment deemed appropriate for them, they had made a significant contribution to sectors outside the realm of waged work. However, in the official imagination, it was male youth who constituted a potentially insurrectionary unemployed class, who were more visible 'loitering' on urban streets. The absence of female unemployed in surviving commentary reflects the gendered occupation of urban space. By contrast to young men, whose street presence has remained a concern up to the present, women were more restricted to the home and/or the workplace, or else they simply did not constitute a threat in the eyes of the male colonizer.[66]

How important were the labour question and the construction of an African working class in the decision of European powers to leave Africa? The decisive power over African affairs ultimately lay at higher levels of European public and private sectors, reacting to their own perceptions of Africa's role in the international economy. It was the crises of the Depression and post-Second World War eras, rather than colonialist understandings of what were still very small African urban populations and African working classes, that drove the modernization and development policies. It was also the recognition, by the mid-1950s, of Africa's relative irrelevance to the reinvigorated European and global economies that made the cost of misconceptions about managing newly growing African cities and African workers so unacceptable.[67] On the other hand, the efforts of the French

---

[65] Quoted in Andrew Burton, 'Raw Youth, School-Leavers and the Emergence of Structural Unemployment in Late-Colonial Tanganyika', *Journal of African History*, 47.3 (2006), 375.

[66] On gendered images of youth, see Andrew Burton and Hélène Charton-Bigot, eds, *Generations Past: Youth in East African History* (Athens, OH: Ohio University Press, 2010).

[67] Ralph A. Austen, 'Africa and Globalization: Colonialism, Decolonization and the Postcolonial Malaise', *Journal of Global History*, 1.3 (2006), 403–8.

government to develop Eurafrica through 1957 or even later suggest that the French had not immediately given up on Africa, even after they recognized how costly it was.[68]

WHERE HAVE ALL THE WORKERS GONE?

Around independence, the overall number of wage workers in sub-Saharan Africa was still rather small, as the ILO statistics reproduced in Table 1.1. show.[69] Nevertheless, in a number of African countries, labour movements played an important role in the road to independence, though not necessarily because of strong ties between trade unions and nationalists. Rather, the link lay in the murkier realm of colonial politics. Union demands and effective strike action helped expose the competing claims that the colonial state made to development, progress and civilization. In effect, the colonial state could not respond to demands for increased benefits and rights from organized labour – which would put its members on a par with metropolitan workers – without dismantling the justification of colonialism. There is an ironic charm – but also a kind of Pyrrhic victory – in the African success in defeating European developmentalist logic. The decision by the Europeans to accept union demands that African labourers be treated on the same basis as their European counterparts was a mutual failure to comprehend African social reality. It was a consequential failure, since the cost of providing European-scale wages and benefits under African economic conditions could not be borne by either colonial or postcolonial regimes. Reluctant European governments were thus encouraged to withdraw from Africa, while their local successors co-opted some of the labour leadership regime but rather quickly suppressed the unions as an autonomous force.[70]

Political leaders of the newly independent states claimed to harness all social and economic energies to build political unity and promote economic advancement. Trade unions, on the other hand, usually represented the relatively privileged 4 or 5 per cent of the population who worked for wages. They were largely concentrated in the civil service and the new state-led

[68] Marie-Thérèse Bitsch and Gérard Bossuat, eds, *L'Europe unie et l'Afrique: de l'idée d'Eurafrique à la convention de Lomé I* (Brussels, 2005).

[69] For more statistical data, see John Sender and Sheila Smith, *The Development of Capitalism in Africa* (London: Methuen, 1986). Their claim that 'by the end of the colonial period, capitalist labor markets had become predominant, and that a working class had emerged as a major social and political force' (p. 129) seems difficult to sustain.

[70] Cooper, *Decolonization*. See the chapter by Freund in this volume.

Table 1.1. Numbers of wage earners in the main branches of economic activity

Territory & year	Agriculture & forestry	Mining & quarrying	Manufacturing	Building & construction	Transport	Commerce	Domestic & other services	Government services	Total
Angola									
1955	–	22,758	47,255	–	–	30,902	–	–	–
Belgian Congo									
1950	238,835	114,350	134,466	84,869	62,211	62,050	265,228	–	962,009
1956	300,791	84,287	152,758	124,319	91,789	81,548	362,404[2]	–	1,179,896
French Cameroons									
1952	32,307	4,706	4,713	12,000	9,295	13,718[3]	10,052[4]	28,822[5]	115,613
1955	40,000	2,000	10,900	18,100	8,000	16,400[3]	11,000[4]	37,500[5]	143,900
French Equatorial Africa									
1952	47,586	24,305	11,129	57,140	7,988	12,216[3]	13,000[4]	28,626[5]	201,990
1955	39,945	19,575	14,941	22,089	15,713	13,042[3]	15,150[4]	21,374[5]	154,754
French Togoland									
1952	1,874	–	686	2,691	1,243	11,690[3]	1,400[4]	8,338[5]	26,401
1955	2,584	105	380	456	850	11,814[3]	1,212[4]	7,065[5]	24,466
French West Africa									
1952	63,622	11,225	24,578	55,363	25,733	37,589[3]	24,071[4]	114,032[5]	356,213
1955	73,600	11,700	31,000	42,800	33,300	52,000[3]	20,500[4]	107,600[5]	372,500
Gold Coast									
1948–49	19,901	35,898	2,130	20,033	9,983	15,758	7,682	19,544	130,930
1954	33,929	36,959	14,755	49,690	21,775	24,486	30,275	32,547	244,417
Kenya									
1950	203,500	8,500	43,400	19,200	31,900	28,500	40,800	84,700	460,500
1956	235,200	9,000	57,700	29,500	47,800	37,900	45,700	134,100	596,700
Madagascar									
1952	80,828	9,595	24,000	12,477	5,925	15,239[3]	36,253[4]	44,325[5]	228,642
1955	96,693	7,996	21,489	19,554	9,528	22,913[3]	26,985[4]	42,404[5]	247,562
Mozambique									
1953	117,912	5,138	29,866[6]	16,882[7]	9,408[7]	–	58,879[8]	–	–
Nigeria									
1953	53,850[9]	50,342	16,022	54,434	36,951	35,837	24,742	51,656	323,834[10]

Northern Rhodesia									
1951	57,025	37,709	19,375	46,424	6,158	9,305	52,670[11]	—	228,676
1656	40,602	37,582	24,585	64,094	7,838	14,477	73,951[12]	—	263,132
Nyasaland									
1956	68,589	530	18,203	25,094	4,144	11,156	36,542	—	164,278
Ruanda-Urundi									
1956	25,594	20,546	5,610	14,390	15,514	10,982	30,264	—	123,401
Sierra Leone									
1948	2,686	6,581	—	8,511	3,705	5,477	1,910[13]	7,976	36,846[14]
1954	2,288	4,901	—	10,963	5,004	4,962	2,688[13]	11,162	41,968[14]
Southern Rhodesia									
1946	225,835	63,805	57,227	54,079	11,207	22,023	96,027[15]	—	530,203
1956	248,346	60,658	73,117	58,084	13,705	30,006	124,037[15]	—	609,953
Tanganyika									
1952	234,317	16,529	22,539	21,253	6,951	14,327	37,862	89,519	443,597
1955	201,350	14,346	19,014	12,161	6,204	11,267	49,390[16]	49,390	413,100
Uganda									
1951	64,868[17]	9,258	23,619	39,063	7,076	4,445	14,329	44,471	207,132[18]
1956	62,034[17]	5,375	24,868	37,107	8,913	5,326	32,384	49,722	225,729[18]
Union of South Africa	700,00[19]	527,991[7]	641,775[20]	147,878[20]	204,090[21]	100,000[19]	300,000[22]	—	—

Source: ILO, African Labour Survey (Geneva, 1958), 667.

[1] Including women and young workers. The figures given for the Belgian Congo, Mozambique, Nigeria, Northern Rhodesia, Nyasaland, Sierra Leone, Southern Rhodesia, Tanganyika and Uganda are for African labour; in other cases the figures are for all labour. [2] Including 39,699 office workers. [3] Including employees in banking and professions. [4] Domestic workers only. [5] General administration and technical services, excluding civil servants. [6] Including cotton ginning and processing of agricultural produce such as tea, sisal and sugar cane. [7] 1950 figures. [8] Domestic workers only (1950 figures). [9] Including fishing. [10] Figures for undertakings employing more than ten workers. [11] Including 20,528 domestic workers. [12] Including 30,805 in domestic service, government and local government, electricity, water and sanitation, etc. [13] Seafarers and dockworkers only. [14] Figures for undertakings employing more than six workers. [15] Including domestic workers (53,874 in 1951, 71,578 in 1956), government and local government, electricity, water, sanitation, etc. [16] Including 30,000 domestic workers. [17] Including cotton ginning, forestry and fishing. [18] Figures for undertakings employing more than five workers. [19] Department of Native Affairs estimates for 1953. Africans only. [20] 1952–53 figures. [21] 1953 figures. [22] Department of Native Affairs estimates for 1953. African domestic workers only.

enterprises. Having seen the capacity of unions to foment discord against colonial administrations, African political leaders worried that trade unions could serve as the vanguard of opposition to their own regimes, especially in the urban centres.[71]

Three elements militated against this. The colonial state, through its policies of registration and welfarism that were only directed towards certain sectors of the economy, had already succeeded in breaking the unity of the working class before the end of the colonial period. Hence, independent African states inherited an already fragmented and increasingly weakened working class. Second, many workers considered 'stabilized' were in fact able to maintain links with rural areas, which continues to this day. This ensured a certain continuously shrinking level of security beyond their jobs. Thus, jobs have been less crucially important for basic survival than for European or American workers, and militancy has suffered. Third, the period of effective strikes in Africa in the final decades of colonialism was coterminous with a period of general economic expansion, whereas the economic contraction that independent African states have experienced has given workers naturally worried about their position in a faltering economy little opportunity to strike. Still, some parts of Africa did experience intense labour conflicts for many years, involving illegal strikes and bloodshed, between trade unions and ruling parties.[72] Even in the 1990s one finds moments when labour mobilization challenged a state.[73]

It should be noted that during the late 1950s, 1960s and into the 1970s, many African countries experienced at least modest growth, life expectancy rose considerably, and education became more accessible. Workers in copper mines or railwaymen, for instance, had reasonable expectations that they could get something out of participation in economic activities. This did not necessarily mean that these workers simply accepted the notion of the European welfare state. They partly invested their salaries in social networks and relationships, often in the rural home areas.[74] When the oil shocks and worldwide recession ate into jobs and pensions, these personal relationships became crucial to survival. In most African countries, the regulated wage

---

[71] Craig Phelan, 'West African Trade Unionism Past and Present', in *Trade Unions in West Africa: Historical and Contemporary Perspectives*, ed. C. Phelan (Oxford: Peter Lang, 2011), 10.

[72] For the case of Senegal, see Babacar Fall, *Le travail au Sénégal au XXe siècle* (Paris: Karthala, 2011).

[73] Julius Ihonvbere, 'Organized Labor and the Struggle for Democracy in Nigeria', *African Studies Review*, 40.1 (1997), 77–100.

[74] Lisa Lindsay, *Working with Gender: Men, Women, and Wage Labor in Southwest Nigeria* (Portsmouth, NH: Heinemann, 2003); Ferguson, *Expectations*.

labour sector contracted. 'Structural adjustment' undermined the very sectors of African economies in which labour had become the most stabilized, and it sharply reduced state services that might have equipped younger generations with the skills they needed for a changing world economy. Instead, international institutions such as the World Bank celebrated the erosion of stable and protected waged employment and the rise of informal activities as pathways to successful entrepreneurship.[75]

The new combination of precariousness and flexibility that has emerged since the 1970s is usually captured by the highly problematic term 'informality'. Informal sectors, however, were often highly structured; there was a considerable movement of people between regular jobs and unregulated income earning, and numerous 'formal sector' companies displayed a strong interest in the interplay of different forms of production. In essence, the term pointed to the continuing and growing 'importance of forms of work that lay outside the form of labour legislation which African countries inherited at independence and outside the limits of the imagination of policy makers who thought they were modernizing Africa'.[76] The number of people who fitted into the category of wage worker in independent Africa did not grow as expected, while it was the category of the excluded – comprising customary labour, informal labour and precarious labour – that largely increased.[77] The recent economic growth of the early years of the twenty-first century has not translated into high levels of waged employment.

It would be misleading to see informal and precarious work as only a new phase in capitalism, in which workers in many parts of the world and most notably in Africa have become unnecessary and disposable. Multinational capital might still need workers from Africa, as long as they are cheap,

---

[75] See the chapter by Barchiesi in this volume.

[76] Cooper, *African Labor History*, 111; also Janet Roitman, 'The Politics of Informal Markets in Sub-Saharan Africa', *Journal of Modern African Studies*, 28.4 (1990), 671–94. For a useful review of the literature on 'informality', see Kate Meagher, *Identity Economics: Social Networks and the Informal Economy in Nigeria* (Woodbridge: James Currey, 2010), 11–26. For critical reflection on the concept, see Jan Breman, 'A Bogus Concept?', *New Left Review*, 84 (2013), 130–8.

[77] Frederick Cooper, 'From Enslavement to Precarity? The Labour Question in African History', in *The Political Economy of Everyday Life in Africa: Beyond the Margins*, ed. Wale Adebanwi (Woodbridge: James Currey, 2017), 152. For recent case studies, see Miles Larmer, 'Permanent Precarity: Capital and Labour in the Central African Copperbelt', *Labor History*, 58.2 (2017), 170–84; Ian Phimister and Rory Pilossof, 'Wage Labor in Historical Perspective: A Study of the De-proletarianization of the African Working Class in Zimbabwe, 1960–2010', *Labor History*, 58.2 (2017), 215–27.

Table 1.2. Wage and salaried workers in sub-Saharan Africa, 2000–10

Country	2000	2001	2002	2003	2004	2005	2006	2007	2008	2009	2010
Angola	33.7	34.3	31.6	32.9	32.2	35.0	37.6	40.5	42.9	44.6	44.5
Benin	10.1	10.1	10.5	10.4	8.5	8.5	8.6	8.6	8.7	8.8	8.6
Botswana	62.1	82.6	75.8	76.2	79.2	79.4	79.8	79.1	80.7	82.1	81.3
Burkina Faso	4.8	5.4	5.8	5.7	5.3	6.1	6.1	5.7	7.1	6.4	6.5
Burundi	5.6	5.5	5.5	5.4	5.3	5.2	5.2	4.9	5.1	5.1	5.1
Cabo Verde	48.7	48.2	48.5	48.7	50.5	51.0	51.5	53.8	54.7	56.0	55.8
Cameroon	20.5	20.8	18.7	18.9	18.7	18.9	19.2	20.3	20.8	21.0	21.1
Central African Republic	30.3	30.8	31.2	31.7	31.0	30.7	31.1	31.4	32.0	31.9	31.8
Chad	4.2	4.3	4.5	4.8	5.1	6.9	7.1	7.1	7.1	7.3	7.4
Congo, Dem. Rep.	15.5	14.8	14.4	14.5	13.9	15.3	15.9	16.4	16.8	17.6	17.7
Congo, Rep.	22.6	23.0	23.2	23.2	22.6	23.4	23.9	24.1	23.7	24.5	25.0
Côte d'Ivoire	21.3	21.4	21.8	21.7	19.6	19.2	19.3	19.1	19.5	19.1	20.5
Equatorial Guinea	56.8	64.5	68.7	69.7	68.2	71.8	72.8	72.7	72.9	74.3	74.5
Eritrea	76.6	78.6	77.2	76.3	76.0	80.8	81.2	80.9	78.2	76.4	78.4
Ethiopia	7.1	7.2	6.8	6.4	6.9	7.9	5.9	6.4	7.5	8.1	8.1
Gabon	44.2	43.7	43.7	43.5	43.7	44.8	66.4	65.9	66.5	65.5	66.2
Gambia, The	22.5	23.4	22.9	23.6	25.6	25.9	23.5	23.0	25.1	26.1	27.4
Ghana	20.9	21.2	21.5	22.2	23.1	23.4	20.4	17.3	18.3	19.3	19.2
Guinea	28.8	29.7	30.5	30.5	31.8	31.8	32.2	33.1	33.3	33.9	31.9
Guinea-Bissau	36.1	34.7	36.3	35.9	35.4	35.9	35.7	35.8	36.9	36.5	37.1
Kenya	34.7	34.2	33.2	33.3	33.2	33.2	31.3	32.2	33.9	34.8	36.7
Lesotho	65.3	65.7	66.0	67.2	67.5	68.2	68.0	69.0	70.4	72.2	73.1
Liberia	17.2	20.2	20.9	19.1	16.1	16.3	16.4	17.1	18.1	18.7	18.8
Madagascar	16.0	15.8	16.9	15.1	9.3	9.4	8.7	8.7	8.9	10.0	9.3

Malawi	33.3	32.7	32.0	32.0	32.7	33.3	33.2	33.2	34.1	35.7	36.3
Mali	9.7	10.3	9.8	11.6	11.9	11.8	11.9	10.3	11.2	11.1	11.6
Mauritania	53.8	53.0	52.2	52.4	53.4	52.6	51.3	54.8	54.8	54.6	52.7
Mauritius	79.4	80.0	79.9	79.9	80.2	80.6	80.8	79.8	80.3	80.2	79.9
Mozambique	7.3	7.2	8.5	9.0	9.2	9.7	10.4	11.0	11.9	12.6	12.8
Namibia	63.8	71.6	72.0	72.2	72.5	62.7	64.1	64.4	64.7	64.4	64.1
Niger	7.2	7.1	7.1	7.2	5.8	5.8	7.3	7.3	7.6	7.4	7.5
Nigeria	54.5	55.0	54.1	56.0	59.9	60.6	61.3	62.0	62.7	63.3	63.5
Rwanda	7.2	7.5	7.8	13.8	14.1	14.5	15.5	15.4	15.6	16.7	16.9
Saõ Tomé and Principe	46.9	47.4	48.0	47.9	47.8	47.8	60.7	62.0	62.1	63.3	63.2
Senegal	22.1	22.3	24.8	26.2	26.2	27.7	27.3	26.7	28.3	29.2	29.5
Seychelles	N/A	N/A	N/A	N/A	N/A	N/A	N/A	N/A	N/A	N/A	N/A
Sierra Leone	6.3	5.5	6.4	7.4	7.4	7.5	7.5	7.9	8.5	8.9	8.9
Somalia	58.4	58.5	58.3	58.1	58.4	59.0	59.9	60.7	60.7	60.9	61.4
South Africa	81.5	81.8	81.9	81.8	81.9	80.9	80.0	82.0	84.4	84.8	84.5
South Sudan	N/A	N/A	N/A	N/A	N/A	N/A	N/A	N/A	N/A	N/A	N/A
Sudan	50.4	51.1	52.1	51.7	51.5	52.3	51.7	52.3	54.0	53.0	53.3
Swaziland	78.4	78.5	78.3	78.6	78.7	78.5	78.8	79.0	79.1	79.0	79.6
Tanzania	6.8	6.9	9.4	9.8	10.3	10.3	10.7	7.5	11.5	12.3	12.6
Togo	26.3	27.0	26.8	25.6	26.1	27.4	26.0	26.3	28.3	25.3	24.9
Uganda	14.6	14.7	14.1	14.7	14.1	14.9	15.7	16.0	16.3	17.7	18.6
Zambia	17.1	17.5	14.7	15.0	15.7	16.5	16.8	16.0	17.5	19.1	19.6
Zimbabwe	39.7	33.5	32.2	30.4	29.1	28.2	27.6	27.2	25.1	23.0	23.8

Source: https://data.worldbank.org/indicator/SL.EMP.WORK.ZS?end=2010&locations=ZG&start=2000 (accessed 29 December 2017)

particularly to reach customers of modest means.[78] Moreover, precarity could be seen as a constitutive feature of capitalist labour, inasmuch as uncertainty and instability have always been inherent characteristics of wage labour, in Africa as elsewhere. Jan Breman and Marcel van der Linden even argue that 'the real norm or standard on global capitalism is insecurity, informality or precariousness'.[79] If this is the case, then Africa in the twentieth century could even be seen as a model case for global capitalism.

[78] Kate Meagher, 'The Scramble for Africans: Demography, Globalisation and Africa's Informal Labour Markets', *Journal of Development Studies*, 52 (2016), 487.

[79] Jan Breman and Marcel van der Linden, 'Informalizing the Economy: The Return of the Social Question at a Global Level', *Development and Change*, 45.5 (2014), 920.

TWO

Precarious and Informal Labour

FRANCO BARCHIESI

Department of African American and African Studies and
Department of Comparative Studies, Ohio State University

The concepts of 'precarity' and 'informality' have become prominent
ways of characterizing the adverse employment impacts of global market
liberalization. In sociological terms, the word 'precariat' is often used to
identify vulnerable populations forced to depend on unprotected and
unstable jobs.[1] By referring to both the insecurity of employment conditions
and related broader social dislocations and inequalities, 'precarity' has tended
to mirror the notion of the 'informal economy', largely applied to societies
in the global South. The International Labour Organization initially used
'informal', with a focus on juridical norms, to define undocumented and
unregulated activities, largely performed as self-employment. More recently,
however, 'informality' has come to characterize unprotected occupations in
a broader sense, or jobs lacking security and social provisions, even when
performed within a legally 'formal' sector or in a subordinate relationship
towards certified enterprises.[2] In older capitalist countries and emerging
economies alike, the expansion of informal employment is crucially shaped
by outsourcing and casualization in established companies, which explains
the conceptual convergence of informality and precariousness.[3] Such changes
decisively question the idea, which played an important role when the notion

[1] Guy Standing, *The Precariat: The New Dangerous Class* (London: Bloomsbury, 2011).

[2] Franco Barchiesi, 'Casual Labor and Informal Economy', in *Sociology of Work: An
    Encyclopedia*, vol. I, ed. Vicki Smith (Thousand Oaks, CA: Sage, 2013), 74–8.

[3] Richard Devey, Caroline Skinner and Imraan Valodia, 'Definitions, Data and the
    Informal Economy in South Africa: A Critical Analysis', in *The Development Decade?
    Economic and Social Change in South Africa, 1994–2004*, ed. Vishnu Padayachee
    (Pretoria: HSRC Press, 2006), 302–23.

of the 'informal sector' first emerged in the 1970s, that a socio-economic dualism exists between waged and irregular employment.

In the early twenty-first century, precarious and informal work have spurred policy interventions and political strategies by labour and social movements. Collective mobilizations of precarious workers have emphasized that wage labour is failing as a conduit to and guarantor of social integration, citizenship rights, redistributive compacts and subjective stability. Yet the alternative, broadly inspired by a once-triumphant Keynesianism, of a harmonious and equitable wage-based social order has also faded as critics of the welfare state point to its environmentally damaging productivism, gender biases in favour of male breadwinning and narrow national focus of citizenship.[4]

To the extent that they question the idea of wage labour as a standard and universal social norm, the concepts of precarity and informality usefully introduce this chapter's discussion of Africa in the twentieth and early twenty-first centuries, a context in which capitalist production regimes have not led to employment relations typically characterized by stable and protected wage earning. The history of precarious, casual and informal labour in Africa rather brings into sharp relief the exceptionality and contingency of the social conditions through which capitalist employment can be conducive to socially inclusive deals. The penetration of wage labour across the continent was uneven, delayed and contested, as it responded to highly localized social processes and coexisted with complex, non-capitalist relations. Even where wages relatively quickly became the dominant form of income, as in mining or transportation nodes in urban centres, African workers chose casual labour, despite its precariousness, in preference to more regular workplace rhythms. Although capital drew significant advantages from such arrangements, which allowed for remarkable flexibility and containment of labour costs, they also persistently challenged capitalist control of the labour force. Finally, work in the capitalist sector was enabled by considerable degrees of coercion, usually carried out by authoritarian colonial states armed with racial ideologies of domination and hierarchical visions of the social order, in which African elders and notables played despotic roles while colonized working populations were relegated to manual labour.

---

[4]   André Gorz, *Reclaiming Work: Beyond the Wage-Based Society* (Cambridge: Polity Press, 1999); Kathi Weeks, *The Problem with Work: Feminism, Marxism, Antiwork Politics, and Postwork Imaginaries* (Durham, NC: Duke University Press 2011); see the chapter by Scully and Jawad in this volume.

Only in late colonial experiments after the Second World War, and mostly in French and British possessions, was the option of 'stabilizing' wage labour through social benefits and the recognition of trade unions pursued, and even then it remained largely confined to more 'formal' employees in the urban areas and did not provide for the entrenchment of democratic rights or political equality.[5] Postcolonial independent states inherited an explosive combination of strong-arm governance, workers' expectations of improved living conditions and persistent refusal or evasion of wage labour, which new African rulers addressed through political solutions that led to further authoritarianism and instability. Even before the devastating impact on workers' lives of the neoliberal structural adjustment programmes of the 1980s, the limited extent of formal employment and the political weakness and subordination of trade unions rendered wage labour unavailable as a foundation of egalitarian and democratic social compacts.

The following pages will outline and analyse the precariousness of African labour in different periods and specific locales. My emphasis on precarity as an enduring condition of wage labour in the continent's history requires a departure from a notion of precarious and informal labour as identified with specific employment relations and actors, such as fast-food workers or street vendors. Labour historians must instead face the challenge of confronting uncertainty and instability as constitutive features of wage relations, whereby compulsion to depend on unrewarding jobs amplifies and deepens the social vulnerability undergirding liberal ideas of 'free' economic conduct.

The rest of this chapter provides therefore a complex historical picture of how precarious, casual, intermittent and unprotected labour has shaped African workers' lives, practices, identities and strategies. The empirical material is structured into four sections. The first (1900–18) is set in the early and contested advance of proletarianization as an explicit project of commodity-producing colonial systems. The second (1919–39) deals with the expansion of casual employment in a context in which the use of forced labour met increasing international opposition, and its complexities at the intersection of the strategies of states, capitalists, local communities and workers. The third (1940–75) is focused on casual and informal employment as responses to, and outcomes of, late colonial and postcolonial attempts to stabilize and discipline wage labour through institutional reforms, social provisions and political coercion. The fourth section (1976–2015) discusses the precariousness of labour in Africa in a period when the 'informal

---

[5]   Frederick Cooper, *Decolonization and African Society: The Labor Question in French and British Africa* (Cambridge: Cambridge University Press, 1996); see the chapter by Freund in this volume.

economy' has become an explicitly formulated social and economic concept and a contested reality between ordinary workers' experiences and attempts by a now triumphant neoliberal discourse to establish informality as a new norm of African entrepreneurship.

THE PRECARIOUSNESS OF WAGE LABOUR AND CONTESTED PROLETARIANIZATION, 1900–18

Under colonial governance and imperatives to produce primary export commodities, wage labour profoundly disrupted and restructured African economic formations and modalities of accumulation. Such impacts were most evident in extractive industries and agricultural sectors where European capital presided over the transition to cash crops, but also affected cultivations, such as cocoa in West Africa, largely introduced by African initiative. Local producers were generally quite resourceful and inventive in adapting, across the continent, pre-colonial social and economic relations to the requirements of colonial capitalism, which African notables and emerging elites could even turn to their advantage. Even the transition from slavery to wage labour, especially in the western and eastern portions of the continent, did not necessarily obliterate the power of slave-holding landlords, as they often managed to mutate into employers of migrant, largely casual or seasonal, workforces. Across these diverse experiences, wage labour was marked by social vulnerability, especially to the extent that the racial ideologies of colonial states defined the African as a natural manual labourer in constant need of white supervision administered through a mix of authoritarian and paternalist means.[6]

In the language of European colonialism, wage labour was not only an economic necessity but also a moral imperative, as colonialism legitimized itself as the continuation of a civilizing move from slavery towards 'free labour'.[7] Yet Africans were institutionally denied the ability to shape or signify their own incorporation into the wage economy. In fact, capitalist work routinely took the form of coerced employment – including 'masters and servants' legislation and measures against vagrancy and 'desertion'

---

[6]   Belinda Bozzoli, *The Political Nature of a Ruling Class: Capital and Ideology in South Africa, 1890–1933* (London: Routledge and Kegan Paul, 1981); Crawford Young, *The African Colonial State in Comparative Perspective* (New Haven, CT: Yale University Press); Opolot Okia, *Communal Labor in Colonial Kenya: The Legitimization of Coercion, 1912–1930* (New York: Palgrave Macmillan, 2012).

[7]   Catherine Hall, *Civilising Subjects: Metropole and Colony in the English Imagination 1830–1867* (Chicago: University of Chicago Press, 2002).

– which blurred the normative divide between 'free' and 'unfree' labour and structured African experiences of working for wages as constitutively and quintessentially precarious. Etymologically, 'precarious' refers to one's uncertainty-generating dependence on the will of another to which, in the absence of alternatives, pleas (*preces*) are addressed. The term thus fits a reality in which not only did colonial exploitation offer very limited opportunities of monetary income as substitutes for low-skill work, but wage labour had a tendency to erode the viability of subsistence agriculture as an independent economic alternative.

When new market opportunities developed, they often took the form of delivering goods and services to emerging areas of waged employment in modalities that would later come to be called the 'informal sector'. African women felt the vulnerabilities generated by the wage economy in particularly acute ways, especially in regions – such as East African estates and central and southern African mining districts – where female roles were increasingly identified with maintaining plots and cattle in rural areas deemed native 'reserves'. The arrangement was advantageous for employers aiming to shift reproduction costs towards African homesteads, but it placed women under specific pressures. Apart from being kept in a subordinate status by the operations of colonial administrators, abetted by African elders and patriarchal discipline, women were still needed in the urban and mining areas where 'working men in the mines and towns, low-paid migrants though they were, still wanted cooked food, clean clothing, and sexual services'.[8] The contradiction inherent in this predicament was often solved by women themselves by escaping male authority in rural areas and moving without authorization to cities where intermittent occupations in the crevices between legality and illegality were available in the form of petty trade, domestic services, sex work, food distribution or brewing.

The existential precariousness of waged work was amplified by the disruptions of migrant labour in African family life, against which the semi-legal world of female urban employment often offered sex work as a simulacrum of domesticity.[9] Female 'prostitution', which in the case of Nairobi as studied by Luise White was almost entirely self-employed, inhabited an indeterminate boundary between exploitation and women's agency in pursuit of autonomous livelihoods. Other routinely criminalized contingent female economic activities – such as hawking, distilling liquor and washing

---

[8]   Teresa A. Barnes, 'The Fight for Control of African Women's Mobility in Colonial Zimbabwe, 1900–1939', *Signs*, 17.3 (1992), 588.

[9]   Luise White, *The Comforts of Home: Prostitution in Colonial Nairobi* (Chicago: University of Chicago Press, 1990).

clothes in the urban and mining areas – defied normative categorizations of 'waged' and 'unwaged' or 'respectable' and 'disreputable' occupations, as they reclaimed a space 'to exist at a distance from the disciplines of time, productivity, and monotony that the more deeply proletarianized sections of the work force were experiencing'.[10] They also provided alternatives to jobs traditionally defined as female, such as housework.

Gender dynamics structured the formation of intermittent urban employment and its multifarious strategies, which ambivalently aided proletarianization while offering income opportunities outside the wage relation. Charles van Onselen documented the significance of masculinity for the *amaWasha*, a guild of Zulu migrant laundry workers in the Witwatersrand gold mines of the early 1900s.[11] The self-employed *amaWasha* were part of an informal economy providing clean clothes or food to a burgeoning and chaotically growing metropolis with still patchy infrastructure and escalating costs of living. Such solutions were temporary, and unregistered laundry operators declined as the sector came under the control of capitalist firms, even if informal food distribution would prove more resilient. Yet while they lasted, these economic modalities were integral to broader, usually unpredictable and often illegal social practices of evasion of wage labour, such as the 'ninevites' and other urban gangs, also studied by van Onselen in Johannesburg. Although the underlying subjectivity was generally apolitical, it was nonetheless steeped in widespread aversion to the labour regime with which a segregationist state attempted to shape African workforces.

Much historical research on precarious work and casual employment is focused on South Africa, especially in light of the linkages between those sectors and the country's early capitalist industrialization and wage economy. South African processes were not, however, exceptional or uncommon on a continent-wide scale. In general, early colonialism heralded a pattern destined to shape twentieth-century African labour history: African workers did not necessarily become a 'working class' in order to confront capital and the state, especially to the extent that their societies were only partially and unevenly incorporated in circuits of capitalist production and exchange.[12] Casual, impermanent, undetected occupations at the crossroads of multiple economic activities and forms of livelihood provided opportunities to *resist*

---

[10] Belinda Bozzoli, *Women of Phokeng: Consciousness, Life Strategy and Migrancy in South Africa, 1900–1983* (Johannesburg: Ravan Press, 1991), 145.

[11] Charles van Onselen, *New Babylon, New Nineveh: Everyday Life on the Witwatersrand, 1886–1914*, 2nd edn (Johannesburg: Jonathan Ball, 2001).

[12] Frederick Cooper, 'Africa and the World Economy', *African Studies Review*, 24.2/3 (1981), 1–86.

incorporation into waged employment and develop alternative identities, strategies and demands. Working conditions that Western, labour-centred social compacts would negatively connote as 'precarious' – for example, the simultaneous performance of contingent employment, informal trade and a temporary waged occupation – were widespread in early colonial capitalism. Such combinations could facilitate value extraction, although they usually implied for the employers some loss of authority in the production process. Colonial policies sustained exploitation by offloading workers' living costs on to household-based agriculture, which was nonetheless also a buffer allowing workers to negotiate, delay or oppose entrance into capitalist production relations. In the end, 'casual labor – the work men could do a few days a week or a month to eke out a living – might have been exploited, but it was beyond employers' control'.[13] The persistence of casual employment suggested that wage labour did not advance uniformly; workers could prefer it as an alternative to forced labour, but also resisted it by choosing 'precarious' jobs.[14] The penetration of wage labour was neither the outcome of a higher form of economic rationality nor a linear and logical movement, dictated by income and productivity differentials, from pre-capitalist to capitalist production. Colonized populations were rather pushed towards wage labour by a mix of economic coercion, land expropriation, taxation and unequal access to capital and infrastructures. Even in a relatively capitalized business, such as copper mining in Katanga,[15] the oppressive conditions of which made African labour recruitment an almost insurmountable challenge, it was casual rather than 'permanent' work that opened vast tracts of territory to capitalist production relations. Capitalist labour markets and African participation in them took a predictable course, as Cooper put it, 'only after the game was over',[16] or once the erosion of independent peasant production had eliminated all viable economic alternatives to working for wages.

Migrant labour in mining, transportation and commercial agriculture underpinned the overlap and mutual imbrication of casual and regular work.[17]

---

[13] Luise White, 'Cars Out of Place: Vampires, Technology, and Labor in East and Central Africa', in *Tensions of Empire: Colonial Cultures in a Bourgeois World*, ed. Frederick Cooper and Ann Laura Stoler (Berkeley, CA: University of California Press, 1997), 437.

[14] On precarious workers in the urban transport sector, see the chapter by Bellucci in this volume.

[15] John Higginson, *A Working Class in the Making: Belgian Colonial Labor Policy, Private Enterprise, and the African Mineworker, 1907–1951* (Madison, WI: University of Wisconsin Press, 1989), 29.

[16] Cooper, 'Africa and the World Economy', 40.

[17] See the chapter by Pérez Niño in this volume.

Mozambican miners, who made up more than two-thirds of the workforce for the Witwatersrand gold mining industry, toiled under oppressive labour contracts in a racially despotic environment. For them, therefore, the defence of a deeply embattled peasant agriculture, not proletarianization, was the main conduit to agency and identity.[18] In fact, in southern Mozambique – where by the late nineteenth-century Portuguese anti-vagrancy provisions had legally imposed work as the core means of African subsistence, and Africans subject to *indigenato* statutes could be inducted into forced labour – migration to South Africa was not the only escape. The Chopi night soil collectors studied by Jeanne Penvenne, for example, preferred precarious work in the city.[19] The female-headed households of male migrants provided casual work (*ganho-ganho*) for commercial farming, which led to renewed exploitation as older women employed their daughters-in-law, thus reproducing precarity along gender and age lines.[20]

In West African cash-crop agriculture, migratory flows were facilitated by the gradual abolition of slavery but did not result in a smooth transition to 'free' labour, rather remaining in a precarious balance of continuity and change.[21] British and French administrations outlawed slavery and ended the slave trade, but also allowed in their possessions the persistence of practices of personal servitude, which only became marginal in the 1930s. In the early twentieth century, massive movements towards areas fallen under European control, such as the Sokoto caliphate in northern Nigeria, involved perhaps more than one million former slaves seeking in commodity production an escape from their masters.[22] Former slave holders, however, often restructured themselves, also with the aid of new colonial administrators, into large landlords. Lord Lugard, the British High Commissioner in northern Nigeria, was concerned that a direct transition from slavery to wage labour could encourage casual work or subsistence farming, which he regarded as

---

[18] Patrick Harries, *Work, Culture, and Identity: Migrant Laborers in Mozambique and South Africa, c.1860–1910* (Portsmouth, NH: Heinemann, 1994).

[19] Jeanne Penvenne, *African Workers and Colonial Racism: Mozambican Strategies and Struggles in Lourenco Marques, 1877–1962* (Portsmouth, NH: Heinemann, 1995).

[20] Bridget O'Laughlin, 'Proletarianisation, Agency and Changing Rural Livelihoods: Forced Labour and Resistance in Colonial Mozambique', *Journal of Southern African Studies*, 28.3 (2002), 511–30.

[21] Dennis Cordell, *Hoe and Wage: A Social History of a Circulatory Migration System in West Africa* (Boulder, CO: Westview Press, 1996); Thomas J. Bassett, *The Peasant Cotton Revolution in West Africa: Côte d'Ivoire, 1880–1995* (Cambridge: Cambridge University Press, 2001).

[22] Martin A. Klein, *Slavery and Colonial Rule in French West Africa* (Cambridge: Cambridge University Press, 1998).

recipes for idleness and sloth. He thus envisaged a system of reconstituted labour coercion in which old masters would remain in control of their slaves even if personal servitude would no longer be recognized or enforced in European courts.[23]

Rather than abruptly disappearing with the advent of cash crops, slavery in West Africa blurred into, and overlapped with, different types of precarious labour, in the literal sense of employment depending, often coercively, on personal subjection. Only gradually and unevenly did the production of export commodities lead to actual labour contracts. In the cocoa cultivations of the Ashanti territory of the Gold Coast, where slavery was finally abolished in 1908, colonial policy was explicitly aimed at labour recruitment from populations forced to move from the north. Migrants, even those who managed to establish their own small-scale cocoa cultivations, worked as casual, seasonal or task labourers on African-owned estates, which benefited from this early experiment with the state-assisted deployment of precarious wage labour.[24] Entrenched reluctance to working for wages in Ashanti, on the other hand, pushed wages to levels that made only casual work viable as a non-slave labour market.[25] Temporary agricultural labourers were not only employed in cultivation. Migrants to northern Nigeria from the Ader region of southern Niger performed a range of casual jobs, such as water and wood carrying or household goods' repairs, necessary to the reproduction of the workforce. Labour mobility and flexibility offset the risks of highly uncertain employment prospects, but also determined new vulnerabilities. Itinerant workers of slave descent lacked juridical status or rights, which made their survival depend on networks of patronage. Yet despite its precariousness, migrant labour could produce new solidarities and refashioned ethnic identities.[26]

Even in sectors where wage labour was more straightforwardly established, such as the Enugu colliery in Nigeria's Igboland, studied by Carolyn Brown, local labour recruiters often came from former slave-trading families, which reinforced resistance to proletarianization by migrant

---

[23] Louise D. Lennihan, 'Rights in Men and Rights in Land: Slavery, Wage Labor, and Smallholder Agriculture in Northern Nigeria', *Slavery & Abolition*, 3.2 (1982), 111–39.

[24] Gareth Austin, *Labour, Land, and Capital in Ghana: From Slavery to Free Labour in Asante, 1807–1956* (Rochester, NY: University of Rochester Press, 2005).

[25] Gareth Austin, 'Cash Crops and Freedom: Export Agriculture and the Decline of Slavery in Colonial West Africa', *International Review of Social History*, 54.1 (2009), 12–14.

[26] Benedetta Rossi, 'Migration and Emancipation in West Africa's Labour History: The Missing Links', *Slavery & Abolition*, 35.1 (2014), 23–46.

outsiders for whom wage earning was a continuation of slavery.[27] Therefore, until the 1920s, workers' protests consisted of desertion and withdrawal to village economies as much as strike action. Across the region, former slaves hired as waged employees hardly fit the description of proletarians as they maintained some access to households' land and cattle. As in the case of mining, the impermanence and precariousness of waged work in export agriculture satisfied capitalist accumulation but also offered African labourers opportunities to resist working for wages.

Plantation systems in East Africa confirmed the emerging pattern thus far noticed, in which workers used uncertainty and instability as weapons to negotiate or subvert wage labour. Cooper's landmark analysis of the end of slavery in Kenya and Zanzibar showed that indigenous farmers participated in the capitalist economy largely as day labourers, which allowed for the survival of independent agriculture for local markets.[28] 'Squatting' was also a way for migrants to preserve plots of their own. Before the First World War, Kenya's developing European-owned tea and coffee estates attempted a shift in modes of exploitation of African labour from rent extraction from semi-independent cultivators ('kaffir farming') to the use of 'squatters' as labourers residing within European properties and often employed in temporary and even casual occupations such as bush clearing.[29] Similarly to other forms of contingent employment, then, squatting served the landlords' cost-cutting goals by keeping wages low and avoiding expensive recruitment from labour reserves, while providing casual workers with income sources in preference to wage labour.

As in West Africa, East Africa's former slave societies knew no uniform economic logic driving workers into waged employment. Similarly to northern Nigeria, British rule in the Sudan opposed immediate and full slave emancipation and boosted the masters' claims, often legitimized by the use of Islamic legal codes, to their servants' subjugation. Yet escaping slaves sought autonomy not in 'free' labour contracts but in the casual and informal jobs of a blossoming urban society.[30] Coercion accompanied the development of cash crops across the region, but also stimulated labour migration in search

---

[27] Carolyn A. Brown, *'We Were All Slaves': African Miners, Culture, and Resistance at the Enugu Government Colliery* (Portsmouth, NH: Heinemann, 2003).

[28] Frederick Cooper, *From Slaves to Squatters: Plantation Labor and Agriculture in Zanzibar and Coastal Kenya, 1890–1925* (New Haven, CT: Yale University Press, 1980).

[29] John Overton, 'The Origins of the Kikuyu Land Problem: Land Alienation and Land Use in Kiambu, Kenya, 1895–1920', *African Studies Review*, 31.2 (1988), 109–26.

[30] Ahmad A. Sikainga, *Slaves into Workers: Emancipation and Labor in Colonial Sudan* (Austin, TX: University of Texas Press, 1996).

of independent income opportunities. German authorities in Tanganyika extensively used servile and forced labour in sisal plantations, which often hired slaves on a seasonal basis from Indian or Arab intermediaries.[31] In Ethiopia, a fragile imperial state, albeit committed to abolition, could not stop the revival of slave raiding in the 1910s or the aggressive strategies of surplus extraction by Abyssinian aristocrats enforcing labour *corvées* to cater for the global demand for coffee grown in recently conquered southern territories. Precarious working conditions also resulted from the attempt of incoming settlers to turn former rent-paying tenants into wage labourers.[32] In response to worsening living and working conditions, peasants in the south-west of the country embraced *shifta* banditry as a form of rebellion and surplus reappropriation. In the eastern and western parts of the continent, then, abolition seldom meant stable economic opportunities, land access and bargaining power for the formerly enslaved. Their continuing precariousness reflected severely constrained options, belying the image of a simple, linear transition from 'unfree' to 'free' labour.

The development of monocultures for export, with or without plantation-type economies, also underscored the precariousness of employment – extending from rural to urban areas – in North Africa. Egypt's growth was driven by cotton grown on land owned by local landlords but coming increasingly under the pressure of foreign financial institutions. The resulting squeeze on tenants contributed to a situation in which, by 1907, 90 per cent of rural families had no or inadequate land for subsistence. Migration was a recurrent solution, but also reproduced gendered hierarchies, as men chose to leave rural waged jobs at 'women's rates'.[33] Many sought employment in the cities, where the most likely outlets were informal work as pushcart vendors or self-employed transport operators, or temporary and casual jobs in the docks or construction sites, where workers were hired by contractors (*khawli*) also operating as moneylenders, thus pushing precarious labourers towards debt peonage.[34] Since very few enterprises, such as the railways or the Suez Canal,

---

[31] Jan-Georg Deutsch, *Emancipation without Abolition in German East Africa, c. 1884–1914* (Oxford/Athens, OH: James Currey/Ohio University Press, 2006); Hanan Sabea, 'Mastering the Landscape? Sisal Plantations, Land, and Labor in Tanga Region, 1893–1980s', *International Journal of African Historical Studies*, 41.3 (2008), 411–32.

[32] Timothy D. Fernyhough, *Serfs, Slaves and Shifta: Modes of Production and Resistance in Pre-Revolutionary Ethiopia* (Addis Ababa: Shama Books, 2010).

[33] James Toth, 'Pride, Purdah, or Paychecks: What Maintains the Gender Division of Labor in Rural Egypt?', *International Journal of Middle East Studies*, 23.2 (1991), 213–36.

[34] Joel Beinin and Zachary Lockman, *Workers on the Nile: Nationalism, Communism, Islam, and the Egyptian Working Class, 1882–1954* (Princeton, NJ: Princeton University Press, 1987), 24–5.

had large contingents of regular waged employees, the oppressive labour contracting system, which became the target of early strike actions, absorbed many who held little hope of jobs in eroded and degraded artisanal production. Old craft 'guilds', which had once played an important fiscal role in the now declining Ottoman state, collapsed, while small workshops of shoemakers, tanners or blacksmiths joined informal barbers or laundry workers in a still prosperous yet increasingly embattled *bazaar* economy. Craft traditions survived among highly skilled artisans, while a section of former guilds' *shaykhs* became labour contractors, thereby shifting downward the precariousness of a rapidly changing world of work that they themselves experienced.

In North Africa, however, as in the rest of the continent, the instability of the workforce served both employers' needs and employees' strategies. Peasants resisted proletarianization by clinging to their plots while entering urban employment (as in Egypt) or by migrating away from plantations on expropriated land (as in Algeria) or work in the mines (as in Morocco's phosphate industry). A preferred alternative was unskilled casual work in the railways and ports run by the Société Sfax Gafsa in Tunisia. The precariousness of city jobs was, nonetheless, heightened by the fact that Spanish, Italian and Greek nationals controlled skilled and high-waged unskilled positions, especially in construction, cigarette making or carpentry.[35] Despite the absence of colour bars as in South Africa, non-European employees were pushed into low-wage and insecure occupations whose vulnerability was ensured by the colonial use of 'native law' to curtail the labour rights of Muslim subjects.

Colonial North Africa mirrored, however, the labour landscape of the opposite end of the continent to the extent that precarious and informal labour found new impetus in the process of urbanization. The next section will show how the expansion of casual employment in the interwar years brought new opportunities for workers to contest wage labour discipline, thereby amplifying the instability and precarity of the colonial economy.

URBANIZATION AND CASUAL WORK, 1919–39

After the First World War coercive labour regimes came under increasing international scrutiny and sanction, especially with the 1926 Slavery Convention and the 1930 ILO Forced Labour Convention. Although colonial

---

[35] Claude Liauzu, 'The History of Labor and the Workers' Movement in North Africa', in *The Social History of Labor in the Middle East*, ed. Ellis J. Goldberg (Boulder, CO: Westview Press, 1996), 163–92.

powers continued to practise forced labour by delaying the ratification of the conventions (for example, Belgium and Portugal) and exploiting exceptions and loopholes in the ILO statutes, capitalist accumulation also confronted the challenge of managing the formation of waged employment, not only in export agriculture and raw materials but in cities whose functions as transportation nodes had expanded in wartime. Urbanization seemed to promise new opportunities and alternative sources of livelihood for Africans, especially when escaping compulsory and precarious work in the rural areas. The urban jobs available were, nonetheless, inadequate to satisfy demand, forcing many residents, often with uncertain property or tenure rights, to eke out their survival in largely unregulated small-scale manufacturing, service or trade. In the early 1930s the negative impacts of the Great Depression on African exports only exacerbated the predicament of precarious urban sectors, while swelling their size.

British and French strategies of managing urbanization generally regarded casual employment as preferable to the formation of a permanent, city-based working class. The contingent nature of most urban jobs open to Africans served the goals of colonial policymakers, as did the linkages that urban workers maintained with rural networks of production and income and the African migrants' reluctance to move permanently to the cities.[36] Among major employers of African workers, the shipping industry had highly mutable schedules, depending on variable commodity flows, while municipalities reserved only the most unskilled operations to 'natives'.[37]

Occupational, and sometimes legal, segregation, the break-up of migrants' families, inadequate housing, utilities and infrastructures, and gendered productive hierarchies determined the fundamental fragility of urban African employment. Yet casual and informal workers were not mere victims of socio-economic forces. In 'settler' colonies and labour reserves, whose rural productions were increasingly unable to provide the youth with the means to personal and family independence, urban employment was an opportunity to earn bride payments outside the control of headmen, who rather used their influence to recruit labourers for the mines or agricultural estates. The city could thus become a repository for alternative cultural norms and social

[36] James Ferguson, *Expectations of Modernity: Myths and Meanings of Urban Life on the Zambian Copperbelt* (Berkeley, CA: University of California Press, 1999).

[37] Justin Willis, '"Men on the Spot", Labor, and the Colonial State in British East Africa: The Mombasa Water Supply, 1911–1917', *International Journal of African Historical Studies*, 28.1 (1995), 25–48.

practices, which were also ridden with conflict.[38] South African studies have shown that, as older generations of migrants saw in the ethics of regular work an avenue to stability and recognition in urban areas, they also regarded their respectability as threatened by younger arrivals who preferred casual occupations and were often stereotyped as criminals.[39]

Alarm at the criminality of the urban 'underclass' was deeply connected, in the mind of colonial administrators, to the imperative of controlling masses of precarious workers whose urban lifestyles had lost the restraints of 'tribal' life while remaining recalcitrant to white rule. In the case of Dar es Salaam, whose population rapidly increased after Tanganyika passed from German to British rule, Burton shows that by the early 1930s the most common urban occupations for Africans were domestic servants, self-employed petty traders or service providers – such as hawkers selling fish, vegetables, milk and charcoal by the roadside or carpenters, water carriers and rickshaw operators – and unskilled or casual labourers, especially in the docks and the city government.[40] The state's criminalization and repression of those engaged in these contingent and informal jobs, which threatened to escape official controls, exacerbated their precariousness.[41] By the 1940s the word *wahuni* was used to negatively connote casual workers as well as wandering and shiftless vagrants. Locatelli's work on Eritrea, a society where wage labour was much more widespread than elsewhere in East Africa, similarly points out that colonial authorities defined criminals as a quasi-anthropological category defined by an aversion to regular work.[42]

The regulation of informality and casualization was therefore for colonial authorities not only an economic matter of value extraction but also a political issue of social control. Cooper's celebrated study of dockworkers in Mombasa demonstrated that casual workers were attracted to the port by the

[38] Frederick Cooper, 'Urban Space, Industrial Time, and Wage Labor in Africa', in *Struggle for the City: Migrant Labor, Capital, and the State in Urban Africa*, ed. Frederick Cooper (Beverly Hills, CA: Sage, 1983), 7–51.

[39] Jeff Guy and Motlatsi Thabane, 'The Ma-Rashea: A Participant's Perspective', in *Class, Community and Conflict: South African Perspectives*, ed. Belinda Bozzoli (Johannesburg: Ravan Press, 1987), 436–56; David Goodhew, 'Working-Class Respectability: The Example of the Western Areas of Johannesburg, 1930–55', *Journal of African History*, 41.2 (2000), 241–66.

[40] Andrew Burton, *African Underclass: Urbanisation, Crime and Colonial Order in Dar es Salaam, 1919–1961* (Athens, OH: Ohio University Press, 2005).

[41] See the chapter by Fourchard in this volume.

[42] Francesca Locatelli, '"Oziosi, Vagabondi e Pregiudicati": Labor, Law, and Crime in Colonial Asmara, 1890–1941', *International Journal of African Historical Studies*, 40.2 (2007), 225–50.

employers' preference for day labourers over unskilled contract employees.[43] Yet local officials were afraid that large numbers of casual workers could turn into a semi-employed or unemployed 'underclass'. Attempts to formally register the docks' labour force followed its spectacular expansion in the wake of the First World War, but casual workers resisted or evaded registration, often with the connivance of African gang leaders. Even when contingent employment dried up during the Great Depression, African dockworkers preferred casual jobs, which escaped capital's tight control of workers' lives and allowed the maintenance of rural income sources. Only by the 1940s, after casual workers had started to organize and strike, did the Kenyan colonial state regard contingent labour and migrant work as threats to be minimized through a mix of repression and social policies geared at stabilizing a more predictable, full-time, waged working class.

In the interwar years, precarity in urban jobs and commercial agriculture reinforced each other, and both informed the agency of casual and informal workers. In Tanganyika, a 1923 masters and servants ordinance envisaged a strengthening of wage labour in sisal plantations by punishing vagrancy and constraining workers' mobility. Yet as the country's officially recorded waged labour force rose from 172,000 in 1913 to 435,000 in 1954, the vast majority remained, by the Second World War, 'non-attested', or not recruited through written contracts (*manamba*), which workers considered akin to slavery. 'Non-attested' labourers, women in large numbers, preferred work as casuals on tea and coffee plantations or clearing and weeding land for sisal, activities compatible with small village farming by unwaged household labour.[44]

In Kenya, by the late 1920s, between half and 75 per cent of the African agrarian workforce was estimated to be engaged in waged employment for at least part of the year. Yet 'squatting' remained widespread, as it allowed European estates access to large numbers of cheap casual or temporary workers, even if capital's recognition of limited and precarious forms of African agriculture reduced white settler control of the labour force.[45] For Kikuyu peasants, 'squatting' was, on the other hand, a form of precariousness far preferable to the labour reserves and coerced migration under the *kipande* system. In the reserves, broken households and inadequate prospects for

[43] Frederick Cooper, *On the African Waterfront: Urban Disorder and the Transformation of Work in Colonial Mombasa* (New Haven, CT: Yale University Press, 1987).

[44] Marjorie Mbilinyi, 'Agribusiness and Casual Labor in Tanzania', *African Economic History*, 15 (1986), 107–41.

[45] Bruce J. Berman and John M. Lonsdale, 'Crises of Accumulation, Coercion and the Colonial State: The Development of the Labor Control System in Kenya, 1919–1929', *Canadian Journal of African Studies*, 14.1 (1980), 66–7.

rural subsistence also forced women into poorly paid casual employment for neighbouring better-off families.[46] Although Kenya may be regarded as a case of specific rural hardship, colonial attempts to improve and stabilize African agricultural work did not make it less precarious. The Gezira scheme in Sudan, started in 1925, was the most ambitious project of colonial social engineering to date, and responded to African refusal to work for wages, which had undermined plans for settler-owned cotton estates. The project lured African peasants into irrigated tenant farming through protected and inheritable occupancy rights. Yet compulsory production requirements exposed African growers to large debts, while heavy taxation eroded their autonomy.[47] In the end, despite the increasing use of incentives aimed at stimulating the peasants' economic initiative, forced cotton cultivation expanded dramatically in the interwar period throughout Congo, northern Mozambique and French West Africa, providing new stimulus to the movement of casual and informal workers to the cities.

In the rapidly growing urban areas, it was usually difficult to differentiate between casual work or precarious occupations and wage labour as such. African wages were low across the board, as colonial policies assumed that migrants were 'target' workers looking for short-term jobs to satisfy elementary needs. Employers took advantage of rural households, imagined as rudimentary social safety nets, to cut wages and deny benefits. In the port city of Lagos, where by 1931 almost 60 per cent of residents were rural migrants,[48] only 10 per cent of workers on the railways, a major employer of wage labour, were considered 'permanent establishment', with monthly salaries and limited benefits. Official statistics did not distinguish permanent from casual labour, and the vast majority of senior waged workers were 'daily rated', hence legally hired as casuals with little or no job security.[49] Yet, similarly to the Kenyan case, casual work on the Lagos docks did not

---

[46] Gavin N. Kitching, *Class and Economic Change in Kenya: The Making of an African Petite Bourgeoisie 1905–1970* (New Haven, CT: Yale University Press, 1980), 50.

[47] Victoria Bernal, 'Cotton and Colonial Order in Sudan: A Social History with Emphasis on the Gezira Scheme', in *Cotton, Colonialism, and Social History in Sub-Saharan Africa*, ed. Allen F. Isaacman and Richard L. Roberts (Portsmouth, NH: Heinemann 1995), 96–118.

[48] Ayodeji Olukoju, 'The Travails of Migrant and Wage Labour in the Lagos Metropolitan Area in the Inter-War Years', *Labour History Review*, 61.1 (1996), 51.

[49] Lisa A. Lindsay, *Working with Gender: Wage Labor and Social Change in Southwestern Nigeria* (Portsmouth, NH: Heinemann, 2003), 54–55.

necessarily dampen working-class consciousness, which drew strength from rural as well as urban claims.[50]

The development of self-employed petty trade, along lines that would later be defined as the 'informal sector', catered to the needs of migrants and nascent working classes for cheap food staples, but also extended urban precarity beyond wage labour. Women played, across the continent, prominent roles in small-scale commerce, which had roots in pre-colonial food economies.[51] Thus, in Ghana, urban 'market women' seized economic opportunities as Asante men moved into cocoa farming and waged work, but could also benefit from long-standing cultural and family norms allowing for some autonomous female legal status.[52] The strengthening of women's economic independence in the context of expanding urban markets could also lead, however, to gender conflicts over the control of such assets.[53] The economic empowerment that resulted for women from informal markets was far from widespread. In cases such as Ghana or Côte d'Ivoire, the hire of seasonal migrants from arid northern regions boosted, especially after the First World War, an expanding, small-scale, cash-crop sector, allowing women to focus on food production and exchange. But in south-eastern and south-western Nigeria, work in commercial agriculture was increasingly done by local women and youth, who had previously spurned this activity. While in the early 1930s two-thirds of all casual labour in Yorubaland was performed by locals,[54] female trade in food, handicrafts and bush products was concentrated in less prosperous rural areas near cash-crop cultivations.

In southern Africa, urban casual and informal activities were most markedly reconfigured as sites of insecurity and gender inequality. The white-ruled segregationist states in Southern Rhodesia and the Union of South Africa presided over a society-wide enforcement of black precariousness. Salisbury's African location was designed to control its vast 'native' population, nearly half of which had arrived from neighbouring colonies. Limited income opportunities, in domestic services or self-employed

[50] Peter Waterman, *Division and Unity among Nigerian Workers: Lagos Port Unionism, 1940s–1960s* (The Hague: Institute for Social Studies, 1982).

[51] Claire C. Robertson, 'Invisible Workers: African Women and the Problem of the Self-Employed in Labour History', *Journal of Asian and African Studies*, 23.1–2 (1988), 180–200; Claire C. Robertson, *Trouble Showed the Way: Women, Men, and Trade in the Nairobi Area, 1890–1990* (Bloomington, IN: Indiana University Press, 1997).

[52] Bill Freund, *The African Worker* (Cambridge: Cambridge University Press, 1988), 82–7.

[53] Gracia Clark, *Onions are My Husband: Survival and Accumulation by West African Market Women* (Chicago: University of Chicago Press, 1997).

[54] John Iliffe, *The African Poor: A History* (Cambridge: Cambridge University Press, 1987), 151–2.

brewing or urban gardening and cattle herding, reflected the social volatility of unregulated and informal settlements. Rather than an orderly site for the reproduction of wage labour, the location was a repository of resistive politics, steeped in rural and urban cultural formations and amplified by soccer clubs, mutual aid societies and *beni* dance associations, which challenged easy categorizations of 'proletarian' identities.[55]

In South Africa, legislation passed in the 1920s allowed municipalities to deport non-white residents to racially segregated 'locations', as African workers were cast as temporary sojourners in 'white' cities. It was a system of institutionalized precariousness tying black urban residence to labour contracts in highly insecure, poorly remunerated jobs. Occupational racial segregation, officially termed 'civilized labour' policy in 1924, restricted black employment prospects, as whites-only jobs were created through publicly owned enterprises in transportation, electricity and steel. Precarious and low-wage jobs in the city or informal activities in the African locations reflected therefore the transient state of black urban life that the racial state intended. Most occupations were exploitative, vulnerable and, as in the case of domestic work, socially fragmented, which impeded the type of collective organizing that precarious workers were capable of elsewhere in the continent.[56] Yet African urbanization proved a far more complex challenge than white social engineers envisaged. Youth escaping work in the mines and women leaving impoverished rural reserves moved to the cities, usually in defiance of legal restrictions and police repression. Self-employed women were especially stigmatized as disorderly and immoral, since they challenged the authority of state institutions and African notables seeking to confine African females to the tasks of rural reproduction.[57] Women's informal work thus thrived in the crevices between legality and illegality, sustaining the world of shebeens, the liquor trade and sex work.[58] Unwaged work also underpinned, however, defiant cultural repertoires responding to the oppressive conditions under which Africans entered wage labour.

[55]   Tsuneo Yoshikuni, *African Urban Experiences in Colonial Zimbabwe: A Social History of Harare before 1925* (Harare: Weaver Press, 2007).

[56]   Jacklyn Cock, *Maids and Madams: A Study in the Politics of Exploitation* (Johannesburg: Ravan Press, 1980); see the chapter by Bryceson in this volume.

[57]   Philip L. Bonner, '"Desirable or Undesirable Basotho Women?" Liquor, Prostitution and the Migration of Basotho Women to the Rand, 1920–1945', in *Women and Gender in Southern Africa to 1945*, ed. Cherryl Walker (Cape Town/London: David Philip/James Currey, 1990), 221–50.

[58]   Christian M. Rogerson and D. M. Hart, 'The Survival of the "Informal Sector": The Shebeens of Black Johannesburg', *GeoJournal*, 12.2 (1986), 153–66.

UNCERTAIN WORLDS OF WORK THROUGH WAR, DECOLONIZATION AND INDEPENDENCE, 1940–75

During the Second World War and in the immediate post-war period, surging African working-class organization and action exemplified the socio-economic importance of urban waged workers. According to Freund, it was at this time that an actual African proletariat emerged as a political force.[59] The war requirements of the Western powers led to further exploitation and worsening living conditions for African workers, triggering unprecedented strike waves in Dar es Salaam, Mombasa, Freetown and the Gold Coast. Nigeria was affected by a general strike in 1945, protesting South African mineworkers faced deadly police repression in 1946, and railway workers in French West Africa spectacularly struck in 1947. It was not only formal trade union organizations, however, that spurred industrial action but also casual and precarious workers with little hope of advancement under colonial capitalism. While full-time, relatively secure jobs were reserved to a minority, Cooper writes:

> Capital and the state had not created a reserve army of the unemployed, but a guerrilla army of the underemployed. Employers fought to establish control with restrictive contracts, pass laws, compounds, and oppressive supervision; workers fought back with desertion, slow downs, and efforts to shape their own work rhythms and social structures.[60]

Facing the challenges of domestic reconstruction, France and Great Britain responded to African workers' insurgency by lessening repression and attempting reforms geared at 'stabilizing' urban waged populations.[61] No longer seen only as a threat, the African working class was then represented, in the imagination of colonial administrators, as a potential partner for development. In the late 1940s and early 1950s, the French government abolished forced labour and extended to some colonized workers the protections of the Labour Code. Britain's Colonial Office envisaged the recognition of African trade unions as a move towards a modern system of industrial relations, which London often fostered against considerable opposition from local officials and settler opinion.[62] The last legal vestiges of forced labour disappeared by 1961, when they were relinquished even by conservative Portuguese colonialism.

---

[59] Freund, *The African Worker*, 37.

[60] Cooper, 'Africa and the World Economy', 41.

[61] Cooper, *Decolonization and African Society*.

[62] Andreas Eckert, 'Regulating the Social: Social Security, Social Welfare and the State in Late Colonial Tanzania', *Journal of African History*, 45.3 (2004), 467–89.

Late colonial reforms were, nonetheless, noticeably limited and emerged not so much as a result of comprehensive capitalist planning (despite exceptions such as the Zambian Copperbelt) but as patchy and unevenly implemented legal measures. European governments wanted to reduce their financial exposure and maximize the economic usefulness of their colonies; thus benefits such as retirement, family allowances, medical aid or collective bargaining were reserved to officially recorded, urban waged workers, deemed to be actual 'employees', and disregarded informal and rural activities. The stabilization of portions of waged employment in transportation, local government or limited manufacturing industries reinforced, as a result, the precariousness of wage labour for most African commodity producers.

An important contradiction became evident. On one hand, the labour stabilization agenda was determined by the struggles of precarious workers to a far greater extent than in the coterminous welfarist experiments in western Europe, which were rather shaped by established working-class organizations. On the other hand, late colonial reforms elevated the model of full-time wage labour into a norm of social order, individual conduct and family relations, which hardly corresponded to the material experiences and practices of casual and informal workers. In the context of decolonization, that contradiction heralded the labour problems that independent rulers would face. Like late colonial governments, the postcolonial nation state showed little concern for casual or informal workers. Instead,

> the world of shanty towns, of corner stalls and makeshift sweatshops, of women selling little packets of flavouring for stew, individual cigarettes and bars of soap did not belong to the structures that it proposed and planned. It was supposed to be a mark of backwardness and a temporary phenomenon only.[63]

Several independent governments kept in their statutes legislation against 'vagrancy' or for the recruitment of 'emergency' labour, which the French and the British had used to justify coercive employment even after the abolition of forced labour.[64] Authoritarian regimes committed to nation building glorified waged employment, yet, as they subjugated trade unions and confronted widespread poverty, made it impossible for wage earning to foster societal cohesion and progressive social compacts.

---

[63] Freund, *The African Worker*, 75.

[64] Alexander Keese, 'Slow Abolition within the Colonial Mind: British and French Debates about "Vagrancy", "African Laziness", and Forced Labour in West Central and South Central Africa, 1945–1965', *International Review of Social History*, 59.3 (2014), 377–407.

The shift towards 'stabilization' in late colonial and postcolonial policies signalled new official concerns with urban informal and casual workers, increasingly depicted as troubling elements liable to degenerate into 'dangerous' classes. In Dar es Salaam, street vending, begging or alcohol production and distribution, in defiance of ordinances against 'native liquor', fed the government's crime scare, resulting in the second half of the 1950s in the deportation of 'undesirables' from the city.[65] Yet official statistics documented that labour in the colony remained 'largely agricultural, unspecialized and impermanent'. Despite projects such as the Groundnut Scheme in the Southern Province, by 1952 only one seventeenth of the total African population in Tanganyika was recorded as 'employees', 20 per cent of whom were in casual positions.[66] The precariousness of rural labour and the coercion visited upon those not covered by 'stabilization' policies stood out in stark relief in Kenya. After the war, attempted agricultural modernization and the enforcement of wage labour in the Kikuyu highlands caused the eviction of 'squatters', which, together with the crisis of the reserves, deepening urban unemployment and the bureaucratic authoritarianism of the settler state, contributed to the Mau Mau insurrection.[67]

The criminalization of informal work and official suspicion towards those not engaged in wage earning were not confined to oppressive East African plantations and settler colonies. In West Africa, the stigma placed on irregular economic activities was integral to the language of colonial reforms. Thus, Lagos authorities aimed the expanding punitive repertoire of juvenile justice at young female street hawkers, routinely assumed to be prostitutes, hence a double threat to the work ethic and virtuous domesticity.[68] Yet in many West African societies, small-scale self-employment drew strength and vitality from deeply entrenched cultural formations and new opportunities provided by wartime industrialization. Emily Osborn shows that the fortunes of craftsmen casting aluminium pots, an item of large consumption, took off in Senegal after the Second World War, as waged employees in newly

[65] Burton, *African Underclass*, 153–63, 241–73.

[66] Karin Pallaver, 'Labor Relations and Population Developments in Tanzania: Sources, Shifts, and Continuities from 1800 to 2000', *History in Africa*, 41 (2014), 307–35.

[67] Bruce J. Berman, 'Bureaucracy and Incumbent Violence: Colonial Administration and the Origins of the "Mau Mau" Emergency', in Bruce J. Berman and John M. Lonsdale, *Unhappy Valley: Conflict in Kenya and Africa. Book 2: Violence and Ethnicity* (Oxford: James Currey, 1992), 227–64.

[68] Abosede A. George, *Making Modern Girls: A History of Girlhood, Labor, and Social Development in Colonial Lagos* (Athens, OH: Ohio University Press, 2014).

established metal plants decided to start their own workshops.[69] Linkages between formal and informal were evident not only in the use of wage income as investment but also in the creative adaptation of industrial sand-casting techniques to a sector otherwise undercapitalized and without access to electricity, water or proper furnaces. The spread of this industry across French West Africa, including Guinea and Mali, was nonetheless enabled by complex networks of apprenticeship and diffusion of knowledge underpinned by long-standing caste-like artisanal associations or religious affiliations. Other studies in West Africa confirm the significance of spiritual connections, often along migration routes, for self-employment. Paul Lubeck, for example, documented how Islamic patronage and social support allowed itinerant preachers in the Kano region of northern Nigeria to combine casual and informal employment with devotional duties, with the result that religion itself informed a critique of wage labour while underpinning strong working-class identities.[70]

South Africa under apartheid was the notable exception to wage labour stabilization policies. In the wake of wartime manufacturing expansion, black workers moved into stable semi-skilled factory jobs, experiencing increases in wages and working-class organization. The brutal repression of the 1946 African mineworkers' strike signalled that the state would not further accommodate labour's demands. Two years later, the National Party rose to power with an agenda averse to incorporating black workers in 'white' cities through the extension of residential protections, unemployment benefits or social security.[71] Apartheid gave shape to a strict, systematic, nationally implemented racial ordering of society, deepening the institutionalized precariousness of non-white workers. African internal migrants, in particular, were envisaged as not merely temporary urban sojourners, which in many ways they already legally were, but actual alien labourers and citizens of putatively self-governing ethnic 'homelands'. To manage black populations who were already urbanized, the regime attempted an 'urban labour preference' policy, encouraging employers to hire youths from the segregated townships, which would absorb sectors engaged in informal economies, resented by the government as pathways to idleness and crime. Yet by the

---

[69] Emily L. Osborn, 'Casting Aluminium Cooking Pots: Labour, Migration and Artisan Production in West Africa's Informal Sector, 1945–2005', *African Identities*, 7.3 (2009), 373–86.

[70] Paul M. Lubeck, *Islam and Urban Labor in Northern Nigeria: The Making of a Muslim Working Class* (Cambridge: Cambridge University Press, 1986).

[71] Franco Barchiesi, *Precarious Liberation: Workers, the State, and Contested Social Citizenship in Postapartheid South Africa* (Albany, NY: State University of New York Press, 2011), 34–40.

1950s, the urban labour preference had failed, as young township dwellers continued to prefer casual and informal jobs to factory work.[72] Since black workers were also escaping the mines and farms, seeking a better life in the cities, white employers had increasingly to rely on circular labour migration, believing workers from the 'homelands' to be more pliable and exploitable given their lack of residential rights. It was therefore ironic that, in the early 1970s, migrant workers themselves became the driving force in the renascent black trade unions.

Contrary to the image of an African 'labour aristocracy' of secure and well-paid employees, the condition of waged workers after independence – with some exceptions, as in Nigeria during the oil boom and copper mining in Zambia – was not favourable. Studies in the 1970s revealed a constant erosion of wage levels and real earnings among urban workers in Accra and Kinshasa, where, well before the age of structural adjustment, male workers moonlighted in self-employment and women's petty trading sustained the survival of households.[73] In countries where 'Africanization' of landholdings replaced European-owned estates, African wage labourers were still largely hired as casuals. In Tanzania, nationalization and state support for communal-based smallholding increased precariousness and casualization in sisal cultivations. As international prices started to decline in the late 1960s, new regulations reduced the size of plots for food staples and slashed food rations, medical care and housing provisions.[74] In Kenya, local authorities were ready to recognize street vending as a source of cheap food and jobs for low-income and unskilled workers, and the state sought to license urban informal traders and establish formal marketplace structures. Shopkeepers, however, opposed the registration of most hawkers – such as shoe-shiners, blacksmiths, mechanics and barbers – who remained in a precarious and semi-legal position. The government also maintained a repressive stance towards the alleged 'immorality' of unmarried women, whose informal occupations were extensively punished.[75] West African social and cultural structures proved more favourable to informal work, also as an alternative to wage labour. Yoruba-speaking workers in Lagos, even unionized employees, for example, eschewed full-time waged work and retained multiple occupations on a

---

[72] Deborah Posel, *The Making of Apartheid, 1948–1961: Conflict and Compromise* (Oxford: Clarendon Press, 1991), 82–90, 158–64.

[73] Richard Sandbrook, 'The Political Potential of African Urban Workers', *Canadian Journal of African Studies*, 11.3 (1977), 411–33.

[74] Sabea, 'Mastering the Landscape?', 432.

[75] Mary N. Kinyanjui, *Women and the Informal Economy in Urban Africa: From the Margins to the Centre* (London: Zed Books, 2014), 23–6.

casual or informal basis, often with plans for a future of self-employment.[76] Expectations of individual entrepreneurship characterized workers' orientation to informal employment and would become central, as the next section will show, to theories of the 'informal sector' that accompanied market liberalization and its devastation of the waged working class.

VULNERABLE LABOUR IN THE AGE OF NEOLIBERALISM AND 'INFORMALITY', 1976–2015

In the 1970s the informal economy became an explicit object of scholarly inquiry. In his pioneering study of urban employment in Accra, Keith Hart categorized as 'informal' activities that eluded state attempts at bureaucratic regulation.[77] The world of street vendors and small repair shops seemed to indicate an untapped economic vitality deriving strength from its exclusion from official systems of registration, licensing, statutory employment conditions and revenue collection. The informal sector encompassed both the provision of goods or services and the production of shelter, food or clothing outside factories.[78] Off-the-books activities could deliver livelihoods and jobs to the poor, but were also underpinned by social networks that eluded state power and planning.[79] Informal work also questioned established conceptual boundaries, since it did not necessarily correspond to casual labour or petty commodity production, nor was it simply coincidental with social marginality.[80]

With the advent of structural adjustment programmes in the late 1970s and 1980s, the World Bank, the International Monetary Fund and Western donors shaped the debate on the informal economy. Public-sector retrenchments and cutbacks in social programmes and subsidies eroded the numbers of waged employees while making the lives of the poor and contingent workers increasingly precarious. Households were forced to diversify their sources of income, and women and children took precarious occupations of all kinds, often to replace wages lost by retrenched family

---

[76] Adrian J. Peace, *Choice, Class, and Conflict: A Study of Southern Nigerian Factory Workers* (Atlantic Highlands, NJ: Humanities Press, 1979).

[77] Keith Hart, 'Informal Income Opportunities and Urban Employment in Ghana', *Journal of Modern African Studies*, 11.1 (1973), 61–89.

[78] Freund, *The African Worker*, 75–81.

[79] Iliffe, *The African Poor*, 243–4.

[80] Alejandro Portes, 'The Informal Sector: Definition, Controversy, and Relation to National Development', *Review (Fernand Braudel Center)*, 7.1 (1983), 151–74.

members.[81] International institutions propagandized informal work as an avenue to successful business initiatives, but informal workers saw their opportunities severely restricted. Andræ and Beckman showed that textile factory employees in Kaduna and Kano (northern Nigeria) could no longer counterbalance, as they used to, declining wages with self-employment in small-scale manufacturing or transportation, also adversely impacted by liberalization.[82] Rather than upwardly mobile entrepreneurialism, informal jobs turned, with few exceptions such as urban food agriculture, into survivalist self-exploitation.

The precariousness of informal activities was exacerbated by their uncertain juridical status, which made them highly dependent on protection and patronage from state officials, and the volatility of their finances, which subjected informal workers to the power of household elders, artisanal 'guilds' or religious associations. Thus, in Senegal, for example, the Islamic Sufi order of the Muridiyya, whose work ethic had configured the relationship between *marabout* and *talibé* (disciple) into one fusing the imperatives of piety and commodity production, legitimized the increasing use of young followers in begging and street trade.[83] Morice's work among artisanal foundrymen in Kaolack (Senegal) indicated that the seeming traditional stability of professional 'castes' allowed a remarkably elastic use of 'apprentices', a term that in the end broadly characterized young workers subjected, often without actual access to training, to age hierarchies rather than labour contracts.[84] In the informal sector, flexible employment reinforced precariousness by compensating for the lack of capital and the difficulty of investing in highly volatile markets, but the exploitation of a flexible workforce was aided by the youths' dependence, for the means of their livelihood, on the will of their elders. At the same time, however, as Julia Elyachar demonstrates in the case of craft production in Cairo,[85] informal social webs steeped in long-standing artisanal identities allowed craftsmen

---

[81] Robertson, 'Invisible Workers'; Kate Meagher, 'Crisis. Informalization and the Urban Informal Sector in Sub-Saharan Africa', *Development and Change*, 26.2 (1995), 259–84.

[82] Gunilla Andræ and Björn Beckman, 'Textile Unions and Industrial Crisis in Nigeria: Labour Structure, Organization and Strategies', in *Workers in Third-World Industrialization*, ed. Inga Brandell (New York: St Martin's Press), 161–4.

[83] Laurence Marfaing and Mariam Sow, *Les opérateurs économiques au Sénégal: entre le formel et l'informel, 1930–1996* (Paris: Karthala, 1999).

[84] Alain Morice, 'Ceux qui travaillent gratuitement: un salaire confisqué', in *Classes ouvrières d'Afrique noire*, ed. Michel Agier, Jean Copans and Alain Morice (Paris: Karthala, 1987), 45–76.

[85] Julia Elyachar, *Markets of Dispossession: NGOs, Economic Development, and the State in Cairo* (Durham, NC: Duke University Press, 2005).

and their young employees to survive the competition of actors entering the sector in response to more recent dislocations.

Belying the informal entrepreneurial paradigm celebrated by international agencies and non-governmental organizations are often severely undercapitalized and unskilled businesses as a frequent destination for mobile populations facing de-agrarianization – the loss of agricultural self-sufficiency – the decay of rural–urban support networks, or the erosion of household safety nets. Structural adjustment policies have been particularly detrimental to market women due to the falling incomes of poor and working-class customers and the growing competition from men engaged in street selling after losing waged jobs.[86] It is a paradox of economic liberalization that ideas of empowerment centred on the informal sector became widespread precisely when neoliberalism undermined the very social institutions – family, education, employment, political patronage – upon which informal economic initiatives depend.[87] Thus, for example, the itinerant preachers and informal workers whom Lubeck studied in northern Nigeria suffered as relations of solidarity and almsgiving faded as a result of the hardships of liberalization. Once respected, preachers thus became embodiments, derogatorily called *gardawa* (unmarried wandering youth), of a new *lumpenproletariat*, which, as earlier working-class discourse was weakened, turned to Islamist politics.[88]

At the turn of the twenty-first century, debates on informal work significantly shifted. In the 1970s and 1980s dualistic perspectives had represented the informal sector in opposition to the formal. In ultimately rejecting dualism, Keith Hart criticizes its simplified polarization between a 'Weberian' attempt to make the economy calculable and predictable through bureaucratic means, and the risks and unpredictability arising from unregulated capitalism.[89] The focus of analyses then turned from the informal activities' regulatory status to their modalities of production and accumulation. Small-scale workshops were portrayed as characterized by low surplus and fierce competition, which undermined the prospects, in Marxian terms, of expanded reproduction of capital.[90] Studies of transportation in

---

[86] Clark, *Onions are My Husband*.

[87] Brad Weiss, 'Contentious Futures: Past and Present', in *Producing African Futures: Ritual and Reproduction in a Neoliberal Age*, ed. Brad Weiss (Leiden: Brill, 2004), 1–20.

[88] Paul M. Lubeck, 'Islamic Protest Under Semi-Industrial Capitalism: 'Yan Tatsine Explained', *International Journal of African Historical Studies*, 55.4 (1985), 369–89.

[89] Keith Hart, 'On the Informal Economy: The Political History of an Ethnographic Concept', Centre Emile Bernheim, Working Paper 09/042, Brussels, Solvay School of Economics and Management, 2009.

[90] Emmanuel Grégoire, 'Les perspectives d'accumulation dans la petite industrie de transformation. L'exemple de la menuiserie métallique à Maradi (Niger)', *Cahiers*

Tananarive[91] and Dar es Salaam[92] found that the paternalist control of vehicle owners deprived operators of the means to start their own businesses. Rather than taking a risk against such volatile investment prospects, workers often preferred to use their earnings to return to the land.

Yet the fact that small-scale, unregistered activities were not reliable paths to independent accumulation did not deny their resilience or significance in the social reproduction of the poor and the irregularly employed.[93] Theories of 'informalization' pointed, as reasons for the viability of informal businesses, to the social practices of the urban poor living in zones that eluded governmental controls.[94] Consumption and the maintenance of social connections thus appeared stronger motivators for informal work than accumulation and investment.[95] Research on artisanal mines in Tanzania reveals, for example, that these uncertainly regulated, often unlicensed, manual and low-technology operations employ youths who, even when working full-time, see mining mostly as a chance to buy into expensive urban lifestyles.[96]

Other scholars see informal labour as merely one facet of 'informality' as an emerging social paradigm in which not only are boundaries between regulated and unregulated economies blurred by liberalization, but entire fields of production, exchange and governance are taken over by non-state

---

d'études africaines, 81/83 (1981), 221–35; Tola Olu Pearce, Olufemi O. Kujore and V. Aina Agboh-Bankole, 'Generating an Income in the Urban Environment: The Experience of Street Food Vendors in Ile-Ife, Nigeria', *Africa*, 58.4 (1988), 385–400.

[91]   Philippe Hugon, 'Le développement des petites activités à Antananarivo. L'exemple d'un processus involutif', *Revue canadienne des études africaines*, 16.2 (1982), 293–312.

[92]   Matteo Rizzo, '"Life Is War": Informal Transport Workers and Neoliberalism in Tanzania 1998–2009', *Development and Change*, 42.5 (2011), 1179–206.

[93]   Claude de Miras, 'De l'accumulation de capital dans le secteur informel', *Cahiers des sciences humaines*, 23.1 (1987), 49–74.

[94]   Michaeline Crichlow, 'Under the Shadows of Capital', in *Informalization: Process and Structure*, ed. Faruk Tabak and Michaeline Crichlow (Baltimore, MD: Johns Hopkins University Press, 2000), 166–86; Ilda Lourenço-Lindell, *Walking the Tight Rope: Informal Livelihoods and Social Networks in a West African City* (Stockholm: Almqvist and Wiksell, 2002); Abdoumaliq Simone, *For the City Yet to Come: Changing African Life in Four Cities* (Durham, NC: Duke University Press, 2004).

[95]   Alain Morice, 'Les vélos de Kaolack', *Cahiers d'études africaines*, 81/83 (1981), 197–210.

[96]   Deborah Fahy Bryceson, 'Youth in Tanzania's Urbanizing Mining Settlements: Prospecting a Mineralized Future', in *African Youth and the Persistence of Marginalization: Employment, Politics, and Prospects for Change*, ed. D. Resnick and J. Thurlow (London: Routledge, 2015), 85–108.

actors and processes.[97] As a result, ambivalence penetrates the discourse of states and international organizations. While still committed to informal entrepreneurialism, they are also increasingly concerned by overlaps of informality and illegality in the form of smuggling, counterfeiting, piracy, and trade in drugs, weapons or minerals from war zones, which exploit opportunities created by porous national borders and global migration routes.[98]

The positioning by theories of informality of unprotected and precarious labour within broader changes in capitalism and state forms could, however, be at the cost of underestimating differentiations – according to gender, class, access to institutions and patronage or exposure to state repression – in informal work itself.[99] On the other hand, informal jobs are not antithetical to wage labour as such, despite their possible meaning as an alternative to waged employment. Informality does not, therefore, envisage a clear-cut break with older forms of commodity-producing work, since global capital can enforce undocumented and unprotected working conditions through decentralization and outsourcing. The vulnerabilities of small-scale industries or self-employed contractors can hardly be understood outside the deepening precariousness of capitalist employment writ large. In rural areas and plantation economies, which tend to be neglected by studies of informal work focused on the cities' poor, the exploitation of casual labour is still rife, offering scant prospects of petty entrepreneurship. 'Land grabs' by large biofuel corporations and industrial cultivations facilitate the degradation of agricultural employment, often abetted by the abuse of undocumented cross-border migrants.[100] Presenting the results of their research on daily-paid sisal and cotton workers in Mozambique's Nampula province, Cramer, Oya and Sender make observations with broad applicability:

> Employer discretion over labour contracts is exercised within a context of widespread poverty, a generally weak presence of trade unions and labour inspectors, low levels of literacy and education and, by the accounts of large farmers, a huge excess in the supply of labour. As local monopsonists, most

---

[97] Karen T. Hansen and Mariken Vaa, eds, *Reconsidering Informality: Perspectives from Urban Africa* (Uppsala: Nordic Africa Institute, 2004); Kate Meagher, *Identity Economics: Social Networks and the Informal Economy in Nigeria* (Woodbridge: James Currey, 2010).

[98] James Ferguson, *Global Shadows: Africa in the Neoliberal World Order* (Durham, NC: Duke University Press, 2006).

[99] Ilda Lourenço-Lindell, 'Introduction: The Changing Politics of Informality. Collective Organizing, Alliances and Scales of Engagement', in *Africa's Informal Workers: Collective Agency, Alliances and Transnational Organizing in Urban Africa*, ed. Ilda Lourenço-Lindell (London: Zed Books, 2010), 1–30.

[100] Blair Rutherford and Lincoln Addison, 'Zimbabwean Farm Workers in Northern South Africa', *Review of African Political Economy*, 114 (2007), 619–35.

rural employers are in a strong position to shape labour relations by using an array of discretionary gambits in setting wage levels, imposing payment methods, offering and threatening to withhold incentives, and by choosing what combination of male and female permanent, seasonal and casual labour to employ.[101]

The rural hierarchies determined by structural adjustment can also greatly constrain – as O'Laughlin argues in the case of Botswana[102] – the range of activities available to former peasants in urban informal sectors. Smallholders, more poorly capitalized, thus cluster around highly competitive and lower-wage activities such as hawking, load carrying, wood collection and barber shops, while better-off peasants have more propitious chances in high-skilled, capital-intensive jobs such as mechanical repairs and tailoring. Women tend to specifically suffer from the gendered differentiation of precarious work, since their opportunities are further limited to occupations, such as street vending, on schedules that are compatible with reproduction and child rearing.

Finally, to ground the study of informal labour in the constitutive precariousness of African commodity-producing employment would highlight connections with the worsening conditions of wage labour in the many realities in which, although eroded by market liberalization, it remains socially and politically significant.[103] Privatization and increasing global competition have put labour on the defensive in erstwhile bulwarks of working-class identity and organization, from the Zambian Copperbelt[104] to South Africa.[105] Continent-wide trends to casualization do not seem, on the other hand, to have abated as a result of attempted export-oriented industrialization or renewed resource-driven growth, processes that accompany Africa's turn to East Asia or Latin America as sources of investment and aid. Strategies to attract foreign direct investment in

---

[101] Christopher Cramer, Carlos Oya and John Sender, 'Lifting the Blinkers: A New View of Power, Diversity and Poverty in Mozambican Rural Labour Markets', *Journal of Modern African Studies*, 46.3 (2008), 380.

[102] Bridget O'Laughlin, 'Missing Men? The Debate over Rural Poverty and Women-Headed Households in Southern Africa', *Journal of Peasant Studies*, 25.2 (1998), 1–48.

[103] See the chapter by Neveling in this volume.

[104] Alastair Fraser and Miles Larmer, eds, *Zambia, Mining, and Neoliberalism: Boom and Bust on the Globalized Copperbelt* (New York: Palgrave Macmillan, 2010).

[105] Jonathan Crush, Theresa Ulicki, Teke Tseane and Elizabeth Jansen van Veuren, 'Undermining Labour: The Rise of Sub-Contracting in South African Gold Mines', *Journal of Southern African Studies*, 27.1 (2001), 5–31; Bridget Kenny, 'From Insurrectionary Worker to Contingent Citizen: Restructuring Labor Markets and Repositioning East Rand (South Africa) Retail Sector Workers', *City & Society*, 15.1 (2003), 31–57; Barchiesi, *Precarious Liberation*.

production for export may in fact encourage extreme employment flexibility, high turnovers and subcontracting to the informal sector, as the case of Tunisian call centres with a relatively highly educated workforce indicates.[106] On the other hand, the intervention of Chinese capital in the mining districts of southern Africa or agricultural areas in West Africa has facilitated the fragmentation of industries and labour processes to take advantage of vulnerable workers[107] and the proliferation of informal markets in the commercialization of imported goods.[108]

By the second decade of the twenty-first century, actors and international institutions that are still committed to wage labour as a pillar of an equitable and fair globalization have regarded informal, precarious and casual work as challenges. As an alternative to probably outdated juridical categories grounded in the formalities of labour contracts, scholars have proposed new distinctions that are attentive to the sociological dimensions of informalized labour, such as employment through family recruitment *versus* reciprocal exchange within socially constructed networks,[109] or the differentiation between informal 'networks of accumulation' and 'networks of survival'.[110] The adoption by the ILO of a 'decent work' agenda has energized attempts by trade unions to organize contingent workers and bridge the formal–informal divide.[111] The underlying difficulties are, however, evident, for example in West Africa, where the share of informal employment ranges from 76 per cent (Senegal) to 93 per cent (Benin) of the labour force; only

[106] Béatrice Hibou, 'Work Discipline, Discipline in Tunisia: Complex and Ambiguous Relations', *African Identities*, 7.3 (2009), 327–52.

[107] Gillian P. Hart, *Disabling Globalization: Places of Power in Post-Apartheid South Africa* (Berkeley, CA: University of California Press, 2002); Ching Kwan Lee, 'Raw Encounters: Chinese Managers, African Workers and the Politics of Casualization in Africa's Chinese Enclaves', *The China Quarterly*, 199 (2009), 647–66.

[108] Suzanne Scheld, 'The "China Challenge": The Global Dimensions of Activism and the Informal Economy in Dakar', in *Africa's Informal Workers: Collective Agency, Alliances and Transnational Organizing in Urban Africa*, ed. Ilda Lourenço-Lindell (London: Zed Books, 2010), 153–68.

[109] Yvan Guichaoua, 'Non-Protected Labour in One West African Capital: Characteristics of Jobs and Occupational Mobility in Abidjan, Côte d'Ivoire', Queen Elizabeth House Working Papers, 132, Department of International Development, University of Oxford, 2006.

[110] Meagher, *Identity Economics*.

[111] Piet Konings, 'Organised Labour and Neo-Liberal Economic and Political Reforms in West and Central Africa', *Journal of Contemporary African Studies*, 21.3 (2003), 447–71; Gundula Fischer, 'Revisiting Abandoned Ground: Tanzanian Trade Unions' Engagement with Informal Workers', *Labor Studies Journal*, 38.2 (2013), 139–60.

2 per cent of informal workers in the Economic Community of West African States (ECOWAS) are union members; and the total unionization rate was 12.8 per cent in 2007.[112]

Not only do the fragmentation and vulnerability of informal and casual jobs pose formidable problems to recruitment and collective bargaining, but trade unions are often discredited as a result of their connections to unpopular politicians or former ruling parties in authoritarian governments. When they do mobilize in response to adverse socio-economic and political conditions, African precarious workers are often more likely to side with equally unprotected social strata, such as students, than with the unions. The fact that, with all its diversity and complexity, and in spite of its vulnerability and fragility, African precarious work continues to elude efforts to make it organizable, manageable and governable reinforces the case, on which this chapter has insisted, for placing precarity at the core of critical inquiry into the problematic place of wage labour in contemporary African history.

---

[112] Craig Phelan, 'Trade Unions, Democratic Waves, and Structural Adjustment: The Case of Francophone West Africa', *Labor History*, 52.4 (2011), 461–81.

THREE
Forced Labour

BABACAR FALL

Université Cheikh Anta Diop, Dakar, and
Freeman Spogli Institute for International Studies,
Stanford University

RICHARD L. ROBERTS

Department of History and Center for African Studies,
Stanford University

In its 1930 Convention on Forced Labour, the International Labour Organization defined 'forced or compulsory labour' as 'all work or service which is exacted from any person under the menace of any penalty and for which the said person has not offered himself voluntarily'.[1] Representatives at the Geneva Convention further clarified forced labour as a particular 'practice of compulsory labour exacted by a state or by agencies of a state, other than as a punishment for a criminal offence or for the purpose of the military defence'.[2] Colonial powers faced enormous pressure to sign up to the 1930 ILO Convention, and several states delayed ratifying it. Despite this general agreement on the abolition of forced labour, despite increased pressure from non-governmental humanitarian groups and despite efforts by colonial reformers – including Jules Marcel de Coppet, the Governor General of French West Africa (1936–38), and Henrique Galvão, inspector of the Portuguese colonies and former governor of Huila Province in southern Angola – forced labour in colonial Africa persisted in many

---

[1]   Forced Labour Convention, 1930 (No. 29), Article 2.1.
[2]   Joseph Folliet, *Le travail forcé aux colonies* (Paris: Éditions du Cerf, 1934), 5.

regions through the period of decolonization and into the present.[3] Forced labour in twentieth-century Africa was a widespread means of building and maintaining infrastructure, supporting the mining sector and developing and servicing the export-oriented agricultural sector in French, German, Belgian, Portuguese, Italian and Spanish colonies, and, to a lesser degree, in the British colonies, where public labour ordinances, compulsory labour ordinances and communal labour ordinances served similar goals. Decolonization did not, however, end forced labour. Several postcolonial states have continued this practice, often under thinly disguised forms of military recruitment.

This chapter examines the variety of practices of forced labour during the colonial period on the African continent and its persistence into the postcolonial period. It provides a framework for understanding the context in which Western colonial powers engaged in forced labour and describes the major forms of forced labour used by both the colonial powers and the newly independent African nations. Forced labour was part of a wider set of practices using coerced labour. This chapter focuses on forced labour as a practice of state mobilization of labour in Africa during the twentieth century. As Frederick Cooper reminds us, during 'the five hundred years in which Europeans and Africans have known each other rather well, no element has been more central in their relationship than work'.[4] Forced labour was a central part of that relationship.

THE ILO AND THE DEBATE AROUND FORCED LABOUR IN THE INTERWAR PERIOD[5]

The ILO was founded together with the League of Nations following the Paris Peace Conference in 1919, during a heady time when social theory and social engineering provided the means to imagine that societies and economies were malleable and could be changed to promote humane treatment of workers and general well-being. One of the ILO's first actions was designed to regulate and protect female workers' health and maternity

---

[3] Jeremy Ball, "'I Escaped in a Coffin'": Remembering Angolan Forced Labor from the 1940s', *Cadernos de Estudos Africanos – Memórias Coloniais*, 9/10 (2006), 4, http://cea.revues.org/1214 (accessed 10 January 2019); National Archives of Senegal, Dakar, 1/K8, Letter of General Governor of French West Africa Federation to the Ministry of Colonies, 25 January 1937.

[4] Frederick Cooper, *On the African Waterfront: Urban Disorder and the Transformation of Work in Colonial Mombasa* (New Haven, CT: Yale University Press, 1987), 1.

[5] For a more detailed account of the ILO in Africa, see the chapter by Maul, Puddu and Tijani in this volume.

during the post-war era of pro-natalist thought and policy.[6] This reflected ILO concerns with vulnerable labouring populations, especially at a time when a large proportion of the world's population resided in colonies and colonial possessions. Moreover, the ILO's founding also coincided with the 1919 Treaty of St-Germain-en-Laye, which required the League of Nations to investigate 'slavery in all its forms regardless of geography or sovereignty'.[7]

The ILO's mandate to investigate and regulate forced labour emerged out of the debates held at the Temporary Slavery Commission of the League of Nations. The ILO was represented on the Commission from 1924. In particular, the Commission received a report written by the American sociologist Edward Alsworth Ross detailing rampant abuses of Africans being forced to work in the Portuguese colonies of Angola and Mozambique.[8] The League and the ILO received reports of similar abuses in the Belgian Congo, the French mandates of Cameroon and Togo, as well as New Guinea and the Dutch East Indies.[9] Being forced to work was similar but not identical to the definition of slavery used in the 1926 Slavery Convention and thus the League directed the ILO to oversee the process of drafting regulations to deal with those types of coerced labour that did not stem from the property relationship inherent in the Slavery Convention's definition.

From the mid-1920s the ILO's Native Labour Section actively collected information on forced labour and its abuses and became a node in a network of individuals and non-governmental organizations pursuing slavery and labour abuses in the colonies. As the ILO worked on the forced labour Convention, colonial powers exerted influence at every step of the deliberations. Representatives of these colonial powers argued that any restrictions on forced labour would hinder their civilizing missions

---

[6] Mary Louise Roberts, *Civilization without Sexes: Reconstructing Gender in Postwar France, 1917–1927* (Chicago: University of Chicago Press, 1994); Nora Natchkova and Céline Schoeni, 'The ILO, Feminists and Expert Networks: The Challenges of Protective Policy (1919–1934)', in *Globalizing Social Rights: The International Labour Organization and Beyond*, ed. Sandrine Kott and Joëlle Droux (Basingstoke and Geneva: Palgrave Macmillan and ILO, 2013), 49.

[7] Suzanne Miers, *Slavery in the Twentieth Century: The Evolution of a Global Problem* (Walnut Creek, CA: Altamira Press, 2003), 58–65.

[8] Edward Alsworth Ross, *Report on Employment of Native Labor in Portuguese Africa* (New York: Abbott Press, 1925). See also Dr Oliveira Santos's official Portuguese reply to Ross's accusations, *Reply to the Accusation Addressed to the League of Nations by Mr. Edward A. Ross, Against the Portuguese in Angola* (Lisbon: Tipografia inglesa, 1930).

[9] J. P. Daughton, 'ILO Expertise and Colonial Violence in the Interwar Years', in *Globalizing Social Rights: The International Labour Organization and Beyond*, ed. Sandrine Kott and Joëlle Droux (Basingstoke and Geneva: Palgrave Macmillan and ILO, 2013), 85–6.

and their work in promoting economic and social development in their colonies. Such interventions yielded the Convention on Forced Labour in 1930, which committed each signatory to 'suppress the use of forced or compulsory labour in all of its forms within the shortest possible time', but offered a five-year transitional period during which forced labour could only be used for public purposes and only on an exceptional basis, 'subject to the conditions and guarantees provided by the Convention'.[10] Of the major colonial powers, only Great Britain, France and the Netherlands signed the Convention in 1930. France did not hesitate to use the loophole in the Convention that permitted members to employ compulsory military recruitment, in principle only for 'work of a military character' (Article 2), to supply compulsory labour mostly for public works. France only abolished forced labour in 1946 as part of its broader post-war commitment to extend metropolitan political, economic and social legislation to its colonies.[11] Belgium did not ratify the Convention until 1944, and Portugal ratified only in 1956, but did not abolish forced labour until 1961 with the outbreak of anti-colonial revolts in Angola. The ILO added new regulations to protect agricultural workers in 1936 and 1939, which were designed to suppress compulsory rural labour exerted through contracts with the assistance of colonial officials, and sought to extend protections to rural areas where abusive working conditions persisted by mandating labour inspections.[12]

The ability of the ILO to influence conditions within colonies, however, reflected the influence of imperial powers on the Governing Body of the ILO and the institution's general lack of enforcement capacity. Article 35 of the ILO's original Constitution was framed within these tensions and thus provided signatories with wide latitude of action regarding the implementation of ILO regulations and conventions. Members of the ILO 'undertook to apply' the conventions that they signed and that were designed for metropolitan contexts

> to their colonies, protectorates, and possessions which are not fully self-governing, (a) except when owning to the local conditions its provisions are inapplicable; or (b) subject to such modifications as may be necessary to adapt its provisions to local conditions. Each Member shall notify to the

---

[10]   *Ibid.*, 85–97; G. A. Johnston, *The International Labour Organisation: Its Work for Social and Economic Progress* (London: Europa, 1970), 234–5.

[11]   Frederick Cooper, *Citizenship Between Empire and Nation: Remaking France and French Africa, 1945–1960* (Princeton, NJ: Princeton University Press, 2014).

[12]   Daniel Maul, *Human Rights, Development and Decolonization: The International Labour Organization, 1940–70* (Basingstoke and Geneva: Palgrave Macmillan and ILO, 2012), 23–7.

International Labour Office the action taken in respect of each of its colonies, protectorates, and possessions which are not fully self-governing.[13]

The ILO required members to submit reports regularly.

FROM SLAVERY TO FORCED LABOUR: A CONTINUOUS USE OF COERCION IN AN IMPERFECT LABOUR MARKET

Slavery is an ancient and dynamic institution in Africa that has changed over time and in response to market forces and to the coercive capacity of masters to exploit their slaves. Slavery mobilized extra personnel for households and fed growing plantation economies in many parts of Africa. With the gradual decline in the transatlantic, trans-Saharan, Red Sea and Indian Ocean slave trades in the course of the nineteenth century, more slaves became available for use in Africa. Coerced labour persisted in Africa because of demands for such labour and because of profound imperfections in African labour markets.

Gareth Austin argues that, since 1500 at least, most of sub-Saharan Africa had high land-to-labour ratios (an abundance of land) with relatively little available liquid capital that could be invested in appropriate technologies (such as the plough). Moreover, the tropical soils were easily eroded and thus retained relatively little long-term fertility in the absence of easily available green manures, which were themselves limited by livestock diseases.[14] Within this context, African farmers interested in 'raising the rate of return' innovated with new crops and turned primarily to coerced labour to augment output. 'In such context', Austin argues, 'it is not surprising that the internal labour markets of precolonial Africa mostly took the form of slave and pawn rather than wage labour.'[15]

This was the context in which European powers engaged in the 'Scramble for Africa', starting in the last three decades of the nineteenth century.

---

[13] Johnston, *The International Labour Organisation*, 232–3, quoting the original.

[14] There were exceptions, of course, including the 'closed-cropped zone' surrounding Kano, where large herds and slave labour promoted intensive agriculture rather than the more common extensive practices. See especially Polly Hill, *Population, Prosperity, and Poverty: Rural Kano, 1900 and 1970* (Cambridge: Cambridge University Press, 1977).

[15] Gareth Austin, 'Resources, Techniques, and Strategies South of the Sahara: Revising the Factor Endowments Perspective on African Economic Development, 1500–2000', *Economic History Review*, 61.3 (2008), 609. See also Gareth Austin, *Labour, Land, and Capital in Ghana: From Slavery to Free Labour in Asante, 1807–1956* (Rochester, NY: University of Rochester Press, 2005), ch. 8.

While securing claims to African territory involved various means, including signing treaties of protection, all colonial powers relied on conquest to some degree. Many African soldiers fighting in colonial armies were recruited from volunteers, including runaway slaves and informal auxiliaries hoping to share in the booty of conquest. All colonial armies required additional armies of porters to carry the material of war as well as food. Few porters volunteered for this labour and most were recruited through coercion. Some were recruited from liberty villages that housed 'freed' slaves rescued from African enemies and strategically situated along the routes the armies traversed. Thus, the very foundation of colonies largely rested on coerced labour.

When the active phase of the Scramble for Africa ended around 1898, nearly all sub-Saharan Africans were engaged in agricultural, pastoral, fishing and hunting pursuits. Most of these pursuits were seasonal and provided significant opportunities for diverse commercial, artisanal, mining and small-scale manufacturing work that fed regional and long-distance trade in Africa and overseas. There were scattered pockets of dense, urban, political and religious agglomerations that supported full-time military, bureaucratic, religious, commercial and mining specialists. With its much longer history of colonization, South Africa had already developed major centres of mining and urban development. Nascent colonial states had also established burgeoning central places of bureaucracy, harbours, commerce and communication. In general, these urban pockets swelled seasonally, as rural workers streamed in to add labour to infrastructural projects only to dwindle again when the planting, herding or fishing demands resumed.

The discovery of diamonds and gold in South Africa in 1867 and 1886, respectively, stimulated Africa's 'gold rush' and inspired European imperialists to think of Africa as a vast treasure trove with fortunes waiting to be discovered. Gold and diamonds were discovered elsewhere in Africa, but the large, concentrated and lucrative mines of South Africa were not found elsewhere. Nonetheless, gold mines were established in Southern Rhodesia, the Gold Coast, the French Sudan and Tanganyika, among other places. Additional gold and diamond sources were discovered later during the colonial era.[16] The great potential of other minerals, such as copper, which was to crucial to the global electrification and communications of the twentieth century, helped stimulate enclaves of development in Africa, especially in the aptly named Copperbelt of the Congo and Northern Rhodesia.

[16] Raymond Dumett, *El Dorado in West Africa: The Gold-Mining Frontier, African Labor, and Colonial Capitalism in the Gold Coast, 1875–1900* (Athens, OH: Ohio University Press, 1998).

Mining required labour. Whether there was little investment in heavy mining machinery or significant investment in capital-intensive mining, mining capitalists wanted cheap labour. The cheaper the labour, the higher were the potential profits. Conditions of mine work were often so onerous that few workers wanted to stay on beyond the terms of their contracts. In this manner, the colonial pattern of circular migration was born. Moreover, since the pay for mine work was so low, few African workers could support their families on their wages. Many Africans preferred to return to their wives and families in their rural homelands as soon as possible.

Colonial economists advanced the concept that African workers were motivated by certain 'targets' – such as sufficient cash to pay taxes, to buy a bicycle, or enough for bridewealth – and once they achieved their goals, they quit working and returned home. This concept of the target worker, which was phrased in economic terms as 'the backward-sloping supply curve of labour', became an excuse for employers to keep wages low; if they paid higher wages, workers would achieve their goals sooner, quit, and thus leave employers scrambling for new workers. Some workers did indeed have targets in mind, but the conditions of work and the poor pay meant that few had a long-term interest in remaining in their jobs.[17]

The circular migration of Africans was a rational response to a bad situation. Pressure to generate cash, pressure to leave dangerous and demeaning work as soon as possible, pressure to return home to invest in the future: all this contributed to the peculiar forms of migration generated by colonial capitalism. Even though agricultural work was hard and the profits usually slim, at least African peasants worked for themselves or their families. By working for their families, these Africans also invested in their futures, because they expected that their sons would also work for them. For others, migrant labour became a new rite of passage signifying the transition to adulthood.[18]

With the end of slavery in Africa, which occurred at an uneven pace on the continent, some former slaves remained with their former masters, while others left to return to their homelands to build new communities

---

[17] See, for example, Elliott Berg, 'The Backward-Sloping Labor Supply Function in Dual Economies: The Africa Case', *The Quarterly Journal of Economics*, 75.3 (1961), 468–91; Marvin Miracle and Bruce Fetter, 'Backward-Sloping Labor-Supply Functions and African Economic Behavior', *Economic Development and Change*, 18.2 (1970), 240–51.

[18] See Sara Berry, *Fathers Work for Their Sons: Accumulation, Mobility, and Class Formation in an Extended Yorùbá Community* (Berkeley, CA: University of California Press, 1984) and Paul Ocobock, 'Earning an Age: Migration and Maturity in Early Colonial Kenya, 1895–1952', *African Economic History*, 44 (2016), 44–72.

or to establish independent households. Far from swelling the ranks of the unemployed and thus being willing to sell their labour, former slaves most often chose to work for themselves or their new communities.[19] Colonial officials, European employers and African capitalists continued to face a profound labour shortage. To justify the compulsion to labour, which resembled slavery, colonial officials argued that coercion was necessary to overcome Africans' inherent 'inertia and laziness' by claiming that such obligatory labour was 'educational'. Officials also implemented administrative, legal and disciplinary regulations to produce streams of forced labourers. Throughout Africa, legal distinctions separated citizens from subjects and subjected the latter to often coercive legal regimes, including some aspects of customary law that put villagers under the control of village chiefs, and 'administrative law', such as the French *Code de l'indigénat*, which put African subjects under the control of colonial officials and subject to a range of punishments for minor infractions, including obligatory labour. In the British colonies, the obligation to provide labour for communal public works legitimized forced labour. To enhance their coercive capacities, colonial states throughout Africa worked through systems of indirect rule, incorporating African chiefs into their wider systems of taxation and labour mobilization. Ironically, in exploiting the moral influence and authority of chiefs, colonial administrations progressively undermined them by transforming them into instruments of colonial policy. In addition, all colonial powers employed various forms of a paramilitary police, sometimes called *gardes de cercles* in French colonies or *cipaes* in Portuguese colonies.

WEAK COLONIAL STATES AND TAXES AS FORCED LABOUR

Reliance on forced labour was one of the outcomes of the transition from slavery and the imperfections of the labour supply in colonial Africa. Africans sought whenever possible to avoid employment in the mines, plantations and fields of European capital and settlers. Precisely because Africans had alternatives for much of the colonial period to selling their labour at the poor rates offered by employers, settlers, capitalists and colonial administrators, colonial states were obliged to organize cheap labour outside

---

[19] Frederick Cooper, *From Slaves to Squatters: Plantation Labor and Agriculture in Zanzibar and Coastal Kenya, 1890–1925* (New Haven, CT: Yale University Press, 1980); Martin A. Klein, *Slavery and Colonial Rule in French West Africa* (New York: Cambridge University Press, 1998); Suzanne Miers and Richard L. Roberts, eds, *The End of Slavery in Africa* (Madison, WI: University of Wisconsin Press, 1988).

of the labour market. Compulsion thus became a central feature in the operation of colonial labour markets. This manifested itself differently in response to demands for labour in different parts of the continent and for different economic sectors.

This is how the International Labour Office understood the emergence of forced labour in colonial Africa:

> It is well known that in the early stages of European economic penetration Africans showed little inclination to look for paid employment of their own accord. They went about their customary activities according to the traditional rules of the society to which they belonged; they had not experience of the European system of work in return for pay, and memories of the slave trade, which lived on in some territories, encouraged them to keep away from European undertakings.

As a result the offer of labour may be said to have been practically non-existent. This was the dominant feature of the labour market with which governments and private enterprise were faced. In order to carry out public works such as roads and railways and to satisfy the manpower needs experienced by undertakings such as plantations and mines, various methods of direct and indirect pressure were adopted.

The result was the more or less widespread and systematic imposition of forced labour on the African population ... Native chiefs were required periodically to supply contingents of able-bodied men, the numbers of which were fixed by the authorities. These men were used primarily for public works, although some of them might be turned over to private employers. Moreover, even in the case of recruitment by private individuals, coercion played a large part since such operations were carried out with the help and direct participation of the authorities.[20]

The ILO report also argued that head or hut taxes constituted an 'indirect form of forced labour, since only through paid employment could many Africans hope to find the necessary money'. By the time this report was published in 1958, during the last phase of empire, the ILO argued that forced labour had more or less disappeared, as 'normal economic incentives' had proven 'increasingly effective in inducing Africans to seek paid employment of their own accord'. This last statement underestimated the profound social, economic and political changes in most of colonial Africa that had by the beginning of decolonization deeply eroded the viability of the rural sector. Taxation was a central element in forcing Africans to work.

---

[20] International Labour Office, *African Labour Survey* (Geneva: ILO, 1958), 295.

The process of colonial conquest and building colonial states was uneven and drawn out over the course of nearly fifty years. Building colonial states was not easily accomplished. On the one hand, there was the 'weak' colonial state: 'the paternalistic mediator struggling to maintain a precarious sovereignty over contending interests' and hobbled by inadequate resources and little coercive force. It had only a 'facade' of power. On the other hand, the 'strong' colonial state continually expanded its bureaucratic apparatus and 'intervened in ever-widening areas of colonial political economy, directing change to serve the interests of metropolitan (or, in the case of Kenya, settler) capital, and containing and suppressing indigenous social forces'.[21] With the backing of white officials, rural chiefs in South Africa became 'decentralized despots' and contributed to the creation of an authoritarian colonial regime that relied on divisions of urban and rural, white and black.[22] In other parts of colonial Africa, the state's ability to intervene significantly in the lives of its subjects varied temporally and spatially and depended upon the colonial state's capacity to 'broadcast' its power. Colonialism was therefore a process open to contradictions, fragilities and deep structural weaknesses and faced the constant struggle to generate sufficient revenue locally to pay for itself without relying on metropolitan resources.[23] Despite their different native policies, all the colonial powers developed forms of indirect rule that responded to the need to construct a colonial administration 'on the cheap'. All colonial states became dependent upon African chiefs, intermediaries and employees.[24]

Few metropolitan governments were willing to pay the direct costs of governing colonies. Instead, colonial administrations were ordered to generate various forms of revenue locally. Some revenue came from excise taxes collected on imports and exports, but the bulk of revenue came

---

[21] Bruce Berman and John Lonsdale, *Unhappy Valley: Conflict in Kenya and Africa. Book One, State & Class* (Athens, OH: Ohio University Press, 1992), 140–76.

[22] Mahmood Mamdani, *Citizen and Subject: Contemporary Africa and the Legacy of Late Colonialism* (Princeton, NJ: Princeton University Press, 1996); Crawford Young, *The African Colonial State in Comparative Perspective* (New Haven, CT: Yale University Press, 1994).

[23] Jeffrey Herbst, *States and Power in Africa: Comparative Lessons in Authority and Control* (Princeton, NJ: Princeton University Press, 2014); Sara Berry, *No Condition is Permanent: The Social Dynamics of Agrarian Change in Sub-Saharan Africa* (Madison, WI: University of Wisconsin Press, 1993).

[24] Benjamin N. Lawrance, Emily Lynn Osborn and Richard L. Roberts, eds, *Intermediaries, Interpreters, and Clerks: African Employees in the Making of Colonial Africa* (Madison, WI: University of Wisconsin Press, 2006).

from direct taxes.[25] Collecting taxes was, however, not easily accomplished. Colonial aggression manifested itself in the episodic or systematic use of violence to force Africans to work for the new colonial economies and pay taxes. All colonial states imposed direct taxes on Africans, either in the form of head, hut or native taxes (*impoto indigena* in Portuguese colonial Africa), or labour taxes (discussed below). Africans often experienced colonialism first through taxes, which drew them more closely into the new colonial order.

By the beginning of the twentieth century the annual tax campaign had become a regular part of life under colonial rule and pulled Africans into wider worlds of commodity and labour markets. Africans had five primary means of generating the cash needed to pay the taxes: they could sell their crops, assuming that there was demand for them; they could plant new crops that had market demand within the colonial economies; they could extort commodities and cash from their neighbours or underlings; they could sell their labour to the emerging mining, urban and capitalist agricultural sectors; or they could migrate to regions where the pressures to pay taxes were, at least temporarily, less acute. These five options were not evenly dispersed throughout the continent. The range of crops that the colonial markets wanted was narrow, and not all crops flourished well in all areas. In zones of settler agriculture, the colonial state coerced Africans not to grow crops that would compete with settlers' output. Whenever they could, Africans preferred to farm for themselves in order to meet their tax commitments.

Within this context, forced labour was a prominent feature in all of colonial Africa. Africans had to be pried from their rural occupations in order to labour for wages not because they were somehow backward and lazy. Instead, they were forced into the colonial labour market because they understood all too well how dangerous, unhealthy and poorly compensated they would be there. Although compulsion took place in rural areas through pressure from village chiefs, through the barrel of a gun from colonial officials, or through pressure from colonial officials who were assisting private labour recruiters, the conditions in which African workers found themselves differed depending upon the sector that employed them: public works, mining, concession companies that controlled vast tracts of land or settler agriculture. The means of recruitment also differed.

[25] Ewout Frankema, 'Colonial Taxation and Government Spending in British Africa, 1880–1940: Maximizing Revenue or Minimizing Effort?', *Explorations in Economic History*, 48.1 (2011), 136–49.

VARIETIES OF FORCED LABOUR IN COLONIAL AFRICA

In 1930 the ILO Convention on Forced Labour identified five types of compulsory work: requisitioned labour, which was generated by direct pressure on African chiefs to provide male labour; prestation, which was a form of direct labour tax often for a fixed number of days per year; the so-called 'second portion' of the annual military draft, selecting those who were not quite able-bodied for public works labour, with some labour funnelled towards private enterprises; penal labour, which was a form of coerced labour widely used for public works but sometimes also hired out for private enterprise; and forced cultivation of certain crops, especially those deemed essential for 'national security' and colonial development. We should also include two additional categories: indentured labour and, more generally, military conscription. Although Africa was often a source of indentured labour recruitment, indentured labourers were also imported into South and East Africa in the mid-nineteenth and early twentieth centuries.[26] Military conscription was a mechanism of coerced recruitment into the military and widely used throughout the world. Both voluntary enlistment and coerced conscription took place in Africa, especially during conquest and around the two world wars. Forced labour always involved extra-economic pressures, but the nature of the forced labour differed according to the context in which it was performed and the length of service required. Moreover, the forms of forced labour changed over time, especially with the development of international scrutiny during the interwar period after the establishment of the League of Nations and the International Labour Organization. Colonial states and many postcolonial independent states used forced labour as punishment for what they considered vagrancy.

REQUISITIONED LABOUR

Once primary African resistance to conquest was crushed, colonial officials found themselves in charge of vast territories with few natural waterways and harbours. The colonial state immediately confronted the need to build

---

[26]   Peter Richardson, 'The Recruiting of Chinese Indentured Labour for the South African Gold-Mines, 1903–1908', *Journal of African History*, 18.1 (1977), 85–108; David Northrup, *Indentured Labor in the Age of Imperialism, 1834–1922* (New York: Cambridge University Press, 1995); Jelmer Vos, '"Without the Slave Trade, No Recruitment": From Slave Trading to "Migrant Recruitment" in the Lower Congo, 1830–90', in *Trafficking in Slavery's Wake: Law and the Experience of Women and Children in Africa*, ed. Benjamin N. Lawrance and Richard L. Roberts (Athens, OH: Ohio University Press, 2012), 45–64.

infrastructure: ports, railways, roads, dams, bridges, telegraphs, barracks, etc. Colonial officials were also confronted by the need to transport materials over long distances, thus requiring porters. Porterage and infrastructure construction required labour.[27] Some labour could be drawn from colonial troops, but the bulk of the work of building infrastructure fell to Africans forced into service. Most of the infrastructure was built using simple hand tools, meaning that the labour was hard and dangerous. All colonial states used some form of requisitioned labour for this purpose. The most common method was for colonial officials to approach village chiefs, who were then instructed to produce a certain number of workers. In French West Africa, Africans requisitioned for labour received a daily ration of food if their work took them more than five kilometres from their homes. Sometimes requisitioned labourers received token cash payments, especially if they were obliged to travel far from home. In British colonial Africa, women and children formed part of the requisitioned labour on infrastructure, especially road work. Few formal rules governed requisitioned labour during first two decades of colonial rule. Britain abolished the provision of requisitioned labour for private enterprises in 1908, but retained it for the building and maintenance of roads, bridges, sanitation and irrigation. By 1912, however, colonial governors began to enact legislation to control requisitioned labour by limiting the numbers of days per year that individuals could be required to work for the colonial state and prohibiting women's and children's labour on state projects.

Most requisitioned labour flowed from chiefs, who responded to pressures from the colonial administration. Chiefs often had wide latitude in choosing recruits for requisitioned labour, and some chiefs used such authority to favour friends and kinsmen and harm rivals. In Kenya, chiefs thus became 'big men' and essential allies of the colonial state. In 1919 the governor issued a circular, instructing government officials in charge of native areas to use all lawful means to 'induce' able-bodied males into the labour market, especially the labour-scarce settler agricultural sector. The Colonial Office ultimately repudiated this circular, although other mechanisms of coercive labour, including the *kipande* or identity card, and restrictions on breaching labour contracts effectively limited free labour. In French colonies, chiefs requisitioned labour for infrastructure but also for use on private plantations and for concession companies in French Equatorial Africa. Here, chiefs requisitioned over 127,000 workers to build the Congo–Océan railway, where mortality rates were upwards of 25 per cent. Chiefs in Upper Volta requisitioned 22,000 workers to build the Thiès–Kayes railway

---

[27] See the chapter by Bellucci in this volume.

in the early decades of the twentieth century, and then thousands more to build the massive irrigation works of the Office du Niger in the 1930s.[28] In Senegal, requisitioned workers were also used to haul barges and unload shipments belonging to European and Lebanese traders. On other occasions they were mobilized as porters, particularly in areas where access was difficult. Porters had to carry administrators on hammocks, with their luggage. In Guinea, where before 1914 portage was the main mode of transportation, the entire output of rubber, from the Région Forestière to Conakry on the coast, was carried by porters. About 55,000 porters were annually enrolled in this *corvée*. Chiefs in Gabon requisitioned labour for the private lumber concessions.[29] In Portuguese colonial Africa, forced labourers were mobilized under the status of *contratados* (contract labourers). Edward Ross described in 1924 how the labour system was functioning as 'virtually state serfdom': government recruited the *contratados* and sold them to private employers for several months without any guarantee of their pay. Jeremy Ball recalled the complaints of a former *contratado*: 'You were not able to buy cloth for your wife with what we were paid, much less a shirt for your child. It was obligatory work, we did it not because we wanted to, but because they wanted us to, hence it was not good.'[30] Unscrupulous recruiters duped southern Nigerians into boarding their canoes only to place them in forced labour on the harsh plantations on the island of Fernando Po (now Bioko) in Equatorial Guinea.[31]

France turned to a mix of different types of forced labour to build the port of Dakar and the Dakar–St Louis railway during the second half of the nineteenth century. Finding both skilled and unskilled labour and retaining such labour long enough to build these public works projects proved a challenge. Some skilled labour for the port project came directly from the Navy, but unskilled labour flowed mostly from the nearby prison. During the planting season, the French recruited Kruman from Liberia to augment the supply of prisoners. To secure workers for the railway project, the French negotiated with Lat Dior, the Damel of Kayor, to supply labour. Lat Dior

---

[28] Myron Echenberg and Jean Filipovich, 'African Military Labour and the Building of the *Office du Niger* Installations, 1925–1950', *Journal of African History*, 27.3 (1986), 533–51; Monica van Beusekom, *Negotiating Development: African Farmers and Colonial Experts at the Office du Niger, 1920–1960* (Portsmouth, NH: Heinemann, 2001).

[29] Jeremy Rich, *A Workman is Worthy of His Meat: Food and Colonialism in the Gabon Estuary* (Lincoln, NE: University of Nebraska Press, 2007).

[30] Ball, 'I Escaped in a Coffin', 8.

[31] Enrique Martino, '*Panya*: Economies of Deception and the Discontinuities of Indentured Labour Recruitment and the Slave Trade, Nigeria and Fernando Pó, 1890s–1940s', *African Economic History*, 44 (2016), 91–129.

in turn pressed village chiefs along the railway line to supply unskilled labour. In return, the French helped Lat Dior to return to the throne, only to be faced with a rebellion once he realized that the railway was an instrument of conquest. The employment agents of the Société des Batignoles, which organized the construction, were forced to bring in carpenters from the south of France, bricklayers and workmen from Spain and the Italian Piedmont, and foremen from Morocco. Chiefs along the railway line continued to provide unskilled labourers, most often by forcing them to work.[32]

Although we cannot draw a direct causal connection between the rubber scandal in the Congo Free State and the enactment of rules limiting requisitioned labour, the timing suggests that the scandal had significant implications for labour regimes in the rest of Africa. Despite huge global demand for ivory and rubber, which was plentiful in the Congo, the Congo Free State did not have the capacity to collect these commodities. In 1891 King Leopold decreed the *régime dominal*, by which the state acquired all vacant land and all the products of that land. Central Africans did not have land rights in the terms that Europeans understood, and thus they were considered trespassers on state land, subject to fines and imprisonment. In 1892 the Congo Free State began to provide vast tracts of state land to European companies in exchange for rents. Leopold gave himself an enormous tract in the heart of the colony. Concession owners needed labour to collect rubber and ivory. Demand for rubber and ivory in Europe was booming due to the transportation revolution (bicycles, cars, trucks) and middle-class leisure consumption (pianos and billiards) and for use as false teeth. Not surprisingly, the concession owners and Leopold turned to requisitioned African labour, eventually requiring Africans to work for the state or the concession companies for up to 280 days per year. Such labour requirements threatened Africans' agrarian economies, which had been eroded by the land alienation act. Few Africans came forward willingly. The state turned to the *Force Publique*, the African army of the Congo Free State, to secure African labour, resulting in horrendous crimes and a massive death toll. Reports from men on the ground and journalists including Roger Casement, E. D. Morel and William Henry Sheppard raised awareness in Europe and caused a public outcry. The Belgian Parliament held an independent inquiry into the abuses in the Congo in 1905, and in 1908 the Parliament voided Leopold's claim to the Congo and annexed the territory. Concerned about the continued loss of African population, the Belgian Congo introduced laws limiting requisitioned labour and prohibiting labour recruitment from regions suffering extreme depopulation. Old Congo

[32] Babacar Fall, *Le travail forcé en Afrique-Occidentale française, 1900–1946* (Paris: Karthala, 1993).

Free State concessions were disbanded, but new ones were auctioned off. Concession companies remained a significant feature of the Belgian Congo's economy, and they continued to requisition labour.[33]

We know surprisingly little about forced labour in North Africa. Jacques Berque only mentions in passing that 'the working masses were sometimes engaged in large-scale public works, such as the Algerian dams, or that harbor at Casablanca', but he does not explore the issue more deeply.[34] Requisitioned labour was certainly used to build the Suez Canal and other major public works in Egypt, and in building and maintaining the railways, harbours and road networks in North Africa, but scholars have focused on other aspects of labour mobilization, such as 'semi-feudal' peasant relations and conscription during wartime.[35] North Africa remains an area where important comparative research still needs to be conducted.

It is important to distinguish between requisitioned labour for public works projects and that for private enterprises, even if few Africans understood the difference. The work was harsh and brutal in both sectors. Demand for requisitioned labour put direct state pressure on village chiefs, who mediated between colonial states and broader African communities, and who had to balance state pressures for workers and the well-being of the village. Alexander Keese describes how chiefs in Congo-Brazzaville used requisitioned labour to fulfil the demands of the state but also forced labourers to work on their own fields.[36] An updated history of African

---

[33] Jean Stengers, 'The Congo Free State and the Belgian Congo before 1914', in *Colonialism in Africa, 1870–1960*, ed. Louis H. Gann and Peter Duignan, vol. II (Cambridge: Cambridge University Press, 1969), 261–92; Adam Hochschild, *King Leopold's Ghost: A Story of Greed, Terror, and Heroism in Colonial Africa* (New York: Houghton Mifflin, 1998). See also John Higginson, *A Working Class in the Making: Belgian Colonial Labor Policy, Private Enterprise, and the African Mineworker, 1907–1951* (Madison, WI: University of Wisconsin Press, 1989).

[34] Jacques Berque, *French North Africa: The Maghrib between Two World Wars*, trans. Jean Stewart (London: Faber and Faber, 1962), 42.

[35] See, for example, Ellis Goldberg, 'Peasants in Revolt: Egypt 1919', *International Journal of Middle East Studies*, 24.2 (1992), 265–80; Nathan Brown, *Peasant Politics in Modern Egypt: The Struggle Against the State* (New Haven, CT: Yale University Press, 1990); Reinhard Schulze, 'Colonization and Resistance', in *Peasants and Politics in the Modern Middle East*, ed. Farhad Kazemi and John Waterbury (Miami, FL: Florida International University Press, 1991), 171–202; Zeinab Abul-Magd, *Imagined Empires: A History of Revolt in Egypt* (Berkeley, CA: University of California Press, 2013), 82–93.

[36] Alexander Keese, 'Slow Abolition within the Colonial Mind: British and French Debates about "Vagrancy", "African Laziness", and Forced Labour in West Central and South Central Africa, 1945–1965', *International Review of Social History*, 59.3 (2014), 377–407.

chiefs is still to be written, but the debate on the invention of tradition has suggested that chiefs were actively complicit in this process, and that they benefited from the augmented authority that it provided. In many areas of colonial Africa, village and canton chiefs used unpaid requisitioned labour for the state to increase the size of their own fields. Village chiefs often had wide latitude in whom they recruited for requisitioned labour. The freed slave villages in French West Africa during the era of conquest, where slaves of France's enemies were sent, often formed a reserve army for the military's need for porters and infrastructure workers.

INDENTURED LABOUR

Africans were recruited into various systems of indentured labour that fed labour needs in the Atlantic world, the Indian Ocean world and on various plantation sectors in or near Africa. In addition, Indian and Chinese indentured labour flowed into Africa as part of a global movement of unfree labour in the aftermath of the abolition of slavery. Indentured labour was a public–private system that funnelled millions of workers around the world from the 1840s to the 1930s to meet the demand for labour largely in tropical agriculture. Hugh Tinker and other scholars have labelled indentured labour a 'new system of slavery', wherein labourers worked for little more than maintenance in brutal conditions not of their own choosing.[37] Other scholars have argued that workers 'freely' entered into indenture agreements that were carefully overseen by British officials.[38] In general, however, few labourers were made aware of the conditions they were to enter or the exact terms of their contracts, nor were their decisions to accept indenture made without coercion, since many faced significant poverty and had few alternatives.

Indentured labour was not a significant part of the African coerced labour scene; its most significant presence was in the sugar sector of Natal, South Africa, where South Asian indentured workers were recruited to build this new sector in the absence of a steady stream of African wage labour. More than 145,000 Indian indentured workers were imported into Natal between 1875 and 1911 to augment the 6,450 Indian indentured workers who had been imported at the beginning of the sugar boom there. In the

---

[37] Hugh Tinker, *A New System of Slavery: The Export of Indian Labour Overseas, 1830–1920* (London: Oxford University Press, 1974).

[38] David Northrup, 'Overseas Movements of Slaves and Indentured Workers', in *The Cambridge World History of Slavery, Volume 4: AD 1804–AD 2016*, ed. David Eltis, Stanley L. Engerman, Seymour Drescher and David Richardson (Cambridge: Cambridge University Press, 2017), 20–48.

late nineteenth century and the early decades of the twentieth century, nearly 40,000 Indian indentured workers were imported into East Africa for railway construction. Between 1904 and 1907, 63,695 indentured Chinese labourers was recruited to work the gold mines of the Witwatersrand in an effort to keep them operating and to undercut the growing tendency of African workers to resist the mine owners' demands for disciplined low-wage workers. During this period, Chinese indentured labourers constituted 35 per cent of the total labour force on the Rand, but the Chinese proved more demanding about labour protections than African labour, and the experiment was abandoned.[39]

By far the largest numbers of indentured workers were imported into the Indian Ocean islands of Mauritius and Reunion, which emerged as major sugar producers in the aftermath of the decline of sugar production in the Caribbean. Together, these Mascarene islands imported 527,402 indentured Indians, of whom 86 per cent went to Mauritius; 34,219 indentured Africans, almost all of whom went to Reunion; and slightly over two thousand indentured Chinese. Conditions on these sugar islands varied by plantation and the price of sugar. Some indentured workers renewed their contracts, others returned home, and a significant number sought out other forms of livelihood on the islands once their contracts ended. In all cases, during the period of indenture, these workers had no right to leave their employers and many were subject to harsh conditions and brutal punishments. By 1922 indentured labour was largely ended.[40]

PRESTATION OR LABOUR TAX

Prestation became a more formal means of forcing Africans to labour on public works projects. In both French and British colonial Africa, the number of days required for *corvée* began to be fixed in the years before the First World War. In French colonial Africa, prestation was a form of annual labour tax, by which all able-bodied men were required to work for a set number of days on public work projects. Legislation set the maximum number of days of obligatory labour but gave the various colonies latitude in setting the exact

[39] Rachel K. Bright, *Chinese Labour in South Africa, 1902–10: Race, Violence, and Global Spectacle* (Basingstoke: Palgrave Macmillan, 2013).

[40] Richard B. Allen, *European Slave Trading in the Indian Ocean, 1500–1850* (Athens, OH: Ohio University Press, 2014); Gwyn Campbell, ed., *Abolition and its Aftermath in Indian Ocean Africa and Asia* (New York: Routledge, 2007); Alessandro Stanziani, *Sailors, Slaves, and Immigrants: Bondage in the Indian Ocean World, 1750–1914* (New York: Palgrave Macmillan, 2014).

duration, which ranged from eight to thirteen days every year. In Senegal, Africans were obliged to work eight days per year, while in the French Sudan the period was fixed at twelve days. Prestation labour in Senegal was reduced to four days in 1922. About 90 per cent of 35,000 kilometres of roads were built under the supervision of the *commandants de cercles*. In Senegal, in 1923 alone, prestation labour generated 4,969,840 workdays.

Workers mobilized under the regime of prestation were not remunerated. Only a daily portion of food was given to each worker, and even this was not guaranteed. Among the frequent abuses of prestation were the retention of the *prestataires* for longer than the allowed period and the practice of using the same workers twice. The regulation that workmen would not be sent to work on sites located more than five kilometres from their villages was routinely ignored. In French Equatorial Africa, a labour tax was introduced in 1918, set at seven days per year, but due to continued labour shortages, in 1925 it was raised to fifteen days to help recruit workers for railway construction. Food was supplied only to those working more than thirty kilometres from their homes. Although Britain abolished requisitioned labour for private companies in 1908, it left intact obligatory 'communal labour' under village chiefs. Women and children were forced to maintain roads and sanitation works in the Gold Coast as well as in other British colonies.[41] Obligatory communal labour persists to this day in rural South Africa.

In 1906 Henry Nevinson published a scathing critique of the abuses in organizing and using forced labour in Angola that came just on the heels of the Congo scandal. Nevinson was particularly incensed by how Africans were enslaved for 'debts' and marched to the coast, where they were 'freed' by Portuguese officials only to be sent to São Tomé as 'voluntary' labour.[42] Elsewhere in Portuguese colonial Africa, labourers in Angola were forced to work for two weeks out of every six weeks or until the 'quota is maintained by shift'. Edward Ross – who interviewed hundreds of workers and whose report on forced labour in Portuguese Africa shamed the League of Nations into taking action – mentioned in 1924 a case in one of the villages he had visited: 'The soldiers come, catch the people, children included, and tie them up. They take about half of the family, leaving the other half to change off with' when the soldiers returned.'[43] The paradox was that the Portuguese,

---

[41] Kwabena O. Akurang-Parry, '"The Loads Are Heavier than Usual": Forced Labor by Women and Children in the Central Province, Gold Coast (Colonial Ghana), ca. 1900–1940', *African Economic History*, 30 (2002), 31–51.

[42] Henry Nevinson, *A Modern Slavery* (London and New York: Harper, 1906).

[43] Edward Alsworth Ross, *Report on Employment of Native Labor in Portuguese Africa* (New York: Abbott, 1925) cited in William H. Worger, Nancy L. Clark and Edward

under Prime Minister António de Oliveira Salazar, were finally gaining control over the vast interior of their colonies and imposing increasingly harsh labour requirements just as France, Britain and Belgium were restricting *corvée* labour, including the establishment of a prohibition on recruiting forced labour during the active agricultural calendar.

In French West Africa, the first real reform of forced labour coincided with the Popular Front government and, more specifically, the appointment of De Coppet as Governor General of French West Africain 1936. In 1937 De Coppet instituted the system of *rachat des prestations*, which allowed wealthier Africans to redeem their labour taxes in cash. Prior to his appointment, only a few people had the right to do this. The *rachat* policy swelled local budgets so that administrators could hire skilled workers for the construction of roads. At the Brazzaville Conference in 1944, Charles de Gaulle rewarded Africans for their support of the Free French with the promise of an eventual repeal of the hated labour tax and the *indigénat*. De Gaulle also promised to introduce a modified form of representative government by permitting political parties and establishing colonial legislatures to advise on colonial rule.[44]

MILITARY CONSCRIPTION

Demand for men to fight, to carry war materiel and to grow crops that were essential to conquest, especially during the First World War, led to significant and sustained intervention in African economies.[45] Britain, France and Belgium increased the recruitment of African soldiers. France turned to conscription to recruit Africans for the front in Europe; Britain increased its voluntary recruitment of soldiers in West Africa and in East Africa primarily for the military campaigns in Cameroon and East Africa. All colonial powers recruited far more labourers than soldiers, since fighting in Africa was labour intensive. In the absence of railways serving the military fronts, war materiel, food and shelter had to be carried overland. David Killingray argues that far more Africans were forcibly recruited as labourers for the war effort than all of the workers forcibly recruited for the mines, concessions, plantations and settler farms. Coercion to fill the pressing need for carriers during wartime was widespread. Britain

---

A. Alpers, *Africa and the West: A Documentary History. Vol. 2: From Colonialism to Independence, 1875 to the Present* (New York: Oxford University Press, 2010), 51.

[44] Fall, *Travail forcé*; Frederick Cooper, *Decolonization and African Society: The Labor Question in French and British Africa* (Cambridge: Cambridge University Press, 1996).

[45] See the chapter by Moyd and Glassman in this volume.

turned to forced recruitment for the East African Carrier Corps that ultimately proved essential in defeating the Germans, but it also resulted in an extraordinarily high mortality rate due to disease and malnutrition. Killingray argues that forced recruitment 'stripped bare' the African populations in large areas of eastern Belgian Congo, Rwanda, Uganda, Kenya, German East Africa, Northern Rhodesia, Nyasaland and the northern regions of Portuguese East Africa. He estimates that half of the total male population of the African reserves in Kenya had been forcibly recruited; overall, Britain had conscripted over half a million men in its African colonies by 1918.[46] Belgium increased recruitment of Africans for the *Force Publique* and the carrier corps, which played crucial roles in the defeat of Germany in Rwanda and Burundi. By 1918, however, pressure for recruitment decreased everywhere, with the exception of French Africa.

France, which had suffered a massive loss of young men as soldiers during the First World War, decided to continue with the annual military recruitment in colonial Africa. Throughout the 1920s and into the 1930s, French colonial states discovered that they could use the annual military draft to identify two categories of young men: able-bodied recruits for the military and those deemed too unhealthy to serve. Those considered healthy were subject to a lottery system out of which would flow military recruits for a three-year stint in the *Tirailleurs sénégalais*.[47] Those not selected were placed in a vague 'reserve army' category, but not conscripted. During the interwar period, France sought to promote colonial economic development through massive public works projects but faced the challenge of finding adequate labour for these projects. A decree dated 31 October 1926 authorized the enlistment of men from among those examined and found fit, but not needed by the military authorities, to be used for public work. They constituted the *tirailleurs la pelle* – soldiers with tools. Men in the second portion, which was the largest share of this population, were drafted into two-year 'contracts' for public service. The French West African model of the 'second portion' was fashioned on one started in Madagascar two years earlier. In 1928 French officials used this 'reserve army' of healthy recruits for public works, including the massive irrigation scheme of the Office du Niger, which was building huge irrigation works using largely manual labour, and for building the Thies–Niger railway. Between 1928 and 1946 nearly

---

[46] David Killingray, 'Labour Exploitation for Military Campaigns in British Colonial Africa 1870–1945', *Journal of Contemporary History*, 24.3 (1989), 483–501.

[47] See Myron Echenberg, *Colonial Conscripts: The Tirailleurs Sénégalais in French West Africa, 1857–1960* (Portsmouth, NH: Heinemann, 1991) for the classic study of the *Tirailleurs sénégalais*.

three thousand men were conscripted into the 'second portion' annually. The peak in recruitment occurred under the Vichy administration in 1941 and 1942, when 4,700 and 5,550 men, respectively, were conscripted as soldier-workers in the colony.[48] The decree of 1926 also provided the legal basis for sending workmen to private cotton and sisal plantations in eastern Senegal and French Sudan. The inhuman working conditions of the 'second portion' are illustrated by the August 1945 report of a committee headed by the former Governor General (1936–39) of French Equatorial Africa, Joseph-François Reste de Roca: 'Out of a thousand soldier-workers employed, 921 suffered from general morbidity and 19 died of dysentery over a four and half month period.' The report concluded that the Office du Niger was a complete failure in both human and economic terms.[49]

Military recruitment resumed with the outbreak of the Second World War. Following a decade of slackening commitment to African development during the Great Depression, wartime mobilization of men and commodities led to far more intensive colonial interventions in the economy. Commodity marketing boards, 'grow more' campaigns and coerced labour in all sectors were hallmarks of this new interventionism. Innovations in aircraft and weapons led to a frenzied search for the minerals needed for advanced technologies. This greater intervention during the war led immediately afterwards to an era of enhanced commitment to development, public and higher education, healthcare and infrastructural investments.[50]

FORCED CULTIVATION

Most Africans farmed for at least part of the year and for parts of their lives. Most African farmers responded positively to price incentives and innovations in transportation by increasing their output and bringing their crops to market. This was certainly the case, for example, with palm oil, peanuts and cocoa in West Africa and with sesame and coffee in East

---

[48] Echenberg and Filipovich, 'African Military Labour'.

[49] Babacar Fall, *Social History in French West Africa: Forced Labour, Labour Market, Women and Politics* (Amsterdam/Calcutta: South-South Exchange Programme for Research on the History of Development/Centre for Studies in Social Sciences, 2002), 11. See also Amidu Magasa, *Papa-commandant a jeté un grand filet devant nous: les exploités des rives du Niger, 1900–1962* (Paris: Maspero, 1978).

[50] Frederick Cooper, *Africa since 1940: The Past of the Present* (New York: Cambridge University Press, 2002).

Africa.[51] Why then did colonial states resort to compulsion to force Africans to cultivate certain crops?

Most of the crops or commodities that colonial authorities required as part of this regime of coercion were those in high demand in Europe. Rubber was one of these in the late nineteenth and early twentieth centuries, to feed the growing demand for bicycle tyres, among other products. This demand put downside pressure on the regions of Africa where wild rubber flourished, especially the Congo. Among the worst abuses was the forced collection – a variant of forced cultivation – of wild rubber in the Congo Free State, discussed above. Africans individually or as collective villages were assigned quotas of wild rubber, and failure to meet these quotas led to severe punishments that ultimately led to the collapse of the Congo Free State and its annexation by Belgium. Vegetable oils derived from palm kernels and peanuts did not seem to warrant coercion, since peasant producers responded with alacrity to price incentives. Cotton, however, proved to be the crop most susceptible to coerced cultivation and most consistently in demand in metropolitan economies.[52]

Demand for cotton in Europe expanded exponentially with the industrialization of the textile industry during the second half of the nineteenth century. Since cotton does not grow in temperate European climates, industrialists had to draw on supplies from thousands of miles away. This was true of all the major European colonial powers: Britain, France, Germany, Italy, Belgium and Portugal. Some promoted cotton production for export in the late nineteenth century, but the era of intensified cotton production occurred in the interwar period.

Coerced cotton production took many forms. In peasant zones of West and East Africa, colonial officials expected market forces to yield sufficient cotton to feed metropolitan demand. Metropolitan cotton mills wanted higher-quality product, lower prices and steadier supplies than were available on the world market. Because African peasants had a keen sense of the labour demands for various crops, they often devoted their efforts to crops that had higher yields and better market prices. Cotton was usually not their choice, since it was labour intensive, often interfered with food crops and sometimes fetched higher prices locally than in the export market. Colonial officials were mostly disappointed by the quality and quantity of cotton delivered for export, and they increasingly turned to more coercive means:

---

[51] See the chapter by Tischler in this volume.

[52] For the range of colonial efforts to promote cotton, see Allen Isaacman and Richard L. Roberts, eds, *Cotton, Colonialism, and Social History in Sub-Saharan Africa* (Portsmouth, NH: Heinemann, 1995).

forcing peasants to cultivate cotton, forcing them to bring their harvest to market and often forcing them to sell their harvest at fixed prices.

Among the most coercive cotton regimes emerged in Portugal's colonies of Angola and Mozambique. Despite the relatively small metropolitan cotton textile industry, colonial officials were under significant pressure to produce colonial supplies. In 1928 Angola and Mozambique provided only 2 per cent of Portugal's cotton demand. The Portuguese cotton lobby played an important role in Salazar's *Estado Nuovo* and pushed Portuguese colonial officials to turn to forced labour to increase colonial cotton production in Angola and Mozambique.[53] By 1946 these colonies were producing 95 per cent of Portugal's demand for raw cotton. But the cost to African peasants was extremely high. As Allen Isaacman has described, the colonial state put enormous pressure on African chiefs and headmen to force African peasants to cultivate cotton despite its low yield and its interference with subsistence crops. By 1944 vast tracts of Mozambique were formally directed as cotton concessions, and well over 800,000 Mozambicans were forced to cultivate cotton and bring their harvests to official markets even as prices fell. Mozambique achieved such results only through a brutal regime of labour control and punishments exerted by African headmen and police.[54]

In the Ivory Coast, the development of coffee and cocoa plantations after 1930 was accomplished by compulsory cultivation and by the conscription of workmen for the benefit of French settlers. In Italian Somaliland, Italian settlers and colonial officials along the fertile Juba River responded to the scarcity of agricultural labour by introducing a unique recruitment approach. In a system that was locally referred to as 'Italian marriage', girls and women were forcibly married to men on the condition that they worked on the settlers' farms for a set number of years.[55]

Africans faced forced cultivation on smaller scales everywhere. Most prominent were the 'chief's fields', sometimes called the *champs du commandant* (fields of the colonial district officer). Some of these fields were designated as experimental fields, where new crops were grown to assess their economic

[53]   Alexander Keese, 'Searching for the Reluctant Hands: Obsession, Ambivalence and the Practice of Organising Involuntary Labour in Colonial Cuanza-Sul and Malange Districts, Angola, 1926–1945', *Journal of Imperial and Commonwealth History*, 41.2 (2013), 238–58.

[54]   Allen Isaacman, *Cotton is the Mother of Poverty: Peasants, Work, and Rural Struggle in Colonial Mozambique, 1938–1961* (Portsmouth, NH: Heinemann, 1996).

[55]   Francesca Declich, 'Italian Weddings and Memory of Trauma: Colonial Domestic Policy in Southern Somalia, 1910–41', in *Marriage by Force? Contestation over Consent and Coercion in Africa*, ed. Anne Bunting, Benjamin N. Lawrance and Richard L. Roberts (Athens, OH: Ohio University Press, 2016), 109–34.

and agronomic viability. But chiefs throughout colonial Africa benefited from their control over requisitioned labour and directed village labour to their own fields, which benefited them directly.[56] This was a central part of the 'bargains of collaboration' that provided the incentive for Africans to serve their colonial overlords.[57]

PRISON LABOUR

Created to discipline and punish, prisons in colonial Africa provided a stream of coerced labour for public works and private enterprise. Prisoners everywhere were under compulsion to work on the maintenance of the prison itself. Female as well as male prisoners worked in gendered roles in the prisons. Minors were increasingly separated from adults and sometimes sent to agricultural colonies, where they worked as part of their rehabilitation. In no cases were prisoners consulted as to whether they wished to work or not. They were compelled to do so. In most colonies, the law obliged prisoners to labour as part of their sentences. In French colonial Africa, prison labour was commonly used to provide supplementary manpower for public works projects. Prisoners were mobilized to build and repair harbours, in railway construction and in the maintenance of government buildings. Generally, mandatory penal labour did not involve the mobilization of large numbers of people. However, arbitrary arrests by the *commandants de cercle* under the *indigénat* usually resulted in assignment to work sites. In French Guinea, prisoners were obliged to work five days a week, with weekends and holidays off. In French Equatorial Africa, prisoners were transferred to work for expatriate logging companies and into the hands of concession owners. In British colonial Africa, a parallel system of prisons – one under native administration and the other under the central government – funnelled prisoners into different labour pools: one for native authorities' public and often private needs and the other primarily for public works. In some cases, as in South Africa, where the prison labour system was highly developed, prisoners working for private enterprise were paid a nominal wage, but this was actually paid to the prison administration as a way of financing the prison system.

South Africa developed the most comprehensive prison labour system. From the founding of the Cape Colony, prisoners had worked on public works. South African prisons developed two models for using prison labour

---

[56] Berman and Lonsdale, *Unhappy Valley*; Keese, 'Slow Abolition'.

[57] Lawrance, Osborn and Roberts, eds, *Intermediaries, Interpreters, and Clerks*, 3–34.

for other than public works. The first was the contract system, under which light manufacturing was conducted in the prisons. On Robben Island, for example, prisoners produced dried seaweed that was sold internationally. The second model was the lease system, whereby prisoners were hired out to private enterprises. At the beginning of the twentieth century, De Beers diamond mines at Kimberley were the largest employers of leased prison labour in South Africa. After the South African War, the gold mines of Witwatersrand increasingly used prison labour. After the 1913 Natives Land Act, white farmers found it difficult to recruit cheap African labour. With the massive increase in incarceration due to pass law violations, especially after the introduction of apartheid, the South African prisons faced severe overcrowding and escalating expenses. To reduce both, the prisons increasingly used the lease system to funnel prison labour to white farmers. In the 1950s more than 200,000 prisoners annually were released on parole to white farmers for whom they were forced to work. These were termed 'farm jails'.[58]

In French West Africa, colonial authorities provided prison labourers to a private company, the Société des Salins du Sine-Saloum, between 1943 and 1956, and confined them to the disagreeable, harsh and underpaid task of salt extraction. Colonial officials justified this action as necessary in order to provide salt for the wider community of the French West Africa Federation, given that no free labour was willing to work under the prevailing conditions and for the low wages being offered.[59] The use of penal labour and government-assisted recruitment lasted until 1956, ten years after the provisions of the Houphouët-Boigny law that legally prohibited the use of forced labour.

AFRICANS' RESISTANCE TO FORCED LABOUR AND ITS IMPACT ON AFRICAN SOCIETIES

The height of forced labour recruitment occurred between 1920 and 1936. Until 1936 the only significant form of African response to forced labour was desertion. We should consider desertion to be a form of spontaneous rebellion that sometimes involved individuals and sometimes groups. Jeremy Ball has argued that in Portuguese colonial Africa, 'the only clear act of

---

[58]   Allen Cook, *Akin to Slavery: Prison Labour in South Africa* (London: International Defence and Aid Fund, 1982).

[59]   Ibra Sene, 'Colonisation française et main-d'œuvre carcérale au Sénégal: de l'emploi des détenus des camps pénaux sur les chantiers des travaux routiers (1927–1940)', *French Colonial History*, 5 (2004), 153–71.

resistance was to flee'.[60] Colonial officials assumed that at least 20 per cent of forced labour would desert. At notoriously abusive labour sites such as Samé, Diakandapé and Marakala in French Sudan, Kindia and Coyah in Guinea, and Wassadou and Koutal in Senegal, forced labour deserted at much higher rates. For these workers, desertion was probably the only viable form of resistance against oppression. Over time, Africans turned to other forms of resistance to forced labour, namely sabotage, refusal to work and songs that shamed African police, chiefs and officials.[61] Since recruitment of forced labour drew from widely dispersed regions, workers rarely developed the consciousness necessary to stage more organized labour stoppages. In the late 1930s resistance to forced labour became widespread. Workers complained more frequently about the quality of food, working conditions, failure to remit promised pay and the brutality of the supervisors. Between 1937 and 1945 we begin to see the occupation of work sites, including management headquarters. Despite these organized labour actions, resistance to colonial forced labour was primarily passive. Jeremy Ball argues that 'work songs lamented suffering the work regime', but the forced labourers 'did not directly challenge the system'.[62]

The long history of forced labour had a significant impact on the long-term health and sustainability of African populations. French Equatorial Africa gained notoriety for the widespread use of forced labour. Colonial authorities forced the able-bodied male population of Gabon and the Middle Congo to work in the timber camps whose products formed a large part of the colonies' exports. On arriving at the lumber sites, Africans were forced to sign binding long-term contracts with European employers. The expansion of cocoa on São Tomé, Principe and Fernando Po depended upon coercing workers into contracts, often by subterfuge and other forms of coercion.[63] With so many able-bodied males away from their home villages, food shortages became endemic, leading to increased poverty and malnutrition, which in turn increased the villagers' susceptibility to diseases including malaria, sleeping sickness and tuberculosis. In the timber-working districts, where there were few women, prostitution and syphilis spread, and drunkenness mounted catastrophically.

---

[60] Ball, 'I Escaped in a Coffin', 2.

[61] See the classic statement by Leroy Vail and Landeg White, 'Forms of Resistance: Songs and Perceptions of Power in Colonial Mozambique', *American Historical Review*, 88.4 (1983), 883–919.

[62] Ball, 'I Escaped in a Coffin', 2.

[63] Catherine Higgs, *Chocolate Islands: Cocoa, Slavery, and Colonial Africa* (Athens, OH: Ohio University Press, 2012).

Around ten thousand forced labourers worked annually on the Congo–Océan railway from 1921 to 1934, linking Brazzaville to Pointe-Noire. Work on this railway was brutally hard, and mortality among the workers enormous. According to official data, in the early 1920s, 25 per cent of the workers perished annually from starvation, dysentery, other diseases and mistreatment. In response to international criticism and the flight of workers to neighbouring colonies, the French improved the labour conditions, and mortality declined to 12 per cent. This figure, however, did not include porters and those who perished *en route* before reaching the construction site. As work progressed, colonial authorities could no longer recruit labour regionally. Instead, they were forced to recruit from as far away as Ubangi-Shari and Chad, where workers had to travel over a thousand kilometres before reaching Brazzaville. Other workers from Ubangi-Shari and Chad who did not travel to Brazzaville were often forced to work on European-owned concessions growing cotton. Africans did not wait around to be conscripted by their chiefs into the ranks of forced labour. Those Africans close to colonial borders fled to different colonies where the labour demands were less strenuous. This was the case in the French Congo, where Africans could flee to both neighbouring Angola and the Belgian Congo. Fugitives from forced labour, however, found themselves under even more draconian labour demands in Angola after the intensification of Portuguese colonial rule and forced labour demands in the 1930s, and from increasing vigilance against 'vagrancy' in the Belgian Congo.[64]

In French West Africa, the people the Mossi region of Upper Volta (now Burkina Faso) found themselves in an unenviable situation, in which they were targeted by colonial authorities as an important labour reserve. From 1932 to 1946, fifty thousand workers were recruited annually for the coffee and cocoa plantations in Ivory Coast, and another fifty thousand were recruited forcibly to settle the cotton-growing areas of the Office du Niger in neighbouring French Sudan. Increased labour coercion stimulated emigration to the neighbouring British colony of Gold Coast (now Ghana). Such emigration increased to 100,000 and should be considered a form of resistance to increased forced labour recruitment.

In the areas considered labour reserves where forced labour recruitment was especially intense, the absence of so many young men who formed the bulk of the able-bodied workers and who were off working in the mines, the cities or the zones of capitalist agriculture, led to declining agricultural output

---

[64]   Alexander Keese, 'The Constraints of Late Colonial Reform Policy: Forced Labour Scandals in the Portuguese Congo (Angola) and the Limits of Reform under Authoritarian Colonial Rule, 1955–61', *Portuguese Studies*, 28.2 (2012), 186–200.

in the villages. Care for the weak, the infirm, the very young and the very old became precarious. Moreover, since the cash that these migrating young men brought back was most often turned over to elderly male household heads and circulated within tight bounds of matrimonial exchange, few resources remained to be invested in agricultural modernization, such as new technologies of production and new crops. In all cases, the powers of these rural despots also involved the ability to approve or deny access to new land to farm. In some parts of Africa, especially where European settlers arrived, access to new and more fertile lands was blocked even more fully. Since relatively few women participated in these labour markets, the many women who remained in rural areas experienced increasing poverty precisely because so much male labour was absent working in the capitalist sectors. This is what Ester Boserup called the feminization of poverty, and it increased dramatically during the course of the twentieth century in Africa. Progressive impoverishment of rural areas pushed more men and women into the labour force and into the expanding urban areas of mid-century colonial Africa.[65]

INTERNATIONAL SCRUTINY, NEW HUMANITARIAN SENSIBILITIES AND THE END OF FORCED LABOUR

The interwar period introduced new pressures that senior colonial administrators and metropolitan governments could not easily ignore. The establishment of the League of Nations and the ILO in 1919, regardless of how ineffective they were in many areas, nonetheless changed the nature and the level of scrutiny to which the colonies were now exposed. In addition, new forms of documentary reporting exposed abuses throughout the colonial world. These international organizations and individuals put pressure on colonial ministries, which in turn put pressure on colonial administrators, to address these practices and abuses.[66]

In response to pressures from the League of Nations and from non-governmental organizations and journalists, the ILO established a Committee of Experts on Native Labour in 1927. These experts included colonial administrators, some of whom had served on the Temporary Slavery Commission, which had been appointed by the League in 1924. It also included representatives from labour and business interests. Befitting

---

[65] Ester Boserup, *Woman's Role in Economic Development* (London: Earthscan, 1970).

[66] J. P. Daughton, 'Behind the Imperial Curtain: International Humanitarian Efforts and the Critique of French Colonialism in the Interwar Years', *French Historical Studies*, 34.3 (2011), 503–28.

such a committee, among its first tasks was to assemble a questionnaire to be sent out to member governments. Just as with the Temporary Slavery Commission, these requests for information sent bolts of activity up and down the administrative ladder from various ministries of colonies to local governors and from local governors to district officers. Coincident with efforts to frame international conventions regarding slavery and forced labour, the 1920s also witnessed the emergence of a new humanitarian sentiment that was linked to the growing international women's movements and to the maturation of new forms of documentary reporting, which further opened colonial practices to wider scrutiny and debate. Such new forms of documentary reporting included travel accounts, such as those by André Gide on the labour abuses in Chad in the late 1920s, and journalistic reporting that sometimes embarrassed colonial officials and often sparked public outrage.[67]

By 1930 the Committee of Experts on Native Labour had pounded out the ILO Forced Labour Convention (No. 29), which defined forced or compulsory labour as 'all work or service which is exacted from any person under the menace of any penalty and for which the said person has not offered himself voluntarily'. The Convention exempted military conscription, service in the event of an emergency, penal labour and 'minor communal services' that could be considered 'normal civic obligations incumbent upon the members of the community'. Forced labour for private enterprise and for underground work in mines was expressly forbidden. The 1930 Geneva Convention aimed 'to suppress the use of forced or compulsory labour in all its forms within a shortest possible period'.[68] Not all colonial powers agreed to the 1930 Convention. It was ratified in 1931 by Britain and the Netherlands. Italy ratified it in 1934 and France in 1937. But ratification of the Convention was delayed in Belgium until 1944 and in Portugal until 1956. Some leading colonial officials, including René Mercier for the French side, argued strongly for the need to modify but maintain temporary forms of forced labour as a way of 'educating' Africans about the value of work.[69] France passed a bill on 21 August 1930 to regulate its coercive labour policies. *Travail forcé* was formally abolished, although it was replaced with *travail obligatoire*. Portugal, under the Salazar regime, chose instead to augment compulsory labour in its effort to promote the economic development of its African colonies.

[67]   See André Gide, *Voyage au Congo* (Paris: Gallimard, 1927), and Albert Londres, *Terre d'ébène (la traite des noirs)* (Paris: A. Michel, 1929).

[68]   Forced Labour Convention, 1930 (No. 29), Article 1.

[69]   René Mercier, *Le travail obligatoire dans les colonies africaines* (Paris: Larose, 1933).

In 1930 the League began to investigate complaints of compulsory labour recruitment and the shipment of labour under government oversight from Liberia to Fernando Po. This commerce in coerced labour was at least three decades old and fed the growing demand for labour on the cocoa plantations on Fernando Po. Liberians were forcibly recruited and effectively sold to Fernando Po planters. The League's investigation revealed widespread government complicity in this trade in coerced labour, resulting in a scandal that rocked the Liberian government. The investigation did not, however, look into the emerging compulsory labour recruitment for the Firestone rubber plantations. In 1926 76 per cent of the 10,500 workers on the rubber plantations had not signed on voluntarily.[70]

The deepening of the Depression in the 1930s and the rumblings of war blunted the potential reforms in Africa regarding forced labour and slavery. In some areas of colonial Africa, the Depression, which often reduced sharply the incomes of peasants and workers, led to the resurgence of forced labour practices such as pawning in order to secure cash for taxes. In the absence of significant other sources of wealth, the pawning of people in payment of loans was a well-established but declining practice in much of West Africa. During the Depression, however, there was a resurgence of pawning.[71] In response to the crises of the Depression, reformist governments were elected in several European metropoles. They contributed to increased attention to colonial reforms. In France, under the Popular Front, which came to power in 1936, the hypocrisy inherent in abolishing forced labour but retaining obligatory labour was increasingly emphasized. In 1937 Governor General De Coppet denounced the persistence of forced labour:

> We are lying in France, in Europe, in the entire world, in Geneva and at the International Labour Organization when, regulations and circulars in hand, we speak of the organization of public works labor in the colonies. We dishonor our colonial administration and we demoralize our civil servants by asking them to apply, on paper only, regulations inapplicable in practice.[72]

---

[70] League of Nations, Secretariat (1930), *Report of the Liberian Commission of Enquiry* (C.658.M272), http://biblio-archive.unog.ch/Dateien/CouncilMSD/C-658-M-272-1930-VI_EN.pdf (accessed 10 January 2019). See also I. K. Sundiata, *Black Scandal: America and the Liberian Labor Crisis, 1929–1936* (Philadelphia, PA: Institute for the Study of Human Issues, 1980), and Emily S. Rosenberg, 'The Invisible Protectorate: The United States, Liberia, and the Evolution of Neocolonialism, 1909–40', *Diplomatic History*, 9.3 (1985), 191–214.

[71] Paul E. Lovejoy and Toyin Falola, eds, *Pawnship, Slavery, and Colonialism in Africa* (Trenton, NJ: Africa World Press, 2003).

[72] Quoted in Cooper, *Decolonization and African Society*, 31.

The outbreak of the Second World War witnessed the return of military conscription and forced cultivation in many African colonies. With the fall of France in 1940, most of colonial Africa remained under the Vichy regime (French Equatorial Africa sided with the Free French), and Vichy's corporatist ideology provided justification for forced labour for the 'public good'. Under Vichy rule, forced labour in French West Africa reached unprecedented levels. The French were not alone in intensifying compulsory labour requirements during the war. Fascist Italy also intensified compulsory labour. Wartime demand for both manpower and tropical commodities increased the use of forced labour throughout the continent. In Southern Rhodesia, all males between the ages of 18 and 45 who were unemployed (i.e. not working for someone else) for three months or longer were conscripted by the state and funnelled to settler farms. In both Rhodesias, Africans were conscripted both in the military and into the Labour Corps to be used as deemed necessary by colonial officials for building of new air bases, which trained pilots and crew for the Royal Air Force, food production, commodity production and for public works more generally. Scholars estimate that between fifty thousand and one hundred thousand Africans were conscripted into the various Labour Corps each year from 1942 to 1945. While labour policies during wartime differed from colony to colony, Britain's loss of its Far Eastern colonies in Asia to the Japanese led to an intensified focus on Britain's African colonies for increased food and commodity production through the mobilization of 'non-combatant labour', the conditions of which were purposely left vague. This was especially true in East and Central Africa, where this region's production of rubber, sisal and pyrethrum led to labour conscription, working under harsh penalties for desertion and resistance to recruitment.[73] In Nigeria, conscripted labour was used in the Jos tin mines.[74] Compulsory labour coincided with sustained droughts and crop shortfalls in East and Central Africa, which contributed to recruitment resistance and anti-colonial agitation.

With the end of the Second World War, the situation become more favourable in French colonies for the implementation of the changes recommended by the Brazzaville Conference in 1944. Thus, when the French National Constituent Assembly commenced its work in October

---

[73] Killingray, 'Labour Exploitation for Military Campaigns'.

[74] Bill Freund, *Capital and Labour in the Nigerian Tin Mines* (Atlantic Highlands, NJ: Academic Press, 1980); see also Gavin Bridge and Tomas Frederiksen, '"Order out of Chaos": Resources, Hazards and the Production of a Tin-Mining Economy in Northern Nigeria in the Early Twentieth Century', *Environment and History*, 18.3 (2012), 367–94.

1945, the representatives of France's overseas territories argued that there was a fundamental contradiction between the concept of the French Union and the persistence of inequality and discrimination which characterized relations between the colonies and France.[75] Following initiatives by its African parliamentarians, the Assembly voted for a succession of reforms. Decrees dated 22 December 1945 and 20 February 1946 abolished the system of penalties that had been a centrepiece of the *Code de l'Indigénat*. A bill presented by Ivory Coast's Félix Houphouët-Boigny abolished forced labour altogether on 1 April 1946. With the end of forced labour, voluntary wage labour became the principal mode of recruiting workers in the colonial territories. By the late 1940s, with significant migration to urban centres, the shortage of manpower that had prevailed for much of the colonial period was reduced, and a free labour market appeared. The accelerated development of a free labour market also gave a strong boost to the struggles of trade unions for progressive social legislation, which climaxed with the passage of the Overseas Labour Law Code on 15 December 1952.

Various forms of officially coerced labour persisted well after the formal abolition of forced labour. All colonial powers retained provisions to punish vagrancy and idleness with periods of forced labour. Even Britain, which prided itself on its early abolition of forced labour, permitted chiefs to organize villagers for obligatory labour on roads and for other public works. All colonial powers had laws that permitted the mobilization of forced labour under emergency conditions. Some colonial officials invoked such emergency provisions when free labour was not available to carry crops to market well into the late 1950s.[76]

The Second World War, meanwhile, had accelerated the development of African nationalism and had provided the European powers with a context for reassessing their colonial policy. The end of the war also led to the creation of new international organizations, such as the United Nations, which, following the revelations of Nazi war crimes and the widespread use of forced labour, contributed to the new international conventions on human rights. The United Nations' Universal Declaration of Human Rights (1948) called yet again for the abolition of all forms of slavery, servitude and the trade in slaves. The first acknowledgement of the continued presence of forms of unfreedom among UN member states was achieved in 1956, when the General Assembly passed the Supplementary Convention on the Abolition of Slavery, the Slave Trade, and Institutions

---

[75] Cooper, *Citizenship between Empire and Nation*.

[76] Keese, 'Slow Abolition'.

and Practices Similar to Slavery, which included debt bondage, serfdom, unfree marriages and exploitation of child labour among the prohibited acts. Defining the relationship between ordinary and exploitative child labour led to the 1989 Convention on the Rights of the Child and to the 1999 ILO Convention No. 182, Concerning the Prohibition and Immediate Action for the Elimination of the Worst Forms of Child Labour. And by way of recognizing that the problem of trafficking in persons was a global human rights problem, in 2000 the UN passed the Protocol to Prevent, Suppress and Punish Trafficking in Persons, Especially Women and Children. The 1990s and the first decade of the twenty-first century witnessed the proliferation of both international conventions against trafficking, the development of international case law regarding trafficking and individual countries' efforts to legislate and enforce anti-trafficking laws.

NEW FORMS OF FORCED LABOUR IN POSTCOLONIAL AFRICA

Decolonization accelerated the end of colonial-era forced labour. In the face of the persistent use of forced labour, the ILO adopted a second Abolition of Forced Labour Convention (No. 105) in 1957 that 'specifically aimed at the abolition of the compulsory mobilization and use of labour by the State for economic development purposes, as well as of forced labour as a means of political coercion or as punishment for the infringement of labour discipline'.[77] Nonetheless, during the postcolonial period, coerced labour was a prominent feature of many state-sponsored development schemes.

Many African nationalists heralded the end of colonial rule as the liberation of Africans from the chains of colonialism and forced labour and promised that independence and economic development would benefit all. Within a decade of the first wave of independence in the late 1950s and early 1960s, however, civil wars, military coups, economic mismanagement and corruption had undermined these promises and bred deep resentments. Liberation movements struggled against the remaining colonial and settler colonies of Guinea Bissau, Angola, Mozambique, Southern Rhodesia, South Africa, South West Africa and Ethiopia, which had annexed Eritrea. Secessionist movements broke out in Nigeria, the Congo and Ethiopia, among other states. In this context, nation states, secessionist movements and rebel movements turned to varieties of coerced labour. Virtually all

---

[77]   Quoted in International Labour Office, *Strengthening Action to End Forced Labour*, Report IV (1), International Labour Conference, 103rd Session, 2014, 7.

independent states retained various forms of coercion in rural areas to sustain the production of export crops and the supply of cheap food to feed the expanding urban centres in an effort to buy peace from politically volatile urban dwellers. This pressure on rural areas encouraged the persistence of various forms of coerced labour including forced marriages, slavery and child labour to augment production. In this section, examples of coerced labour in economic development and in rebel movements will illuminate the range of coerced labour in postcolonial Africa.

Leaders of independent African nations faced many of the same problems of mobilizing labour that their colonial predecessors had faced. Many turned to old colonial methods of mobilizing labour through anti-vagrancy laws. Others exhorted and then obliged underemployed youth to join newly created Labour or Workers' Brigades – such as in Senegal under the county's first president, Mammadou Dia, or in Ghana under its first president, Kwame Nkrumah. Newly empowered chiefs in independent Mali, Guinea and the Congo turned to 'communal' labour to mobilize reluctant villagers to work and harvest crops to help build the new nation.[78] Other independent nations turned to even more draconian forms of forced labour under the guise of promoting development.

In 1967 independent Tanzania launched an ambitious economic development programme that President Julius Nyerere called *ujamaa*, a Swahili term referring to 'community' or 'extended family'. It became a shorthand for a linked set of political and economic reforms that was to yield prosperous and self-reliant rural villages centred on the provision of clean water and sanitation, access to community-owned farming machinery and public education. Tanzanian peasants, however, were less convinced about the value of moving from their farms, where they understood the micro-endowments of various terrains, to the new *ujamaa* villages which were often far from their farms. Frustrated with the tepid response from peasants to take advantage of programmes designed to help them, the state turned to violence to compel peasants to move to the *ujamaa* villages. By 1973, under Operation Ujiji, the weight of the military was being used to uproot peasants and force them to relocate to *ujamaa* villages. Faced with the continued deterioration of rural and urban standards of living and under pressure from World Bank and International Monetary Fund structural adjustment programmes, in 1985 Tanzania finally abandoned many aspects of *ujamaa*.

---

[78] Keese, 'Slow Abolition', 404–5; Klaus Ernst, *Tradition and Progress in the African Village: Noncapitalist Transformation of Rural Communities in Mali* (New York: St Martin's Press, 1976).

In 1961 the Eritrean Liberation Front (ELF) began a thirty-year war of liberation against Ethiopia's annexation of Eritrea. The ELF created a highly disciplined army and support system that ultimately prevailed against a much stronger Ethiopian military. In 1991 Eritrea became an independent country with an ambitious economic development agenda. To further build a sense of national identity, Eritrea instituted compulsory military service for all men and women between the ages of 18 and 40. This consisted of six months' military training and twelve months of active service. Eritrea was making considerable strides towards its goals when war with Ethiopia broke out again in 1998. Reservists were called out to augment the active military recruits. The border war was enormously costly to the state's investment in economic development. In 2000 peace accords were signed to end the border war, but the Eritrean government did not demobilize its vast military. Instead, the government extended compulsory military service indefinitely under the label of the Warsai-Yikaalo Development Campaign (WYDC). Designed to be a 'school of the nation', WYDC was supposed to provide labour for economic development projects in the national interest, but it morphed into a 'modern form of slavery'. Men and women in WYDC worked 'under menace of penalty' (which is the classic ILO formulation of forced labour) and were subject to periodic police round-ups of deserters and draft dodgers.[79]

Smaller-scale forced labour continues in many rural areas of independent Africa where chiefs continue to exert 'traditional authority' over prestation. Some of the most egregious cases can be found in post-apartheid South Africa, where basic human rights are enshrined in the constitution. However, the constitution continues to recognize the authority of rural chiefs, who claim traditional authority to call upon unpaid 'tribal levies' to work on village projects, including the chiefs' own fields. Tribal levies are essentially forced labour, which, given male migration patterns, tends to fall most heavily on women.[80]

---

[79] Giam Kabreab, 'Forced Labour in Eritrea', *Journal of Modern African Studies*, 47.1 (2006), 41–72; Tricia Redeker Hepner and Samia Tecle, 'New Refugees, Development-Forced Displacement, and Transnational Governance in Eritrea and Exile', *Urban Anthropology and Studies of Cultural Systems and World Economic Development*, 42.3/4 (2013), 377–410.

[80] Ineke van Kessel and Barbara Oomen, '"One Chief, One Vote": The Revival of Traditional Authorities in Post-Apartheid South Africa', *African Affairs*, 96 (1997), 561–85; Christina Murray, *South Africa's Troubled Royalty: Traditional Leaders after Democracy*, Law and Policy Paper 23 (Australian National University, 2004).

In a review of the persistence of forced labour legislation in 1979, labour attorney David Ziskind surveyed the existence of forced labour legislation in independent Africa and identified which nations had provisions for exacting compulsory labour for which kinds of issues. At the time, the Central African Empire (now the Central African Republic), Kenya, Liberia, Tanzania and Uganda had laws that made it possible to imprison and to impose forced labour on individuals who opposed the 'established political, social or economic order'. Liberia retained provisions allowing it to forcibly mobilize labour under its 'Rules and Regulations Governing the Hinterland'. In Kenya, officials could require work for the conservation of natural resources. In Sierra Leone, the state could impose compulsory cultivation in cases of extreme famine. Workers on strike faced imprisonment and forced labour in Benin, Gabon, Ghana, Kenya, Nigeria, Tanzania and Uganda. Zaire, under President Mobutu, and Chad had provisions to force individuals to labour if they failed to pay their taxes. In Lesotho, chiefs could still require villages to act as 'messengers', a vague category of work.[81]

Failed states, widespread corruption, neo-patrimonialism and economic mismanagement fuelled resentment among Africa's independent populations. Rebellions and insurrections occurred in many regions throughout the continent. Some were supported by Cold War rivalries that used rebel movements as proxies. Some were supported by white settler regimes eager to destabilize neighbouring states that harboured guerrilla groups fighting for majority rule. But rebel movements drew on deep resentments about the failed promises of independence. Some were secessionist movements seeking to separate territory from the nation state, some sought to topple current regimes, and others were more inchoate movements against the status quo without a clear political agenda. All rebel movements required financing and new recruits to sustain themselves.[82]

A central feature of the late twentieth-century roving rebel movements in Africa has been the 'civilianization' of armed conflict. Organized militaries have traditionally sought to protect civilian populations, although rape and pillage by victorious troops has been common. The civilianization of armed conflict in Africa has meant that civilians are targeted directly and continuously. This is especially true with regard to the 'reproduction' of the rebel bands. Rebel movements in Sierra Leone, Liberia, Mozambique,

---

[81] David Ziskind, 'Forced Labor in the Law of Nations', *Comparative Labor Law*, 3 (1979–80), 253–83.

[82] Thandika Mkandawire, 'The Terrible Toll of Post-Colonial "Rebel Movements" in Africa: Towards an Explanation of the Violence against the Peasantry', *Journal of Modern African Studies*, 40.2 (2002), 181–215.

northern Uganda, Somalia and the Democratic Republic of the Congo (DRC) have preyed particularly on boys and often girls as child soldiers and girls as 'bush' wives. Founded in 1975 by Ian Smith's white minority government in Southern Rhodesia and later supported by South Africa, Renamo became a roving rebel band that led to a civil war and devastated vast tracts of Mozambique before agreeing to a ceasefire in 1992. Among its tactics was the abduction of girls who became bush wives and were forced to perform domestic and sexual labour. Evidence from the rebel movements of the 1990s has documented that some 120,000 children were forcibly recruited. In the Ugandan Lord's Resistance Army, which abducted 25,000 children, child recruits constituted 70 to 80 per cent of the force, with girls composing about a third. Two to three thousand girls were forcibly recruited into the Revolutionary United Front (RUF) in Sierra Leone. While some girls fought, most were forced into marriages to provide sexual, domestic and reproductive services to the rebels. Fifty per cent of the bush wives in the RUF were under 15. In Somalia and northern Nigeria, the al-Shabaab and Boko Haram rebel movements have abducted school girls and forced them into marriages to rebel fighters as a means of undermining Western education and of providing sexual and domestic labour. In the eastern regions of the DRC, girls and young women abducted by combatants have been taken to bases in the forest where they are forced to provide sexual services and domestic labour.[83]

CONCLUSION

Forced labour was a subset of a wider set of practices using coerced labour. The focus of this chapter has been on forced labour as a practice of state mobilization of labour in Africa during the twentieth century. The mobilization of labour by the state has been a feature of African labour history since the beginning of colonial conquest. In their efforts to conquer territory, build infrastructure and promote economic development (especially for export), colonial states in Africa faced populations unwilling to work for the state or private enterprises at the wages offered and under the prevailing conditions. To compensate for deficiencies in the labour market, the state

[83] See Stacey Hynd, "'To Be Taken as a Wife Is a Form of Death": The Social, Military, and Humanitarian Dynamics of Forced Marriage and Girl Soldiers in African Conflicts, c. 1990–2010', in *Marriage by Force? Contestation over Consent and Coercion in Africa*, ed. Anne Bunting, Benjamin N. Lawrance and Richard L. Roberts (Athens, OH: Ohio University Press, 2016), 290–310.

turned to formal means of compulsion to generate workers for its various goals. This chapter has identified seven prominent forms of forced labour in twentieth-century Africa: requisitioned labour, indentured labour, prestation (labour tax), military conscription, military conscription for non-military uses, forced cultivation and penal labour.

Although African nationalists promised that independence would end colonial-era forms of forced labour and bring wealth and well-being to all, many independent African states retained or modified colonial-era laws that permitted forced labour. Rebel groups throughout postcolonial Africa also turned to forced labour to provide soldiers, as well as girls and women to provide sexual and domestic services.

Almost ninety years after the adoption of the ILO Forced Labour Convention in 1930, which called on 'member States to suppress the use of forced labour and to criminalize the offense', the practice still exists, albeit in different forms from those that provoked such concern in the early twentieth century.[84] In 2010 the ILO estimated that 20.9 million people were victims of forced labour worldwide.[85]

[84] ILO, *Strengthening Action to End Forced Labour*, 1.

[85] International Labour Office, *Global Estimate of Forced Labour: Results and Methodology* (Geneva: ILO, 2012), 2.

PART II

KEY SECTORS

FOUR
Agriculture

JULIA TISCHLER

Department of History, University of Basel

Agriculture has been the most important economic activity and socially structuring force around the world until very recently – and it still is for many people. While the ratio of urban residents is constantly rising in Africa, 63.9 per cent of its population were still living in rural areas as recently as 2011.[1] However, neat statistical divisions into urban and rural areas, agricultural and non-agricultural occupations do not capture the much more intertwined reality of African labour relations. Today and throughout history, households have adopted diversified livelihood strategies combining food production and the selling of agricultural surpluses with non-farming activities, which are becoming increasingly important. However, compared to other regions of the world, agricultural work still looms large on the African continent.

Agricultural labour has not been at the core of conventional labour history, which was for a long time preoccupied with industrial and urban work, class formation and proletarianization. Agricultural history in its early variants focused on commercialization and colonialism, outlining how agricultural production and labour relations transformed under capitalism. Case studies showed how companies and colonial governments drove Africans towards producing particular cash crops, entangling peasantries in global networks of production and consumption under often disadvantageous terms of trade. On the other hand, important studies showed that African farmers were also active agents of commercialization[2]

---

[1]   Food and Agriculture Organization, *Statistical Yearbook 2014, Africa* (Accra: Food and Agriculture Organization of the United Nations, Regional Office for Africa, 2014).

[2]   P. Hill, *The Migrant Cocoa-Farmers of Southern Ghana: A Study in Rural Capitalism* (Cambridge: Cambridge University Press, 1963); C. Bundy, *The Rise and Fall of the South African Peasantry*, 2nd edn (Oxford: Oxford University Press, 1988); G. Austin,

and complicated existing models of agrarian capitalism, arguing, for instance, that accumulation and differentiation among farmers occurred unhindered by communal tenure or expectations of kin. In line with broader trends in African labour history, studies from about the 1980s and 1990s shifted away from the earlier structural focus towards asking how African producers experienced, shaped and resisted commercialization and colonial agricultural planning.[3]

Some of the still-existing lacunae pertain to categories of dependent agricultural work, particularly agricultural wage labour, since historians have focused on peasants. Moreover, environmental historians have rightly deplored the lack of systematic engagement with ecological factors, as only a few studies address the ways in which agricultural labour has been shaped by climate, topography, soil quality or short-term events such as droughts or pests.[4] Recently, global or transnational perspectives, also under the umbrella of Global Labour History (GLH), have opened up new research fields for the history of agricultural work, including transnational entanglements in terms of agricultural knowledge and technology.[5] The following, necessarily selective, overview provides a brief chronological sketch of how agricultural labour and policy have evolved before and since 1950. The third section examines particular types of agricultural labour and production systems in greater detail.

AGRICULTURAL LABOUR DURING THE FIRST HALF OF THE TWENTIETH CENTURY

More than any other type, agricultural work has been shaped by environmental factors. Scholarship has stressed the particular 'difficulty' of

---

Labour, Land and Capital in Ghana: From Slavery to Free Labour in Asante, 1807–1956 (Rochester, NY: University of Rochester Press, 2005).

[3] See W. Beinart and C. Bundy, *Hidden Struggles in Rural South Africa: Politics and Popular Movements in the Transkei and Eastern Cape, 1890–1930* (London: James Currey, 1987); C. van Onselen, *The Seed is Mine: The Life of Kas Maine, a South African Sharecropper, 1894–1985* (Oxford: James Currey, 1997); S. Feierman, *Peasant Intellectuals: Anthropology and History in Tanzania* (Madison, WI: University of Wisconsin Press, 1990); M. van Beusekom, *Negotiating Development: African Farmers and Colonial Experts at the Office du Niger, 1920–1960* (Portsmouth, NH: Heinemann, 2002).

[4] J. McCann, *People of the Plow: An Agricultural History of Ethiopia, 1800–1990* (Madison, WI: University of Wisconsin Press, 1995).

[5] A. Zimmerman, *Alabama in Africa: Booker T. Washington, the German Empire, and the Globalization of the New South* (Princeton, NJ: Princeton University Press, 2012).

Africa's climate, soils and topography[6] – including soils too thin for deep ploughing, sleeping sickness that prevented the use of draught animals in vast areas, irregular rainfall or aridity in many parts of the continent. On a comparatively high proportion of the continent, soils are inherently low in nutrients and the ability to hold water. Only 8 per cent of Africa's land mass is considered high-quality agricultural land, while 55 per cent is deemed unsuitable for cultivation altogether. Secondly, the relative abundance of land until very recently and the low labour-to-land ratio has been found to account for agricultural practices that were extensive rather than intensive, focusing on land-saving rather than labour-saving technology.[7]

In different regions on the continent – including the Sahara, the Nile Valley and North Africa, the Inner Niger Delta, the Ethiopian highlands, and the forest and savannah regions in West Africa – African communities developed sedentary lifestyles and food production systems several thousands of years ago, extending more widely throughout sub-Saharan Africa from about 3000 BC. Iron working, developing around 1000 BC, and the use of ox-ploughs, which has been proven for two Eritrean sites in the first millennium BC, were important technological changes in the way agricultural labour was performed, allowing for more intensive production and urbanization.[8] Economic differentiation remained at a comparatively low level in much of sub-Saharan Africa, as control over land was established via kin-based communal groups rather than private property. However, gendered divisions of labour marked agricultural production from the start. In much of southern and eastern Africa, households centrally depended on agricultural labour performed by women, while animal husbandry was in the hands of men. Men rich in livestock were able to acquire more wives and, having rights over their wives' labour, cultivate larger areas.[9]

[6] J. Iliffe, *Africans: The History of a Continent*, 2nd edn (Cambridge: Cambridge University Press, 2007).

[7] G. Livingston, S. Schonberger and S. Delaney, *Sub-Saharan Africa: The State of Smallholders in Agriculture* (Rome: International Fund for Agricultural Development, 2011), 2–3; T. Reardon, 'African Agriculture: Productivity and Sustainability Issues', in *International Agricultural Development*, ed. C. Eicher and J. Staatz, 3rd edn (Baltimore, MD: Johns Hopkins University Press, 1998), 457.

[8] G. Maddox, *Sub-Saharan Africa: An Environmental History* (Santa Barbara, CA: ABC-CLIO, 2006), 31–7; McCann, *People of the Plow*, 39.

[9] I. Berger, 'Women in East and Southern Africa', in *Women in Sub-Saharan Africa: Restoring Women to History*, ed. I. Berger and F. White (Bloomington, IN: Indiana University Press, 1999), 5–6.

Agricultural commercialization, conventionally dated to the last quarter of the nineteenth century, was intertwined with intensifying local and long-distance trading activities in several regions in Central and southern Africa, and especially in West Africa, which preceded the onset of formal colonial rule. Studies have highlighted how groups of peasants in West Africa and southern Africa tapped into emerging new markets, producing export commodities such as groundnuts, palm oil or rubber, or, in the case of South Africa, foodstuffs and raw materials required by the rising mining industry. In western and Central Africa, increased agricultural commercial activity was, furthermore, linked to the abolitionist movement and European powers' mission to replace the trade in people with the trade in cash crops. Paradoxically, this emphasis on so-called legitimate commerce often led to an increased use of slave labour, as intensified production caused higher labour demands, and plantation owners were often not able to pay competitive wages.[10] In addition, European extraction of cash crops often brought forth different new forms of forced labour (see below).

Analysing agriculture under colonialism, research has differentiated between different models, depending on the incorporation of African peasants or white settlers, respectively, and the degree to which colonial agricultural policy was grafted on to pre-existing labour relations or else transformed them. Commonly, distinctions are made between 'peasant' and 'settler' colonies, while the latter are further differentiated as to the degree to which they relied on settler-based cash cropping or industrial production. The first category is usually associated with West Africa. Here, the onset of formal colonial rule implied a significant expansion in scale and diversification of agricultural production, but there were strong continuities with the 'legitimate commerce' period. More generally, in parts of tropical West, Central and East Africa, production remained in the hands of African peasant producers, as they often proved more efficient than European-run plantations. In such cases, colonialism did little to change African farmers' production processes but was geared at extracting the produce of the latter and increase export production. Given African farmers' initiative, market demand, the need to acquire cash to pay taxes and the newly erected transport infrastructure, this strategy often succeeded. The prototypical example of successful smallholder cash cropping under colonialism is the cocoa production by the Akwapim in the Gold Coast, which was introduced in the 1880s and expanded considerably in subsequent decades. Akwapim farmers, some of whom moved into Akim territory, used a variety of labour

---

[10] R. Law, S. Schwarz and S. Strickrodt, eds, *Commercial Agriculture, the Slave Trade and Slavery in Atlantic Africa* (Woodbridge: James Currey, 2013), 1–27.

forms for cocoa cultivation, initially relying on women and children, possibly slaves, and later also attracting local labour.[11]

In East Africa, export-oriented agriculture had not made much headway by the nineteenth century, except for Zanzibar and a few other coastal communities. Commercialization and colonialism hence transformed agrarian labour relations more profoundly, as exemplified by the case of coffee production around Mount Kilimanjaro. Initially a chief-centred activity, coffee cultivation became more entrenched in smallholder production and, necessitating large-scale recruitment of non-domestic labour, led to the development of a labour market.[12] Change was also profound in the centralized kingdom of Buganda, which – following the decline in the slave and ivory trade in the last two decades of the nineteenth century – became a major producer of cotton. Here, in contrast to Akwapim cocoa farming, however, the colonial state (particularly its railways) played an important transformative role.[13] Compared with West Africa, administrators in East Africa were more invested in encouraging European farming. In Kenya, where the white settler population constituted a powerful political force, commercial production came to play a more substantial role in the colony's economy. While African farmers expanded their production in the early twentieth century, European settlers meanwhile pressed the colonial government to assist them in their request for cheap labour. As a result, Africans were squeezed into reserves on poor soils and excluded from important markets. On the other hand, this division was not neatly upheld, as white farmers were often unable to recruit the necessary labour and hence depended on African families cultivating on their land, the so-called squatters. Officials generally sympathized with settler demands but were not prepared to suppress African commercial farming, which accounted for the bulk of Kenyan export earnings.[14] Similar policy conflicts and adjustments occurred in other parts of East Africa. In German East Africa, influential officials came to embrace the concept of *Volkskultur*

---

[11] Hill, *Migrant Cocoa-Farmers of Southern Ghana*.

[12] A. Eckert, 'Comparing Coffee Production in Cameroon and Tanganyika, c. 1900 to 1960s: Land, Labor, and Politics', in *The Global Coffee Economy in Africa, Asia, and Latin America, 1500–1989*, ed. W. G. Clarence-Smith and S. Topik (Cambridge: Cambridge University Press, 2003), 286–311.

[13] A. I. Richards, F. Sturrock and J. M. Fortt, eds, *Subsistence to Commercial Farming in Present-Day Buganda: An Economic and Anthropological Survey* (Cambridge: Cambridge University Press, 1973).

[14] N. E. Makana, 'Metropolitan Concern, Colonial State Policy and the Embargo on Cultivation of Coffee by Africans in Colonial Kenya: The Example of Bungoma District, 1930–1960', *History in Africa*, 36 (2009), 315–29.

or were at least reluctant to give in to European planters' demands to curb competition by African cultivators.[15] While policies varied, in most cases a general understanding emerged that commercial farming through African smallholders (or plantation owners) could be at least as profitable as working with inexperienced European planters.

African producers' position in colonies with a powerful settler population and a significant urban-industrial sector differed markedly from the contexts discussed so far. Here, agricultural policy left little scope for, or was even hostile towards, African peasant farming. South Africa is an extreme case of how a powerful settler minority was able to assert itself as planters and commercial farmers, while Africans were forced into a labour market that serviced the white-run economy. Scholars have highlighted the centrality of both economic and extra-economic coercion in the emergence of agrarian capitalism, which rested on (imported) slave labour and later also on indentured labour and migrant contract labour (see below). African peasants who had taken advantage of the new markets of the mining industry in the later decades of the nineteenth century quickly came to suffer from systematic state discrimination.[16] Measures to assist agricultural production, including tariffs, credits, transport or marketing, favoured whites, while African access to land was increasingly circumscribed – most centrally by the infamous Native Land Act of 1913, which limited African landownership to 7–8 per cent of the Union's land mass and put restrictions on sharecropping and tenure. In colonial Zimbabwe, a similar situation emerged. Subsistence-oriented labour allowed most Shona and Ndebele cultivators and livestock keepers to remain economically independent from the colonial state, while trading surpluses with the often struggling settler population. When the settler colonial state consolidated, however, African producers' self-sufficiency was continuously undermined, as land appropriation and taxation forced them into selling their labour.[17] Here, too, the reserves served as labour pools, forming part of larger southern African networks of circular labour migration. In the 1940s both South African and Southern Rhodesian bureaucrats came to question the system of circular labour migration – men oscillating between subsistence production and wage work in mines or on farms owned by whites – proposing

---

[15] J. Koponen, *Development for Exploitation: German Colonial Policies in Mainland Tanzania, 1884–1914* (Hamburg: LIT, 1994), 416–17. For the case of *Volkskultur* in Togo, see also A. Zimmerman, 'German Alabama in Africa: The Tuskegee Expedition to German Togo and the Transnational Origins of West African Cotton Growers', *American Historical Review*, 110.5 (2005), 1379.

[16] Bundy, *Rise and Fall of the South African Peasantry*.

[17] R. Pilossof, 'Labor Relations in Zimbabwe from 1900 to 2000: Sources, Interpretations, and Understandings', *History in Africa*, 41 (2014), 337–62.

instead a policy of 'professionalization'. In both settler colonies, however, the suggested separation between agricultural and industrial workforces did not become a reality, and large parts of the urban populations have maintained their rural connections until the present day.

Several cases, however, do not fit into the settler vs. peasant typology and/or reflect a different chronology. Egypt, one of the oldest agricultural systems in the world, is a particularly early case of revenue-oriented agricultural intensification. When the British established an Egyptian protectorate in 1914, the country had already seen large-scale agricultural reforms. In the early nineteenth century, Muhammad Ali, pasha and viceroy of Egypt from 1805 to 1848, introduced new crops and irrigation systems, and transformed cultivation practices and land ownership for the sake of export-oriented cotton growing – a process that ultimately led to the emergence of a landowning oligarchy and impoverished peasantry, which became a source of political conflict.[18] Ethiopia, successfully resisting colonization, equally defies the above typology. In Ethiopia's northern highlands, an area of rich soils and high population density taking advantage of a specific ox-plough system, decisions on what to grow, or what tools, labour relations and techniques to employ, had been taken primarily at farm level during Melenik's reign (1889–1913). Here, it was the central state under Ras Tafari's regency since the early 1920s that intervened in local agricultural economies, incorporating farmers into the national economy on the basis of exportable products, including coffee, hides and gold. In the course of the twentieth century, farming became closely connected to the emerging towns and cities and their consumption needs. Italian colonialists intensified some of these trends, studying and intervening in farming during the period of Italian occupation from 1935 to 1941 in order to meet urban and metropolitan requirements.[19]

Many of the changes wrought by colonial governments were launched within a framework of 'development'. The interwar period, and particularly the 1930s, constituted a turning point, as policy shifted from the previous philosophy of laissez-faire towards a more interventionist approach with the professed aim of raising living standards in the colonies. In a context of global economic depression and social unrest in the colonies, 'development' was to give new legitimacy to the colonial project. Confident in the scientific manageability of African societies and environments, European powers invested in agricultural research and planning and implemented a range of

[18] A. R. Mustapha and G. Williams, 'Agrarian Change', in *Encyclopedia of Twentieth-Century African History*, ed. P. T. Zeleza (London: Routledge, 2003), 21–2.

[19] McCann, *People of the Plow*.

schemes to transform subsistence farming into profit-making systems that would generate cash-crop-based revenue on international markets. Contrary to their proclaimed aim of benefiting the metropolis and the colony alike, such interventions more often than not disturbed local agricultural economies and went along with coercion and hardship. At the same time, studies have pointed to the limits of colonial development, pointing to examples of African producers retaining control over their households' labour and production.

The Office du Niger, a large cotton- and rice-growing scheme in French Sudan, and the Gezira scheme on the Sudanese Nile exemplify these dynamics. The former project, initiated in the 1920s in the Middle Niger valley, followed the policy of colonial *mise en valeur* by providing cotton for the French textile industry and rice for French Senegal. The scheme's mobilization of labour was a concession to colonial realities and the difficulties of recruiting (wage) labour. Rather than working through plantations, the Office pursued a policy of *colonisation indigène*. Peasant families were – in most cases forcibly – settled at the scheme to cultivate their own plots under close supervision. In different ways, including disobedience and avoidance strategies, farmers showed that they disagreed with many aspects of the scheme, pushing Office authorities to adjust their aims accordingly – for instance, to make conscious use of the farmers' local knowledge and to drop the focus on cotton in favour of rice.[20] Similar characteristics – export orientation, discrepancies between rhetoric and reality and local contestations – emerged in the context of the Gezira scheme, a large-scale irrigation and cotton-production enterprise launched in the 1920s under British-Egyptian rule. Again, colonial authorities worked through highly controlled peasant families in trying to produce a raw material – cotton – for the sake of the metropolitan economy, in this case the British textile industry. Peasants contested the operation of the scheme. Rather than relying solely on unpaid family work, as planners had expected, many entered sharecropping arrangements or hired (migrant) labour, hence undermining the ideal of the 'yeoman farmer'.[21]

Some case studies have argued that agricultural development became a catalyst for nationalist resistance, antagonizing rural people and drawing them into the anti-colonial struggle, for instance in Northern Rhodesia and Nyasaland. In the late 1940s colonial officials started with a new initiative

---

[20] Van Beusekom, *Negotiating Development*.

[21] V. Bernal, 'Cotton and Colonial Order in Sudan: A Social History with Emphasis on the Gezira Scheme', in *Cotton, Colonialism, and Social History in Sub-Saharan Africa*, ed. A. Isaacman and R. Roberts (Portsmouth, NH: Heinemann, 1995), 96–118.

in rural development, investing considerable sums for bold programmes. Forced resettlements, redesigned landscape usages and labour-intensive conservation measures, such as in the Lower Shire valley in Nyasaland and parts of Northern Rhodesia, however, led to widespread resentment among African producers.[22]

Indeed, despite its benign rhetoric of ending slavery and modernizing agrarian labour relations, colonial interventions in numerous instances relied on coercion. Colonial officers and European landowners often found it impossible to recruit and maintain labour forces by wages alone. Cotton is a well-studied example of how a commercialized crop led to new coercive labour regimes. In German East Africa in the early 1900s and in French Central Africa from the mid-1920s, cotton production was based on forced labour. Similar observations hold true for the Belgian Congo and the Portuguese colonies of Angola and Mozambique. Research has pointed to the contradictions involved, as colonial officers claimed to facilitate free markets and 'rational' economic behaviour, but were at the same time deeply prejudiced about Africans' capacities for work.[23] This translated into paradoxical theories about liberating Africans from an earlier condition of slavery by forcing them to work. Force affected the production process, as peasants and agricultural workers were closely supervised and punished if they did not produce the required amounts of crops. Moreover, it was central to recruitment, as seen in the example of the Office du Niger, to which only a minority of tenants came voluntarily. Besides physical force, taxes and/or land dispossession were further means of mobilizing labour. Despite this legacy of coercion, however, Africans would also associate agricultural work with freedom. Many preferred independent livelihoods rather than wage labour, and an elaborate ideology around farming as a form of material progress and emancipation – inspired by the model of Booker T. Washington in the United States – emerged, particularly among the wealthier strata.[24]

Colonial development interventions aimed to transform African agriculture at many levels – crops, technology, property relations, family structures as well as labour relations and labour practices. Colonial agricultural development usually combined productivity increases with far-reaching efforts at transforming rural lifeworlds, including health,

[22] M. Vaughan, 'Exploitation and Neglect: Rural Producers and the State in Malawi and Zambia', in *History of Central Africa: The Contemporary Years since 1960*, ed. D. Birmingham and P. Martin (London: Longman, 1998), 167–202.

[23] A. Isaacman and R. Roberts, eds, *Cotton, Colonialism, and Social History in Sub-Saharan Africa* (Portsmouth, NH: Heinemann, 1995).

[24] Zimmerman, 'German Alabama in Africa'.

nutrition and gender relations. As seen in the examples of the Gezira scheme and the Office du Niger, agricultural development in the interwar period rested on the ideal of a nuclear family household, led by a male head who would command the labour of his wife and other dependants. This ideal was conservative and transformative at the same time, in that it sought to build upon existing structures rather than implant new labour relations, while simultaneously going against the perceived evil of polygamy (see below), promoting individualism and limiting the power of extended kin. On the level of crops, the emphasis was on the production of marketable produce (including coffee, cocoa, cotton, rice, groundnuts), while both the Gezira scheme and the Office du Niger made (limited) provisions for tenants to produce food for their own consumption as well. In sum, such schemes translated into a reduction in the number of crops grown, often resulting in monocropping systems.[25]

On the level of technology, irrigation assumed major importance in colonial development programmes. Dams and canals were built to increase cultivation areas and facilitate a year-round productive cycle, independent from annual floods. This new labour regime, however, often meant an increased workload, distracting farmers from food production and other economic activities that were part of many families' risk-balancing strategies. Besides polyculture, colonial officers took issue with practices of shifting cultivation and extensive farming, which were cast as inefficient and environmentally harmful, and promoted intensive and sedentary farming (or rotational farming within special limits and according to a pre-defined sequence) instead. Induced technological change furthermore revolved around the introduction or increased use of ploughs. At the Office du Niger, officials tried to move African farmers ahead on an imagined evolutionary line by undoing the 'backward' practice of extensive hoe-farming, encouraging instead the use of ploughs to allow for a more intensive use of the land – a practice that has been shown to have caused serious soil damage in many cases. Ploughing furthermore affected gendered divisions of labour. Colonial officers often promoted the increased use of ploughs as a way to involve men more intensively in cultivation and decrease women's workload. In an earlier, non-colonial context, the system of ox-ploughing, which first emerged in the Ethiopian northern highlands and then spread more widely in Menelik's late nineteenth-century state, led to a male monopoly of much of the cultivation process. As ploughing remained an exclusively male activity, women's labour and economic position in agriculture was marginalized.[26] Relatedly, colonial

---

[25] Van Beusekom, *Negotiating Development*; Bernal, 'Cotton and Colonial Order in Sudan'.

[26] McCann, *People of the Plow*, 74–5.

administrators frequently found fault with the way households used their cattle. Officials criticized farmers' and pastoralists' 'irrational' accumulation of cattle and pleaded for quality rather than quantity. In their eyes, cattle were to be put to use either as draught animals or for beef production, ignoring or overriding the long-standing social-economic functions that cattle had in many communities as means of accumulation and bridewealth.

Despite the diverse shapes that agricultural policy took in the first half of the twentieth century, some commonalities in terms of its effects and responses on the ground can be made out. Before the age of 'development', colonial agricultural policy was unreservedly geared towards metropolitan interests, with cash-crop production generating tax incomes and supplying cheap raw materials to Europe. As an effect, African producers were increasingly integrated into larger markets, allowing a few privileged individuals to prosper. The majority, however, remained on a level of semi-subsistence, forced to neglect food production for the sake of cash crops.[27] Moreover, African farmers became entrenched in a system of global trade, in which colonial territories provided agricultural raw materials, while processing and manufacturing, and hence higher-value generation, took place in the metropolises. African cultivators' responses were diverse. While some agricultural interventions led to open defiance, scholarship has pointed to the manifold instances of more 'hidden' protest, such as continuing with prohibited practices, acts of sabotage, or what reads in colonial sources as 'laziness', 'apathy' or 'cheating'. Since peasants rarely formed class-based collectives, and since they had access to the means of production and thus partial autonomy, 'everyday struggles' have been found to be more characteristic of their protest than large-scale, organized defiance. Forms of less explicit protest could have profound effects on colonial development schemes, as for instance in the above-discussed case of the Office du Niger. Some African agriculturists also seized opportunities arising from colonial development and made significant economic gains. As several cases have shown, successful farmer-entrepreneurs usually hailed from the traditional or formally educated elites and had privileged access to land and labour, showing how agricultural development often reinforced existing social-economic differences.[28]

Moreover, colonial agricultural policy was shaped by pre-fixed notions of gender and affected the way women and men worked the land. Women's central role in cultivation, typically including both production for the family and for the marketplace, in most cases translated into social recognition and

---

[27] Isaacman and Roberts, eds, *Cotton, Colonialism, and Social History.*

[28] Koponen, *Development for Exploitation*, 417.

a degree of economic independence. Colonial agricultural policy, however, focusing on men as commercial agents, excluded women from commercially lucrative activities. Instead, colonial (and missionary) policy promoted the patriarchal household with a clearly demarcated domestic sphere that was cast as female. Notions of female domesticity could find common ground among African males, who wished to control women and bar them from emerging markets.[29] Research has highlighted various examples of how externally induced commercialization subjected women to greater exploitation. In colonial Togo, for instance, cotton growing, spinning and ginning had been in the hands of women, while men had only a subsidiary role in these activities. German agricultural officers, however, created new opportunities for Ewe males and undermined the relative economic independence of women.[30] Similarly, women were marginalized in the Gezira scheme, as they were not eligible to hold tenancies, even when they had owned land before it was appropriated for the scheme.[31] Moreover, many women in southern Africa were faced with increased workloads and disintegrating families given the fact that able-bodied men were away on labour migration for a good part of the year. In West Africa, by contrast, some women were able to defend or even improve their position in the agricultural economy, for instance by forming credit cartels or commodity and trade associations. Even mass protests, as those against price fixing and taxation in colonial Lagos (1930s–1950s), have been shown to go back to the initiative of market women organized in guild-like unions.[32]

Similar trends of women's exclusion in agricultural commercialization and an increasingly rigid demarcation between the (female) household and outside work have been observed for northern Africa as well. In Egypt, Muhammad Ali's politics in the first half of the nineteenth century had disruptive effects on the family labour unit, as state-led infrastructure projects, large estates and the military siphoned off great numbers of male peasants and increased rural women's workload immensely. Rural women's economic marginalization continued in the twentieth century, as they were largely held back from wage labour on private or state farms and from urban areas. In North Africa at the

---

[29] C. Johnson-Odim, 'Women and Gender in the History of Sub-Saharan Africa', in *Women's History in Global Perspective*, ed. B. G. Smith, 3 vols (Urbana, IL: University of Illinois Press, 2005), vol. III, 9–67; J. Comaroff and J. L. Comaroff, 'Home-Made Hegemony: Modernity, Domesticity, and Colonialism in South Africa', in *African Encounters with Domesticity*, ed. H. K. Tranberg (New Brunswick, NJ: Rutgers University Press, 1992), 37–74. See the chapter by Bryceson in this volume.

[30] Zimmerman, 'German Alabama in Africa', 1381–2.

[31] Bernal, 'Cotton and Colonial Order in Sudan'.

[32] Johnson-Odim, 'Women and Gender in the History of Sub-Saharan Africa', 48.

time generally, women's work was restricted and devalued, as they performed the largest part of the agricultural tasks as unpaid family labour, but were excluded from wage labour and commercial production.[33]

AGRARIAN LABOUR IN THE SECOND HALF OF THE TWENTIETH CENTURY

The first couple of decades in the second half of the twentieth century were a rather prosperous period in many parts of Africa, as most regions experienced rapid economic growth thanks to high commodity prices. In this context of optimism, African leaders took over after independence and set out to establish modern nation states along the models of the industrialized world, with strong bureaucracies in charge of extensive development schemes. Given the continued cash-crop boom, agriculture constituted a major growth area and was hence pushed by national governments as well as the international donor community. In the forests of Côte d'Ivoire and in Kenya, smallholders were thus able to increase areas under cultivation and expanded, respectively, their tea and coffee production. Senegal and Ghana continued exporting groundnuts and cocoa on an increased scale.[34] However, many economists and officials conceptualized agriculture to be contributory to the supposedly more modern industrial sector – resulting in often misguided development agendas.

The phase of optimism ended in the later 1970s in the face of serious economic and environmental challenges. In the late 1960s and early 1970s, drought in the Sahel caused serious food shortages, hundreds of thousands of deaths and refugees as well as social and political turmoil. Similar effects of drought and environmental degradation came to affect the semi-arid areas of the African Horn and parts of eastern and southern Africa well into the late twentieth century. Pressure on land and environmental resources increased in the face of rapid population growth, which reached 4.1 per cent in the 1970s. Land scarcity in northern Ethiopia, North Africa, parts of West Africa and in high-rainfall areas of eastern and southern Africa led many people to cultivate marginal lands and reduce pasture areas. In addition, rising oil prices, affecting motor-dependent African transport systems, had adverse effects, in

---

[33] J. Tucker, 'Women in the Middle East and North Africa: The Nineteenth and Twentieth Centuries', in *Women in the Middle East and North Africa: Restoring Women to History*, ed. G. Nashat and J. Tucker (Bloomington, IN: Indiana University Press, 1999), 73–131.

[34] Iliffe, *Africans. The History of a Continent*, 260.

addition to falling revenues for minerals and agricultural export crops.[35] At this stage, the detrimental effects of Africa's role in the global economy, providing agricultural and mineral raw materials, really came to the fore.

Political factors further exacerbated the decline of the agricultural sector. In the late 1970s and early 1980s, Robert Bates and Michael Lipton drew attention to the 'urban bias' in many national governments' spending policies, arguing that rural producers were exploited to finance industrialization and the development of urban areas. Not only were the latter identified as sources of economic growth, but many African leaders deemed urban electorates to be more central to the stability of their governments. Such policy biases in many countries meant that peasant farming was discouraged by artificially low producer prices, ill-maintained transport systems and labour shortages.[36] If governments did support agricultural production in this period, they often favoured large-scale schemes, including socialist villages, state farms, irrigation schemes or private estates. In Zambia, for instance, President Kaunda's government concentrated on the copper industry and used rural development mainly to ensure urban food supplies. Credits, state farms, extension services and other measures concentrated on wealthier farmers and maize production, while women and their cultivation of traditional food crops such as millet and cassava were neglected. When copper prices collapsed in 1974, agricultural policy had achieved little to improve the living standards of poor rural people.[37] International development institutions mirrored this policy focus, placing their emphasis on industrialization. Structural adjustment in the 1980s re-emphasized the agricultural sector; however, such policies effectively pushed peasant producers further into non-agricultural work and accelerated urbanization in many countries.

Many leaders of independent African nations consciously tried to cut colonial ties, but their agricultural policies and initiatives often displayed striking continuities with the colonial period. These included monopolistic structures and a high degree of state intervention in the sector in terms of export, pricing and marketing.[38] Moreover, coercion and authoritarianism as well as notions of top-down, large-scale planning continued to characterize agricultural development programmes. Julius Nyerere's *ujamaa* policy in the late 1960s and 1970s exemplifies the ambivalences of development

---

[35] *Ibid.*, 260–7.

[36] R. H. Bates and S. S. Block, 'Revisiting African Agriculture: Institutional Change and Productivity Growth', *The Journal of Politics*, 75.2 (2013), 373–4, 383.

[37] Vaughan, 'Exploitation and Neglect'.

[38] Mustapha and Williams, 'Agrarian Change', 23.

and decolonization. While the president's aim was to enhance Tanzania's economic autonomy, the implementation of *ujamaa* increasingly relied on force to move peasants into villages, get them to adopt communal farming and enhance cash-crop production. The Ethiopian land reforms under the Derg regime, initiated in 1975, present another case of socialist agricultural development *cum* forced villagization. To transform the existing feudal-like production relations, the ruling military council appropriated land without compensation and prohibited the use of wage labour on private farms. Most farms were thus run by individual peasant families, next to a range of state and cooperative ventures. Newly formed rural institutions (peasant associations possessing a large degree of autonomy), resettlements and mandatory quotas were meant to transform agriculture so as to increase rural income, lead to greater equality and serve as a basis for industrialization at the same time.[39] After the 1952 revolution, Egypt pursued a similar path to increase agricultural output through peasant production under a socialist agenda. Nasser's land reforms sought to curb the huge disparity between peasants and big landowners by confiscating large estates, limiting sizes for holdings and setting up compulsory state cooperatives.

Other countries adopted more free-market strategies. In Kenya, Africans took over most of the commercial enterprises after 1963; valuable cash crops were adopted in highland areas, and smallholder incomes grew. All of this happened, however, at the expense of a growing landless class. The country's agricultural economy was hence marked by an increasing degree of stratification, with a divide that was no longer racial but ran between black commercial farmers or rich peasants on the one hand, and the majority of poor peasants on the other. Similarly pursuing a path of capitalist development, leaders in Côte d'Ivoire emphasized economic growth through agricultural modernization. To increase and diversify agricultural exports, peasants were encouraged to settle in the forest zone and put it under cash cropping. While focusing on the peasant sector, the Ivorian state also encouraged private and state plantations. As in Kenya, agricultural policy enhanced social-economic inequalities. A class of Ivorian commercial farmers emerged, including President Félix Houphouët-Boigny himself, many of whom would later invest in manufacturing, trade and urban real estate. However, the Ivorian 'miracle' was not to last; by the end of the 1970s the

---

[39] M. wa Githinji and G. Mersha, 'Untying the Gordian Knot: The Question of Land Reform in Ethiopia', in *Land, Poverty and Livelihoods in an Era of Globalization: Perspectives from Developing and Transition Countries*, ed. A. H. Akram-Lodhi et al. (London: Routledge, 2007), 310–43.

economy had declined, not least due to falling commodity prices and global overproduction of coffee and cocoa.[40]

South Africa constitutes a rare example of agricultural modernization through a large-scale, high-tech commercial sector. This development, however, was crassly racialized, as commercial farming was exclusively white, promoted by generous state support. So-called 'betterment projects' for black peasants, enforced after the Second World War, were part of the state's overall strategy of pushing Africans into the role of workers (for white agriculture or industry) and/or subsistence producers. Betterment allocated land according to its intended economic function – as woodland, arable, grazing, residential areas – relocated large numbers of Africans into concentrated villages, and undermined land renting and labour tenancy on white farms. Land restitution and land reforms introduced after 1994 are yet to deliver substantial change. By contrast, post-independence land reforms in neighbouring Zimbabwe, which had experienced similar dynamics of settler-dominated agricultural commercialization, led to a significant growth of the black peasant sector. Ten years after independence, Zimbabwe peasants produced 55 per cent of the marketed maize and 70 per cent of the total national maize production.

South Africa and Zimbabwe were further exceptional in terms of technology use. While both countries were slow to mechanize by international standards, as the availability of cheap workers reduced the need for labour-saving technologies, their adaptation of agricultural technology went further than in other African nations. By the 1970s increased levels of mechanization in South Africa, bolstered by state subsidies, had ended the chronic shortage of unskilled labour and led to numerous lay-offs.[41] On the other hand, mechanization in combination with the country's policy of providing an inferior education for the black majority ('Bantu education') caused serious shortages of skilled agricultural labour able to operate heavy machinery. In other nations, technology use remained at a rather low level, which has been seen as a major reason why peasant agriculture has been less productive than, for instance, in Asia or Latin America.[42] Mechanization and chemical fertilizers did become more important during and after the Second World War, but several difficulties hampered the adoption of globally widespread technologies, including those related to economies of scale. At the Office

---

[40] P. Nugent, *Africa since Independence: A Comparative History*, 2nd edn (Basingstoke: Palgrave Macmillan, 2012).

[41] D. Atkinson, *Going for Broke: The Fate of Farmworkers in Arid South Africa* (Cape Town: HSRC Press, 2007), 53–8.

[42] Reardon, 'African Agriculture', 449.

du Niger, for instance, mechanized ploughing proved too expensive, leaving farmers indebted. Similarly, chemical fertilizers failed to take root given their high costs.[43] Generally, irrigation and fertilization remained significantly lower in Africa than in Asia, while the two continents were in 1965 on a par in terms of tractor usage, a labour-saving rather than land-augmenting technology. Structural adjustment programmes, reducing input subsidies, further contributed to the low-tech nature of African farming.[44]

The slow adaptation of technology has also been linked to environmental conditions, as soil qualities and climates in sub-Saharan Africa and in tropical regions generally are very different from the temperate zones, where most research takes place. Given Africa's enormous variations in soil quality and climates, the multitude of crops grown under diverse ecologies and significant weather instability, large areas furthermore did not lend themselves to Green Revolution technologies (improved seeds, fertilizer, irrigation), which were designed mainly for standardized agricultural systems such as India's floodplains.[45] At present, the low technological standard in many sections of African agriculture is linked to a labour market in which low-skilled, underpaid and casual wage labour predominates.

The 1980s saw a shift in development economics, when the World Bank and the International Monetary Fund critically reassessed the previous approach of concentrating on urban areas as centres of growth. The resulting liberalization policies were intended to put 'the rural producer in a more direct relationship with "the market"',[46] thereby making the agricultural sector more efficient, competitive and export oriented. However, scholars have judged structural adjustment policies to have benefited large-scale producers and fostered concentration, while proving harmful or even devastating to smaller-scale peasants.[47] Cutbacks on subsidies and public spending, state retreat in marketing, liberalization of prices, markets and trading policies all had adverse effects on peasant production. In addition, state farms and parastatals collapsed.[48] Scholarship has discussed structural

[43] Van Beusekom, *Negotiating Development*, 128–9.

[44] Reardon, 'African Agriculture', 452.

[45] Iliffe, *Africans. The History of a Continent*, 266.

[46] Vaughan, 'Exploitation and Neglect', 170.

[47] D. F. Bryceson, 'De-Agrarianisation: Blessing or Blight?', in *Farewell to Farms: De-Agrarianisation and Employment in Africa*, ed. D. F. Bryceson and V. Jamal (Aldershot: Ashgate, 1997), 240–1.

[48] Mustapha and Williams, 'Agrarian Change', 24; F. Hendricks, 'Peasants', in *Encyclopedia of Twentieth-Century African History*, ed. P. T. Zeleza (London: Routledge, 2003), 428–34.

adjustment in a larger context of 'de-agrarianization' and 'de-peasantization', processes by which 'peasantries lose their economic capacity and social coherence and demographically shrink in size'.[49] While labour migration and complementary non-agricultural work have constituted important economic strategies for a long time, structural adjustment catalysed these trends. Smallholders' *commercial* agricultural activities suffered in particular, while they combined subsistence production increasingly with non-farm incomes.[50] Similar trends have been observed for Latin America and Asia; however, in the latter cases, redundant agricultural labour was absorbed by the growing industrial sector. This has happened to a much lesser extent in Africa. De-agrarianization and the decline in social-economic significance of agricultural work are thus not a result of increased opportunities outside farming, but of constraints within the sector. Unlike in Europe, Latin America and Asia, moreover, the overall trend for rural people is not one of occupational specialization but rather the contrary, as small-scale producers continue to diversify their livelihoods to make ends meet.[51]

Structural adjustment, income diversification and the growing importance of rural wage labour have had mixed effects for women. In some cases, women have found agricultural wage labour preferable to unpaid family work, for instance in the sugar estates in Morogoro in Tanzania. Here, women associate wage labour on the estates, even if casual, with increased economic power and social advancement.[52] More generally, however, rural occupational diversification and wage labour seem to exacerbate power imbalances within households, as women are often on the lowest rank of the workforce, receive lower wages than men and suffer from an extremely heavy workload. A case study on Uganda shows that women who work as coffee graders generally spend up to ten hours daily, six days a week, in the factory, using breaks to feed their children and elderly relatives with food they prepared in early morning, and facing further domestic chores upon their return. Within the factory, working conditions for women were found to be particularly poor and badly paid.[53]

[49] Vaughan, 'Exploitation and Neglect', 170; D. F. Bryceson, 'Africa at Work: Transforming Occupational Identity and Morality', in *How Africa Works: Occupational Change, Identity and Morality*, ed. D. F. Bryceson (Bourton on Dunsmore: Practical Action Publishing, 2010), 9.

[50] *Ibid.*, 10; Mustapha and Williams, 'Agrarian Change', 19.

[51] Bryceson, 'De-Agrarianisation'; Bryceson, 'Africa at Work'.

[52] M. Mbilinyi, 'Sweet and Sour', in *How Africa Works: Occupational Change, Identity and Morality*, ed. D. F. Bryceson (Bourton on Dunsmore: Practical Action Publishing, 2010), 165–84.

[53] K. Wedig, 'Capitalist Labor Regimes in Uganda's Coffee Sector: Intersections of Social Divisions and Corporate Labor Strategies', paper presented at the conference 'Africa in a Capitalist World', Berlin, July 2017 [unpublished].

The current trend of increasing workloads for women has its roots in the colonial period, as seen above. In the post-independence era, the previous policy of 'domesticating' women's work continued, highlighting their obligations as homemakers and food producers. Agricultural development policy intended to attach men more closely to the rural areas,[54] but such attempts did not stop the dynamics of male labour migration and the economic dualism it created, with men earning wages and women shouldering the burden of the family's subsistence. The decreasing returns of agricultural production from the 1980s onwards increased pressure on all household members to earn an income; hence, many women were drawn into commercial production and wage labour outside the household. While this process undermined men's previous monopoly on cash cropping and export production, women still perform the largest bulk of the domestic chores.[55] In sum, postcolonial agricultural policy and structural adjustment, with its focus on larger-scale, input-heavy and men-dominated commercial farming, increased gendered labour divisions and power imbalances.[56]

TYPES OF AGRICULTURAL LABOUR AND PRODUCTION SYSTEMS

Following historical and social science research, among the most distinct characteristics of sub-Saharan African agrarian labour relations are, respectively, the endurance of peasant production and the comparatively limited use of wage labour in agriculture. Instead, access to land is mostly organized via communal arrangements, with family labour as the predominant form. This view will be commented on in greater detail, and partly qualified, in what follows. This section examines particular types of agricultural labour, which emerged in the chronological account above, in greater detail. The distinction between the categories discussed here is by no means absolute, as many forms blurred into each other.

The category of agrarian labour that has received the most attention – in research as much as in colonial and postcolonial state policy – is that of the peasant. Part of the fascination stems from the fact that the African continent seems to defy the grand narrative of the 'agrarian transition', a radical restructuring of the countryside under capitalist encroachment by which some peasants would become commercial farmers and some

---

[54] Vaughan, 'Exploitation and Neglect', 172.

[55] Bryceson, 'Africa at Work'.

[56] C. Gladwin, 'Introduction', in *Structural Adjustment and African Women Farmers*, ed. C. Gladwin (Gainesville, FL: University of Florida Press, 1991), 1–22.

agricultural wage labourers, while the majority would leave the countryside to be absorbed into the industrial sector. Given the continent's relative abundance of land and the fact that peasants confronted neither widespread land alienation (except for 'native reserves') nor its conversion into private property, many Africans have retained a foothold in the countryside until the present. Their preference for the 'peasant option',[57] farming for one's own sustenance rather than being proletarianized, has been found to constitute a determining factor in labour relations on the continent.

In the early years after independence, African peasantries attracted significant scholarly attention. Different strands of peasant studies emerged in Tanzania, in Kenya and in South Africa. Prominent topics were the relations of peasants to the nation, their revolutionary potential, and their neo-colonial situation. Controversial questions concerned their 'uncaptured' status, which some scholars interpreted as a reason for the agricultural sector's 'backwardness', and which others viewed as an asset. The South African discussion centred on the class character of the rural population and its nature as a peasantry or rather displaced proletariat, also in view of its role in the liberation movement.[58] At the same time, the term 'peasantry' itself is controversial. Recent research has stressed the heterogeneity within this category, comprising producers with diverse sources of income, constraints and objectives. Also, peasants' access to land, usage of labour, production processes, crops grown as well as their degree of market integration has been found to differ too much to speak of such producers as constituting a common class.[59]

Most frequently in historical studies, 'peasants' denote producers working mainly for their own subsistence and consumption, selling surpluses on the market (though not being primarily exchange oriented) and using predominantly household labour.[60] Historically, and especially in recent decades, a large number of smallholder peasants, or even the majority, have been women. Most scholarship agrees that peasants existed before colonization, particularly in parts of North Africa, Sudan, Ethiopia and West Africa. As seen above, colonialism in many cases meant their further integration into international markets. While the colonial state

---

[57] T. O. Ranger, *Peasant Consciousness and Guerilla War in Zimbabwe: A Comparative Study* (Berkeley, CA: University of California Press, 1985).

[58] Hendricks, 'Peasants', 431–3.

[59] C. Oya, 'The Empirical Investigation of Rural Class Formation: Methodological Issues in a Study of Large- and Mid-Scale Farmers in Senegal', *Historical Materialism*, 12.4 (2004), 289–326.

[60] Hendricks, 'Peasants', 428.

undermined peasant production in the settler colonies, the overall trend of commercialization and colonial policy in the late nineteenth and the first part of the twentieth centuries has been one of 'African peasant formation'. Since independence, however, peasant production has undergone a steady process of erosion.[61] A prominent theme in historical research on peasants is the latter's relation to capitalism. Giving the lie to common stereotypes, scholars have shown peasants as entrepreneurs and agents of capitalism rather than as its antithesis. Studies on West Africa's 'cash crop revolution' starting in the late nineteenth century – for example, Senegalese groundnut farming, palm oil production in Côte d'Ivoire and cocoa cultivation in the Gold Coast – found that the first leaps towards commercial production were achieved predominantly through family and dependent labour. Only later, if at all, would peasant farmers employ farm labourers on a grander scale.[62] Similarly, peasants in South Africa played an important role in agrarian commercialization in the later decades of the nineteenth century, even though this was successively undermined.[63] Not all of these peasants were independent producers, but worked on white-owned land for a share of the crop they produced. Such forms of sharecropping were at the foundation of the developing agrarian capitalism on the South African Highveld in the late nineteenth and early twentieth centuries.

Sharecropping afforded African families some degree of autonomy. Implying interaction and interdependence between white landlords and their black tenant families, sharecropping went against segregationist ideology but was a necessary concession to reality, as many white farmers lacked the financial means to employ wage labour. For African families, sharecropping provided an opportunity to retain access to land, avoid wage labour and preserve some degree of independence. Besides having to share the produce, African sharecroppers were left alone in their daily routines, sometimes even working for absentee landlords. Labour organization within the household was patriarchal, as the male family head negotiated the terms of the shareholding agreement, was in charge of finances and commanded the labour of his wife or wives and children. Sharecropping continued, more or less covertly, well into the 1950s, even though its outlawing by the 1913 Native Land Act dealt a blow to the institution and changed the terms of negotiation for the worse for African farmers. The South African state

---

[61] Bryceson, 'De-Agrarianisation', 255.

[62] G. Austin, 'Vent for Surplus or Productivity Breakthrough? The Ghanaian Cocoa Take-Off, c. 1890–1936', *Economic History Review*, 67.4 (2004), 1035–64; P. Hill, *Studies in Rural Capitalism in West Africa* (Cambridge: Cambridge University Press, 1970).

[63] Bundy, *Rise and Fall of the South African Peasantry*.

preferred labour tenancy to cash-and-kind tenancy – a widespread system under which families would provide labour for three, six or nine months per year, for very little or low payment. The contract (written or oral) included the labour of the wife/wives and children, while the male head of household himself would commonly not work for the white farmer. In return, tenants received access to land to graze their cattle and plant crops for subsistence (or sometimes for sale). Due to Africans' preference for employment in the cities, labour tenancy was on the decline after the 1930s.[64]

While sharecropping and labour tenancy in South Africa were particular outgrowths of settler-colonial and race-based land alienation, they also existed in other contexts in which access to land was highly differentiated. In postcolonial Malawi, for instance, the state encouraged estate agriculture for tobacco production, leading to a complex system of different forms of estates relying predominantly on tenant labour – from huge estates owned by international companies, whites or President Hastings Banda and his entourage, to middle-sized holdings of Malawian civil servants, politicians or businessmen, to so-called 'progressive smallholders'. Not all of these tenants were landless, nor were they entirely dependent on the estate for their living, but rather they chose this form of work for its income. In other regions in Malawi, however, tenants fared much worse, working for landlords because of a lack of alternatives and being bound to the employer by debts for seeds, fertilizer and the food they received upon their arrival.[65] Sharecropping existed also in the northern highlands of Ethiopia, based on a communal land tenure system before the 1975 reform. A family that lacked the labour power or oxen necessary to cultivate its land would engage another family to work on it in return for one-quarter to one-half of the harvest. In the south, sharecropping and other tenancy arrangements were prevalent as well, but in a context of big estates owned by absentee landlords, which were divided into small plots worked by sharecroppers.[66]

---

[64] I. Ochiltree, "'A Just and Self-Respecting System'"? Black Independence, Sharecropping, and Paternalistic Relations in the American South and South Africa', *Agricultural History*, 72.2 (1998), 354–5; C. van Onselen, 'The Social and Economic Underpinning of Paternalism and Violence on the Maize Farms of the South Western Transvaal, 1900–50', *Journal of Historical Sociology*, 5.2 (1992), 127–60; A. Jeeves and J. S. Crush, 'Introduction', in *White Farms, Black Labor: The State and Agrarian Change in Southern Africa, 1910–50*, ed. A. Jeeves and J. S. Crush (Oxford: James Currey, 1997), 15–27.

[65] Vaughan, 'Exploitation and Neglect', 195, 197–8.

[66] G. Ellis, 'Land Tenancy Reform in Ethiopia: A Retrospective Analysis', *Economic Development and Cultural Change*, 28.3 (1980), 523–45.

Slavery constituted a widespread form of obtaining agricultural labour, although decreasingly so in the period covered in this chapter. Most relevant for the processes described here is the link between slavery and agrarian commercialization. Several studies showed slave labour to have been at the core of early capitalist production, rather than a remnant of an old order. According to Robert Ross, it was slave labour that facilitated 'initial accumulation' in the wine and wheat areas of the Cape under the Dutch East India Company. Slaves were brought to the Cape via the Indian Ocean, mostly hailing from Mozambique, Madagascar, India and East Indonesia. In addition, the Khoikhoi population was forced into farm labour through dispossession, the pass system and apprenticeships. While large plantations with a substantial slave workforce were rare, two-thirds of the farmers had at least one slave labouring under regimes that were characterized by violence and brutality.[67] Similarly, as seen above, research on the rise of agricultural commerce in West Africa has pointed to the fact that, despite abolition and the gradual decline of the transcontinental slave trade in the nineteenth century, 'legitimate commerce' often involved enslaved labour well into the colonial period.

While 'traditional' slave work in many cases involved domestic chores or work for a household's cultivation and animal husbandry, it also emerged in conjunction with the plantation economy. As Frederick Cooper has shown, slaves constituted a crucial labour force for the clove plantations in Zanzibar and Pemba and the grain and coconut plantations run by African and Arab masters in Malindi/Mombasa. While the British tried to undermine the slave trade after the 1860s, here – as in West Africa – abolition did not mean an abrupt end of enslaved labour, and planters continued to obtain sufficient numbers of slaves to uphold their production. While some former slaves of Arab and Swahili landowners did become proletarians in the early colonial period (for example, seeking work on the Mombasa labour market), many did not. As in South Africa, masters usually did not own large numbers of slaves and often worked alongside them. Slaves would work for 40–50 hours per week and were not uniformly organized in gang labour systems. In Zanzibar, they were even paid for overtime.[68]

---

[67] R. Ross, 'The Origins of Capitalist Agriculture in the Cape Colony: A Survey', in *Putting a Plough to the Ground: Accumulation and Dispossession in Rural South Africa 1850–1930*, ed. W. Beinart, P. Delius and S. Trapido (Johannesburg: Ravan Press, 1986), 56–100.

[68] F. Cooper, *Plantation Slavery on the East Coast of Africa* (New Haven, CT: Yale University Press, 1977); F. Cooper, *From Slaves to Squatters: Plantation Labour and Agriculture in Zanzibar and Coastal Kenya, 1890–1925* (New Haven, CT: Yale University Press, 1980).

Slavery-based plantations were also common in West African Islamic societies up to the late nineteenth/early twentieth centuries. Separated from kin and often acquired through raids, slaves constituted a significant part of the population. Although the exact contribution of plantation slavery to the 'cash crop revolution' is not entirely clear, several scholars have argued that it was pivotal to the emerging specialized production.[69] As a recent case study of the Sokoto caliphate has shown, numerous estates were run through gang labour provided by slaves, closely supervised by headmen or officials.[70] Gradually in the course of the twentieth century, enslaved work in plantation agriculture took a backseat, while various other forms of (coercive) labour mobilization became important. In settler colonies, a combination of land alienation and taxation ensured that plantation labour was forthcoming (though often not considered to be sufficient); in other cases, chiefs were used to recruit labour, while the sugar plantations in Natal relied on imported contract workers from India. Eventually, coerced labour on plantations decreased while wage labour became more dominant.[71]

Even though they have been referred to as a 'relatively insignificant' form of production in tropical Africa,[72] plantations – large-scale agricultural units, specialized and geared towards market production, using a relatively large labour force – have been a long-standing phenomenon on the African continent and were important in the development of exports and the introduction of new crops. As seen, plantation labour was often enforced, or enslaved, low-skilled, subject to harsh conditions, closely supervised, and mostly worked in gangs. In the early colonial period, plantations constituted enclaves of intensive capitalistic production competing with peasant production. By the late nineteenth century, plantations existed in almost all parts of Africa, from the Islamic states in West Africa and East African clove cultivation, to the North African coastal belt, where plantations were run by indigenous planters or European colonists, to rice production in Madagascar and sugar production in South Africa.

[69] For instance, P. Lovejoy, *Transformations in Slavery: A History of Slavery in Africa*, 3rd edn (Cambridge: Cambridge University Press, 2012).

[70] M. B. Salau, *The West African Slave Plantation: A Case Study* (New York: Palgrave Macmillan, 2011).

[71] R. Goodridge, 'Plantations and Labor, Colonial', in *Encyclopedia of African History*, vol. III, ed. K. Shillington (London: Fitzroy Dearborn, 2005), 1201–2; P. T. Zeleza, 'Plantation Agriculture', in *Encyclopedia of Twentieth-Century African History*, ed. P. T. Zeleza (London: Routledge, 2003), 434.

[72] E. Walker, 'Peasant Production, Colonial: Cash Crops and Transport', in *Encyclopedia of African History*, vol. III, ed. K. Shillington (London: Fitzroy Dearborn, 2005), 1188.

Under colonial rule in the twentieth century, plantations came to focus more narrowly on export crops, while the former variants had also produced food for local consumption. This went along with changes in ownership from local ruling and commercial elites to foreigners, as the old plantations in West and East Africa lost their labour in conjunction with abolition. Colonial authorities (when they did not opt for peasant agriculture and against expatriate-run plantations in the first place) fostered foreign ownership by settlers or corporations, including Unilever with its large concessions in Congo (and later also Nigeria and Gabon), or Firestone Rubber in Liberia.[73] Such new colonial plantations equally rested on labour that was – at most – nominally free. The first decade of the twentieth century constituted the heyday of colonial plantations. On São Tomé and Príncipe, in Mozambique and Angola, Portuguese planters produced, respectively, coffee, cocoa, sugar, cotton and coconut. In South Africa, Swaziland, Mauritius and Réunion, sugar plantations were important, while German companies established cocoa, banana and coffee plantations in Cameroon and Togo, as well as sisal and coffee in Tanzania. Kenyan settlers controlled large coffee and tea estates.[74]

Many foreign merchants and companies, however, failed in their attempts to establish plantations, especially so in West Africa. Not only was there already a robust peasant production, which traders did not want to relinquish; planters also suffered from a structural lack of labour and were rarely competitive internationally. In East Africa, European settlers were encouraged to set up plantations, and in many cases plantation and peasant economies existed side by side. In North Africa, settler plantation farming was probably most promoted in the settler colony of Algeria, which saw large-scale land dispossession, while rural Algerians became increasingly proletarianized.[75] Plantation agriculture expanded after independence, with state-supported increases in cash-crop farming, including under socialist governments, as in Angola, Mozambique or Tanzania. At the same time, the sector 'Africanized', that is, it came into national hands in socialist-oriented states or became dominated by African agrarian elites, as in Kenya and Malawi.[76] However, many nationalized plantations achieved only low production levels and did not improve incomes for workers or state profits. In the present era, plantations are exceptions in a context of smallholder production, and many of them are

---

[73] Goodridge, 'Plantations and Labor, Colonial', 1201; Zeleza, 'Plantation Agriculture', 434.

[74] P. Eyzaguirre, 'Plantation Economies and Societies', in *New Encyclopedia of Africa*, vol. IV, ed. J. Middelton and J. Miller (New York: Charles Scribner's Sons, 2008), 151–5.

[75] Zeleza, 'Plantation Agriculture', 434, 435.

[76] *Ibid.*, 436.

owned by multinational corporations. Labour mobilization continues to be a problem, as plantation work is avoided when other options exist. Research mostly agrees that plantations will continue to decline, as prices for export crops fall and global competition increases.[77]

Wage labour is probably the category least associated with Africa's agricultural history and present. However, several scholars have criticized the fact that rural wage labour, while not at all insignificant, is rather seriously under-represented in both research and policy. While African labour history has produced nuanced studies on wage labour in other sectors, such as mining, manufacturing or transport, agrarian wage labour seems to be a somewhat unwieldy category. The agrarian wage worker was and still is hardly ever a 'full' proletarian, but combined and combines rural wage labour with subsistence production or other sources of livelihood. Moreover, family labour seems to have predominated until the present. In the 1970s historical research debated rural proletarianization in a discussion that stressed these complexities and the limitations on the use of hired labour.[78] The fact that so many rural producers withstood full proletarianization seems to have been, among other factors, a matter of personal preference. In his study on farm labour in South Asante, Gareth Austin showed how (migrant) wage labour became increasingly widespread in the more established cocoa farms from the 1920s onwards. However, these workers would in the 1930s reverse 'the trend towards greater separation of labour from control of the land', demanding sharecropping arrangements rather than wage contracts in order to obtain a higher degree of autonomy and income. Similar observations have been made for the Gold Coast and the eastern Côte d'Ivoire, where wage contracts were partly replaced by sharecropping agreements.[79]

On the continent, South Africa seems to stand out as an exception. Whereas the labour-to-land ratio was low here as well, land appropriation facilitated the emergence of a highly mechanized and commercialized farming sector in which, eventually, wage labour predominated. Here, as in other countries, however, this transition was far from linear and complete. In the course of South Africa's 'agricultural revolution' following the formation of the Union in 1910, large-scale white farmers increasingly relied on a workforce of highly exploited, mostly migrant wage labourers, who contributed to the commercial sector's significant growth. However, migrant wage labour was 'neither an inevitable move beyond tenancy

---

[77] Eyzaguirre, 'Plantation Economies and Societies'.

[78] See the chapter by Eckert in this volume.

[79] G. Austin, 'The Emergence of Capitalist Relations in South Asante Cocoa-Farming, c. 1916–33', *Journal of African History*, 28.2 (1987), 275.

and sharecropping, nor an intermediate stop on the road to a proletarian, settled labor force'.[80] Earlier tenancy relations were only gradually and unevenly replaced by wage work; in addition, such work could hardly be termed 'free' in many instances, as workers were subjected to a coercive and highly exploitative contract system. As farm labour recruiters faced tough competition from the mining industry, many commercial farmers came to turn to long-distance migration, drawing labour from Mozambique, Southern Rhodesia and Malawi. These workers would labour on the farms for a specified period (often six months), living in barracks or compounds without their families, receiving below-subsistence wages. Work regimes were characterized by tough discipline, surveillance and violence – even though this could be tempered by paternalism. Propositions to divide the South African black labour force permanently between rural and urban areas popped up repeatedly, but only a small minority of commercial farmers shifted towards using settled wage labour when supplies became critical in the 1930s.[81] By the 1960s, however, supply and demand for agricultural labour assumed a more balanced position, and commercial agriculture focused on mechanization and a smaller but better-trained black labour force.[82]

Up to the present day, South African commercial farming is notorious for its often dismal working conditions, and similar observations have been made for commercial farms and 'agribusinesses' across the continent. This is particularly the case for smaller employers, whereas larger and more technologically advanced enterprises can often afford higher wages and are subject to monitoring by local authorities, trade unions and non-governmental organizations.[83] Recent research has deplored the lack of scholarship and understanding of the rural wage labour market. Arguing against the notion of Africa's 'uncaptured peasantry' and the impression that rural dwellers successfully resisted proletarianization, several scholars point to the ubiquity of agricultural wage labour, which, for most people, does not constitute the only source of livelihood but is nonetheless a very important one, especially for the poorest. Case studies of rural Mozambique, Mauritania, Senegal and Uganda have highlighted the significance of rural labour markets, even though the great majority of wage workers combine various

---

[80] Jeeves and Crush, 'Introduction', 3.

[81] *Ibid.*; van Onselen, *The Seed is Mine.*

[82] Atkinson, *Going for Broke*, 58–9.

[83] C. Oya, 'Rural Inequality, Wage Employment and Labour Market Formation in Africa: Historical and Micro-Level Evidence', Policy Integration Department, International Labour Office, Working Paper No. 97 (Geneva: ILO, 2010), 26–7; Wedig, 'Capitalist Labor Regimes'.

sources of income, including own-account farming, and are hardly a 'pure landless proletariat'. While most people do prefer independent farming, rural dwellers with little or no land, but also peasant farmers, value the wages they gain by working in agribusinesses, companies or casual labour on wealthier neighbours' farms as a reliable source of income.[84]

In most African countries, rural wage labour markets are poorly regulated, as rules on health and safety standards, working hours and minimum wages, if they exist in the first place, are hardly enforced. Agricultural wage labour may serve as a buffer against economic hardship, but it rarely leads to upward social mobility. A case study on Uganda, for instance, shows that wage work in the coffee sector is not only of a low standard, but also builds upon and reinforces existing social differentiation and inequality. Access to waged positions and working conditions depends crucially on gender, kinship and ethnicity, as labour gang leaders recruit casual workers from their own areas, assigning almost all skilled and better-paid work to men. Moreover, these workers regard their engagement as casual and temporary and barely identify as wage workers, which explains the lack of formal organization and collective action.[85]

Much of this wage labour today takes place in the context of 'agribusinesses', a rather loose term referring to agricultural production by large, often transnational corporations. Historically, some of these grew out of the pre-colonial and early colonial concession companies, which had far-ranging rights in terms of levying taxes, enforcing cash-crop cultivation among peasant communities and/or establishing plantations. In southern Africa, large- and medium-scale settler farms can also be seen as early variants of agribusiness, such as the 'factories in the field' that emerged in the early decades of the twentieth century in the South African maize triangle. Capitalized farmers founded large-scale estates and employed semi-permanent workers on long-term contracts, supplementing this settled core of staff with migrant workers. Recruitment and work routines have been likened to those of the mining industry. Mostly young men were recruited, who were housed in barrack compounds, worked around the clock under the supervision of African intermediaries, and often did piece work.[86]

[84]   Oya, 'Rural Inequality'; Wedig, 'Capitalist Labor Regimes'; M. Rizzo, 'Rural Wage Employment in Rwanda and Ethiopia: A Review of the Current Policy Neglect and a Framework to Begin Addressing It', Policy Integration Department, International Labour Office, Working Paper No. 103 (Geneva: ILO, 2011).

[85]   Wedig, 'Capitalist Labor Regimes', 16–23; on similar dynamics in Ethiopia and Rwanda, see Rizzo, 'Rural Wage Employment in Rwanda and Ethiopia'.

[86]   M. Murray, 'Factories in the Fields: Capitalist Farming in the Bethal District, 1910–1950', in *White Farms, Black Labor: The State and Agrarian Change in Southern Africa, 1910–50*, ed. A. Jeeves and J. S. Crush (Oxford: James Currey, 1997), 75–92.

After independence, some governments nationalized large agricultural estates or plantations, while others tried to control these companies more tightly. Moreover, given the decreasing profitability of plantation agriculture, companies took over more and more functions in the value chain. Modern agribusinesses, such as Unilever, Nestlé or British American Tobacco, are often in charge of manifold aspects of food or commodity business, controlling not only production, but also processing, transport, marketing and distribution. Hence, some companies own estates, management companies, consultancies, fertilizer and chemical plants, export and import companies, research institutions, food-processing factories or packaging plants.[87] In particular, South Africa-based farms and agribusinesses are spearheading such trends towards concentration, capital-intensive farming and diversification, expanding on the continent and becoming important players in food processing, logistics and distribution.

In 2000 the large-scale agricultural sector employed about 1.4 million full-time workers.[88] Research has drawn attention to changes in labour management from 'older' to (parts of) modern agribusiness. Under colonial paternalism – a management style denoting a mixture of 'paternal' protection and violent sanctioning, orchestrated through a narrative of parent–child, that is, farmer–worker, relations – the farm was seen as a private space, with workers residing near the farmer's household and being closely monitored. Work scheduling and cash payments were often irregular and subject to a considerable amount of discretion. Research on large-scale agriculture in Zimbabwe and South Africa has highlighted changes in this system following majority rule, when resident farm workers acquired permanent employment status, which led to more regular wages and working hours as well as a more impersonal management system. Corporal punishment receded, as farmers placed greater emphasis on providing incentives. Similar developments have been noted for the Kenyan cut-flower industry, which is placing more and more emphasis on formal qualifications, stabilization and worker motivation. Many studies have, however, highlighted the negative aspects of this decline or transformation of agrarian paternalism towards a system that emphasizes the wage relation over the personal one, is more strictly market oriented, and contributes to an overall trend of casualization, labour contracting and flexibilization.[89]

[87] Zeleza, 'Plantation Agriculture', 436.

[88] P. Gibbon, B. Daviron and S. Barral, 'Lineages of Paternalism: An Introduction', *Journal of Agrarian Change*, 14.2 (2014), 165.

[89] P. Gibbon and L. Riisgaard, 'A New System of Labour Management in African Large-Scale Agriculture?', *Journal of Agrarian Change*, 14.1 (2014), 94–128.

In the past two decades, contract farming has attracted significant policy and academic attention, as a form of production that links smallholders in agribusiness chains. Under contract systems, smallholders (but also capitalized family farms and commercial enterprises) produce on the basis of an agreement with the buyer – agro-processing companies, parastatals, exporters or retailers – which specifies quantity, quality and price. The World Bank and other development agencies promote contract farming as a commercially oriented form of smallholder production that interferes little with the way producers organize their labour and offers reliable markets and technological support. More critical studies, however, have pointed to the detrimental effects of contracting, as producers have suffered from monopsonistic structures and are doing little to improve their condition of poverty. While the producers under contract are nominally independent, scholars have argued that they – often the wives and children of male contract partners – are de facto hired hands on their own land.[90]

CONCLUSION

Agricultural labour has constituted an ambivalent category of work. It has meant hard toil in often unfavourable environmental conditions and exploitation by colonial and postcolonial elites. At the same time, it could lead to autonomy and self-determination, allowing producers to resist wholesale proletarianization and subjection to the market. Agricultural work has been an integral component of capitalist development in Africa, as well as an exit option.[91] At the threshold of domestic and extra-household work, agricultural activities centrally revolve around gendered and age-specific divisions of labour.

Interpreting historical changes in agricultural labour throughout the twentieth century depends very much on one's perspective. On the one hand, rural Africa does seem to confirm global trends – such as the spreading of capitalist modes of production, producers' integration into larger markets, concentration, de-agrarianization and a gradual shift towards free wage labour – albeit with a certain time lag. From another perspective,

[90] C. Oya, 'Contract Farming in Sub-Saharan Africa: A Survey of Approaches, Debates and Issues', *Journal of Agrarian Change*, 12.1 (2012), 1–33; P. Little and M. Watts, 'Introduction', in *Living under Contract: Contract Farming and Agrarian Transformation in Sub-Saharan Africa*, ed. P. Little and M. Watts (Madison, WI: University of Wisconsin Press, 1994), 3–18.

[91] See the chapter by Eckert in this volume.

however, the persistence of peasant and family labour and the significance of agricultural work generally is significant. Both interpretations are also echoed in current debates about the future of agrarian labour in Africa. There is a clear tendency in parts of academic research and donor policy to side with smallholder cultivation as the preferred pro-poor policy and means of ensuring food security. Other scholars, however, stress the reality of de-peasantization and/or emphasize improvements in agricultural wage labour conditions as a way to enhance living conditions. Most prominently, Deborah Bryceson has argued that Africa's 'uncapitalised ... peasant producers' are rather a 'historical anachronism' and that '[p]easant farming' is not, as previously imagined, the 'continent's ticket to modernization'.[92] Seen in the context of the long history of Western policy towards and intervention in African agriculture, there are certainly parallels in today's notion of the self-sufficient peasant and colonial stereotypes of the quintessentially rural African.

[92] Bryceson, 'De-Agrarianisation', 255, 240.

FIVE
Mining

CAROLYN A. BROWN

Department of History and Center for African Studies,
Rutgers University , New Brunswick

[T]he integrity with which ... black migrant working men, disciplined
and controlled, ... retained their senses of identity, measuring them not
only against those of the white men who employed them, and those who
supervised them but also against those of black officials in the compounds
and black supervisors underground. Migrant masculinity was sustained in
solidarity with fellow mineworkers and in partnership with women and other
men at home.

Dunbar Moodie and Vivian Ndatshe[1]

The paradox of Africa's mineral (and indeed, natural resource) wealth, on the
one hand, and the pervasive poverty of its people, on the other, remains a
deep and oft-noted feature of its economic landscape.

United Nations Economic Commission for Africa[2]

The development of [the] coal industry did a lot to my village. But for the
coal industry civilization would have not reached us as early as it had reached
us. The coal industry initiated me into Ozo title. Now I am Ozo Samuel N.

---

[1] Dunbar Moodie and Vivienne Ndatshe, *Going for Gold: Men, Mines and Migration*
(Berkeley, CA: University of California Press, 1994), 2–3.

[2] United Nations Economic Commission for Africa, *Minerals and Africa's Development:
International Study Group Report on Africa's Mineral Regimes* (Addis Ababa: United
Nations Economic Commission for Africa, 2011), 9.

Onoh. I was able to train up my children, build good houses. We contributed money and built schools and churches.

Samuel N. Onoh, Miner, Enugu Government Colliery[3]

Mineworkers are an important sector in the political economy of colonial and postcolonial Africa. In some areas, mining introduced wage labour.[4] The miners in South Africa and elsewhere shaped the formation of African labour studies in the 1970s and 1980s. Miners are in the economic sector that attracts the most foreign capital and that lends itself to production systems familiar to Europeans. Industrial mining appears to draw upon 'universal' (i.e., European) processes of labour deployment and control. Mining impacts on the state in varied and numerous ways. It encouraged colonialists to intervene in the African home in ways that agricultural production would not allow, except in cases of mass relocations such as the Gezira project (Sudan) and the Office du Niger (Mali).[5] With mining, the state 'imagined' that it could change the intricacies of African family life to push Africans into the 'modern' nuclear family. Policymakers felt that the conjugal family, with a male breadwinner and one housewife, was the key to social stability and a bulwark against working-class radicalism. But African miners had their own ideas of 'modernity' that drew upon (and modified) gendered ideologies about manhood and families from the village. As Ferguson notes of Zambian Copperbelt workers, men 'were never as "migrant" as colonial conservatives imagined, neither were they so permanently urbanized as … colonial liberals claimed'.[6]

---

[3] The Ozo society was a secret society signifying wealth and spiritual purity. Onoh also had six wives, a conspicuous show of wealth. The expenditure on his children's education showed the compatibility of 'traditional' and 'modern' symbols of elite male status. Onoh began work in 1915 as a tubman and worked his way up through the ranks until he became an underground foreman after the Second World War. Interview with Samuel N. Onoh, Ngwo-Etiti, Nigeria, 9 August 1975.

[4] See the chapter by Eckert in this volume.

[5] V. Bernal, 'Colonial Moral Economy and the Discipline of Development: The Gezira Scheme and "Modern" Sudan', *Cultural Anthropology*, 12.4 (1977), 447–79; J. Filipovich, 'Destined to Fail: Forced Settlement at the Office du Niger, 1926–45', *Journal of African History*, 42.2 (2001), 239–60; M. van Beusekom, 'Disjunctures in Theory and Practice: Making Sense of Change in Agricultural Development at the Office du Niger, 1920–60', *Journal of African History*, 41.1 (2000), 79–99.

[6] James Ferguson, *Expectations of Modernity: Myths and Meanings of Urban Life on the Zambian Copperbelt* (Berkeley, CA: University of California Press, 1999), 177.

In the nineteenth century, the discovery of diamonds and gold deposits in South Africa initiated a scramble for resources by foreign companies seeking investments in minerals and valuable gemstones. Today the increased prices of minerals fuelled by the demand from China and the West has encouraged new foreign investment in Africa and caused an explosion in artisanal mining by individuals and violent militias seeking 'blood minerals'. The experiences of the men – and, to an increasing degree, women and children – who work these minerals are a critical element of the history of the continent's engagement with the various phases of globalization.

In some respects, Africa's mineral history is a tragic chronicle of the paradox quoted above: the presence of rich mineral wealth is accompanied by deepening poverty and exploitation. One narrative is that this paradox has not weakened but intensified, pulling into desperate poverty the continent's millions. Another is the remarkable initiative taken by individual miners to make artisanal mining one of the most dynamic sectors of many African economies. Most states attained independence in the 1960s, when it appeared that mineral wealth would pull a nation to modernity. But by the second decade of independence, these states saw the opportunities for development slip away, as oil prices climbed, mineral prices plunged and debt surpassed national budgets. The conditionalities of loans from the World Bank and the International Monetary Fund devalued currencies, eliminated state subsidies and facilitated foreign investment. Some states struggled to preserve some modicum of economic control against powerful mining and financial interests, while others succumbed to violent conflict by militias and armies financed by 'blood minerals'. The instability of mining states such as the Democratic Republic of the Congo (DRC), Sierra Leone and Liberia is as much a political consequence of neoliberal policies as is the desperate, doomed flight of tens of thousands of African migrants crossing the Mediterranean.

This chapter is a brief introduction to the history of African mineworkers in smallholder, private foreign and state-owned enterprises. It is a broad survey of the history of labour in both North and sub-Saharan Africa during the colonial and postcolonial periods. It includes a brief description of pre-colonial mining as it shaped modern mining operations and systems of labour mobilization. It surveys labour in the most advanced mining areas – in southern Africa and the Copperbelt of Zambia and the DRC (i.e., gold, diamonds, copper, uranium, cobalt, coltan, etc.) – as well as in mining complexes in West Africa: the iron mines of Liberia, tin in Nigeria, gold in Ghana, diamonds in Sierra Leone and Angola and a variety of metallic and base metals and gemstones in North Africa, which has 85 per cent of the world's phosphate reserves.[7]

This chapter uses gender – masculinity – as a lens to analyse the ways in which African workers shape, and are shaped by, the work experience in Africa's mining industries. It sees masculinity as an important theoretical framework for interpreting the social history of the industry's workforce *from the perspective of working men* in the mines and as social actors in the associated communities and the nation. Despite the recognition of mining as a predominantly male occupation, few studies of workers' activism explicitly identify the ideology of masculinity as a useful category for analysing the experiences and activism of workers in the industry. But masculinity is the 'hidden' illusion in discussions of 'honour', 'respect', 'dignity', 'humiliation', racial epithets, etc.[8] Mining is associated with men and masculinity; even though it appears to be 'gender neutral', it incorporates numerous attributes that many societies associate with adult manhood.

We use Lindsay and Miescher's definition of masculinity as 'a cluster of norms, values and behavioural patterns expressing explicit and implicit expectations of how men should act and represent themselves to others'. Ideologies of masculinity are 'culturally and historically constructed, their meanings continually contested and always in the process of being renegotiated in the context of existing power relations'.[9]

The mine was a space of intense renegotiation between categories of men: between black workers and white management, between various categories of workers, between workers and 'native managers'. Ultimately, these struggles were between workers and mining capital, an opposition that appears 'genderless', but these were often struggles over the dignity *of* work and *at* work and the aspirations of men who wanted to be respected household heads and members of communities and the nation. Although it is beyond the scope of this chapter, an analysis of the gendered and racial expectations of European men, as 'bosses', brings crucial insights into the power dynamics of workplace control. John Tosh, a former Africanist, and others have explored the role of 'empire' in shaping the 'modern' British

---

[7] See Bill Freund's chapter on African trade unions in this volume for more substantial coverage of continental mine unions.

[8] With the exception of one chapter on gender, John Iliffe's book on *Honour in African History* (Cambridge: Cambridge University Press, 2005) is explicitly about African men, with chapters on 'Men on Horseback', 'Honour and Islam', 'Honour in Defeat', 'Urbanisation and Masculinity', etc.

[9] Lisa A. Lindsay and Stephan F. Miescher, 'Introduction: Men and Masculinities in Modern African History', in *Men and Masculinities in Modern Africa*, ed. L. A. Lindsay and S. F. Miescher (Portsmouth, NH: Heinemann, 2003), 1–32.

(imperial) man and explain his proclivity to use extreme violence against 'native' men in the colony.[10]

Because men form the predominant population in mining, articulations of and struggles over masculinity are deeply implicated in its work relationships. Masculinity is a 'silent' category, seldom problematized or analysed.[11] However, masculinity is routinely articulated in the discourses of labour and management in the mines and is evoked in ways that articulate the power relationships in production.[12] European 'men' routinely called African men 'boys' and institutionalized this subordination in the titles – 'boss boys' – of the 'native' supervisors who assisted them in controlling the workplace. Miners, despite these demeaning titles, were called upon to do a job that meets the major expectations of manhood – strength, physical endurance and willingness to incur risks and danger.

The skill hierarchy overlapped with race and made the workplace a volatile space where men with competing masculine identities ('imperial' vs. 'working class') reflected the power relations between labour and management. Colonial forms of labour control differed significantly from those in European mines.[13] Brutality and violence held great purchase and intersected with racial ideas about African abilities that were formed in the intellectual culture of imperialism and scientific racism. These skill/racial distinctions hardened into occupational hierarchies that were protected by systems of racial control – the colour bar and job reservation – both developed initially in South Africa's gold and diamond industries. As industrial mining spread in Africa, these patterns were replicated throughout the continent.

Lindsay and Miescher also argue that, in contrast to R. W. Connell's original claim of the social dominance of 'hegemonic' masculinity,[14] African men can at any given moment assume one of a complexity of masculinities, some indigenous (i.e., the father, the successful farmer, the 'Big Man') and others foreign (i.e., Christian man, industrial man, 'imperial' man).[15] Thus, a young miner (junior man) can be forced into the mine by elder men, become

[10] John Tosh, 'Imperial Masculinity and the Flight from Domesticity in Britain, 1880–1914', in *Gender and Colonialism*, ed. T. P. Foley et al. (Galway: Galway University Press, 1995), 72– 85; see also John Tosh, 'Masculinities in an Industrializing Society: Britain, 1800–1914', *Journal of British Studies*, 44.2 (2005), 330–42.

[11] Lindsay and Miescher, 'Introduction', 4.

[12] Michael Burawoy, *The Politics of Production: Factory Regimes Under Capitalism and Socialism* (London: Pluto Press, 1985), 209–52.

[13] *Ibid.*

[14] R. W. Connell, *Masculinities* (Cambridge: Polity Press, 1995), 76–80.

[15] Lindsay and Miescher, 'Introduction'.

an 'industrial man' through his experience, use his wages to become an elite 'Big Man' with many wives and children (see the opening quote by Samuel Onoh) and, when jobs disappear, become an artisanal miner like the reckless *orpailleur* (gold diggers).[16] Thus, although all the 'men' were white and all the 'boys' were African, the work experience, permanent wages and status of industrial mining as a 'modern' industry gave African miners a self-perception as vital, progressive men and the social identity of prominent, influential members of the community and nation.[17]

The story begins with the conquest and the association of wage labour (forced labour) with defeat and ends with the desperate, yet innovative, embrace of artisanal mining as a survival strategy and an effort to reclaim lost social prestige.[18] Initially, as the quote by Samuel Onoh notes, miners used jobs to acquire rural symbols of male prestige: marrying many wives, heading large families and acquiring (usually foreign) commodities that brought status and standing within the community, drew clients and allowed for the dispensation of patronage. They vacillated between these new and 'traditional' masculinities, as they attempted to 'reconcile for themselves the opportunities and constraints of their situations with the expectations of parents and other community members'.[19] Men's ability to juggle old and new masculinities based on fatherhood, work and status and the invention of new forms is one of the ways that workers mediate the power of capital in the workplace and the colonial state in the broader society. This ability to create forms of masculinity that accrue social dividends in their communities attests to the rich veins of personal construction that workers evoke to resist Western narratives of African backwardness and helplessness.

---

[16] Jeroen Cuvelier, 'Men, Mines and Masculinities: The Lives and Practices of Artisanal Miners in Lwambo (Katanga Province, DR Congo)', PhD dissertation, University of Leuven, 2011, 295. Artisanal mining has led Katanga men to create a trans-Atlantic masculine subculture; see chapter 5, 'Rastaman goes mining', 216–86.

[17] For a comparison with labour in the industrial sector, see the chapter by Neveling in this volume.

[18] See the chapter by Fall and Roberts in this volume.

[19] Lindsay and Miescher, 'Introduction', 13. McKittrick's contribution to this volume notes an instance among Ovambo men in which the fathers' power in transitioning their sons to social maturity was strengthened and expressed in ritualistic form. Meredith McKittrick, 'Forsaking Their Fathers? Colonialism, Christianity and Coming of Age in Ovamboland, Northern Namibia', in *Men and Masculinities in Modern Africa*, ed. L. A. Lindsay and S. F. Miescher (Portsmouth, NH: Heinemann, 2003), 33–51.

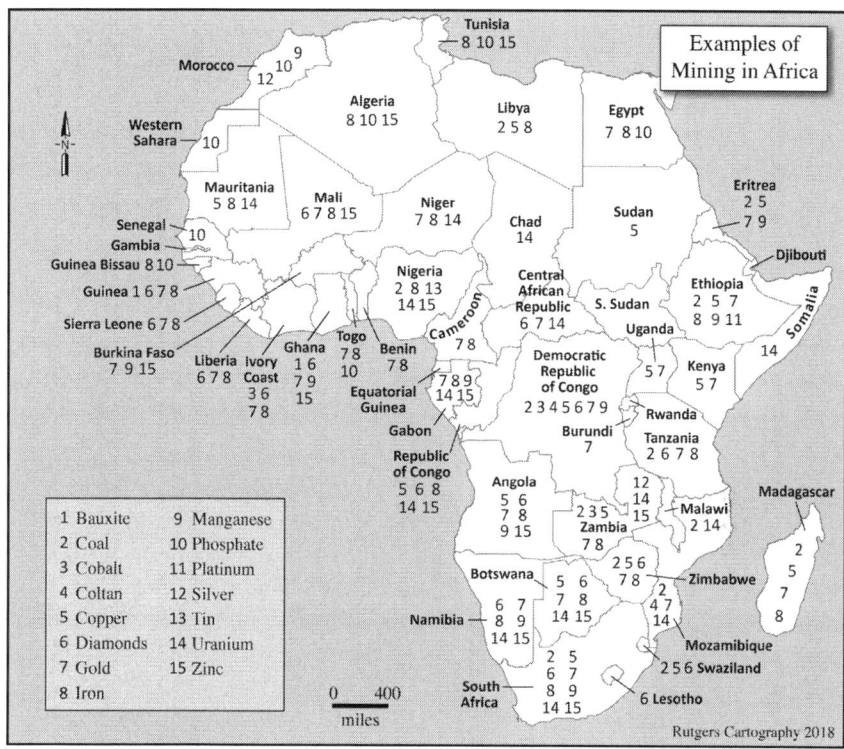

Map 5.1. Africa's main natural resources (Mike Siegel of Rutgers Cartography)

PRE-COLONIAL MINING PRECEDENTS

Minerals were associated in Africa with the rise of centralized states that were marked as 'Iron Age' because of the extraordinary consequences of iron for agricultural as well as weapons production, such as in the Mande state of Mali[20] and the powerful Nubian state of Meroe.[21] Colonial and contemporary mining companies have used the historic workings of African states, empires and communities to determine the location of minerals and gemstones for mining. For millennia, Africans had extracted metallic and non-metallic minerals.[22]

[20] D. T. Niane, *Sundiata: An Epic of Old Mali*, rev. edn (Harlow: Pearson Longman, 2007).

[21] Graham Connah, *African Civilizations: An Archaeological Perspective*, 4th edn (Cambridge: Cambridge University Press, 2007), 23.

[22] Paul T. Zeleza, *A Modern Economic History of Africa, Volume 1: The Nineteenth Century* (Oxford: CODESRIA, 1993), 174–80.

Today, Egypt's most profitable gold mine, Sukari,[23] is located in the Nubian Desert at the site of mines worked by hundreds of slaves during the Roman and early Christian centuries.[24]

Archaeologists, ethnologists and anthropologists have also determined that mining and the smelting of ore, such as iron, reinforced rural gendered patterns and gave men physical and spiritual power over both extraction and processing.[25] Iron was associated with the founder of the Mali Empire, Sundiata Keita, who was a cripple until he was assisted by a blacksmith who belonged to an endogamous caste or *nyamakala*.[26] The story is immortalized in the *Epic of Sundiata*, a poem performed by a *griot* (poet, storyteller) throughout the Mande-speaking areas. The smelting of iron, for example, is considered a spiritual process, only performed by men, and often when isolated from women.[27]

These indigenous production systems were surprisingly resilient in supplying mineral needs through local production and trade even into the mid-nineteenth century. Before the First World War, local miners, working under labour contractors, were the major source of tin in northern Nigeria.[28] In southern Africa, 'virtually all the modern mines of Rhodesia were sited on such old workings' of the Kingdom of Great Zimbabwe (AD 1100–1400) and the Mapungubwe Kingdom (AD 1075–1220),[29] which were exporting into the Indian Ocean trade.

Before the colonial era, mining was part of a diversified and integrated economy that incorporated farming, handicraft production and trade. A

---

[23] The Sukari project is a joint venture between the Egyptian government and Centamin, the Australian mineral exploration, development and mining company; see 'Sukari Gold Mine, Egypt', https://goo.gl/a5iouF (accessed 23 July 2016).

[24] F. Millar, 'The Condemnation to Hard Labour in the Roman Empire, from the Julio-Claudians to Constantine', *Papers of the British School at Rome*, 52 (1984), 124–47; Connah, *African Civilizations*, 55.

[25] Eugenia Herbert, *Iron, Gender and Power: Rituals of Transformation in African Societies* (Bloomington, IN: Indiana University Press, 1993).

[26] Patrick R. McNaughton, *The Mande Blacksmiths: Knowledge, Power, and Art in West Africa* (Bloomington, IN: Indiana University Press, 1993).

[27] Blacksmiths were *always* male and had a skill so strategically important that their technological knowledge was restricted by membership in endogamous castes, *nyamakala*. They were also associated with monarchical power. *Ibid.*, 1–21.

[28] Bill Freund, *Capital and Labour in the Nigerian Tin Mines* (Atlantic Highlands, NJ: Humanities Press, 1981), 14–24.

[29] Charles van Onselen, *Chibaro: African Mine Labour in Southern Rhodesia 1900–1933* (London: Pluto Press, 1976), 11; Connah, *African Civilizations*, 237, 252.

multitude of extractive systems was used, possibly based on the same conditions – geography, ore quality and labour resources – that shape colonial and modern mining. For shallow deposits of gold, for example, alluvial washing or surface mining was employed, while deeper deposits led to underground workings of varied depths. All used a variety of labour systems, ranging from family labour to gangs of slave labour.[30]

In addition to the Indian Ocean trade, African gold entered networks in the Muslim states of North Africa and on to Europe from the West African Sahel and forest belts, the Nubian hills and the southern plains. Today, Ghana, Africa's second largest exporter of gold, produces the majority of its output from mines originally worked by the Ashanti.[31] The variety of mining systems indicates levels of technological sophistication and labour utilization with deep historical roots. Today, some of the most violent struggles between artisanal miners and industrial companies have erupted in these fields. The elaborate chiefly system of the Ashanti Empire gave chiefs the right to demand communal and family *corvée* (forced) labour for both *placer* (alluvial) and shallow pit systems.[32]

In the eighteenth century, Ashanti gold was exchanged for salt *pound for pound* in the trans-Saharan trade.[33] This trade introduced Europeans to the medieval states of Ghana, Mali and Songhai in the western Sahel. This knowledge is captured in a fourteenth-century Italian map, which has a drawing of Mansa Musa (AD 1280–1337), King of Mali, holding a golden orb. Musa was so wealthy that, on his way to Mecca in 1324, he put so much gold into the Cairo economy that it destabilized the markets.[34]

---

[30] Van Onselen, *Chibaro*, 11; Raymond E. Dumett, *El Dorado in West Africa: The Gold-mining Frontier, African Labor, and Colonial Capitalism in the Gold Coast, 1875–1900* (Athens, OH: Ohio University Press, 1998), 51–81; UNECA, *Minerals and Africa's Development*, 11–12.

[31] Anglogold Ashanti, a South African and Ghanaian company which was formed in 2004, is the third largest gold company in the world. It has both deep-level and open pit mining. For a discussion of pre-colonial mining methods, see Dumett, *El Dorado in West Africa*, ch. 3, 'Traditional Gold Mining in the Southwestern Akan Region', 41–79.

[32] *Ibid.*, 51–71.

[33] E. Anne McDougall, 'Salts of the Western Sahara: Myths, Mysteries and Historical Significance', *International Journal of African Historical Studies*, 23.2 (1990), 231–57; Paul Lovejoy, *Salt of the Desert Sun: A History of Salt Production and Trade in Central Sudan* (Cambridge: Cambridge University Press, 2003); Edward W. Bovill, *The Golden Trade of the Moors: West African Kingdoms in the Fourteenth Century* (Princeton, NJ: Markus Wiener, 1995), 119–31.

[34] He had over five hundred slaves, each carrying gold, and one hundred camels with 300 pounds of gold each. Bovill, *The Golden Trade of the Moors*, 5, 87.

Salt was as valuable as gold within the continent, as demonstrated by its pound for pound exchange rate. It was a preservative for food, a supplement for animals, and was used for medicinal purposes and for dyeing textiles and leather. Multiple methods of production were used, including slaves working rock salt deposits in the Sahara and communities gathering crystals from the borders of salt lakes and ponds.[35] Thousands of tons of salt were sent throughout West Africa and deep into Central Africa, creating trade networks that integrated regional trade.

Copper was associated with ancient Egypt, as well as with the formation of states in Central and southern Africa, such as Ingombe Illede (fourteenth century)[36] in the Copperbelt region of central Zambia and the DRC. Northern Nigeria was a source of tin, an important element in the production of bronze weapons, tools and the magnificent court art of the Benin Kingdom.[37] To the north, Algeria is rich in metallic minerals, including iron, which the Phoenicians mined in the second millennium BC.[38] All of these pre-colonial mining systems were integrated into indigenous economies, played a role in state formation and demonstrated an ongoing process of technological development and commercial engagement with the global economy. This would all end under colonial occupation, which would redirect and restructure African mining, outlaw indigenous miners and reduce the people who created centuries of knowledge and skill to 'unskilled' workers. This industrial mining was an enclave owned by and directed towards global markets. Africans continue to struggle to recover their former control.

IMPLANTING COLONIAL MINING: THE STATE, CAPITAL AND YOUNG AFRICAN MEN

When defeat and colonial rule fragmented African notions of honour, elements were absorbed not only into the ethics of colonial armies and

---

[35] Lovejoy, *Salt of the Desert Sun*, 15–32.

[36] Connah, *African Civilizations*, 260.

[37] *Ibid.*

[38] Algeria (Tindouf province) has one of the largest iron ore reserves of over 300 million tons. There are zinc and lead mines in the north, in Bejaia, which also has the third largest lead reserves (60 million tons) in the world. Mohammad Abu Abdullah, 'Algerian Government Pushes to Improve Miners' Rights', *The New Arab*, 6 April 2015, https://goo.gl/LXaJQi (accessed 22 July 2016).

respectable Christians but also into a working-class ethic designed to ensure survival and dignity in towns and workplaces.[39]

The first large-scale foreign investments in African mineral extraction were in the nineteenth-century South African gold and diamond industries. Subsequent exploration suggested other viable sites in Central and North Africa. Mining under early conditions was fraught with difficulties and required the intense involvement of the new state to secure land, labour and capital for mining and the supportive infrastructure. The state created a legal framework to block African prospecting and mining rights, to seize land, to secure and control labour, if necessary through force, and to draft fiscal policies that threw the burden of capital formation on to the same population whose labour was being appropriated. In the case of South Africa, the industry relied on a strong state to disrupt neighbouring economies, create a regional labour pool and supply large numbers of unskilled labourers.

Elsewhere, labour mobilization generally followed conquest, and the first contingents were prisoners of war from unsuccessful resistance. In southern and Central Africa, the military defeated the most powerful states and seized land, coerced workers and terrorized villages into accepting authority. In Algeria, the French launched a brutal war of attrition that killed thousands and destroyed villages and cities. They even chopped down olive trees to deprive communities of an alternative to wage labour. The result was a near proletarianization of the peasantry and the urban classes.[40]

Conquest allowed the manipulation of social institutions, such as the monetization and exploitation of the bride price, to push young men in the cattle-based economies of southern Africa to do wage labour.[41] In other regions, land seizures and mandatory taxes, as well as the promotion of foreign goods, incentivized the young to work for wages. 'Traditional' labour systems were co-opted as in northern Nigeria, where 'native' labour contractors supplied the men when Britain seized the tin mines.[42] Compliant chiefs used their authority to call up young men for stints in the mines.[43] In areas where labour obligations were already established through clientage,

---

[39] Iliffe, *Honour in African History*, 281.

[40] M. Bennoune, 'Socio-Economic Changes in Rural Algeria: 1830–1954', *Peasant Studies Newsletter*, 11.2 (1973), 14–15.

[41] Jeff Guy, 'The Destruction and Reconstruction of Zulu Society', in *Industrialisation and Social Change in South Africa: African Class Formation, Culture and Consciousness 1870–1930*, ed. S. Marks and R. Rathbone (New York: Longman, 1982), 181–2, 187.

[42] Freund, *Capital and Labour in the Nigerian Tin Mines*, 89–95.

[43] Carolyn A. Brown, *'We Were All Slaves': African Miners, Culture, and Resistance at the Enugu Government Colliery* (Portsmouth, NH: Heinemann, 2003), 76–80.

pawnship or slavery, labour was merely redirected to the mines. Local headmen functioned as recruiters, bringing in crews and collecting the pay for their output. In many areas, the conscription of marginal populations – slaves, pawns and other subordinates – led to protests that erupted in violence.[44]

Mining benefited from the rural process through which young men became 'adult men'. A respected adult man was successful in farming or cattle raising and headed a large homestead or compound with 'wealth in people' – many wives, descendants and clients.[45] Young men depended on their fathers and other senior men to direct them through the process of social maturity.[46] Marriage and wives were key to this process and required resources – for some cattle, for others farmland – to make the bride wealth payment for an independent household/homestead.[47] Until then, a young man was a 'social minor', reliant on his father's largesse and obliged to perform strenuous labour, conduct warfare and execute, but not participate in, village governance.

Mine work changed this process. It both strengthened and jeopardized the authority of senior men. While seniors could send young men to the mines, the wages earned allowed the young to escape the control of the seniors. Mining jobs brought prestige and financed social rituals that were important for village cohesion and personal status. Mineworkers experimented with forms of association that enabled them to discuss work conditions, strategize on forms of protest and pursue village development projects that expressed their position as 'new' progressive men. They built modern houses, schools and hospitals, financed potable water and educated their children.[48] In this way, wage labour destabilized the customary transitions of generational masculinities. Miners earned prominence as a new category of social beings – industrial men – within kinship networks and rural communities. While, to the state and the mining companies, they were only 'units of labour', to the men themselves and their communities they were successful social

---

[44] In Nigeria, again, slaves – miners who earned wages – led an uprising in the 1920s to protest the freeborns' refusal to allow them to perform rituals reserved for men of wealth. Carolyn A. Brown, 'Testing the Boundaries of Marginality: Twentieth-Century Slavery and Emancipation Struggles in Nkanu, Northern Igboland, 1920–29', *Journal of African History*, 37.1 (1996), 51–80.

[45] Guy, 'The Destruction and Reconstruction of Zulu Society', 169–72.

[46] Brown, *'We Were All Slaves'*, 41–3; Luise White, 'Matrimony and Rebellion: Masculinity in Mau Mau', in *Men and Masculinities in Modern Africa*, ed. L. A. Lindsay and S. F. Miescher (Portsmouth, NH: Heinemann, 2003), 177–91.

[47] McKittrick, 'Forsaking Their Fathers?', 33–4; Brown, *'We Were All Slaves'*, 41–3; White, 'Matrimony and Rebellion', 180.

[48] Brown, *'We Were All Slaves'*, 289.

beings. These conflicting conceptions of labour – as abstract units and as social beings – were major factors in the continent's tumultuous mining history. Managers' objectification of 'the African worker' locked them into erroneous assumptions and racial stereotypes about African men. Violence and industrial brutality were the only assurance that Africans could 'adapt to the work rhythms of industrial capitalism: to the idea that work should be steady, and regular and carefully controlled'.[49] The workplace was the site of this struggle between men.

LAND, LABOUR AND TECHNOLOGY: MIGRANT MEN AND 'MODERN' MINES

The colonial state was profoundly affected by the transformation of African pre-colonial artisanal mining to industrial mining controlled by expatriates.[50] The project was a public–private partnership in which the public – the African population – actually had no advocates. The myth was that African interests were represented by the paternalistic colonial state for whom the 'civilizing' mission conflicted with many African cultural practices and social institutions. Wage labour was an important 'marker' of personal and societal 'progress', and the state provided support for an export enclave that met the needs of foreign industry.[51]

As industrial mining spread in Africa in the early twentieth century, companies adopted South Africa's two-tier labour model, which reflected the racial hierarchies of colonial society: a small number of privileged expatriate (European) skilled miners and a large pool of rotating, unskilled migrant (African) labourers. In states with settlers, the political cost was high in trying to reconcile the demands of whites with the avoidance of violent conflict with 'natives'. In both the workplace and the broader society, 'whiteness'

---

[49] Frederick Cooper, 'Colonizing Time: Work Rhythms and Labor Conflict in Colonial Mombasa', in *Colonialism and Culture*, ed. N. B. Dirks (Ann Arbor, MI: University of Michigan Press, 1992), 209.

[50] Local mining efforts in Ghana, Zimbabwe and the Congo were destroyed. UNECA, *Minerals and Africa's Development*, 13.

[51] Mining operations were often the only industrial enclaves requiring wage labour in the colony. Colonial economic policies guaranteed that mines would have very weak links with the rest of the economy, because most of the minerals were exported in raw form or subject to only basic processing. *Ibid.*

conferred special power and authority while 'native' meant subordination and oppression.[52]

There was a gathering consensus in the early twentieth century towards uniform labour standards for colonial populations. The 1930 Forced Labour Convention (No. 29) of the International Labour Organization was one example. However, governments assiduously deceived the reporting mechanism.[53] Administrators such as Sir Frederick Lugard, former Governor General of Nigeria, who represented Britain on the League of Nation's Temporary Slavery Commission, cynically claimed that coercion was the best way to introduce Africans to the values of 'free [i.e. wage] labour'.[54] This increased tensions between generations and strata that sometimes erupted into violence.

There were two systems of African labour utilization: migrant labour, consisting of unskilled, single men on contracts often living in compounds and single-sex hostels; and a 'stabilized' labour force of skilled and semi-skilled men, living for extended periods with their families in company housing. The decision to use either system was shaped by population densities, production technologies, the relative costs and ratio of skills and the geographical composition of the ore field. Geography was a 'fixed' input, as a mine could not be 'moved' to a more suitable location. The position of mineral deposits in relation to faults and other geographical interruptions, high- or low-grade deposits and the depth of workable sites shaped decisions about whether to use mechanization or intensive labour. Surface ore deposits suggested open pit methods, which became increasingly popular in late colonial Africa. A large field of deep-level, low-grade deposits, as in the South African goldfields, could be worked profitably with large numbers of unskilled workers, a small body of skilled workers and supervisors. In the early 1920s, two companies, Union Minière du Haut Katanga and Companhia de Diamantes de Angola (Diamang), copper and diamond producers, respectively, shifted from migrant to stable labour with the intention of monitoring and transforming African family life.[55] Both companies realized

[52] It is Michel Burawoy's contention that the 'power in production' was always legitimized by the legal system governing the broader colonial society. See Burawoy, *The Politics of Production*.

[53] For a discussion of how colonial governments subverted this Convention, see Brown, *'We Were All Slaves'*, ch. 4.

[54] *Ibid.*, 82–3.

[55] The social scientists at the Rhodes-Livingston Institute in Northern Rhodesia assumed that African women were the cause of promiscuity, and that urban immorality but would soon accept the modern 'nuclear' family structure. Ferguson noted that, despite the expectations of these scholars, African workers were not living in nuclear families. Ferguson, *Expectations of Modernity*, ch. 5.

that married workers were more permanent, had lower mortality and absenteeism rates and worked for longer periods, which permitted skills accumulation.[56]

An intersecting series of conditions determined the forms of labour, the degree of workers' industrial power and the system of extraction of industrial mining.[57] In coal mining, the pillar and stall system of many separate 'rooms' allowed hewers (miners) to escape supervision and set their own pace of production. In gold mining, the isolation was provided by the creation of 'stopes', separate passages of extraction connected to the shaft that followed the line of gold deposits. A mine could have many of these stopes branching off at various points from the shaft. These disparate stopes, in turn, gave the miners' workplace autonomy, decreased managerial supervision, and complicated the management's ability to regulate the rhythms and productivity of labour. This allowed workers to use subversive, non-confrontational or 'hidden forms of resistance'.[58] Thus, when workers use sabotage to regulate the pace of production, they are expressing worker consciousness.

In the late colonial and postcolonial period, underground mining was replaced by open cast or open pit mining. The labour requirements of any particular mine depended on variable and constant factors: input prices, the range of production technologies, the scale and location of pits and underground workings, ore concentration and the relative cost and skills ratio of white and black labour. Companies had to assess the productive costs and benefits of raising African skill levels through training, in comparison to hiring skilled white labour. These choices depended on the degree of state control over skilled and unskilled labour markets. Recruitment costs were not always under state control and, in southern Africa, reflected competition with settler farms and regional mining.

---

[56] William H. Worger, *South Africa's City of Diamonds: Mine Workers and Monopoly Capitalism in Kimberley 1867–1895* (New Haven, CT: Yale University Press, 1987); Todd Cleveland, *Diamonds in the Rough: Corporate Paternalism and African Professionalism on the Mines of Colonial Angola, 1917–1975* (Athens, OH: Ohio University Press, 2015).

[57] For a description of these conditions, see Charles Perrings, *Black Mineworkers in Central Africa: Industrial Strategies and the Evolution of an African Proletariat in the Copperbelt 1911–41* (Portsmouth, NH: Heinemann, 1979), ch. 1.

[58] R. Cohen, 'Resistance and Hidden Forms of Consciousness Among African Workers', *Review of African Political Economy*, 19 (1980), 8–22.

THE HIDDEN ABODE OF PRODUCTION: POWER AND RESISTANCE IN THE COLONIAL MINE, 1914–39

The First World War cemented the colonial status of African territories and caused inflation in the colonies. A post-war economic contraction depressed the demand for and price of gold. White workers, despite their small number, moved to the forefront in demanding higher wages and job protection. In South Africa, they launched a violent strike against a Randlord proposal to reduce the ratio of white to cheaper black labour. They occupied the mines, barred black workers from them, seized areas of Johannesburg and engaged in pitched battles with police and government troops. The government retaliated with a warlike onslaught and bombed areas of Johannesburg, killing 153 and wounding over 500.[59]

The colonial mine was more than an extractive institution. It was a male socialization space for the gendered racial and power hierarchies of the colonial world. Workplace authority was in the hands of white expatriate miners and managers, which made the workplace a volatile site of men ('imperial' vs. 'native boys') competing over the power in production.[60] European supervisors and African 'boss boys' ('native' foremen) used coercion, extortion and corporal punishment to discipline the men and reach production goals. But the very 'male' nature of mine work, with its physical demands, celebration of skill and technological knowledge, encouraged the men to solidify their self-identity as 'industrial men' in an industry that played a major role in the colonial and global economy. They initially used indirect means of protest – malingering, absenteeism and even desertion – to control the pace and intensity of work and the frequency with which they presented themselves at the mine. Denied the right to form unions, they used indigenous associations to organize strikes. Embedded in their actions were their beliefs in what constituted meaningful work.[61]

[59] Robert Davies, *Capital, State and White Labour in South Africa, 1900–1960: An Historical Materialist Analysis of Class Formation and Class Relations* (New York: Humanities Press, 1979). For a less successful series of strikes by a smaller number of white miners in coal, see Ian Phimister, *Wangi Kolia: Coal, Capital and Labour in Colonial Zimbabwe 1894–1954* (Harare: Baobab Books, 1994), 52–4.

[60] For an analysis of the important role of the colony in British masculinity and an explanation of the behaviour of colonial men, see Tosh, 'Imperial Masculinity'; see also Brown, *'We Were All Slaves'*, 63–4, 291.

[61] For a discussion of pre-colonial work cultures relative to wage labour and what constituted 'work', see Keletso E. Atkins, *The Moon is Dead! Give Us Our Money! The Cultural Origins of an African Work Ethic, Natal, South Africa, 1843–1900* (Portsmouth, NH: Heinemann, 1993); see also Keletso E. Atkins, '"Kaffir Time": Preindustrial

The negligence of managers regarding safety and occupational health led the men to include 'survival' as an occupational skill that defined an 'industrial man'.[62] An industrial 'folk knowledge' developed – including the recognition of sounds ('talking rocks') that preceded a mine collapse, the detection of methane gas, the conservation of energy in high humidity and temperatures – and became an essential element of skill.[63] Surviving the workplace itself was the ultimate skill, and most miners recognized it as such. These challenges served to reinforce their identities as 'industrial men', heroic figures who could confront danger, exhibit physical endurance and perform tasks that others feared.

Underground mining generates a spirituality that is not found in other industries. Factory workers do not claim to have 'cheated' death whenever they leave the workplace alive. But when men enter the mines, they are 'swallowed' by the earth and enter a dangerous cosmic place.[64] They enter the unknown, the burial space inhabited by their ancestors. The mine is a place of hidden danger, of unexpected catastrophe and possibilities of wealth, extraordinary tests of male resolve and endurance of pain, and an unwavering commitment to honour. Death hangs over mining as much more than a 'possibility'. Death dares workers to confront the mine and goads them to increasingly risky behaviour to demonstrate their bravery to other men, to increase production and to become 'working men'. That many mining spirits are gendered female suggests that their deeper meaning may concern men's ideas and anxieties over gender. Until recently, it was taboo for women to enter the Enugu coal mines.[65] Cuvelier argues that the complicated meanings that artisanal miners attach to female spirits who control access to minerals express anxieties about gender, mining and death.[66]

Temporal Concepts and Labour Discipline in Nineteenth-Century Colonial Natal', *Journal of African History*, 29.2 (1988), 229–44.

[62] Brown, *'We Were All Slaves'*.

[63] There were other hazards such as the radiation found in copper mines and phosphate deposits.

[64] In Nigeria, men from a rich agricultural area adjacent to the mines refused to go underground, noting that 'a man may as well be buried alive'. Brown, *'We Were All Slaves'*, 189.

[65] Personal communication when visiting a mine, July 1975.

[66] Cuvelier, 'Men, Mines and Masculinities', 163–215.

In the 1930s the most liberal colonial powers had reached a consensus that abrogated extreme forms of violence, supported labour stabilization[67] and declared these to be the most 'enlightened' ways to mobilize and control African workers. Colonial labour conditions had become the subject of increasing levels of international surveillance by the ILO and other organizations, and some semblance of 'international standards' had emerged, at least at the level of discourse.

The stock market crash of 1929 caused a precipitous drop in the demand for minerals, resulting in a severe crisis for the continent's mineworkers. Retrenchments and wage cuts followed, throwing men and their families into indefinite destitution. The rural economy, buffeted by ever lower prices for agricultural products, offered no respite. In the mid-1930s the pent-up grievances erupted into an escalating series of 'dangerous' protests. Zambian miners demanded restoration of pre-Depression wages and attacked white managers, a clear rejection of the racial hierarchy of authority.[68] In Morocco, phosphate workers in state-owned mines in Yousouffa and Khouribga formed clandestine unions and joined with French workers in demanding wage increases.[69] But this unity was fragile, as 'whiteness' was a powerful factor preventing European workers from collaborating with Africans. The most formidable strikes came from the plantation and oil (Trinidad) workers in the West Indies, whose protests became anti-colonial uprisings.[70] These actions sounded the alarm that dangerous levels of discontent lay

[67] Some governments were arguing that migrant labour caused lawlessness, family breakups and promiscuity. See Major G. St. J. Orde Browne, *Labour Conditions in West Africa*, Cmd. 6277 (London, 1941).

[68] In both the Northern Rhodesian Copperbelt and the Enugu (Nigeria) coal mines, miners adapted indigenous associations to industrial needs: the *Mbeni* dance societies in Northern Rhodesia and the *nzuko ifunaya* (workers groups modelled on urban 'tribal' associations) in Enugu. See Perrings, *Black Mineworkers in Central Africa*; Brown, *'We Were All Slaves'*, 127–8.

[69] J.-F. Clement and Jim Paul, 'Trade Unions and Moroccan Politics', *Middle East Research Information Project (MERIP) Reports*, 127 (October 1984), 19–24.

[70] On the Copperbelt, see Ian Henderson, 'Early African Leadership: The Copperbelt Disturbances of 1935 and 1940', *Journal of Southern African Studies*, 2 (1975), 83–97; Ian Henderson, 'Wage-Earners and Political Protest in Colonial Africa: The Case of the Copperbelt', *African Affairs*, 72.288 (1973), 288–99; Perrings, *Black Mineworkers in Central Africa*; Peter Weiler, 'Forming Responsible Trade Unions: The Colonial Office, Colonial Labor and the Trades Union Congress', *Radical History Review*, 28–30 (1984), 367–92. On the British Caribbean, see W. Arthur Lewis, *Labour in the West Indies: The Birth of a Workers' Movement* (London: New Beacon Books, 1977); Ken Post, *Arise Ye Starvelings: The Jamaican Labour Rebellion of 1938 and its Aftermath* (The Hague: M. Nijhoff, 1978).

beneath the surface of the British Empire. The protests shocked colonial administrators throughout the Empire because of their strategic timing, levels of organization, effectiveness in identifying targets and demographic scope. The ominous consolidation of Nazi power in Germany led imperial states to include colonial workers, at least partially, in industrial relations systems current in Europe.

This unrest in the 1930s attracted imperial attention to the state of labour relations in the colonies. The initiatives of the ILO to monitor the conditions of colonial labour suggested an international consensus over the most appropriate ways of treating colonial workers. While miners in developed mining enclaves such as South Africa, North Africa and Sierra Leone had trade unions, others experimented with forms of collective action to challenge the workplace.[71] Until this wave of strikes, few governments allowed Africans to form unions, so workers adapted indigenous associations – guilds, mutual aid associations, urban progressive unions – to industrial functions and secretly organized protests. Workers targeted the points of vulnerability and timing in the mines' productive systems. This dangerous sign of worker autonomy was a political threat and forced an adoption of industrial relations systems to prevent strikes from evolving into broad militant populist movements that would make political demands on the colonial government.[72] But the war was looming.

Thus, Africa's mining industry entered the Second World War with 'controlled' unionization that had, however, 'colonial' restrictions (i.e. lack of autonomy, close state monitoring, fiscal supervision, etc.) as state-controlled channels for worker discontent.

STRATEGIC MINERALS, MILITANT MINERS AND STATE CONTROL: AFRICAN MINERS DURING THE SECOND WORLD WAR[73]

Please note that in future the designation 'men' must be substituted for 'boys' in all communications referring to the Colliery labour either collectively or

[71] In Nigerian mines, workers' organizations resembled the urban (tribal) unions established by 'sons abroad'. For discussion, see Brown, *'We Were All Slaves'*, ch. 8; cf. Higginson, *A Working Class in the Making*. For comparable historical examples, see the chapter by Freund in this volume.

[72] Lewis, *Labour in the West Indies*; Post, *Arise Ye Starvelings*; Weiler, 'Forming Responsible Trade Unions'; Perrings, *Black Mineworkers in Central Africa*.

[73] For the role of African labour during the Second World War, see Carolyn Brown, 'African Labor in the Making of World War II', ch. 3 in *Africa and World War II*, ed.

individually. No person employed by this department must be addressed as 'boy'.[74]

Pearl Harbor (1941) and Japan's victory over British Singapore (1942) deprived the Allies of their primary source of tropical products and the strategic mineral tin. Nigerian tin mines became a strategic necessity, and Britain conscripted over 100,000 men a month to work in them. Poor work conditions, inadequate rations and disease increased morality rates by 4.4 per 1,000 to an astronomical 25.6 per 1,000.[75]

Miners increased productivity in supplying essential minerals, despite rampant inflation and strike prohibitions. There was some labour stabilization to reduce work stoppages and facilitate output. But in 1942 strikes erupted in virtually every major industry, with a ferocity and determination that shocked state officials. Predictably, they tightened constraints on workers' freedom of movement, arrested leaders, banned the right to strike and reduced the power of trade unions. But it was difficult to support racist labour practices in a political environment dominated by the fight against fascism, and the state withdrew support for racial forms of labour control.

German attacks on shipping lanes brought African minerals to the forefront of the Allied campaign. South Africa, the Belgian Congo, Northern and Southern Rhodesia, the Gold Coast and Nigeria became key sources of the majority of strategic minerals. South African and Sierra Leonean diamonds[76] for industrial manufacture, and the uranium for the atomic bomb (Belgian Congo), were the most vital contributions.[77] The state increased the surveillance of mineworkers, trying to isolate them from the political movements demanding independence. But the state strategy of bureaucratizing industrial conflict led workers to select as leaders educated men who could help them navigate the bureaucratic industrial

J. Byfield, C. Brown, T. Parsons and A. Sikainga (New York: Cambridge University Press, 2015), 43–67.

[74] Nigerian Coal Corporation Files, New No. P.1, 'Letter from Colliery Department to All Officials and Staff-European and African', Colliery Manager (Enugu) to Staff, 23 December 1941, quoted in Brown, *We Were All Slaves*', 225.

[75] Freund, *Capital and Labour in the Nigerian Tin Mines*, ch. 5.

[76] Raymond E. Dumett, 'Africa's Strategic Minerals during the Second World War', *Journal of African History*, 26.4 (1985), 381–408. For an analysis of Britain's strategy to obtain US dollars from selling to the United States diamonds polished in the Palestine Mandate, see David de Vries, *Diamonds and War: State, Capital and Labour in British-Ruled Palestine* (New York: Berghahn Books, 2010).

[77] United States Government, Department of the Interior, Bureau of Mines, *The Minerals Yearbook for 1943* (Washington, DC: Government Printing Office, 1943), 1567.

relations procedures that the state had developed to thwart worker activism. These men often held deeply nationalist sentiments and ignored the state's attempt to depoliticize African unions. They were often accused of manipulating the illiterate rank and file and maligned by government officials as 'scoundrels'.[78]

War conditions and the coordinated planning and execution of labour policies collapsed the distinction between European 'working men' and African 'native labourers'. This encouraged African workers to compare their sacrifices and conditions of service to those of expatriate government staff and European and American miners.[79] Some metropolitan labour policies were applied, in 'colonial' form, to Africa and its workers. Propaganda alleged a shared – metropole–colony – sacrifice,[80] with expectations of fair treatment, while common mining technologies encouraged African miners to identify with an international brotherhood of miners.[81] Having played a major role in wartime production, some miners participated in the rash of post-war general strikes sparked by transport workers.[82] They complained that low wages prevented them from being 'breadwinners'. But in reality, few wives were housewives, as most worked on their own account.[83] Nationalist discourse indicated a racialized class consciousness that demanded dignity, social justice and racial parity in the face of the dehumanizing and abusive systems of industrial discipline. It became an affront for a respected man to be excluded from national politics, and many miners' unions were in the vanguard of the post-war nationalist struggles. But it was an uneasy collaboration.

[78] See Brown, *We Were All Slaves'*. For a full discussion, see chapter 6, 'The Politics of "Productivity": Unions, the War and Changes in the Political Apparatus of the Mines 1940–1945'. The emergence of this type of educated and militant leader was a natural consequence of the state's attempt to entangle worker grievances in a morass of bureaucratic procedures.

[79] *Ibid.*, 54.

[80] R. Smyth, 'The British Colonial Film Unit and Sub-Saharan Africa, 1939–1945', *Historical Journal of Film, Radio and Television*, 8.3 (1988), 285–98.

[81] David Frank, 'The County of Coal', *Labour/Le Travail*, 21 (Spring 1988), 233–48.

[82] T. Oberst, 'Transport Workers, Strikes and the "Imperial Response": Africa and the Post World War II Conjuncture', *African Studies Review*, 31.1 (1988), 117–34.

[83] For a discussion of men's manipulation of the breadwinner discourse despite their wives' financial autonomy, see Lisa Lindsay, 'Domesticity and Difference: Male Breadwinners, Working Women and Colonial Citizenship in the 1945 Nigerian General Strike', *American Historical Review*, 104.3 (1999), 783–812.

WHEN WORK HAS GONE: ARTISANAL MINING, RECONFIGURED GENDER AND SURVIVAL STRATEGIES IN POSTCOLONIAL AFRICA.

As the nationalist movements mobilized for independence, the future of African mining was being negotiated by the late colonial state. The goal was to use increased African mineral exports for the reconstruction of Europe. Both France and Britain established 'development' agencies to increase the output of mineral production focused on new mineral prospecting and capital support for private companies in mineral development.[84] The results were a rapid growth in production of African minerals: a 200 per cent increase in manganese, phosphates and iron, a 150 per cent increase in copper and a 350 per cent increase in cobalt.[85] The last years of colonialism featured a modern 'scramble for African mineral rights', and mines were opened and expanded in a majority of African countries.[86]

The structural impediments to real development were visible within a decade of independence: foreign ownership, weak links between mining and the rest of the economy, imported inputs, repatriation of virtually all profits and a reproduction of the same racial labour force of colonial rule – most important skilled jobs were held by expatriates, while Africans occupied low-skilled and unskilled jobs. Additionally, mining was the biggest source of public revenue. When the mineral market plunged in 1980,[87] state revenues declined, compounded by the oil crisis. In the 1990s Zambia's imports cost three times the revenue generated from copper in the 1970s. The crisis forced state mines to reduce production; many mines were closed and thousands of men were out of work. In the 1980s the security of mining jobs evaporated. The crisis also crippled the continent's agricultural sector and sent a significant portion of the rural population into the cities.

The price for gold, copper and diamonds began to increase again in the mid-1990s,[88] but the intervention of powerful international financial

---

[84] In Britain, public–private partnerships, largely in mining, were financed by the Colonial Development Corporation and in France by the Fonds d'Investissement et de Développement Économique et Social (FIDES), with targeted mining support from the Bureau Minier de la France d'Outre-Mer (BMIFOM). See UNECA, *Minerals and Africa's Development*, 13.

[85] *Ibid.*, 14–15.

[86] Iron (Guinea, Liberia, Mauritania and Sierra Leone), uranium (Gabon, Niger and South Africa), bauxite (Guinea), manganese (Mauritania). *Ibid.*, 14.

[87] *Ibid.*, 15.

[88] For a description of the factors generating Zambia's collapse, see Ferguson, *Expectations of Modernity*, ch. 1: 'The Copperbelt in Theory: From "Emerging Africa" to the Ethnography of Decline'; on the impact of the prescriptions of the World

organizations deepened the crisis. In 1992 the World Bank presented a package of reforms to Zambia and other mining nations which it claimed would help African mining meet projected demand for minerals and attract foreign investment. The programme reduced state participation, offered a wide range of incentives, made taxes more competitive, liberalized exchange rate policies and introduced assurances of a stable fiscal regime.[89] Foreign investment increased, but the conditions of life for broad sectors of the population declined precipitously. Not all countries complied with World Bank prescriptions. Egypt, for example, is accused of having 'outdated policies', because it requires mining companies to pay 'at least half' of their profits to the government, in addition to annual royalties.[90]

In 2007 global mineral demand and mineral prices reached a peak and led to increased investment by China and Western countries in African minerals. Many nations became new mineral producers: one-third of the top fifty metallic mineral-producing countries and 60 per cent of the world's largest diamond-producing nations are in Africa.[91] Increased prices also stimulated individual miners throughout the continent to engage in artisanal mining as a strategy of personal survival.[92] The division of labour in the artisanal industry varied with the product and the local conditions. In many areas, mining involved a working group of four to six male diggers, who subcontracted from pit holders, working under claims secured by 'claim holders' with financial support from financiers.[93]

As former miners moved into the field, they used the attributes of artisanal mining, which had great similarities to industrial mining, to fashion new masculine identities. Men who engage in small-scale mining are challenging the former perception that paid work and 'personal success in

Bank and the International Monetary Fund on Zambia and the whole continent, see *ibid.*, ch. 7: 'Global Disconnect: Abjection and the Aftermath of Modernism'.

[89]   UNECA, *Minerals and Africa's Development*, 17.

[90]   'There's Gold in Them Dunes, Miners Say of "Geological Disneyland" Egypt', *The Japan Times*, 29 April 2016, https://goo.gl/JZ2X1L (accessed 7 July 2016).

[91]   Deborah Fahy Bryceson and Jesper Bosse Jønsson, 'Mineralizing Africa and Artisanal Mining's Democratizing Influence', in *Mining and Social Transformation in Africa: Mineralizing and Democratizing Trends in Artisanal Production*, ed. D. F. Bryceson, E. Fisher, J. B. Jønsson and R. Mwaipopo (London: Routledge, 2014), 5–6.

[92]   Bryceson and Jønsson estimate that, in Africa, about nine million people engage in mining, with an additional 54 million benefiting from the industry. *Ibid.*, 6.

[93]   *Ibid.*, 9.

the workplace' are important for masculine identity.[94] In 2005, when Jeroen Cuvelier conducted his research in Katanga on the role of artisanal mining on constructions of masculinity, he noted that former industrial miners had used their new experiences as artisanal miners to construct respectable masculine identities. He argues that artisanal mining was not just an economic activity but a 'gender-specific lifestyle' that allows men 'to rethink and reshape the relationship between work and masculinity'.[95] They transformed artisanal mining – a humiliating, subservient job – into a profession that celebrated personal wealth, physical strength, technical skill, efficiency and courage.[96] They are self-made men who exhibit a lifestyle of 'ostentatious consumption', 'public performance' and a swagger to validate their status as innovative and entrepreneurial. In this way, they 'regain a sense of masculine working pride' under conditions of uncertainty and impoverishment. These miners created their own commodity chains linked to global markets and a hierarchy of production that delivered their copper to China and other markets.[97]

CONCLUSION

> Then all African workers were titled boy, for example, timber man was called timber boy, peak [sic] called peak boy, tub man called tub boy. Everything, boy, boy! Only the Europeans were called overman and foreman.[98]

Since the beginning of the colonial period, mining has been a defining industry that has shaped the development *and* underdevelopment of Africa. Minerals and valuable gemstones were the major attraction for imperial acquisition in the late nineteenth century and remain the central target of foreign investment today. Despite the millennia of productive mining controlled by African societies, Westerners assumed that the people who

---

[94] Cuvelier, 'Men, Mines and Masculinities', 28. Cuvelier notes that members of producers' associations are connected to *négociants* who arrange transport of the ore to warehouses in several main cities. Mineral buyers are tied to *maisons* (buying houses) or independent buyers of copper and cobalt. Ore from the DRC goes through Zambia to South Africa, where it is dispatched from the port of Durban to Asia. *Ibid.*, 20.

[95] *Ibid.*, 293.

[96] *Ibid.*, 293–4.

[97] Bryceson and Jønsson, 'Mineralizing Africa', 7.

[98] Eze Ozogwu, Mine Supervisor, Enugu Government Colliery. Interview with Eze Ozogwu, Amankwo-Ngwo, 2 June 1975.

produced copper, gold, iron and tin, and traded it with the world, were incapable of organizing production of minerals for modern use. To the managers and state officials, the workers who laboured in these industrial mines were only subordinate, immature beings, not deserving of the title 'industrial man' and requiring extraordinarily brutal forms of discipline to ensure that they were productive, diligent and reliable. The mines were an enclave of modernity located in an environment of rural 'tradition' and 'superstition' that gave colonialists the illusion that they could successfully launch a process of social engineering within the context of industrial production. Mining companies and the colonial state assumed that the African societies from which they drew their labour could be manipulated to imitate a 'modernity' defined by patterns in Europe. To colonialists and, to some extent, Western policymakers today, African miners were an inchoate, malleable mass of undistinguishable bodies that could be manipulated and controlled at will.

But this chapter and the intellectual resources on which it is based concern human beings for whom work had meaning that allowed them to create gendered identities reflecting their priorities, aspirations and social goals. Masculinity enables us to frame the significance of the work experience in the context of historical trends that shape the history of contemporary Africa today. Mineworkers constituted a subculture that was relatively isolated from general society, operated within a moral code that often challenged the societal norms and created an occupational community that enabled them to manoeuvre in a dangerous environment. That this experience, which was marked by abuse, racism and violence, could become the basis of a new male identity is attributable to the men's insistence on being acknowledged as respectable men. If we examine the reasons for their activism, the instances when they challenged the state or risked their lives to protest against poor treatment, we will understand the importance they gave to respect, dignity and honour.

Miners played an important role in the struggles for political rights in the closing decades of colonialism, in accelerating the collapse of the South African apartheid regime and in opposing neoliberal reforms. In the narrow export-oriented economies of Africa, they know well the power that they can wield to pressurizee governments for political and economic rights. After the 25 January Revolution in Egypt in 2012, workers in the Sukari gold mine led multiple protests and strikes against the implementation of neoliberal reforms.[99] In 2011 miners were among the over two million Egyptian

---

[99] 'Mineral Authority Reject Firing of Sukari Gold Mine Workers', *Al-Masry Al-Youm* (*Egypt Independent*), 27 July 2012, https://goo.gl/RkJ6QA (accessed 7 July 2016).

workers who participated in nearly four thousand strikes as part of the 'Arab Spring'.[100] They developed sophisticated strategies to remind government of its obligation to create a social and economic environment of growth, social justice and development. In 2009 the United Nations Economic Commission for Africa convened a taskforce to develop a new *Africa Mining Vision*.[101] The document was approved by the First African Union Conference of Ministers Responsible for Mineral Resources Development. This was one result of the agitation of Africa mineworkers and political activists throughout the continent.

---

[100] J. Beinin, 'Egyptian Workers and January 25th: A Social Movement in Historical Context', *Social Research*, 79.2 (2012), 323–48.

[101] UN Economic Commission for Africa, 'Africa Mining Vision', http://www.africaminingvision.org/ (accessed 8 July 2016).

SIX
Industry and Manufacturing

PATRICK NEVELING

Department of Social Anthropology, University of Bergen,
and Historical Institute, University of Bern

The 2010s have seen abundant predictions that African economies may soon industrialize on a large scale. Leading economists such as Justin Lin identify low wages and emerging infrastructures as important locational advantages for African nations to benefit from 'flying geese' effects, which will come in the form of industrial relocations from middle-income countries such as China, India, Brazil and Russia.[1] Then again, the assumption that now it is 'Africa's turn to industrialize' is not a novelty in the continent's history.[2] Indeed, large-scale industrialization projects as a key to a better future have been central to African politics throughout the twentieth century. At the same time, African political initiatives have often required backing from labour and trade unions, and, in the medium term, have had to deliver on promises to improve working and living conditions if postcolonial administrations wanted to stay in power.[3] The impact of such domestic initiatives on labour histories in manufacturing and industry has often been coupled with push and pull factors framed by uneven and multifarious global, transnational and regional political and economic processes.

This chapter maps and analyses the links between such internal and external industrial policies and practices, and the labour histories of wage

---

[1] Justin Yifu Lin, 'From Flying Geese to Leading Dragons: New Opportunities and Strategies for Structural Transformation in Developing Countries', *Global Policy*, 3.4 (2012), 397–409.

[2] Laura Mann, 'Africa's Turn to Industrialize?', *Review of African Political Economy* (ROAPE blog), https://goo.gl/RCn3Uj (accessed 20 June 2016).

[3] Ukandi Godwin Damachi, Hans Dieter Seibel and Lester Trachtman, eds, *Industrial Relations in Africa* (New York: St Martin's Press, 1979).

workers in African manufacturing industries. The aim is to outline a 'history of globalized work' for African manufacturing and industry since around 1900 rather than to elaborate a 'universal history of work' that introduces microhistories of the lives and times of individual trade unionists or shop floor workers in a given number of African manufacturing locations.[4]

The following gives an overview of the various labour histories that have emerged across manufacturing industries in African colonies and nations since around 1900. The first section takes stock of export substitution industries linked with agriculture as well as of early import substitution industries before the Second World War. The second section considers the continent-wide turn towards import substitution under wartime production and under colonial and postcolonial development policies before the 1970s. The third section focuses on changes to manufacturing workers' histories triggered by the non-aligned movement's policies and the many structural adjustment programmes since the 1980s. The conclusion discusses the contribution of historiographies of African industrial labour to the future of industrial development policies in Africa.

COLONIAL EXPORT AND IMPORT SUBSTITUTION INDUSTRIES BEFORE THE SECOND WORLD WAR

Periodizations of twentieth-century global (economic) developments associated with Fordism, Keynesianism, post-Fordism or neoliberalism have little applicability in African history. If anything, colonial policies before the Second World War created economic realities aimed at 'peasantization rather than proletarianization'.[5] In fact, European colonial powers considered African labourers to be 'temporary wage earners at risk of becoming "detribalized" if allowed to stay away too long' from their villages.[6] In line with the colonizers' view of Africans, histories of African industrial labour before the onset of modernization policies in the late colonial era have for many decades been neglected, as 'scholars seem[ed] to be following in the footsteps of earlier colonial administrations which, until World War II,

---

[4]   Willem van Schendel, 'Stretching Labour Historiography: Pointers from South Asia', *International Review of Social History*, 51.S14 (2006), 229–61; Marcel van der Linden, 'The "Globalization" of Labor and Working-Class History and its Consequences', *International Labor and Working-Class History*, 65 (2004), 136–56.

[5]   Andreas Eckert, 'Regulating the Social: Social Security, Social Welfare and the State in Late Colonial Tanzania', *Journal of African History*, 45.3 (2004), 467.

[6]   Frederick Cooper, *Decolonization and African Society: The Labor Question in French and British Africa* (Cambridge: Cambridge University Press, 1996), 2.

were mainly concerned with promoting agriculture and mining, considering manufacturing not to be vital'.[7]

More recent research tells a different story, however. An early industrialization phase began in the 1830s, when prices for African tropical raw materials and for their transport were comparatively high. Increased access to second-hand machinery facilitated the part-processing of bulk exports, especially for reducing bulk materials, such as converting ores into semi-refined metals, sawing logs into planks and reducing groundnuts to oil.[8] Such African appropriations of nodal points in commodity chains were especially pronounced in the plantation sector, where much agricultural produce required part-processing, at least, before export to imperial markets. Therefore, a considerable proportion of labourers commonly considered part of the agricultural sector were, in fact, employed in manufacturing industries. As many African colonies depended on plantations, their manufacturing industries would play a considerable role in the formation of local bourgeoisies and capital. Regimes of worker control and the organization of production would have a lasting impact on the lives and times of labourers in later manufacturing industries inasmuch as the inflow and outflow of labourers on the plantations would shape class composition, spatial segregation and ethnic divisions central to African labour histories to this day.

Sugar cane pioneered African manufacturing industry, as the canes 'could not spatially be separated from the manufacturing process'.[9] The invention of vacuum pans in the 1830s and the introduction of steam-driven crushing and milling technologies a few decades later made sugar mills Africa's first global factories. These factories advanced under regimes of forced and coerced labour in a competitive global market. Regions missing out on automation and efficiency would quickly decline as plantation and milling enterprises went bankrupt. At the same time, elaborate systems of managerial control developed, and divide-and-rule politics at work in the mills and on the plantations radiated out into colonial societies.[10]

---

[7] A. S. Mlambo and E. S. Pangeti, 'Introduction', in *Zimbabwe: A History of Manufacturing, 1890–1995*, ed. A. S. Mlambo, E. S. Pangeti and I. R. Phimister (Mount Pleasant, Harare: University of Zimbabwe Publications, 2000), 2.

[8] William Gervase Clarence-Smith, 'Colonial Industrialisation, 1840s–1960s', paper presented at the Global Economic History Network (GEHN) Conference 2, Irvine, CA, 15–17 January 2004, LSE Research Online, https://goo.gl/5Urssy (accessed 17 June 2016).

[9] Ulbe Bosma and Roger Knight, 'Global Factory and Local Field: Convergence and Divergence in the International Cane-Sugar Industry, 1850–1940', *International Review of Social History*, 49.1 (2004), 11.

[10] On capitalists in colonial societies, see the chapter by Austin in this volume.

Throughout much of the nineteenth and the first half of the twentieth centuries, Mauritius was the frontrunner in the African sugar cane industry. Cane cutters and day labourers as much as a growing number of independent smallholders in Mauritius absorbed the risks of an increasingly volatile world market. The global recessions of the 1870s and the 1930s drove many descendants of liberated slaves and former indentured labourers into abject poverty and thereby created a huge reserve of only apparently free wage labourers, bound, in fact, by clearly defined positions in commodity chains and by debts. Those who remained in the countryside became dependent on the plantations' job contractors hiring labour at the lowest rate by the hour, the day or the week. Those who left for the cities became urban slum dwellers and filled the ranks of a reserve army ready to work on the docks and in the emerging manufacturing industries of the 1930s.[11]

While such households had no access to social welfare provisions up to the Second World War and lived in ramshackle dwellings with no access to the emerging infrastructures of twentieth-century modernity such as electricity, running water, sewerage, public transport and schools, manufacturing workers in the industrial sugar mills lived a very different life.[12] They were the first generations of skilled workers. Corporations invested in their training, their contracts often ran over several years, they earned higher wages than cane cutters, and they had rights to housing, free healthcare and schooling provided by the mills.[13] The lives of this manufacturing labour aristocracy were detached from the worlds of rural and urban slum dwellers, and the expansion of Mauritian plantation and milling ventures into the Natal region and beyond from the 1880s onwards brought similar ethnic and class divisions to other parts of Africa.

Import substitution industries were a second aspect of African manufacturing before the Second World War. In most cases, they led to similar, highly flexible and precarious labour markets. As early as the 1920s and 1930s, governments in South Africa and Rhodesia, for example, introduced import substitution industrialization backed by revenues from mining and cheap labour. In Uganda, the British administration protected smallholding cotton growers but prohibited the opening of textile mills

---

[11] Patrick Neveling, 'Manifestationen der Globalisierung. Kapital, Staat und Arbeit in Mauritius, 1825–2005', PhD dissertation, Martin Luther University, Halle/Saale, 2012.

[12] On mining and transport, see the chapters by Brown and by Bellucci.

[13] M. D. North-Coombes, *Studies in the Political Economy of Mauritius* ([Moka, Mauritius]: Mahatma Gandhi Institute, 2000).

and the production of bicycles.[14] Despite such policies, several Indian family firms expanded after the First World War to become early large-scale manufacturing businesses, opening sawmills, sugar factories, soap works and steel re-rolling mills across eastern Africa. Around the same time, British development corporations opened state-backed printing, brewing and food-processing industries to provide jobs for the unemployed in East African colonies. Western Africa had a higher variation of industrial activities, as port cities and landlocked urban transport hubs required local workshops, while Lebanese entrepreneurs successfully established groundnut milling, sawmills and food-processing industries in the 1920s.[15]

If little is documented about the labour relations and labour histories in West Africa's emerging industries, export substitution industries set up to support agricultural exports in East Africa have received more attention. In Mauritius and Tanganyika, for example, aloe fibres and sisal had been planted for rope making since the early 1900s, and the sector became a full-fledged hemp industry in the 1920s and 1930s. As the plants grew by themselves, the lion's share of labour input was for cutting, cleaning, weaving and processing. Extracting fibres from aloe leaves required technological advances, and skilled workers were in ever higher demand as workshops and factories now processed hemp into bags for sugar. Corresponding with the rapid development of the industry, labour relations were in constant flux. Especially in the early years of sisal manufacturing, businesses were of makeshift nature, and otherwise clear-cut racist colonial divisions of labour were less pronounced. Owners and labourers collaborated closely in small workshops, jointly struggling, for example, to adjust second-hand Krupp machines to the specifics of local plants. As business expanded and large-scale industrial operations with elaborate divisions of labour and numerous job titles developed in the years after 1945, so too did hierarchies diversify. On Tanganyikan estates, for example, headmen, overseers and factory workers would look down on hard-working cutters, who had immigrated by

---

[14] Will Kaberuka, *The Political Economy of Uganda, 1890–1979: A Case Study of Colonialism and Underdevelopment* (New York: Vantage Press, 1990).

[15] Peter Kilby, 'Manufacturing in Colonial Africa', in *Colonialism in Africa 1870–1960, Vol. 4: The Economics of Colonialism*, ed. L. H. Gann and Peter Duignan (Cambridge: Cambridge University Press, 1975), 476–98; Gareth Austin, Ewout Frankema and Morten Jerven, 'Patterns of Manufacturing Growth in Sub-Saharan Africa: From Colonization to the Present', Utrecht University, Centre for Global Economic History, CGEH Working Paper No. 71, 2015, https://goo.gl/FhC1qX (accessed 17 June 2016).

the thousands from Rwanda. These migrants were often organized in gangs who brought home knowledge for unionization and resistance.[16]

COLONIAL AND POSTCOLONIAL IMPORT SUBSTITUTION INDUSTRIES BEFORE THE 1970S

Unionization and increasingly pronounced workplace hierarchies would be defining features of the second phase of African industrial manufacturing and the labour histories this produced. Again, developments across the continent were varied and uneven, with some colonies and young nations having a much higher concentration of manufacturing industries, and these industries often concentrated in particular regions.

Statistics emerge as a central tool for historians examining colonial rule in the 1940s. They are of limited value for labour histories of industrial manufacturing in Africa, however, because of the somewhat distorted and overly rigid three-sector division into agricultural, non-agricultural and service industries.[17] This leads to a mislabelling of mills for groundnuts or sugar not as manufacturing industries but as agricultural production, which comes at the analytical cost of excluding the very sites where technology in manufacturing as well as social technologies for controlling labour developed.

With or without statistics, there is overwhelming evidence of the exceptional scope and duration of South African industrialization. This was the 'only Sub-Saharan African country that achieved a more extended period of accelerated manufacturing output growth', which lasted from around 1924 to 1978 and saw the nation diversify from garments and electronics into car manufacturing and other heavy industries in the post-1945 period.[18] Economic historians agree that South African policies promoting the growth of a manufacturing workforce emerged because the many disenfranchised whites put pressure on government to fund import substitution industry programmes with revenues from the booming mining sector from 1924 onwards.[19]

Racist policies such as the Native Title Act of 1913, however, served to dispossess many black families and created an urban *lumpenproletariat*, which

---

[16] John Iliffe, *A Modern History of Tanganyika* (Cambridge: Cambridge University Press, 1979), 308–11.

[17] Daniel Speich Chassé, *Die Erfindung des Bruttosozialprodukts: Globale Ungleichheit in der Wissensgeschichte der Ökonomie* (Göttingen: Vandenhoeck & Ruprecht, 2013).

[18] Austin, Frankema and Jerven, 'Patterns of Manufacturing Growth', 2.

[19] *Ibid.*, largely replicating the argument in Kilby, 'Manufacturing in Colonial Africa'.

was subjected to (what today is called) industrial and vocational training for garment making and food processing.[20] Import substitution policies acknowledged the need for job creation across racist segregation, which is why the South African industrial workforce not only differed in scale from those of other colonies but also incorporated a diverse array of men and women from various social strata and of various origins. Since the early 1900s, wages had been differentiated by racist and sexist ideologies, with 'white men' earning around twice as much as 'white women' and the latter earning twice as much as 'non-European men', who, again, earned twice as much as 'non-European' women and children.[21]

South African labour histories thus are possibly the first where the 'myth of the male breadwinner' came to dominate gender relations. Discrimination came as a devaluation of women's labour through lower wages on the one hand and by declaring their income superfluous for households depending largely on male incomes.[22] Such double discrimination came to a head as wartime production ended after 1945. As white industrial workers had been conscripted and as wartime shortages had required industrial expansion, 'black men' and 'daughters of the depression' – women who had lost their jobs during the 1930s – had arrived on the shop floor. Both groups were pushed out of many industries when soldiers returned home and demanded jobs, and when competition from imports returned, as industrial production picked up in western Europe in the 1950s.[23]

Global wars and depressions were not the only factors that created highly disruptive labour histories and working-class biographies in South Africa's manufacturing industries and beyond. The 1930s also marked the heyday of African labour movements, with many of the new comprehensive worker organizations filing appeals to the International Labour Organization for support against racist colonial labour legislation because of their obvious ignorance of the League of Nations Covenant. Although African workers quickly found out that the colonial powers had no interest in making regulations designed for northern workers available to them,[24] their protests

---

[20] Iris Berger, *Threads of Solidarity: Women in South African Industry, 1900–1980* (Bloomington, IN: Indiana University Press, 1992), 20–9.

[21] *Ibid.*, 35.

[22] Helen Icken Safa, *The Myth of the Male Breadwinner: Women and Industrialization in the Caribbean* (Boulder, CO: Westview Press, 1995).

[23] Berger, *Threads of Solidarity*, 70, 132.

[24] Brian Nicol, 'Industrial Relations in Uganda', in *Industrial Relations in Africa*, ed. U. G. Damachi, H. D. Seibel and L. Trachtman (New York: St Martin's Press, 1979), 274.

were manifestations of the increasingly transnationalized nature of labour relations and of the transnationalized biographies of many trade unionists.

The fight for unionization involved further transnational dimensions, not least in the realm of law itself. South African legislation was the first to recognize rights to association for individual professions. Strikes and riots in Mauritius won the Mauritian Industrial Associations Ordinance No. 7 of May 1938, which for the first time granted a universal right to unionization, and which would serve as a blueprint for many colonial territories in Africa and beyond. Mauritius became a hotspot for unionization, with officials from the small island colony among the few delegates from the colonized world who co-founded the International Conference of Free Trade Unions (ICFTU) at the Free World Labour Conference in 1949.[25]

The plantation system, mining industries and other large-scale colonial ventures had established ethnicization policies across Africa, and these became a crucial policy tool of colonial and later postcolonial governments to fend off movements demanding a more just distribution of wealth. Such policies, obviously, had significant impact on workers' lives and labour relations across the continent. French and British 'modernization camps' that forced populations into settlements in Algeria and Kenya so they would help defeat anti-colonial uprisings were the extreme end of colonial divide-and-rule policies.[26]

A divide-and-rule policy of less inhumane quality accompanied the seamless transition from late colonial to early postcolonial industrialization policies in many African colonies. This involved the collaboration of incoming governments, unions and factory management to facilitate labour exploitation and curb workers' initial enthusiasm for economic justice in postcolonial states. The cornerstones of this transition are evident in an outstanding study of an African manufacturing enterprise from the end of the Second World War to the 1970s, Bruce Kapferer's historical anthropology of relations between African workers and Indian management in a Zambian textile factory.[27] Kapferer's ethnographic field research from 1964 to 1966 coincided with the final steps towards Zambian independence. In the 1910s Kabwe had been Northern Rhodesia's first mining centre and had

---

[25]   Richard Croucher and John McIlroy, 'Mauritius 1938: The Origins of a Milestone in Colonial Trade Union Legislation', *Labor History*, 54.3 (2013), 223–39.

[26]   Moritz Feichtinger and Stefan Malinowski, "'Eine Millionen Algerier lernen im 20. Jahrhundert zu leben". Umsiedlungslager und Zwangsmodernisierung im Algerienkrieg 1954–1962', *Journal of Modern European History*, 8.1 (2012), 107–35.

[27]   Bruce Kapferer, *Strategy and Transaction in an African Factory: African Workers and Indian Management in a Zambian Town* (Manchester: Manchester University Press, 1972).

since retained good transport connections as a major town on the 'line of rail' from the Copperbelt to Livingstone. The segregation of settlements was similar to those of towns in other African settler colonies. Although the incoming postcolonial administration sought to break down 'residential separation on racial lines' across Zambia,[28] for the time being Kabwe's manufacturing workers lived in municipal housing areas and farm settlements on the western side of town and crossed a colour line on their way to work in the Indian-owned Narayan Bros. Factory and General Store located on the high street in Kabwe's town centre. The double use of the building as store and factory is reminiscent of Indian family business histories in East Africa that often combined merchant and manufacturing activities.

Indian owners and management used the factory layout to control shop floor relations. Three assembly lines defined a pecking order. Workers on line one enjoyed close contact with foremen and managers, which meant perks and better wages. Workers on assembly lines two and three performed the same tasks as their better-off colleagues, albeit for lesser pay; they would, therefore, constantly aim to be moved up to the next line. The factory was in many ways a miniature version of the British colonial divide-and-rule regime. Workers referred to those among them who were closest to management as *chichawa*, a term otherwise used for informers reporting on African nationalist leaders to the colonial administration. At Narayan Bros., the term was given to the head tailor, the cutter and the lead tailor – individuals who worked closest with the management and kept the 'cotton boys' in check. While the 'cotton boys' (some of whom were, in fact, girls who picked loose cotton ends from finished garments) worked long hours, the *chichawa* had a high number of absentee hours during which they looked after their own tailoring businesses or engaged in larger scale political projects, such as loan applications and disbursement of government grants for cooperative farming.[29] This happened with the consent of an otherwise fairly draconian management regime, for such high-profile side projects consolidated the *chichawas'* political power networks, and thereby the factory hierarchy.

Ethnic divisions were a complementary structuration to maintain inequality in the factory and the city. Migrant workers had to rely on personal and kinship networks to establish themselves in Kabwe. This created ethnic networks and dependencies on the shop floor, as those already in employment helped newcomers find accommodation and jobs. Such political and ethnic networks were put to the test when independence came. Workers at the bottom of the factory hierarchy demanded better pay and

---

[28] *Ibid.*, 11, n. 7.

[29] *Ibid.*, 36–55. On cooperative labour, see the chapter by Nyanchoga in this volume.

better working conditions. They sought support from the National Union of Commercial and Industrial Factory Workers' representatives in Kabwe, only to find out that the union officials' ties to Zambia's United National Independence Party also meant that union officials supported the cause of the Indian factory owners and not that of the workers.[30]

Similar regimes were in place in many factories across the continent, as a turn towards import substitution industries backed by colonial and postcolonial development policies changed the landscape of economic activity. New ventures, such as East Africa's first integrated cement factory set up by the British Uganda Development Company, altered the composition of workforces for good. The bargaining power of new manufacturing labourers often depended as much on an industrial activity's position in regional and international markets as it did on local and national political settings. Jobs in tea processing and fertilizer production initiated by the colonial state in Southern Rhodesia[31] came with lesser bargaining power for workers than boom industries such as the textiles and clothing factories that mushroomed in Southern Rhodesia to supply the South African market after independent India had targeted South Africa with an embargo due to its apartheid policies.[32]

Such boom industries meant a high demand for manufacturing labour and thus high wages and better working conditions. However, pre-colonial and colonial world market position cast a long shadow on spatial variations in the intensity and nature of African industrial manufacturing activity. Well into the 1960s the North African Arab states and the Republic of South Africa had higher shares of industrial activity in their gross domestic products not only because they were 'old commercial economies',[33] but also because of their strategic importance in the first decades of the Cold War. A nation such as Egypt enjoyed capital investment and so-called development aid from both the socialist and the capitalist blocs from the 1950s. This is vividly illustrated in the history of the Egyptian Iron and Steel Company plant in the vast industrial region of Helwan, built with West German support in 1954 and expanded in 1967 with support from the Soviet Union.[34]

---

[30] *Ibid.*, 125–45.

[31] Kilby, 'Manufacturing in Colonial Africa', 476–8.

[32] Ian Phimister, 'From Preference towards Protection: Manufacturing in Southern Rhodesia, 1940–1965', in *Zimbabwe: A History of Manufacturing, 1890–1995*, ed. A. S. Mlambo, E. S. Pangeti and I. R. Phimister (Mount Pleasant, Harare: University of Zimbabwe Publications, 2000), 38.

[33] Kilby, 'Manufacturing in Colonial Africa', 470.

[34] Dina Makram Ebeid, 'Manufacturing Stability: Everyday Politics of Work in an Industrial Steel Town in Helwan, Egypt', PhD dissertation, London School of Economics and Political Science, 2012, 17.

Internal markets constituted another crucial factor in the development of import substitution industries in subtropical and tropical African colonies and nations. Accordingly, labour histories of manufacturing and industry are particularly relevant in political units with large populations and with higher per capita income. Tens of millions of Nigerians and Ethiopians, for example, provided sufficient consumer demand for construction materials and simple manufactured goods such as textiles, beer and cigarettes, even if per capita income was low. This created efficient factories producing for a growing regional market, and with these factories came urbanization and proletarianization. After 1945 large European companies, such as Nestlé, Imperial Chemicals, Associated Portland Cement Manufacture and Philips, set up shop, attracted by the sizeable Nigerian market and by local government industrial investment incentives such as income tax holidays and import duty relief for 'pioneer industries'.[35] Tropical and subtropical African colonies and postcolonial nations with higher gross income levels often had comparatively larger European resident communities whose wealth meant higher levels of inequality and, at the same time, secured consumer demand for sophisticated manufactured goods. This stimulated private capital investment, specialization in manufacturing, and an education system that nurtured industrial workers. Accordingly, Southern Rhodesia headed the pre-Second World War ranking of manufacturing output in tropical and subtropical African colonies with a 9 per cent share of total output, and retained this position well into the 1950s. Kenya and the Belgian Congo expanded manufacturing output from a 5 per cent pre-war share to around 9 per cent in 1954, and Uganda achieved a ratio of around 7 per cent in the same year.[36]

Not all African nations moved forward on the industrial growth trajectories of the late colonial era. This was, again, for different reasons. In the mid-1950s Tanganyika had the lowest manufacturing share of the entire continent at 2.6 per cent, and the nation's economic situation would depend well into the 1980s on how its sisal industry fared on the global market.[37] In the Belgian Congo, by contrast, mining industries and palm oil production demanded export substitution industries for part-processing of raw materials. Given the colony's unique position as a supplier of wartime raw materials, these industries grew rapidly since the 1930s and exponentially during the

---

[35] Kilby, 'Manufacturing in Colonial Africa', 493–503.

[36] Ibid., 470–5.

[37] Hanan Sabea, 'Reviving the Dead: Entangled Histories in the Privatisation of the Tanzanian Sisal Industry', Africa: Journal of the International African Institute, 71.2 (2001), 286–313.

Second World War. But they did so because the Belgian colonizers had set up a draconian system of forced labour. This virtually split the colony in two. Outside the export-oriented regions around Leopoldville and Katanga, agriculture remained in the hands of smallholders, who received little attention except as a pool of forced labourers. Export substitution industries, on the other hand, had access to vast capital and were mainly powered by expatriate engineers from the Walloon region, where mining had been the main driver of Belgian industrialization in the nineteenth century. Because its colonial industrialization policies relied on expatriate expertise, Belgium was able to withdraw the linchpins of industrialization after independence, with the effect that the Mobutu regime lacked access to skilled workers and export substitution industries quickly collapsed.[38]

Another important aspect to be added here is that, whereas the Belgian Congo had achieved independence through an alliance of the middle class and poor peasants and in open antagonism to the colonizers, other postcolonial nations had emerged as independent by way of peaceful negotiations. In smaller nations such as Ghana and Mauritius, for example, colonial administrations brought in high-profile academics (W. Arthur Lewis and James Edward Meade, respectively) to survey existing industries and recommend diversification strategies. A large number of estate housing units were erected in Ghana following an earthquake in 1939 and in Mauritius following two cyclones in 1960. In both cases, these housing estates would provide workers for new import substitution industries in the 1960s, and in both cases these industries benefited from port modernization and large-scale development projects for electrification. Although the University of Ghana, founded in 1948, predates the University of Mauritius by more than twenty years, both colonies had an educated local petty bourgeoisie already in the 1940s, which pushed for independence.[39]

In one of the earliest comprehensive studies on factory workers in an African nation, Margaret Peil interviewed Ghanaian factory workers in sixteen firms in Accra, Kumasi, Tema and Takoradi. Although this early 1970s study somewhat awkwardly searches for evidence of modern 'industrial man', it offers insights into the lives of Ghana's manufacturing workers. The emergence of a hierarchy was visible not only in wage differences between

---

[38] Frans Buelens and Danny Cassimon, 'The Industrialization of the Belgian Congo', in *Colonial Exploitation and Economic Development: The Belgian Congo and the Netherlands Indies Compared*, ed. Ewout Frankema and Frans Buelens (London: Routledge, 2013), 229–50.

[39] Margaret Peil, *The Ghanaian Factory Worker: Industrial Man in Africa* (Cambridge: Cambridge University Press, 1972), 1–23; Neveling, 'Manifestationen der Globalisierung', 248–346.

trained and untrained workers but also in untrained workers' identification by background ('from Bawku') and trained workers' identification by profession ('polisher at Pioneer Plastics'). Ghanaian factories of the 1960s were located in cities, predominantly, and while the older workers hoped for a return to their villages as men of wealth and prestige, younger workers hoped for a good life in the bustling cities. Despite a high degree of unionization, workers were reluctant to voice discontent with their labour conditions, and employment remained precarious irrespective of the size of the factory. There was little protection from dismissal, so that even a broken machine for which there were no spare parts could mean the loss of employment.[40]

EXPORT-ORIENTED INDUSTRIALIZATION SINCE THE 1970S

Nearly all the African postcolonial nations would join the non-aligned movement (NAM) and its call for a new international economic order (NIEO) which would change global terms of trade and strengthen postcolonial sovereignty. One central demand of the NAM was for development aid to be considered as reparation for colonial exploitation, and for such aid to generate an industrial manufacturing basis for nations across the global South. Importantly, the NAM's leverage across Africa in the late 1960s had much to do with the involvement of trade union and labour movements in anti-colonial and independence movements.[41] This consolidated and nurtured a political desire to establish national industries – to move African production, to quote a popular Egyptian slogan, 'from the needle to the rocket'.[42] However, the global economic crises of the 1970s forced many African nations into what is now known as the Third World debt crisis of the 1980s. Structural adjustment programmes from the World Bank and the International Monetary Fund brought a sudden death to demands for an NIEO, which meant that, as much as the initiative's short-lived success, the backlash that followed constituted a key moment in African manufacturing labour histories.

---

[40] Peil, *The Ghanaian Factory Worker*, 218–37.

[41] Priya Lal, 'African Socialism and the Limits of Global Familyhood: Tanzania and the New International Economic Order in Sub-Saharan Africa', *Humanity: An International Journal of Human Rights, Humanitarianism, and Development*, 6.1 (2015), 17–31.

[42] John Waterbury, *The Egypt of Nasser and Sadat: The Political Economy of Two Regimes* (Princeton, NJ: Princeton University Press, 1983), 81, quoted in Ebeid, 'Manufacturing Stability', 16.

These trajectories of a rapid rise and fall of NIEO industrialization ventures are evident, for example, in the labour relations in Nigerian vehicle assembly plants. Nigeria's post-civil war economic strategy sought to transfer a large share of wealth to Nigerians by way of 'a capital goods sector-led industrialisation which would raise … value added in the manufacturing sector'.[43] Vehicle assembly plants featured prominently in the second national development plan of 1970–74, which was influenced strongly by the NIEO agenda. Truck assembly ventures in the 1950s, for example, had combined parts from trucks discarded locally with imports of spare parts to reduce the costs of imports of new vehicles. After the oil boom of the 1970s, the Nigerian state was flush with money and sought to oblige companies to source all parts locally. Wages improved and production of trucks and cars expanded. When an economic crisis hit in 1981, automotive assembly had not made a significant contribution to Nigeria's gross domestic product. Now cheap imports also threatened the larger Volkswagen and Peugeot plants in Nigeria, and the government was forced by international lenders to waive protective countermeasures as the crisis deepened in the years after. Austerity measures were introduced in the factories, with overtime reduced, shifts cut, temporary staff released and compulsory holidays all targeting the workforce as the major disposable budgetary item. Workers' options for resistance were severely limited because the government had established the Nigerian Labour Congress as recently as 1978, and entry into this new umbrella union exposed a lack of experience and cohesion among automotive unions. Other limiting factors were, as in the case of the Zambian textile factory discussed above, structures of patronage in recruitment policies that worked to the benefit of politicians and bureaucrats and enabled a 'patronising ideology of the ruling class', telling the workers 'to be thankful for being on the payroll when millions of Nigerians are jobless'.[44]

South African manufacturing workers had an exceptional position, in part because of the nation's much longer history of large-scale industrial activity and in part because apartheid had prevented any genuinely postcolonial turning point in politics and labour relations. Even in such a repressive system, strike action could end with a workers' victory, however. For example, a 1980 strike in Uitenhage, near Port Elizabeth, saw the National Union of Motor Assembly and Rubber Workers of South Africa (NUMARWOSA) organizing for a living wage. The general strike that erupted had very different outcomes across the city's manufacturing enterprises. The workers

---

[43] Yusuf Bangura, 'The Recession and Workers' Struggles in the Vehicle Assembly Plants: Steyr-Nigeria', *Review of African Political Economy*, 39 (1987), 5.

[44] Bangura, 'The Recession and Workers' Struggles', 11.

of the Goodyear plant were locked out and re-employed under police guard. Volkswagen workers, by contrast, kept their jobs, won wage increases and strengthened the union's position in the factory, because they joined forces across the apartheid system's dividing lines, with 'African' and 'coloured' workers united in strike action for three weeks. In contrast, workers in the Port Elizabeth plants of Ford and General Motors split on racial lines, with Africans refusing to join NUMARWOSA's strike initiative. Such unity and disunity came despite the fact that, in all the factories, working conditions were equally harsh for all groups. Spatial segregation across the city was the key to successful organizing. When workers in other factories split along the racist divisions imposed by the apartheid state, workers' organization in the Volkswagen factory could overcome these divisions because African and coloured workers had long-established social relations due to their joint use of a rugby field that separated their housing compounds.[45]

As for the sugar mills becoming Africa's first global factories and for colonial legislation allowing for universal unionization, Mauritius again offers paradigmatic insights into the history of austerity politics in Africa. Rights to unionization had boosted the bargaining power of some Mauritian professions. Clerks and manufacturing workers organized successfully in the 1950s and 1960s to win universal pension rights, free schooling and healthcare for the colony.[46] The high hopes that many members of the Mauritian workforce had for a better life in the postcolonial state after 1968 would be shattered in the 1970s, however. Without the London Colonial Office underwriting loans for the development of industry and infrastructure on Western financial markets, state-owned factories were the first to close, and the postcolonial state became highly dependent on World Bank loans. Money was spent in part on building more estate housing, motivated by the fact that the ruling elite was under massive pressure from an insurgent socialist movement with strong trade union links. A second major budget item was for establishing and running Africa's first Export Processing Zone (EPZ). Parliamentarians debating the 1970 Export Processing Zone Act unequivocally agreed that employment in zone factories producing textiles, garments, watches, light consumer electronics and so forth would be for young, unmarried Mauritian women. A minimum wage was deemed unnecessary because women workers' income would be for households with male breadwinners. EPZ mass employment instead would be an initial

[45] Glenn Adler, 'Shop Floors and Rugby Fields: The Social Basis of Auto Worker Solidarity in South Africa', *International Labor and Working-Class History*, 51 (1997), 96–128.

[46] Jeremy Seekings, 'British Colonial Policy, Local Politics and the Origins of the Mauritian Welfare State, 1936–50', *Journal of African History*, 52.2 (2011), 157–77.

wage-depressing sacrifice, turning Mauritius into an African Singapore, where export industries and an EPZ had created the archetypical new industrializing economy of the late 1960s and 1970s with rising wages and an expanding urban middle class.

Mauritian EPZ labour policies thus repeated the myth of the male breadwinner that had shaped the gender relations of South African import substitution policies since the 1920s. The harsh reality was rather that many of the 20,000 workers entering into EPZ employment during the 1970s were single mothers well above the age of 25 and heading households. They now depended on manufacturing labour shaped by shift work, noise pollution, sexism and bullying and lacked the constitutional right to unionization, which had been waived for the zone in the EPZ Act of 1970. When Mauritian state expenditure for social housing and industrial infrastructure could no longer be met from income from sugar exports during the global crisis of 1979, World Bank structural adjustment policies brought down the gender imbalance in the EPZ. As global markets picked up steam in the mid-1980s, the EPZ turned Mauritius into a boom economy: growth rates matched those of the leading Asian economies, full employment was reached by the early 1990s, and 'Africa's first tiger' was born. In the process, EPZ workers began to see their biographies as global ones, as foremen and factory management constantly reminded them of the production output of workers in Asian and Latin American zones.

During the boom years, workers enjoyed rapid wage increases, and labour became so scarce that factories hired headhunters to bring in production engineers as well as machinists. The nation's increasing income levels were reflected in a housing construction boom, the spread of shopping malls and the purchase of motorcycles, automobiles, washing machines, microwaves, dishwashers and other items that changed life on the island for good. Job security was not reflected in employment contracts, however. When the 'flying geese' companies relocated to other African zones with cheaper labour that had been established because of the structural adjustment programmes in Kenya, Lesotho or Madagascar, many Mauritian households were dependent on EPZ income and could no longer service their debts for the purchase of new housing, consumer items and so forth. At the same time, Mauritian government investment, in a second phase of supposedly high-tech-based industrialization, largely attracted call centre and financial sector processing activities to the island. Neither of these new sectors, nor the robust tourism sector, could absorb the first and second generation of EPZ workers who re-entered the job market.[47]

---

[47] Neveling, 'Manifestationen der Globalisierung'.

CONCLUSION

The experience of Mauritian EPZ workers has been replicated many times in Africa since the 1980s, though no African zone has gone through a boom and bust cycle of similar scale. Despite evidence to the contrary, EPZs and the more recent re-labelling of the zones as SEZs (Special Economic Zones) continue to be portrayed as the best solution for creating employment in manufacturing industries across the continent. Structural adjustment programmes of the 1980s and 1990s enforced the creation of EPZs in all African nations affected. This, coupled with bilateral and multilateral trade preferences to boost industrialization, such as the United States' African Growth and Opportunities Act and its various amendments since 1999, has created pockets of rapid EPZ-based industrialization in Egypt, Ghana, Kenya, Lesotho, Tunisia and more recently in some South African EPZs and in the new SEZs in Ethiopia, Nigeria, Tanzania and elsewhere. Labour relations remain very precarious in such zones, and rapid movements of capital have disrupted the lives of many workers. Whether such industrialization policies could ever generate overall and lasting success remains questionable.[48]

Strikingly, many African industrialization efforts since around 1900 have had little or no regard for what they would mean for the lives of workers, let alone in what ways they could be embedded into existing political economies. Instead, and despite evidence to the contrary, the thrust of development policies focused on industrialization has too often been to rely on outside actors and local bourgeoisies, whether the joint ventures of import substitution's heyday or the 'flying geese' repeatedly conjured in EPZ promotion policies since the 1970s.

Labour histories that capture and compare the experiences of Africans in manufacturing industries throughout these different periods could be an important corrective for how to establish and run industries. Such labour histories remain rare, especially for the period before 1960. What such histories reveal is that, if industrialization prognoses refer to low wage levels as comparative advantages, this has meant and may most likely mean relocation of labour-intensive manufacturing industries to African regions.

---

[48] United Nations Development Programme, *If Africa Builds Nests, Will the Birds Come? Comparative Study on Special Economic Zones in Africa and China*, Working Paper Series No. 06 (2015), https://goo.gl/8jrTsj (accessed 14 July 2016); Patrick Neveling, 'Export Processing Zones, Special Economic Zones and the Long March of Capitalist Development Policies during the Cold War', in *Decolonization and the Cold War: Negotiating Independence*, ed. Leslie James and Elisabeth Leake (London: Bloomsbury, 2015), 63–84.

Large-scale employment in such industries has a particular (and most likely not positive) impact on social mobility. At the same time, labour histories themselves may offer the best service to African efforts to industrialize the continent if they have a combined interest in the trajectories of individual workers' biographies as well as in the changing shape of social formations and political economies in industrializing regions. This way, labour histories of African manufacturing and industry consider the differences between past and present industrialization policies and how they succeeded and/or failed because of changes in global and regional political economies since 1900. The changing labour relations in African factories, changing machinery and management technologies, changing chains and cycles of industrial production, changing social mobility, aspirations and life cycles of African industrial workers are not only futures past to be recorded and studied, but also a source for developing future development policies.

SEVEN
Transport

STEFANO BELLUCCI

International Institute of Social History, Amsterdam, and
Institute for History, Leiden University

In contemporary Africa, the development of transport labour is intrinsically connected to the expansion of the typical, capitalist form of labour relations: free wage labour.[1] Historically, labour power in transport has proven to be particularly prone to be exploited in exchange for wages: the transport worker of twentieth-century Africa, from the porter to the aviation pilot, is usually a wage worker.

In the twentieth century, caravan routes made up of porters or camels began to be used by trucks and cars; additionally, the sailing boats of the Nile and along West African rivers were joined by motorized vessels. In response to the increasing use of motor vehicles and trucks, colonial governments put emphasis on road construction – albeit on a small scale and using fairly rudimentary tools commensurate with that period. The colonial authorities were keen to make headway in the hinterland primarily to extract and transport raw materials to seaports for onward transmission to their European capitals; thus, the driving force for road construction was not to provide a public service for African colonial subjects. Another important transport initiative of the twentieth century was the construction of railways.[2] The African railway network's main lines were completed by the 1930s. Often, mining and the export of agricultural crops were the almost exclusive reasons for the construction of railways. Seaports and paved roads also developed significantly in the twentieth century. Unlike railways, seaports and roads

---

[1]   On the expansion of wage labour in Africa, see the chapter by Eckert in this volume.

[2]   This chapter excludes from the transport labour sector those workers employed in the building of railways, ports and roads. These labourers are considered to be working for the construction industry.

had existed for centuries in Africa. What changed was the introduction of the steam engine, and later the petrol engine, imported from Europe and North America to Africa during the colonial years – especially in the period encompassing the two world wars and the introduction of lorries and cars, which introduced driving as an important type of job. Railways also required new labour and mechanical expertise. Commercial air transport expanded in the second half of the twentieth century. The air transport industry in Africa directly generated an estimated 400,000 jobs in 2012.[3] A good portion of these workers are highly skilled and well paid.[4]

TRANSPORT AND THE ORIGINS OF FREE WAGE LABOUR

The workers who make the transport of goods and people possible are not restricted to the types we usually think of, such as dock workers/longshoremen, sailors, train drivers or pilots. Workers in this sector include operators and maintenance crews, as well as ticket collectors, flight attendants and so on. A last category is made up of workers involved in the maintenance of the infrastructure, as well as administrators, clerks, cleaners, etc.[5]

The twentieth century experienced a revolution in the transport sector in the African continent. In this period, along with porters and boatmen, there were railway and dock workers as well as lorry and car drivers. New technologies allowed for the construction of infrastructure such as railways, roads, harbours and ports. Although, according to some scholars, some porters and boatmen were already wage earners and constituted the embryonic element of the free wage worker in Africa, it was with the advent of the new transport systems that wage labour spread throughout the continent.[6] At the very least, it is safe to say that transport, together with

---

[3] See Aviation Benefits beyond Borders, http://aviationbenefits.org/around-the-world/africa (accessed 9 May 2015).

[4] In today's Africa, road transport is the most dominant mode of motorized transport, accounting for 80 per cent of the goods traffic and 90 per cent of the passenger traffic on the continent. See United Nations Economic and Social Council, *Africa Review Report on Transport*, E/ECA/CFSSD/6/6, Addis Ababa, 29 September 2009, 2–3. On skilled labour, see the chapter by van den Bersselaar in this volume.

[5] Marcel van der Linden, 'Transport: A Work of Globalization', paper given at the workshop 'Working on Globalisation: Work and Transport in Global History after 1945', International Research Centre 'Work and the Human Life Cycle in Global History', Humboldt University, Berlin, 25–27 October 2013 [unpublished].

[6] John Iliffe, *The Emergence of African Capitalism* (Minneapolis, MN: University of Minnesota Press, 1983).

other modern economic sectors, led to the development of modern, capitalist labour exploitation in Africa, through wages paid in cash.

Human porterage, animal caravans and river boatmen have always been present in African history.[7] The history of these traditional transport sectors dates back centuries, all the way to the ancient world. These workers represented the core of economic activity and trade in Africa. However, although porterage, caravans and boatmen exist to this day, the advent of the steam engine and petrol engines in the twentieth century resulted in their decline in importance. Workers in new sectors came to the fore within African economies, challenging the social status or those employed in more traditional sectors.

Historically, caravans had been organized and porters recruited on behalf of European travellers, whose comings and goings provided the East African economy with the start of a tourist industry. A basic change took place beginning in the late nineteenth century, when the International African Association and various missionary agencies began to establish continuously occupied stations.[8] These were harbingers of low-paid wage labour and spread Western, capitalist ideologies and cultural values.

Labour in the traditional transport sectors was both unfree and free. Sometimes, it was carried out by slaves and other times by free men who received different types of wages: in money or in kind. At the turn of the century, in the Niger Delta, the British Consul H. H. Johnston reported that, among the trading communities, slave labour, that is, unfree labour, was dominant. Slave workers were domestic slaves who worked as porters or boatmen because this was the will of the family leader.[9] In northern Igboland,

---

[7] Peter C. W. Gutkind, 'The Canoemen of the Gold Coast (Ghana): A Survey and an Exploration in Precolonial African Labour History', *Cahiers d'études africaines*, 29.115 (1989), 339–76; David Northrup, 'Porterage in Eastern Zaire, 1885–1930: Labor Use and Abuse in War and Peace', paper presented at the 25th Annual Meeting of the African Studies Association, Washington, DC, 1982; Stephen J. Rockel, *Carriers of Culture: Labor on the Road in Nineteenth-Century East Africa* (Portsmouth, NH: Heinemann, 2006); Kenneth Swindell, 'The Struggle for Transport Labor in Northern Nigeria, 1900–1912: A Conflict of Interests', *African Economic History*, 20 (1992), 137–59.

[8] Norbert Dodille, *Introduction aux discours coloniaux* (Paris: PUP, 2011), 84–7.

[9] As Consul Johnston wrote: 'It is a curious fact and an evidence of the mild character of the slavery in the Niger Delta, that nearly all the leading men in the oil rivers at the present time are ex-slaves, – such as Yellow Duke of Old Calabar, Ja Ja of Opobo, Waribu and Oko Jumbo of Bonny, and William Kia of Brass.'
    H. H. Johnston, 'Report on the British Protectorate of the Oil Rivers (Niger Delta)', 1888, cited in David Northrup, *Trade Without Rulers: Pre-Colonial Economic Development in South-Eastern Nigeria* (Oxford: Clarendon Press, 1978), 222; and A. E.

slaves were used not only in yam plantations but also as porters to carry these agricultural products from the areas of their production to the markets where they were traded.

On the Swahili Coast, slavery continued well after its official abolition – the practice remained legal in parts of East Africa until the 1900s – as freed slaves, for a variety of reasons, were not able to enjoy their new status unconditionally. Although the majority of slaves were used on agricultural plantations, a smaller number were employed as soldiers as well as porters. Slave porters were granted freedom of movement because of the nature of their work. They also developed special skills and competences that allowed them certain other privileges, such as the right to retain a portion of their earnings. These privileged half-slaves, half-salaried porters developed strong ties with their masters. When Europeans arrived, professional porters, known as *pagazi*, were reluctant to serve them, as they perceived that these foreigners were more interested in cost cutting and short-term commercial relationships. According to some, a proletarian and nationalist Swahili consciousness originated among these hired slave workers.[10]

In the Congo river basin, when the construction of the Matadi–Kinshasa railway started in 1890, porters around Matadi were employed *en masse* in the new trade by the Compagnie du Congo pour le commerce et l'industrie. However, there are no records of forced labour. The porters were enticed to work with the promise of wages, and, when these were not paid or did not meet the expectations of the porters, unrest erupted. High mortality rates and dire working conditions were also a cause of unrest. Between 1890 and 1894 about 1,800 Africans died in construction-related activities.[11]

During the twentieth century, transport came to represent modernity, and consequently the wage workers who worked in this sector were considered 'modern Africans'. With some notable exceptions, such as, for example, South Africa and Egypt, railway workshops and harbour installations constituted the beginning of a process of industrialization. In Sudan, Atbara and Port Sudan became important centres where labour was skilled, free and paid in wages. In the Horn of Africa, it was with the import, from the late 1920s, of thousands of trucks that an industry of garages and motor

---

Atmore, 'Africa on the Eve of Partition', in *The Cambridge History of Africa, Volume 6: From 1870 to 1905*, ed. Roland Oliver and G. N. Sanderson (Cambridge: Cambridge University Press, 1985), 44.

[10] Jan-Georg Deutsch, *Emancipation without Abolition in German East Africa, c. 1884–1914* (Athens, OH: Ohio University Press, 2006), 19–20.

[11] Kiobe Lumenga-Neso, 'La question du chemin de fer Matadi-Kinshasa au 19e siècle', *Zaïre-Afrique*, 18.126 (1978), 343–63.

workshops was established, mainly run by Italians with Eritrean wage workers as employees – especially so after the Fascist invasion of Ethiopia in 1935 which brought into the region a mass of FIAT trucks.

The modern transport sector was highly driven by European – but also American – capital, and therefore its typical mode of production was capitalist in the western European and North American sense: capital that employed salaried or wage labour. The reasons why many 'free' Africans were attracted to earn wages varied – from the need to earn cash in order to pay taxes to the transformation of societies into consumerist ones (the commodification process); from the need to pay for services to the possibility of obtaining credit in order to start one's own business or acquire land; or from customary mobility during dry seasons to curiosity and the will to self-empower.

In the 1910s the French colonial administration began to refuse to accept local currencies, such as cowries or lengths of copper, and from 1917 onwards taxes had to be paid in hard currencies, that is, in those denominations recognized by European powers.[12] The cash economy steadily grew roots. This was when thousands of porters began to be paid in cash. In 1905 the poll tax represented 45 days' wages and sometimes absorbed the entire cash income. In the period 1909–11 the colonial government began to regroup the population into hamlets of not less than thirty dwellings and to suppress shifting slash-and-burn cultivation. Taxation was frequently levied in the form of labour dues, which, in the case of Madagascar, drove many locals into a kind of feudal servitude with the settlers; the only way to escape was for Africans to acquire cash by selling their labour power.[13] One effect of the colonial transport revolution was to discharge vast numbers of Africans from porterage into less skilled, more menial work, which was, however, paid in hard currency.

The passage from unfree labour to free wage labour is not clear-cut, and is subject to many variations. At the beginning of the twentieth century, on the one hand, unfree labour was still being used in transport activities such as porterage and construction; on the other hand, in technologically advanced sectors such as the railways, steam boats and motor vehicle transport, free wage labour – similar to that present in Europe at that time – was the norm. It was in the construction of railways and harbours as well as in the porterage and caravan sectors that unfree labour mixed with free wage labour, giving to

[12] Marc Michel, *Les Africains et la Grande Guerre: L'appel à l'Afrique (1914–1918)* (Paris: Karthala, 2014).

[13] Jean Fremigacci, *État, économie et société coloniale à Madagascar: De la fin du XIXe siècle aux années 1940* (Paris: Karthala, 2014).

the capitalist mode of production a different face which was neither typical western European nor traditionally African.

During the First World War, labour was forcibly recruited by all warring sides on a huge scale, especially for porterage in the East African campaign.[14] Porters recruited through the mediation of local chiefs were often paid in cash, and, where this was the case, the amount of money in circulation in the local economy increased as a result (soldiers were also salaried workers). At the end of the First World War, wage earners in eastern Africa numbered about one hundred thousand. This number included civilian porters. The mass conscription of Africans as porters had broad effects throughout the region. Many areas were virtually emptied of men, and food production was crippled due to this loss of manpower. A few thousand so-called Cape Coloureds, that is, persons of mixed race, served in France as drivers and labourers during the war.[15] Back in South Africa, many continued in the transport trade as both free wage workers as well as self-employed labourers.

In short, three typical situations in the grey zone between free and unfree labour can be identified: 1) a person enters work unfreely but is paid a wage in return; 2) a person is attracted to wages and enters freely but cannot freely leave the work position; 3) a person is forced to work for free (unpaid), but for a limited period of time (he or she is not a slave). These characteristics are dominant in the first part of the twentieth century in Africa. According to the unchallenged Nieboer–Domar hypothesis on the structural existence of slavery in market economies, forced and unfree forms of labour occur when there is a shortage of cheap labour.[16] This was a problem in German Togo and Cameroon, where car-accessible roads and railways reduced transport costs and liberated labour hitherto engaged in porterage, their construction required large levies of 'political labour'. Forced labour therefore applied more to the construction sector for the public good, including transport infrastructure; much less did it involve African transport workers: porters, drivers, railway and port operators, etc.

---

[14] Robert J. Cummings, 'A Note on the History of Caravan Porters in East Africa', *Kenya Historical Review*, 1.2 (1973), 109–38; Jan-Bart Gewald, *Forged in the Great War: People, Transport, and Labour, the Establishment of Colonial Rule in Zambia, 1890–1920* (Leiden: African Studies Centre, 2015).

[15] Albert M. Grundlingh, *War and Society. Participation and Remembrance: South African Black and Coloured Troops in the First World War, 1914–1918* (Stellenbosch: Sun Press, 2014), 97.

[16] Herman J. Nieboer, *Slavery as an Industrial System* (The Hague: Martinus Nijhoff, 1900); Evsey D. Domar, 'The Causes of Slavery or Serfdom: A Hypothesis', *Journal of Economic History*, 30.1 (1970), 18–32.

The coexistence of free wage labour, in transport but not only in this sector, and forms of unfree labour is a complex matter. At the turn of the twentieth century, the increasing demand of the French authorities for porters and workers for the railways threatened to erode domestic slavery and deprive the Baule, a large group of farmers in Ivory Coast, of their labour force.[17] This caused a series of rebellions and generated unrest that lasted for years in the first two decades of the twentieth century. Gabriel Louis Angoulvant, the Governor of French Ivory Coast, resorted to arms in order to 'pacify' the region. But more than guns, it was the increasing opportunities to earn wages in railway construction that dampened the commitment of many Africans to follow their local leaders in the rebellion. Domestic slaves were tempted to leave even the most compassionate of households to become wage workers. The upshot was the evolution of a group of people more faithful to the new imperialist forces than to the local powers. These proto-wage workers were unwittingly exploited by the French authorities; initially, they only saw as significant who was paying them rather than recognizing who was exploiting them.

In addition to periodic demands by administrative authorities for short-term and often unpaid, coerced labour to fill the need for porters for officials and for workers on projects such as the construction of roads, government rest houses and even railways, new migratory labour patterns were established, occasionally by direct government recruitment for the commercial sector. In the Gold Coast (today's Ghana), chiefs of the Northern Territories were paid a head tax of five shillings for every man sent to labour underground in the gold mines of the colony, where the mine companies were in direct competition with indigenous cocoa cultivators. When such incentives failed to produce sufficient 'recruits', district commissioners resorted to coercion.[18] There was even discussion of implementing a system based, as in South Africa, on pass laws, a labour bureau and a revised Master and Servant Ordinance to ensure greater stability and control over mine labour.

The coming of railways and roads did not mean the end of porterage of course. In Madagascar, after the construction of the Fianarantsoa railway between 1925 and 1933, porterage was still regularly levied wherever there

---

[17] Fabio Viti, 'Colonialismo e liberazione degli schiavi nel Baule (Costa d'Avorio)', *Africa: rivista trimestrale di studi e documentazione*, 61.1 (2006), 30–65.

[18] Samuel A. Ntewusu, 'Settling in and Holding on: A Socio-Economic History of Northern Traders and Transporters in Accra's Tudu, 1908–2008', PhD dissertation, African Studies Centre, Leiden University, 2012.

was neither a railway line nor a road for motor vehicles.[19] Some unfree forms of recruitment also survived in the modern transport sector. The system, called labour service for works in the public interest (*Service de la main-d'œuvre des travaux d'intérêt général* or SMOTIG), was introduced in French West Africa in the early 1920s. In Senegal, SMOTIG was sometimes used in the maintenance work on the Thiès–Niger railway. It recruited workers who did not enter freely into work but were wage workers. In the Horn of Africa, by 1940 the daily wage of transport workers was higher than that of workers in other sectors in the region.[20]

Yet one should not exaggerate the speed with which the transformation of labour relations occurred – from slave to wage work or from unfree to free labour – especially at the beginning of the twentieth century. In particular, in more economically advanced countries such as Egypt, a new class division was in the making with the rise of a working class or urban proletariat. This was more apparent in the cities, where a cosmopolitan class of *nouveaux riches* had started to inhabit the recently constructed, fashionable quarters of Cairo, Alexandria and Port Said, while the urban poor lived as slum dwellers in the ancient parts of the cities.[21] The transport revolution, which in Egypt coincided with the opening of the Suez Canal in 1869, was at the centre of this transformation – together with the plantation industry.[22]

By the 1920s, urban transport of goods – at a micro level especially – throughout the continent started to be increasingly dominated by Africans.[23] In Accra, with more than two hundred African owners of motor cars, this

---

[19] Gwyn Campbell, *An Economic History of Imperial Madagascar, 1750–1895: The Rise and Fall of an Island Empire* (Cambridge: Cambridge University Press, 2008), 252–6.

[20] See Stefano Bellucci and Massimo Zaccaria, 'Wage Labor and Mobility in Colonial Eritrea, 1880s to 1920s', *International Labor and Working-Class History*, 86 (2014), 89–106; Stefano Bellucci and Massimo Zaccaria, 'Engine of Change: A Social History of the Car-Mechanics Sector in the Horn of Africa', in *Transforming Innovations in Africa: Explorative Studies on Appropriation in African Societies*, ed. Jan-Bart Gewald, André Leliveld and Iva Peša (Leiden: Brill, 2012), 237–56.

[21] Daniel Panzac, 'The Population of Egypt in the Nineteenth Century', *Asian and African Studies*, 21.1 (1987), 11–32; Joel Beinin and Zachary Lockman, *Workers on the Nile: Nationalism, Communism, Islam and the Egyptian Working Class, 1882–1954* (Princeton, NJ: Princeton University Press, 1987), 5–7.

[22] For a general history of the transformation of Egyptian society between the nineteenth and twentieth centuries, including the impact of the opening of the Suez Canal and the world economy on the Egyptian economy, see Ehud R. Toledano, 'Social and Economic Change in the "Long Nineteenth Century"', in *The Cambridge History of Egypt, Vol. 2: Modern Egypt, From 1517 to the End of the 20th Century*, ed. M. W. Daly (Cambridge: Cambridge University Press, 1998), 252–84.

[23] On African capitalists, see the chapter by Austin in this volume.

local group held a significant position in the goods transport sector.[24] In the second half of the twentieth century, taxis and minibuses, which dominated urban public transport, were mainly in the hands of Africans, some of whom became important capitalist entrepreneurs. In Addis Ababa, the first bus company was owned by Emperor Haile Selassie himself. The road transport sector saw greater involvement of African locals than the railway sector. In part, this was because the local workforce was used to build the roads, together with the fact that less technology and capital was needed to prepare and run the road transport system. In West Africa, the vehicles themselves soon passed into African ownership. Road haulage was for many the second step, after produce buying, up the capitalist ladder, and everywhere it was mostly Africans who drove the vehicles and maintained them. The internal combustion engine initiated many into modern technology, and the lorry driver became the new type of African self-made man, the adventurer who, like the traders and porters of earlier times, dared to travel beyond tribal horizons and even beyond colonial ones.

There were, however, instances of the involvement of European settlers in the transport sector. Between 1935 and 1939, after the Fascist invasion of Ethiopia, perhaps 200,000 Italians either volunteered or were conscripted for temporary wage labour in East Africa. The newcomers were concentrated in the towns, especially in Eritrea. Many found work in offices or motor-vehicle repair shops. Italy initiated a huge road construction programme, which gave employment to unskilled Italian immigrants as well as Africans. An all-weather road was built from Addis Ababa to Assab and Massawa, which became once more the chief port of north-east Africa.[25]

THE CONTROL OF SKILLED LABOUR

As eloquently explained by Berman, labour must be 'controlled'.[26] All forms of labour relations, from free to unfree, from tributary to wage labour, need laws. In colonial labour relations, for colonial administrators and many African colonial ruling classes, labour legislation legitimacy was sometimes

---

[24] In the 1920s Accra was significantly smaller than today. The city had a population of less than 18,000 in 1901 and about 62,000 in 1931; see Jennifer Hart, *Ghana on the Go: African Mobility in the Age of Motor Transportation* (Bloomington, IN: Indiana University Press, 2016), 61. In this historical period, when cars were a rarity, a few hundred motor cars could dominate the goods' transport system.

[25] Bellucci and Zaccaria, 'Engine of Change'.

[26] Bruce Berman, *Control and Crisis in Colonial Kenya: The Dialectic of Domination* (Oxford: James Currey, 1990).

divine and sometimes political, depending on the case. A great deal of force and violence was also necessary to exercise control over labour, with enclosure systems, and criminal or physical penalties for those who did not respect the legal systems. However, free wage labour is controlled more surreptitiously, often with regulations presented as rational acts but always with the purpose of satisfying the needs of capital to exploit labour power.

In many parts of Africa, skilled transport workers were attracted from Europe, America and even Australia by the lure of high wages, precisely to work on railways, ports and later at airports as technicians and managers. These skilled, white workers were costly, partly because of their tendency towards unionism and collective action. This meant that efforts on the part of employers to keep the costs of labour as low as possible – thereby investing capital in as profitable a manner as feasible – were primarily borne by the African workers, who were paid considerably less than their white colleagues.

The central problem facing employers was one of productivity: how to employ labour in order to meet industrial demand, while, at the same time, preventing workers from using their collective muscle to press for improvements in their livelihoods. This was the basis of the capitalist mode of production as it was applied in the African colonial context. Laws and force were solely used during colonial times to satisfy the needs of capital. With independence from colonialism, the interests of capital vis-à-vis labour remained the same, but the new African leadership found it quite problematic to support capital (still overwhelmingly European) against labour (overwhelmingly African). This was true for transport as well as other sectors.[27]

Many sectors were affected by the new policies adopted by the independent African governments. The challenges posed by development efforts and the fact that most African countries did not possess enough capital to improve their economic structures meant that several transport infrastructures were not maintained and either declined in importance or were abandoned. This was the case of the railways, which, in colonial times, played an important role in the African transport revolution.

Since the 1960s, road and air transport – along with the omnipresent porterage and water transport – have had a real boom across the entire continent, although in relative terms Africa has remained the continent with the least developed transport system (see Table 7.1). Air transport workers are skilled, free wage workers *par excellence*. There is basically no account of any other type or form of labour relations within this sector. Much

[27]   See the chapters by Brown and Neveling in this volume.

more complex is the situation of the motor vehicle transport sector. Here, the categories of jobs multiply: from taxi drivers to lorry drivers; from city minibus to long-range coach drivers; from taxi bikers to chauffeurs for the growing wealthy African elite and for government officials or aid workers. Within these sectors, the premise of African workers' economic obedience to local, 'traditional' intermediaries began to collapse. Loss of command of labour could mean the loss of mastery over women and men.

Table 7.1. Transport and other economic indicators: percentage of distribution of world totals, 1961

	Africa	South America	Europe (excl. USSR)	North America
Population	8.5	4.9	14.0	8.9
Area	22.5	13.2	3.7	18.0
Air transport capacity	2.0	5.0	23.0	62.0
Air traffic	2.3	5.3	24.0	60.0
Rail freight traffic	1.8	1.0	11.0	29.0
Commercial vehicles	2.9	4.8	24.0	55.0
Energy consumption	1.6	2.2	27.0	38.0
Gross domestic product (1958)	3.3	4.7	28.0	51.0

Source: UN Statistical Yearbook, in A. Adedeji, 'The Economic Evolution of Developing Africa', in *The Cambridge History of Africa, Volume 8: From c. 1940 to c. 1975*, ed. M. Crowder (Cambridge: Cambridge University Press, 1984), 223.

In the transport sector, in the years during and following the Second World War, hundreds of thousands of jobs were created, as new docks, roads and airfields were built. The 1960s were not boom years in economic terms, but the national incomes of African countries were growing nonetheless, and unemployment was relatively low.[28] Often, big cities by themselves could not provide enough labour; more workers were therefore diverted from rural areas to those cities in particular which constituted railway or port hubs. Cities expanded and urban transport grew with them. In these urban contexts, Africans increasingly found jobs as car, bus and lorry drivers. Demand for drivers as well as for mechanics continued to expand. Road transport, both urban and long-distance, is still one of the most important branches within the transport sector as a whole. The motorways driven through the hearts

[28] Michael Roemer, 'Economic Development in Africa: Performance since Independence, and a Strategy for the Future', *Daedalus*, 111.2 (1982), 125–48.

of the major cities during the 1960s and 1970s transformed the social and geographical landscape.

In the meantime the number of workers in ports and in maritime transport also grew significantly in the whole continent. Today, labour in the harbours of Africa is many times larger compared to a century or even half a century ago.[29] In South Africa, for example, in the 1960s and 1970s alone, the number of workers in ports increased three or four times.[30] Airports were built, and the number of internal passengers (including some within neighbouring countries) carried by South African Airways grew at an annual rate of more than 10 per cent from about one hundred thousand in the late 1940s to over two million in the 1970s.

In today's Africa, labour in transport is very polarized between those employed in structured, formal systems, and those workers who do not have a written employment contract and are therefore more precarious and weaker vis-à-vis their employer. The first group of workers tends to be more protected by legal provisions; its members have higher wages than those of the second category and they also have a guaranteed pension. These are air and railway transport workers and, to a lesser extent, bus, taxi and lorry drivers. In the second category figure the drivers of minibuses in the ever growing African urban centres. These are usually called by their local name – *molue, bolekaja, ongoro, daladala, matatu, boda boda, bajaj*, just to mention a few. The private minibus system is truly a 'mass transit system', which efficiently moves hundreds of thousands of city dwellers. The private minibuses exist because of the inefficiency of the public transportation and road systems.

From the labour history point of view, the workers in this industry are very cheap, and there is no interest, therefore, on the part of the state in regulating this sector too much. If labour was made more 'formal', prices would immediately rise. Therefore, conductors, call boys, mechanics, money collectors, cleaners, etc. are employed without a written contract, that is, casually. They can be sacked at any given moment by the owner of the minibuses – that is, they are precarious workers.[31] The working conditions are appalling, and this often results in accidents and unsafe working practices

---

[29] Darren Fraser and Theo Notteboom, 'Port Development in Sub-Saharan Africa: Competitive Forces, Port Reform, and Investment Challenges', in *Dynamic Shipping and Port Development in the Globalized Economy, Vol. 1: Applying Theory to Practice in Maritime Logistics*, ed. Paul Tae-Woo Lee and Kevin Cullinane (Basingstoke: Palgrave Macmillan, 2016), 53–78.

[30] Bernard Dubbeld, 'Breaking the Buffalo: The Transformation of Stevedoring Work in Durban between 1970 and 1990', *International Review of Social History*, 48, Special Issue 11 (2003), 97–122.

[31] See the chapter by Barchiesi in this volume.

in order to meet targets. The heavy pollution affects these workers, leading to lung problems – problems that are exacerbated because they do not have health benefits or insurance coverage. These workers tend to be paid wages, that is, they are free wage workers – unless they are relatives of the owner, which reduces their 'freedom' to enter or leave the business. Although variable, evidence suggests that informal transport workers live on very low and insecure wages. They are the typical 'working poor'. Their wages are paid either by the hour or daily – almost never weekly or monthly. Sometimes, wages depend on revenues and fluctuate accordingly.[32]

Table 7.2. Percentage of public transport journeys

City	Formal/public+private transport	Informal/private transport
Abidjan	33	67
Algiers	6	94
Cairo	48	52
Cape Town	74	26
Dakar	5	95

Source: R. Cervero and A. Golub, 'Informal Transport: A Global Perspective', *Transport Policy*, 14 (2007), 447.

In a few cases, drivers can also rent or lease their vehicles. In this case, they have no regular wage. Their income consists of what is left from the 'takings' after rent has been given to the vehicle owners and other expenses have been paid. These expenses may include maintenance, spare parts, petrol, parking fees, fines and bribes.

---

[32] Information on workers in the minibus sector can be found in the vast literature that exists on the subject; in addition to the literature cited in other parts of this chapter, see Xavier Godard, *Les transports et la ville en Afrique au sud du Sahara: le temps de la débrouille et du désordre inventif* (Paris: Karthala, 2002); Joe L. P. Lugalla, 'The Informal Urban Transport System in Tanzania: The "Dalla-Dalla" Buses of Dar-es-Salaam', *Internationales Afrika-Forum*, 26.4 (1990), 353–60; Mark Ingle, 'An Historical Overview of Problems Associated with the Formalization of the South African Minibus Taxi Industry', *New Contree: A Journal of Historical and Human Sciences for Southern Africa*, 57 (2009), 71–87; Carlos M. Lopes, '"Hug me, hold me tight!" The Evolution of Passenger Transport in Luanda and Huambo (Angola), 1975–2000', in *The Speed of Change: Motor Vehicles and People in Africa, 1890–2000*, ed. Jan-Bart Gewald, Sabine Luning and Klaas van Walraven (Leiden: Brill, 2009), 107–26.

ON THE ROAD

During colonialism, until the 1920s, road systems, railway lines and ports did not constitute networks aimed at serving the interests of the African people. These networks did not link African people or places to each other. Rather, the transport system constituted an element of the economic drainage – from the African interior to the coast and to Europe – of primary and agriculture commodities. Ultimately, colonial transport served the economic interests of companies in European metropoles. This is why labour actions in the transport sector affected in greater measure the colonial power and interests and in lesser measure the African people. The whole situation changed with the demographic boom and urban expansion that occurred after the Second World War.

In the second half of the twentieth century, road transport and road workers became crucial in terms of Africa's economic interests, as well as for African societies. Cities and villages grew along these transport lines and hubs. The transport system inherited from colonialism had transformed the demographic settlement of African people. At the same time, in the growing African cities, the bus industry, and especially the minibus industry, boomed.

In the last few decades, African societies have become increasingly dependent on motor transport, and overwhelmingly on road transport. Drivers constitute the main actors in this social transformation. Theoretically, this situation should give road workers enormous political bargaining power. For example, strikes by drivers could affect the entire population of a country. Nevertheless, the reality is quite different. The road transport sector is extremely fragmented, it is in private hands, and it is constituted of small firms, each with few employees. These employees are usually recruited following family, village or friendship patterns and are less prone to unionizing than railway or dock workers. This difference is crucial in order to understand the historical changes that occurred in the vertical relations between workers and employers within the transport sector in general – to the advantage of the employers. For these reasons, workers in the road transport sector are particularly vulnerable and subject to the whims of their employers. Two notable exceptions are bus drivers working for public companies, and taxi drivers, who are normally self-employed.[33]

The two dominant categories of workers in the road transport sector are the urban minibus drivers and lorry drivers. Lorry drivers are particularly

---

[33] Meshack M. Khosa, 'Accumulation and Labour Relations in the Taxi Industry', *Transformation: Critical Perspectives on Southern Africa*, 24 (1994), 55–71; J. D. Jordan, 'Public Transport in Harare', *Zambezia: A Journal of Social Studies in Southern and Central Africa*, 11.2 (1983), 127–38.

skilled workers, as they are often not only drivers but also semi-professional or professional mechanics. Lorry drivers need to be able to repair their vehicles in case of a mechanical breakdown during their journeys.

Self-employment is supposedly the aspirational goal of many road transport workers. As cogently explained by Mb□gua wa M□ngai, writing on the subculture surrounding the minibus world in Nairobi, a young person who joins the trade of informal urban transport usually comes from a very poor and marginalized urban background. Looking up to the *nouveau riche* and their tacky displays of wealth, the aspiration of these young drivers is to become a so-called 'big man' as well.[34] Their motto is 'get rich or die trying'.[35] The story of minibus drivers in Nairobi reflects the story of the transport workers in many other African cities, in which a fragmented, neoliberal society produces new patterns of individualistic aggrandisement.[36] Similar aspirations are harboured by lorry drivers, although these are normally more experienced and mature workers than those in the minibus industry and therefore less 'aggressive' in pursuit of their goal. They receive a salary if they work for a big company or, less commonly, they are self-employed and paid by the trip. A negligible minority of these workers becomes self-employed, because the initial investment necessary to buy a truck or a bus is very difficult to acquire through the poor wages received. Tips taken by minibus drivers from clients or tricks carried out by lorry drivers, such as the transport of passengers in lorries designated for the transport of goods, do not make any real difference.

There exists a certain amount of recent academic work on the role and working conditions of minibus workers, but there is much less on lorry drivers.[37] It is therefore easier to have a more informed idea about the working conditions of minibus workers. Minibus workers can be divided into

---

[34] On entrepreneurship, see the chapter by Pilossof in this volume.

[35] Mbũgua Wa Mũngai, *Nairobi's Matatu Men: Portrait of a Subculture* (Nairobi: Twaweza Communications, 2013), 44–93.

[36] Tim Gibbs, 'Becoming a "Big Man" in Neo-liberal South Africa: Migrant Masculinities in the Minibus-Taxi Industry', *African Affairs*, 113.452 (2014), 431–48.

[37] Matteo Rizzo, 'Informalisation and the End of Trade Unionism as We Knew It? Dissenting Remarks from a Tanzanian Case Study', *Review of African Political Economy*, 40.136 (2013), 290–308; Gaston M'Bemba-Ndoumba, *Transports urbains publics et privés au Congo: enjeux et pratiques sociales* (Paris: L'Harmattan, 2010); Piet Konings, 'Solving Transportation Problems in African Cities: Innovative Responses by the Youth in Douala', *Africa Today* 53.1 (2006/07), 35–50; Klaas van Walraven, 'Vehicle of Sedition: The Role of Transport Workers in Sawaba's Rebellion in Niger, 1954–1966', in *The Speed of Change: Motor Vehicles and People in Africa, 1890–2000*, ed. Jan-Bart Gewald, Sabine Luning and Klaas van Walraven (Leiden: Brill, 2009), 75–103.

three main categories: drivers, conductors (in charge of collecting fares from passengers) and stage workers (cleaning, selling tickets, attracting passengers, controlling passenger queues, etc.). Overwhelmingly, their work contract is a verbal one – in some cases this is because family, village and friendship relationships play a central role in the recruitment of drivers and conductors.[38] The written contract, which is rarely given, consists of the mere recording of name, phone number and national identity – occasionally the ethnic group – and, where possible, the address of the worker, on either a loose piece of paper or in a register in the hands of the employer. The majority of workers in the minibus industry are employed as precarious workers, subject either to temporary terms or given an indefinite commitment on the part of the owner of the minibuses, who can nonetheless discharge the worker at any time. Workers in the minibus industry may work from ten to fifteen hours per day. Stage workers work normally fewer hours than conductors and drivers and are normally paid on a daily basis. Wages are very low but tend to be within the national averages of the working poor in other sectors of the economy. No benefits are provided and, contrary to what many of these youngsters believe, no possibility of career advancement exists. To summarize, today's urban transport workers are the typical product of neoliberalism. They are vulnerable to exploitation and conduct a precarious life.

WORKING IN A STRATEGIC SECTOR

Historically, workers in the transport sector have had a fair amount of bargaining power vis-à-vis both their employers and the state. Transport is a key economic and civil sector in every society, and a relatively small number of organized workers could be effective in blocking it, creating a stranglehold on a society's economic and human activities. There have been many strikes and instances of unrest among unionized and non-unionized transport workers in twentieth-century Africa. Transport strikes have been more effective than those in other sectors. In more than one case they have brought down governments, like the taxi strike in Addis Ababa in 1974, which led to the Marxist revolution. Therefore while, on the one hand, employers have had to keep these workers under control, on the other hand, they have had to concede a certain number of the workers' demands.

---

[38] Meleckidzedeck Khayesi, 'Matatu Workers in Nairobi, Thika and Ruiru: Career Patterns and Conditions of Work', in *Negotiating Social Space: East African Microenterprises*, ed. Patrick O. Alila and Poul O. Pedersen (Trenton, NJ: Asmara World Press, 2001), 79.

Moreover, this strategic position of transport workers has produced a process of de-casualization of labour. Unrest and walkouts among transport workers have served to persuade employers that they are better off with full-time staff than with occasional labour. De-casualization meant the introduction of new rules limiting or blocking entry into dock work in order to maintain high economic standards for workers and thereby keep them more attached to the business, whether private or government-owned.

According to Charles A. Orr, African 'transport workers were the first to organise trade unions' in many African countries.[39] European railway workers were the first to bring trade unions and collective bargaining to Rhodesia, early in the twentieth century. Railway workers were trade union pioneers in Dahomey, Ivory Coast, Sudan and Ethiopia. A strike of African railway workers in Southern Rhodesia in 1945 was the first important sign of labour unrest in that territory.[40] In the 1940s dock workers were the first to organize themselves in Mauritius and in Libya, and they were among the earliest to do so in Tanganyika. At the same time, motor vehicle drivers were the first to set up unions in Uganda, Liberia, Tanganyika and Nyasaland. Transport unions, while not actually the first in existence, were established relatively early on in the following countries: Egypt (tram workers in 1908), South Africa (African dock workers in 1919), Gambia (seamen in the late 1920s), Nigeria (railway and port workers in 1931), Gold Coast (motor vehicle drivers in 1931); during the 1940s, Kenya and Uganda (Asian railway staff), Tanganyika and Nyasaland (railway workers), Kenya (port, railway and motor transport workers) and Zanzibar (cart coolies and seamen) followed.[41] Although instances of unrest and walkouts were common among porters, a proper beginning of trade unionism among black African workers can be traced to the 1910s. These workers' organizations began as small-scale associations among groups of relatively skilled and settled urban workers. Transport was the key sector of this historical development, and it owed much to the advice and assistance of communists and socialists throughout the continent.

Before the advent of socialism in Africa, there were strikes by skilled personnel, such as those of the railway clerks in the Lagos Colony of

[39] Charles A. Orr, 'Trade Unionism in Colonial Africa', *Journal of Modern African Studies*, 4.1 (1966), 65–81.

[40] Kenneth Powers Vickery, 'The Rhodesia Railways African Strike of 1945, Part I: A Narrative Account', *Journal of Southern African Studies*, 24.3 (1998), 545–60; Kenneth Powers Vickery, 'The Rhodesia Railways African Strike of 1945, Part II: Cause, Consequence, Significance', *Journal of Southern African Studies*, 25.1 (1999), 49–71.

[41] Orr, 'Trade Unionism', 78.

1904, joined by unskilled railway workers.[42] The reaction of the British authorities was invariably inflexible. Worker unrest was viewed as a direct challenge to colonial authority. Scab labour and violence were used to break strikes; workers were fired upon during the 1919 Sierra Leone railway strike.[43] Although it was rare to see the demands of skilled workers being granted, some small concessions were occasionally made – in Sierra Leone, there was a wage increase after the strike.[44] However, the concerns of non-unionized and unpoliticized workers were generally disregarded. Even worse, the risk for the most vociferous and activist workers was imprisonment and even extrajudicial execution. In this context, the political protection and class-consciousness that the spread of socialist ideals engendered gave enormous strength to African workers. Among the most politicized were the transport workers.

Once the railways had been built, the people who maintained them were in a strategic position, as they could have a huge impact on the economy if they withheld their labour. Following the First World War, communism and socialism spread in Africa, starting in the Arab-speaking North and in South Africa. Between 1919 and 1921 at least eighty-one instances of labour unrest were recorded in Egypt alone. The Cairo tramwaymen were the first to go on strike. Almost immediately thereafter they were joined by Egyptian state railway workers, taxi and carriage drivers; dock workers in Port Said, tramwaymen in Alexandria, customs officials in the Suez Canal, etc. all joined the struggle. The labour unrest affected other economic sectors as well, but the transport workers were the most crucial for the success of the workers' struggle.[45] Not only did the outbreak of labour unrest put an end to the British protectorate – Britain unilaterally granted partial independence in 1922 – but it also showed how socialist ideals were spreading among workers. After this limited independence, the new labour legislation did not improve the situation of Egyptian workers, but those in strategic sectors such as transport, and in particular tramway workers, managed to fight their cause and obtain some victories, despite harsh repression. According to Beinin and

[42] Antony G. Hopkins, 'The Lagos Strike of 1897: An Exploration in Nigerian Labour History', *Past & Present*, 35.1 (1966), 133–55.

[43] Akintola J. G. Wyse, 'The 1919 Strike and Anti-Syrian Riots: A Krio Plot?', *Journal of the Historical Society of Sierra Leone*, 3.1/2 (1979), 1–14.

[44] Eliphas G. Mukonoweshuro, *Colonialism, Class Formation, and Underdevelopment in Sierra Leone* (Lanham, MD: University Press of America, 1993), 111.

[45] Marius Deeb, 'Bank Misr and the Emergence of the Local Bourgeoisie', *Egypt Middle Eastern Studies*, 12.3, Special Issue: Middle Eastern Economy (1976), 74.

Lockman, tramway workers were the most organized and politicized in Egypt. Indeed, they were instrumental in the victory of the Wafd Party in 1924.[46]

The popular appeal of nationalism to workers was demonstrated in 1911, when Tunisian workers protested against the Italian invasion of Libya. The birth of Tunisian nationalism is very much linked not only to these political events but also to workers' concerns, with the transport workers once more taking centre stage. In February 1912 an Italian tram driver knocked down and killed a child; the trams were then boycotted and Tunisian employees of the company claimed equal pay with Italian personnel.[47] The government declared that there had been a political plot and exiled some nationalist activists of the Young Tunisians party. The combination of workers' demands and political agitation was the first clear manifestation of a Tunisian independentist consciousness.[48]

In 1919, in Sierra Leone, government employees, workers from the Public Works Department – together with local policemen – initiated the 'strike week'. A reporter of those days described the events:

> This has been a very exciting week. What a pity we haven't daily papers in Freetown. By this time it's rather stale to talk of the splendid fight which Railway and Public Works Men have put up for their war bonuses (given to Indian and European mechanics) … If R. Barker, the blundering Acting General Manager and locomotive Superintendent of the Railways did think once that Sierra Leoneans could only bark without biting, then he is shockingly disillusioned. It is grand the way the fellows have stuck together.[49]

Demands for higher wages and better working conditions were at the root of this labour unrest, and socialist ideals were able to give these concerns political guidance. In 1916 and 1918 Abdoulaye Mara, an ex-soldier of Senegalese origin, encouraged strikes in the docks at Conakry, Guinea, and in 1920 there was a strike in the port of Dakar.[50] In 1919 and 1920 there were strikes on the Dakar–St Louis railway, where for the first time black workers began to voice their claims separately from white workers. In May

---

[46] Beinin and Lockman, *Workers on the Nile*, 128–37.

[47] Andrew Borowiec, *Modern Tunisia: A Democratic Apprenticeship* (Westport, CT: Praeger, 1998), 17–18.

[48] See Phillip C. Naylor, *North Africa: A History from Antiquity to the Present* (Austin, TX: University of Texas Press, 2009), 141–67.

[49] *Sierra Leone Weekly News*, 19 July 1919, 'Rambling Talks' by the Rambler, https://goo.gl/AJU5FQ (accessed 27 April 2013).

[50] Catherine Coquery-Vidrovitch, *Africa: Endurance and Change South of the Sahara*, trans. David Maisel (Berkeley, CA: University of California Press, 1988), 227 [originally published as *Afrique noire: permanences et ruptures* (Paris: Éditions Payot, 1985)].

1919 the government of French West Africa was sufficiently concerned to legislate for an eight-hour day, though the law was not implemented, and even the *Code du travail* (Labour Code) continued to refer to a ten-hour day for Africans. After decades of struggle, the government was forced to listen to the workers' demands. This was also because, in 1924, a Dahomeyan lawyer, Kodjo Tovalou-Houenou, had founded in Paris the Universal League for the Defence of the Black Race, backed by the French Communist Party and the Intercolonial Union.[51]

Before the advent of modern transport and other industrial developments in Africa, there was very limited working-class consciousness among black African wage workers. This was due, above all, to the prevalence of migrant labour: long-term commitment to wage labour, and to particular industries, was still highly unusual. A generalized sense of class distinction was more common in towns. Before politics and legislation, it was music and dancing that could express the grievances of this new class in the making. As Orr put it:

> The leading role of transport workers can also be easily explained. They, too, constitute a large fraction of the African labour force and they enjoy many advantages over other workers. Transport workers usually work for large employers. They are drawn from a variety of places and backgrounds. Their travel and their contacts help them to break through the boundaries of isolation, fear, and ignorance. They must be alert and technically skilled, and they must assume responsibilities in the course of their work. They tend to pick up new ideas and new techniques en route and thus quite naturally find themselves in the vanguard of union organisation.[52]

The 1930s were the years of the global economic crisis, and the 1940s saw the Second World War and the subsequent reconstruction. Workers in the transport sector in Africa felt, more so than their equivalents elsewhere, the reduction of investment in this industry. The Depression had a snowball effect, and the European reaction was to shift the burden increasingly on to Africans: wages deteriorated, and this resulted in strikes by both skilled and unskilled workers. In 1934 drivers went on strike in Lagos against the Lebanese-owned Zarpas transport company. They were reproved by Herbert Macaulay's *Lagos Daily News*: 'At this time of economic depression, workers ought to know that there are many unemployed ready to take their place

---

[51] Babacar M'Baye, 'Marcus Garvey and African Francophone Political Leaders of the Early Twentieth Century: Prince Kojo Touvalou Houénou Reconsidered', *Journal of Pan African Studies*, 1.5 (2006), 2–19.

[52] Orr, 'Trade Unionism', 80; see also Kurt Beck, 'Roadside Comforts: Truck Stops on the Forty Days Road in Western Sudan', *Africa*, 83.3 (2013), 426–45.

if they foolishly go out on strike.'[53] As usual, scab labour and police action against pickets broke the drivers' strike. In an attempt to protect the railways from more competitive African-owned motor transport businesses, licensing, road inspection and restrictive legislation were introduced. The Gold Coast Carriage of Goods Road Ordinance of 1934 provided for the 'prohibition' of the transport of particular commodities over routes identified by the colonial administration.[54] The result was a series of fruitless boycotts and petitions by lorry owner-operators. Class and sectional interests divided the African response, yet the reality of the situation was increasingly at variance with British assertions of inherently superior political and economic competence.

In South Africa, the Industrial and Commercial Workers' Union, founded by Clements Kadalie, had its stronghold among the dock workers in the Cape Town harbour facilities. Their successful 1919 strike led to the establishment of trade unionism in South Africa.[55] In 1936 the communists helped 'coloured' and African workers to form a single union in the docks and railways at Cape Town. In 1938 the National Liberation League created a workers' Non-European United Front, and, in 1939, a demonstration by the Front in Cape Town induced the government to veto provincial plans to enforce urban segregation. Meanwhile, the Front also attracted younger activists who were tired of the intensely communal politics of the South African Indian Congress; when Indian rights in the Transvaal, already curbed in 1932, were further circumscribed in 1939, the Front organized passive resistance. In the meantime, the white railway workers' union, the Spoorbond, was involved in the Afrikaner-Broederbond, a secret society of Afrikaans-speaking white men wielding extensive political power, in efforts to pass anti-Jewish laws – in other words, they were not concerned with salaries and working conditions, since white workers in South Africa had all the rights a worker of the time could hope for.[56]

---

[53] A. Hughes and R. Cohen, 'An Emerging Nigerian Working Class: The Lagos Experience, 1897–1939', in *African Labour History*, ed. P. W. C. Gutkind, R. Cohen and J. Copans (London: Sage, 1978), 48.

[54] Ernest Aryeetey and Ravi Kanbur, 'Ghana at Sixty: Learning from a Developing African Nation's Past', in *The Economy of Ghana Sixty Years after Independence*, ed. E. Aryeetey and R. Kanbur (Oxford: Oxford University Press, 2017), 5–6; and G. B. Kay and Stephen Hymer, *The Political Economy of Colonialism in Ghana: A Collection of Documents and Statistics, 1900–1960* (London: Cambridge University Press, 1972), 194.

[55] Bengt G. M. Sundkler, *Bantu Prophets in South Africa* (London: Lutterworth Press, 1948; 2nd edn, Oxford: Oxford University Press, 1961), 86.

[56] Baruch Hirson and Yael Hirson, *History of the Left in South Africa: Writings of Baruch Hirson* (London: I.B.Tauris, 2005), 103; Uma Shashikant Mesthrie, 'Indian Responses in Natal to Non-European Unity Moves, 1927 to 1945', in *Natal 1909–1961: A*

Transport was the sector that gave birth to trade unionism in the Horn of Africa. In the 1940s labour unions were formed in Eritrea and among the Djibouti–Addis Ababa railway workers. The first strike reported in the region occurred in 1947 among the railway workers. Economic transformations fostered social changes, and new kinds of associations came into being, generating a new occupational structure. An urban version of the traditional self-help association emerged among the urbanized Ethiopian workers, known as *iqub, yedir* and *mahaber*.[57] These represented a very small proportion of workers until at least the 1990s, when Ethiopia began to experience an urbanization boom.

In Ghana, it was the railwaymen who, with their strikes, voiced the concern of the people vis-à-vis the corrupt practices of the once popular Convention People's Party led by Kwame Nkrumah. They did so with a strike in 1961, which caused Nkrumah to make his dramatic speech known as the 'Dawn Broadcast', with which the socialist president accused the party's officials of abusing their offices and replaced them with non-corrupt but radical young activists – a move that was later reversed by a military coup.

In neighbouring Ivory Coast, through the 1960s and 1970s, President Félix Houphouët-Boigny was able to contain periodic labour unrest. Backed by France, the Ivorian strongman managed to retain political power through continuous government reshuffles and, on the labour front, trying to co-opt when possible outspoken opposition leaders. This happened a few times with the lorry drivers, who became an increasingly powerful lobby in the country – and all over the continent. From the 1960s, a petty bourgeoisie or middle class of Africans was in the making. From this sector of society came both socialist and conservative neoliberal activists. Separating the progressive elements from the conservative ones was a task which President Houphouet-Boigny mastered extremely well. The lorry drivers and taxi drivers were the typical expression of this new African class, and in Ivory Coast, as elsewhere, it was a class distressed by the growth of working-class militancy.[58]

A wave of general strikes took place in Africa in the years after the Second World War. Post-war labour unrest had a significant impact on the relationship between weakened European imperialist powers and African

---

Collection of Papers on Developments in Natal in the Union Period, 1910–1961 [presented at a workshop at the University of Natal, 27–28 October 1982] (Pietermaritzburg: Department of Historical Studies, University of Natal, 1983), 111–33.

[57] Gerry Salole, 'Not Seeing the Wood for the Trees: Searching for Indigenous Non-Government Organisations in the Forest of Voluntary Self Help Associations', *Journal of Social Development in Africa*, 6.1 (1991), 5–17.

[58] Corinne Benveniste, *La boucle du cacao, Côte d'Ivoire: étude régionale des circuits de transport* (Paris: Travaux et documents de l'OSTROM, 1974).

colonies in search of independence. General strikes occurred in Senegal in 1946, Tanganyika in 1947, Nigeria in 1945, Sudan in 1947, Tunisia in 1947 and Zanzibar in 1948. They were felt in the colonial administrative capitals, such as Dakar, Tunis and Dar es Salaam, but also in important transport hubs, such as the port of Mombasa or the railway cities of Atbara and Thiès. According to many historians, the post-war wave of labour unrest brought to the fore on the political scene the labour question and its dilemmas. The labour question marked the beginning of the decolonization process in Africa.[59] Transport workers' unions were key actors both in this historical wave of labour and in the political, nationalist struggle. In particular, railway strikes were extremely effective in the process of decolonization in French West Africa in 1947–48, in Ghana in 1947 and in Southern Rhodesia in 1947.[60]

Dock workers' strikes were significantly successful in Durban during the so-called 'strike action' of black employees, from 1937 to 1942. For South Africa, no longer a colony, the strike action proved that a proto-proletariat was in the making. The workers fought a battle for better wages, better working conditions, and at the same time against the state, run by the white ruling class.[61] In colonial Africa, dock workers mobilized in Mozambique in 1947 and in Mombasa in 1955, where the Kenyan workers' fights and anti-colonial struggles coincided.

Although the labour unrest was triggered by motivations linked to the economic and working conditions of the strikers, it was noted that a significant feature of strikes in the transport sector – the blockage of ports and railway hubs – was the large degree of support given by the urban population.[62] Transport workers were so vital for the colonial economies that, on the one hand, the 'imperialist response' was harsh in the face of their insubordination; but, on the other hand, the colonial authorities felt compelled to allow concessions, albeit limited, to the African working class. Trade unions began to be slowly recognized, radical working-class elements were fostered by these organizations, and transport workers played a key role

---

[59] Frederick Cooper, *Decolonization and African Society: The Labor Question in French and British Africa* (Cambridge: Cambridge University Press, 1996).

[60] Frederick Cooper, '"Our strike": Equality, Anticolonial Politics and the 1947–48 Railway Strike in French West Africa', *The Journal of African History*, 37.1 (1996), 81–118; Timothy Oberst, 'Transport Workers, Strikes and the "Imperial Response": Africa and the Post World War II Conjuncture', *African Studies Review*, 31.1 (1988), 117–33.

[61] Tim A. Nuttall, '"Do Not Accept Kaffir Standards": Trade Unions and Strikes among African Workers in Durban during the Second World War', *South African Historical Journal*, 29.1 (1993), 153–76.

[62] Oberst, 'Transport Workers'.

also in this kind of 'institutionalized' labour struggle.[63] However, since then union power has declined, together with the labour conditions of workers in the transport sector in general, as a result of the structural adjustment programmes, which brought about privatization and the closing down of ports and railways, and due to the fact that labour supply – the number of people who can operate cars, minibuses, buses and to a certain extent even lorries – has increased dramatically.

Transport workers in the minibus industry have always been politically weak because of the lack of organized and institutionalized representation. To this day, they are not unionized, and existing transport unions, so far, have not done much to involve them in their activities – because they are 'informal workers' with no contracts.[64] Cervero and Golub associate these workers with the more 'traditional' or pre-modern labour sector.[65] But these traditional-cum-modern workers fare worse than their predecessors, as they do not even benefit from the self-help structures of non-modern societies, leaving them socially excluded and disenfranchised, reflecting the typical lot of urban workers in Africa today.

CONCLUSION

The transport sector is crucial for the understanding of the development of wage labour in Africa. Since the very beginning of European colonial invasion and capitalist expansion, workers involved in every aspect of the vast transport sector have constituted an important factor within every economic system. For this reason, businesses and administrations constantly tried to control transport workers, with varying levels of success. Labour in transport progressed and increased its productivity with the development of new technologies and infrastructures. The work opportunities of African transport workers widened and diversified, from porter to driver, dock or railway worker, clerk, pilot, etc. Today, the sector is dominated by road transport. Drivers constitute by far the largest section of transport workers. Cars, taxis, minibuses and lorries are ubiquitous in the continent.

Historically, with the scarce supply of skilled labour, those workers with such skills became increasingly aware of being not only important but irreplaceable for employers and society at large. This is why transport

---

[63] See the chapter by Freund in this volume.

[64] On informal and precarious labour, see the chapter by Barchiesi in this volume.

[65] Robert Cervero and Aaron Golub, 'Informal Transport: A Global Perspective', *Transport Policy*, 14.6 (2007), 445–57.

workers, more than others, managed to organize themselves in unions. Their unrest threatened to create widespread disruption, as their strikes and boycotts could block the entire chain of production. Today, in the neoliberal era, with the dominance of the driving industry, the informalization of industrial relations, self-employment and abundance of labour, the strategic position of transport workers has diminished dramatically. The consequence is a deterioration of living and working conditions as well as a decline in the wages of the once 'elite' transport workers.

PART III

INTERNATIONAL DIMENSIONS AND MOBILITY

EIGHT
The International Labour Organization

DANIEL ROGER MAUL

Department of Archaeology, Conservation and History,
University of Oslo

LUCA PUDDU

Department of Cultures and Civilizations at the University
of Bologna, and Department of History, Cultures and
Religions, Sapienza University of Rome

HAKEEM IBIKUNLE TIJANI

Department of History,
National Open University of Nigeria, Lagos

AFRICA AND THE ILO'S FOUNDATIONAL YEARS

The relationship between the International Labour Organization and Africa during the first decades after the Organization's founding in Versailles in 1919 was, first and foremost, shaped by the ILO's strong European bias. The ILO built on the European labour experience in more than one aspect: its roots lay in the demands of late nineteenth-century European social reformers and proponents of international labour law, and it had grown out of the immediate effects of the First World War in Europe. The integration of the reformist part of the European labour movement into the war effort in many countries, and the Russian October Revolution of 1917, had created the political environment in which the ILO was founded. Its establishment was in a sense both a reward for European workers' contributions to the war effort and a safety valve to calm the revolutionary potential of the working class. In the same sense, the ILO's tripartite structure, in which workers' and employers' delegates took part next to government representatives in the decision-making process, built on the practical experiences and institutions created by some European countries during the war, which were for the first time institutionalized at the international level by the ILO.[1]

While the ILO's mandate was not restricted to any world region or political and social environment, a tension between the universalistic claims of the ILO's Constitution and a definite bias towards European industrial labour permeated the work of the Organization from the start. Initially, the ILO catered primarily to the needs of industrial wage labourers (including seafarers) in the industrialized countries of the West. Both the standard-setting activities and the technical work in which the ILO engaged during the interwar period reflected this bias.[2] From 1919 onwards, the annual sessions of the International Labour Conference (ILC) adopted international labour standards in the form of Conventions and Recommendations (the latter being instruments that are not binding under international law), dealing with a broad range of issues, from protection of children and women workers in industry through labour inspection to social insurance and employment policies. The common denominator of these activities was that the great majority of these standards dealt with problems specific to the industrialized world. Non-industrial labour, including agricultural labour – although within the competence of the ILO – was given much less attention.[3] Seen from this perspective, the ILO initially was poorly equipped to deal with the problems of the great majority of working people on the African continent. The 'industrial bias' by and large also permeated all other areas of the ILO's work, from research and the production of statistics to the early technical assistance

[1]   For an account of the period leading up to the establishment of the ILO and the early days of the Organization, see Anthony E. Alcock, *History of the International Labour Organisation* (London: Macmillan, 1970), 1–49; Bob Reinalda, *Routledge History of International Organizations: From 1815 to the Present Day* (London: Routledge, 2009), 137–77, 221–8; Olga Hidalgo-Weber, 'Social and Political Networks and the Creation of the ILO: The Role of British Actors', in *Globalizing Social Rights: The International Labour Organization and Beyond*, ed. Sandrine Kott and Joëlle Droux (Basingstoke and Geneva: Palgrave Macmillan and ILO, 2013), 17–31.

[2]   While the standards adopted in the early years were intended predominantly to protect workers in the physical performance of their work, as early as the 1930s the ILO began to extend its standard setting to a wider field of social policy, covering areas ranging from systems of social security to employment policy. In the period after the Second World War, human rights issues such as freedom of association and protection from discrimination at work increasingly became the subject of the ILO's normative activities.

[3]   Amalia Ribi Forclaz, 'A New Target for International Social Reform: The International Labour Organization and Working and Living Conditions in Agriculture in the Inter-War Years', *Contemporary European History*, 20.3 (2011), 307–29.

projects that the ILO started to implement during the 1930s. This bias was reflected clearly in the lack of resources committed to the study of African labour issues at the level of the International Labour Office, the ILO's secretariat in Geneva, itself. During the interwar years, a tiny Native Labour Section (consisting of only one to three people) accounted for all the ILO's work not only on Africa, but the entire colonial world.

Another fundamental problem, which affected the relationship between the ILO and Africa during these early years, was rooted in the poor representation of African countries and their interests within the Organization. Apart from the South African Union,[4] which, due to its status as a 'white' British Dominion, occupied a peculiar position, only two sub-Saharan African countries, Liberia and Ethiopia, were members of the Organization before the Second World War. Whatever influence they might have exerted, it was effectively constrained by the fact that they were hardly ever in a position to send full delegations to the ILC.[5]

The single most important obstacle to the ILO's engagement with African labour and social affairs clearly was to be found in the political status of vast parts of the continent, which were still under the formal colonial rule of European powers. During the ILO's first two decades of existence, the colonial powers' claim to sovereignty over African affairs was essentially never disputed within the bodies of the Organization, an acquiescence in which its predominantly European character at this point played an important part.[6] All colonial powers, except for Portugal, held permanent seats on the ILO's Governing Body. The initial absence of the two major powers that were critical of colonialism, the United States and the Soviet Union, further contributed to an environment in which the colonial powers met very little

[4] Jeremy Seekings, 'The ILO and Welfare Reform in South Africa, Latin America and the Caribbean, 1919–1950', in *ILO Histories: Essays on the International Labour Organization and Its Impact on the World During the Twentieth Century*, ed. Jasmien van Daele, Magaly Rodríguez García, Geert van Goethem and Marcel van der Linden (Bern: Peter Lang, 2010), 145–72.

[5] Susan Zimmermann, '"Special Circumstances" in Geneva: The ILO and the World of Non-Metropolitan Labour in the Interwar Years', in *ILO Histories: Essays on the International Labour Organization and Its Impact on the World During the Twentieth Century*, ed. Jasmien van Daele, Magaly Rodríguez García, Geert van Goethem and Marcel van der Linden (Bern: Peter Lang, 2010), 221–50.

[6] *Ibid.*

resistance in their attempts to keep their territorial possessions out of the international spotlight.[7]

One of the most important decisions regarding the ILO's constitutional treatment of the colonies was taken at the Second Session of the ILC in 1920. The issue under debate was whether and how the provisions of international labour standards could be applied to overseas territories as stipulated in Article 35 of the ILO's Constitution. This article, known as the 'colonial clause' gave the colonial powers freedom to exempt their colonies from certain international labour standards, without these territories automatically falling outside the scope of ILO standards in general. In practice, the 'colonial clause' provided the colonial powers with an effective means to ensure, up to the Second World War, that all initiatives aimed at achieving more rapid social progress in the colonies, or securing the larger-scale implementation of ILO standards, would come to nothing.

The exclusion of colonial issues from the ILO's proceedings was further highlighted by the absence of direct representation from the colonies in the Organization's meeting rooms. India, which became a full member of the Organization as early as 1919, was the only exception to this rule.[8] In no other case before 1939 did metropolitan governments ever include a representative of a colonial territory as a direct participant in their delegations, although prominent figures from the colonies were very sporadically called upon in an advisory capacity to help with the ILO's standard-setting work.[9] In the absence of direct representation from the colonies during the annual session of the ILC, it fell mainly to the workers' group to put colonial issues on the agenda.[10]

Paradoxically, when the Organization first took steps to broaden its outlook towards the non-European world during the 1930s, the marginal position that Africa occupied within the ILO became even more pronounced. Against the

---

[7]   The United States did not join the ILO until 1934, under the presidency of Franklin D. Roosevelt. The membership of the Soviet Union, which established relations with the ILO that same year, was exclusively the result of its accession to the League of Nations. The Soviet Union had no involvement in the Organization's work, nor did it send delegations to the ILC. Harold K. Jacobson, 'The USSR and ILO', *International Organization*, 14.3 (1960), 402–28.

[8]   India was represented from the start, although up to 1929 its delegations were effectively dictated to by the British delegation, though afterwards they became more independent. On India's early role, see G. Rodgers, 'India, the ILO and the Quest for Social Justice', *Economic and Political Weekly*, 46.10 (2011), 45–52.

[9]   See International Labour Office, *Social Policy in Dependent Territories* (Geneva: ILO, 1944), 56ff., nn. 2, 3.

[10]   Zimmermann, '"Special Circumstances" in Geneva'.

background of fundamental political, economic and social crises, the ILO attempted to widen its portfolio and move beyond standard-setting into the field of socio-economic planning and technical assistance. As part of this new direction, the ILO developed a growing awareness of the needs of the less industrialized parts of the world, followed by the first practical steps to regionalize its work.[11] While Latin America (a first ILO Regional Conference – for Latin America – took place in Santiago de Chile in 1936), and to a certain degree also Asia,[12] now became target areas of ILO activities, Africa remained widely untouched by these new endeavours. Instead, the ILO's overall approach to Africa remained for most of the time a merely humanitarian one. The focus of these efforts was less on matters of labour and social policy in the broader sense, but instead concentrated, first and foremost, on the worst abuses of 'native labour' in the colonies. In other words, when ILO discussions touched upon African labour and social issues during the interwar period, they stayed clear of one particular problem: forced labour.[13]

The systematic use of forced labour in many parts of colonial Africa during the interwar years was the result of a complex interplay between the colonial powers' aim of making their colonies more profitable (*mise en valeur*) and their parallel unwillingness to commit resources for a social infrastructure capable of ameliorating the damaging effects of this policy. The reluctance to get involved in social development was not based on financial considerations alone. According to the prevailing colonial doctrines of the time, it would have been a mistake, for example, to promote a policy which provided the indigenous population with an incentive to leave rural areas and move permanently into 'European' working conditions. Wherever the need for labour arose, short-term, migratory forms were favoured, and the social costs were left to be shouldered by the indigenous workers' 'natural environment' – that is, the rural areas and the 'tribal' structures from which they came and to which they were expected to return when their labour was no longer required.[14]

[11] Véronique Plata-Stenger, '"To Raise Awareness of Difficulties and to Assert their Opinion": The International Labour Office and the Regionalization of International Cooperation in the 1930s', in *Beyond Geopolitics: New Histories of Latin America at the League of Nations*, ed. Alan McPherson and Yannick Wehrli (Albuquerque, NM: University of New Mexico Press, 2015), 97–114.

[12] A first Asian Regional Conference would eventually take place in Delhi in 1947.

[13] J. P. Daughton, 'ILO Expertise and Colonial Violence in the Inter-War Years', in *Globalizing Social Rights: The International Labour Organization and Beyond*, ed. Sandrine Kott and Joëlle Droux (Basingstoke and Geneva: Palgrave Macmillan and ILO, 2013), 85–97.

[14] See M. Mamdani, *Citizen and Subject: Contemporary Africa and the Legacy of Late Colonialism* (Princeton, NJ: Princeton University Press, 1996).

Until the Second World War, it was general policy, at least in the British Empire, to avoid, as far as possible, 'stabilization' at the place of work and permanent migration to the cities. Labour shortages were often bridged by coercive measures, and private and public interest often went hand in hand in order to meet demand in the labour force. The brutality of the recruitment methods and working conditions, and the socially disruptive effects that the mass recruitment of men of employable age inflicted on the indigenous communities, repeatedly caught the attention of the public in Europe and North America. As a result, the topic of forced labour systems pervaded all aspects of contemporary debate on colonial policy. From the early 1920s onwards, the International Labour Office and its first Director, Albert Thomas, acted as part of an 'international colonial issue network' opposing forced labour in the colonies.[15]

When the League of Nations began preparations for a convention against slavery in 1924, the International Labour Office, which was also represented on the League's Permanent Mandate Commission, seized the chance to use this as a lever for its own campaigns. In the wake of the League's debates on the Slavery Convention, which was passed in 1926, the ILO was given the task of conducting a study into possible steps 'to prevent compulsory labour or forced labour from developing into conditions analogous to slavery'.[16] Its mandate was constrained, however, by the colonial powers' unwillingness to expose their ruling practices to any significant degree of international scrutiny, and the ILO went a long way to accommodate them. The installation of a non-tripartite Committee of Experts on Native Labour underpinned the patronizing character of this work. It consisted mainly of colonial administrators and colonial economic interests, among them Sir Frederick (later Lord) Lugard, British colonial administrator and Governor General of Nigeria (1914–19), Albrecht Gohr from the Belgian Ministry of Colonies, Martial Marlin, former governor of various French colonies, and Albrecht Freiherr von Rechenberg, former governor of German East Africa.[17]

---

[15] Daughton, 'ILO Expertise and Colonial Violence'; Luis Rodríguez-Piñero, *Indigenous Peoples, Postcolonialism, and International Law: The ILO Regime (1919–1989)* (Oxford: Oxford University Press, 2005). For a summary of the debate, see Daniel Roger Maul, 'The International Labour Organization and the Struggle against Forced Labour from 1919 to the Present', *Labour History*, 48.4 (2007), 477–500.

[16] Susan Pedersen, *The Guardians: The League of Nations and the Crisis of Empire* (New York: Oxford University Press, 2015).

[17] Daughton, 'ILO Expertise and Colonial Violence'.

The four conventions and a whole series of recommendations which the ILO passed between 1930 and 1939 as a result of this work revolved around the problem of forced labour. In the end, the ILO defined colonial labour as a special form of labour, referred to as 'native labour', to which separate norms applied. It drafted a special Native Labour Code (NLC), distinct from the International Labour Code which comprised all ILO conventions.[18] The discourse which culminated in the development of the NLC underpinned this distinction; it rested on the widely shared assumption that colonial policies had a duty to 'educate' the native population. The main area of controversy was the question of whether the abolition of forced labour and related phenomena helped or hindered the performance of this educational duty. Thomas, who was arguing for far-reaching measures to abolish forced labour, saw the ILO's role as 'lift[ing] the chains that still bind the native so as to prepare him for the next educative step',[19] a position that was widely supported by the workers' group within the ILO. Among the colonial powers, however, only Great Britain supported the immediate abolition of forced labour for private purposes. In contrast, the French, Belgian, Dutch, Portuguese and South African delegations were critical of the distinction between forced labour for public purposes and forced labour for private interests, which both seemed acceptable to them, at least for a transitional period.[20]

The Forced Labour Convention of 1930 called for the abolition of forced labour 'in all its forms' and only permitted transitional periods with regard to work performed for 'public purposes'.[21] However, provisions that laid down what was *not* to be deemed forced or compulsory labour (among them military service and forced labour as a consequence of a court conviction) provided loopholes for the colonial signatories. The conventions also exempted any work or service forming part of the 'normal civic obligations of citizens', as well as 'minor communal services'. This offered further opportunities to make exceptions for certain coercive practices widely

---

[18] In addition to the 1930 Forced Labour Convention, ILO instruments dealing with recruitment practices (Recruiting of Indigenous Workers' Convention, 1936 (No. 50)) and working contracts (Contracts of Employment (Indigenous Workers) Convention, 1939 (No. 64)) tackled the problem of long-term contracts, the latter mostly aiming at widespread systems of indentured labour.

[19] Quoted in Daniel Roger Maul, *Human Rights, Development and Decolonization: The International Labour Organization, 1940–70* (Basingstoke and Geneva: Palgrave Macmillan and ILO, 2012), 24.

[20] For a summary of this discussion, see Maul, 'The ILO and the Struggle against Forced Labour', 480–5; see also Alcock, *History of the ILO*, 81–93.

[21] Forced Labour Convention, 1930 (No. 29).

used in colonial Africa.[22] Notwithstanding their indisputable humanitarian achievements, the ILO conventions of the 1930s dealing with forced labour underlined that Africa and other parts of the colonial world were still deemed an area where a set of rules applied that was different from the realm of regular international labour standards.

Parallel to this normative effort to tackle forced labour, the world economic crisis and the social and political turmoil it had caused triggered an opening for new, more comprehensive ways of thinking about social problems in the colonial territories, in the ILO as well as in the official colonial mind. In particular, those parts of the colonial world that had – under the premises of *mise en valeur* – expanded their export-oriented sectors after the First World War faced social turbulence in the latter part of the 1930s. A series of strikes affecting strategically important functions of the colonial economy broke out, not only in the British Caribbean but also, for example, in Northern Rhodesia in 1935, in the ports of Mombasa (Kenya) and Dar es Salaam (Tanganyika), and among railway workers in the Gold Coast (Ghana) in 1939. Taken together, they became the impetus for the British Colonial Development and Welfare Act (CDWA) of 1940, which first embraced an active colonial development policy and an unprecedented admission of financial responsibility for the welfare of the people of the Empire.[23] This new course of action relied on a series of official reports that had related the social and political instability in the colonies to the lack of colonial social policy (and restrictions on the right to organize in trade unions).[24] Furthermore, the development of trade unions in the colonies now became a goal of British colonial policy, in the hope of 'taming' the colonial workforce by creating a predictable and thus controllable negotiating power. Signs that a new perspective on social issues was beginning to open up, and above all indications of the willingness to commit financial resources to the colonies, were also visible in the policies of other colonial powers. The French Popular Front Government (1936–38) broke with the utilitarian policy of *mise en valeur* and espoused instead the altruistic development of the colonies by the French state, although a lack of time and insurmountable

[22]   Despite the far-reaching concessions that all parts of the NLC made to the wishes of the colonial powers, very few, apart from Britain, were prepared to ratify the documents until the early 1950s. See K. K. Norsky, *The Influence of the International Labour Organization on Principles of Social Policy in Non-Metropolitan Territories* (Oxford: Oxford University Press, 1951), 88–103.

[23]   See Frederick Cooper, *Decolonization and African Society: The Labor Question in French and British Africa* (Cambridge, MA: Harvard University Press, 1996), 58–65.

[24]   For example, Malcolm W. (Lord) Hailey, *An African Survey* (London: Oxford University Press, 1938).

institutional resistance within the colonies prevented this policy from ever getting far beyond the drawing board.[25]

The ILO's Native Labour Section tried for most of the 1930s to sustain this official change of mind with its own activities. While its initial task was mainly to support the struggle against forced labour, it increasingly collected data and produced surveys on African social affairs in order to support the reform of colonial social policy. Taken together, and although modest in scale and thoroughly paternalistic in outlook, these initiatives would prove to be a platform which enabled the ILO soon afterwards to become a driving force behind a change of attitude and action vis-à-vis the social problems of colonial territories in Africa and elsewhere.[26]

A PEOPLE'S PEACE FOR THE COLONIES: THE ILO AND AFRICA DURING THE SECOND WORLD WAR

The Second World War worked as a catalyst for this new thinking. In its hallmark Declaration of Philadelphia (1944), the ILO, on the side of the Allied powers, claimed a comprehensive role in social and economic post-war planning based on the idea of universal social rights. Parallel to the Declaration of Philadelphia, the ILO promoted a programme of colonial reform under the programmatic title of 'social policy in dependent territories'. This programme became the basis for a series of recommendations and conventions to be adopted between 1944 and 1948, which committed the colonial powers to developing their territories in line with a broad social objective. These instruments, adopted by International Labour Conferences in the immediate post-war period, reflected the growing influence of colonial reformist development thinking on the official mind. The majority of the colonial powers also saw the propaganda value such a commitment would have, both vis-à-vis their critical American allies and the colonial populations.

From its exile in Montreal, where the Organization had moved its headquarters after the German invasion of France in May 1940, the ILO had done its part to moderate discussions and synthesize colonial reform initiatives. The provisional head of the Native Labour Section, Wilfrid Benson, had spent the first years of the war in London, where he had entertained close relationships with British colonial reformers as well as with the colonial governments-in-exile of Belgium, the Netherlands

---

[25] Cooper, *Decolonization and African Society*, 73–107.

[26] International Labour Office, *Social Policy in Dependent Territories*, 32–42.

and the Free French. Towards the end of the war, when an Allied victory seemed imminent, he came up with a blueprint for a post-war social reform programme for the colonial territories.

Benson's considerations culminated in the publication of a programmatic article entitled 'A People's Peace in the Colonies', published in the *International Labour Review* in February 1943.[27] The article had significant diplomatic motives. Benson's programme was firmly connected to colonial reform initiatives that rested on the dual experience of the colonial powers' wide-scale defeat in South-East Asia by the Japanese and the parallel mobilization of colonial resources for the war effort, in particular in Africa. But it was also not by coincidence that Benson connected his considerations on colonial social policies to the general promise by the British Minister of Labour, Ernest Bevin, of a 'people's peace' that would be the necessary outcome of a 'people's war' being fought on a global scale and that would bring greater welfare and a more just post-war order for all. Benson built on the universalistic discourse established by the Atlantic Charter and Roosevelt's Four Freedoms speech.[28] From the perspective of the ILO, the colonial reform programme was part of a wider 'parallel operation' in which the colonial world would become part of an overall global programme of social reform based on the idea of universal social rights. Benson's suggestions for a 'people's peace in the colonies' rested on the idea of a future order built on four programmatic pillars: 1) the subordination of all colonial policy to a superordinate social objective; 2) a move away from the laissez-faire of the pre-war period to a commitment on the part of the colonial state to active economic and social development; 3) the safeguarding of the indigenous populations' participation, first and foremost through the promotion of trade unions, as a contribution to social development 'from the ground up'; and 4) the increased 'internationalization' of colonial social policy, with a mandate for the ILO for the development of a global social policy. Benson argued that justice and worldwide economic and military security could only be achieved if the war brought a 'people's peace' also for people under colonial rule.

According to 'A People's Peace in the Colonies', all future policy would have to be subordinated to an overriding social objective. The colonial state needed to become 'the most active agency for promoting social welfare'.[29]

---

[27] Wilfrid Benson, 'A People's Peace in the Colonies', *International Labour Review*, 47.2 (1943), 141–68.

[28] Townsend Hoopes and Douglas Brinkley, *FDR and the Creation of the U.N.* (New Haven, CT: Yale University Press, 1997).

[29] *Ibid.*, 155.

There were humanitarian and economic justifications for such policies, since they would help to improve the livelihoods of colonial people by raising their living standards and thus ultimately the productivity of their work. Emphasis, however, was put once again on the positive effect that social policy measures would have on the maintenance of order and control in the colonies.[30] In the same context, Benson's article once more suggested promoting trade unions and other forms of democratic representation of interests and integrating more indigenous representatives into the institutions of reconstruction.[31]

A good part of this programme eventually ended up in the guidelines for a new colonial social policy enshrined in the programmatic Recommendation on Social Policy in Dependent Territories adopted by the International Labour Conference in Philadelphia in 1944.[32] Its adoption against the background of the famous Declaration of Philadelphia, by which the ILO claimed to assume a leading part in the construction of the new global post-war order, gave additional weight to the document. It linked the debate on colonial reforms to the more general debate on the coordination of economic and social policy, the use of socio-economic planning and the increased interventionist role of the state in general.[33]

While the ILO thus drew the colonial world closely into a discourse about social rights, the concrete programme of colonial reform never became fully integrated in the overall programme of the Declaration of Philadelphia. At a closer look, it rather reflected ideas of a gradual and qualified universalism. The colonial powers, for instance, successfully resisted the full application of the International Labour Code in the colonies. They did so mainly for two reasons: first, applying schemes of social security wholesale to the colonies – in other words, building the colonial welfare state in parallel with European post-war reforms – was regarded as far too costly; secondly, there were political reasons, which became evident in the area of trade union freedoms. Here, the attitude of the colonial powers was particularly ambivalent.[34] Although trade unions were encouraged, both the colonial bureaucracies and the officials on the ground did their utmost to limit union activities to such an extent that they could not grow into a political threat. As a result, even after

---

[30] *Ibid.*, 167.

[31] *Ibid.*, 161.

[32] Social Policy in Dependent Territories Recommendation, 1944 (No. 70).

[33] Benson, 'A People's Peace'.

[34] See the chapter by Scully and Jawad in this volume.

the Second World War, the remaining colonies continued to represent a world apart, or, in other words, a sphere to which less stringent rules applied.[35]

THE BUMPY ROAD TO LAGOS, 1945–60

From the early post-war period onwards the ILO's centre of gravity began to shift away from Europe to those regions of the globe that were increasingly labelled as 'underdeveloped' or 'developing'. From 1948 onwards, under a new Director-General, the American David A. Morse, the ILO, which had joined the United Nations in 1946, reinvented itself as one of the UN's agencies to provide technical assistance programmes to underdeveloped countries.[36] In the first decade under Morse, technical assistance attained the role of a second pillar of the Organization, next to the ILO's classic standard-setting activities. However, while the ILO began vigorously to reach out to Asia, Latin America and the Middle East with its vocational training and other programmes, sub-Saharan Africa remained somewhat beneath the radar of its technical services (and standard-setting activities) for almost another decade.[37]

In fact, nowhere did the ILO face more barriers to entering the scene than in Africa. The main reason could once again be found in the colonial powers' dedication to heading off any further 'internationalization' of colonial policy and the increased accountability they feared it would bring – especially in light of the growing strength of independence movements in the colonies. The forum which the United Nations offered at the same time to critics of colonialism, such as the newly independent India, only served to reinforce the colonial powers' sensitivity to 'interference' by international organizations.[38]

Not that the colonial powers were opposed to developing their possessions socially and economically. Colonial economic and social policy in post-1945 Africa started partly with ambitious schemes designed to make the colonial territories more productive and ultimately enable them to play a significant part in the reconstruction of war-torn European economies and

[35] Maul, *Human Rights, Development and Decolonization*, 59–118.

[36] Sunil Amrith and Glenda Sluga, 'New Histories of the United Nations', *Journal of World History*, 19.3 (2008), 251–74.

[37] Daniel Roger Maul, 'The ILO, Asia and the Beginnings of Technical Assistance', in *The ILO from Geneva to the Pacific Rim: West Meets East*, ed. Jill M. Jensen and Nelson Lichtenstein (Basingstoke and Geneva: Palgrave Macmillan and ILO, 2015), 110–33.

[38] Roland Burke, *Decolonization and the Evolution of International Human Rights* (Philadelphia, PA: University of Pennsylvania Press, 2010).

the construction of the welfare state at home. Such was the rationale behind the often-cited 'second colonial occupation' of Africa after 1945.[39] However, French and British colonial politicians, who had started with ambitious schemes of social and economic development after 1945, came around very quickly to more sober calculations in the face of failed expectations, political unrest and growing demands by fledgling trade unions and nationalist leaders. Welfare colonialism soon reached its limits.[40] The more Africans, against this background, began to turn the language of human rights and social reform – provided by the Declaration of Philadelphia and the ILO's colonial conventions – into social and political claims, the more hesitant the colonial powers grew to tolerate any international organization's 'meddling'.[41] Instead, they started to build up alternative bodies of inter-colonial cooperation among themselves, such as the Commission for Technical Co-operation in Africa South of the Sahara (CCTA), to prevent the 'internationalization' of colonial social policy. As a result, the ILO found itself banging on closed doors for the major part of the 1950s.

THE DEBATE ABOUT AN ILO AFRICAN FIELD OFFICE

The degree of resistance was illustrated particularly well by the long history of the ILO's attempts to establish a field office in sub-Saharan Africa. As early as 1951 the ILO had started to promote the idea of setting up a field office which, like those already existing in Asia, Latin America and the Middle East, would be used mainly to coordinate technical assistance programmes on the African continent. The idea was not met with much enthusiasm from the colonial powers. The British Colonial Office asked the ILO to proceed 'very carefully'.[42] While Britain pleaded for a firm but diplomatic approach, the other CCTA powers were more categorical in their rejection of the ILO's

---

[39] On the theory of the 'second colonial occupation of Africa', see J. Hargreaves, 'Toward the Transfer of Power in British West Africa', in *The Transfer of Power in Africa: Decolonization 1940–1960*, ed. Prosser Gifford and W. Roger Louis (New Haven, CT: Yale University Press, 1982), 131ff.

[40] See the chapter by Scully and Jawad in this volume.

[41] Cooper, *Decolonization and African Society*; Andreas Eckert, 'Exportschlager Wohlfahrtsstaat? Europäische Sozialstaatlichkeit und Kolonialismus in Afrika nach dem Zweiten Weltkrieg', *Geschichte und Gesellschaft*, 32.4 (2006), 467–88.

[42] Watson (MOL) to Gavin, 19 January 1952, in Archives of the International Labour Organization, Geneva (ILOA), ILOA-NL 1002: Second Session of the Committee of Experts on Social Policy in Non-Metropolitan Territories 1951.

plans.[43] The hostility towards 'interference' by the ILO was so strong that it led on occasion to serious tensions among the colonial powers themselves.[44] In 1953, for instance, the British were reproached bitterly by the French for permitting an ILO mission to West Africa to investigate, among other things, industrial relations and union freedoms.[45] When the ILO took first stock at the end of 1953, it found that 'in no case has there been the slightest indication that any of them [Britain, France, Belgium] would give any support to the idea of establishing an ILO field office in Africa'.[46]

This first setback was met with a new set of diplomatic activities. The ILO tried, for example, to use the imminent accession of the Soviet Union to membership in the Organization (due in 1954), and thus the prospect of another strong anti-colonial voice among its members, as an argument to convince the colonial powers to make concessions.[47] In the end, it was the workers' group within the ILO's Governing Body that opened the discussion again. At a meeting on colonial policy which the ILO organized in Lisbon at the end of 1953, the representatives of the Western-oriented International Confederation of Free Trade Unions (ICFTU) caused a stir by lodging an open protest against the ILO's lack of involvement on the African continent.[48] To prevent the ILO from being put in an embarrassing position again, Wilfred Jenks, the Assistant Director-General of the ILO, travelled to London, Paris and Brussels to campaign among colonial politicians for an agreement concerning the ILO's future policy on Africa. Cautiously, in these

---

[43] While the French reacted sceptically, the Belgians, Portuguese, Rhodesians and, above all, the South African government simply would not hear of any direct involvement in Africa by international organizations in general. Lee (Dept. of Labour, South Africa) to Martin, Colonial Office, UK (CO), 21 March 1952, in Public Record Office, National Archives, London (PRO), PRO-CO 859/364: Activities of the ILO Committee of Experts on Minimum Standards of Social Policy in Non-Metropolitan Territories 1952.

[44] Watson to Tennant, Ministry of Labour, UK (MOL), 25 February 1953, in PRO-CO 859/367: International Labour Organization, Committee of Experts on Social Policy in Non-Metropolitan Territories, 3rd Session, Lisbon 4–19 December 1953.

[45] *Ibid.*

[46] Gavin to David A. Morse, 21 November 1952, in Archives of the International Labour Organization, Geneva, Morse Files (ILOA-MF) Z 11: Africa General.

[47] When, for instance, Wilfred Jenks, the ILO Assistant Director-General, met the Portuguese dictator António Salazar on the fringes of the meeting on Colonial Social Policy in Lisbon at the end of 1953, he tried to convince Salazar of the benefits of a 'positive policy of international action'. In practical terms, the results of this and other initiatives remained meagre. Jenks to Morse, 23 December 1953, in: ILOA-MF Z 1/1/1/13: Mr. Jenks – Africa.

[48] *Ibid.*

talks Jenks tried to make clear that an agreement of this nature, which he argued would be in the colonial powers' own best interests with a view to avoiding future conflicts, could not be reached 'unless the metropolitan powers felt able to make a substantial contribution towards securing it by offering a positive programme'.[49]

The next year, 1955, marked a change in the ILO's Africa policy. In the run-up to another expert meeting on colonial social policy, which took place at the end of the year in Dakar (then in French West Africa), the ICFTU, which represented most of the members of the ILO's workers' group, took the initiative. It demanded that the Committee of Experts on Social Policy in Non-Metropolitan Territories (COESP), the main ILO body dealing with colonial social policy since the immediate post-Second World-War period, be transformed into a representative African equivalent of the tripartite Asian Advisory Committee (AAC) that had been set up at the beginning of the 1950s.[50] This was an ingenious proposal, as such an African Advisory Committee would incorporate under the same auspices both the African colonial territories and the independent states of the region, and thus, in a roundabout way, effectively integrate the colonies formally into the Organization. The second demand brought the idea of an African field office back on to the agenda.[51] The ILO leadership was uneasy about these initiatives, and Morse complained on more than one occasion about the lack of understanding shown by the critics of the Organization's apparently soft approach to colonialism. 'The ILO', he stated, 'cannot deal with African issues like a pressure group. It cannot overreach the realities of the political situation.'[52] On the other hand, the ILO did try to capitalize on the accusations against it and the prospects of its workers' group becoming 'increasingly restless and liable at any time to suggest far-reaching proposals'.

---

[49] Jenks to Morse, 24 January 1954, in *ibid*.

[50] Among the factors behind this demand were the disputes within the ICFTU regarding its position on colonial issues in Africa. The American trade union federation, the AFL-CIO, believed that the ICFTU, and the British Trades Union Congress in particular, were not doing enough to actively counter the presumably growing influence of the Soviet Union in Africa. Anthony Carew, 'Conflict within the ICFTU: Anti-Colonialism and Anti-Communism in the 1950', *International Review of Social History*, 41.2 (1996), 147–81. For a more in-depth treatment, written mostly from the American perspective, see the biography of the Afro-American trade unionist and civil rights activist Maida Springer: Yvette Richards, *Maida Springer: Pan-Africanist and International Labor Leader* (Pittsburgh, PA: University of Pittsburgh Press, 2000).

[51] Governing Body (GB) 131 (1956), 41.

[52] Cabinet meeting 12 January 1956, in ILOA-MF Z8/1/32: Meetings of the Director-General, Notes, Minutes, 1951–1957.

If the colonial powers wanted to avoid Africa turning into the 'sport of political forces', Wilfred Jenks admonished them, they would have to take on a more conciliatory position.[53]

The increased pressure from the international trade union movement was not the only factor behind this change. More significant was the fact that, in the early years of the decade, the very foundations of colonial rule had started to crumble in Africa. Against the backdrop of conflict and outright war, the French North African protectorates of Morocco and Tunisia attained independence around the middle of the decade. At about the same time, the British grudgingly initiated a transfer of power in sub-Saharan Africa, where Ghana would become the first country to gain independence, with Nigeria following soon after.[54]

These developments not only provided further inspiration for nationalist movements in the remaining colonies, they also opened up opportunities for the newly independent African and Asian states in international fora. The Bandung Conference of African and Asian States in 1955 was only one among many occasions on which this new voice could be heard. With independence looming across the continent, the Pan-African movement intensified its anti-colonial agitation, and countries such as India and Egypt were ready to lend their voices in international fora to those who had still no representation. As the Afro-Asian bloc grew in numbers, so did the demand it raised within the ILO and all the other parts of the UN system for an outright end to colonial rule. The new strength of this group of states, and the ammunition they got from ongoing colonial conflicts in Kenya and Algeria, inevitably affected the colonial powers' approach to colonial questions.[55]

In parallel, the debates that surrounded the adoption of some of the ILO's human rights standards during the 1950s offered yet another chance for the Afro-Asian countries to put the colonial powers in the dock. The Abolition of Penal Sanctions (Indigenous Workers) Convention, 1955

---

[53] The minutes of the meetings of 19 June 1956 and 26 June 1956 are recorded by the Office in ILOA-MF Z 11: Africa General, and in Public Record Office, Ministry of Labor, UK (PRO-LAB) 13/984: ILO and Africa 1955–1957.

[54] On the complex interplay of metropolitan, colonial and international factors, which accelerated the political decolonization process in the mid-1950s, see W. David McIntyre, *British Decolonization, 1946–1997: When, Why and How Did the British Empire Fall?* (Basingstoke: Palgrave Macmillan, 1998), 79–101; Raymond F. Betts, *France and Decolonisation, 1900–1960* (Basingstoke: Palgrave Macmillan, 1991), 78–114.

[55] The thought-provoking view on the alliances within the postcolonial world under the banner of Afro-Asian or 'Third World' solidarity is taken from Vijay Prashad, *The Darker Nations: A People's History of the Third World* (New York: The New Press, 2007).

(No. 104), was a case in point, since it shed some light on the survival, in some places, of 'old-style' colonial labour regimes that distinguished between different spheres of law for Europeans and indigenous labourers by selectively using penal sanctions for breach of labour contracts against the latter. In this case, but even more so with regard to the Abolition of Forced Labour Convention, 1957 (No. 105), and the Discrimination (Employment and Occupation) Convention, 1958 (No. 111), the debates gained additional momentum precisely because Cold War and anti-colonial discourses became inseparably intertwined. While the Soviet Union and the United States saw themselves under attack in the debates surrounding the conventions on forced labour and racial discrimination, respectively, the Afro-Asian countries seized the opportunity to shed light on the continued abuses of colonial labour in both fields.[56]

At the International Labour Conference in 1956, this background music blended in with the ongoing debates on the ILO's position in Africa. What was most worrying for the colonial powers was the fact that US government representatives joined the ranks of those who asked them to stop obstructing plans for an ILO African field office.[57] The debates made the ILO realize that it would now have to give up its previous caution, as any further delay could do severe damage to the ILO and its future position in Africa. A meeting of the ICFTU in the Ghanaian capital Accra in January 1957, marked again by harsh anti-colonial criticism, provided further impetus for the ILO to take action. The ICFTU condemned the CCTA in no uncertain terms and demanded that the colonial powers in Africa open up to international organizations. It renewed calls for the establishment of an ILO field office in Africa as soon as possible and asked for speedy preparations for a Regional Conference.[58] Shortly thereafter, a British Colonial Office memorandum spoke in entirely new tones of the ILO, lauded its technical work as 'first-rate' and proposed no longer to 'insulate our dependent territories from the Organization'.[59]

Similar developments were observed with regard to the creation of a tripartite African Advisory Committee (AFAC) on the model of the one already in place in Asia. After having fought such an idea for many years, the

---

[56] For a broader UN context, see Daniel Roger Maul, 'International Organizations and Globalization of Human Rights', in *Human Rights in the Twentieth Century: A Critical History*, ed. Stefan-Ludwig Hoffmann (New York: Cambridge University Press, 2011), 301–20.

[57] ILC 40 (1957), Record of Proceedings (RoP), 235–6.

[58] Carew, 'Conflict within the ICFTU', 162.

[59] Memorandum from the CO (anon.), 'The ILO and Africa', 22 January 1957, in PRO-LAB 13/984: ILO and Africa 1954–1957.

British now came around to the opinion that such a committee could well serve as a 'safety valve for the expression of African hopes and aspirations'.[60] In the course of 1957, most of the other CCTA powers also changed their attitude and aligned their positions accordingly. The increasing interest in African issues which the Soviet Union was displaying in international fora might have been a decisive factor for this change of mind. The colonial powers saw the danger that, if they remained inflexible, the communist-dominated World Federation of Trade Unions (WFTU) might get a hold on the fledgling trade union movement in Africa. Eventually, the question of an African field office came up again. Something resembling a contest broke out among the colonial powers over where this office should be located. Both the British and the French made it clear to Morse that they would like to see it situated in one of their territories. Even Brussels declared its desire to play host in the Belgian Congo.[61] The Portuguese had no particular intentions in this respect but were by no means dismissive either, and even issued an invitation for the first meeting of the AFAC to be held on Portuguese territory in Africa.[62]

Morse's final choice of location for the field office was Lagos, Nigeria, where it took up its work in January 1959.[63] This choice was motivated by the fact that Nigeria was shortly to become independent and its leaders, unlike those of the alternative location, Ghana, displayed no ambitions to spearhead the anti-colonial movement. Establishing the office in Ghana may, in this light, have led to a re-politicizing of the issue of the ILO's involvement in Africa, which was the last thing it wanted.[64]

---

[60] *Ibid.*

[61] Jenks's notes on the meeting about Morse's trip to Brussels with the ministers Troclet Fafchamps, Auguste Buisseret (colonies), 14 January 1958 (Note 16/1), in *ibid.*

[62] Jef Rens's notes on the meeting with the Portuguese foreign minister Paula Cunha and the colonial minister Ventura, 5 February 1958 (trip 1–4.2.), in *ibid.*

[63] Morse's note to George Tobias informing the US government about the Office's African plans, 21 August 1958, in National Archives, Washington, DC (NA) – RG 174.5 (Bureau of International Labor Affairs), B 20: General Correspondence, 1953–1967.

[64] It should be noted that ILO officials had engaged nationalists in colonial Gold Coast and Nigeria before their independence in 1957 and 1960, respectively. Undoubtedly, it successfully persuaded most labour leaders to eschew a leftist ideology for the Western model tagged 'sound industrial relations'. See Hakeem Ibikunle Tijani, 'McCarthyism in Colonial Nigeria: The Ban on the Employment of Communists', in *The Foundations of Nigeria: Essays in Honor of Toyin Falola*, ed. Adebayo Oyebade (Trenton, NJ: Africa World Press, 2003), 647–68; Hakeem Ibikunle Tijani, 'Building

In August 1958 Morse announced his decision on the office's location to the governments. The same year that the ILO opened its office, the AFAC held its first meeting in the Angolan capital, Luanda, and preparations began for the first African Regional Conference, to be held as soon as logistically possible. On a long trip to Africa in 1959, Wilfred Jenks noted with satisfaction that the ILO's expansion into Africa now had the wide support of all the main powers represented on the continent.[65]

FROM THE COESP TO THE AFRICAN ADVISORY COMMITTEE

While the ILO struggled hard on the diplomatic level to get a foothold in Africa during the 1950s, there were constant claims for the ILO's competence in social affairs on the continent, mostly through the so-called Committee of Experts on Social Policy in Non-Metropolitan Territories (COESP). Founded in 1947, its mandate included all remaining colonial ('non-metropolitan' in the UN nomenclature) territories, most of which happened to be located in Africa. The COESP met four times between 1951 and 1957. Until the new African Advisory Committee eventually took up its work in 1959, these gatherings – along with the meetings of the Governing Body which discussed the COESP's reports – were the only regular occasions at which late colonial social policy was addressed at all within the ILO. During this period, the COESP remained the lone 'colonial voice' of the ILO. This gave its findings a particular significance. The COESP looked into a broad variety of subjects, ranging from the regulation of migratory labour to the introduction of initial schemes of social security in the colonial territories, and it issued recommendations for the colonial powers which served as a guideline for their policies.[66]

The composition of the COESP was – very much like the opening of the African field office – a highly politicized question and the result of a hard-fought battle between the various political forces in the Governing Body, which had a final say on the nominations. In order to secure the colonial powers' commitment to the work of the ILO, its members had to be appointed in close collaboration with these powers themselves. As a result,

"Sound" Industrial Relations in Nigeria: The British and Organised Labour, 1940s to 1960', *Lagos Historical Review*, 11 (2011), 21–36.

[65] Report by Jenks, 29 April 1959, in ILOA-MF – Z 1/1/1/13: Report on Mr Jenks Mission to Africa, Dec. 1958–Feb. 1959.

[66] The first preliminary and the first official meetings took place in 1947 and 1951, respectively, in Geneva, followed by Lisbon in 1953, Dakar in 1955 and Geneva again in 1957.

in many ways the face of the Committee strikingly resembled its predecessor from the interwar years. It was predominantly white, and the great majority of its members came from the metropolitan/administrative side.[67] Against the background of a growing anti-colonial mood, heated discussions on the composition of the Committee took place, and the colonial powers resisted repeated demands by India and other non-European countries on the Governing Body for more 'colonial' African and Asian experts to be appointed. As early as 1947, when the composition of the COESP was first discussed, the workers' group on the Governing Body joined the ranks of those who criticized its colonial bias.[68]

The ILO, in the meantime, did its best to shift the focus of the COESP's work to the treatment of specifically African problems. The colonial powers were reluctant to change the orientation of the Committee, precisely because they wanted to prevent the COESP from functioning as a substitute for the lack of regional ILO structures in Africa. The colonial work of the Office itself had been almost exclusively directed at Africa since the beginning of the 1950s. Via the topics selected for discussion and the formulation of the problems to be solved, the ILO attempted to insert this internal focus in the proceedings of the COESP. By 1955, when it met in Dakar, the Committee's transformation into a body concerned more with African problems than with colonial problems in general was complete. At this point, almost all the resources of the Non-Metropolitan Territories Division, which had assumed the work of the Native Labour Section after the war, were being taken up by a large-scale 'African Labour Survey'. The COESP's task in its last session was, in fact, simply to evaluate this (900-page) report, which looked at every

---

[67] Of the twelve members of the COESP in 1951, nine were colonial administrators and three were academics. In Lisbon, in 1953, eight of ten members were administrators. In 1955, in Dakar, the Committee was again dominated by administrative figures, apart from the employers' and workers' representatives appointed specifically for the purpose. Of the twelve members present, nine were involved in colonial administration. GB 118 (1952), RoP, App. III: Report of the Second Session of the Committee of Experts on Social Policy in Non-Metropolitan Territories, 71; GB 124 (1954), RoP, App. V: Report of the Third Session of the Committee of Experts on Social Policy in Non-Metropolitan Territories, 77; GB 131 (1956), RoP, App. XIV: Report of the Fourth Session of the Committee of Experts on Social Policy in Non-Metropolitan Territories, 147; GB 138 (1958), RoP, App. III: Report of the Fifth Session of the Committee of Experts on Social Policy in Non-Metropolitan Territories, 70.

[68] The political considerations that came into play are summarized in a letter from Robert Gavin to Wilfred Jenks, 18 December 1950, in ILO-NL 1001 – Committee of Experts on Social Policy in Dependent Territories, 1944–1954.

aspect of labour and social policy in Africa.[69] The presentation of this survey in 1957 reinforced the ILO's interest in the African continent at a time when it still found itself confronted with closed doors on the ground.

What was striking about the majority of the Committee's findings on colonial (i.e. African) social policy was the universalistic consensus they expressed. Evidently, the framework which the ILO had laid down in this respect in its colonial reform opus of the mid-1940s had been accepted and now served as a guideline for evaluating colonial social policy. More than anything, this meant that no one – apart from outsiders such as South Africa – now argued in terms of the otherness of colonial populations or of 'native' labour. It was a generally recognized premise of colonial social policy that, with the right set of measures in place, colonial populations were able to become universal workers who could be fully integrated into the development process. The break with the particularism of the pre-war period was visible in a whole series of COESP recommendations, and nowhere more so than in the revision of the migrant labour issue.[70] It had a great symbolic value and significance, since it separated those who defended systems of migrant labour along a racial or culturalist rationale and those in favour of a stabilization of the labour force in the workplace, a position that came with ideas of basic social security, trade union rights and family wages. The Committee on more than one occasion came out, with South Africa as the sole dissenting voice, in favour of stabilization.[71] Accordingly, the COESP's findings also embraced the concept of the family wage. A passage on wage policy in the report of the Dakar meeting in 1955 found that workers in the colonies needed to earn wages that were 'sufficient to support stabilised family life without the need for assistance from outside sources away from the place of employment, such as distant land holdings'.[72] This was a clear sign that, in the view of the experts, the solution to the social problems of colonial Africa or elsewhere was no longer to be sought in the conservation of the colonial populations' 'traditional' ways of life and work.

The universalistic tenor of the COESP's findings was not entirely free from overtones of doubt, however. The majority of the experts were sceptical, for example, about whether methods to increase productivity, which had proved their worth in the developed world, would always be

---

[69] International Labour Office, *African Labour Survey* (Geneva: ILO, 1958).

[70] See the chapter by Pérez Niño in this volume.

[71] GB 118 (1952), RoP, App. III: Report of the Second Session of the Committee of Experts on Social Policy in Non-Metropolitan Territories, 69 *et seq.*

[72] GB 131 (1956), RoP, App. XIV: Report of the Fourth Session of the Committee of Experts on Social Policy in Non-Metropolitan Territories, 145.

suitable for Africa. They believed there were 'special factors affecting productivity in Africa, due perhaps to climate, human traditions or attitudes, which might tend to limit the successful application of new methods to Africa'.[73] There were also disagreements within the Committee on whether forcibly promoting an industrial, urban way of life was always the best way forward.[74] In the discussions surrounding the wage issue, for example, some of the experts warned of the undesirable results of a wage policy that made influx into industrial centres too attractive. They argued that this in turn could have devastating effects on the economic structures in the colonies. In territories where most of the inhabitants lived in subsistence-economic conditions and worked mainly in agriculture, a mass departure to the modern sectors of the economy would probably destroy rural areas. Equally, a wage policy that promoted urbanization would contribute to 'detribalization', which would necessarily be accompanied by the 'disintegration of the family and the social structure'.[75] 'Particular conditions' in Africa repeatedly invoked were the backwardness of the continent and the 'magnitude of the problems to be treated'.[76]

In the view of the experts, the stage of development Africa had reached, or not reached, also called for restrictions of the universalistic model on issues such as trade union freedoms.[77] When the debate turned to industrial relations in 1955, the majority of the Committee's members were convinced that the level of development in Africa and the embryonic stage of most of the African trade unions would, at best, permit only a gradual application of ILO standards. The COESP was therefore willing to tolerate extensive interference by the colonial powers in union freedoms, as long as this served the long-term goal of creating independent organizations and institutionalizing structures of collective bargaining.[78]

ILO officials tended, through their reactions to the discussions of the COESP, to cement the qualified universalism of the Committee's findings. The main concern of ILO officials was to gain legitimacy for the Organization's colonial activities through the Committee's work. They

---

[73] GB 124 (1954), RoP, App. V: Report of the Third Session of the Committee of Experts on Social Policy in Non-Metropolitan Territories, 81.

[74] On labour in industry, see the chapter by Neveling in this volume.

[75] GB 131 (1956), RoP, App. XIV: Report of the Fourth Session of the Committee of Experts on Social Policy in Non-Metropolitan Territories, 152.

[76] *Ibid.*

[77] See the chapter by Freund in this volume.

[78] GB 131 (1956), RoP, App. XIV: Report of the Fourth Session of the Committee of Experts on Social Policy in Non-Metropolitan Territories, 151f.

accordingly tried to smooth out existing tensions in the Committee and uphold an image of unity. This could mean, as a UN observer noted in Lisbon in 1953, that ILO officials tried frantically behind the scenes to shield the South African representative from attacks launched by the Committee itself and by observers who had been sent by the trade union movement.[79] It also meant that politically explosive issues, such as racial discrimination or workers' rights, which the members of the COESP argued about heatedly while discussing more technical problems such as vocational training, workers' housing and productivity, were not mentioned in the summaries of the COESP's results. The Office tried, in these summaries, to cover up the controversial points and to mask differences of opinion inside the Committee by using vague formulations that could be viewed as a compromise. The fear of losing what little influence on the future of colonial social policy it had made the ILO very cautious in this respect.[80]

In essence, then, the ILO's colonial work in the 1950s was fully compatible with the two main objectives that the majority of colonial social policymakers were pursuing with regard to the international public. These objectives were to present colonial social policy at all times as being consistent with the international modernization discourse and, at the same time, to justify the continuation of colonial rule and the inevitable compromises with ILO principles that this implied. The findings of the COESP were conducive to both these aims. The colonial powers were able to claim that the basic consensus between the experts of the COESP was more or less identical with the dominant official thinking on colonial social policy. Not only were identical issues debated under the same universalistic premises at the meetings of the CCTA, with regard to matters of stabilization, family wages and housing, but the CCTA even came to the same conclusions as the COESP. Furthermore, Britain and France now supported the creation of trade unions in their territories and openly endorsed the ideal of good industrial relations as the basis of social progress. The emphatically anti-universalistic position of the South African representatives isolated them on virtually all issues, in the COESP and the CCTA alike.[81]

The findings of the COESP experts also legitimized the actions of the colonial powers when it came to the application of labour standards.

[79] Report Wilfrid Benson (UN) on the third meeting of the COESP, 6/1/1954, in UN Archives, New York – Registry Archive Group (RAG) 5/3.1 Department of Political Affairs, Trusteeship and Decolonization: ILO Committee on Social Policy – Lisbon 1953.

[80] See *ibid.*

[81] See Cooper, *Decolonization and African Society*, 362–9.

None of the colonial powers was prepared to bear the cost of establishing welfare systems in their territories to the extent demanded by ILO standards. Furthermore, their willingness to support trade union movements ended as soon as these movements threatened to become organizations capable of challenging the colonial administrations politically. This was just one of the points on which the universalistic rhetoric employed by the colonial powers rang particularly hollow. The vexatious experience of colonial social policymakers – that political and social movements in the colonies and critics of colonialism in international fora never missed an opportunity to demand the redemption of colonial promises and to point out the contradictions inherent in colonial rule – made them all too aware of the fundamental dilemma they faced. The same universalistic discourse that the colonial powers had subscribed to after the war in order to maintain control was now threatening to undermine, socially and politically, the foundations of colonial rule. The findings of the COESP came in particularly handy for bridging the continuing gulf between universalistic language and the dilution of this universalism that was necessary if the colonial powers wanted to maintain control.

INDEPENDENT AFRICA AND THE ILO

The gradual decolonization of African territories opened up new opportunities for the ILO to uphold its position within the emerging network of international organizations. To some extent, decolonization restored the Organization's original mandate as envisaged by Clemenceau, Wilson and Lloyd George at the Paris Peace Conference in 1919: improving working conditions throughout the world to counter the revolutionary challenge and the alternative development models offered by the Soviet-led socialist bloc to recently independent African states.[82] In this respect, the ILO assumed the same position as other UN agencies: it was supposed to become part of a growing non-coercive international political realm 'linking governments and citizens throughout the liberal world economy'.[83] Decolonization also authorized the Organization to diversify its scope of action, which would gradually move from focusing exclusively on international standard setting to the provision of advisory services to new African members. In the 1960s

---

[82] Guy Ryder, 'The International Labour Organization: The Next 100 Years', *Journal of Industrial Relations*, 57.5 (2015), 749.

[83] Craig N. Murphy and Enrico Augelli, 'International Institutions, Decolonization, and Development', *International Political Science Review*, 14.1 (1993), 80.

the ILO would appear more and more as a typical development agency committed to spreading all over the world the values enshrined in the 1964 Employment Policy Convention.[84]

At the beginning, the Organization found in Africa a new audience eager to obtain technical assistance from abroad to speed up the process of institution building and economic growth. Indeed, at its inception, UN technical assistance was welcomed by countries in the developing world as a fair and non-colonial way of development that promised enduring links between North and South on the basis of cooperation rather than exploitation.[85] In this respect, the ILO's formal detachment from the rivalries of Cold War politics made it an ideal partner for African rulers: they could rely on the advice of international experts in the preparation of national development plans and the organization of manpower through the ILO's Vocational Training and Management Development programmes, whatever the international affiliation or domestic macro-economic orientation of the country looking for advice. The ILO's technical assistance in the field of institution building and manpower training did fit well with the technocratic ethos embedded in the dominant development paradigms of the 1960s, which framed the path towards modernization as the outcome of the acritical reproduction of abstract models that could be exported all over the world, irrespective of the social and political characteristics of the country of destination.[86] Key ILO themes such as the fight against unemployment were not yet on the Organization's agenda, since there was widespread consensus that large-scale investment and capital accumulation in the so-called modern sector would gradually lead to the 'take-off' of national economies, thereby absorbing human manpower displaced from the 'traditional' sector.[87]

In spite of the end of formal colonial linkages, however, the relationship between the ILO and sub-Saharan Africa was characterized by several elements of continuity. The double standard continued to shape the Organization's attitude towards the continent, with the only difference that its advocates were no longer metropolitan governments in Europe

---

[84] Guy Standing, 'The International Labour Organization', *New Political Economy*, 15.2 (2010), 307–18.

[85] David Webster, 'Development Advisors in a Time of Cold War and Decolonization: The United Nations Technical Assistance Administration, 1950–1959', *Journal of Global History*, 6.2 (2011), 249–72.

[86] David C. Engerman and Corinna R. Unger, 'Introduction: Towards a Global History of Modernization', *Diplomatic History*, 33.3 (2009), 375–85.

[87] W. Arthur Lewis, 'Economic Development with Unlimited Supply of Labour', *The Manchester School*, 22.2 (1954), 139–91; W. W. Rostow, *The Stages of Economic Growth: A Non-Communist Manifesto* (Cambridge: Cambridge University Press, 1990).

but the new African rulers who had inherited colonial structures of control and remained heavily dependent on the consent of the former colonial powers for major domestic policy decisions. A case in point was the debate surrounding the application of the Abolition of Forced Labour Convention, adopted in 1957: a topic that resurfaced again at the height of the ILO's agenda in correspondence with the restructuring of power relations within the ILO's Governing Body in favour of recently independent Asian and African countries. As a consequence, the issue of economic development and labour conditions in the 'Third World' became one of the main concerns of the Organization, which found itself trapped in the debate between those who advocated economic growth as a pre-condition for the improvement of working conditions and those who accorded priority to the protection of basic human rights. The Abolition of Forced Labour Convention was immediately ratified by the great majority of African countries, which framed forced labour as one of the most blatant examples of colonial crime. However, while local governments enthusiastically embraced the ILO's human rights regulations in the realm of free labour, they were much more reticent when it came to turning these conventions into domestic law.[88] This reticence could be explained in light of the civilizing mission that postcolonial regimes felt entrusted to implement in their attempt to address the injustices of colonialism. African leaders framed this discourse in exceptional terms, as if the fight against poverty was comparable to a state of war that authorized them to suspend ordinary laws in order to overcome the burden of underdevelopment. The underlying argument was that the liberation struggle was not over: the *locus* of conflict had simply moved from the national arena to the international stage, where African countries faced trading conditions aimed at reproducing political subordination in a more subtle but enduring form.[89] ILO officials were not of the same opinion, however, since they argued that adherence to fundamental human rights norms was an essential prerequisite on the path towards authentic long-term development.[90]

The 1962 annual report of the Committee of Experts on the Application of Conventions and Recommendations (COE) provides a clear illustration of the clash of perspectives between the ILO and African governments. The COE argued that forced labour had not disappeared, in spite of the ratification of the Abolition of Forced Labour Convention, but was

---

[88] Maul, 'The ILO and the Struggle against Forced Labour', 488.

[89] Immanuel Wallerstein, *The Politics of the World Economy: The States, the Movements, and the Civilizations* (Cambridge: Cambridge University Press, 1984); Colin Leys, *The Rise and Fall of Development Theory* (London: James Currey, 1996).

[90] Maul, 'The ILO and the Struggle against Forced Labour'.

resurfacing in new forms under the guise of compulsory labour. This statement was particularly true for West Africa, where various regimes were establishing specific programmes aimed at conscripting African youth into public development projects with the objective of pushing economic growth and creating a sense of national belonging. Many African governments reacted vehemently to this statement, arguing that their young citizens should be prepared for the extreme sacrifice of defending their nation, which not only consisted of the protection of the national territory but also of safeguarding their country's economic independence.[91] This early debate highlights how the ILO largely looked at the continent without an in-depth contextualization of the political and social struggles that were affecting newly independent African countries. To a certain degree, the COE's observations reflected the dominant understanding of Africa as an empty space that could be remodelled through the infusion of Western technologies and organizational norms. In the case of the ILO, these norms took the form of universal principles and sets of assumptions about what it considered to be ideal labour relations. The dispute about the applicability of the Abolition of Forced Labour Convention also underscores how the Organization was not universally perceived as an apolitical entity. Indeed, the ILO's idea of equalizing working conditions around the world was implicitly perceived in several circles as an attempt to freeze the existing division of labour to the advantage of industrialized countries, since it restrained African rulers' freedom to exploit the only factor of production where Africa had a comparative advantage: manpower.[92]

THE ILO AND THE RIGHT PATH TO DEVELOPMENT

The ILO's specific attention to the world of work rapidly turned it into a clearing house between the supporters of liberal macro-economic theory and Marxist critics who considered contemporary development models as attempts to reproduce Africa's economic subordination to the industrialized world. Indeed, the crisis of modernization theory that started to emerge at the end of the first 'Development Decade' authorized the ILO to assume a leadership role within the network of development agencies, with Africa at the centre stage. The Organization devoted renewed attention to the issue of rural development in sub-Saharan Africa, which had so far been marginalized

---

[91] *Ibid.*, 490.

[92] Guy Standing, 'The ILO: An Agency for Globalization?', *Development and Change*, 39.3 (2008), 357.

in official policy discourses: in 1968, two years after the World Conference on Land Reform held by the ILO in collaboration with the Food and Agriculture Organization of the United Nations, the International Labour Conference adopted a Recommendation that called on member states to improve the well-being of tenants and sharecroppers. The 1968 Recommendation was in line with the overall philosophy of the Organization, since it proposed the reproduction of the ILO's tripartite model through the establishment of ad hoc organizations with representatives of local governments, agricultural workers and landowners.[93]

Another programme that played a central role in the ILO's quest to influence the elaboration of overall development policies for sub-Saharan Africa was the World Employment Programme (WEP). The WEP was launched in 1969 by Director-General Morse, with the ambition of promoting full employment on the global stage; however, at the same time, it sanctioned a net departure from earlier assumptions on the positive link between economic development, capital-intensive projects and the presence of an unlimited supply of labour in the African countryside. Although weakened by the budgetary crisis provoked by the decision of the United States to leave the ILO in 1977, the programme was a response to the growing criticism surrounding mainstream development thinking in sub-Saharan Africa: according to its first Director, Louis Emmerij, the WEP stemmed from the consciousness that economic growth *per se* was not conducive to full employment and better working conditions, and he proposed a shift from capital to labour as the central component of the development effort.[94]

From its inception, the WEP focused on developing research programmes on employment issues and providing advice to African countries such as Chad, Burundi, Malawi, Sierra Leone and Somalia, just to cite a few. Nevertheless, it was in East Africa that the ILO largely focused its attention on finding a solution to the skyrocketing level of unemployment among the youth. The most renowned WEP mission in East Africa was without doubt the 1972 Comprehensive Mission to Kenya, because it introduced for the first time the concept of the 'informal sector' into the intellectual debate on development. Kenya was a perfect case study for the WEP, since it exemplified the contradictions of a country that had achieved rapid economic growth but also showed high levels of inequality across the population.

---

[93] Tenants and Share-croppers Recommendation, 1968 (No. 132).

[94] Ashwani Saith, 'Reflections: Louis Emmerij', *Development and Change*, 36.6 (2005), 1163–76; Paul E. Bangasser, 'The ILO and the Informal Sector: An Institutional History', International Labour Office, Employment Paper 2000/9, Geneva, 2000.

The mission did not abandon the binary map that featured in dominant understandings of the African economic landscape, but reframed it in a new fashion through the substitution of the modern/traditional dichotomy with the formal/informal one. According to its report, poverty in Kenya was the outcome of the exclusion of the large majority of the population from the modern sector of the economy, in this case refashioned as the formal sector. Another innovation lay in the fact that the ILO mission did not cast the informal sector exclusively in pejorative terms, but also highlighted how informal activities, albeit ignored and not supported by the government, were one of the main providers of employment and potentially a source of Kenya's future wealth. At the same time, however, the report reproduced conventional wisdom about development as a teleological process: informality was just a temporary step that would disappear with the creation of links between the formal and informal sector, so as to 'ensure a dynamic growth of this large segment of the Kenyan economy'.[95]

Another relative weakness of the Kenya report was that it looked at the informal sector largely as an urban phenomenon, without paying attention to the problem of unemployment and poverty alleviation in the countryside. The Ethiopian mission of 1972/73, in this respect, was another milestone in the process of the ILO's engagement with African development, since it repositioned the agricultural sector and the issue of land reform at the centre stage of macro-economic analysis. Land reform and rural development were topics that ranked first on the political agenda of imperial Ethiopia at that time.[96] For this reason, in 1970, Addis Ababa sent a request for an ILO technical assistance mission from the Jobs and Skills Programme in Africa. This demand produced some perplexity among the middle ranks in the Organization, who deemed the Ethiopian economy to be structurally different from those of its neighbours and not suitable as a basis for further WEP action on the African continent. The second request in 1972, however, found a ready audience in Wilfred Jenks, by then ILO Director-General, who was eager to maintain a close relationship with one of the most important diplomatic powers in sub-Saharan Africa.[97]

[95] International Labour Office, *Employment, Incomes and Equality: A Strategy for Increasing Productive Employment in Kenya* (Geneva: ILO, 1972), 7.

[96] Temesgen Gebeyehu, 'Land Tenure, Land Reform and the *Qalad* System in Ethiopia, 1941–1974', *Journal of Asian and African Studies*, 46.6 (2011), 567–77.

[97] Nick Bernards, 'Actors and Entanglements in Global Governance: The ILO in sub-Saharan Africa', PhD dissertation, McMaster University, Hamilton, Ontario, 2016, 124.

The conclusions of the mission showed very clearly how ILO experts were somewhat disenchanted by conventional wisdom on development as a linear path of expansion and absorption of surplus labour by the modern sector of the economy in urban centres. According to the Ethiopian mission:

> In the 1950s and 1960s it was common to view the existence of rural underemployment in LDCs as a potential reservoir for economic growth … the older view has in fact been rendered obsolete both by the rapid growth of the population in LDCs in recent years and by the labour displacing character of growth in the modern sector … The question is no longer that of drawing labour out of agriculture but rather that of finding a way to keep it in agriculture … The new interest in agricultural development as the key to economic growth is thus seen as a reaction to the disappointing employment record of import substitution growth policies.[98]

Contrary to their colleagues in Nairobi, the ILO experts in Ethiopia did not advocate the launch of a Comprehensive Employment Strategy Mission on the ground, since they were of the opinion that such a mission would merely replicate the work of the Ethiopian Planning Commission. The Ethiopian report was nonetheless interesting insofar as it revived the basic assumptions made by the ILO Kenya mission one year earlier:[99] the idea that the problem of unemployment was the result of the artificial 'modern' versus 'traditional' dichotomy that informed much of modernization theory.[100] The recommendations of the Ethiopian mission focused on the introduction of land reform and additional land taxes to finance public investments in labour-intensive sectors of the economy, moving away from the dogma of capital-intensive development projects and exchange parity with international currencies.[101]

[98] Food and Agriculture Organization Library, Report of the Exploratory Employment Policy Mission organized by the International Labour Organization and Financed by the United Nations Development Program, Employment and Unemployment in Ethiopia, Geneva, 1974, 1; for a summary of the report, see Mark Blaug, 'Employment and Unemployment in Ethiopia', *International Labour Review*, 110.2 (1974), 117–43.

[99] See Nick Bernards, 'The Global Governance of Informal Economies: The International Labour Organization in East Africa', *Third World Quarterly*, 38.8 (2017), 1831–46.

[100] S. N. Eisenstadt, 'Studies of Modernization and Sociological Theory', *History and Theory*, 13.3 (1974), 225–52; Colin Leys, 'African Economic Development in Theory and Practice', *Daedalus*, 11.2 (1982), 99–124.

[101] Bernards, 'The Global Governance of Informal Economies', 1833–4.

The relevance of the two East African missions in shaping the global debate on development became apparent in 1976, when the World Employment Conference officially introduced the 'basic needs approach' and the idea that development should pass first through the satisfaction of basic needs in terms of food, housing and education. Satisfaction of basic needs, redistribution with growth and full employment became fundamental tenets of the new development agenda, finding an enthusiastic audience at the World Bank. One of the experts who had worked on the Kenya mission in 1972, Frances Stewart, was engaged by World Bank President Robert McNamara in 1977 to elaborate a new basic needs strategy for the organization – a proof of the global relevance of the two East African missions in shaping the intellectual debate on the right way to development.[102]

THE ENTANGLEMENT BETWEEN INTERNATIONAL AND INTERNAL POLITICS

In spite of the apparent apolitical nature of the ILO's advisory role in sub-Saharan Africa, the Organization's attempt to promote abstract policy ideas and turn them into domestic regulations was often thwarted by hidden struggles within the political arena of African countries. In this respect, the relationship between the African continent and the ILO was not so different from the relationship between Africa and other bilateral donors or international organizations such as the World Bank and the International Monetary Fund: it was a history of extraversion, marked by continuous attempts on the part of local actors to turn the ILO's technical assistance into a powerful tool in the quest for state territorialization, political centralization and marginalization of local competitors.[103]

The Kenyan mission, in this regard, is a case in point of how the introduction of abstract policy ideas backed by the seal of international donors could be appropriated by local rulers to legitimize specific forms of statehood and state–society relations.[104] The Kenyan government readily appropriated the conclusions of the 1972 ILO report to legitimize itself as the guardian of the interests of informal workers: in this way, the

---

[102] Howard Stein, *Beyond the World Bank Agenda: An Institutional Approach to Development* (Chicago: University of Chicago Press, 2008), 22.

[103] Jean-Francois Bayart, 'Africa in the World: A History of Extraversion', *African Affairs*, 99 (2000), 217–67.

[104] On the relationship between labour and state, see the chapter by Britwum and Dakhli in this volume.

government in Nairobi not only presented itself as a political force that stood on the side of the poorest among the poor, but also prevented the emergence of alternative trade unions or grassroots organizations that could challenge the authority of the Kenyan state through the mobilization of marginalized urban masses. In fact, Nairobi selectively appropriated several measures advocated by the ILO and rejected others that threatened the government's grip on power, while also making use of diplomacy to discipline the ILO's officers who tried to reveal this paradox.[105] In 1975, for instance, a junior ILO research officer wrote a working paper that accused Nairobi of resisting the suggestions of the mission in order to protect the vested interests of the dominant classes in Kenyan society. In response, the Kenyan Ministry of Labour wrote a letter of complaint and obtained an official apology from the Director-General's office, which prevented the paper from being distributed further outside of the Organization's circles.[106]

Opposition to recommendations of technical assistance missions that challenged conventional wisdom or advocated reform of the status quo did not stem only from Africa, however, but could also emerge from interest groups within the ILO's tripartite structure in Geneva. This was the case with the 1973 Ethiopian mission report in the section where the ILO consultants suggested the reduction of urban wages and salaries for public servants in order to discourage in-migration from the countryside.[107] These observations were vehemently contested by the head of the Workers' Relations Department in Geneva, who was also giving voice to the concerns of the Confederation of Ethiopian Labour Unions about a draft version of the mission report that threatened the economic and social benefits achieved by Ethiopian workers in the past fifteen years.[108] In the case of both Kenya and Ethiopia, the ILO could not act as if it was a mere pressure group but had to take into account the political situation on the ground.

---

[105] Bernards, 'The Global Governance of Informal Economies', 1838.

[106] Bernards, 'Actors and Entanglements', 132–3.

[107] According to ILO consultants, 'A wage policy which reduces differentials between urban and rural income … has the advantage of reducing the attractiveness of urban residence for potential migrants.' See Food and Agriculture Organization Library, Report of the Exploratory Employment Policy Mission organized by the International Labour Organization and Financed by the United Nations Development Program, Employment and Unemployment in Ethiopia, Geneva, 1974, 28.

[108] Bernards, 'Actors and Entanglements', 124.

THE ILO AND AFRICA AT THE TURN OF THE CENTURY

The status of the ILO in sub-Saharan Africa suffered a setback in the 1980s in correspondence with the emergence of the Washington Consensus and the launch of structural adjustment programmes (SAPs) by the World Bank and the IMF. The weakness of the ILO largely lay in the fact that its historical objectives – such as the improvement of labour rights, standard setting and collective bargaining – were increasingly perceived as detrimental to economic growth, since they were believed to hinder the flexibility of the labour market called for by the new political economy of neoliberal wisdom.[109] This clash of perspectives persisted throughout most of the 1990s and emerged clearly from the conclusions of the World Bank's 1995 *World Development Report* and the ILO's 1995 *World Employment* publication.[110] The former rejected the conditional link between international trade agreements and enforcement of core workers' rights, recommending a labour relations regime characterized by decentralized negotiation to thwart the bargaining leverage of trade unions. In fact, the *World Development Report* supported the idea that growing unemployment was a by-product of inflexible labour markets and excessive workers' rights, which in turn increased labour costs for employers.[111] The *World Employment* report, on the other hand, rejected the idea of a causal relationship between labour market rigidities and labour market performance, arguing that the deterioration of the latter was also provoked by such external factors as shifts in technology, trade and investment between different regions of the world.[112]

The argument put forward by the ILO in the *World Employment* report gave voice to the concerns of many African countries that were also beneficiaries of SAPs. This clearly emerges from the conclusions of a symposium held by the ILO in Arusha in February 1993, with the participation of several African scholars, labour ministers and trade union representatives. Experts from African countries such as Kenya, Uganda, Lesotho, Nigeria and Zimbabwe argued that SAPs had often been introduced without the consultation or input of trade unions and employers'

---

[109] Leys, *Rise and Fall of Development Theory*.

[110] The World Bank, *World Development Report 1995: Workers in an Integrating World* (New York: Oxford University Press, 1995); International Labour Office, *World Employment 1995 – The ILO Report* (Geneva: ILO, 1995).

[111] On capitalists and employers, see the chapters by Austin, by Pilossof and by Berry in this volume.

[112] Jerome I. Levinson, 'A Missed Opportunity: The World Bank's World Development Report 1995: Workers in an Integrating World', International Labor Rights Fund, 1995, https://goo.gl/x88vv5 (accessed 17 October 2017).

organizations, stressing the need for tripartite bargaining to make the policy prescriptions of the Washington Consensus more effective. Most importantly, they maintained that SAPs should be country-specific and take into account the level of development of the beneficiary, thereby challenging the orthodox approach of the World Bank and its attempt to apply given prescriptions to all countries without any differentiation.[113]

This debate also highlights how the ILO gradually detached itself from the early approach adopted in the 1960s, when the Organization looked at sub-Saharan Africa without an in-depth contextualization of the political and social struggles that were affecting the continent and supported the idea of remodelling labour relations according to abstract principles that could be potentially applied everywhere. The idea that policy recommendations should take into account the particular situation of African countries and that social forces should be involved in the process of implementation was successfully advanced by the ILO in the debate over pension reform in sub-Saharan Africa, which became a fierce site of ideological conflict with the World Bank in the 1990s. The restructuring of African pension systems was strongly advocated by the Bretton Woods organization because it deemed the prevailing systems to be unsustainable in the long term under the pressure of intergenerational conflict, while the ILO rejected these neo-Malthusian arguments and emphasized that 'pay-as-you-go' programmes were more suited to the needs of African societies.[114] To contain the spread of the World Bank-supported defined contribution schemes in sub-Saharan Africa, the ILO adopted three strategies: first, it cited SAPs as the driving force behind the breakdown of pension income while attacking the supposed efficiency of privately managed schemes; secondly, it exploited its long-term connection with African policymakers and trade unions, involving different stakeholders in line with the spirit of tripartite bargaining; finally, it highlighted how its pension reform programme was more suited to the specific features of sub-Saharan Africa, whereas the alternative proposed by the World Bank was built on universal assumptions and without any attention

---

[113] International Labour Office, *Political Transformation, Structural Adjustment and Industrial Relations in Africa: English-speaking Countries: Proceedings of, and Documents Submitted to, a Symposium (Arusha, 1–4 February 1993)*, Labour Management Relations Series No. 78 (Geneva: ILO, 1994), 230.

[114] Kurt Weyland, 'External Pressures and International Norms in Latin American Pension Reform', Kellogg Institute for International Studies, Working Paper No. 323, 2006, https://goo.gl/3uJaQA (accessed 20 October 2017); M. Cichon and P. Karuna, 'Financing Social Protection', in *Reflections on Reform Strategies for Social Protection in English-speaking African Countries* (Geneva: ILO, 2000).

to African 'exceptionality'.[115] This strategy proved to be successful: in the 1990s, countries such as Ghana, Uganda and Nigeria gradually turned from the pension system advocated by the World Bank to ILO-sponsored social insurance schemes.[116] The underlying reason for this shift was twofold: it reflected growing dissatisfaction with the macro-economic policies of the Washington Consensus, but it was also a natural response to the attempt of new African democracies to appease trade unions and popular electoral support before national elections.[117]

Success in the struggle for reform of the African pension system did not prevent the ILO from reforming itself during the mandates of Directors-General Michel Hansenne (1989–99) and, since 1999, Juan Somavia. Hansenne, and later Somavia, repositioned the ILO at the centre of the economic and social debate on globalization, pushing for the definition of core labour conventions that would be gradually recognized as universal human rights.[118] The 1997 International Labour Conference, the 1998 Declaration of Fundamental Principles and Rights at Work, the 2008 Declaration on Social Justice for a Fair Globalization and the 2009 Global Jobs Pact introduced new distinctions between rights and general principles, with the former giving rise to precise legal obligations and the latter consisting of more general expectations that member states would conform to international regulations.[119] This move was welcomed by African countries, which were eager to attract direct investment from abroad and unwilling to improve working conditions for fear of being less attractive to foreign capital. While critics argued that the voluntary approach to labour regulation worked to the benefit of the neoliberal development paradigm, Hansenne justified this shift with the argument that the adoption of soft law would guarantee a minimum of fundamental rights everywhere, even if it did not entail the

---

[115] Michael Kpessa and Daniel Béland, 'Transnational Actors and the Politics of Pension Reform in Sub-Saharan Africa', *Review of International Political Economy*, 19.2 (2011), 267–91.

[116] *Ibid.*, 282.

[117] *Ibid.*, 285.

[118] Steve Hughes and Nigel Haworth, 'Decent Work and Poverty Reduction Strategies', *Relations industrielles / Industrial Relations*, 66.1 (2011), 38.

[119] Steve Hughes and Nigel Haworth, *The International Labour Organization (ILO): Coming in from the Cold* (London: Routledge, 2010); Lucio Baccaro and Valentina Mele, 'Pathology of Path Dependency? The ILO and the Challenge of New Governance', *ILR Review*, 65.2 (2012), 195–224.

equalization of social conditions among countries at different levels of development.[120]

A landmark of the ILO's new trajectory was the elaboration of the 'decent work' concept in 1999 and the subsequent launch of the Decent Work Agenda (DWA) for sub-Saharan Africa, whose main target so far has been the improvement of workers' rights in the informal sector. The term 'informal economy' as elaborated by the 2002 International Labour Conference refers to 'all economic activities by workers and economic units that are – in law or in practice – not covered or insufficiently covered by formal arrangements. Their activities are not included in the law, which means that they are operating outside of the formal reach of the law.'[121] Attention to the informal has stemmed from the fact that, in spite of the steady economic growth experienced by the African continent over the past fifteen years, progress towards poverty reduction targets enshrined in the Millennium Development Goals has not been satisfactory enough, while 90 per cent of the African labour force still depend on the informal economy for their livelihood.[122] The DWA is an attempt to strengthen the social dimension of globalization and contain its 'adverse impact on conditions of employment … [that], at their extreme, can lead to forced labour'.[123]

The connection between the DWA and the improvement of working conditions in the informal economy was reiterated again by the 2008 Declaration on Social Justice for a Fair Globalization,[124] which reaffirmed the commitment of the ILO and its member states to achieve the four strategic goals embedded in the concept of 'decent work'.[125] The adoption of Recommendation 204, Transition from the Informal to the Formal

---

[120] Baccaro and Mele, 'Pathology of Path Dependency?', 202; Felix Hauf, 'The Paradoxes of Decent Work in Context: A Cultural Political Economy Perspective', *Global Labour Journal*, 6.2 (2015), 138–55.

[121] International Labour Office, 'Resolution Concerning Decent Work and the Informal Economy', report of the Committee on the Informal Economy, Geneva, 2002, 53.

[122] International Labour Office, 'The Informal Economy in Africa: Promoting Transition to Formality: Challenges and Strategies', Geneva, 2009, 6.

[123] International Labour Organization, 'A Global Alliance against Forced Labour: Report of the Director-General', International Labour Conference, 93rd Session, Geneva, 2005, 63, https://goo.gl/99GwYM (accessed 15 October 2017).

[124] International Labour Organization, 'ILO Declaration on Social Justice for a Fair Globalization', adopted by the International Labour Conference at its 97th Session, Geneva, 2008, https://goo.gl/sF7QCK (accessed 25 October 2017).

[125] ILO, 'The Informal Economy in Africa', 17.

Economy,[126] at the 2015 International Labour Conference was another milestone in the historical trajectory of the ILO's efforts to extend labour rights to informal workers and enterprises. The core of the recommendation consists of the idea that problems associated with the informal economy can be tackled by facilitating the transition of workers and economic units from the informal to the formal economy, while promoting the creation of decent jobs in the formal economy and preventing the informalization of already existing formal jobs. The attempt to improve workers' conditions through incorporation of the informal into the formal economy does not always take into account the root causes of informality, however, such as the fact that formality bears a cost or that the continuum between the formal and informal economy is often underpinned by specific power relations within the society.[127]

The new approach advocated by the ILO towards the world of informality nonetheless sanctions a radical change from the original understanding of the informal economy elaborated by the Kenya report in 1972. While ILO experts in Kenya looked at the informal world as an economic arena defined by creativity and resilience, over the years the concept of informality has gradually become a synonym for poverty, thereby reproducing in a new form the old bias against that which falls beyond the immediate reach of the African state.[128] In this respect, the ILO's emphasis on the informal world is a blueprint for the Organization's ability to reposition itself within the framework of the post-Washington Consensus: the lack of social protection and workers' rights in the informal sector has turned the fight against poverty into a fight against informality, which in turn has increasingly overlapped with the attempt to improve African governance by bringing the state back into the equation after the neoliberal turn of the 1980s and 1990s.[129]

[126] R204 – Transition from the Informal to the Formal Economy Recommendation, 2015 (No. 204), https://goo.gl/47yqkm (accessed 20 January 2018).

[127] Donald L. Sparks and Stephen T. Barnett, 'The Informal Sector in Sub-Saharan Africa: Out of the Shadows to Foster Sustainable Employment and Equity?', *International Business & Economics Research Journal*, 9.5 (2010), 1–11; Supriya Routh and Vando Borghi, eds, *Workers and the Global Informal Economy: Interdisciplinary Perspectives* (New York: Routledge, 2016); Nick Bernards, 'The International Labour Organization and the Ambivalent Politics of Financial Inclusion in West Africa', *New Political Economy*, 21.6 (2016), 606–20.

[128] Bangasser, 'The ILO and the Informal Sector', 16.

[129] John Harold Sande Lie, *Developmentality: An Ethnography of the World Bank-Uganda Partnership* (Oxford: Berghahn Books, 2015).

DECENT WORK, GLOBALIZATION AND AFRICAN DEVELOPMENT

The implementation process of the DWA in sub-Saharan Africa highlights how the ILO cannot be regarded merely as a decision-making arena for member states but rather 'as an international organization for the conceptualization, diffusion, and transmission of ideas and policies on labour issues in a broader transnational network of diverse actors ... and interest groups acting beyond the nation state'.[130] In this respect, the DWA offered a new opportunity to expand the ILO's influence in the elaboration of a development agenda for sub-Saharan Africa and to encourage stronger institutional links with other international organizations – such as the World Bank, the IMF or the World Health Organization – thanks also to the parallel 'Delivering as One' initiative promoted in the 2000s by the UN secretary general in an effort to prevent the fragmentation of UN agencies.[131]

A sign of the ILO's effectiveness in shaping the debate on economic development lies in the integration of the DWA into the Poverty Reduction Strategy Papers (PRSPs) promoted by the Bretton Woods organizations in sub-Saharan Africa as a substitute for SAPs since the late 1990s. This led to the incorporation of full employment as a strategic objective of the PRSPs.[132] Another area of confrontation with the World Bank and the International Finance Corporation (IFC) concerned the content of the *Doing Business* report, an annual publication launched by the IFC in 2004 to rank countries according to a composite index describing business regulations and their enforcement. The debate surrounding the *Doing Business* report recreated in a refashioned form the clash of perspectives between the World Bank's *World Development Report* and the ILO's *World Employment* publication in 1995: the original version of the *Doing Business* report largely repeated the idea that labour market regulations were detrimental to economic growth, assigning higher scores to countries with minimal labour law and implicitly promoting labour deregulation. This contradiction was highlighted by a study of the ILO's Economic and Labour Market Analysis Department in 2007, which argued that the

> index clearly does not encourage countries to abide by many of the
> International Labour Conventions of the International Labour Organization

---

[130] Jasmien van Daele, 'The International Labour Organization in Past and Present Research', *International Review of Social History*, 53.3 (2008), 506.

[131] Erica Di Ruggiero, Joanna E. Cohen and Donald C. Cole, 'The Politics of Agenda Setting at the Global Level: Key Informant Interviews Regarding the International Labour Organization Decent Work Agenda', *Globalization and Health*, 10.56 (2014).

[132] Hughes and Haworth, 'Decent Work and Poverty Reduction Strategies'.

(ILO). In many instances, countries score worse if their national labour legislation reflects the provisions set forth in the ILO conventions ... even though these are international treaties ratified and adopted by many countries.[133]

By challenging the idea that legal systems were only a burden to efficient business, as well as the methodological choices that underpinned such a conclusion, the study called for a revision of the index that would take into account the positive externalities produced by labour rights and tripartite bargaining. Indeed, one year later, in the midst of the 2008 global economic crisis, the World Bank announced changes to the indicators of its *Doing Business* publication, aligning the methodology in order to assign higher scores to those countries that had adopted regulations in compliance with the most relevant ILO conventions.[134] Further changes were introduced in 2011, following two years of work by the consultative group convened by the World Bank and composed of experts from the ILO, the Organization for Economic Co-operation and Development and civil society and employer organizations.[135] The consultative process added modifications to the methodology for employing workers indicators in line with relevant ILO conventions – for example, the Weekly Rest (Industry) Convention, 1921 (No. 14) – affecting, in particular, minimum wage, paid annual leave and the maximum number of working days per week.[136]

Another arena in which the ILO has attempted to advance its own social policy ideas in sub-Saharan Africa in recent years is the rural sector, which has received renewed attention from international experts and development practitioners after a widespread decline of interest in the 1990s. The Organization has shown interest in the rural sector since the early 2000s, with the resumption of standard-setting activities particularly relevant to the rural context, such as the Safety and Health in Agriculture Convention, 2001 (No. 184), the Promotion of Cooperatives Recommendation, 2002 (No. 193),

[133] Janine Berg and Sandrine Cazes, 'The Doing Business Indicators: Measurement Issues and Political Implications', Economic and Labour Market Paper 2007/6, International Labour Office, Geneva, 2007, 3, https://goo.gl/tsof8f (accessed 19 October 2017).

[134] Hughes and Haworth, 'Decent Work and Poverty Reduction Strategies'; see also World Bank, 'Doing Business: Changes to the Methodology, 2005–2017', https://goo.gl/nnThPA (accessed 15 October 2017).

[135] 'Doing Business Employing Workers Consultative Group, Final Report, April 25, 2011', https://goo.gl/dZMGhX (accessed 10 October 2017).

[136] World Bank, *Doing Business 2011: Making a Difference for Entrepreneurs* (Washington, DC: International Bank for Reconstruction and Development, 2010), 93–5.

and the Work in Fishing Convention (No. 188) and Recommendation (No. 199) in 2007.[137] The necessity of focusing on rural employment for the purpose of poverty reduction was then clearly articulated at the 2007 ILO African Regional Meeting in Addis Ababa and reiterated at the 97th Session of the International Labour Conference in 2008.[138] The approach proposed by the ILO occupies a middle ground between the neoliberal agenda advocated by the World Bank and the critical position of several NGOs and radical thinkers that have dismissed the World Bank's recent initiatives in the rural sector, such as the *Benchmarking the Business of Agriculture* initiative, as tools to advance the interests of large agribusinesses and the dispossession of smallholders and other marginalized groups in the developing world.[139]

The 2007 report of the Director-General underlined that decent jobs in the rural sector could be created only in a context of improved agricultural productivity, advocating the integration of smallholder farmers into international markets through global value chains.[140] The idea that commercial farming and integration into global value chains could be a pathway out of poverty fitted perfectly with the new agenda for agricultural development proposed by the World Bank in its 2008 *World Development Report*, but the ILO position differed in certain key aspects.[141] In fact, the DWA provided an integrated framework for promoting institutional change in order to address the adverse effects of globalization on the poorest sectors of African societies, thereby combining the goal of increased productivity and better information exchange prescribed by the dominant consensus on market primacy with the concerns of those critics who argued that poverty

---

[137] For these Conventions and Recommendations, see https://www.ilo.org/normlex.

[138] International Labour Office, *Unleashing Rural Development through Productive Employment and Decent Work: Building on 40 Years of ILO Work in Rural Areas*, Committee on Employment and Social Policy, Governing Body, 310th Session (GB.310/ESP/1), Geneva, 2011, https://goo.gl/GrdXPZ (accessed 19 October 2017).

[139] Henry Veltmeyer, 'The World Bank on "Agriculture for Development": A Failure of Imagination or the Power of Ideology?', *Journal of Peasant Studies*, 36.2 (2009), 393–410; Alice Martin-Prével and Frédéric Mousseau, *New Name, Same Game: World Bank's Enabling the Business of Agriculture* (Oakland, CA: The Oakland Institute, 2014).

[140] International Labour Organization, 'The Decent Work Agenda in Africa: 2007–2015, Eleventh African Regional Meeting, Report of the Director-General', Addis Ababa, April 2017, 37, https://goo.gl/ux5Nr3 (accessed 20 October 2017).

[141] World Bank, *World Development Report 2008: Agriculture for Development* (Washington, DC: The International Bank for Reconstruction and Development/World Bank, 2007), 91, https://goo.gl/worTFi (accessed 22 October 2017).

alleviation and improvement of working conditions should be at the centre of any development initiative.[142]

The UN Secretary General's 'Delivering as One' initiative for a more cohesive UN approach towards Africa offered another opportunity 'to integrate the priorities of Decent Work Country Programmes into other development frameworks and agendas at country level'.[143] An example of this integration is the ILO's involvement in the Social Protection Floor (SPF) initiative in Africa in partnership with the World Health Organization, created in 2009 out of the consciousness that economic growth alone could not address economic insecurity and promote decent work.[144] The SPF initiative was motivated by the attempt to contain the most adverse effects of globalization on marginalized groups in the developing world by ensuring access to basic social services and the realization of minimum essential levels of rights embodied in human rights treaties to every sector of the population.[145]

CONCLUSION

In summary, the ILO's position on colonial social policy during the 1950s essentially remained the one it had taken during the reform phase of the war and the immediate post-war period. Its success in having integrated the colonial territories into a generally universalistic discourse was countered by its long-term failure to vanquish the double standard which the colonial powers continued to apply within their domains. After the First World War the double standard had been on display in the adoption of specifically colonial conventions on 'native labour', while now it was reflected in the very existence of a separate committee concerned with social policy in dependent territories. The double standard continued to manifest itself in the 'gradual universalism' which characterized the findings of the committee, and in the ILO's inability to overcome the colonial powers' resistance to its

[142] Murat Arsel and Anirban Dasgupta, 'Critique, Rediscovery and Revival in Development Studies', *Development and Change*, 46.4 (2015), 644–65; ILO, 'Decent Work Agenda in Africa: 2007–2015', 14–16.

[143] ILO, 'Decent Work Agenda in Africa: 2007–2015', 21.

[144] International Labour Office, *Efficient Growth, Employment and Decent Work in Africa: Time for a New Vision* (Geneva: ILO, 2011) 44–5, https://goo.gl/5SzaNp (accessed 23 October 2017).

[145] International Labour Office and World Health Organization, 'The Social Protection Floor', Geneva, October 2009, 4, https://goo.gl/P1zfEV (accessed 25 October 2017).

involvement in Africa. Almost until the very end of their rule in Africa, the colonial powers thus managed to uphold their contention that, under colonial conditions, a different set of rules applied from those the ILO claimed to be of a universal nature. In addition, until the eve of African independence, the ILO remained a forum in which African actors hardly had a say about their own affairs.

The ILO's stance on the extension of labour rights to sub-Saharan Africa after decolonization was marked by the same contradictions that had featured the immediate post-war period. The ILO's success in providing technical assistance to independent African countries and shaping the global debate on development was countered by its failure to reverse the double standard of which new African rulers continued to make use in the name of the struggle against economic underdevelopment and neocolonialism. Following the establishment of the Washington Consensus, the ILO resorted again to the double standard to contain the ongoing attack on labour rights by the Bretton Woods organizations and its gradual loss of influence within the international aid arena. Whereas the World Bank and the IMF supported the reproduction of abstract economic models aimed at deregulating African economies, thereby serving the 'bureaucratic need to simplify and universalize local social systems'[146] according to the rules of the market, the ILO argued that African problems should be tackled by taking into account the specific features of African societies and their unequal insertion into the international economic system. By doing so and giving voice to African concerns, the ILO regained a central role in the global debate on economic development and labour policies in the African continent of the twenty-first century.

[146] David Mosse, 'Colonial and Contemporary Ideologies of "Community Management": The Case of Tank Irrigation Development in South India', *Modern Asian Studies*, 33.2 (1999), 304.

NINE
Labour Migration

HELENA PÉREZ NIÑO

Centre of Development Studies, University of Cambridge

The history of labour migration in twentieth-century Africa is inextricable from the process of articulation of the continent to the global economy and the development of capitalist relations of production and exchange. In comparison with other regions with a history of colonial occupation, African agrarian structures at the beginning of the twentieth century were distinctive, with the exception of settler colonies of East and southern Africa, for the absence of a proprietary class concentrating and monopolizing land. Over the following decades, this sustained access to land by direct producers would prove at times an obstacle and at times an advantage in capital's attempt to mobilize a large labour force to develop large-scale mining, export-oriented agriculture and infrastructure projects. As a consequence, the massive mobilization of long-distance, periodic migrant labour had a lasting influence on the organization of production as well as on the character of labour relations across Africa, albeit in context-specific ways.

Labour migration had become one of the predominant forms of labour mobilization by the late nineteenth century. It has been argued that all African societies experienced the effects of labour migration in one way or another during the twentieth century.[1] As will be discussed in this chapter, extra-economic coercion played no small part in ensuring that a workforce was eventually made available, frequently at low cost to employers. *Chibalo* in southern Africa, *prestation* in French West Africa, bonded labour and *corvée* were among the idioms of unfree labour. Poll taxes and raw violence, however central to these forms of labour mobilization, do not explain all forms of labour migration: millions of Africans migrated for work through

---

[1] D. D. Cordell, J. W. Gregory and V. Piché, *Hoe and Wage: A Social History of a Circular Migration System in West Africa* (Boulder, CO: Westview Press, 1996).

channels – informal, clandestine or voluntary – that ran parallel to those that mobilized forced labour and that largely remained unrecorded. Over time, labour mobilization transformed the foundations of domestic agriculture and progressively locked households into commodity relations, which in turn cemented the emergence of forms of 'free labour' as well as of new forms of 'unfree labour'.

This chapter is concerned with providing an overview of experiences of labour migration within the broader historical process of labour commodification. A neat distinction between free and unfree labour as well as between labour migration and other forms of migration is not always possible or analytically helpful. While some migrated for wages, others migrated as sharecroppers, and some forms of wage labour derived from earlier forms of forced and slave labour.[2] To the extent that other contributions to this volume touch on such issues, this chapter focuses on migrant wage labour and to a lesser extent on specialized commodity production by migrants.

The drivers and outcomes of the mobilization of migrant labour are at the centre of debates in African labour history. In the literature on large-scale mining in southern Africa, the incorporation of migrant workers is widely seen as a historical attempt of employers to depress wages and lower labour costs by means of mobilizing migrants to constitute a segment of the workforce with lower reservation wages. Migrant labour recruitment in the development of export-oriented agriculture has been recognized as a mechanism for adjusting the labour supply to the markedly seasonal rhythms of production. Other accounts have stressed that the recruitment of labour migrants attempted to segment and fracture the workforce politically, to thwart the emergence of class consciousness and collective mobilization. In still other cases and regions, labour migration was found to be actively sought by migrants themselves as an opportunity for improved living standards, for accumulation or for evading local forms of oppression.[3] The long-term effects of labour migration have also been assessed variously. In some cases, migrant remittances are credited as having triggered processes of 'accumulation from below', ultimately leading to social mobility and

---

[2]   *Ibid.*; F. Manchuelle, *Willing Migrants: Soninke Labor Diasporas, 1848–1960* (Athens, OH: Ohio University Press, 1997).

[3]   See C. Meillassoux, *Maidens, Meal and Money: Capitalism and the Domestic Community* (Cambridge: Cambridge University Press, 1981); J. S. Crush, A. Jeeves and D. Yudelman, *South Africa's Labor Empire: A History of Black Migrancy to the Gold Mines* (Boulder, CO: Westview Press, 1991); Cordell et al., *Hoe and Wage*; J. P. Chauveau and P. Richards, 'West African Insurgencies in Agrarian Perspective: Côte d'Ivoire and Sierra Leone Compared', *Journal of Agrarian Change*, 8.4 (2008), 515–52.

socio-economic differentiation. Other cases suggest that labour migration extended the direct producers' access to land by way of providing the cash income necessary to sustain family-based agriculture in a period of rapid commodification, or emphasize the impact of migration on changing cultural identities and social norms.[4]

A survey of the literature suggests that, although labour migration was once considered merely a transitional form preceding generalized proletarianization, instead it remained numerically relevant in some regions and sectors, even as the labour migration systems broke down in the wake of independence and liberalization. Labour migration did not invariably result in the emergence of a fully proletarianized working class, but it certainly contributed to the monetization of rural areas and to the progressive commodification of livelihoods.

As the arc traced by these varied accounts of labour migration in African societies suggests, continent-wide generalizations are best avoided when accounting for labour migration. The combination of diverse and even contradictory tendencies has resulted in complex regional and local labour histories. Accordingly, experiences of migration translated into impoverishment for some households and accumulation for others. In certain cases, labour migration brought about a revolution of social structures, while in others it reinforced those that were pre-existing: 'Migration ... is perhaps best viewed as a structure in which various kinds of relationships with various outcomes can occur, depending on other social and economic contexts.'[5] An exhaustive continent-wide survey of these drivers and outcomes could not be covered in a single chapter. Instead, this chapter outlines the challenges of accounting for labour migration and traces the history of the most salient dynamics around labour migration systems.[6] The chapter concludes by discussing emerging themes in the study of African labour migration.

---

[4]   For example, in drought-hit colonial Upper Volta, integration to labour markets was a form of protecting the autonomy of domestic agriculture (Cordell et al., *Hoe and Wage*), while in the case of the migrant homesteads of Pondoland, labour migration seems to have been triggered by the colonial squeeze of African livelihoods and the resulting need for labour-saving durable consumables and mass-produced tools – iron hoes, firearms, cloth, soap, blankets. See W. Beinart, 'A Century of Migrancy from Mpondoland', *African Studies*, 7.33 (2014), 387–409.

[5]   B. Freund, 'Labor and Labor History in Africa: A Review of the Literature', *African Studies Review*, 27.2 (1984), 1–58.

[6]   On labour migration systems as an analytical category, see A. H. Jeeves, *Migrant Labour in South Africa's Mining Economy: The Struggle for the Gold Mines' Labour Supply, 1890–1920* (Kingston and Montreal: McGill-Queen's University Press, 1985), and Cordell et al., *Hoe and Wage*.

ACCOUNTING FOR LABOUR MIGRATION: METHODOLOGICAL AND THEORETICAL DEBATES

Starting from the 1950s, scholars from a wide range of disciplinary and political traditions contributed to the study of migratory labour and its impact on the transformation of societies, markets and political systems in Africa. Early contributors – such as Monica and Godfrey Wilson, who worked on southern and Central Africa, Margaret Read on Nyasaland, scholars in the Rhodes-Livingston Institute working on the Copperbelt, and Polly Hill's classical work on the migrant cocoa farmers of Ghana – examined the impact of migratory cycles on family life, on kin structures, on local authority and on identities and traditions, and engaged critically with the arguments around 'detribalization' and extra-economic pressures.[7]

From a very different perspective, insights from classical and neoclassical economics were also applied to the study of labour migration in developing economies in the post-war period. From a classical perspective, Arthur Lewis theorized the effect of the transfer of surplus labour from traditional to capitalist sectors; the impact of capital accumulation on wage levels over time and the likely effect of continued immigration of unskilled labour that would depress wages.[8] For behaviouralist models, wage differentials and labour demand in urban areas were considered variables that informed the individual's decision to migrate. Migration was understood as a mechanism to clear the labour market and allow for the optimal redistribution of the factors of production, assumed to be unevenly distributed between, on the one hand, developing countries and traditional sectors (which concentrated labour surpluses) and, on the other hand, developed economies and modern sectors (which concentrated capital). In the work of influential neoclassical development economists such as Todaro, migrants were assumed to be rational, self-interested maximizers, responsive to market signals, who would choose to go where the commodity they sold (labour) was best remunerated.[9]

---

[7]   For a detailed reconstruction of the early historiography of labour migration, see Freund, *The Making of Contemporary Africa*; Cordell et al., *Hoe and Wage*; D. Potts, *Circular Migration in Zimbabwe and Contemporary Sub-Saharan Africa* (Woodbridge: James Currey, 2010); P. Delius and L. Phillips, 'Introduction', in *A Long Way Home: Migrant Worker Worlds, 1800–2014*, ed. P. Delius, L. Phillips and F. Rankin-Smith (Johannesburg: Wits University Press, 2014), pp. 1–16.

[8]   W. A. Lewis, 'Economic Development with Unlimited Supplies of Labour', *The Manchester School of Economic and Social Studies*, 22.2 (1954), 139–91.

[9]   M. P. Todaro, 'A Model of Labor Migration and Urban Unemployment in Less Developed Countries', *The American Economic Review*, 59.1 (1969), 138–48.

Critics questioned these models early on for taking the uneven distribution of labour and capital as a given and thereby disregarding historical processes of dispossession and coercive mobilization of the migrant workforce. By portraying migration as resulting from individual choice, these models fail to account for the constellation of political and social relations that shaped and constrained individual motivations.[10] Limited as these ahistorical and voluntarist models were when accounting for the functioning of African labour migration, they remain the conceptual foundation of policy and practice, as exemplified by the wide acceptance of the push and pull factor analysis and the human capital framework.

TOWARDS A HISTORICALLY GROUNDED POLITICAL ECONOMY OF LABOUR MIGRATION IN AFRICA

In the 1970s, Marxist, Third-Worldist and anti-imperialist scholars revisited debates about labour migration in Africa. In *dependentista* accounts, labour migration was a component of the articulation of the modes of production. For Marxists, it was to be understood as a form of super-exploitation characteristic of the African transition to capitalism. Labour mobilization among groups whose links to land were not completely severed was given careful consideration. It was proposed that, through coercively mobilized labour migration, peasant farmers and family-based agriculture were forced to subsidize capitalist accumulation by allowing for the periodic mobilization of their labour force at rates below the costs of labour reproduction. Farming households were made to shoulder the costs of reproducing the labour force for the benefit of capital.[11]

Broadly speaking, this new framing of the question contributed to unveil the extent to which late twentieth-century labour migration in Africa remained rooted in longer histories of slave and forced labour. Capitalist penetration and the development of large-scale mining and agriculture in the late nineteenth century had triggered a spike in demand for labour in

[10] S. Amin, *Modern Migrations in Western Africa: Studies Presented and Discussed at the Eleventh International African Seminar, Dakar* (Oxford: Oxford University Press, 1974); J. Banaji, 'The Fictions of Free Labour: Contract, Coercion, and So-Called Unfree Labour', *Historical Materialism*, 11.3 (2003), 69–95.

[11] H. Wolpe, 'Capitalism and Cheap Labour Power in South Africa: From Segregation to Apartheid', *Economy and Society*, 1.4 (1972), 425–56; M. L. Morris, 'The Development of Capitalism in South African Agriculture: Class Struggle in the Countryside', *Economy and Society*, 5.3 (1976), 292–343; Meillassoux, *Maidens, Meal and Money*.

the context of the recent abolition of chattel slavery. The labour regimes that emerged around the new centres of accumulation were profoundly dependent on political and extra-economic pressures for mobilizing labour. Hut and poll taxes went hand in hand with forms of forced labour and forced cultivation in compelling people into labour migration as a coping or avoidance strategy. In southern Africa and in other settler colonies, these measures were introduced against the background of land evictions and an overlapping array of measures to restrict the development of black commercial farmers while controlling the resettlement of communities and the movement of migrant workers. However, the drivers and methods of labour recruitment varied across regions and periods, with important differences in West Africa, where African farmers prospered through agricultural booms.[12]

It followed from these accounts that African labour was mobile before it was 'free' in Marx's terms, that is, either separated from the means of production or unable to reproduce itself based on its own production. In some cases, the use of long-distance migrant labour allowed employers to emulate functionally the labour-disciplining effects of proletarianization, such as the spatial separation that prevented workers from partaking in domestic agriculture and the growing dependence on wages for social reproduction. But similarly, new demands transformed patterns of consumption, and through labour migration, hinterlands became inextricably bound in the cash economy. The appeal for employers of recruiting migrant labour in different regions of Africa counteracted and complicated the pressures towards the

[12] G. Arrighi, 'Labour Supplies in Historical Perspective: A Study of the Proletarianization of the African Peasantry in Rhodesia', *The Journal of Development Studies*, 6.3 (1970), 197–234; Wolpe, 'Capitalism and Cheap Labour Power in South Africa'; Amin, *Modern Migrations in Western Africa*; T. Kanogo, *Squatters and the Roots of Mau Mau, 1905–63* (Nairobi/London: East African Publishers/James Currey, 1987); G. Austin, *Labour, Land and Capital in Ghana: From Slavery to Free Labour in Asante 1807–1956* (Rochester, NY: University of Rochester Press, 2005). From a different perspective, Cross drew on D. Harvey, *The New Imperialism* (Oxford: Oxford University Press, 2003), to propose that West African social formations would have gone through a period of accumulation by dispossession (ABD) that resulted in a landless peasantry obliged to sell their labour as a commodity. H. Cross, *Migrants, Borders and Global Capitalism: West African Labour Mobility and EU Borders* (Abingdon: Routledge, 2013), 12–17. A problem with the ABD thesis is that land dispossession was not prevalent in many of the regions where migrant labour originated and that access to land was powerfully mediated by other social hierarchies and relations (of kin, seniority and gender), with consequences for the formation of labour markets.

proletarianization of labour, where such existed, and cemented the process of expansion of commodity relations.[13]

However, the categories that attempted to capture how surplus was extracted from migrant workers (categories such as 'migrant-peasants' and 'semi-proletarians') were also problematic. They presumed that periodic migration would eventually result in the full proletarianization of the workers. By calling instead for an approach that was open to considering the agency of workers themselves, the critique of the structuralist literature expanded the analytical horizons to encompass groups whose labour migration experiences had remained invisible. Case-based studies have incorporated a more sophisticated understanding of the complexity of migration as a driver of class formation, for example in the study of the accumulation from below based on migrant remittances; of overlapping ethnic, generational and gender relations around labour migration; and of the 'political economy of affliction' inflicted by the labour process.[14]

From a period in which labour was at the centre of the study of African migrations, academic interest shifted to the study of more loosely defined migrant livelihoods.[15] Some authors in this tradition reject the assumption that labour migration is inherently exploitative and propose that mobile lives are a norm rather than an aberration of African labour markets. In this approach, also popularized in the study of remittances as a link between migration and development, mobility creates the conditions for valued exchanges and potentially for poverty reduction.[16] As the following section will show, these changing accents and inflections in the study of labour migration themselves reflect the transformation of the world of labour and employment taking place in Africa over the past decades.

---

[13] G. N. Kitching, *Class and Economic Change in Kenya: The Making of an African Petite Bourgeoisie, 1905–1970* (New Haven, CT: Yale University Press, 1980); Meillassoux, *Maidens, Meal and Money*; H. Bernstein, 'Considering Africa's Agrarian Questions', *Historical Materialism*, 12.4 (2004), 115–44.

[14] Kitching, *Class and Economic Change in Kenya*; M. Neocosmos, *The Agrarian Question in Southern Africa and 'Accumulation from Below': Economics and Politics in the Struggle for Democracy* (Uppsala: Nordiska Africainstitutet, 1993); Chauveau and Richards, 'West African Insurgencies in Agrarian Perspective'; B. O'Laughlin, 'Land, Labour and the Production of Affliction in Rural Southern Africa', *Journal of Agrarian Change*, 13.1 (2013), 175–96; Delius and Phillips, 'Introduction'.

[15] B. O'Laughlin, 'Proletarianisation, Agency and Changing Rural Livelihoods: Forced Labour and Resistance in Colonial Mozambique', *Journal of Southern African Studies*, 28.3 (2002), 511–30.

[16] O. Bakewell, 'Keeping Them in Their Place: The Ambivalent Relationship between Development and Migration in Africa', *Third World Quarterly*, 29.7 (2008), 1341–58.

SOME METHODOLOGICAL CONSIDERATIONS ON AFRICAN LABOUR MIGRATION

The complex nature of migration itself poses some methodological problems. Historical records on migratory flows are uneven and fragmentary, even for the most recent decades.[17] Furthermore, available data is better at tracing the highly institutionalized colonial flows than accounting for clandestine labour migrations in the same period.[18] More recently, labour informalization and casualization have made it increasingly difficult to distinguish labour from other types of migrations.

Existing aggregate statistics should be approached with caution, because labour relations have changed over time and there are no homogeneous units of analysis. Snapshot observations from demographic surveys can measure the stock of migrant workers in a given period but cannot capture change and movements over time (migrant flow). Cut-off points and categorization rules are highly arbitrary.[19] Furthermore, distinguishing categorically between refugees, economic migrants and labour migrants is daunting, as are efforts to account for the labour experiences of refugees and internally displaced persons (IDPs) in humanitarian emergencies. In this respect, the study of labour migration has been greatly enhanced by the use of ethnographic methods, case studies and detailed small sample surveys, which to an extent compensate for missing cross-country and longitudinal data.

LABOUR AS A MOBILE COMMODITY: THE MAKING OF AFRICAN LABOUR MIGRATION SYSTEMS

The study of labour migration in Africa is the study of a mechanism with multiple moving parts. Casual, seasonal, periodic and permanent labour migration patterns coexisted and shaped one another. The palimpsest of labour migration circuits in the period of capitalist penetration and

---

[17]   J. M. Shitundu, *A Study on Labour Migration Data and Statistics in East Africa* (Geneva: ILO, 2006); O. Bakewell and H. de Haas, 'African Migrations: Continuities, Discontinuities and Recent Transformations', in *African Alternatives*, ed. P. Chabal, U. Engel and L. de Haan (Leiden: Brill, 2007), 95–118; C. Oya, *Rural Inequality, Wage Employment and Labour Market Formation in Africa: Historical and Micro-Level Evidence* (Geneva: ILO, 2010); G. J. Abel and N. Sander, 'Quantifying Global International Migration Flows', *Science*, 343.6178 (2014), 1520–22.

[18]   Crush et al., *South Africa's Labor Empire*.

[19]   D. Posel, 'Have Migration Patterns in Post-Apartheid South Africa Changed?', *Journal of Interdisciplinary Economics*, 15.3–4 (2004), 277–92.

development in Africa results from overlapping experiences with varying durations and distances travelled. Labour migration circuits could be domestic, regional or international but also institutionalized, spontaneous or clandestine.[20] This constellation of movements had several epicentres during the twentieth century, the so-called labour migration systems. Around these epicentres, but not exclusively, millions of working lives were involved in one or different types of migration against the background of economic boom and crisis, as well as political coercion, struggle and resistance.

Labour migration systems constructed a socio-spatial division of labour between labour-sending areas and centres of capitalist accumulation.[21] Due to its volume, labour outmigration was a central component of economic and political processes in the main sending areas in southern Africa as well as in the West African labour reserves. In Togo, approximately 20 per cent of the population was engaged in labour migration in the 1960s; 30 per cent of the workforce migrated from Mozambique in the 1970s, and, in the same period, Upper Volta provided 60 per cent of the migrant workforce in the West African system. In labour-sending countries such as Mali, Guinea and Niger, the rate of migration within the country was never as significant as the outward migration to other West African countries.[22] However, trans-border labour recruitment similarly shaped the political processes of the main labour migration destinations. In the gold mines in Transvaal, foreign migrant workers accounted for 70 per cent of the workforce in the 1970s. In the coffee and cotton plantations of Buganda, labour migrants from Tanzania, Rwanda and other parts of Uganda accounted for one-third of the total population in the late 1940s. About a quarter of the population of Côte d'Ivoire consists of oscillatory and settled labour migrants. Similar dynamics took place in the other large epicentres of labour migration: the Libyan oil sector, the Central African Copperbelt, the groundnut basin in Senegal, etc. During the twentieth century, the recruitment of labour migration became a distinctive feature of most African economies, with consequences for the broader struggles between labour and capital.[23]

---

[20] See the chapter by Fourchard in this volume.

[21] However, cases of labour-sending areas that also recruited labour migrants have been documented across the continent. Cordell et al., *Hoe and Wage*; Potts, *Circular Migration in Zimbabwe*.

[22] Amin, *Modern Migrations in Western Africa*; Potts, *Circular Migration in Zimbabwe*.

[23] Crush et al., *South Africa's Labor Empire*; Austin, *Labour, Land and Capital in Ghana*.

MINING AND THE 'LABOUR EMPIRE' IN SOUTHERN AFRICA

The development of the mining industry and other ancillary sectors in the South African Transvaal and in Rhodesia brought about a spatial reorganization of production on a scale unforeseen in southern Africa. Of all the transformations introduced by capital accumulation based on mining, few were as socially significant as the effort to mobilize workers. This involved the largely coercive integration of African peasantries from within the Union of South Africa and Rhodesia as well as from neighbouring colonies. Mozambicans had been recruited to the sugar cane plantations of Natal and the diamond mines of Kimberley, but by the 1920s all recruitment of foreign workers in South Africa was redirected to the mining sector. South Africans who had lost land to massive evictions and many of those who remained as tenants on white-owned farms were further removed on to homelands that would function as labour reserves.[24] The mobilization of migrant labour was complemented by the introduction of an array of measures that restricted the productive autonomy and mobility of the population, including the generalization of poll taxes to be paid in cash, restrictions on access to land, new evictions, forced resettlement and legislative measures to supersede labour tenancy and commercial agriculture by African farmers.[25]

In the following decades, and amid continuous tension between factions of farming and mining white capital, with conflicting interests regarding labour mobilization, the mining lobby and the state would lay down the conditions for the creation of the largest labour migration system in Africa on the basis of the native reserves and the neighbouring colonies. Extra-territorial migrants would be pitted against migrants from the homelands.[26]

[24]   S. Trapido, 'Landlord and Tenant in a Colonial Economy: The Transvaal, 1880–1910', *Journal of Southern African Studies*, 5.1 (1978), 26–58; M. Legassick and F. de Clercq, 'Capitalism and Migrant Labour in Southern Africa: The Origins and Nature of the System', in *International Labour Migration: Historical Perspectives*, ed. S. Marks and P. Richardson (London: Temple Smith, 1984); P. Harries, *Work, Culture, and Identity: Migrant Laborers in Mozambique and South Africa, c. 1860–1910* (London: Pearson Education, 1994).

[25]   Arrighi, 'Labour Supplies in Historical Perspective'; Morris, 'The Development of Capitalism in South African Agriculture'.

[26]   Jeeves, *Migrant Labour in South Africa's Mining Economy*; Crush et al., *South Africa's Labor Empire*. The labour question also pitted industrial and commercial capital that favoured workers' stabilization and would benefit from the expansion of domestic demand against uncompetitive Afrikaner farming capital that depended on subsidies and immobilized cheap labour to subsist. S. Trapido, 'South Africa in a Comparative Study of Industrialization', *Journal of Development Studies*, 7 (1971), 309–20. Contradictions were also rife in labour-sending colonies. The consolidation

This required continuous adjustments of the volumes of labour recruited, to avoid becoming dependent on a single source of workers and to ensure that foreign migrant labour effectively counteracted domestic labour supply fluctuations. The resulting labour system was designed to exploit black labour, to protect white skilled and semi-skilled jobs in mining, and to assist the reproduction of white capital on the basis of cheap labour.[27]

State-sponsored labour recruitment agencies (the Native Recruiting Corporation, NRC; the Witwatersrand Native Labour Association, WNLA; and the Rhodesian Native Labour Bureau, RNLB) recruited domestic and foreign migrant workers throughout southern Africa and as far as Angola and Tanzania. The agencies enacted international labour migration agreements that sought to optimize recruitment from the region. Although this did not prevent the development of clandestine labour migration channels, it helped regulate the migrant labour supply by making workers dependent on transport provided by the employers to reach their work destination. Throughout the period, the mining industry relied increasingly on the state to mediate labour relations and recruitment via repatriation clauses, which helped recruiters adjust supply, and regulations on deferred payments, which also created a stream of revenue and taxation for the states where migrant labour originated. The number of foreign migrant workers in South African mines increased from 100,000 in the 1920s to 265,000 in 1970.

The crisis of the 1930s illustrates how the employment and shedding of precarious foreign labour was used to compensate for volatility and risks. While, before the crisis, foreign workers constituted up to 50 per cent of the mining workforce (and up to 70 per cent in gold mining alone), by 1932 this had come down to 26 per cent. The sharp reduction in the demand for labour disproportionately hit the most flexible and vulnerable segments, the foreign workers.[28]

---

of Portuguese East Africa in the late nineteenth century was funded by the taxes and fees charged to Mozambican migrant workers, but the massive migration to the mines in the Transvaal for wages or to evade *chibalo* was resented by Portuguese plantations and other domestic sectors. M. Newitt, *A History of Mozambique* (Bloomington, IN: Indiana University Press. 1995).

[27] Crush et al., *South Africa's Labor Empire*. Shift wages in gold mining remained unchanged between 1911 and the Second World War. Legassick and de Clercq, 'Capitalism and Migrant Labour in Southern Africa', 147.

[28] Legassick and de Clercq, 'Capitalism and Migrant Labour in Southern Africa'; Crush et al., *South Africa's Labor Empire*.

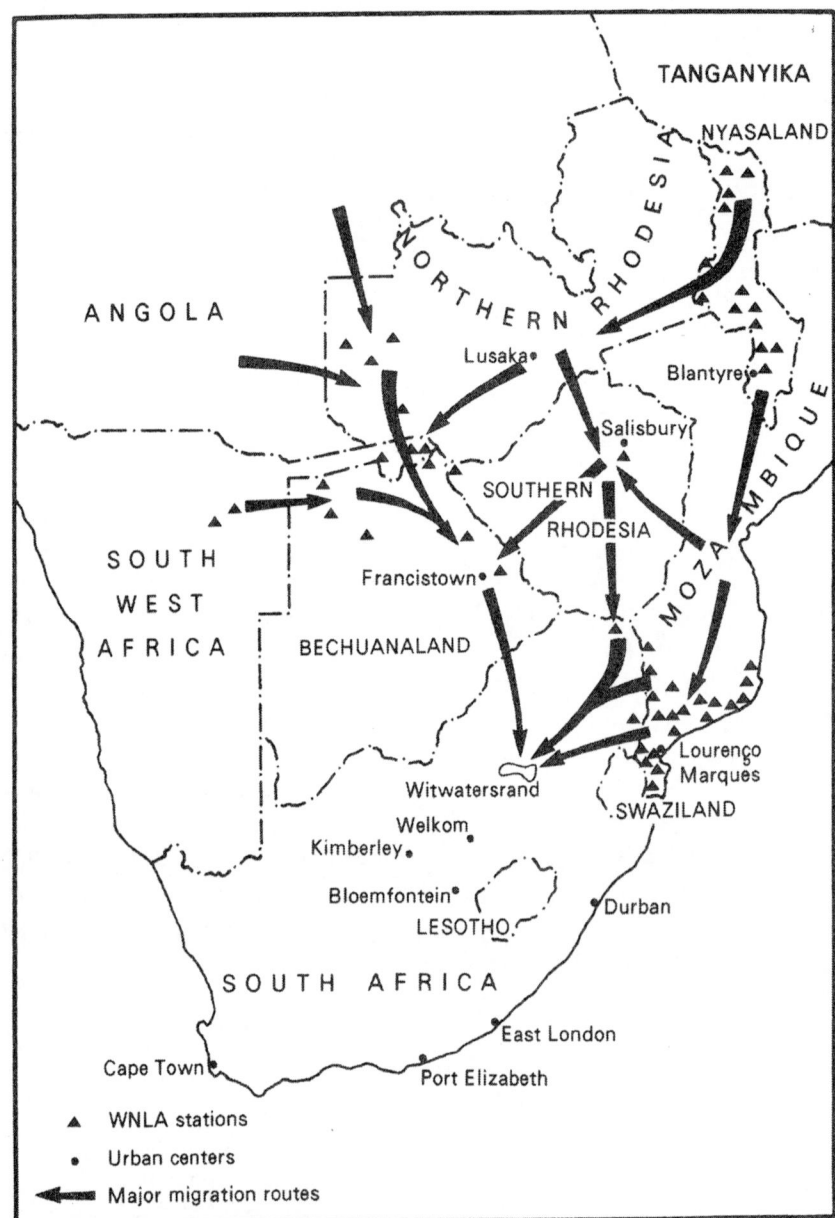

Map 9.1. Major migration routes to South African gold mines, 1940–70 (source: adapted from Francis Wilson, *Labour in the South African Gold Mines, 1911–1969* (Cambridge, Cambridge University Press, 1972), ix)

Workers were divided along racial, ethnic and national lines by a range of official measures and employer practices. Internal and foreign migrant workers were subjected to different contractual conditions and separate jurisdictions, which ultimately entrenched a segmentation of the mining workforce. By the 1970s, 97.3 per cent of the foreign migrant workers were categorized as non-skilled workers, and for decades their employment was restricted to non-skilled jobs.[29]

Central to the mobilization of foreign and internal migrant workers was the time-bound nature of the migration, the prohibition on settling permanently in the mines and the periodic return of workers to their homesteads. The employers discharged most of the costs of the physical and social reproduction of the labour force on to the family economy. Whether this amounted to the articulation of capitalist and pre-capitalist modes of production or whether it expressed the particular nature of capital accumulation in southern Africa has been at the centre of debate. However, reproduction based on the combination of wage-work and domestic agriculture became unsustainable by the 1940s. The squeeze was felt both by those relying on agriculture in the homelands and by the growing black urban population with no access to land for farming or means for autonomous production. The fall in real wages motivated the creation of the first African and multiracial trade unions.[30]

In the post-war years, the employment of foreign migrants resumed and recovered its pre-war levels. Foreign workers would, for the most part, still have access to land and to families engaged in farming, so that their wages could be further depressed and their recruitment used in this period as a means to counteract the growing militancy of the trade unions.[31] By the 1950s a rift between agriculture and other sectors had developed. The scaling up of commercial farming and land concentration allowed for mechanization and the shedding of agricultural jobs. Despite high levels of employment in mining, between 1960 and 1977 the unemployment rate went from 18.3 to 22.4 per cent, highlighting the profound crisis of social reproduction in the labour reserves. Chronic levels of unemployment and underemployment became a structural characteristic of the contemporary South African economy.

Price inflation and falling real wages set off a series of strikes in the Rand during the 1970s, a decade of sustained social unrest around labour conditions and against the apartheid regime, but also of fierce repression on the part of the apartheid state. The liberation struggles and independence of Zimbabwe, Mozambique and Angola and the rise to power of socialist parties throughout

[29] Crush et al., *South Africa's Labor Empire*.

[30] Wolpe, 'Capitalism and Cheap Labour Power in South Africa'; Morris, 'The Development of Capitalism in South African Agriculture'.

[31] See the chapter by Freund in this volume.

Africa effectively threatened to upset capitalist accumulation in mining by breaking apart the labour system on which its profits rested. However, the hollowing out of the migrant labour system was neither sudden nor a linear process. Foreign labour migration to the South African mines, which never regained its previous magnitude, nevertheless remained central to sustaining the economies of southern Mozambique, Lesotho, Zimbabwe and Swaziland.[32] In the past decade, South Africa has become the epicentre of international migration from different African countries. As shown in Table 9.1, the immigration of Zimbabweans to South Africa is currently one of the largest cross-border population movements in the continent.[33]

Table 9.1. Flows of over 100,000 migrants over the 2005–10 period from countries in Africa

Country of origin	Destination	Migrant flow in 2005–10
Zimbabwe	South Africa	495,779
Tanzania*	Burundi	294,595
Morocco	Spain	265,763
Uganda*	South Sudan	187,684
Morocco	France	172,019
Egypt	United Arab Emirates	169,580
Guinea*	Liberia	164,677
Burkina Faso	Côte d'Ivoire	153,283
Kenya*	South Sudan	153,018
Algeria	France	140,523
Zimbabwe	United Kingdom	130,647
Ethiopia*	South Sudan	125,524
Côte d'Ivoire	Burkina Faso	119,154
Nigeria	United States	103,012
Somalia*	Kenya	100,646

* Cases involving humanitarian crises or refugee repatriation

Source: author with data from G. J. Abel and N. Sander, 'Quantifying Global International Migration Flows [Supplemental material], Science, 343.6178 (2014), 1520–2.

[32] Bakewell, 'Keeping Them in Their Place'.

[33] Table 9.1 allows us to discern between flows predominantly related to refugees and returnee flows (Burundi, South Sudan, Liberia and Somalia); countries with large outward migration to Europe and to the countries of the Gulf Cooperation Council, GCC (Morocco, Egypt); and established migratory flows within Africa (Burkina Faso, Côte d'Ivoire and Zimbabwe).

LABOUR MIGRATION TO THE CENTRAL AFRICAN COPPERBELT

Copper mining transformed the world of labour in the Belgian Congo and in Northern Rhodesia, starting from the late 1910s. On the back of sustained international demand for copper, by 1930 Northern Rhodesia had one of the world's largest and most profitable copper sectors. Copper exports grew by 130 per cent between 1936 and 1941, and the number of workers increased from 7,459 in 1933 to 26,023 in 1940.[34] In order to mobilize the labour force necessary, an array of economic and extra-economic measures was introduced, including the imposition of taxes and the promise to workers of access to consumer goods. African farmers were mobilized as migrant labour for the mines, and some white South Africans were hired as skilled workers.

Labour relations in the Copperbelt soon resembled those in the Transvaal mines, where methods of recruitment and opportunities were segmented along racial lines. Poll taxes, coupled with the growth of mining-related employment, resulted in the rapid monetization of the non-mining economy. The Northern Rhodesian state attempted to control the mobility, residence and domestic links of the migrant labour force. Restricting permanent settlement was not always necessary but was harder to enforce than in the highly institutionalized system of South Africa. Nevertheless, the continued mobilization of oscillatory migrant labour was the foundation of the profitability of the sector and was justified at the time by employers and the state on the grounds of preventing detribalization.[35]

Ferguson rejected accounts from the 1970s that proposed a linear progression from circular migration towards a fully settled and proletarianized labour force. On the contrary, he argued that, from the very beginning, large-scale mining relied on a combination of different forms of labour mobilization: rural migrant workers, voluntary workers and contract labour recruited through agents. The majority of the workforce during the boom years of the late 1920s and early 1930s consisted of contract workers, but voluntary workers overtook those contracted after the crisis in the 1930s.[36] In fact, during certain periods, employers had allowed the permanent settlement of workers and their families before the crisis, not least because

---

[34] M. Larmer, *Mineworkers in Zambia: Labour and Political Change in Post-Colonial Africa* (London: I.B.Tauris, 2007).

[35] J. Ferguson, 'Mobile Workers, Modernist Narratives: A Critique of the Historiography of Transition in the Zambian Copperbelt (Part One)', *Journal of Southern African Studies*, 16.3 (1990), 385–412; H. Macmillan, 'More Thoughts on the Historiography of Transition on the Zambian Copperbelt', *Journal of Southern African Studies*, 22.2 (1996), 309–12; Larmer, *Mineworkers in Zambia*.

[36] Ferguson, 'Mobile Workers, Modernist Narratives'.

they needed to secure experienced labour and faced competition for workers from the Transvaal mines, which paid comparatively higher wages.[37]

The Great Depression and the profound crisis in the international price for copper translated in the early 1930s into rising unemployment in the Copperbelt: up to 79 per cent of the jobs for African miners disappeared between 1930 and 1932. Falling living standards and the attempt to raise taxes led to major strikes by African workers' unions in 1935 and 1940. Demands focused on improvements in wages and working conditions and against job reservation. The vast number of workers that, at the time of the strike of 1935, could no longer conceive a return to rural livelihoods evidenced the irreversible effects of migrant stabilization. The realization that mobilization and resistance had been organized in compounds and settlements led employers in the aftermath of the strike to reintroduce pass laws along with other measures to restrict and reverse labour stabilization.[38]

In the 1970s a new period of price instability eroded the viability of the mining sector. Copper mining would no longer be the undisputed engine of the Zambian economy, and the migrant labour system came to a standstill. Former labour-sending regions were forced to refashion their livelihoods in the absence of wages and remittances. Petty trade, smuggling and other commercial pursuits absorbed part of the former migrant labour: 'Forced to find alternative means of participation in the money economy, the former low-cost industrial reserve has turned itself, at the height of a nationwide economic crisis, into a no-cost redistribution unit.'[39]

MIGRANT LABOUR AND AGRICULTURAL FRONTIERS IN WEST AFRICA AND THE SAHEL

The history of labour migration in twentieth-century West Africa was similarly shaped by processes of economic articulation to export circuits, in this case predominantly of tropical agricultural commodities. But it was also shaped by the specific cultural, political and demographic characteristics of the region and by the different power balances in the struggles unleashed by producers' demand for labour. Colonial penetration destroyed and reconfigured pre-colonial mercantile circuits and rested on resource accumulation in coastal areas as well as on slave and migrant labour mobilization from the West African hinterlands.

---

[37] *Ibid.*; Larmer, *Mineworkers in Zambia.*

[38] Larmer, *Mineworkers in Zambia.*

[39] J. Pottier, 'Defunct Labour Reserve? Mambwe Villages in the Post-Migration Economy', *Africa*, 53.2 (1983), 17.

Two different circuits of labour migration towards agricultural frontiers coexisted in the twentieth century, one from within the savannah and forested regions predominantly subjected to poll taxes by the British administration, and a second stemming from the French West African Sahel, where labour migration was driven by taxes and attempts to evade forced labour. Sahelian migrants, from regions with unreliable and limited agricultural production, provided seasonal and permanent agricultural labour to the emerging cocoa, coffee and cotton plantations of Côte d'Ivoire, Ghana and Nigeria as well as for manufacturing and other non-agricultural employment.[40] Access to land in the cocoa belt through an array of sharecropping arrangements attracted massive migration from within Côte d'Ivoire and Ghana but also, importantly, from Upper Volta. Similar sharecropping arrangements characterized migrations to Senegambia from the savannahs and the Sahel. The productive reinvestment of revenue from groundnut and cotton via Muslim fraternities in the Sudanese savannahs and northern Nigeria considerably increased the demand for agricultural and non-agricultural wage labour, as did major infrastructural works linked to all these agricultural booms.[41]

With the exception of the Nigerian oil sector and, more recently, other extractive sectors in the Gulf of Guinea, the prominence of export agriculture shaped the formation of classes of migrant labour. The periods of mobilization and return followed the seasonality of agricultural production, but the less regulated mobility of the labour force – compared to southern Africa – meant that increases in demand for labour could effectively contribute to tightening the labour market and pressuring wages upwards, as was the case during the phase of agricultural expansion in northern Ghana. Therefore, employers continued to recruit migrant labourers to challenge the conditions of settled workers and sharecroppers. Both in cocoa and in groundnut production, daily and casual contracts became the norm in the period in which the expansion of the agricultural frontier reached its limit, and production was intensified via mechanization. This gave the employers greater flexibility to adjust the supply of labour. In response, migrant workers in Senegambia took to joining work gangs to improve their bargaining position.[42]

---

[40] J. A. Arthur, 'Labor Migration Patterns in West Africa', *African Studies Review*, 34.3 (1991), 65–87; Cordell et al., *Hoe and Wage*.

[41] Cordell et al., *Hoe and Wage*; Manchuelle, *Willing Migrants*. See the chapter by Tischler in this volume.

[42] K. Swindell, 'People on the Move in West Africa: From Pre-Colonial Polities to Post-Independence States', in *The Cambridge Survey of World Migration*, ed. R. Cohen (Cambridge: Cambridge University Press, 1995), 196–202.

Population resettlement through labour migration did, however, reverse the political economy of the hitherto powerful hinterland kingdoms and caliphates, which progressively gave way to coastal domination. Accordingly, the population, which until the 1920s was more or less evenly distributed between the coast, the forest and the Sahel, had become by the 1970s predominantly concentrated around the coastal centres of accumulation.[43] Migrations in West Africa became more complex after independence, in the context of, first, commodity cycles, and then liberalization and political crisis. However, while in the 1960s rural-to-urban migration gave impetus to rapid urban growth, by the 1990s circular and urban-to-rural migration was the dominant pattern. Overall, the rate of urbanization was slower in West Africa than elsewhere in the continent, and periods of economic crisis triggered episodes of reverse migration into rural areas.[44]

Sahelian Migrants and the Development of the Groundnut Basin

In the mid-nineteenth century, coastal plantations in Senegal and along the Gambia river started to supply a growing export market for groundnut – the main source of vegetable oil – and rice. The growing demand for agricultural labour coincided with the process of manumission, which had created groups of floating land-poor and landless populations that could not subsist on their own farming and engaged in periodic labour migration. Former slave traders from the hinterlands of Mali, Mauritania and Guinea became seasonal sharecroppers in Senegambia in order to raise capital to finance the trading activities that brought them to the ports. Former slaves became an available source of independent seasonal labour on groundnut estates, and some used their wages to buy their freedom or to establish themselves in patronage relations with former masters. Monetization, the introduction of colonial taxes and the expansion of the groundnut economy in the first decades of the century contributed to attracting new streams of labour migrants from Senegal's hinterlands and the Sahel. Outmigration became generalized among Malinke, Bambara and Soninke

---

[43] Amin, *Modern Migrations in Western Africa*. It has been argued that, before infrastructure and logistical developments, the transport costs of migrant labour would have been lower than the costs of exporting commodities produced in hinterlands. Cordell et al., *Hoe and Wage*; Amin, *Modern Migrations in Western Africa*.

[44] C. Beauchemin and P. Bocquier, 'Migration and Urbanisation in Francophone West Africa: An Overview of Recent Empirical Evidence', *Urban Studies*, 41.11 (2004), 2245–72.

men, predominantly as groundnut sharecroppers – the Navétanes in Senegal and the 'stranger farmers' of the Gambia.[45]

Among the Soninke, migration involved both poor and former slaves as well as the maraboutic and non-clerical aristocracy. The latter used trading networks and Islamic schools to seek opportunities for employment as *laptots*, commercial agents and colonial officers throughout the first half of the twentieth century. These varied forms of circular outmigration reaching all social groups among the Soninke transformed social relations by subverting the elders' power and depriving local production of labour. The development of the Bamako–Dakar railway and of port infrastructure changed the spatial organization of the groundnut economy and created jobs in construction, transport and services.[46] Soninke men, among others, were migrating for longer periods and were more likely to settle in their labour destinations. In the 1970s accumulation on the basis of groundnut slowed down, with land and seed becoming increasingly scarce. This eroded the foundation of the sharecropping arrangements with the Navétanes, resulting in a switch to wage-labour migrants. Manchuelle has proposed that the migration of unskilled West African workers to France came from among the ranks of these migrant and increasingly urbanized workers.[47]

Labour Migration to the West African Cocoa Belt

Migrant labourers were instrumental in the introduction of cocoa, coffee, rubber and cotton agriculture to internal agrarian frontiers in the Gold Coast, Nigeria and Côte d'Ivoire. However, the development of wage-labour relations took place in the presence of forms of unfree labour, such as slave labour and *corvée*, which were prevalent before the introduction of wage labour.[48] The continued coexistence of forms of free and unfree labour belies the assumption that pre-capitalist relations of production would be inexorably overcome by the logic of capital and resulted in processes of negotiation, struggle and resistance.[49]

---

[45] P. David, *Les navétanes: histoire des migrants saisonniers de l'arachide en Sénégambie des origines à nos jours* (Dakar: Nouvelles Éditions Africaines, 1980); Swindell, 'People on the Move in West Africa'; Manchuelle, *Willing Migrants*; C. Oya, 'Stories of Rural Accumulation in Africa: Trajectories and Transitions among Rural Capitalists in Senegal', *Journal of Agrarian Change*, 7.4 (2007), 453–93.

[46] Manchuelle, *Willing Migrants*.

[47] *Ibid.*

[48] See the chapter by Eckert in this volume.

[49] Freund, *The Making of Contemporary Africa*; Swindell, 'People on the Move in West Africa'; Austin, *Labour, Land and Capital in Ghana*.

During the early stages of the expansion of cocoa in Asante, for example, growers relied on slave labour, despite the administrative prohibition of forced and slave labour. Growers with access to land used household labour, but larger plantations relied on pawns and previously enslaved people from the Northern Territories, which reduced the supply price of labour and ultimately boosted the accumulation of a 'forest rent'.[50] Between the late 1910s and the mid-1930s, male slave labour was replaced by migrant wage workers from the same northern savannahs, although women and children often remained subjected to pawning. However, by the mid-1930s wage labour was being progressively replaced by sharecropping. The contractual arrangements for the sharecroppers were originally stringent but became more favourable over time, as the expansion of cocoa to other parts of Ghana and the growth of the non-cocoa economy multiplied sources of employment and strengthened the bargaining position of labour within the sector. That the pressure for a change from wage labour to sharecropping came from the workers themselves problematizes accounts of sharecropping as a merely transitional form on the path towards wage employment.[51]

Requisitioned labour and the introduction of poll and hut taxes accelerated monetization and the commodification of labour across French West Africa. Mossiland, in the dry savannahs of Upper Volta, was not suitable for extensive cash cropping and provided most of the large contingent of migrant workers for cocoa farming in Ghana and Côte d'Ivoire. By crossing into the Gold Coast in the first half of the century, Mossi men were evading *corvée* labour (in place until 1946), forced cotton cultivation (introduced in the 1920s) and – at least temporarily – poll taxes. The international, circular and massive Mossi migration to the cocoa belt could still be accommodated in the calendar of sorghum and millet farming at home and became an avenue for the social empowerment of the youth. The French colonial authorities first encouraged this migration as a source of fiscal revenue, but soon felt the heightened difficulty of recruiting workers for the Ivorian plantations. In order to divert the 'voltaic' migrants into French colonies, Upper Volta was parcelled out to the neighbouring colonies between 1932 and 1947.[52] Once forced labour was abolished and Ivorian cocoa farming offered better conditions, Mossi migratory streams were redirected to western Côte d'Ivoire where many remained as settled farmers and where thousands of Burkinabe still migrate every season (see Table 9.1).

---

[50] Austin, *Labour, Land and Capital in Ghana*.

[51] *Ibid.*

[52] Cordell et al., *Hoe and Wage*.

Along with wage-labour migrants, another stream of migrants was decisive in the development of the cocoa economy: those who gained access to land and set up cocoa farms in their own right. The social norms, institutions and political processes that granted access to forested frontiers to migrant farmers from northern Ghana, eastern Côte d'Ivoire, Nigeria and the Sahel had influential long-term effects on the politics of autochthony in the cocoa belt. The emblematic cases include the migrant cocoa farmers of Akwa Pim in Ghana, who crossed the Densu river at the turn of the century to negotiate access to plots and set up burgeoning independent cocoa operations; as did the Mossi and Baoulé (from central Côte d'Ivoire) who obtained land in the western Ivorian forest through the *tutorat*, a set of social norms that encouraged forest lineages to grant land to strangers.[53] Côte d'Ivoire's first president, Félix Houphouët-Boigny, and the Democratic Party of Côte d'Ivoire, in power from the 1960s until 1999, represented the interests of Ivorian migrant farmers and articulated a development strategy that rested on the westward expansion of cocoa. By 1960 over a third of all the labour force in Côte d'Ivoire came from Burkina Faso, Mali, Niger and Guinea, but other tenant farmers came from eastern and central Côte d'Ivoire. The 'Houphouëtian compromise' encapsulated the way in which state revenue was mobilized to compensate the original owners of the land through investment and employment opportunities; to mobilize cocoa farmers' political support through guaranteed prices and subsidies; and to garner political strength by giving foreign migrants the right to vote. In the 1990s, however, structural adjustment and the crisis in the cocoa sector resulted in the shedding of thousands of jobs in the state and in parastatal agencies.[54] Pressure from urban unemployment and agrarian crisis brought the end of the 'Ivorian miracle', and the old compromise could not be sustained. Mounting political instability resulted in violent struggles over land ownership, migration and conflicting ideas of autochthony and *ivoirité*.[55]

The expansion of cocoa production in the early twentieth century contributed to making the Gold Coast the world's largest producer. Accumulation based on cocoa exports created jobs in agriculture but also

[53] P. Hill, *The Migrant Cocoa-Farmers of Southern Ghana: A Study in Rural Capitalism* (Cambridge: Cambridge University Press, 1963); J. P. Chauveau, 'How Does an Institution Evolve? Land, Politics, Intergenerational Relations and the Institution of the *tutorat* between Autochthons and Migrant Farmers in the Gban Region (Côte d'Ivoire)', in *Land and the Politics of Belonging in West Africa*, ed. R. Kuba and C. Lentz (Leiden: Brill, 2006), 213–40.

[54] See the chapter by van den Bersselaar in this volume.

[55] Chauveau, 'How Does an Institution Evolve?'; Beauchemin and Bocquier, 'Migration and Urbanisation in Francophone West Africa'.

in construction, manufacturing, services and mining.[56] Furthermore, the construction of the Akosombo Dam and the development of the Port of Tema contributed to boosting other productive linkages as well as development in the manufacturing sector that employed workers from Niger, Nigeria, Togo, Benin and Upper Volta.[57] Crises in the cocoa economy had different effects for foreign migrant workers in Ghana, where migrants were more readily scapegoated. In 1969, for example, between 55,000 and 213,000 workers in cocoa agriculture – for the most part Nigerians – were forcibly repatriated. However, these evictions did not solve the price crisis and may have aggravated it by constraining the labour supply and raising production costs.[58]

In independent Ghana and Côte d'Ivoire, the agricultural dynamism of the cocoa belt took part of the pressure off rural-to-urban migration. Efforts to diversify the Burkinabe economy and create local sources of employment had limited success. Periods of crisis in the cocoa belt led to relatively rapid growth of Ouagadougou from the 1970s via internal migration. But seasonal labour migration stemming mainly from Burkina Faso as well as from within Ghana and Côte d'Ivoire continued well into the 1980s (see Table 9.1).

The Nigerian Exception?

Labour migration in Nigeria followed a different trajectory. A considerable proportion of the migrant labour that was recruited in the expansion of cotton and cocoa in central Nigeria after the 1920s came from southern and northern Nigeria. Rather than the creation of separate labour reserves, there was significant resettlement in the middle belt, and groups of skilled workers and officials from the south settled in northern Nigeria. Outmigration was also significant: contract and clandestine Nigerian migrants worked in the cocoa plantations of Fernando Po, Spanish Guinea and Ghana until the 1969 evictions. However, unlike in other West African economies, by the 1950s over 70 per cent of migrant labour was internal, partly moving to the cotton belt, but also taking up jobs in Lagos, Ibadan and the Delta.[59]

The discovery of oil deposits in the 1970s transformed the patterns of labour migration. In the period of development of the oil sector, between two and three million migrants entered Nigeria from Ghana, Niger, Chad, Cameroon, Burkina Faso, Togo and Benin. Not all were labour migrants,

---

[56]   See the chapters by Brown, Neveling and Berry in this volume.

[57]   Arthur, 'Labor Migration Patterns in West Africa'.

[58]   Swindell, 'People on the Move in West Africa'; Bakewell, 'Keeping Them in Their Place'.

[59]   *Ibid.*

but all sought to benefit from opportunities in and around the oil economy, including access to commodities, subsidized prices and higher wage levels. A number of ambitious infrastructure projects, such as the construction of Abuja and the Kainji Dam, required considerable labour mobilization and improved wages. Ghanaian teachers and professors staffed the new polytechnic universities. However, the oil sector was hit by the 1979 crisis, and the Nigerian economy suffered as a consequence. Nationalist narratives of retribution led to the expulsion of over two million unskilled foreign migrant labourers, half of them Ghanaian.[60]

The end of colonial rule brought a hardening of the national borders that made migration more onerous for workers. Both in Ghana and Nigeria, post-independence crises were dealt with by decreeing the expulsion of masses of labour migrants. In contrast, in Mali, Liberia and Sierra Leone, post-independence was a period of rapid expansion of urban activity in which rural–urban migrants sought the jobs and opportunities that were concentrated in and around capital cities. However, structural adjustment in the 1980s hollowed out the state, reducing public-sector employment and indirect sources of livelihoods and jobs. This had the effect of slowing down the rate of urban expansion and contributing to instances of urban–rural migration in West African countries.[61] Large migratory flows continue to characterize West Africa in the early twenty-first century. Nigerian outmigration and the circular flow of the Burkinabe into Côte d'Ivoire constitute some of the largest contemporary continental flows within Africa, and there is a large diaspora from Ghana, Nigeria and Liberia living in the United States (see Table 9.1). As in the case of East Africa, armed conflict and political instability in the region have been at the root of massive cross-border population flows. Furthermore, there is a more recent diversification of the migration destinations, with a growing number of West Africans migrating to the United Kingdom, the Gulf states but also to South Africa.[62]

EAST AFRICAN LABOUR MIGRANTS AND SQUATTERS

Less systemic patterns of labour migration characterized the expansion of agricultural commodities in East Africa. Their different histories

---

[60] Arthur, 'Labor Migration Patterns in West Africa'.

[61] A. Adepoju, 'The Politics of International Migration in Post-Colonial Africa', in *The Cambridge Survey of World Migration*, ed. R. Cohen (Cambridge: Cambridge University Press, 1995), 166–71; Beauchemin and Bocquier, 'Migration and Urbanisation in Francophone West Africa'.

[62] Bakewell and de Haas, 'African Migrations'.

notwithstanding, Kenya, Tanzania and Uganda were important epicentres of internal and transnational labour migration during the twentieth century. One particularity that stands out in comparison with the labour migration systems reviewed so far was the shorter distance of displacements and the clear predominance of internal migration.

Evictions and land dispossession coupled with the institutionalized attempt to create labour reserves paved the way for the development of settler farming in Kenya. Here, the contrast of the coastal plantations and highland settler estates is telling. Unlike white settlers who benefited from the state's active involvement in mobilizing and fixing the workforce after the abolition of slave labour in 1907, powerful large Arab and Swahili landholders – denied the assistance of the state – were unable to sustain high rates of surplus extraction and sustained accumulation. Former slaves and Mijikenda migrants became squatters and occasional workers in the production of food and cash crops. In contrast, circular labour migration was the main channel for mobilizing workers to the tea plantations of Kericho. Workers also migrated from Burundi and Rwanda, but mostly from densely populated areas of Nyanza and the Western Province, to the plantations and estates of the Rift Valley and the Central Province, and from the densely populated Kikuyu areas, for work in agriculture, transport, construction and the state. Migration contributed numerically to what was probably one of the largest contingents of wage labourers in the continent by the late 1920s.[63] By the 1930s up to a quarter of the male adult population in parts of Nyanza was engaged in labour outmigration. Large-scale agricultural development and the growth of food markets opened options for labour migration and cash cropping, but migration stemmed predominantly from districts where land was relatively scarce and cash cropping less viable. Over time, profitable cash cropping would require bought inputs, and many households then opted for the comparatively higher returns of wage labour.[64]

In contrast, settler farms in the 'white highlands' relied on Kikuyu migrant 'squatter' tenants. Instead of the dynamic white commercial farming that the administration envisioned, white absentee farmers in the highlands depended on labour extracted from squatters and their successful production. To overcome this, the state and the farmers agreed to increase the demands for labour from squatters and to preclude independent herding and farming.

---

[63] F. Cooper, *From Slaves to Squatters: Plantation Labor and Agriculture in Zanzibar and Coastal Kenya, 1890–1925* (New Haven, CT: Yale University Press, 1980); B. Berman and J. Lonsdale, *Unhappy Valley: Conflict in Kenya and Africa*, 2 vols (London: James Currey, 1992).

[64] Kitching, *Class and Economic Change in Kenya*.

Their strategy pitted squatters against migrant contract labour on the farms. The ensuing resentment and grievances led to desertion but also to violent resistance by Kikuyu squatters during Mau Mau.[65] In the post-independence period, there was some resettlement and the emergence of successful accumulation in agriculture by African farmers in the Central Province. For the most part, however, labour migration patterns remained in place, although more stringent border controls negatively affected the migration prospects of the foreign workforce.[66]

In colonial Tanganyika, internal migrant workers as well as migrants from Rwanda and Burundi had been recruited in the production of coffee in estates around Kilimanjaro and cotton plantations south of Lake Victoria. In the coastal sisal plantations, labour migrants from Mozambique and the interior dominated over local workers. Migrant workers from Tanganyika instead engaged in long-distance migration to the mines of the Rand and to the Copperbelt. During the late 1940s, attempts to develop large-scale commercial agriculture, notably the groundnut scheme, stretched labour supplies to the limit. The administration response was to subdivide Tanganyika into areas of labour outmigration and areas of peasant agriculture, which did not prevent a 'scramble for wages' that pitted agricultural projects against other labour-intensive sectors. In periods of rising food prices during the 1950s, wage workers had every incentive to return to their land to become commodity producers instead.[67]

However, after independence, *ujamaa* and villagization attempted to discourage long-distance labour migration and to stimulate the resettlement of former migrant labourers. This was reinforced by the nationalization of agricultural estates that further reduced the sources of employment for migrants. As the economic situation deteriorated in the 1970s, falling real incomes forced large groups of urban dwellers into self-employment and informal livelihoods. Petty trade, artisan production and informal service provision became the means of social reproduction.[68] The socialist state's governments tended to reject this development, because it was contrary to their ideology of virtuous and productive village life against unproductive

[65] Kanogo, *Squatters and the Roots of Mau Mau*.

[66] W. T. S. Gould, 'Regional Labour Migration Systems in East Africa: Continuity and Change', in *The Cambridge Survey of World Migration*, ed. R. Cohen (Cambridge: Cambridge University Press, 1995), 183–9.

[67] M. Rizzo, 'What Was Left of the Groundnut Scheme? Development Disaster and Labour Market in Southern Tanganyika 1946–1952', *Journal of Agrarian Change*, 6.2 (2006), 205–38.

[68] See the chapter by Barchiesi in this volume.

urban self-employment. A concerted effort on the part of the state was made to ban, relocate and prosecute self-employed and informal workers. These conflicts reflected the irreversible effects of expanding commodity relations and the strategies that former labour migrants deployed when labour migration streams ceased to offer viable livelihoods.[69] During the 1990s, armed conflict in the Great Lakes region produced the largest population movements of refugees and IDPs in the continent. Over 1.3 million refugees settled in western Tanzania, at times increasing the local population by up to 50 per cent. However difficult it was to discern seasonal and oscillatory labour migration from refugee and IDP flows, it is noteworthy that the routes of forced migrants mirrored the colonial routes of labour migration to western Tanganyika.[70]

NORTH AFRICA AND OUTWARD MIGRATION STREAMS

The formation of a migrant labour force in North Africa during the twentieth century was founded on the displacement of nomadic herders out of the plains and the formation of estates headed by *colons* (colonial settlers). Colonial land concentration had different effects in Morocco and Tunisia and was perhaps more disruptive of the pre-existing production regimes and trading routes in Algeria. Displaced from the plains, Berbers retreated into mountainous regions, where the prospects for reproduction based on agriculture were precarious, and subsequently became a reserve army of labour for settler agriculture. People in the Rif and Kabylia started to combine household agriculture with long-distance seasonal migration to the plains and the cities. This pattern of labour migration involved for the most part unmarried men, but in areas of more acute dependence on off-farm income it would involve all men of working age.

The inability of the settlers to raise agricultural productivity on the estates led to the adoption in the 1920s of sharecropping arrangements and to replacing cereals by more profitable but labour-intensive citrus, vine and olive orchards in both Tunisia and Morocco. The system was upset by different crises. In the 1930s generalized unemployment among seasonal migrants

---

[69] A. M. Tripp, 'Defending the Right to Subsist: The State vs. the Urban Informal Economy in Tanzania', WIDER Working Paper 59, World Institute for Development Economics Research, United Nations University, 1989, 28–31.

[70] Gould, 'Regional Labour Migration Systems in East Africa'; R. Black, L. M. Hilker and C. Pooley, 'Migration and Pro-Poor Policy in East Africa', Working Paper C7, University of Sussex, Development Research Centre on Migration, Globalisation and Poverty, 2004; Bakewell and de Haas, 'African Migrations'.

destabilized the financial foundations of family agriculture and caused the relocation of villagers to urban slums and urban-based livelihoods, including employment in the emerging manufacturing and construction sectors. The operation of the ports, transport logistics and the array of infrastructural projects under construction in the first half of the century created a demand for labour outside agriculture.[71]

From the 1920s onwards, Algerians from Kabylia also started to migrate for work to France. To compensate for the reduced labour supply, the estates of Oran and Algiers began to recruit Moroccan migrants as seasonal wage workers. Later on, labour shortages in France, Germany and Belgium triggered labour recruitment from Tunisia and Morocco, and the 1950s was a period of rapid expansion of North African emigration. As North African migrants stabilized in France and became skilled workers, new frontiers of recruitment for unskilled labour were developed, notably in Senegal.[72] European demand for labour slowed down with the oil crisis. Whether this reflected highly restrictive immigration policies in Europe after the 1970s or alternative patterns of migration within Africa is open to debate. Active recruitment gave way to more restrictive migratory regulations, but the Moroccan population in Europe continued to grow through spontaneous migration from 400,000 in 1975 to three million by 2004, which corresponded to 10 per cent of the total population. Similarly, migrants living outside Tunisia amounted to 9 per cent of the population by 2003. In contrast, emigrants account for less than 3 per cent of the Algerian population, while Libya's large oil economy made it into a labour migration destination for workers from Egypt, Sudan and from across the Maghreb.[73] At present, Egypt, Algeria, Tunisia and Morocco all have large migrant populations living in Europe and account for the largest share of African outward migration (see Table 9.1).

[71] N. MacMaster, 'Labour Migration in French North Africa', in *The Cambridge Survey of World Migration*, ed. R. Cohen (Cambridge: Cambridge University Press 1995), 190–5. See the chapter by Bellucci in this volume.

[72] Manchuelle, *Willing Migrants*.

[73] M. Baldwin-Edwards, 'Between a Rock and a Hard Place: North Africa as a Region of Emigration, Immigration and Transit Migration', *Review of African Political Economy*, 33.108 (2006), 311–24; Bakewell and de Haas, 'African Migrations'.

THEMES IN AFRICAN LABOUR MIGRATION

URBANIZATION AND THE LINKAGES BETWEEN LABOUR MIGRATION AND DEVELOPMENT

While different labour migration experiences contributed to the consolidation of urban centres in Africa, migrant stabilization was actively discouraged when not banned outright in different periods and sectors by employers and states, for example in the Northern Rhodesian Copperbelt and the mines of the Transvaal. Similarly, migration to booming agricultural districts (sugar plantations in Natal, tea and coffee estates in Kenya, tobacco farms in central Malawi, to cite some examples) did not directly result in pressures towards urbanization. If agricultural exports contributed to urbanization, it was indirectly, by triggering employment in construction, transport, agro-processing and in the state apparatus.

The growth of peri-urban settlements in the late twentieth century owed more to the loss of jobs and the overall squeeze of subsistence in the countryside than to surges in demand for labour in urban areas. During agricultural crises, migration to peri-urban settlements allowed distressed migrants to engage in new livelihoods by straddling urban and rural economies.[74] Finally, urbanization was not a linear process in twentieth-century Africa, and economic crises resulted also in some instances of falling urban growth rates and urban-to-rural migration.

Since the 1990s the literature on labour migration has reinterpreted spatial mobility as a driver of societal change rather than as an economic malfunction. This work has produced a different, frequently positive, understanding of the linkages between migration and development – for example, as experiences and remittances that are accrued via migration enhance the human capital of the migrants and unlock sources of finance for domestic economies with potential poverty-reduction effects.[75] However, there is also a new recognition that migration is not an avenue open to all, and that the uneven distribution of the streams of revenue generated by migrants can reinforce inequality and social differentiation at the local level. Examples of remittance-fuelled processes of reinvestment resulting in agricultural dynamism coexist side-by-side with instances of stagnation and distress migration.[76]

---

[74] Potts, *Circular Migration in Zimbabwe*.

[75] N. Nyberg-Sorensen, N. van Hear and P. Engberg-Pedersen, *The Migration–Development Nexus: Evidence and Policy Options* (Geneva: International Organization for Migration, 2002); Bakewell, 'Keeping Them in Their Place'.

[76] S. Orvis, 'The Kenyan Agrarian Debate: A Reappraisal', *African Studies Review*, 36.3 (1993), 23–48; Oya, *Rural Inequality, Wage Employment and Labour Market Formation in Africa*.

INFORMAL WORK AND LABOUR CASUALIZATION

The informalization and casualization of formal labour in Africa has had a double effect on labour migration.[77] In relative terms, it has resulted in a deterioration of the conditions of settled labour, thereby reducing the comparative appeal of recruiting migrant workers in the eyes of employers. In absolute terms, it has also contributed to a greater precarity for the remaining migrant workers. Labour flexibilization, deregulation, outsourcing and subcontracting have translated into greater employment instability, losses in terms of real wages and statutory benefits and lack of legal and social protection for migrant workers.

The use of migrant labour in formal employment seems to have experienced a steep reduction in the period of liberalization. Structural adjustment reduced the employing capacity of the public sector, with dire consequences for countries such as Tanzania, Kenya and Angola, in which labour demand in the private sector was already sluggish during the 1990s.[78] Foreign migrant labour in the South African mining sector, which represented 60 per cent of the total workforce in the 1970s, accounts nowadays for less than 30 per cent. Part of this shift reflects the removal of settlement restrictions after the end of apartheid, but the downward trend continued thereafter. In the platinum mines alone, the number of migrant Mozambican workers (the largest contingent among foreign migrants) halved between 2003 and 2012, and there are fewer than 10,000 migrant workers from Lesotho, Swaziland and Botswana. This happened at the same time as there was an overall rise in the hiring of contract labour, which now represents almost 40 per cent of the workforce. The rise of contract labour, disparities between formal and informal employment and conflicts between different types of workers present their own challenges for workers' collective action. In some cases, the fight for decent jobs has been couched implicitly as a fight against jobs for migrants.[79]

Horticultural sectors in East and southern Africa are experiencing similar tendencies towards labour informalization and casualization. Trade liberalization, increased competition and vertical integration in production have reduced the role of the state in the regulation of the labour market

---

[77] See the chapter by Barchiesi in this volume.

[78] C. M. Rogerson, 'Globalization or Informalization? African Urban Economies in the 1990s', in *The Urban Challenge in Africa: Growth and Management of its Large Cities*, ed. C. Rakodi (Tokyo: United Nations University Press, 1997), pp. 337–62.

[79] Posel, 'Have Migration Patterns in Post-Apartheid South Africa Changed?'; K. Forrest, 'Rustenburg's Fractured Recruitment Regime: Who Benefits?', *African Studies*, 73.2 (2014), 149–68.

and work conditions. In its place, corporate responsibility and self-regulation have become the guiding mechanisms in expanded global value chains. On the other hand, stringent competition linked to transnational outsourcing and subcontracting has introduced renewed pressures for cost reduction via the flexibilization of labour. This has resulted in a greater scope for temporary, casual and contractual labour, contract farming, the proliferation of labour brokers as well as the growing participation of women in the workforce, including as migrant workers.[80]

The informalization of the more permanent and secure types of employment has coincided with the expansion of informal work. According to the ILO, unemployment increased by 0.3 per cent between 1999 and 2004 in sub-Saharan Africa, despite an average annual GDP growth rate of 3.3 per cent and a 2.7 per cent annual growth rate of the workforce in the same period. By 2004 the unemployment rate stood at 10.1 per cent, but the rate in southern African countries can be three times as high.[81] It was estimated that about 93 per cent of the new jobs created in Africa during the 1990s were in the informal sector and its contribution to GDP seems on the rise across the continent. ILO data from the 1990s indicated that up to 63 per cent of the urban workforce was employed in the informal sector. However, the majority of these jobs were in very small family or individual enterprises, with minimum protection and in informal activities, including hawking, scavenging, petty trade, as well as in low-cost services such as transport.[82] The feminization of informal work led to the initial praising of the informal sector as being more receptive of women, but as Meagher warned,

> high levels of female entry into informal activity should not be confused with high levels of opportunity. Many of the same factors that disadvantage women in the formal sector operate as obstacles to success

---

[80]   Posel, 'Have Migration Patterns in Post-Apartheid South Africa Changed?';
C. S. Dolan, 'Benevolent Intent? The Development Encounter in Kenya's Horticulture Industry', *Journal of Asian and African Studies*, 40.6 (2005), 411–37;
S. Barrientos and A. Kritzinger, 'Squaring the Circle: Global Production and the Informalization of Work in South African Fruit Exports', *Journal of International Development*, 16.1 (2004), 81–92.

[81]   J. D. Schmidt, 'Flexicurity, Casualization and Informalization of Global Labour Markets', in *Globalization and the Third World*, ed. B. N. Ghosh and H. M. Guven (London: Palgrave Macmillan, 2006), 129–47. Here a note of caution is necessary: standardized statistical indicators on labour and employment were not developed with African labour markets in mind and lead to frequent measurement biases. See Oya, *Rural Inequality, Wage Employment and Labour Market Formation in Africa.*

[82]   Rogerson, 'Globalization or Informalization?'.

in the informal sector, particularly limited access to capital and low levels of education and skills.[83]

The combined effect of the informalization of employment and the growth of the informal sector have resulted in a blurring of the distinction between formal and informal employment, with implications for migrant workers. There are also problems with criteria for categorization in labour surveys: many of those classified as self-employed tend to be dependent workers who are working on commission or on outsourced jobs.[84]

OUTWARD LABOUR MIGRATION AND THE 'BRAIN DRAIN'

Between 2005 and 2010 over 3.6 million people engaged in trans-border migration within Africa. No other region in the world has such large, dynamic and concentrated internal migration. Although this figure also includes the movement of refugees and returnees, the distinctive internal nature of migratory flows owes much to a long and consequential history of labour migration in Africa. Contrary to the impression created by current media narratives, Africa is not a large contributor to trans-regional migration, and migration within Africa surpasses outward migration in volume.[85] What is distinctive about African migratory patterns in global perspective is that Africa has the largest internal migration flow of all regions and the highest concentration of overall migration within the same region.[86] Unlike in most other regions, the volume of internal migration is slightly larger than that of outward migration. Figure 9.1 compares migratory movements in Africa and other continents and Table 9.1 includes the largest migratory movements between 2005 and 2010.

The best existing estimates indicate that migration originating in Africa accounted in 2005 for only 14 per cent of all migrants in the EU and only 3 per cent in the US, and there is no solid evidence for arguing that upward trends in outward migration will be sustained. 'Absolute numbers of African

[83] K. Meagher, 'Crisis, Informalization and the Urban Informal Sector in Sub-Saharan Africa', *Development and Change*, 26.2 (1995), 271.

[84] *Ibid.*

[85] In fact, if North African countries – the largest continental contributors to outward migration – were omitted, migration within Africa would surpass outward migration by a large ratio.

[86] Even in West Africa, the only sub-region in which the rates of migration surpass the rate of population growth, the migration flow within Africa is seven times larger than the outward flow. Bakewell and de Haas, 'African Migrations'.

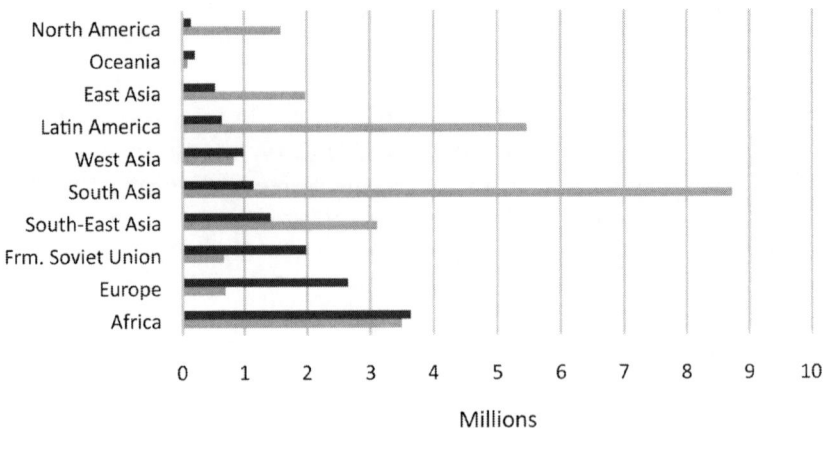

Figure 9.1. Internal and outward migratory movements by region, 2005–10 (source: based on data by Abel and Sander, *Quantifying Global International Migration Flows* [Supplementary material], 1 December 2015.)

migrants to Europe might be increasing but falling as a percentage of overall immigration level.'[87] Furthermore, outward migration stemming from Africa is highly concentrated among North African countries.

Another frequent misrepresentation relates to the characteristics of African migrants. Highly skilled immigrants are a large share of all migrants of African origin. In Europe, 13.5 per cent of all highly skilled foreigners are Africans. In the United States, African migrants have among the highest rates of high school completion of all immigrant groups.[88] While the emigration of Africans out of the continent is less numerically significant than other global and intra-African flows, the concentration of highly skilled migrants among those who relocate poses serious problems in terms of 'brain drain', the disproportionately high rate of emigration of people with tertiary level education as a share of all migrants.[89]

An important share of professionals from countries with well-regarded higher education, particularly in health sciences, have emigrated within

---

[87] *Ibid.*, 112.

[88] O. Bakewell, 'Migration and Development in Sub-Saharan Africa', in *Migration in the Global Political Economy*, ed. N. Phillips (Boulder, CO: Lynne Rienner, 2011).

[89] Adams defines as 'brain-drain' outward migratory flows involving more than 10 per cent of the population with tertiary education in a given country. R. H. Adams, 'International Migration, Remittances, and the Brain Drain: A Study of 24 Labor-Exporting Countries', Policy Research Paper 3069, The World Bank, Poverty Reduction and Economic Management Network, Washington, DC, 2003.

Africa and overseas. African migrants account for 7.8 per cent of doctors and 8.4 per cent of nursing personnel working in OECD countries. It has been estimated that the number of African doctors, nurses, lab technicians and pharmacists practising abroad far surpasses the total national health personnel in countries such as Ethiopia, Malawi and Zambia. Periods of political instability have contributed to the accelerated emigration of skilled workers. For example, under Idi Amin, an important share of the practitioners in the Ugandan health sector fled the country, and it is estimated that up to 50 per cent of Zimbabwean health workers have relocated since 2001.[90] With up to 60 per cent of its medical doctors abroad, Ghana has experienced a veritable exodus of health professionals. Many skilled Ghanaians migrated within Africa in the 1970s and 1980s, but Europe and North America have become preferred destinations thereafter.[91] In countries with long histories of migration, such as Senegal and South Africa, the exodus of highly skilled migrants has coincided with the arrival of skilled foreign workers. The overall impact of the outmigration of highly skilled populations is, however, still poorly understood. Analysts debate whether the macroeconomic impact of the disproportionate outmigration of skilled personnel could be offset by the potential positive effect of revenues remitted. Liberia, Morocco and Tunisia are the countries with the highest rate of remittances as a share of GDP.[92]

CONCLUSION

Labour migration is hardly a peculiarity of capitalism in Africa. Circuits of labour migration have been important in other periods and in other regions. However, examined in the historical context of the different African trajectories of development of productive forces, expansion of commodity relations and articulation to international circuits of trade and finance, the movement of workers and the spatial stretch of labour relations appears under a different light. In a vast continent in which, for the most part, the colonial encounter did not succeed in dissolving the very strong relationship between people and the land, changes in production involved massive movements of oscillatory labour migration.

[90] A. Adepoju, *Migration in Sub-Saharan Africa* (Uppsala: Nordiska Afrikainstitutet, 2008).

[91] M. Bump, 'Ghana: Searching for Opportunities at Home and Abroad', *Migration Information Source* (March 2006), https://goo.gl/YwdKTW (accessed 15 December 2015).

[92] Baldwin-Edwards, 'Between a Rock and a Hard Place'.

Labour relations in twentieth-century Africa took a range of forms, remarkable in their extreme heterogeneity and impossible to chart using the instruments provided by standardized categories in labour studies. Many of these contractual forms – formal and informal, coerced and 'free', institutionalized or clandestine – involved relocation and separation from the homestead, at times over very long distances. These dynamics introduced durable change in social relations, balances of power and identities within households, kin groups and communities and shaped agrarian class structures, processes of urbanization and labour struggles throughout the continent. Labour migration trajectories, their drivers and their effects encapsulate the contradiction of processes that were exploitative in nature, that were put into motion through coercion, and yet – by virtue of being contested, avoided or reshaped by those who confronted them – resulted in an array of contingent outcomes.

PART IV

VARIETIES OF WORK

TEN
Domestic Work

DEBORAH FAHY BRYCESON

Centre of African Studies, University of Edinburgh, and
International Gender Studies Centre, University of Oxford

Throughout African history, domestic labour time, directed at meeting the basic consumption needs of family members, has dwarfed any other labour time allocation. Yet it has received scant historical documentation because of its diffuse, home-based nature and the repetitive work of daily basic need provisioning – all readily observable in the here and now but defying analytical attention over time and space.

Domestic labour, commonly termed 'housework', is conventionally conflated with 'women's work'.[1] Housework encompasses childcare, cooking, washing, cleaning and general household maintenance. It is perceived as a jumble of multitasking activity dominating women's daily lives, motivated by love, duty, care and concern for family and lineage rather than monetary gain. This chapter attempts to piece together a historical narrative of the changing nature of domestic labour since 1900 based on social science literature.

Rural African women, notably the millions engaged in hoe production of staple food crops, were responsible for a triple workload of agricultural production, household drudgery and childcare responsibilities.[2] Pro-natalist norms, in conformity with agrarian labour needs, ordained frequent

---

[1] R. Dixon-Mueller, *Women's Work in Third World Agriculture* (Geneva: ILO, 1985); A. Whitehead, 'Rural Women and Food Production in Sub-Saharan Africa', in *Political Economy of Hunger, Volume 1: Entitlement and Well-Being*, ed. J. Drèze and A. Sen (Oxford: Clarendon Press, 1991), 425–73. Whitehead remarks that 'what invisibilizes women's work as "family labour" is its "family" or "domestic" character. This conflation could best be addressed with clear female and male delineation of agency of all ages in the performance of household basic needs provisioning' (p. 449).

[2] D. F. Bryceson, 'Wishful Thinking: Theory and Practice of Western Donor Efforts to Raise Women's Status in Rural Africa', in *Women Wielding the Hoe: Lessons from Rural*

childbearing. A voluminous literature on African rural women and work was informed by an earlier theoretical debate about domestic labour centred on the unequal gender division of household labour and the devalorization of women's work within the home.[3] These themes struck a chord with Western donor agencies' efforts to ameliorate poverty and power asymmetries in the African countryside. The World Employment Programme of the International Labour Organization commissioned a number of rural labour studies during the 1980s, amassing evidence of women's domestic labour patterns.[4]

The following section traces domestic labour's evolution with respect to domestic labour performance, the household division of labour, and how unmonetized, family-based domestic labour is affected by the general expansion of labour commodification in African economies through time. The next section establishes the analytical context, drawing attention to productive and reproductive spheres encompassing housework, rural subsistence agriculture and urban production patterns, as well as childcare demands. African domestic labour's evolution is periodized as follows: the colonial period, 1900–49; the nationalist and early postcolonial period, 1950–79; economic crisis, de-agrarianization and income diversification, 1980–99; and the neoliberal economic boom, urbanization and sectoral realignment towards natural resource extraction in African national economies from 2000 to the present.

AFRICAN DOMESTIC LABOUR'S CONTENT AND CONTEXT: FAMILY NEED PROVISIONING, COMMODIFICATION AND FOUNDATIONAL PRE-COLONIAL SOCIAL RELATIONS

Domestic labour is defined as the provisioning of household basic needs including cooking, cleaning, childcare and direct subsistence food production for family farming households, unmediated through the market. With respect to women's input, its scope and intensity can contract or expand depending on women's involvement in paid work outside the home and childcare

Africa for Feminist Theory and Development Practice, ed. D. F. Bryceson (Oxford: Berg Publishers, 1995), 201–22.

[3] S. James and M. Dalla Costa, *Power of Women and the Subversion of the Community* (Bristol: Falling Water Press, 1972); A. Oakley, *Housewife* (London: Allen Lane, 1974).

[4] L. Benaría, ed., *Women and Development: The Sexual Division of Labor in Rural Societies* (New York: Praeger, 1982); R. Anker, M. Buvinic and N. H. Youssef, *Women's Roles and Population Trends in the Third World* (London: Croom Helm, 1982); L. Goldschmidt-Clermont, *Economic Evaluations of Unpaid Household Work: Africa, Asia, Latin America and Oceania* (Geneva: ILO, 1987).

responsibilities related to the fertility rate. It diminishes to the degree that women have fewer children and/or join the wage labour force, but cannot disappear without jeopardizing the labour supply and survival of families, communities and nation states.[5]

The changing nature of African domestic labour since 1900 relates to transformation of African household membership. At the outset of the twentieth century, African family structure was tremendously varied, rarely approximating a Western nuclear household model. The overlap between the household as a familial residential unit as opposed to units of production, reproduction, decision making and consumption is not precise. Ekejiuba, writing about eastern Nigeria, charts the fluidity of everyday rural familial ties, comprised of 'negotiated relationships that result in interdependence and relative autonomy between the sexes'.[6] Rather than the term 'household' she refers to the 'hearth-hold', defined as a unit 'demographically consisting of a woman and all her dependents whose food security she is either fully or partially responsible for'. Men were part of one hearth-hold or oscillated between several wives, mistresses and a mother. A woman's hearth-hold constituted a domestic unit where consumption, production and reproduction came together; it formed the pivotal centre of domesticity, with the cooking hearth symbolizing food, comfort, well-being and safety. In monogamous or polygamous marriages, men were considered 'heads of household' while women were 'heads of hearth-hold' with clearly differentiated responsibilities.

The male head facilitated rather than acted as a direct agent of hearth-hold production. He provided the residential dwelling and assets such as land, fruit trees and livestock, used to support women's productive hearth-hold activities. Men paid school fees and hospital bills and provisioned meat to augment women's staple food contribution from their farming. Whitehead, writing about a Muslim agrarian society in northern Ghana, describes a similar pattern centred on the 'mother–child dyad', while the husband's and wife's mutually agreed 'conjugal contract' was nonetheless subject to negotiation, sometimes of a conflictual nature.[7]

[5] D. F. Bryceson and U. Vuorela, 'Outside the Domestic Labor Debate: Towards a Theory of Modes of Human Reproduction', *Review of Radical Political Economy*, 16.2/3 (1984), 137–66.

[6] F. I. Ekejiuba, 'Down to Fundamentals: Women-Centred Hearth-Holds in Rural West Africa', in *Women Wielding the Hoe: Lessons from Rural Africa for Feminist Theory and Development Practice*, ed. D. F. Bryceson (Oxford: Berg Publishers, 1995), 50–1.

[7] A. Whitehead, 'I'm Hungry Mum: The Politics of Domestic Budgeting', in *Of Marriage and the Market*, ed. K. Young, C. Wolkowitz and R. McCullagh (London: CSE Books, 1981), 88–111.

Variations of this pattern were prevalent over the broad swathe of agrarian sub-Saharan Africa. Ester Boserup identified African hoe agriculture as a largely 'female farming system' based on shifting cultivation that generated relatively low output per land unit but optimized output per labour unit.[8] Women specialized in staple food crop production, generally with separate farm plots, agricultural tasks and crops from their husbands. Along with their heavy agricultural labour input, the importance of women's childbearing role and high fertility was accentuated by the labour-demanding nature of hoe agriculture and the high incidence of child mortality.[9] Boserup has been critiqued for overstating the role of female farming in Africa,[10] but its relevance for understanding African rural labour patterns endured during the twentieth century.

In the drier climates of North Africa characterized by patrilineal descent and heavier penetration of Islam, plough agriculture or pastoralism prevailed. The adoption of seclusion practices meant far less agricultural work and labour expenditure of any description for women outside the home.[11] This, however, was counteracted in rural societies where men were inclined to travel away from the household for paid employment or business. For example, Berber peasant women in the Atlas mountains of Morocco had full working days directly engaged in agricultural production of household foodstuffs, water and firewood collection, childcare, tending the sick and carpet production.[12]

---

[8]   E. Boserup, *Woman's Role in Economic Development* (London: Earthscan, 1970).

[9]   African 'natural fertility regimes' had no conscious fertility control, with girls' early marriage soon after puberty and a tendency for women to give birth to between six and eight children during their reproductive years. Breastfeeding practices until the child was weaned at three to four years of age were associated with amenorrhea, postpartum sexual abstinence and women getting pregnant approximately every four to five years. J. Bongaarts, O. Frank and R. Lesthaeghe, 'The Proximate Determinants of Fertility in Sub-Saharan Africa', *Population and Development Review*, 10.3 (1984), 511–37.

[10] D. F. Bryceson, 'African Women Hoe Cultivators: Speculative Origins and Current Enigmas', in *Women Wielding the Hoe: Lessons from Rural Africa for Feminist Theory and Development Practice*, ed. D. F. Bryceson (Oxford: Berg Publishers, 1995), 3–22; J. Guyer, 'Women's Farming and Present Ethnography: Perspective on a Nigerian Restudy', in *ibid.*, 25–46.

[11] R. Longhurst, 'Rural Development Planning and the Sexual Division of Labour: A Case Study of a Moslem Hausa Village in Northern Nigeria', in *Rural Development and Women in Africa* (Geneva: ILO, 1984), 117–22.

[12] V. Maher, 'Work, Consumption and Authority within the Household: A Moroccan Case', in *Of Marriage and the Market*, ed. K. Young, C. Wolkowitz and R. McCullagh (London: CSE Books, 1981), 69–87.

Slave trading in the pre-colonial, conflict-ridden nineteenth century created mayhem in domestic life and labour patterns in many parts of sub-Saharan Africa. Where male slaves were seized, women were left to provision their families' food needs; alternatively the impact of indigenous slavery and slave raiding could result in women withdrawing from farming for security and/or the adoption of and strict adherence to Islamic practices.[13] The trans-Atlantic slave trade in West Africa was drawing to a close by the mid-nineteenth century. On the other hand, slavery was escalating in East and Central Africa.[14] The East and Central African trade was less directed at foreign export and more heavily targeted at women and children than the trans-Atlantic trade.[15] Women served as pawns to chiefs or Swahili traders along the slave trade routes.[16] Their commodified value rested primarily on supplying agricultural products, cooked food and sex. Seized women, who reached the urban coastal towns and Zanzibar, were destined to become domestic labourers and, frequently, concubines bearing children for their masters.

With exceptionally rapid economic and social change since 1900, transitions from coerced to paid labour, from agricultural to service-sector work and from formal to informal employment underpin the rising commodification of labour and goods in society and the valuation or devaluation of domestic labour.[17] The sections that follow track the evolution of domestic labour relations, revealing the interplay of forced, obligatory and volitional labour that can be further disaggregated into six distinct forms of labour relations (Figure 10.1). Pre-colonial labour relations are concentrated in segments A, B and C.

Despite rapid changes in production unfolding within African households, the reproductive sphere has been less volatile. Women's total fertility rates started to decline in the 1980s. Pro-natalist attitudes have held sway particularly in Africa's rural areas. High fertility rates are most prevalent in places where women shoulder a disproportionate share of the societal workload, and where household food provisioning, cleaning and maintenance are taken for granted as women's work. The following sections probe why this is so.

---

[13]   B. Cooper, 'Reflections on Slavery, Seclusion and Female Labour in the Maradi Region in the 19th and 20th Centuries', *Journal of African History*, 35.1 (1994), 156–65.

[14]   F. Cooper, *Plantation Slavery on the East Coast of Africa* (New Haven, CT: Yale University Press, 1977); A. Sheriff, *Slaves, Spices and Ivory in Zanzibar* (London: James Currey, 1987).

[15]   P. Manning, *Slavery and African Life: Occidental, Oriental, and African Slave Trades* (Cambridge: Cambridge University Press, 1990).

[16]   M. Wright, *Strategies of Slaves and Women: Life Stories from East/Central Africa* (London: James Currey, 1993).

[17]   Bryceson and Vuorela, 'Outside the Domestic Labor Debate'.

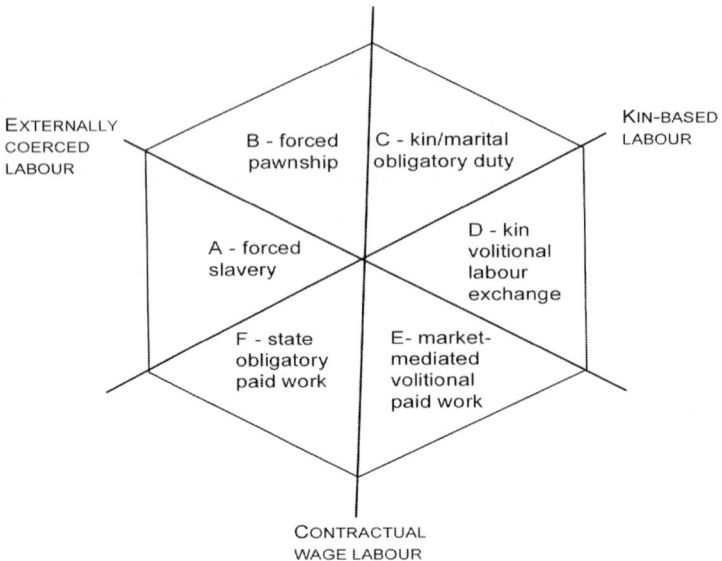

Figure 10.1. Hexagon of domestic labour relations (author's depiction)

COLONIAL RULE, 1900–49

By the dawn of the twentieth century, European colonial conquest and governance of the continent was nearing completion, justified largely in terms of stabilizing a strife-torn continent in the aftermath of the slave trade. The existence of slave trading for centuries in East and West Africa contributed to the formation of new ethnic identities associated with geographical dispersion of the enslaved as well as sexual liaisons between male masters and female slaves, which literally gave birth to creolized populations.[18] Slavery did not end with the official banning of the slave trade and slavery or the imposition of colonial government.[19] Large numbers of erstwhile slaves continued to work in servile labour conditions for people who occupied social positions related to the old order.[20] This was especially true for female slaves performing domestic labour in homes; many married their masters in reconstituted households. The dominant form of domestic

[18] D. F. Bryceson, 'Swahili Creolization: The Case of Dar es Salaam', in *The Creolization Reader: Studies in Mixed Identities and Cultures*, ed. R. Cohen and P. Toninato (London: Routledge, 2010), 364–75.

[19] J.-G. Deutsch, *Emancipation without Abolition in German East Africa c.1884–1914* (Oxford: James Currey, 2006).

[20] C. Robertson and M. Klein, eds, *Women and Slavery in Africa* (Madison, WI: University of Wisconsin Press, 1983).

labour in Africa at the turn of the century was the labour of wives-cum-mothers, residing in the countryside in farm households.

'MOTHER AFRICA': RURAL WOMEN'S DOMESTIC LABOUR PATTERN

European colonial policies were directed at economic profit and political stabilization in the continent's vast rural hinterland. Women as hearth-holders became central to colonial stabilization strategies. The distinction between male-headed households and female-headed hearth-holds was not lost on the colonial bureaucracy. Colonial policies encouraging European settler-led enterprises drew African male household heads away from their female hearth-holds into the expanding cash economy. Male labour needed to be transported and employed in plantations and mines, but women, who had been shunted about, used as pawns and traded as slaves at the will of men during the slave trade, entered a new era of residential immobility through being entrusted to tribal authorities under colonial governments' indirect rule policies. Native authorities facilitated the colonially imposed taxation system that created men's need to generate cash income, propelling male labour migration, the activities of labour recruitment agencies and the creation of physically divided households.[21] Colonial and native authority governance shared the objective of deterring women from migrating to their husbands' place of work or the city, keeping women *in situ* in their marital home areas.[22]

Considered capable of independently caring for their offspring and provisioning their basic needs for water, energy and food, rural women were cast in the role of 'Mother Africa', serving as *de facto* female heads of households. A wife's domestic labour and food production maintained the children and beckoned back their migrant husbands from distant plantations and mines. Meagre portions of the bachelor earnings of the male migrants trickled back to home areas in the form of purchased consumer goods such as tin roofing, bedding, pots and pans. Above all, bridewealth payments were migrants' major expenditure, affording ritual-officiating local elders a means of wealth accumulation. Although women were not directly involved in the cash economy, their use value as domestic labourers and childbearers

[21] C. Murray, *Families Divided? The Impact of Migrant Labour in Lesotho* (Cambridge: Cambridge University Press, 1981).

[22] M. Mbilinyi, 'Resistance in "Customary" Marriage: Tanzania's Runaway Wives', in *Forced Labour and Migration: Patterns of Movement within Africa*, ed. A. Zegeye and S. Ishemo (London: Hans Zell, 1989), 211–54.

was commodified in such payments. In traditional rituals, their value as childbearers and agricultural producers was repeatedly acknowledged.[23]

While tribal gender divisions of labour differed in terms of their allocation of tasks, functionally the workday had a remarkable constancy throughout the continent. In East Africa, Monica Wilson observed in the mid-1930s the banana-growing, patrilineal, virilocal Nyakyusa living in a lush highland area of Tanganyika.[24] They practised polygyny and arranged early marriages of girls at puberty. Dutifully, a wife had to 'cook and brew beer, fetch water and firewood, clean the house and byre, mud the walls and floor, work in the fields, and make bark-cloth and mats. Cooking was the primary duty of a wife, closely identified with sexual intercourse, the most conspicuous activity of the favourite [wife].'[25]

In southern Africa, among the Bemba who occupied the dry savannah in Northern Rhodesia, Audrey Richards noted:

> Cooking is an occupation, which has to be fitted into a seasonal as well as a daily routine. The Bemba housewife has to cleanse and tidy her hut and look after her children as well as prepare the daily meals ... Over and above, she is responsible ... for more than half of the agricultural work of the year, and therefore the time she has free for cooking varies from month to month.[26]

The preparation of an evening meal was estimated to occupy two to three hours per day. Girls learned housekeeping skills primarily by observing their mothers. By the time of their marriage at fourteen or fifteen years of age, they could cook the full range of Bemba dishes.

In West Africa, the Bamenda women of Cameroon positioned food farming in the foreground of their daily activities. Women skilfully cultivated several plots spanning different soils and agronomic conditions to provision food variety and minimize the possibility of total crop failure. Walking to and from these plots added to the time and effort involved in collecting firewood and water, pounding grain, preparing meals and childcare. Kaberry records women visiting their fields between two-thirds and three-quarters of all days

[23] For example, P. M. Kaberry, *Women of the Grassfields: A Study of the Economic Position of Women in Bamenda, British Cameroons* (London: HMSO, 1952).

[24] M. Wilson, *For Men and Elders: Change in the Relations of Generations and of Men and Women among the Nyakyusa-Ngonde People 1875–1971* (Boston, MA: Beacon Press, 1977).

[25] *Ibid.*, 129.

[26] A. I. Richards, *Land, Labour and Diet in Northern Rhodesia* (Oxford: Oxford University Press/International African Institute, 1939), 100.

of the calendar year.[27] Pregnant women farmed until the day of delivery, and then rested for three to four weeks after the birth of the baby.

Colonial governments operated with a double standard towards rural women's work. While taking advantage of the female farming system as a support to male labour migration, they gave women little credit for their economic self-reliance and hard work, placing emphasis on the role of the 'male breadwinner'.[28] Government agricultural extension work and the introduction of export crops were pointedly focused on men. Yet the ideology of male patriarchy was used to co-opt wives' labour in their husbands' commercial cash cropping, as exemplified in Ghanaian cocoa and Nigerian rice.[29]

NURTURING WESTERNIZED FEMALE DOMESTICITY

Christian missionary teachings were premised on marital conjugality and male household headship in conformity with a European patriarchal household model. The implicit and increasingly explicit stated aim was to deter women from urban migration, viewed as highly disruptive to African tribal social order. Those women and girls already in urban areas were subjected to Christian missionaries' teachings that equated being a Christian woman with motherhood and good homemaking. Unmarried women in Zambian urban areas were considered 'bad girls'.[30] In South Africa, housewifery was the central pivot of female education at mission schools, women's hostels and correctional institutions.[31]

In the Belgian Congo, the *foyer sociaux* programme, first fostered by Catholic missions in the 1920s, evolved into a 'civilizing' mission to impart

---

[27] Kaberry, *Women of the Grassfields*.

[28] B. Rogers, *The Domestication of Women: Discrimination in Developing Societies* (London: Taylor and Francis, 1981).

[29] J. Allman and V. Tashjian, *'I Will Not Eat Stone': A Woman's History of Colonial Asante* (Oxford: James Currey, 2000); J. Carney and M. Watts, 'Disciplining Women: Rice, Mechanization and the Evolution of Mandinka Gender Relations', *Signs*, 16.4 (1991), 651–81.

[30] J. L. Parpart, '"Wicked Women" and "Respectable Ladies": Reconfiguring Gender on the Zambian Copperbelt, 1936–1964', in *'Wicked' Women and the Reconfiguration of Gender in Africa*, ed. D. L. Hodgson and S. A. McCurdy (Portsmouth, NH: Heinemann, 2001), 274–92.

[31] D. Gaitskell, 'Housewives, Maids or Mothers: Some Contradictions of Domesticity for Christian Women in Johannesburg, 1903–39', *Journal of Africa History*, 24.2 (1983), 241–56.

a Western model of monogamous nuclear families, home economics and maternal hygiene to urban African women.[32] A small coterie of civil servants and other salaried African men who had converted to Catholicism were permitted to bring their wives and families to the towns. The aim of the programme was to channel women towards housekeeping skills and away from trading and beer brewing activities. As supportive wives to career-minded husbands and mothers of clean and well-dressed children schooled in baby care and the use of forks, knives and spoons, they formed part of an embryonic, monogamously married, urban African elite.[33]

COALESCING URBAN DOMESTIC LABOUR PRACTICES AND WAGED SERVANTS

Given restrictions on African urban migration, most towns and capital cities were primarily inhabited by non-Africans, notably European government administrators, Asian or Lebanese traders and a mix of educated European and Asians working as professional health, education or legal service providers. The occupational division of labour in towns was strongly male-biased for all races. While non-African urban women were rarely engaged in formal sector work, many, if not most, employed domestic servants.

Interestingly, with the exception of *ayahs* hired to mind pre-school children, the majority of domestic servants during colonial rule were men, euphemistically called 'house boys', 'garden boys', even 'nurse boys' to push the pram and wash nappies.[34] African female domestic servants were tainted with notions of slavery, primitivism and promiscuity. In Northern Rhodesia, with its long-standing tradition of hiring houseboys, white women purportedly shunned female servants who they feared might be attractive to their husbands. Domestic service performed in the intimacy of the colonial home sparked sensitivity about the transgression of racial and

---

[32] N. R. Hunt, 'Domesticity and Colonialism in Belgian Africa: Usumbura's Foyer Social, 1946–1960', *Signs*, 15.3 (1990), 447–74.

[33] C. Dickerman, 'City Women and the Colonial Regime: Usumbura, 1939–1962', *African Urban Studies*, 18 (1984), 33–48.

[34] J. Bujra, *Serving Class: Masculinity and the Feminisation of Domestic Service in Tanzania* (Edinburgh: Edinburgh University Press, 2000); K. T. Hansen, *Distant Companions: Servants and Employers in Zambia. 1900–1985* (Ithaca, NY: Cornell University Press, 1989); K. T. Hansen, 'Body Politics: Sexuality, Gender and Domestic Service in Zambia', *Journal of Women's History*, 2.1 (1990), 120–42.

class boundaries.[35] With the labour of houseboys readily at their disposal, many colonial wives became obsessed with maintaining standards of cleanliness. Tea rituals and thoroughness of cleaning procedures became the quintessential mark of being in a British home.

In conclusion, over five decades of colonial rule, labour transformation in the domestic sphere underwent profound transformations from the forced labour of nineteenth-century slavery and pawnship to a more statist form of labour control whereby men were induced to work as migrant labourers or engaged in cash cropping while their wives and mothers were obliged to remain *in situ* in their home areas, shouldering an inordinately heavy workload that served to offset the shortfall of basic needs provisioning from their husbands' cheap migrant wages. Women were a central pivot of domestic labour production and reproduction as food producers, welfare provisioners and childbearers. In Figure 10.1, these dynamics refer to section C (women as dutiful wives and mothers) and F (men as tax-propelled, long-distant migrant workers).

During the colonial period, the colonial state was compelling rather than coercing male wage labour, while relying heavily on women's undervalued rural domestic labour to subsidize the economy's embryonic agricultural and mining enterprises. The colonial male migrant labour system created a stark racial duality of domestic labour performance. African rural women were left with a staggering share of housework, basic needs provisioning and childcare, while European urban women, with hired male domestic labour support at their disposal and children often away at boarding school, were often entirely free from household drudgery.

THE NATIONALIST ERA, 1950–79

After the Second World War, the 'winds of change' brought rising politicization of the African population accompanied by aspirations for improved living standards and working conditions, giving impetus to the African struggle for national independence. Hurried measures were taken by colonial governments to address racial educational access and inequities in wage policies. Primary schools were opened to African children in urban areas, and to a lesser extent in rural areas, vital for the acquisition of work skills needed in the new national economies. The low 'bachelor' wages of the male circular migration system were replaced by a 'family wage' in many

[35] A. McClintock, *Imperial Leather: Race, Gender and Sexuality in the Colonial Context* (Abingdon: Routledge, 2013).

countries, thereby facilitating migration of urban migrants' families to the city. Women, who had hitherto been afforded only a tenuous urban foothold, began migrating with their husbands from rural farms or alternatively made their way independently to towns and cities where they assisted urban relations with domestic labour and childcare, since job markets had yet to welcome them.

Rapid urban growth, improving health facilities and a rising total fertility rate characterized most regions of the continent, except southern African mining economies, where urbanization and fertility decline were already well progressed, and North Africa, where the fertility rate had started to decline during the 1960s (Figure 10.2). A total fertility average of roughly seven indicates that natural fertility practices prevailed.

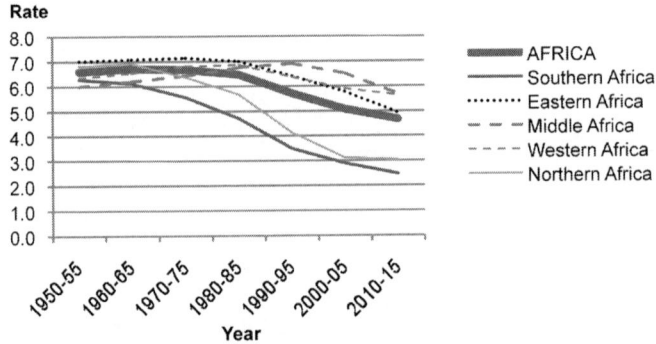

Figure 10.2. Total fertility rates by region, 1950–2012 (source: United Nations, Department of Economic and Social Affairs, Population Division, World Population Prospects: The 2012 Revision, Vol. 1, pp. 214–16).

DRAWING THE SHORT STRAW: CONCENTRATING RESPONSIBILITY FOR RURAL DOMESTIC LABOUR

Post-independent national governments were eager to embark on the development of their economies through mineral extraction or the expansion of peasant export crop production. The new African nation states of the 1960s benefited from a global agricultural commodity price boom. Most exhorted their large peasant populations to leap beyond subsistence agriculture to modern agriculture, targeting the use of agricultural inputs such as fertilizers and improved seeds to raise yields and enhance rural households' standard of living.[36]

---

[36]   See the chapter by Tischler in this volume.

Most long-distance migrant men returned to the farmstead. The postcolonial project to commodify peasant agriculture biased the production of export crops entirely towards men as household breadwinners, while women continued to act in the role of 'Mother Africa', as housewives and food crop producers for direct home consumption.[37] Male heads of households frequently co-opted their wives unpaid into cash-crop production or processing. Generally, men were responsible for provisioning basic purchase needs such as kerosene, soap and protein food items such as meat, fish, eggs and milk. Otherwise, they were free to spend their cash-crop earnings as they saw fit, including leisure time pursuits, investments and payment of bridewealth for additional wives. Whether the benefits of men's cash-crop sales percolated to other household members beyond these purchases was debatable.[38] Many donors thought otherwise and initiated income-generating women's projects to boost women's purchasing power.[39]

African government policies were premised on the continuation of women's family homemaking and food production.[40] Foreign donors took women's domestic labour burden for granted, overlooking women's often intensified workload. In addition to food crop cultivation, they were co-opted to assist their husbands in the cultivation of export crops. Meanwhile, the drive to enrol children in school lessened children's domestic labour chores. Sons reduced their input into herding the household's small animal stock and scaring birds away from crops, whereas girls had less time to assist their mothers with cooking, cleaning, fetching water and the care of younger siblings.

Bukh's meticulous documentation of a normal workday in the life of one Ghanaian rural woman reveals the pressures of domestic work for a single mother with seven children. Out of her 18-hour working day, 8.5 hours were devoted to domestic work, while trading activities occupied 5.5 hours. The remaining time was used for eating meals. She looked after her young children throughout the 24-hour day. Bukh's time measurement of meal preparation over 10 days in 40 households in a Volta region cocoa-producing area by gender and age revealed that females over sixteen years performed

---

[37] Rogers, *The Domestication of Women.*

[38] P. Caplan, '"Children are our Wealth and We Want them": A Difficult Pregnancy on Northern Mafia Island, Tanzania', in *Women Wielding the Hoe: Lessons from Rural Africa for Feminist Theory and Development Practice*, ed. D. F. Bryceson (Oxford: Berg Publishers, 1995), 131–49.

[39] D. F. Bryceson, 'Easing Women's Working Day in Sub-Saharan Africa', *Development Policy Review*, 12.1 (1994), 59–68.

[40] Rogers, *The Domestication of Women.*

most of the cooking (78 per cent), followed by females under sixteen years (13 per cent) and older and younger males (8 per cent).[41]

RECONFIGURING THE TERMS OF DOMESTIC SERVICE FOR AN EXPANDING AFRICAN URBAN POPULATION

Literature on domestic service work is heavily biased towards South Africa,[42] and given the white racism of apartheid policies we must be careful in interpreting the significance of the data for the rest of Africa. Nonetheless, it is interesting to observe that in the Johannesburg–Pretoria area, African women servants only started to equalize with men at the end of the Second World War.[43] Increasingly under apartheid residential zoning, female domestic servants working as cleaners and *ayahs* had to be willing to live away from their own families in accommodation provided by their white employers. Generally, older women with grown children were left accepting such employment conditions. Meanwhile, men employed as cleaners, gardeners or guards commuted long distances daily from their homes to work.

In the rest of the continent, as colonial expatriates departed, a new form of home help surged, displacing waged domestic servants with reliance on extended family assistance for housework and childcare. The usual pattern was to arrange for a young female relation from the family's home area to come to the city to work as an unpaid nanny, receiving room and board. In some cases, the young migrant was afforded opportunities to further her education. Not surprisingly, girls were keen to serve, given that this was a point of entry into city life. Family domestic help from female rural relations became an important conduit for female migration to the city, facilitating the rapid equalizing of what had hitherto been a heavily male-biased urban sex ratio in the African population.

However, as illustrated in Karen Hansen's research on Zambia,[44] this seemingly win-win arrangement often went awry, with a tug of war ensuing between the young girl and her sponsoring female relation. The matron's demand for the girl's concentrated focus on her domestic work

[41] J. Bukh, *The Village Woman in Ghana* (Uppsala: Scandinavian Institute, 1979).

[42] Gaitskell, 'Housewives, Maids or Mothers'; J. Cock, *Maids and Madams: A Study in the Politics of Exploitation* (Johannesburg: Ravan Press, 1980).

[43] Cock, *Maids and Madams*, estimates that 800,000 women were domestic servants in South Africa in the late 1970s. Hansen, 'Body Politics', records a gradual rise of female servants in Zambia – 1951: 30,000 men, 250 women; 1956: 33,000 men, 855 women; 1968: 36,491 men, 1,758 women.

[44] Hansen, 'Body Politics'.

responsibilities were countered by the girl's eagerness to escape the house and enjoy city life. Furthermore, many if not most matrons fell into some form of social monitoring of the girl, anxious that her domestic helper did not become pregnant, a hazardous possibility that could result from liaisons with men outside or within the household. Antagonisms and fears mounted over time. Most girls rarely stayed in the job for more than a year or two. If the family could afford it, the matron tried to circumvent the sexual undertones of this situation by arranging for paid domestic work by older, middle-aged women past their reproductive years, or that of male servants.[45]

In sum, the nationalist era was a period of radical change in production and settlement patterns, but 'Mother Africa' prescriptions prevailed, with continuing expectations placed on rural women to shoulder domestic labour single-handedly and give birth to several children. By contrast, women's urban domestic labour was considerably streamlined, with less arduous and time-consuming work. Like European employers before them, African matrons occupied higher social positions in the urban hierarchy, with fewer demands on their domestic labour time, and they were rarely in salaried labour. Nonetheless, they sought domestic labour assistance. Many found a ready solution in arranging family domestic help from their rural home area.

With reference to Figure 10.1, these labour arrangements fell into the voluntary kin labour exchange category (Section D) and were liable to pose dilemmas arising from the intersection of productive and reproductive issues emanating from having domestic help staying in the intimacy of the household unit. Labour relations were therefore moving forward, with men primarily in waged labour (E), women in familial duty (C) or voluntary kin labour exchange (D) that was unpaid, but overall material conditions were improving. Rural women with heavy familial duties were facing the harshest circumstances, and it is no wonder that their daughters were eager to migrate to the city and engage in extended family relational exchange.

DEBT AND DE-AGRARIANIZATION, 1980–99

The oil crises of the mid- and late 1970s bifurcated the continent into a fortunate few countries that were oil-rich (Angola, Nigeria, Gabon, Congo and Libya) as opposed to the vast majority that were crippled by the oil price rise, trapping them in expensive transportation of their agricultural crops from huge numbers of dispersed smallholder farms to distant coastal ports. The competitiveness of their exports in the global market plummeted and

---

[45] *Ibid.*

inevitably plunged them one by one into debt. African countries forced to seek World Bank and International Monetary Fund loan support faced structural adjustment debt conditionality, severe government cutbacks and economic restructuring. Ongoing agricultural development programmes and input subsidies along the lines of the Asian Green Revolution, which many peasant farmers were introduced to in the 1970s, were phased out, leaving farmers demoralized in the face of yield achievements that were slipping away from them.[46]

During the 1980s the continent's smallholder farmers were largely left to revert to subsistence farming. Men's cash-crop earnings dwindled to negligible amounts. Households that had become accustomed to spending cash on an increasing proportion of their basic needs and school fees faced household finance shortfalls. A scramble for alternative sources of income on the part of all able-bodied members of the household ensued.[47] In the process, the gender divide between male agricultural cash earnings and female unremunerated subsistence agricultural work began to erode. Men, women and many of their offspring, who would have otherwise attended school, attempted to cobble together viable livelihoods. They concentrated on non-agricultural cash-generating activities, setting in train a process of de-agrarianization.[48] As peasant agrarian production declined, the AIDS crisis struck first in East Africa, then southern Africa, and thereafter spread to urban areas, becoming a pandemic of disease, death and despair, concentrated in several cities in southern and eastern Africa and elsewhere on the continent.

'MOTHER AFRICA' AS MULTITASKING SUBSISTENCE FARMER, NURSE AND CASH EARNER

During the crisis years of the 1980s and 1990s, various post-independence trends in domestic labour were reversed. Men switched from cash cropping to non-agrarian pursuits, primarily local services, trade, migrant labour and artisanal mining in mineral-rich areas. Women's work activities became an ever more complex juggling act. Most noteworthy, in addition to their

---

[46] D. F. Bryceson, 'Sub-Saharan Africa's Vanishing Peasantries and the Specter of a Global Food Crisis', *Monthly Review*, 61.3 (2009), 4–62.

[47] D. F. Bryceson, 'The Scramble in Africa: Reorienting Rural Livelihoods', *World Development*, 30.5 (2002), 725–39.

[48] D. F. Bryceson, 'African Rural Labour, Income Diversification and Livelihood Approaches: A Long-Term Development Perspective', *Review of African Political Economy*, 26.80 (1999), 171–89.

domestic labour responsibilities, they crossed the long-held gender boundary between women as household subsistence producers and men as cash earners. Increasingly, women engaged in a variety of cash-earning activities performed outside the home. Most were an extension of their home-making skills. Sales of prepared snacks and beer brewing were mainline activities, followed by a panoply of hair plaiting, knitting, tailoring, soap making, midwifery, etc.[49] Many ventured into petty trade for the first time.

They continued farming to supply their families' subsistence food needs, but increasing numbers were occupied with the heart-breaking care of husbands and sons who had returned home from migrant labour with advanced symptoms of AIDS.[50] In the early stages of the AIDS epidemic, most of the victims were men infected by prostitutes while working away from home, but over time infection inevitably spread to wives in urban and rural areas. As female carers themselves fell victim to the disease, rural areas experienced paralysis. Orphans sought homes with distant relations or attempted to fend for themselves in child-headed households.[51]

In the scramble to find cash earnings, male youths were especially prevalent. Many dropped out of school to work on their own account or for their families. Coincidentally, of those who entered the service sector, some helped to alleviate women's domestic chores in rural and urban areas. Boys with bicycles and specially adapted carriers collected water or firewood from long distances to sell at central distribution points in villages or towns, thereby saving women hours of walking and heavy head- or back-loading.

The AIDS epidemic triggered a demographic downturn. An increase in mortality rates combined with a decline in the total fertility rates in East, southern and West Africa (see Figure 10.2). Higher mortality of men and women of childbearing ages, fear of AIDS and the expanding number of orphans challenged pro-natalist attitudes. The value of children in supporting the rural family's agrarian work effort was being reassessed as peasant agriculture contracted. The erstwhile rationale of having large numbers of children to offset anticipated high rates of infant mortality was superseded

[49] Bryceson, 'The Scramble in Africa'.

[50] C. Obbo, 'What Women Can Do: AIDS Crisis Management in Uganda', in *Women Wielding the Hoe: Lessons from Rural Africa for Feminist Theory and Development Practice*, ed. D. F. Bryceson (Oxford: Berg Publishers, 1995), 165–78; D. F. Bryceson and J. Fonseca, 'Risking Death for Survival: Peasant Responses to Famine and HIV/AIDS in Malawi', *World Development*, 34.9 (2006), 1654–66.

[51] D. F. Bryceson, 'Who Cares? Family and Lineage Coherence and Caring Capacity during Rural Malawi's AIDS Crisis', in *Family, Ties and Care: Family Transformation in a Plural Modernity*, ed. H. Bertram and N. Ehlert (Berlin and Farmington Hill, MI: Barbara Budrich Publishers, 2012), 503–20.

by rising adult mortality. Sex became a dangerous activity. Women began rethinking their sex lives. Some single women avoided marriage and some wives, who feared contracting HIV/AIDS through a promiscuous husband, resorted to divorce.[52] As both production and human reproduction trends took a downturn, the optimism of the preceding two decades of African nationalist achievement dimmed. The 1980s and 1990s were decades of struggle for immediate survival, devoid of a clear sense of direction at household or national levels.

COMMODIFICATION OF URBAN FEMALE LABOUR: JUGGLING DOMESTIC LABOUR AND INCOME DIVERSIFICATION

Migration to urban areas met with the struggle to find employment.[53] Lowly paid, casualized, informal labour became entrenched, accompanied by signs of the feminization of the labour force.[54] Urban women actively sought income-earning opportunities, especially in petty trade and services.[55] Husbands were increasingly supportive of women working to bolster household earnings. Nonetheless, tensions ensued in response to the reduction in time women could devote to cooking and childcare.

Clark observed Ghanaian husbands and wives blaming household income shortfalls on each other. Men's contributions to food money and school fees were less reliable, so they appreciated their wives' earnings but 'regretted the greater personal independence and reduced housework standards needed for wives to work full time'.[56] In Ghana and Tanzania, husbands of urban market women complained that their wives did not have time to take care of

---

52 L. Cloutier, *Income Differentials and Gender Inequality: Wives Earning More than Husbands in Dar es Salaam, Tanzania* (Dar es Salaam: Mkuki na Nyota, 2006).

53 See the chapter by Pérez Niño in this volume.

54 G. Standing, J. Sender and J. Weeks, *Restructuring the Labour Market: The South African Challenge. An ILO Country Review* (Geneva: ILO, 1996).

55 M. Munachonga, 'Income Allocation and Marriage Options in Zambia', in *A Home Divided: Women and Income in the Third World*, ed. D. Dwyer and J. Bruce (Stanford, CA: Stanford University Press), 173–94; A. Larsson, M. Mapetla and A. Schlyter, eds, *Changing Gender Relations in Southern Africa: Issues of Urban Life* (Oxford: African Books Collective, 1998); Cloutier, *Income Differentials and Gender Inequality*.

56 G. Clark, 'Gender and Profiteering: Ghana's Market Women as Devoted Mothers and "Human Vampire Bats"', in *'Wicked' Women and the Reconfiguration of Gender in Africa*, ed. D. L. Hodgson and S. A. McCurdy (Portsmouth, NH: Heinemann, 2001), 307.

their children or cook properly.[57] Most men assumed that they should never be expected to cook.[58] Many men questioned their wives' commitment to motherhood, suspecting them of using birth control or abortion 'to prevent the nuisance that children would pose for their businesses'.[59] Women's earnings were weighed against the opportunity costs of childbearing. The role of women as mothers remained steadfastly central to the valuation of their social worth.

The restructuring of the division of responsibility for household welfare between husbands and wives was pervasive during the 1980s and 1990s.[60] Couples negotiated on a day-to-day *de facto* basis, and despite country diversity, the outcome was generally the extension of women's responsibility for provisioning purchased needs, assisting their husbands who were not able to fully shoulder their long-held responsibility for non-food household expenses. Yet women's purchased contributions to the household tended to be downplayed. They continued to be referred to as 'mothers' and 'housewives' rather than 'breadwinners'. Husbands were still expected to ensure household economic welfare. The gulf between theory and practice gave rise to household tensions over money matters and ambivalence about women's status in the household[61] as illustrated by a male reader's letter to the editor of a Lusaka newspaper warning of:

> a new danger to Zambian marriages, this time not from drunken husbands, but from the working woman. Obviously, the wife who feeds the family including her husband (i.e., if he is not earning) … often humiliates her husband by reminding him that as breadwinner, she is in charge of the house. Which

---

57 G. Clark, 'Money, Sex and Cooking: Manipulation of the Paid/Unpaid Boundary by Asante Market Women', in *The Social Economy of Consumption*, ed. H. Rutz and B. Orlov (Washington, DC: University Press of America, 1989), 323–8; T. Pietilä, 'Drinking Mothers Feeding Children: Market Women and Gender Politics in Kilimanjaro, Tanzania', in *Alcohol in Africa: Mixing Business, Pleasure, and Politics*, ed. D. F. Bryceson (Portsmouth, NH: Heinemann), 197–212.

58 In Cloutier's survey (*Income Differentials and Gender Inequality*) of 68 women in Dar es Salaam, none of the women mentioned receiving help with domestic chores from their husbands even if the husbands were unemployed. Daughters were most likely to give some assistance.

59 Pietilä, 'Drinking Mothers Feeding Children', 204.

60 Munachonga, 'Income Allocation and Marriage Options in Zambia'.

61 N. N. Gwawa, '"Money as a Source of Tension": An Analysis of Low Income Households in Durban', in *Changing Gender Relations in Southern Africa: Issues of Urban Life*, ed. A. Larsson, M. Mapetla and A. Schlyter (Oxford: African Books Collective, 1998), 33–55.

husband can take this kind of insult? Even though a man may be a loafer …
[his] dominant role as traditional head of the family should be respected.[62]

LIFELINE DOMESTIC SERVICE EMPLOYMENT AND EXTENDED FAMILY RECRUITMENT

During this period, as industries closed and many government ministry staff were laid off or hung on to their jobs but found their civil service and service-sector wages being continuously undermined by inflation, the search for supplementary informal work took over. Interestingly, in many towns, where polarized income levels prevailed, domestic service functioned as a reservoir of employment. In depressed mid-1980s Zambia, it was estimated that domestic work constituted the largest sector of the paid labour force, superseding mining.[63]

More broadly, women employers preferred to hire older women as house servants and *ayahs*. Urban circumstances conspired towards the convergence of supply and demand, since older female heads of household, given increasing numbers of widows and divorcees associated with the AIDS crisis, became more numerous. Women's cultural claims on support from male relatives in patrilocal areas depended on whether they were married, widowed or divorced. Those in the latter two cases were often structurally displaced from rural land access. Many, thrown back on their own resources, sought a livelihood in the city, while those without urban relations faced a precarious existence. Domestic service was therefore an attractive livelihood, because it usually provided accommodation at the employer's residence. Those who did not obtain that perk had no other option for shelter than to rent in Lusaka's already crowded low-income settlements. Divorcees with children to support were most likely to be unsuccessful, because female employers perceived them as potentially on the lookout for a husband.[64]

However, most urban households were not in a position to hire domestic servants on formal or informal terms and were apt to seek help from extended families residing in their rural home areas. Nonetheless, they agonized about the sexual threat that female relations' close physical proximity to their husbands posed. Cooking had sexual connotations such that many matrons were not keen to have domestic help cooking in the

[62] Reader's letter to the editor, *Zambian Daily Mail*, quoted in Munachonga, 'Income Allocation and Marriage Options in Zambia', 174.

[63] Hansen, 'Body Politics'.

[64] K. T. Hansen, 'Gender and Housing: The Case of Domestic Service in Lusaka, Zambia', *Africa*, 62.2 (1992), 24–65.

household and restricted female relations' work to childcare and cleaning responsibilities.

The combination of deep economic recession and the AIDS pandemic during the 1980s and 1990s created financial constraints and sexual tensions within African households throughout the class spectrum. Women's working days were lengthened further, as they added cash-earning activities to their daily work schedule. While men's paid work decreased with the involution of peasant cash cropping and urban job layoffs, there is no evidence that they used the time off paid work to help with the domestic labour within their households. Daughters, however, were often observed giving their mothers assistance.

With reference to Figure 10.1, this period marked a profound restructuring of market-mediated paid work (E), in which the formal labour market severely contracted and was replaced with far more amorphous, lowly paid, insecure casualized work and self-employed petty trade with erratic earnings. These circumstances provided a point of entry for women. Many chose informal trade, which afforded time flexibility and the possibility of taking their children to the market. Others sought hired domestic workers and childcare assistance (D) as a means of recruiting labour within the home.

Meanwhile, there were contestable issues regarding marital duties (C) as men's breadwinning role declined and women entered the labour market. Given the time pressures they faced as domestic labourers within the home and income-earners in the market, husbands and wives both had grounds for complaint regarding the failure of their partners to fulfil their traditional home provisioning roles. Added to this was the temptation of domestic servants working in the house, and the fear of AIDS. These were trying times publicly and privately.

OF STATUS AND SERVITUDE: WIDENING RURAL–URBAN AND CLASS DIVIDES IN MINERALIZING AFRICA, 2000–15

The new millennium marked an era of rising optimism. Slowly, over the preceding two decades, the scramble for viable forms of livelihood in the face of the loss of Africa's comparative advantage in agriculture gave way to mounting numbers of income-diversifying, would-have-been farmers finding their way into alternative income-generating activities. Artisanal mining of gold and diamonds offered the possibility of the highest returns.[65] Farmers

---

[65] D. F. Bryceson, J. B. Jønsson, E. Fisher and R. Mwaipopo, eds, *Mining and Social Transformation in Africa: Tracing Mineralizing and Democratizing Trends in Artisanal Production* (London: Routledge, 2014).

and other rural dwellers widely dispersed across the landscape were in the best location for making new mineral deposit discoveries. In the 1990s African governments succumbed to World Bank pressure, and new national mining codes were introduced to encourage foreign investment in large-scale African mining. This launched African countries' pronounced shift to mineral export, boosting service-sector activities and African economic growth from low or negative rates to impressive growth of over 5 per cent in a number of mineral-rich countries in the 2000s.[66]

RURAL AND URBAN DOMESTIC LABOUR JUXTAPOSED

A major step forward in African domestic labour studies is the availability of comparative national time use data for a number of countries at the turn of the millennium.[67] Data collected on the basis of a standardized system of national accounts (SNA) is used for calculating countries' gross national product. These statistics are deemed to represent productive, wealth-generating labour, whereas non-SNA activities are not included in the national accounts and largely encompass domestic labour as reproductive labour involved in maintaining the welfare of people within the household, community and nation state.

Comparative data for Benin,[68] Madagascar[69] and South Africa[70] shows that women's total working day was longer than that of males; measured in female/male ratios as 1.48 in Benin, 1.18 in Madagascar and 1.30 in South Africa.[71] When considering domestic labour tasks, the female/male ratio is far wider: 2.16 in Benin, 2.15 in Madagascar and 2.63 in South Africa. Women's time doing domestic labour was 69 per cent of their total work in Benin, 78 per cent in Madagascar and 66 per cent in South Africa. Strikingly, the classic triad of cooking, cleaning and childcare remains overwhelmingly

---

[66] The World Bank, *Africa's Pulse: An Analysis of Issues Shaping Africa's Economic Future*, vol. 7, April 2013.

[67] J. Charmes, 'A Review of Empirical Evidence on Time Use in Africa from UN-Sponsored Surveys', in *Gender, Time Use, and Poverty in Sub-Saharan Africa*, ed. C. M. Blackden and Q. Wodon (Washington, DC: World Bank, 2006), 39–72.

[68] Benin EIBEP, 'Enqueté Intégrée de base pour l'évaluation de la Pauvreté', Cotonou: INSAE/PNUD, 1998.

[69] Madagascar EPM, Module Emploi du Temps. Antananarivo: INSTAT-DSM/PNUD-MAG/97/007 (2001).

[70] South Africa, A Survey of Time Use 2000 & 2010, Pretoria, Statistics South Africa Statistics 2001, 2013.

[71] Charmes, 'A Review of Empirical Evidence on Time Use'.

women's responsibility. However, calculating male and female labour in terms of SNA-categorized domestic labour, including agricultural production and fire and water collection, is far more equitable, with female to male ratios of 1.33 in Benin, .96 in Madagascar and .81 in South Africa.

Certainly, there are many questions that need to be asked about the data before jumping to any conclusions about African female domestic labour. Have men shifted some of the time they formerly devoted to cash-crop production to subsistence food and livestock production and water and firewood collection? If men are assuming more responsibility for family subsistence farming, they are doing so as the smallholder peasant farming sector is shrinking in size and the countryside is greying. Male and female youth are veering towards an exit from agriculture.

Malawian household survey data[72] was collected just a year after famine prevailed in the country.[73] Gender differentiation in the '4 Cs' of cooking, cleaning, childcare and collection of water and firewood accords with the above-mentioned patterns. The data demonstrates how variation around the mean differs markedly by sex and age. Women have the longest working hours with the least flexibility to reduce their labour input. Fifteen per cent in rural areas exerted themselves beyond 70 hours per week, and only 5 per cent worked less than 10 hours. Rural men were twice as likely to be in the latter category and half as likely to be working over 70 hours. Boys' and girls' workloads were far less onerous, with 73 per cent of boys and 56 per cent of girls working 10 hours or less per week.

A drastic reduction in domestic labour time in urban as opposed to rural households emerged as the most salient pattern from the time use survey data. This could be attributable in some cases to larger family size but, more significantly, lifestyle differences were at play. Households in the highest quartile were more likely to have heads of households who were second-generation city dwellers, educated and part of Africa's burgeoning urban middle class, endeavouring to live in bigger, more comfortable and aesthetically pleasing, if not architecturally designed, houses.[74] Unlike living conditions in the majority of African households, their houses were equipped with cooking stoves, refrigerators, washing machines, vacuum cleaners and

---

[72] Q. Woden and K. Beegle, 'Labor Shortages Despite Underemployment? Seasonality in Time Use in Malawi', in *Gender, Time Use, and Poverty in Sub-Saharan Africa*, ed. C. M. Blackden and Q. Wodon (Washington, DC: World Bank, 2006), 97–116.

[73] Bryceson and Fonseca, 'Risking Death for Survival'.

[74] 'Africa's Growing Middle Class: Pleased to be Bourgeois', *The Economist*, 12 May 2011; C. Mercer, 'Middle-Class Construction: Domestic Architecture, Aesthetics and Anxieties in Tanzania', *Journal of Modern African Studies*, 52.2 (2014), 227–50.

microwaves, purchased at big shopping malls dotted around the capital city or on trips abroad and shipped home, part of a middle-class consumer boom, especially apparent in the countries where mineral exports were rising.

DOMESTIC SERVANTS' CHANGING TERMS AND CONDITIONS

The full count of formally and informally employed domestic workers in Africa, encompassing 'house girls', 'maids', 'houseboys', gardeners and security guards, is impossible to know. Recent ILO figures based on available data from twenty countries suggest that there are 5.2 million domestic workers,[75] but this is likely to be a gross undercount given the lack of published statistics in most countries (see Map 10.1 on p. 332).

In addition to the ongoing domestic labour trends documented in the preceding section, three new tendencies have surfaced in the new millennium. First, the expansion of the African middle class amid economic prosperity has led to increased demand for domestic workers in the capital cities and towns. Second, despite rising demand for domestic workers, de-agrarianization and high urban migration rates have pushed the supply of domestic labourers beyond the level of demand in many countries, compelling some female domestic labourers to look for jobs abroad, especially in wealthy oil-producing countries such as Nigeria, Gabon, the Middle East Gulf States or Europe. Third, the transfer of children from rural to urban areas to serve as domestic labourers in kin and non-kin related households has evolved towards pernicious forms of trafficking and child labour mistreatment in some places.

Women from Sierra Leone, Cameroon, Ethiopia and Eritrea have been migrating to the Middle East in increasing numbers.[76] Fernandez records that approximately 30,000 Ethiopian women were trafficked annually by illegal brokers, enduring harrowing journeys through the Somali desert and sea-crossings to Yemen.[77] The *khafala* system of recruitment in the Gulf involved domestic workers entering a private contract with a hitherto unknown employer with few or no labour safeguards.[78]

[75] International Labour Office, *An Overview of Domestic Work in Africa* (Geneva: ILO, 2013). This excludes child domestic labourers under eighteen years of age, of whom there are profuse numbers in Africa.

[76] 'Women from Sierra Leone Sold like Slaves into Domestic Work in Kuwait', *The Guardian* (London), 2 April 2015.

[77] B. Fernandez, 'Cheap and Disposable? The Impact of the Global Economic Crisis on the Migration of Ethiopian Women', *Migration Review*, 24.2 (2010), 297–322.

[78] On illegal networks, see the chapter by Fourchard in this volume.

However, the vast majority of African domestic labourers found employment in their own countries, mostly informally with indefinite, non-contractual, open-ended terms from their employers. Many came from the countryside to live and work for urban extended family relations. These were well-established patterns, with turns for the better in a few countries. Notably, minimum wage legislation in post-apartheid South Africa brought improved pay and the lifting of the racial colour bar, easing social tension between 'madams and maids'.[79] But wage control intensified the demand for cheap domestic labour options that were disempowering rather than empowering for domestic workers. Notably, children under the age of eighteen became more vulnerable to exploitation as informal workers.[80]

In different parts of Africa, the practice of voluntary kin labour exchange for goods or services (C in Figure 10.1) became more complex and took on an involuntary, forced nature (B), arising from the emergence of a commercial intermediary taking a recruitment fee, or poor rural households, in the name of foster care, pledging their child for labour service in return for payment in cash or kind from more affluent urban kin. Human Rights Watch estimates that 85 per cent of child domestic workers in Africa are girls, associated with the large and ubiquitous supply of rural girls potentially on hand for placement in the urban homes of kin or non-kin. Its Guinea case study demonstrates the influence of increasing wealth disparities between rural and urban areas, revealing three main conduits for girls' placement: 1) extended family ties based on close networking of rural and urban branches of the extended family; 2) extended family ties where the child is an orphan or seen as a burden, leading to offloading the girl on to a third party, pawning her to settle a debt, or an extended family member gaining pecuniary gain as an agent transferring the girl from her natal rural home to a more affluent known or unknown urban home; or 3) parents/guardians entering into agreement with informal or formal non-familial commercial recruiting agents for the girl's placement.[81]

The children are rarely given direct payment for their work. In their placement homes, the girls are likely to be marginalized, working long hours

[79] T. Dinkelman and V. Ranchhod, 'Evidence on the Impact of Minimum Wage Laws in an Informal Sector: Domestic Workers in South Africa', *Journal of Development Economics*, 99.1 (2012), 27–45; F. B. Nyamnjoh, 'Madams and Maids in Southern Africa: Coping with Uncertainties and the Art of Mutual Zombification', *Afrika Spectrum*, 40.2 (2005), 181–96.

[80] D. Thorsen, *Child Domestic Workers: Evidence from West and Central Africa* (Dakar: UNICEF, 2012), https://goo.gl/i8L21i (accessed 16 September 2016).

[81] Human Rights Watch, *Bottom of the Ladder: Exploitation and Abuse of Girl Domestic Workers in Guinea*, vol. 19, no. 8(A), June 2007.

at the beck and call of their guardian and receiving inferior food and lodging. It is not clear that many of the sending households continue to get regular payments. Girls placed in households at a young age are in the worst position, usually out of touch with their natal family, lacking a clear sense of identity, with nowhere to go and lacking the confidence and self-esteem to demand better treatment. Feeling a strong sense of abandonment, as they become older many hope to escape but have nowhere to go.

In addition to being subjected to verbal abuse and corporal punishment, roughly a third of the girls in the Human Rights Watch Guinean survey had been sexually assaulted. Similarly, in Kenya, IRIN reports the story of a sixteen-year-old orphan, Nora, brought to Nairobi by her aunt, who brokered a deal with a household in which Nora would work at the rate of $10/ month, to be received by her aunt. Nora was given food and lodging but no payment. In addition, she contended with the sexual demands of the head of household and consequent AIDS infection.[82]

Child fostering has been an age-old practice between poorer and better-off households in Africa that has served in the past to enhance economic survival, education and socialization of children in need. However, the welfare of those being transferred from their natal home needs to be monitored by a concerned social network of persons dedicated to ensuring the child's well-being in guardianship. Recent evidence suggests that the traditional institution of kin support, while no doubt still present throughout the continent in caring household networks, has transmogrified in some places towards forced labour[83] or indeed slavery.[84]

---

[82] IRIN, 'Domestic Workers Often Do More than Housework', IRIN Humanitarian News and Analysis, 26 May 2009, https://goo.gl/3iXtq8 (accessed 24 April 2015).

[83] 'The Forced Labour Convention defines forced labour as "all work or service which is exacted from any person under the menace of any penalty and for which the said person has not offered himself voluntarily". In addition, more recently, international legal instruments have also elaborated definitions of institutions and practices similar to slavery. Those practices include debt bondage, the practice of required debtors to provide personal services (usually work) that are not equivalent to the amount of the debt, or where the nature and length of the services are not determined … The Trafficking Protocol also states that trafficking might be present where there is exploitation or the prostitution of others or other forms of sexual exploitation.' Human Rights Watch, *Bottom of the Ladder*, 85.

[84] The ILO Worst Forms of Child Labour Convention, 1999 (No. 182), defines this as 'all forms of slavery or practices similar to slavery, such as the sale and trafficking of children, debt bondage and serfdom and force or compulsory labour, including force of compulsory recruitment of children for use in armed conflict'. Human Rights Watch, *Bottom of the Ladder*, 80; International Labour Organization, *World Report on*

In view of such tendencies in Africa and elsewhere in the world, the ILO's Forced Labour Convention has renewed relevance and is bolstered by the ILO's recent passage of a Worst Forms of Child Labour Convention to encourage the formulation of national policies and legislation. More broadly, the ILO's Homework Convention, 1996 (No. 177), extended standard labour rights coverage to home workers, excluding unpaid care workers. However, twelve years later, in 2008, the Convention had been ratified by only four countries, all from Europe.[85] The ILO instituted a Domestic Workers Convention, 2011 (No. 189), but regulation of the sector has been elusive.[86]

All things considered, the African continent's economy has markedly improved at the turn of the twenty-first century under the influence of a mineral boom. This has hastened rather than reversed de-agrarianization tendencies. Rural out-migration of young men and women continues apace, leaving behind an ageing countryside. With recently available time use survey data, the inequalities of the gender division of labour between men and women, girls and boys in the countryside have been confirmed statistically. The data reveals the very large disparity between the long and hard working day of rural people, particularly rural women, relative to their urban counterparts.

Using Figure 10.1 to trace historical labour change, we see that there has been a great deal of revamping of obligatory kin/marital duties as an increasing proportion of the populations of nation states tips towards an urban majority. Gender divisions of labour between husbands and wives are more contestable, and reciprocal relations between poor rural and more well-to-do urban branches of extended families are becoming far less reliable. This is most clearly evidenced in the transfer of young rural girls from rural to urban homes to be domestic helpers. Familial concern for the welfare of such underage children seems to be eroding in some circumstances. The intervention of commercial recruiters placing children in unvetted, unmonitored households looms on the horizon as a tragic throwback to the Atlantic and Indian Ocean slave trades, Africa's darkest moments in labour history.

Child Labour 2015: Paving the Way to Decent Work for Young People (Geneva: ILO, 2015), https://goo.gl/wSwiCx (accessed 6 June 2015).

[85] G. Standing, 'The ILO: An Agency for Globalization?', *Development and Change*, 29.3 (2008), 355–84.

[86] See the chapter by Maul, Puddu and Tijani in this volume.

CRITICAL CHANGES OVER THE CENTURY

The commonplace nature of domestic labour's daily routine of household basic needs provisioning is generally overlooked as a topic of enquiry and omitted from historical records. Yet far from humdrum, it manifests a progression of continental changes in labour supply, motivations and relational ties that are critical to an understanding of African history more broadly. Its grand narrative spans a kaleidoscopic range of human agency from practicality, duty, selfless love and concern to indifference, cruelty and treachery in the case of those perpetrating forced labour, be it bonded or enslaved.

In 1900 Africa was the world's most labour-scarce continent, with a large, underpopulated landmass that had been subjected to slave export for centuries. Between 1900 and 2015 the continent's population expanded, accelerating in size during the post-independence period with the introduction of medical services and technological change. Gradually, labour supply outstripped demand in unskilled labour spheres. More and more men, and increasingly women, engaged in commodified labour activities spurred by the need for cash for proliferating purchased needs. Domestic labour became less arduous in urban as opposed to rural areas, but the sphere remained highly labour-absorbing, left primarily in the hands of women, even though time use data indicates that women's work day is over-burdened with work relative to that of men. This is a paradox that can only be explained by considering a spectrum of motivations and relational ties that do not conform to market logic. To add to the complexity of domestic labour, a duality exists between domestic labour performed by nuclear family members as opposed to domestic workers, be they paid 'servants' earning wages or 'domestic helpers' recruited from the extended family.

During the first decades of the postcolonial period in the 1960s and 1970s, women migrated to urban areas and were initially enveloped in economic dependency on a male wage earner. Those in the salaried classes sometimes had the means to hire domestic servants. However, there is a latent hazard in engaging domestic workers, if their physical presence is deemed to be transgressing boundaries of conjugal intimacy and challenging the stability of the family unit. In those cases, paid or extended family-based domestic labour is viewed as a threat requiring careful management through selective recruitment.

Labour commodification evolved from the brutal, destabilizing influence of the slave trade to a colonial labour force involving men in circular migration to mines or plantations, or *in situ* peasant cash cropping, while women stayed in their tribal areas minding the domestic hearth, shouldering family food production and all domestic labour. A 'Mother Africa' mystique evolved around the belief that women's 'duty' to work for the welfare of their family members, communities, the nation state and continent at large had no bounds. Women's productive and reproductive roles within the household intensified between 1900 and 1980.

However, this pattern was disrupted when women became increasingly involved in the casualized production of goods and service provisioning, which impinged on their domestic labour time during the 1980s and 1990s. Some of women's quintessential domestic labour tasks, notably water and firewood collection, were alleviated by the commodification of services provided by young men using bicycle transport to reduce the arduous nature of the task. In urban areas, growing numbers of middle-class women deployed paid or unpaid domestic workers, which deflected from their domestic labour burden, but not to the extent one might expect in view of higher housekeeping standards that generated more 'necessary' work. But as economic hardships unfolded, women increasingly earned income in their own right as members of the working class or educated middle class.

Class stratification overlapped with intimacy and sexuality in myriad ways, beginning with female slaves who were domestic labourers and often served as sexual partners for their masters. This shifted to a colonial 'Mother Africa' mystique, which ordained women's rightful position as wife and mother, maintaining the agrarian hearth-hold. During the 2000s, African economic prosperity surged but was unequally distributed between and within urban and rural areas. Affluent women arranged domestic help to free up time for their economic activities. Middle-class households absorbed members of the working class as paid female domestic servants or unpaid helpers. In the eyes of the women employers or guardians, the domestic workers' sexuality posed a potential threat to the conjugal stability of the husband and wife in the household. By the 2010s, cases of sexual exploitation of female domestic labourers were being reported. Trafficking of young girls as domestic labourers exposed them to a disturbing range of labour and sexual abuse.

WOMEN'S DOMESTIC LABOUR QUANDARY: WORK, WELFARE AND WEALTH UNDER COMMODIFICATION AND DEMOGRAPHIC TRANSITION

Tracing the interaction between domestic labour and commodification through twentieth-century history, the use value of women's productive labour, sexuality and reproductive capacity has been appreciated and objectified within the home, through slave trade transactions or bridewealth payments. However, the interests of the colonial state and tribal authorities converged towards keeping women *in situ*, producing and reproducing within hierarchical rural societies on an unremunerated basis.

Women more easily circumvented control in the postcolonial period, when they were afforded freedom of movement to migrate to urban areas and the liberty to choose a marriage partner and work outside the home in the cash economy. Nonetheless, the gender division of labour remained largely biased towards women's performance of gratis cooking, cleaning and childcare, even when they were earning cash to provision their households. Given that their labour was valorized in the market and by inference their performance of domestic labour had opportunity costs, why was this the case? After all, there was a financial trade-off between working for monetary payment and doing domestic labour for their families. But wages for housework was never the issue. It was more complicated than that.

The feminist theory of patriarchy argues that women as wives and mothers are subject to male control over their labour, sexuality and children, and the unequal gender division of domestic labour is viewed as an outcome of male dominance. This argument is weakened when men are unable to bring home sufficient income to provision their families' purchased needs. And in the scramble for new sources of income during the 1980s and 1990s, class sometimes trumped gender, with some African women succeeding in earning greater amounts and/or more regularized earnings than their husbands.[87]

But tracing commodification and market valuation is not the whole story. An understanding of demographic change is just as vital for understanding the twists and turns of the changing nature of domestic labour. Women by default, as well as by choice and design, do drudgerous domestic labour. Their volition relates to the value they place on bearing and rearing children. In the words of one Tanzanian rural woman, 'children are our wealth and we want them'.[88] Women gain a sense of achievement, identity, long-term economic security and pleasure from being a mother. Domestic labour performance is an integral part of being a mother.

Men may walk away from household provisioning responsibilities, particularly when they are faced with failure to earn sufficient income, whereas women's nurturing role as mothers is far more imperative to the realization of her self-worth and meaning in life. In other words, the mother–child dyad continues to prevail as the basic household unit. Why? Part of

---

[87] Cloutier, *Income Differentials and Gender Inequality*; D. F. Bryceson, J. B. Jønsson and H. Verbrugge, 'Prostitution or Partnership? Wifestyles in Tanzanian Artisanal Gold-Mining Settlements', *Journal of Modern African Studies*, 51.1 (2013), 33–56.

[88] Cited in Caplan, '"Children are our Wealth and We Want Them"'.

this relates to the strong pro-natalist attitudes that have prevailed on the African continent. Traditionally, having many children was considered vital to ensuring the agrarian household's need for labour. But the fertility rate is now declining in many countries; women's fertility attitudes are altering, not least because of the influence of the AIDS pandemic and declining infant and child mortality rates.[89] The de-agrarianization process has generated a labour surplus in urban areas. Pressures on women to bear children for family farming have eased. Women still want children, but they are prioritizing the quality of their children's lives over the numbers born.

Throughout the centuries, agrarian labour ascription has passed down from generation to generation. People assumed that their work life would approximate that of their parents. Such labour ascription has lifted for men and women. Motherhood is no longer so emphatically attributed to female personhood. 'Mother Africa' and all the arduous domestic labour associated with that term are being re-evaluated by girls and women. Ways and means of avoiding household drudgery are surfacing.

CONCLUSION

Since the hardships of the 1980s structural adjustment and 1990s liberalization policies, ever widening numbers of men and women are piecing together their work lives through occupational experimentation. Under these circumstances, domestic labour is not women's sole preoccupation. Now African women generally have one or more forms of earned income as well. Higher-income women gain leverage through fertility control, hiring domestic servants to free up the time they are obliged to cook and clean, working in the labour market and devising individual businesses or business partnerships, sometimes with their husbands.

Domestic servitude is a key arena for facilitating the 'new African mother'. The supply of domestic workers and helpers is facilitated by de-agrarianization and urbanization processes. The transfer of domestic labourers from rural to urban areas represents complementary opportunities

---

[89] The United Nations Millennium Development Goals programme achieved a reduction in the under-five child mortality rate by 45 per cent from 177 to 98 deaths per 1,000 live births in sub-Saharan African countries between 1990 and 2012. United Nations, *The Millennium Development Goals Report 2014* (New York, 2014), 24, https://goo.gl/noVsQZ (accessed 4 June 2015). For example, in Morocco the average number of children born per woman in urban areas dropped from 7.7 to 2.1. H. Zerari, 'Femmes du Maroc entre hier et aujourd'hui: Quels changements?', *Recherches Internationales*, 77.3 (2006), 70.

for those needing and those offering their labour services. However, in some cases, the nature of child and female domestic service has reverted to the earlier reviled pattern of master–slave relations. With the intervention of domestic labour recruiters or the subversion of traditional kin labour exchange obligations, labour forms have arisen to facilitate and cheapen the costs of domestic servants for the expanding urban middle class. Inescapably, women's and children's roles in paid and unpaid domestic labour are conditioned by simultaneous processes of impoverishment and enrichment.

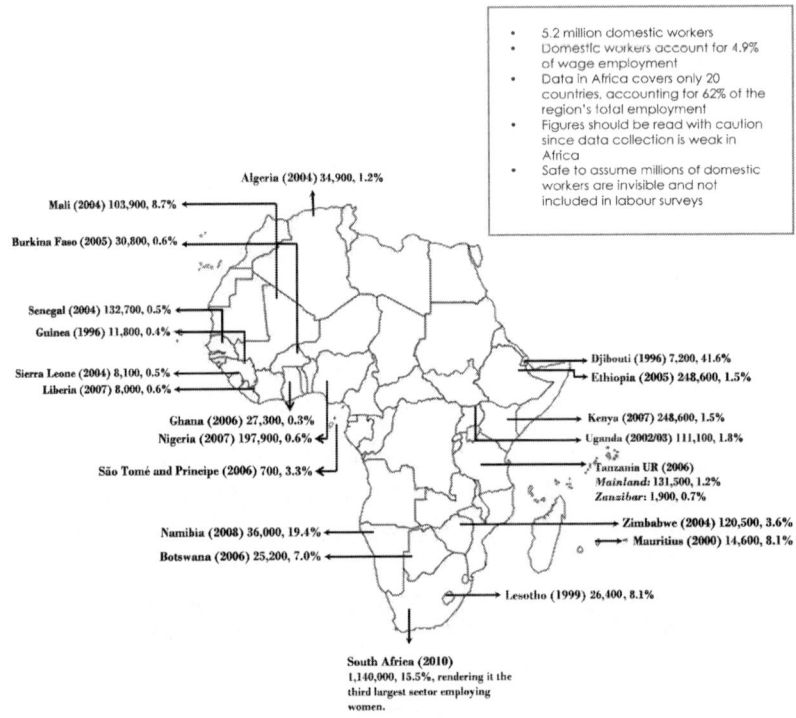

- 5.2 million domestic workers
- Domestic workers account for 4.9% of wage employment
- Data in Africa covers only 20 countries, accounting for 62% of the region's total employment
- Figures should be read with caution since data collection is weak in Africa
- Safe to assume millions of domestic workers are invisible and not included in labour surveys

Algeria (2004) 34,900, 1.2%

Mali (2004) 103,900, 8.7%

Burkina Faso (2005) 30,800, 0.6%

Senegal (2004) 132,700, 0.5%
Guinea (1996) 11,800, 0.4%

Sierra Leone (2004) 8,100, 0.5%
Liberia (2007) 8,000, 0.6%

Ghana (2006) 27,300, 0.3%
Nigeria (2007) 197,900, 0.6%

São Tomé and Principe (2006) 700, 3.3%

Namibia (2008) 36,000, 19.4%

Botswana (2006) 25,200, 7.0%

Djibouti (1996) 7,200, 41.6%
Ethiopia (2005) 248,600, 1.5%

Kenya (2007) 248,600, 1.5%
Uganda (2002/03) 111,100, 1.8%

Tanzania UR (2006)
Mainland: 131,500, 1.2%
Zanzibar: 1,900, 0.7%

Zimbabwe (2004) 120,500, 3.6%
Mauritius (2000) 14,600, 8.1%

Lesotho (1999) 26,400, 8.1%

South Africa (2010)
1,140,000, 15.5%, rendering it the third largest sector employing women.

Map 10.1. Available data on estimates of domestic workers and percentages of female domestic workers in total employment in Africa (Briefing Note 1. An overview of domestic work in Africa (Addis Ababa and Geneva: ILO). Available at: https://www.ilo.org/wcmsp5/groups/public/---africa/documents/meetingdocument/wcms_213683.pdf).

ELEVEN
Military and Police

JOËL GLASMAN

Faculty for Cultural Studies, University of Bayreuth

MICHELLE R. MOYD

Department of History, Indiana University, Bloomington

Colonial ideologues viewed soldiers and policemen as champions of order, strength and discipline. On the other hand, African nationalists and critics of colonial oppression described them as collaborators or traitors to the nationalist cause. Léopold Sédar Senghor spoke about the *Tirailleurs sénégalais* as the 'Black watchdogs of Empire'; Sylvanus Olympio characterized them as 'mercenaries'; and Frantz Fanon named them the 'spokespersons of the colonist and the regime of oppression'.[1] Similarly, Marxist and other radical thinkers came to the conclusion that colonial soldiers were traitors, albeit less to the national cause than to their social class.

Recent historiography, however, uses more nuanced frames for understanding the work of soldiers and policemen. Historians now make use of expressions such as 'men in uniform', 'colonial intermediaries', 'labour aristocracy' or 'violence workers', and increasingly compare military and police labour with other forms of labour.[2] There remain, however, two

---

[1] Senghor, Memmi and Fanon are quoted in Myron Echenberg, *Colonial Conscripts: The Tirailleurs Sénégalais in French West Africa, 1857–1960* (Portsmouth, NH: Heinemann, 1991). 3. Olympio quoted in Comi Toulabor, *Le Togo sous Eyadéma* (Paris: Karthala, 1986), 46.

[2] On the police, see Anthony Clayton and David Killingray, *Khaki and Blue: Military and Police in British Colonial Africa* (Athens, OH: Ohio University Press, 1989); David M. Anderson and David Killingray, eds, *Policing and Decolonisation: Politics, Nationalism and the Police, 1917–1965* (Manchester: Manchester University Press, 1992); Wiliam J. Berridge, "'What the Men are Crying out for Is Leadership': The Khartoum

challenges in addressing the history of policemen and soldiers as workers. The first challenge is to pay tribute both to the historical continuities *and* changes in these types of work. As is well known, several African languages acknowledge the colonial roots of police and soldiers' work, using words of colonial origin to designate them: *polisi* (Bambara), *mupurisa* (Shona), *konstebo* (Swahili), *polisi* (Swahili), *sodja* (Ewe), *soja* (Yoruba) and *musoja* (Shona). However, the work lives of men in uniform have been marked by considerable changes driven by colonial rule, repression, world wars, anti-colonial struggles, military coups, civil wars and democratization.

Throughout the twentieth century, the main distinctive feature of army or police labour has been the use of violence.[3] In war, violence includes the ability to maim or kill without hesitation. It also implies the ability to bear the physical demands of long marches, difficult terrain, harsh weather conditions, poor nutrition, and the ability to transition quickly from the most tedious tasks to the violence of combat and back again.[4] Similar features apply to police work; policemen face analogous conditions in contexts that have many of the same stressors as combat, even if they manifest in different forms

---

Police Strike of 1951 and the Battle for Administrative Control', *Journal of Imperial and Commonwealth History*, 39 (2011), 121–42; Timothy J. Stapleton, *African Police and Soldiers in Colonial Zimbabwe, 1923–80* (Rochester, NY: University of Rochester Press, 2011); on the military, see Marc Michel, *Les Africains et la Grande Guerre: L'appel à l'Afrique (1914–1918)* (Paris: Karthala, 2003); Nancy E. Lawler, *Soldiers of Misfortune: Ivoirien Tirailleurs of World War II* (Athens, OH: Ohio University Press, 1992); Anthony Clayton, *Histoire de l'armée française en Afrique: 1830–1962* (Paris: Albin Michel, 1994); Joe Lunn, '"Les Races Guerrières": Racial Preconceptions in the French Military about West African Soldiers during the First World War', *Journal of Contemporary History*, 334.4 (1999), 517–36; Timothy H. Parsons, *The African Rank-and-File: Social Implications of Colonial Military Service in the King's African Rifles, 1902–1964* (Portsmouth, NH: Heinemann, 1999); Gregory Mann, *Native Sons: West African Veterans and France in the Twentieth Century* (Durham, NC: Duke University Press, 2006).

3   Daniel Hoffman, 'Violence, Just in Time: War and Work in Contemporary West Africa', *Cultural Anthropology*, 26.1 (2011), 34–57; Martha K. Huggins, Mika Haritos-Fatouras and Philip G. Zimbardo, *Violence Workers: Police Torturers and Murderers Reconstruct Brazilian Atrocities* (Berkeley, CA: University of California Press, 2002); Sönke Neitzel and Harald Welzer, *Soldaten – On Fighting, Killing and Dying: The Secret Second World War Tapes of German POWs* (London: Simon and Schuster, 2012); Erik Jan Zürcher, ed., *Fighting for a Living: A Comparative History of Military Labour 1500–2000* (Amsterdam: Amsterdam University Press, 2013).

4   Alf Lüdtke, 'Soldiering and Working: Almost the Same? Reviewing Practices in Industry and the Military in Twentieth-Century Contexts', in *Work in a Modern Society: The German Historical Experience in Comparative Perspective*, ed. Jürgen Kocka (Oxford: Berghahn Books, 2010), 109–30.

and, typically, on smaller scales. Violence, broadly defined, remained a central feature of police and soldiers' work in the twentieth century.[5]

However, violence work has been moulded by a broad variety of social constellations.[6] While many soldiers and policemen have been free men working for regular wages,[7] others have been coerced into this type of work – as was the case for slaves in colonial armies, colonial conscripts during the Second World War or child soldiers in current civil wars. Violence work has been at times a free, but in other circumstances an unfree, type of labour. Furthermore, violence work has not always been wage labour. Some soldiers and policemen have benefited from regular wages and important privileges (free housing, medical treatment, schooling for their children, etc.), but others have barely been paid at all. As in other occupations, police and army work has been highly stratified at times, and the social conditions of violence workers have varied over time and space. Consequently, soldiers' and policemen's everyday experiences vary significantly. Some have enjoyed long careers and achieved high rank and prestige. Some policemen, soldiers, insurgents or militia leaders have even succeeded in becoming part of the economic and political elite, or even heads of state. Others, however, have experienced their work as a risky task in an uncertain and ever-changing political, economic and social environment.

A second challenge in writing the labour history of soldiers and police is the relative scarcity of direct sources. Quantitative data remain scarce and are often unreliable; many questions regarding headcounts, wages or war casualties remain unanswered, and may indeed be unanswerable. Qualitative sources are no easier to use. Soldiers and police forces have strong public identities, as evidenced by the important parts they play in official parades and state ceremonies. They also have a strong impact on public imaginaries. One gets fascinating accounts of soldiers and policemen in African literature (Chinua Achebe's *Anthills of the Savannah*), songs (Alpha Blondy's reggae *Brigadier Sabari*) and even television shows (Missa Hébié's sitcom *Commissariat de Tampy*), but first-hand accounts and ego-documents that might provide access to the thought-worlds of African soldiers and police are few and far between.

Detailed life stories, such as the autobiography of G. A. Chaza, who served as a police officer in the British South Africa Police, or of John Mandambwe, who served in the King's African Rifles (KAR), are rarities.[8]

---

[5]   Zürcher, ed., *Fighting for a Living*.

[6]   See the chapter by Fourchard in this volume.

[7]   On wage labour, see the chapter by Eckert in this volume.

[8]   Gahadzikwa A. Chaza, *Bhurakuwacha: The Story of a Black Policeman in Rhodesia* (Harare: College Press, 1998); John E. A. Mandambwe (with Mario Kolk), *Can You*

Most police remain anonymous workers of the state, with a few exceptions.[9] Many more soldiers have made it to the forefront of politics, but even they seldom write much – Yoweri Museveni's autobiography, which recalls his path from rebel soldier to head of state, is an exception. Thus, our historical understanding of the military and police as work relies on a spectrum of varied though fragmentary sources, ranging from administrative reports to personal files, iconography and, for the most recent period, interviews and direct ethnographic observations.[10] Historians who want to understand soldiers as workers must read between the lines and against the grain to extract such sensibilities, and they must do so without much of a secondary literature to help frame their assessments. This is a field that cries out for further research.

This chapter explores the main features of soldiers' and policemen's work in colonial and postcolonial Africa, while underlining the broad diversity of experiences associated with this type of work across time and space.

THE GENESIS OF COLONIAL MILITARY AND POLICE FORCES

European colonial powers built armies of African soldiers to aid in building empires, and, thus, they were part of the colonizers' original labour pools. These armies conquered territories, forced the inhabitants of those territories to submit to colonial authority and carried out colonial rule following conquest. Police forces, often made up of ex-soldiers, were generally established after the conquest phase. Policing styles varied significantly from one colonial power to the next, with the British employing a more civilian style, for example, and others using a more military style. Colonial policing responsibilities sometimes overlapped with those of the military, even when colonial rulers intentionally constituted military and police organizations as separate entities. Both organizations played parts in building and maintaining colonial states. Their labour took many forms, including violence work (combat, but also the work of policing subject populations), as well as

---

Tell Me Why I Went to War? A Story of a Young King's African Rifle, Reverend Father John E. A. Mandambwe (Zomba: Kachere Books, 2008); Timothy J. Stapleton, *A Military History of Africa*, 3 vols (Westport, CT: Praeger, 2013).

[9] Siaka Probyn Stevens, *What Life Has Taught Me* (London: Kensal Press, 1984).

[10] Berridge, "'What the Men Are Crying out for Is Leadership'"; Stapleton, *A Military History of Africa*; Joël Glasman, 'Unruly Agents: Police Reform, Bureaucratization and Policemen's Agency in Interwar Togo', *Journal of African History*, 55.1 (2014), 79–100; Thomas Bierschenk and Jean-Pierre Olivier de Sardan, *States at Work: Dynamics of African Bureaucracies* (Leiden: Brill, 2013).

physical labour; supervision of subordinates, prisoners and labourers; and ceremonial roles.

Complex processes were at work in building colonial armies. For example, the German colonial army in East Africa (*Schutztruppe*) paid its troops relatively high wages, enticing some men to join as a way of achieving social mobility and relative authority. War spoils supplemented their wages, and prestige bolstered their authority vis-à-vis colonized African peoples. But significant coercive factors also influenced young men's entry into the *Schutztruppe*. Poverty, gender shaming, lack of transferable skills, a desire to escape certain forms of enslavement, and combinations of these and other factors all convinced African men to become colonial soldiers. Even if, on the surface, many of these soldiers looked to be 'volunteers', these less visible forms of coercion influenced their choices.

Colonial recruitment methods differed across time and space, exposing the labour relationships inherent in the making of colonial armies. Different recruitment methods often existed alongside each other within an army. Colonizers also moved back and forth between different styles over the course of an army's recruitment history. The *Schutztruppe*, for example, did not use conscription (that is, compelling soldiers to join) for most of its history. But during the First World War, as Germany's strategic situation devolved, the *Schutztruppe* turned to forced conscription of young men to supplement its numbers as it marched through eastern and south-eastern Africa.[11]

French West Africa offers some contrasts in recruitment patterns and techniques that endured over a longer span of time and greater expanses of territory than other colonial histories. Recruitment of African soldiers in French West Africa during the conquest period (1886–1905) involved coercion that equalled 'the discredited technique of *rachat*' – the practice of 'repurchasing' slaves from their West African masters that characterized the early 1800s.[12] Reforms begun in 1857 produced the standing colonial army for French West Africa (the *Tirailleurs sénégalais*), initiating movement towards a more volunteer army. In this phase, French officers began issuing recruits with colourful new uniforms and opened up infantry training in an effort to attract new recruits who would otherwise have been sceptical, given the physical labour demands made of recruits in the earlier *rachat* period. Still, *rachat* persisted into the conquest period alongside these other recruitment practices.

[11] Michelle Moyd, "'We Don't Want to Die for Nothing': Askari at War in German East Africa, 1914–1918', in *Race, Empire, and First World War Writing*, ed. Santanu Das (Cambridge: Cambridge University Press, 2011), 90–107.

[12] Echenberg, *Colonial Conscripts*.

Beginning in the 1880s, three forms of recruitment emerged in French West Africa. First, colonial officers paid enlistment bonuses to slaveholders to secure their slaves' service. Second, colonial armies incorporated prisoners of war and porters into their ranks. Third, they incorporated West African career soldiers, providing a ready-made mid-level leadership echelon.[13] Multiple recruitment techniques thus existed alongside each other. In 1912, with international tensions high and the threat of war looming, French colonial authorities announced a partial conscription, requiring recruits to serve four years as compared to the five- or six-year service required by volunteers.[14] In 1918 a mass levy brought 63,000 African troops into the *Tirailleurs sénégalais*[15] to fight for France in the First World War. A review of British recruitment practices in the nineteenth century and into the First World War shows similar patterns with regard to an initial reliance on enslaved or otherwise 'unfree' men, followed by a push to recruit 'freeborn' men who supposedly exhibited 'martial race' characteristics suitable for military service.[16] Colonial officers' willingness to use more or less coercive recruitment methods, and in some instances to offer attractive incentives for enlistment, reveals the prevailing conditions under which African recruits cooperated with recruitment efforts or not – in other words, how they were able to sell their labour.

Soldiers in colonial armies worked in many different capacities. They spent their days in training, combat and ceremonial roles, all of which demanded physical stamina and concentration. They also performed physical labour, including work on construction projects in and around the colonial stations. When not engaged in military campaigns or training, colonial troops served as a cheap and captive labour force, and thus served colonial ideals of how local labour regimes should function.

Combat and its inherent violence occupied a central place in colonial soldiers' work lives. During the conquest phase some colonial armies campaigned almost constantly. Colonial armies' methods of war involved long marches across difficult terrain. Scouting, tracking and provisioning for the columns of soldiers, porters and family members also occupied soldiers while on the march. Management of prisoners captured during combat also fell to soldiers, shading into police work. First and foremost, though, violence work meant killing, or threatening to kill, anyone deemed hostile or supportive of enemy combatants. Soldiers also raided and laid siege to

---

13   *Ibid.*

14   *Ibid.*

15   Lunn, '"Les Races Guerrières"'.

16   Samson C. Ukpabi, 'Military Recruitment and Social Mobility in Nineteenth Century British West Africa', *Journal of African Studies*, 2 (1975), 87–107.

villages, seized livestock and goods as spoils of war, and used scorched earth ways of war that rendered local landscapes barren and unproductive for long periods after battle, profoundly disrupting local and regional societies, economies and cultural practices. In all of these ways, soldiers' work was defined by violence.[17]

Soldiers and police both performed constabulary work, including patrols, escorts, carrying messages and summons, making arrests, guarding prisoners and providing security for dignitaries. Soldiers and police in these roles often assisted with tax collection, adding a visible coercive element to the state's interface with its colonized subjects. Senior soldiers and police also filled supervisory roles, including overseeing prisoners and labourers, carrying out punishments and executions, recruiting labourers, organizing and managing porters during expeditions and conducting training for rank-and-file soldiers.[18] In the minds of Africans who lived with the everyday violence of colonial rule, these soldiers and police were the face of the colonial state.[19]

Military work conditions, and soldiers' responses to these conditions, determined the effectiveness of colonial armies when tested in times of stress, as in combat. Thus, studying differences in recruitment practices and work conditions also reveals the conditions under which soldiers resisted their officers' or commanders' authority, expressing themselves against the work being demanded of them. Soldiers' acts of resistance ranged from discrete individual acts of indiscipline, to small acts of collective indiscipline involving more than one soldier, to strikes or all-out mutinies involving many soldiers.[20]

[17] Michelle Moyd, *Violent Intermediaries: African Soldiers, Conquest, and Everyday Colonialism in German East Africa* (Athens, OH: Ohio University Press, 2014). For comparisons, see Benjamin Claude Brower, *A Desert Named Peace: The Violence of France's Empire in the Algerian Sahara, 1844–1902* (New York: Columbia University Press, 2009); David Anderson, 'Massacre at Ribo Post: Expansion and Expediency on the Colonial Frontier in East Africa', *The International Journal of African Historical Studies*, 37.1 (2004), 33–54; Bertrand Taithe, *The Killer Trail: A Colonial Scandal in the Heart of Africa* (Oxford: Oxford University Press, 2011).

[18] Moyd, *Violent Intermediaries*. See also Marie Muschalek, 'Violence as Usual: Everyday Police Work and the Colonial State in German Southwest Africa', in *Rethinking the Colonial State*, ed. Søren Rud and Søren Ivarsson (Bingley: Emerald Publishing, 2017), 129–50.

[19] G. C. K. Gwassa and John Iliffe, eds, *Records of the Maji Maji Rising* (Nairobi: East African Publishing House, 1967).

[20] David Killingray, 'The Mutiny of the West African Regiment in the Gold Coast, 1901', *International Journal of African Historical Studies*, 16.3 (1983), 441–54; Moyd, *Violent Intermediaries*; Taithe, *The Killer Trail*.

Comparative research on colonial army mutinies and strikes illustrates the extent to which soldiers' work conditions affected their willingness to continue working for European officers. In German East Africa, strikes or acts of collective indiscipline occurred infrequently. They took place in the two least stable periods of *Schutztruppe* history – either in its formative years (1889–95) or during the second half of the East African campaign of the First World War, when the *Schutztruppe*'s military disposition took a decisive turn for the worse compared to the first half.[21] Otherwise, the *Schutztruppe* remained largely untouched by disruptive strikes or mutinies. Smaller acts of indiscipline occurred with some regularity, however, in response to day-to-day demands placed on the soldiers by their officers and NCOs. By contrast, the history of colonial armies in French West Africa reveals a wider range of resistance to recruitment over a longer span of time. Widespread resistance to recruitment occurred throughout the French Federation during the First World War.[22] Only the privileged *originaires* – those who by virtue of living in the communes had claims to French citizenship and enjoyed some privilege – cooperated fully with French recruitment drives. Others, considered French colonial subjects, needed more convincing. In the end, French successes in recruiting 63,000 African troops to reinforce French lines on the Western Front in 1918 should not overshadow the significant resistance that recruiters faced in the process.

British recruitment efforts in eastern and western Africa during the same timeframe also brought tens of thousands of troops into the war and also met with resistance in some places, such as in Nyasaland (Malawi) and among the Hausa and Yoruba in Nigeria.[23] More comparative and synthetic analysis linking the work conditions of soldiers and police to their expressions of discontent, whether minor or major, will help us better understand the nature of soldiering as a colonial labour form.

---

[21] Moyd, *Violent Intermediaries*.

[22] Lunn, "'Les Races Guerrières'".

[23] James K. Matthews, 'Reluctant Allies: Nigerian Responses to Military Recruitment 1914–1918', in *Africa and the First World War*, ed. Melvin E. Page (London: Palgrave Macmillan, 1987), 95–114; George N. Njung, 'West Africa', in *1914–1918-Online: International Encyclopedia of the First World War*, ed. Ute Daniel et al. (Berlin: Freie Universität Berlin, 2014), DOI: 10.15463/ie1418.10462 (accessed 14 January 2019); Melvin E. Page, *The Chiwaya War: Malawians in the First World War* (Boulder, CO: Westview Press, 2000).

THE SOCIOLOGY OF COLONIAL MILITARY LABOUR

In building colonial armies, European officers imagined ideal types of soldiers, constructing and then using 'martial race' categories to organize their thinking about recruitment. In short order, however, these racialized criteria revealed inherent inconsistencies. In labelling some groups more martial than others, colonial militaries elevated certain masculine identities to relative positions of authority within nascent colonial states. Men who belonged to such groups stood to gain from the increased status and wealth that accompanied this belonging. The Kamba, a group that became part of the KAR rank-and-file, illustrate this logic. The Kamba began joining the KAR in large numbers in the 1930s, when famine conditions in their reserves, exacerbated by the global Depression, led many Kamba to sell their livestock in order to get cash to pay for basic needs and taxes.[24] Participation in the KAR gave them access to a regular salary, uniforms and social status that they otherwise would not have had. The Kamba thus became a martial race and a privileged group out of a position of relative weakness. Soldiering became a central feature of Kamba masculinity ideals and sociopolitical position in British East Africa.[25] Colonial recruitment needs grew in the mid-1930s with the Italian invasion of Ethiopia, and the Kamba answered the call, providing a 'growing percentage of the KAR' during the late 1930s.[26] Thus, the Kamba became violence workers, their compensation and status coming from their willingness to use violence in service of the colonial state. By the 1960s, however, on the eve of Kenyan independence, Wakamba men no longer needed to rely as much on the KAR for opportunities for upward mobility, although their martial race self-definition continued to play a part in Wakamba 'communal identity' through the independence era.[27]

Recruitment based on martial race categorization also meant that certain groups of men experienced disproportionate levels of coercion and violence, both as part of recruitment processes and in combat situations. *Tirailleurs sénégalais* recruited from purported *races guerrières* in French West Africa during the First World War were deployed as shock troops in some of the worst fighting on the Western Front, particularly at Verdun.[28] At other times, though, when armies became desperate for manpower, this focus on martial

[24] Timothy H. Parsons, '"Wakamba Warriors are Soldiers of the Queen": The Evolution of the Kamba as a Martial Race, 1890–1970', *Ethnohistory*, 46.4 (1999), 671–701.

[25] *Ibid.*

[26] *Ibid.*, 680.

[27] *Ibid.*, 696.

[28] Lunn, '"Les Races Guerrières"'.

race recruiting preference dissipated, with colonial armies coercing men to fight regardless of their origins. This dynamic proves the basic fiction of colonial martial race recruitment strategies, as well as the primacy of colonial labour imperatives, and points to the need to consider how colonial military recruitment intersected with racializing practices within wider colonial labour regimes and ideologies.

Colonial militaries also depended on other kinds of labour to function. Especially during the conquest phase, most logistical functions of these armies were handled by labourers recruited from localities surrounding colonial garrisons. Until the widespread expansion of motorized and rail transport during the interwar period, armies relied on vast numbers of porters to move their supplies and materiel.[29] Soldiers' household members also undertook much of the domestic labour that undergirded soldiering, whether in garrison or during expeditions. Women and children frequently accompanied soldiers' columns on the march, handling cooking, laundry, nursing and the gathering of food, water and firewood. During the interwar period, when urbanized garrison life dominated soldiers' day-to-day activities, women continued to play central roles in supporting the armies' logistical needs.[30] In these ways, soldiers' households served as a basis for building their colonial armies' logistical infrastructures on the cheap.[31] This labour relationship thus also reflected built-in gendered and generational hierarchies that, alongside other labour dynamics such as migrancy, heightened the value of soldierly masculinity as a mechanism for socio-economic mobility.

FIGHTING IN THE WORLD WARS

The world wars provoked unprecedented levels of military recruitment, mobilizing African colonial soldiers to work and fight both on the continent and overseas. In these two global conflicts, African colonial soldiers' roles as violence workers, honed during the decades of colonial conquest, reached new levels of intensity. Built for fighting in the 'small wars' of colonial conquest, these armies now fought against similarly organized and equipped,

[29] Geoffrey Hodges, *The Carrier Corps: Military Labor in the East African Campaign, 1914–1918* (Westport, CT: Greenwood Publishing, 1986).

[30] Parsons, *The African Rank-and-File*; Sarah Zimmerman, 'Mesdames Tirailleurs and Indirect Clients: West African Women and the French Colonial Army, 1908–1918', *International Journal of African Historical Studies*, 44.2 (2011), 299–322.

[31] Michelle Moyd, 'Making the Household, Making the State: Colonial Military Communities and Labor in German East Africa', *International Labor and Working-Class History*, 80 (2011), 53–76.

European-led, colonial armies. Soldiers who fought abroad in Europe and other distant theatres found that warfare could manifest itself in previously unimaginable ways.

Encounters with new devastating technologies, long-distance deployments and racist ideologies constrained soldiers' abilities to determine their own work conditions. In turn, these dynamics influenced their understandings of what it meant to be violence workers. In both wars, examples of soldiers' resistance, ranging from strikes to desertion, illustrate that African soldiers held clear ideas about what constituted appropriate work conditions following their substantial sacrifices for European imperial powers. After both wars, veterans asserted claims for fair compensation and recognition of their labours from indifferent and racist colonial administrations with higher priorities. Viewing African soldiers and veterans of the world wars as workers shows that, despite soldiers' clear ideas about the benefits that should come as a result of their military service, colonial administrators only minimally acknowledged these claims after the war. Viewed through the lens of racist and civilizationist colonial labour ideologies, we see that soldiers' and veterans' struggles paralleled those of other workers for recognition from colonial states that usually failed to honour the promises they had made while they were drumming up manpower to fight in wars with little connection to the day-to-day interests of most African men and their communities.

THE FIRST WORLD WAR

Hundreds of thousands of African colonial soldiers fought in the First World War, both within and beyond the continent. These included 450,000 French West African and North African soldiers who fought on the Western Front in Europe as well as in the Dardanelles campaign. These soldiers fought in some of the bloodiest battles of the war, including at Verdun. Their use as 'shock troops' at Verdun – an outgrowth of the martial race thinking described in the previous section – probably resulted in disproportionate casualty rates for some of these units.[32] Following the Allies' defeat of German colonial forces in Cameroon in 1916, troops from Gold Coast and Nigeria joined with others drawn from the British empire (KAR and Indian soldiers), the Belgian Congo and South Africa to fight against German East Africa's *Schutztruppe*, which was also composed of an African rank-and-file. The colonial powers all had armies of African soldiers at the outset of the war, but these were relatively small: the *Schutztruppe* had a scant 2,000 soldiers in 1914. Recruitment drives rapidly expanded their numbers, so that by 1916

---

[32] Lunn, "'Les Races Guerrières'".

some 16,000 men were fighting for the Germans in East Africa. As early as 1910, French thinkers had advocated an aggressive recruitment strategy in Africa designed to build a 'reservoir of men' to supplement their numbers in Europe. Thus, *Tirailleurs sénégalais* and others fought in some of the earliest engagements of the war on the Western Front in 1914, and men from western and northern Africa continued to participate in Entente offensives throughout the rest of the war, including in the Dardanelles. France mobilized some 192,000 *Tirailleurs sénégalais* during the war. White South African troops fought on the Western Front in Europe and also against the Senussi in the Egyptian–Libyan border region.[33] During the interwar period, these men often experienced long demobilization processes, and their reintegration into the communities they had left behind often did not go smoothly.[34] Although older historiography argued that veterans of the First World War played a significant part in nationalist politics, this contention has proven to be overblown. Most veterans made quite conservative demands of the colonizers – they wanted pensions, land, jobs and care for their families. With a few exceptions, nationalism was not a primary goal of veterans, particularly in comparison to the post-Second World War era, in which their interests took on new importance, as more robust nationalist movements began to draw on a wider selection of interest groups and demographics than had previously been the case.

THE SECOND WORLD WAR

As in the First World War, European imperial powers drew on their existing colonial armies to work and fight in different parts of Africa, and also in overseas theatres. The French again mobilized African colonial troops, and many who helped defend France against the *Wehrmacht's* invasion were massacred by German soldiers in 1940.[35] The *Wehrmacht* took an additional 100,000 of these troops prisoner.[36] African troops fought both in Vichy French armies and in the Free French Forces assembled to defeat Vichy. African troops in the Free French Forces fought in a number of major

---

[33] Bill Nasson, *Springboks on the Somme: South Africa in the Great War 1914–1918* (Johannesburg and New York: Penguin, 2007); Ian Van der Waag, *A Military History of Modern South Africa* (Johannesburg: Jonathan Ball, 2015); Stapleton, *A Military History of Africa*.

[34] Lunn, "'Les Races Guerrières'".

[35] Raffael Scheck, *Hitler's African Victims: The German Army Massacres of Black French Soldiers in 1940* (Cambridge: Cambridge University Press, 2006).

[36] Scheck, *Hitler's African Victims*.

campaigns, including in Gabon, Tunisia and in the campaign against the Italians in eastern Africa. North African troops also fought in the Italian campaign in 1943–44.

Similarly, the British mobilized some 500,000 colonial troops from western and eastern Africa to fight in Africa and abroad during the course of the war.[37] The KAR bore the brunt of the confrontation with Italian forces in Ethiopia and eastern Africa, but soldiers from the Sudan Defence Forces, the Royal West African Frontier Force (RWAFF) and the Somaliland Camel Corps also fought there. White South African troops also fought in the Ethiopian campaign. Despite their relatively small numbers, their presence in the forefront of the victory march into Addis Ababa in April 1941 highlighted the extent to which racist thought influenced soldiers' deployment in particular circumstances.[38] Beginning in 1943, RWAFF and KAR troops were also sent to fight in Burma, a hellish campaign that resulted in significant casualties, including psychological disorders resulting from the particular hardships of warfare in this theatre.[39]

The presence of African soldiers and labourers in the North African theatre of the war warrants further study. In military histories, this theatre features as a series of battles between German and British armies composed of white officers and soldiers. It is thus subsumed into the wider European conflict without much regard to the effects of the war on North Africa itself, much less the presence of African soldiers from across the continent. Yet African soldiers and workers from East Africa, South Africa, parts of equatorial Africa, Sudan and Morocco served there.[40] Moreover, North African troops fought in Europe, especially in the Italian campaign.[41]

In all of these cases, going to war was work. Despite advances in transportation routes and technologies, for example, soldiers often still marched long distances under difficult, treacherous conditions, such as those encountered in Burma and Ethiopia. And combat itself constantly tested the physical and mental endurance and strength of soldiers, wherever they fought. Violence work in war required having one's wits about oneself under stressful conditions, and maintaining concentration on intricate tasks,

---

[37] David Killingray, *Fighting for Britain: African Soldiers in the Second World War* (Woodbridge: James Currey, 2010).

[38] *Ibid.*

[39] *Ibid.*

[40] *Ibid.*; Parsons, *The African Rank-and-File*; Van der Waag, *A Military History of Modern South Africa*.

[41] Driss Maghraoui, 'The *goumiers* in the Second World War: History and Colonial Representation', *Journal of North African Studies*, 19 (2014), 571–86.

such as firing weapons with accuracy. Soldiers in combat might go days and weeks without proper food, water, hygiene or rest, but they still had to remain absorbed in their work in order to avoid injury or death.[42] They shifted rapidly back and forth between boredom and extreme activity. Their work was dangerous and taxing, and many did not live to see the benefits they imagined would accrue to them through their military service.

The Second World War also saw the expansion of numbers of soldiers recruited for use 'specifically as non-combatants (auxiliaries and pioneers), [or] laborers in uniform'.[43] The British in particular recruited vast numbers of soldiers for this purpose. These military labourers were drawn from all over the continent and were deployed in the East and North African campaigns, as well as in the Middle East.[44] Recruitment methods included both enticing volunteers to join and conscripting enough men to fill the ranks. Soldiers' work in these capacities included a variety of 'manual labor and garrison duties' that were physically taxing and intense.[45] According to Killingray, these men 'served as laborers on docks, in stone quarries, building fortifications, and for general construction work; semi-skilled men and tradesmen were employed as signalers, in printing maps, as fire-fighters, and lorry drivers'.[46] As during earlier periods, men in uniform served as a captive and cheap labour force.

SOLDIERS' PROTESTS, STRIKES AND MUTINIES

African soldiers who served in the world wars sometimes protested against their work conditions, though perhaps not as often as one might expect given the scale of their involvement with war work in different theatres. During the First World War, *Tirailleurs sénégalais* participated in the French army mutinies of 1917, the result of widespread anger following the Verdun campaign in 1916, in which some 162,000 French soldiers died.

In November 1944, 1,300 demobilized *Tirailleurs sénégalais* who were stationed just outside Dakar at Camp de Thiaroye mutinied against their commanders. The soldiers, many of whom had been prisoners of war in Germany, demanded back pay, allowances and fair pensions. *Tirailleurs*

---

[42] Huggins et al., *Violence Workers*.

[43] David Killingray, 'Labor Mobilisation in British Colonial Africa for the War Effort, 1939–46', in *Africa and the Second World War*, ed. David Killingray and Richard Rathbone (New York: St Martin's Press, 1986), 71.

[44] *Ibid.*

[45] *Ibid.*, 73.

[46] *Ibid.*

who were guarding the camp fired on the protestors, killing thirty-five and seriously wounding another thirty-five. Hundreds more received less serious wounds.[47] Thirty-five of the soldiers were arrested, tried and convicted on charges of mutiny, although later, in 1947, they received amnesty. The massacre at Camp de Thiaroye is the most famous example of African soldiers protesting against their work conditions, but it is not the only one. The Mauritius Regiment, a unit fighting for the British against Vichy forces in Madagascar, mutinied upon arrival there in December 1943.[48] British colonial troops also participated in small- and large-scale mutinies in Sierra Leone, Gold Coast, Sudan, Burma and elsewhere throughout the war.[49] Soldiers of the *Force publique* garrisoned at Luluabourg in Belgian Congo mutinied in 1944 for a variety of reasons related to their treatment by Belgian officers. The soldiers' actions were also part of a wider set of anti-colonial actions, including a labour strike against Union Minière.[50] These expressions of anger due to unfair treatment from colonial officers stood out, because such actions had been quite rare in African colonial armies. Soldiers' desertions or refusals to undertake particular military missions should also be understood as expressions of dissatisfaction with work conditions generated by racist colonial military hierarchies. These factors combined with the exigencies of war to exacerbate unfair labour relations, which many soldiers refused to continue to tolerate as the war dragged on. We cannot fully understand these protests, strikes and mutinies without analysing soldiers' position at the intersection between colonial racial thought, labour practice and the violence and trauma of combat.

DECOLONIZATION, COUPS AND THE TRANSFORMATION OF MILITARY WORK

The aftermath of the Second World War challenged the role of policemen and soldiers. Urbanization, demographic growth and labour movements exposed the contradictions inherent in colonial rule. On the one hand, the colonizers needed more and more African soldiers and policemen. On the other hand, they were not prepared to give them complete responsibility for

[47] Myron Echenberg, "'Morts pour la France": The African Soldier in France During the Second World War', *Journal of African History*, 26.4 (1985), 363–80.

[48] Killingray, *Fighting for Britain*.

[49] *Ibid*.

[50] Bruce Fetter, 'The Luluabourg Revolt of Elisabethville', *International Journal of African Historical Studies*, 2.2 (1969), 137–47.

colonial order. The number of African officers remained very low. Even though African employees were instrumental in specific duties such as translating, typewriting or copying, most bureaucratic tasks continued to be taken care of by European officers. In French West Africa, for instance, the first African police superintendents were only appointed in the 1950s. In the end, the 'Africanization' of police forces did set in. However, this process was both too slow and too late.

An important impetus for change was the soldiers' and policemen's discontent regarding their working conditions. While some protests had already occurred before the Second World War, they gained a new vehemence afterwards. War veterans were especially vocal. The 1944 mutiny at Thiaroye signalled the tensions to come in the post-war period. The Senegalese politician Lamine Guèye adopted the *Tirailleurs'* cause and politicized the question of war veterans.[51] Policemen also protested against bad working conditions. In 1951 in Khartoum, 700 policemen went on strike in protest against the dismissal of several of their colleagues.[52] For the colonial administration, this kind of strike made it obvious just how heavily colonial domination relied on this particular profession. In the 1950s and 1960s police strikes and army mutinies became more frequent. Members of the Congolese *Force publique* mutinied in 1960, as did the first battalion of the Tanganyikan Rifles in Dar es Salaam in 1964. In all of these cases, soldiers' revolts resulted from the failure of colonial leadership to take seriously their troops' demands for adequate pay and care in exchange for their work. Equally important, however, was the widespread failure to recognize African soldiers as suitable for leadership roles, which in many cases remained in the hands of white officers and NCOs. The degree to which soldiers felt locked out of the potential for upward mobility is another factor that reminds us of the importance of thinking about soldiers through the lens of labour history.

Anti-colonial struggle marked another change in soldiers' labour histories, with many men and women across the continent taking up arms as their primary occupation, even if only for brief periods. The national wars of liberation in Algeria (1954–62), Kenya (1952–63), Cameroon (1955–62), Angola (1961–74), Guinea Bissau (1963–74) and Mozambique (1964–74) resulted in the militarization of societies. During the Algerian war, for instance, the French army recruited massively among the Algerian population. In 1961, in a country of ten million people and against a nationalist army of some 80,000 *moujahidines* (ANL – *Armée Nationale de Libération*, the armed

---

[51]   Gregory Mann, *Native Sons: West African Veterans and France in the Twentieth Century* (Durham, NC: Duke University Press, 2006).

[52]   Berridge, "'What the Men are Crying out for Is Leadership'".

wing of the *Front de Libération Nationale*, or FLN), the French mobilized around 420,000 soldiers and 503,000 auxiliaries. The French troops were made up of soldiers fighting in regular forces (professional soldiers, legionnaires, African soldiers, French conscripts, etc.) as well as *supplétif* forces (*harkis, maghzens, aassès, groupes mobiles de protection rurale*, auto-defence groups, etc.) recruited from the local population.[53] The massive mobilization of the local population went far beyond the mere numbers needed for fighting; it was part of a colonial strategy of counter-insurgency war. This resulted in high casualty numbers – around 30,000 dead French soldiers and 350,000 Algerian casualties (3 per cent of the population) – as well as the emigration of a large number of French settlers and Algerians – including most of the *harkis* who had fought on the French side.

After the national war of liberation, military experience became a political asset: the new political elite frequently came from a military background. In Algeria, commander-in-chief Colonel Houari Boumediene became minister of defence and eventually head of the Algerian state (1965–78). Even for leaders who were trained in civil professions, experience as a 'freedom fighter' was a crucial issue – as it was for José Eduardo dos Santos, a fighter in the People's Movement for the Liberation of Angola (MPLA), who eventually became Angola's head of state in 1979, or João Bernardo Vieira, head of state of Guinea Bissau after his coup in 2005. Another example is Robert Mugabe, who stated that the experience as a freedom fighter gave him, in addition to his seven academic degrees, a 'degree in violence'.[54] Their experiences as violence workers and as wartime leaders lent them credibility as leaders of newly independent nations that were expected to participate in international politics and economics. That many of these leaders remained in power decades later resulted in part from their ability to draw on political language and powerful symbols of struggle not unlike those of labour movements.

Coups and military rule were a third factor that led to changes in soldiers' work lives. Between 1958 and 2001 almost every African nation state – except for Botswana, Cape Verde and Mauritius – experienced at least one military coup or an attempted coup. Coups became a banal political tool in postcolonial Africa: there were two coups per year following independence.[55] In most cases, plotters claimed to be acting in the name of higher national interests, accusing the overthrown leaders of corruption or tribalism. In Togo, Gnassingbè Eyadema and his fellow veterans killed the civil president

---

[53] On other forms of professionalism, see the chapter by Pilossof in this volume.

[54] 'Robert Mugabe: The Man Behind the Fist', *The Economist*, 29 March 2007.

[55] P. Collier, *Wars, Guns, and Votes: Democracy in Dangerous Places* (New York: Harper Collins, 2009).

Sylvanus Olympio in 1963, accusing him of tribalism against the Kabyè. In Uganda, Idi Amin, who had risen through the ranks of the KAR to a high-level advisory position in the Obote regime, used anti-Ganda sentiment to justify his 1971 coup. The Ugandan army became an organization largely dominated by men from northern Uganda, Amin's home region, and especially 'Sudanese' or 'Nubi' soldiers who had long been viewed by the British and others as a martial race. Coups should also be understood, then, as a method of renegotiating military labour. Military coups have their origins in soldiers' discontent about their conditions of work, their relative status compared to other kinds of workers (especially bureaucrats), praetorianism and rivalries between factions of the army. In Togo, for example, soldiers who had fought in Indochina and Algeria were unhappy about their lack of professional prospects in the new national army. Theirs was one of the first military coups in an independent African nation, demonstrating the clear link between wartime military service and expectations of post-war rewards.

Coups had many consequences, the most important of which was state militarization. Coups were followed by rapid career advancement for the plotters and their accomplices, with violence work becoming the basis for political work, and soldiers considering themselves as the best men for the job of leading nations. Privates became sergeants, lieutenants became generals and generals became heads of state. Some of the plotters were high-ranking officers before seizing power, such as Zine el-Abidine Ben Ali of Tunisia (1987–2011) or Omar el-Béchir of Sudan (since 1989); others, such as Gnassingbè Eyadema of Togo (1963/67–2005) or Samuel Doe of Liberia (1980–90) were NCOs who could access higher ranks, and thus prestige, after becoming heads of state. In military regimes, the army complemented the political party as a site of elite formation and selection. Military leaders – such as Moussa Traoré in Mali (1968–91), Lansanna Conté in Guinea (1984–2008) or Jerry Rawlings in Ghana (1981–2001) – established extensive networks of military patronage. In several countries, such as Egypt under Gamal Abdel Nasser (1954–70), Sudan under Gaafar Nimeiry (1969–85) or Libya under Mouammar Kadhafi (1969–2011), the military ransacked the political realm. Even those who attempted to civilianize their power – such as Joseph Désiré Mobutu in the Democratic Republic of the Congo (DRC) (1965–97) or Teodoro Obiang Nguema Mbasogo in Equatorial Guinea (since 1982) – still relied strongly on their armed forces.

In the aftermath of military coups, armies have tended to grow rapidly – both in absolute and relative numbers vis-à-vis other state agencies. Performances of state power and calls for national security communicated new labour paradigms in which the military not only dictated the terms of labour, but argued for its centrality in maintaining sovereignty in an age of

Cold War rivalries and post-independence struggles for political authority. In order to control oversized armies, military leaders kept them divided. They built competing companies, units and factions. They hired foreign consultants and army experts and, in times of real crisis, relied on Western paratroopers and mercenaries. They maintained a strong division between a small and highly privileged officer staff and a massive and underpaid rank-and-file. In turn, officers could deploy a strategy of straddling by holding both military and political positions, as well as economic functions. Uganda is a case in point: under President Yoweri Museveni, many officers became economic entrepreneurs, profiting from everyday corruption through checkpoints, gas smuggling, misappropriation of ghost soldiers' salaries and cattle plunder. Military rulers not only established a new style of ruling, they also embodied a new political subjectivity. Camouflage became a widespread style in the streets and markets of African urban centres as well as in ministerial offices and at international meetings. Simultaneously, military techniques that were common under colonial rule – including coercive measures, physical torture or whipping – made their way into everyday political life. Here again, the links between violence work and political work become evident.

MILITARY WORK AT WAR: SOLDIERS, REBELS AND WARLORDS

Since the 1980s military and police work have been reshaped either by processes of democratization and structural adjustment, as in Benin, Nigeria, Kenya or South Africa, or by civil war in places such as the DRC, Liberia, Sierra Leone or Sudan. After dealing with soldiers at war in this section, we will focus on democratization in the next section. Since the Second World War, one-third (62 out of 178) of the world's wars have been fought in Africa.[56] The Central African region has been the theatre of a succession of mutinies, rebellions and insurgencies since the 1960s. The Horn of Africa has experienced a war of secession in Ethiopia, followed by civil war and interstate war with Eritrea.[57] Chad and Sudan have been countries where war alternated with short periods of peace for decades. However, it was in the 1990s, in the aftermath of the Cold War, that the number of African wars peaked. Separatist movements, armed groups and war entrepreneurs

---

[56] Sven Chojnacki and Gregor Reisch, 'Perspectives on War: Collecting, Comparing and Disaggregating Data on Violent Conflicts', *Sicherheit und Frieden*, 26.4 (2008), 233–45.

[57] Alexander de Waal, *Evil Days: Thirty Years of War and Famine in Ethiopia* (New York: Human Rights Watch, 1991).

mushroomed, relying on light, cheap and highly mobile weaponry such as Kalashnikovs, light rockets and landmines, and challenging conventional definitions of military labour by linking them explicitly to resource extraction and other revenue-generating methods.[58] Beginning in 1996, the 'African World War',[59] fought mainly in the DRC, has involved about ten countries and several non-state armed groups. Non-state armed groups have contributed to shaping African military labour, from Al-Shabaab in Somalia, M23 in Kivu and the *janjaweed* in Darfur, to the Ansar al Dine in northern Mali and the Boko Haram in northern Nigeria. In turn, states have responded to these insurgent militaries with expensive, long-term military deployments and counter-insurgency operations that frequently exacerbate conditions for civilians living in proximity to the conflict areas.

A paradigmatic case for the new role of soldiers in wars were the violent conflicts in Liberia and Sierra Leone in the early 1990s, known for the strategic use of theatrical violence – including horrific acts such as the chopping off of civilians' hands and arms – as a way of persuading local populations to be compliant. In the Mano River, most rebels were former students or peasants who took up arms to enter the labour market and escape the authority of their chiefs.[60] Rebellion was embedded in the long history of slavery, clientelism and colonialism, which reinforced the power of the elderly and big men among young members of the communities. Youth joined militias partly as a result of inadequate work opportunities, as well as an expression of frustration against these elders who had hoarded political and economic authority.

Civil wars had numerous consequences for soldiers' lives. In some regions – Mano River, the Horn, Central Africa and the Great Lakes region – war was no longer exceptional but became a part of normal social and political life. In these 'no peace, no war' situations,[61] peacetime did not imply non-violence, and war was always around the corner. In Chad, for instance – a country whose history has long been shaped by war, starting with pre-colonial *razzias* and the brutal conquest by French colonial troops – the creation of the *Front de Libération Nationale du Tchad* (Frolinat) in 1966 inaugurated a new and

---

[58]   William Reno, *Warlord Politics and African States* (Boulder, CO: Lynne Rienner, 1998).

[59]   Gérard Prunier, *Africa's World War: Congo, the Rwandan Genocide, and the Making of a Continental Catastrophe* (Oxford: Oxford University Press, 2009).

[60]   Paul Richards, 'New Barbarism in Africa?', in *Fighting for the Rain Forest: War, Youth and Resources in Sierra Leone*, ed. Paul Richards (Oxford: James Currey, 1996), xiii–xxxv; Daniel Hoffman, 'The City as Barracks: Freetown, Monrovia, and the Organization of Violence in Postcolonial African Cities', *Cultural Anthropology*, 22.3 (2007), 400–28.

[61]   Paul Richards, ed., *No Peace, No War: An Anthropology of Contemporary Armed Conflicts* (Athens, OH: Ohio University Press, 2005).

long-lasting cycle of rebellion and repression. Marielle Debos has named this period 'interwar',[62] a period in which people are waiting for the next war while hoping that it will not break out. War is intermittent, mostly limited to the dry season, and entails, for soldiers and rebels alike, long periods of waiting.

In these wars, the front lines change quickly, since the distinction between soldiers and combatants is not ideological but rather driven by the imperative to control resources and to demand civilian compliance in labour needs. In Chad, the factions are divided by circumstances and tactical choices rather than by identities or political stances. Combatants may have close ties with several factions, so that civil wars often set brothers and cousins against one another. Thus, the first consequence of civil war is the porosity of conventional boundaries between soldiers, rebels and civilians. 'Those who live by the gun'[63] can be, alternatively, army volunteers, rebels or road bandits. Social scientists have felt obliged to craft new categories to name those who live from war, categories that bypass the distinction between soldiers and rebels (such as 'men in arms' or the neologism *sobels*).[64] In different situations, rebels can become police agents, customs officials or soldiers in the state's armed forces. Similarly, civilians living as farmers, herders or merchants may take up arms and enter the bush for a few months or a year. Different categories of people become rebels: deprived minorities, victims of violence, young men facing socio-economic marginalization or soldiers not getting any salary. Daniel Hoffman, therefore, states that warriors are part of the workforce in the economy of war.[65]

Another consequence of civil wars has been the massive recruitment of children into armed forces, a phenomenon that should be read through the lens of labour history as well. Child soldiering is neither new, nor is it specifically African. But on a continent where half of the population is under eighteen years of age, and in a period characterized by several parallel civil wars, the phenomenon has taken on epic proportions. The United Nations Children Fund (UNICEF) estimates broadly that 300,000 children worldwide are soldiers, most of them in Africa – such as the *kadogo* in the DRC or Nigeria's *sozaboys*. Child soldiers do not require salaries, and they are likely to develop ties to the military as a surrogate family in times of relative insecurity. While we should avoid simplistic renderings of child soldiers as victims of exploitation, we

[62] Marielle Debos, 'Living by the Gun in Chad: Armed Violence as a Practical Occupation', *Journal of Modern African Studies*, 49.3 (2011), 409–28.

[63] *Ibid.*

[64] Catherine E. Bolten, '*Sobel* Rumors and Tribal Truths: Narrative and Politics in Sierra Leone, 1994', *Comparative Studies in Society and History*, 56.1 (2014), 187–214.

[65] Hoffman, 'Violence, Just in Time'.

should keep in mind that armies rely on them because they are perceived to be malleable and docile. The Liberian 'small boys units' of Charles Taylor's National Patriotic Front of Liberia (NPFL) are emblematic of the coercion of children into armed forces. Children are used by rebel forces as cooks, messengers, porters, spies or 'soldiers' wives'; they are also used as fighters, and they have been directly involved in systematic beatings, mutilations, massacres and the rape of civilians. After they had taken Monrovia, Taylor's NPFL reformed as the National Patriotic Party, but around 15,000 minors remained members of Taylor's government forces. Other armed forces – such as the Lord's Resistance Army of Joseph Kony in Uganda – gained a reputation for kidnapping children for soldiering. In some regions of Central Africa, the DRC and south Sudan, child soldiering has become endemic.

A further consequence of civil wars has been the internationalization of military labour. Not only have civil wars entailed the massive movement of troops between neighbouring countries (for instance, between Liberia and Sierra Leone in the early 1990s, from Uganda to Rwanda in 1993, or from Rwanda to the DRC in 1996), they have also witnessed the massive involvement of mercenaries from abroad. Famous mercenary outfits such as Executive Outcomes (South Africa), DSL (United Kingdom), MPRI (United States) or Levdan (Israel) have transformed African wars into 'dog wars' fought by corporate armies. Ukrainian pilots, French legionnaires or South African paratroopers have been part of the African military landscape since the 1960s. Another step towards internationalization has been in the form of international peacekeeping interventions. Since 1960 the United Nations has conducted thirty peacekeeping missions, with troop numbers ranging from 200 to 20,000, in countries such as Angola, Central African Republic, Côte d'Ivoire, the DRC, Ethiopia, Mali, Rwanda, Somalia and Sudan. Africa is currently host to some 80,000 international troops from all continents. Other international organizations such as the African Union, European Union and the Economic Community of West African States, as well as individual states (mainly France, South Africa and the United Kingdom) have also conducted peacekeeping operations. The Ghanaian and Nigerian armies, in particular, have gained reputations as professional peacekeepers, with the Ghanaians also enjoying a vaunted representation as exemplary ones. The African Union is becoming increasingly proactive in peacekeeping operations. Whereas international soldiers have sometimes been welcomed by local populations, they have been harshly criticized at other times for their lack of efficiency. In several cases, peacekeeping operations have been perceived as illegitimate because of the foreign soldiers' behaviour; they have been accused of war crimes – the Africa Mission in Somalia (AMISOM); corruption – the United Nations Organization Mission in the Democratic Republic of the Congo

(MONUC) and AMISOM; or sexual abuses – MONUC and the United Nations Mission in Liberia (UNMIL).[66]

Finally, a further consequence of civil wars has been that the experience of armed struggle has become political training for state leaders. Former rebel soldiers have become heads of state in countries such as Liberia (Charles Taylor, 1997–2003), Central African Republic (François Bozizé, 2003–13), Uganda (Yoweri Kaguta Museveni, 1986–present), Rwanda (Paul Kagame, 1994–present) and the DRC (Laurent Désiré Kabila, 1997–2001). They have not only shaped state armies by reforming them according to their long experience of fighting against them, but they have embodied the new African figure of the strongman. Paul Kagame is a case in point. The former rebel, winner of the 2009 'Clinton Global Citizen Award' for his leadership, became a favourite of global investors. His many hagiographists not only connect the economic success of Rwanda to his military past; they celebrate his military habitus, describing him as spartan, stoic, austere and disciplined, all qualities presumably gained in the army and which are key to his triumph.[67] The picture of the rebel as the new strongman not only attracts the approval of global elites and corporate investors, but it also influences the young urban unemployed who are on the lookout for social models and opportunities.[68]

POLICING AFRICA AFTER DEMOCRATIZATION AND STRUCTURAL ADJUSTMENT

The consequence of the 'third wave' of democratization for police work has been strongly debated. While many countries (for example, Benin, Ghana, Nigeria, Senegal, Tanzania, Zambia and others) witnessed a formal transition from autocratic to liberal rule, some scholars have emphasized the continuities of policing practices. Often enough, policemen trained to protect autocratic regimes and to track political opponents have remained in charge. In countries that experienced harsh police repression, policemen remained 'figures of shame'.[69] The policeman remains 'one who has big boots' (Bambara: *sàbàràbàtìgì*), the 'man with the small stick' (Ewe: *kpovito*), the 'son

---

[66] Hoffman, 'The City as Barracks'.

[67] See, for instance, Patricia Crisafulli and Andrea Redmond, *Rwanda, Inc.: How a Devastated Nation Became an Economic Model for the Developing World* (London: Macmillan, 2012).

[68] On ex-military leaders in politics, see Anders Themnér, ed., *Warlord Democrats in Africa: Ex-military Leaders and Electoral Politics* (London: Zed Books, 2017).

[69] Jonny Steinberg, 'Policing, State Power, and the Transition from Apartheid to Democracy: A New Perspective', *African Affairs*, 113.451 (2014), 173–91.

of the stick' (Hausa: *dan sansa*), 'those who wear a belt' (Mandinka: *koulou siti*) or 'the boys who have guns' (Shona: *vakomana vezvivhorovho*). The public image of policemen is often associated with petty corruption. Alongside guards, soldiers or customs officers, they often have the reputation of being the most corrupt professionals. In Francophone West Africa, drivers call policemen the '*mange mille*' (eaters of banknotes of 1,000 FCFA). Day-to-day policing work in many parts of Africa carries the connotation that police do not work hard but instead, like vampires, exist in a parasitic relationship with their civilian victims.

Certain permanencies notwithstanding, some change has taken place. A case in point is the police in post-apartheid South Africa. Scholars have rightly pointed out that, in spite of the renaming of the 'police force' as the 'police service', key features of today's South African police recall the old apartheid institution: a paramilitary model of control over urban space re-emerged, and arbitrary arrests of young men at night and the use of violence against strikers have remained characteristics of police work. Even the appointment of the first black police commissioner in South Africa in 2000 could not convince observers of a profound change in police work. Nonetheless, some aspects of South African police work did change. A crucial point is the interaction with the public. During apartheid, the main task of the South African policemen was to repress insurgency. Today, policemen do respond to public demand. 'When democracy came', Jonny Steinberg writes, 'a dam wall burst; black civilians began calling police in high numbers and police responded.' For the first time in history, responding to civilians' calls became part of regular police work.[70]

Furthermore, everyday policemen's work is affected by the interaction with other security actors. Police forces often suffer from a lack of training and public support. They are often understaffed, underpaid and underequipped. Offices constantly run out of paper, and citizens have to pay for basic services. Many therefore hire private security companies. In spite of having one of the highest ratios of policemen per inhabitant (200,000 policemen and reservists for 50 million inhabitants, i.e. 1 for every 250), South Africa relies heavily on private security agents. There are around 400,000 registered active private security guards in South Africa, a number that is higher than that of the police and the army combined.[71] The diversification of security actors – private security companies, vigilantes, neighbourhood watches, area boys, etc. – is both a challenge for police agents and a source of revenue. Police agents often become private security agents after retirement. Others practise 'moonlighting', that is,

---

[70] *Ibid.*

[71] See also the chapter by Fourchard in this volume.

working as official cops by day and private cops at night. Others again are employed as 'consultants' for security firms. The plurality of arrangements between the state and private security companies has laid the ground for practices of urban policing that are neither public nor private and have therefore been termed 'twilight policing'.[72] In this context, the question of professionalization and specialization remains a crucial issue. Policing includes a wide range of skills and duties – anti-riot policing, patrolling, raiding, data gathering, paper processing, filing, etc.

Last but not least, democratization did not change a key structural feature of military and police work: gender inequality. A comparative survey in fourteen West African countries found out that on average only 12 per cent of personnel in security sector institutions (armed forces, police, judiciary system and prisons) were women.[73] This figure varies among countries and sectors. Whereas women make up almost 17 per cent of employees in the prison system, they constitute only 10 per cent of police staff and less than 4 per cent of military staff. However, the gender gap exists everywhere. In some countries, women are not allowed to serve in the military. Moreover, if women are allowed to serve, they often remain confined to administrative and subaltern tasks and do not reach the highest ranks.

Of course, the rule admits significant exceptions. Over the past few decades, some African women have served in the highest ranks of the security system, such as Elizabeth Mills-Robertson, who in 2009 was the acting Inspector General of Police in Ghana; Mary Gahonzire, who served as acting Commissioner General of the National Police of Rwanda in 2008; and Mangwashi Victoria Phiyega, who was Commissioner of the National Police in South Africa in 2012. However, these remain isolated cases. And while the police service of Ghana employs almost 20 per cent women, this, too, is an exception.

An emblematic case is Rwanda, a country that is often praised for the significant participation of women in politics. Rwanda has recognized the importance of gender equality and has created 'gender desks' to raise awareness of gender issues in its armed forces. In 2010 the high command promoted women to the ranks of major, lieutenant colonel and colonel, an idea that is anything but new in a country that has a tradition of female combatants and female officers. Rose Kabuye, a former lieutenant of the Rwandan Patriotic Front and a hero of the liberation of Rwanda, was a lieutenant colonel in

---

[72] Tessa D. Diphoorn, *Twilight Policing: Private Security and Violence in Urban South Africa* (Berkeley, CA: University of California Press, 2015); on the relationship of labour with the state, see the chapter by Britwum and Dakhli in this volume.

[73] Miranda Gaanderse and Kristin Valasek, eds, *Le secteur de la sécurité et le genre en Afrique de l'Ouest: une étude de la police, de la défense, de la justice et des services pénitentiaires dans les pays de la CEDEAO* (Geneva: Centre de Genève pour le Contrôle des Forces Armées, 2011).

the Rwandan army and a public figure of strength and the armed struggle against the *génocidaires*. However, even in Rwanda, there is no woman at the top command level of the army, and the proportion of women in the military and the police remains strikingly low, at 0.8 per cent and 10 per cent, respectively.

The under-representation of women in the military and police does not mean that they do not play a role in these sectors. On the contrary, many tasks that are crucial for the functioning of armies are dependent upon women. The presence of women within and around military camps, barracks and police stations is no accident; they are in charge of many logistical duties (food supplies, hygiene, health, patching uniforms, etc.). African armed forces were historically constructed on a gender division of 'man in arms'/'woman in services', which seems hard to undo. This leads to a separation of tasks as well as a hierarchization of duties. The notion that marching in the street with a rifle is a noble duty that deserves status and remuneration whereas feeding and clothing soldiers is informal unpaid labour has been entrenched in military thought since before colonial occupation and has continued through the colonial and postcolonial eras.

Gender inequalities, however, have significant consequences, including the sexualization of work relations. On the one hand, work in armed forces is connected with the construction of specific martial masculinities. Armies and police institutions intervene in the social construction of gender through rules (for instance, it is common in police institutions to employ only unmarried personnel and to accept pregnancy only for married women) as well as through a general discourse of virility and bravery. One effect of this gendered discourse is homophobia, with homosexuality being taboo in military and police organizations. On the other hand, the use of force often bears a link with sexualized violence in contexts as different as dictatorships, civil wars or post-revolutionary systems. In Central Africa, the civil war has been marked by the use of widespread campaigns of rape, battering or genital mutilation as war tactics. More recently, the Egyptian police has been accused of the systematic rape of male and female activists in custody, a practice aimed at stifling opposition. Continuing reports of sexual abuse and the exploitation of vulnerable populations around military posts in peacekeeping operations in Chad, Sudan and elsewhere remind us that the gendered sociology of African militaries relies on gendered assumptions about labour as well.[74]

---

[74] United Nations High Commissioner for Human Rights, *Report of the Mapping Project Documenting Serious Violations of International Human Rights Law and International Humanitarian Law Committed within the Territory of Central African Republic between January 2003 and December 2015* (Geneva, 2017).

CONCLUSION

During the colonial period, military and police forces undertook the work, often violent, of building and maintaining colonial states. Recruits were drawn from myriad backgrounds, but often their origins could be traced to histories of unfree labour or conditions of economic hardship that made such harsh work a viable path to manhood and respectability. Recruitment techniques among the colonizing powers were historically contingent, varying according to labour needs, wartime demands and the availability of those willing to become recruits. Resistance to conscription occurred in many places, most notably during the First World War, when young men across the continent fled from the excesses of European recruitment drives, alongside wider resistance to colonial labour demands. Embedded in European recruitment methods were racist and gendered assumptions about who could perform different kinds of work. Colonial reliance on soldiers' household members – women and children – as a cheap source of labour for logistical needs helped keep armies in the field. This strategy also reinforced patriarchal hierarchies, elevating soldierly masculinity as a preferred mode of labour and socio-economic mobility.

During the two world wars, hundreds of thousands of African soldiers were deployed to fight or labour both within the African continent and overseas. Soldiers and veterans who returned to their homes after the war expected their labours to yield benefits, usually of the most conservative kinds – land, jobs and care for their families. Their disappointment when colonial governments failed to honour these expectations sometimes led to strikes or mutinies. These moments are best understood within a labour history framework that can provide insights into the pliable relationship between soldiering, labour and racial inequalities at different times.

After decolonization, the conditions of labour in armed forces changed. First, African soldiers and policemen could now access the highest ranks formerly reserved for European officers. Secondly, some African officers now played a leading role in political processes, either because they had liberated their country through national wars (in Algeria, Angola, Kenya, Guinea Bissau or Mozambique), or because soldiers had taken power through military coups (Egypt, the DRC, Ghana, Guinea, Libya, Liberia, Mali, Togo, Sudan, Tunisia, Uganda, etc.). Labour in the military could now become a path for personal wealth accumulation and, at times, access to political power. This, however, was only true for a small number of high-ranking officers who could accumulate military positions as well as political and economic positions. Most of the rank-and-file remained poorly paid and worked in continuing poor conditions in the context of rapidly growing army headcounts.

For most of the twentieth century, armed forces in most African countries followed similar paths, for they were, almost everywhere, successively shaped by colonial conquest, colonial rule, decolonization and military rules. In the 1980s, however, the paths of national armies moved apart. In countries torn by civil wars (the DRC, Liberia, Rwanda, Sierra Leone, Sudan, Uganda, etc.), military labour conditions have been reframed by the violent dialectic of rebellions and counter-insurgency. In these countries, the boundaries between soldiers, rebels and civilians became more porous. Living by the gun became an option for many peasants, students or even children seeking labour opportunities.

In contrast, in countries spared (or relatively spared) civil war (Benin, Ghana, Nigeria, Senegal, Tanzania, Zambia, South Africa, etc.), military labour has been framed by the effects of democratization and structural adjustment programmes. In these countries, police work became more complex and diverse, following the general tendency of police specialization (anti-riot policing, patrolling, raiding, data gathering and so on). Simultaneously, the public image of police work remained ambiguous, oscillating between suspicions of corruption and demands for safety and security.

As Daniel Hoffman argues, scholars should 'think of violence as literal work, and think the labor of war as labor'.[75] Thus, despite the centrality of violence as the distinguishing marker of soldiering and police work, it is still 'built on the factors of capital and labour just like any other industry, [which] makes it possible to analyze the activities of the soldier as just another form of work'.[76] As troubling as it is to think in this direction, ignoring soldiers and police as workers perpetuates the notion that military violence is somehow disconnected from markets and capital, when, in fact, they are usually intricately intertwined and mutually supportive. Perhaps even more importantly, we should recognize the ways that fluctuations in socio-economic opportunities within societies often dictate levels of interest in military and police work, as well as the degree to which the state and other powerful actors incentivize these forms of work in order to attract enough people to join them.

[75] Hoffman, 'Violence, Just in Time'.
[76] Zürcher, *Fighting for a Living*.

TWELVE
Crime and Illegal Work

LAURENT FOURCHARD

Centre for International Studies, Sciences Po, Paris

Many expressions in African societies identify groups that operate between the legal and illegal at the frontier of petty and serious crime: *tsotsis* or *skollies* in South Africa; *wahuni* in Tanzania; *jaguda boys, boma boys* or *area boys* in Nigeria. They designate broad categories that embrace the criminal, the delinquent, the young and the jobless. For a large section of society, these common labels represent the embodiment of danger, disorder, crime and delinquency. To consider an unemployed young person and a leader of a gang as belonging to the same category shows the difficulty in disentangling joblessness and crime, the need to investigate the permanently shifting frontier between legal and illegal labour and to recognize the difficulty in capturing what constitutes crime in various African countries.

Crime in the African continent has been shaped by different imperial and national legal histories. In English-speaking countries, the term 'crime' is often used to designate an offence committed by adults, as opposed to 'delinquency', which is associated most of the time with juvenile offenders. By contrast, in French-speaking countries, 'crime' is used to designate the most serious offences which require severe penalties.[1] Instead of emphasizing these particular distinctions, I will use 'crime' as a behaviour or action prosecuted by the law that threatens the perpetrator with a penalty. This conventional definition is complicated by the fact that many African countries have inherited various legal histories of different origins (European and Islamic, as well as local traditions reshaped by colonial and national laws). Studying crime thus implies looking at incriminating processes, that is, the making of criminal codes, but also understanding what is locally perceived

---

[1] Philippe Robert and Laurent Mucchielli, *Crime et sécurité: l'état des savoirs* (Paris: La Découverte, 2002), 6.

as crime in a continent in which the state's monopoly on law and order is far from obvious.

Illegal labour is a notion that is no less ambivalent. Legal definitions are scarce at the global level. For the Organisation for Economic Co-operation and Development (OECD), illegal work concerns persons who are not legally authorized to work. This may involve, for instance, work by children below the prescribed minimum age, migrant workers without work permits or government employees who hold a second job incompatible with the duties of their first job.[2] This definition does not really make sense in Africa, as a majority of people work in activities that are not included in the law, or that operate outside the formal reach of the law, activities that have been labelled the informal economy. If there is an international consensus today on the necessity to distinguish the illegal from the informal, this has not always been the case. Criminalizing various forms of labour has instead been at the core of colonial and postcolonial economic practices and strategies.

To articulate crime and illegal labour thus implies uncovering three key related elements: criminalization of labour by colonial and postcolonial states; activities considered as criminal by national legislations, but which might be regarded as legitimate by the population; and criminal activities that require organized forms of labour and sometimes violence and are perceived as illicit by the majority of citizens. Academic literature is fragmented on these matters. The history and sociology of crime has focused on the perpetuation of crime and violence rather than on a labour history perspective, while criminal organizations have been uncovered in only a few countries (South Africa and more recently Nigeria). The following sections thus partially cover the continent as a whole in looking at four specific historical trends.

First, the definition of crime and illegal labour was determined by the obsession of colonial officials with orderly development and by the need to distinguish between those who were useful and those who were useless for the colonial economy. Numerous forms of labour (trading, brewing, preparing food) and unemployment (seeking jobs, wandering) came to be considered illegal in a number of colonies in the early colonial period. Second, with the uneven expansion of bureaucracy after the Second World War, groups labelled as undesirables consisted mainly of young people, who were increasingly dealt with by the state – a trend that was often kept up by national governments after independence.[3] Third, increasing casualization of work, liberalization of trade and the decline of the bureaucratic state

---

[2]   Organisation for Economic Co-operation and Development, *Informal Employment and Promoting the Transition to a Salaried Economy* (OECD Employment Outlook, 2004).

[3]   See the chapters by Britwum and Dakhli and by van den Bersselaar in this volume.

from the late 1970s onwards saw an increasing smuggling economy in many countries, which further blurred the legal and the illegal. Finally, the more recent global concern with the image of Africa as a place of transnational drug networks and criminal organizations needs to be examined in the light of the limited evidence on the matter.

THE MAKING OF UNDESIRABLES

At the end of the nineteenth century and the early twentieth century, most colonial authorities had a dual vision of Africa consisting of two opposing images: the primitive and the civilized, the pre-capitalist and the capitalist, and the tribal system considered as rural in contrast to the modern urban world.[4] Indirect rule in the British Empire, the *politique des races* in French West Africa or the system of reserves in South Africa were inspired by the idea that African people should be kept where they belonged in order to facilitate ruling them.[5] Colonial officials, however, soon faced the contradiction between keeping the populations on site and their imperative need for a labour force in mining areas, ports, cities and on settler farms. They soon had to deal with an undesirable population.

Illegal labour in the colonial context was very much about the history of criminalization of groups engaged in precarious jobs (petty traders, producers and vendors of alcohol, washers) or those suspected of not working and simultaneously challenging the authority of chiefs, elders and husbands (the 'unemployed', 'idle and undisciplined youth', or 'isolated women'). Rather than being the product of a coherent administrative machinery, these policies of dissociating the legal from the illegal were cobbled together on the basis of the conjectural interests of administrations and companies, and as a result of the uneven development of empirical knowledge, the gradual expansion of bureaucratic services and the uneven support of some influential groups (traditional chiefs, European settlers, enterprises).[6] These were made more complicated by the fact that African workers did not necessarily demand stable

[4]   Frederick Cooper, ed., *Struggle for the City: Migrant Labor, Capital and the State in Urban Africa* (Beverly Hills, CA: Sage, 1983); James Ferguson, *Expectations of Modernity: Myths and Meanings of Urban Life on the Zambian Copperbelt* (Berkeley, CA: University of California Press, 1999), 86.

[5]   Peter Geschiere and Stephen Jackson, 'Autochthony and the Crisis of Democratization, Decentralization, and the Politics of Belonging', *African Studies Review*, 49.2 (2006), 4.

[6]   Laurent Fourchard, *Trier, exclure et policer. Vies urbaines en Afrique du Sud et au Nigeria* (Paris: Presses de Sciences Po, 2018), 32.

waged jobs, but were rather seeking casual, impermanent, 'hidden' labour. If the definition of illegal labour kept changing over time, the criminalization of women's activities and repression of illegal labour in settler colonies strongly shaped early colonialism in Africa.

As the colonial notion of work was mainly based on gainful employment and wage labour, unemployed people soon became criminalized, but unevenly across the continent. Being unemployed had a very particular meaning; most of the time, it referred to men and women without a labour contract in a colonial productive space (mines, farms, towns) or outside a native reserve. This was highly dependent on the capacity of the colonial administrations (or municipalities or private companies) to produce appropriate documents – such as a pass (South Africa, Rhodesia), a temporary residence permit or *kipande* (Kenya) or a *passeport de mutation* (Belgian Congo) – which could be used to dissociate workers from other people.[7] The most restrictive system was created in South Africa, where a 1923 law identified the 'unemployed' as those who were unable to find work within 14 days after their arrival in town, 'women without husbands' as well as 'idle, dissolute and disorderly natives'.[8] Such permits were not common in West Africa, making illegal labour and unemployment more elusive issues.

Criminalization of labour particularly affected women, especially when their activities were perceived as challenging the colonial economy. In most parts of Africa, the legal codification of permanent minority status for women placed them securely under the control of their male relatives.[9] Everywhere they moved – to towns and rural commercial areas to seek jobs to support their families by sending remittances back home – women without husbands were labelled as 'unattached women', 'isolated women' or 'spinsters'. Administrations or local chiefs were suspicious of them, and their activities were often criminalized.[10] They had great difficulties in getting access to the wage labour market, as well as to non-wage activities,

---

[7]   Andrew Burton, *African Underclass: Urbanisation, Crime and Colonial Order in Dar es Salaam, 1919–61* (Oxford/Dar es Salaam/Athens, OH: James Currey/Mkuki na Nyota/Ohio University Press, 2005), 17–43.

[8]   Doug Hindson, *Pass Controls and the Urban African Proletariat* (Johannesburg: Ravan Press, 1987), 39–41.

[9]   Teresa Barnes, *'We Women Worked so Hard': Gender, Urbanisation and Social Reproduction in Colonial Harare, Zimbabwe, 1930–1956* (Oxford: James Currey, 1999), 23.

[10]   Lynette A. Jackson, '"When in the White Man's Town": Zimbabwean Women Remember *Chibeura*', in *Women in African Colonial Histories*, ed. Jean Allman, Susan Geiger and Nakanyike Musisi (Bloomington, IN: Indiana University Press, 2002), 191–218; Jane Allman, 'Rounding up Spinsters: Gender Chaos and Unmarried Women in Colonial Asante', *Journal of African History*, 37.2 (1996), 195–214.

since colonial authorities gave preference to a male workforce in the mines and compounds, infrastructural work and commercial agriculture, while they adopted different attitudes towards women involved in trading, dyeing, brewing, food producing or prostitution. Most of the time prostitution was regulated rather than strictly banned, while beer brewing was often criminalized, mainly because it was seen as challenging the productivity of male workers.

In French North Africa, strict colonial regulations and sanitary reasoning came to replace the more discreet and flexible approach to sexuality of the Ottoman period: registration of all women became compulsory, and they were placed under the supervision of the police and medical doctors and were forced to reside in specific neighbourhoods (*quartiers réservés*) and houses dedicated to sexual services (*maisons closes*).[11] All other forms of prostitution became illegal. The lives of 'clandestine prostitutes' became increasingly precarious. They continued to work as second-hand clothes vendors, market cleaners or domestic workers, but these poorly paid jobs were insufficient to feed a family or to pay the rent, while illegal forms of prostitution were subject to frequent police raids. Official prostitutes had no better working conditions. In Bousbir, the main quarter in Casablanca, most of them were once married before being abandoned. Once in Bousbir, they lost their economic independence and their relationships with the external world, as they came under the tight control of women procurers who did not allow them the profits of their work. Control of casual sex work was less strict in other colonies. In Nairobi, prostitution was tolerated; a professional identity developed in the interwar period to the point that a number of women could accumulate wealth and buy property.[12] Prostitution was never outlawed in Southern Rhodesia, while other forms of contractual engagement (such as *mapoto* or temporary marriages) were recognized. In Nigeria, authorities forbade solicitation and brothel keeping during the Second World War, but regulations were not strictly enforced.[13] With the notable exception of North Africa, criminalization of casual sex work was not a strong colonial concern, and when implemented, it was unable to limit the growing economic, social and sexual autonomy of women.

[11] Christelle Taraud, *La prostitution coloniale: Algérie, Maroc, Tunisie (1830–1962)* (Paris: Éditions Payot & Rivages, 2003).

[12] Luise White, *The Comforts of Home: Prostitution in Colonial Nairobi* (Chicago: University of Chicago Press, 1990).

[13] Saheed Aderinto, *When Sex Threatened the State: Illicit Sexuality, Nationalism, and Politics in Colonial Nigeria, 1900–1958* (Urbana, IL: University of Illinois Press, 2015).

Surprisingly, brewing and selling beer, a common activity of women in pre-colonial Africa, worried the administration much more, especially in British Africa. The progressive monopolization of brewing and the sale of beer in the hands of the colonial authorities and municipalities in South Africa, Southern Rhodesia and eastern Africa led to the proliferation of illegal drinking venues all over the continent: in 1960, 60 per cent of the alcohol trade in South Africa went through the 10,000 illegal taverns known as *shebeens* in Soweto and 30,000 distributors in Cape Town;[14] in the early 1970s, 8,000 of the 44,000 jobs in Nairobi's self-help city were in illegal brewing. Working in the *shebeen* was the female activity that was the most widespread and most profitable of all undeclared activities in South African townships.[15] Brewing beer was compatible with individual economic necessity and the need to take care of children.[16] In Sophiatown (Johannesburg), some brewers could earn 10 pounds per week in the early 1950s, while the vast majority of male workers earned less than 16 pounds a month in 1956.[17] The majority of women, however, were working long hours at night in return for a very unstable revenue, due to the destruction of goods, the imposition of heavy fines and the risk of imprisonment. The illegality of many forms of women's work gave them a highly volatile and precarious life. Reports published by the International Labour Organization in the early 1970s recognized the need to distinguish a non-wage sector labelled the 'informal sector'[18] from illegal work. This had no immediate effect on national governments, which were still very much influenced by post-war development policy and preoccupied with the issues it presented in the area of work; petty trade and women brewers were among those aspects that were not even recognized as 'work'.[19]

---

[14] Anne Mager, 'The First Decade of European Beer in Apartheid South Africa: The State, the Brewers and the Drinking Public, 1962–1972', *Journal of African History*, 40.3 (1999), 371.

[15] Deborah Posel, *The Making of Apartheid, 1948–1961: Conflict and Compromise* (Oxford: Clarendon Press, 1997), 175.

[16] Belinda Bozzoli, *Women of Phokeng: Consciousness, Life Strategy and Migrancy in South Africa, 1900–1983* (London: James Currey, 1991), 145.

[17] Posel, *The Making of Apartheid*, 171.

[18] Keith Hart, 'Informal Income Opportunities and Urban Employment in Ghana', *Journal of Modern African Studies*, 11.1 (1973), 61–89; International Labour Organization, 'Employment, Incomes and Equity: A Strategy for Increasing Productive Employment in Kenya' (Geneva: ILO, 1972).

[19] Justin Willis, *Potent Brews: A Social History of Alcohol in East Africa, 1850–1999* (Oxford/Athens, OH: James Currey/Ohio University Press, 2002), 208–9.

BETWEEN IDLERS AND CRIMINALS

The frontier between idlers, delinquents and criminals became more blurred from the 1940s onwards. This was one of the unexpected effects of the so-called labour stabilization policy introduced after the war to quash the solidarity that had occurred between the 'floating population' and the more permanent urban workers during the 1930s and 1940s riots and strikes in the French and British empires.[20] The aim was to transform a potentially 'anarchic' floating population into a true working class which, it was hoped, would become increasingly differentiated in terms of salaries, promotion and qualification. There was a strong belief that colonial state intervention could address one of the wartime obsessions: disorder and delinquency; the objective was to clearly dissociate workers from loafers, wage earners from temporary migrants and supposedly orderly groups from dangerous populations.[21] In this framework, groups of urban youth committing offences or refusing to work became a central political concern in most parts of the continent. Offences committed by children and young people, as well as alternative ways of life that did not match colonial or nationalist expectations with regard to order and labour, became a central concern for welfare services, late colonial authorities and new national governments.[22] The judiciary and bureaucratic institutions, in combining in the same category the so-called 'won't works' with thieves and more serious offenders, contributed to blurring the frontier between the licit and illicit.

Interestingly, many expressions became common in local parlance to qualify groups or individuals operating between the legal and illegal or between unemployment and crime. Beginning in the 1930s in the South African townships, the designation *tsotsi* was used for a black boy who was unemployed or partially working and who was often suspected of being involved in theft or more serious crimes such as assault, murder and rape.[23] *Tsotsis* saw regular wage labour as undignified, unprofitable and a denial of freedom: as they rejected the idea of steady employment, they were regularly referred to as 'won't works' by officials. A *skollie*, an Afrikaans generic term, referred to a poor and coloured male who refused to work for a living but was most of the time associated with criminal gangs, even if he might not be a member of one of them. In Lagos and Ibadan in the 1930s and 1940s, a

[20] Frederick Cooper, *Decolonization and African Societies: The Labor Question in French and British Africa* (Cambridge: Cambridge University Press, 1996).

[21] *Ibid.*

[22] See the chapter by Scully and Jawad in this volume.

[23] Clive Glaser, *Bo-Tsotsi: The Youth Gangs of Soweto, 1935–1976* (Oxford: James Currey, 2000).

jaguda boy meant a pickpocket or a member of a group of offenders extorting money by violent means, while a *boma boy* denoted a vagrant, a good-for-nothing, an unlicensed guide or a member of an organized group that might be working with prostitutes. In Dar es Salaam, the term *wahuni* identified a jobless youth who might become a delinquent.

Repressive policy towards youths and 'won't works' became increasingly common. This was the case in 1930s Morocco: abandoned children and professional beggars were rounded up and returned to the countryside. In the British Empire, the service and municipalities expelled destitutes or delinquents who were considered unfit for modern labour. In Dar es Salaam, between 1940 and 1960, from 1,000 to 2,000 *wahuni* were rounded up and sent back to their rural 'homes' every year. In Nigeria, the social welfare office criminalized street trading for girls under sixteen years of age, leading to a dramatic increase in the number of girls convicted in Lagos juvenile court, despite strong opposition by market women (from 200 cases a year in 1956 to 1,260 cases a year in 1963 and 1964).[24] In the Northern Region, in the 1960s, British and Nigerian welfare officers decided that 'genuine and deserving beggars' (the handicapped, the *mallam*, deaf beggars and the children helping them) could be assisted as they were considered necessary for political and religious leaders to fulfil religious obligations of almsgiving, while 'professional beggars' (mainly unemployed youth) had to be expelled or forbidden to come to town. In Senegal, the 1960s socialist government, inspired by colonial legislation on vagrancy, wanted to get rid of what it called the *encombrements humains* (human congestion) made up of young beggars, prostitutes, petty traders and 'lunatics'.[25] The government unsuccessfully tried to confine their activities to specific places in and around Dakar (market, asylum) and to send the others back to the country. In South Africa, an expanding punitive state caught more juvenile vagrants, young unemployed and *tsotsis* in the townships: the number of youths appearing before juvenile courts rose from 21,526 a year in 1933 to 177,923 a year in 1957, and an increasing number were sent to prison (around 10,000 a year in 1948 as compared to around 90,000 a year in 1969).[26] This experience of large-scale incarceration became an important factor in producing

---

[24] Laurent Fourchard, 'Lagos and the Invention of Juvenile Delinquency in Nigeria', *The Journal of African History*, 47.1 (2006), 115–37.

[25] Ousseynou Faye and Ibrahima Thioub, 'Les marginaux et l'État à Dakar', *Le Mouvement social*, 204 (2003), 93–108.

[26] Laurent Fourchard, '"Enfants en danger" et "enfants dangereux". Expertises et différenciation raciale en Afrique du Sud, 1937–1976', *Politix*, 99.3 (2012), 175–98.

and reproducing criminal violence. Late colonial administrators and new independent political leaders, imbued with the ideology of modernization and orderly urbanization, used a coercive embryonic welfare state to routinely criminalize more young and destitute people than ever.

ILLEGAL LABOUR AND TRANSNATIONAL SMUGGLING

From the mid-1970s onwards the formal labour market severely contracted and was replaced by a far more amorphous and insecure casualized work environment, characterized by self-employed, petty trade, poorly paid jobs, with erratic earnings: informality and increased precariousness of work became dominant factors in most African economies.[27] Simultaneously, one of the symptoms of the historical transformation of the continent under structural adjustment programmes was the growing involvement of political and economic operators in activities deemed criminal by national legislations and international laws.[28] This occurred in the context of the looting of national resources that resulted from the privatization of state enterprises and services, as well as the liberalization of the banking systems, which helped to convert money of illegal origin (for example, from fraud, corruption, overbilling) into licit assets (for example, real estate, hotels, casinos, lotteries, art objects, fisheries, banks). This development was facilitated by the prevalence of cash in African economies, which was much higher than in other continents. Transnational trade activities, whose criminal character is impossible to evaluate, became increasingly central for a number of states and especially for border societies.

Transnational smuggling of goods has existed in Africa since the establishment of colonial borders. The implementation of different tariffs and taxes on products led to a gradual emergence of groups of professional smugglers. On the West African coast, part-time carriers worked for large smuggling companies moving tobacco, alcohol, gunpowder or imported cloth between Togo and the neighbouring colonies, and smugglers gave up fishing or farming only once they had established themselves in the smuggling trade.[29]

---

[27] See the chapters by Bryceson and Barchiesi in this volume.

[28] Jean-François Bayart, Béatrice Hibou and Stephen Ellis, *La Criminalisation de l'État en Afrique* (Paris: Karthala, 1996), 26.

[29] Dmitri van der Bersseelaar, 'Somebody Must Necessarily Go to Bring this Drink: Gin Smugglers, Chiefs and the State in Colonial Ghana', *Cultural and Social History*, 11.2 (2014), 243–61.

Once in place, the border created strong local interests among transnational smugglers.[30]

In many countries, smuggling considerably expanded with the 1980s liberalization of the economy, particularly the import of products. The liberalization of imports was supposed to decrease the attractiveness of parallel markets and limit the practice of multiple frauds and contraband, but it actually strengthened transnational commercial networks. Since the beginning of the 1980s, states referred to as *entrepôt* states (Benin, Togo, the Gambia, Equatorial Guinea, Burundi) have built a comparative regional advantage by importing products at low prices and re-exporting them, very often illegally from the point of view of importing countries such as Senegal and Nigeria.[31] In this particular case, a set of professional smugglers emerged for a number of specific products that were highly protected and/ or subsidized, such as the importation of sugar in Senegal or used cars in Nigeria.[32] However, the effects of structural adjustment programmes on smuggling were wider.

Nigeria, the primary economy in West Africa, is a significant case. In the 1960s and 1970s the products smuggled were mainly money and crops (cocoa or peanuts) sold at a higher price in neighbourhood countries. But Nigerian outflows to the region increased considerably after the implementation of structural adjustment in 1983, and began to include consumer goods, fuel, construction materials, clothing and fake drugs. The availability of cheap subsidized fuel in Nigeria led to an increase in smuggling activities between Nigeria and its neighbours, which involved tens of thousands of traders, smugglers, carriers and street re-sellers, particularly in Benin and Cameroon. At the same time, with the dramatic cut in the pharmaceutical labour force (from 13,000 workers in 1983 to 7,000 in 1984), the development of fake drugs kick-started and, by the mid-1990s, assumed the majority of all drug sales in Nigeria, while the country became a wholesale supplier for the West and Central African private drug markets.[33] In one particular neighbourhood of Lagos, the industry grew from a few retail shops in the early 1970s to about 1,000 wholesale 'pharmaceutical traders' in 2010. In the process, the

---

[30]   Paul Nugent, *Smugglers, Secessionists, and Loyal Citizens on the Ghana-Togo Frontier* (Athens, OH: Ohio University Press, 2002).

[31]   John Igué and Bio G. Soulé, *L'État entrepôt au Bénin: Commerce informel ou solution à la crise?* (Paris: Karthala, 1992).

[32]   Stephen S. Gotlub, 'Entrepôt Trade and Smuggling in West Africa: Benin, Togo and Nigeria', *The World Economy*, 35.9 (2012), 1139–61.

[33]   Kristin Peterson, *Speculative Markets: Drug Circuits and Derivative Life in Nigeria* (Durham, NC: Duke University Press, 2014), 82.

practices of the so-called legitimate trade and the clandestine illicit one became increasingly intermingled.[34] In this case, the re-exportation of drugs such as cigarettes begins with large formal enterprises that import goods through official channels, before they are trans-shipped through informal or illegal mechanisms involving a network of large and small operators.

The situation is different where there is little possibility of formal trade, in countries such as Sierra Leone, Somalia and the Congo, in which military power and illicit trade have gone hand in hand. The collapse of the government in Somalia in 1991 provided a major stimulus to transnational trade in livestock. At the main market town of Garissa on the Kenya–Somalia border, cattle sales increased about fivefold between the late 1980s and the late 1990s.[35] In autocratic states, smugglers and border societies might perceive themselves as marginalized and consider illicit trade as a mean of economic survival. Contraband activities between Uganda, Congo and Sudan dramatically increased at the end of the Idi Amin regime in 1979, when the population in north-western Uganda that was fleeing repression by the Obote regime started a triangular trade in manufactured goods, oil and gold between Kenya, Uganda and Congo. Smuggling is seen in the local society as a source of economic empowerment, as part of the struggle against oppression and as a way to allow populations to fend for themselves.[36] Not so differently, illicit trade along the transborder road between southern Tunisia and Libya is referred as *el khat*, or 'trade of contraband', which became widespread during the structural adjustment period in Tunisia. Attempts to close the border are much contested by the border societies, who claim the right to do illicit business in the context of perceived national economic marginalization.[37]

Smuggling is illegal, because it escapes taxation or control by the state, but it is perceived as legitimate in many border societies. This is well understood by officials, who often prefer to compromise or negotiate with the local society rather than antagonize them. Traders do not seek to systematically sidestep officials but prefer to pay them off in order to have a *faux semblance* of legality and to avoid losing time and money.[38] In Morocco, *trabendo* is a

[34] *Ibid.*, 5–6, 21.

[35] Peter D. Little, *Somalia: Economy without State* (Oxford/Bloomington, IN: James Currey/Indiana University Press, 2005).

[36] Kristof Titeca and Tom de Herdt, 'Regulation, Cross-border Trade and Practical Norms in West Nile, North-Western Uganda', *Africa*, 80.4 (2010), 573–94.

[37] Hamza Meddeb, 'L'ambivalence de la «course à "el khobza"». Obéir et se révolter en Tunisie', *Politique Africaine*, 121.1 (2011), 35–51.

[38] Paul Nugent and Akim I. Asiwaju, *African Boundaries: Barriers, Conduits and Opportunities* (London: Pinter, 1996); Karine Bennafla, *Le Commerce frontalier en Afrique centrale: acteurs, espaces, pratiques* (Paris: Karthala, 2002).

word adapted from the Spanish *contrabando* to designate contraband trade in oil, alcohol, clothes, shoes, mobile phones and money between Morocco and Algeria since the 1990s. In local parlance, the road between Maghnia and Berkane 'has to be bought' (*Nechrou trig*) from *gendarmes* and customs officials, and the price to be paid could be as high as 15 per cent of the value of the products exchanged.[39] The contraband trade in the north-western Ugandan borderlands is to a large extent dominated by a number of powerful businessmen referred as tycoons, who play an important role in illicit trade (fuel, cigarettes, batteries, minerals, alcohol, pharmacy drugs, sugar, sweets, cloth) and legal activities (hardware or transport), which serve as a cover for their illegal activities. They have a firm grip on this trade through a coalition with particular state officials whom they pay for their services, which allows them to conduct their illegal trade and pushes out potential outside competitors.[40] As state officials regulate cross-border activities, concepts such as 'legality' and 'illegality' have become very blurred, as these 'illegal' practices exist through the protection by the 'legal' authorities.[41]

In a number of border societies, smuggling is clearly not seen as a crime but rather as part of the transnational economy in which the border between legal and illegal is permanently redefined. The *coupeurs de routes*, established since the colonial period in northern Cameroon, present their activities not as robbery but as working, while robbing merchants is not seen any differently from other forms of extortion by the state (fees taken by customs officials, referred as *douaniers combattants*, or border people impersonating customs officials).[42] This practice is rooted in a longer tradition: during the colonial period, a number of local chiefs allowed bandits to operate on their territory on the condition that they paid them a fee. Some chiefs organized cattle theft operations to compensate for the pillages no longer tolerated by colonial administrations.[43] Historically, the extractive practices of the bandits and of the state in different parts of Cameroon are not clearly separable from one another.[44]

---

[39]   Fatima Nabila Moussaoui, 'Le Trabendo ou la mondialisation par la marge', *Politique Africaine*, 137.1 (2015), 117–28.

[40]   Kristof Titeca, 'Tycoons and Contraband: Informal Cross-border Trade in West Nile, North-western Uganda', *Journal of Eastern African Studies*, 6.1 (2012), 47–63.

[41]   *Ibid.*, 58

[42]   Janet Roitman, *Fiscal Disobedience: An Anthropology of Economic Regulation in Central Africa* (Princeton, NJ: Princeton University Press, 2004).

[43]   Issa Saibou, *Les Coupeurs de route: histoire du banditisme rural et transfrontalier dans le bassin du Lac Tchad* (Paris: Karthala, 2010), 103, 113.

[44]   Nicolas Argenti, *The Intestines of the State: Youth, Violence and Belated Histories in the Cameroon Grassfields* (Chicago: University of Chicago Press, 2007), 174.

These examples show that large- and small-scale smugglers often operate in tandem and could cooperate with officials. All over the West Nile and northern Uganda, tycoons provide numerous jobs that are necessary all along the smuggling routes, at collection points, at distribution points, in depots and in hideouts for the smuggled goods, but also in the various formal companies. The specialists in the smuggling of oil, referred to as OPEC boys, in the town of Arua (Uganda) number around 300 to 400, but the whole sector gives jobs to many more players (for example, carriers, spotters).[45] Most of the time border residents are involved in assisting in the routine activities of officials. At the border of Ghana and Togo, they cook, clean and shop for officers, they are the prime informants for officials regarding illicit trade routes, and they assist them in checking on and if necessary disciplining travellers crossing the border. While these relationships are uneasy, for the most part they maintain an equilibrium beneficial to all parties involved.[46]

THE EMERGENCE OF CRIMINAL ORGANIZATIONS

Africa's porous borders have been increasingly perceived as a conducive environment for the development of transnational drug trafficking, which has attracted the growing concern of various UN agencies since the 1990s.[47] Much of this concern has focused on West Africa and its role as a trans-shipment point for South American cocaine destined for Europe. This has been accompanied by the development of the language of the global war on drugs, which labels every person trading or selling drugs as a major drug baron resorting to violence – a stereotypical language that does not reflect the realities of the people using, producing and smuggling drugs in Africa.[48] This new international concern is based on the increase in seizures of cocaine on the continent in the past fifteen years, but as a matter of fact, the quantities sold by African smugglers remain marginal.[49] This last section focuses on Nigerian drug traffickers and criminal gangs in South Africa, which are

---

[45] Kristof Titeca, 'Les Opec boys en Ouganda, trafiquants de pétrole et acteurs politiques', *Politique Africaine*, 103.3 (2006), 143–59.

[46] Brenda Chalfin, *Neoliberal Frontiers: An Ethnography of West Africa* (Chicago: University of Chicago Press, 2010), 68.

[47] Neil Carrier and Gernot Klantschnig, *Africa and the War on Drugs* (London: Zed Books, 2002).

[48] *Ibid.*, 2, 6.

[49] In 2009 the whole continent accounted for merely 0.1 per cent of global seizures. *Ibid.*, 103.

partly covered in an emerging literature on criminal networks. Criminal organizations are sometimes understood as organized groups making a living from activities considered as criminal and violent such as drug trading, kidnapping, embezzlement or large-scale theft.[50] But as the Nigerian and South African cases show, the border is often blurred between highly structured organizations and looser local networks of friends making a part-time living from their criminal activities.

The success of Nigerian criminal groups at the world level in specific illicit markets – notably drugs, human trafficking and advance fee fraud – is to be understood as part of the legacy of widespread forms of slavery and unfree labour, early corruption of the political and bureaucratic elites, the massive growth of a transnational diaspora after the civil war (1967–70) and of unemployed, qualified people after the introduction of structural adjustment programmes in the 1980s.[51] Transnational trafficking of heroin and cocaine developed from the 1980s onwards, but there are no drug barons nor Colombia-style cartels in Nigeria that control large sectors of the business or smuggling routes. Most of the drug-smuggling activities are conducted by local networks made up of three to a few dozen members,[52] which import from tens to hundreds of kilogrammes of drugs from the producer regions in West Africa and repackage them in small quantities for sale in consumer countries. The first generation of heroin and cocaine smugglers in the 1980s came from some of the groups most directly affected by the policies of the International Monetary Fund – urban unemployed, scholars stranded abroad without state scholarships and traders in international goods.[53] Today's 'mules' – people who transport illegal drugs – are not usually from the poorest sections of society but have some experience of international travel, a valid visa and possibly a foreign passport. They receive between 1,000 and 5,000 pounds sterling per trip. The majority are well aware of the freight they are carrying and most of them know the risks they take. Thus, the term 'mule' – someone being tricked or unknowingly taking a risk – should be considered a misnomer in this respect.[54]

---

[50] *Ibid.*, 511.

[51] Stephen Ellis, *This Present Darkness: A History of Nigerian Organized Crime* (London: Hurst, 2016).

[52] Antonio Mazzitelli, 'Transnational Organized Crime in West Africa: The Additional Challenge', *International Affairs*, 83.6 (2007), 1075–95.

[53] Carrier and Klantschnig, *Africa and the War on Drugs*, 90

[54] *Ibid.*, 97.

Smugglers need to have the experience of an import/export entrepreneur to be able to join the trade in heroin and cocaine. Nigerian men and women seem to dominate transnational drug trafficking in heroin and cocaine in a number of African countries today: they clearly introduced it in Ghana and South Africa in the 1990s – partly to avoid state repression after the creation of the National Drug Law Enforcement Agency in 1989.[55] In these countries, however, they deal with existing local criminal organizations that control the drug consumption market. The end of the trade embargo on South Africa has led to a proliferation in the number of retailers and an increase of drug consumers at an unparalleled level. This, in turn, has further fuelled the violence between rival criminal organizations historically rooted in black and coloured townships.

In South Africa, it is not easy to distinguish who is a criminal and who is an idler, especially in areas such as townships, where violent extortion, assault and robbery have become part of daily life. In the Cape Flats, working-class dormitories built in the 1960s and the 1970s on the outskirts of Cape Town, young men and women who were clearly not members of a gang participated in activities associated with the gangs, while many residents disputed the claim of being a gang member: what from the outside could be construed as gangs were loose groups of friends who only hardened and territorialized during conflict.[56] Groups of friends protecting the street did not necessarily have much in common with powerful prison gangs involved in murder and drug trafficking, and having strict hierarchical structures.[57] The same ambivalence could be found in Johannesburg and Soweto *tsotsis* groups, which could include, on the one hand, bigshot gangs running protection rackets, gambling dens and armed robbery, and on the other hand, street-corner friend networks, unarmed, unemployed, engaged in informal employment or petty theft and smoking cannabis.

The development of gangs at the periphery of Johannesburg between the end of the nineteenth century and the early twentieth century has been analysed by Charles van Onselen as the emergence of a black *lumpenproletariat* of peasants without land, nostalgic for rural and peasant life and resisting

---

[55] Mark Shaw, 'West African Criminal Networks in South and Southern Africa', *African Affairs*, 101.404 (2002), 291–316; Emmanuel Akyeampong, 'Diaspora and Drug Trafficking in West Africa: A Case Study of Ghana', *African Affairs*, 104.410 (2005), 438–9.

[56] Steffen Jensen, *Gangs, Politics and Dignity in Cape Town* (Oxford/Johannesburg/Chicago: James Currey/Wits University Press/University of Chicago Press, 2008), 98.

[57] Irvin Kinnes, *From Urban Street Gangs to Criminal Empires: The Changing Face of Gangs in the Western Cape* (Pretoria: Institute for Security Studies, 2000).

the process of proletarization.[58] Other 1980s radical historians have viewed delinquents and gangsters as a labour force that is difficult to absorb. But South African gangs tended to be preoccupied with rival groups within the townships rather than with larger political issues, and it is unlikely that gangs in South Africa could have flourished without a significant degree of support from other sectors of the community.[59] Gangsters often conduct their activities away from their home areas, and township residents share in the spoils of the gangs' criminal exploits, especially stolen goods.[60] Cape Flats gangs in the 1970s could provide incomes for 100,000 people through the illicit economy they controlled, sometimes paying water and electricity bills for the residents. Soweto gangs rarely robbed or assaulted residents of their own township, but they raided schools, *shebeens* and parties, and held up passengers at major railway stations in the city centre. Local women were provided with a certain degree of protection from outside harassment in exchange for sexual services, while the victims of gang rape were almost invariably outsiders.[61]

Insecure environments made gangsters key security providers. Supplying miners with alcohol and commercial sex, and providing them a measure of safety, was the primary business of Russian gangs known as Marashea in East Rand towns and Johannesburg in the second part of the twentieth century.[62] They controlled a large number of female Basotho migrants who dominated the brewing business. Russians were frequently given a woman and had free access to 'unattached women' affiliated with the group. Marasheas had also a number of loafers, who relied on various, often illegal means to survive, in particular the large-scale liquor distribution and prostitution rackets that catered to the needs of African mineworkers. When jobs became more difficult to obtain, men engaged in predatory practices such as robbery, smuggling diamonds and gold, assassinations and hiring out as muscle. In the 1980s, when mining industries declined, Russian groups competed fiercely for meagre resources: they became central players in a series of taxi wars in the 1980s and 1990s, when the sector was deregulated.

[58] Charles van Onselen, *New Babylon, New Nineveh: Everyday Life on the Witwatersrand, 1886–1914* (Johannesburg: Jonathan Bell, 1982), 395.

[59] Gary Kynoch, *We are Fighting the World: A History of the Marashea Gangs in South Africa, 1947–1999* (Athens, OH: University of Ohio Press, 2005), 8.

[60] *Ibid.*, 9.

[61] *Ibid.*; Glaser, *Bo Tsotsis*; Don Pinnock, *Gang Town* (Cape Town: Tafelberg, 2016).

[62] Kynoch, *We are Fighting the World*.

CONCLUSION

Nigeria and South Africa are not unique in terms of crime and illegal activities on the African continent, but they should not be considered as the benchmark against which other countries should be compared. Nor have criminal organizations in these two countries become more widespread with the liberalization of the continent's economy. Instead, criminal organizations in Nigeria and South Africa reveal their historical rootedness and their relative peculiarity at the continental level: the prevalence of gangs and violence in South Africa is a legacy of a brutalizing mining environment, long-lasting legal discrimination and a coercive penal system, while drug and human trafficking in Nigeria have to be seen as part of a longer history of widespread slavery, massive state corruption, large-scale international migration and porous borders. What has become more common at the continental level – even if it difficult to evaluate its scale – is the importance of contraband, one of the unexpected effects of the IMF-dictated liberalization of trade. If this represents today a massive loss of state revenues, it is also perceived as a legitimate means of earning a living for millions of workers and one possible path towards economic integration for those at the bottom. All over the continent, workers living in border societies are vocal in declaring illegal trade as legitimate, while fragmentary evidence shows that state officials are part of local deals that increase the precariousness of these workers.

The promotion of the informal economy by the IMF, the World Bank and some African countries as a solution to massive unemployment and poverty has led to a gradual recognition of its legitimacy, even if some governments are still harassing and criminalizing street vendors. The legacy of excessive colonial bureaucratic control of the unemployed, the young, women selling alcohol or food and internal migrants has been gradually but very unevenly declining in the past two decades or so. This process is working simultaneously with the formalization of the informal economy, which is taking place in many sectors (for example, street vendors, taxi drivers, waste management), especially in millionaire cities.[63] The growing pressure of international migrants and refugees on some African countries (South Africa, Côte d'Ivoire, Morocco, Libya, Nigeria, Kenya) represent one of the key political challenges for the continent as a whole and one of the most thought-provoking aspects in the ongoing academic discussion on the link between crime and illegal labour.

---

[63] Laurent Fourchard and Simon Bekker, eds, *Governing Cities in Africa: Politics and Policies* (Pretoria: HSRC Press, 2013).

THIRTEEN
White-Collar Workers

DMITRI VAN DEN BERSSELAAR

Institute for African Studies, University of Leipzig

The term 'white-collar work' describes a broad spectrum of non-manual paid employment, including relatively low-level clerical jobs, mid-level planning and accounting functions, and high-level managerial roles. White-collar workers are found in trading, banks and other service industries, in the offices of industrial enterprises, and as part of the civil service. The explicit distinction between white-collar workers and blue-collar workers (those engaged in manual labour) is associated with industrial societies.[1] The term's focus on dress does not just refer to the practice that manual workers often have to wear blue overalls while office workers are expected to wear white shirts: it also refers to differing expectations of education, career advancement and habitus. White-collar workers tend to operate in a safer and cleaner working environment, get paid more and are usually better qualified than blue-collar workers. Thus, even those in low-level clerical positions may consider themselves superior to manual workers, as has been frequently the case among African clerks. In twentieth-century Africa, the primary contrast to white-collar work was not necessarily blue-collar work, as most African economies retained large percentages of agricultural labourers and of workers in the informal sector. Indeed, white-collar workers made up only a small percentage – generally less than 5 per cent – of the total number of workers.[2] Their roles, however, tended to make them quite visible, and

---

[1] Jürgen Kocka, *White Collar Workers in America 1890–1940: A Social-Political History in International Perspective* (London: Sage, 1980), 12.

[2] Bill Freund, *The African Worker* (Cambridge: Cambridge University Press, 1988), 39; for more recent statistics, see ILOSTAT database, https://www.ilo.org/ilostat/ (accessed 15 January 2019).

they were over-represented among those who functioned as intermediaries between the (post-)colonial state and the population.[3]

The history of white-collar work in African societies is associated with colonial administrations, postcolonial bureaucracies and expatriate business. However, white-collar work existed in Africa before the coming of colonial rule (although without a dress code involving a white shirt): African merchants employed clerks and managers; some African polities employed bureaucrats and diplomats; and European traders and missionaries employed African clerks and agents. During the nineteenth century, Western-style educated Africans from Sierra Leone and Senegal in particular were recruited as white-collar workers and sent across West and West-Central Africa.[4] When colonial rule was established across Africa during the final decades of the nineteenth century this had a quantitative impact on white-collar work, increasing the demand for such employees. Around the turn of the twentieth century it also had a qualitative impact, bringing three changes to white-collar work: first, the expectation of a Western-style education (initially not up to a very advanced level) rather than an indigenous education as a prerequisite for employment; second, the gendering of white-collar work as work done by males; and third, the limit placed on career progression, as all higher positions in the colonial administrations would be taken up by appointees from Europe.[5]

Throughout the twentieth century, African white-collar workers found themselves at sites of tension. During the colonial period this involved the impact of colonial discourse which impacted upon their relations with colonial administrators, while their relations with other Africans could be problematic too. White-collar workers employed as civil servants, even those who did not take advantage of their position to oppress or take bribes, were seen as instruments of colonial power and could become a focus of resentment against colonial rule. Attempts by white-collar workers to convert the benefits of their jobs into social status and political influence in African communities were frequently contested. Their claims to prominence, based on education and employment, were challenged by elders who based their

[3] Benjamin N. Lawrance, Emily Lynn Osborn and Richard L. Roberts, eds, *Intermediaries, Interpreters, and Clerks: African Employees in the Making of Colonial Africa* (Madison, WI: University of Wisconsin Press, 2006).

[4] Jonathan Derrick, 'The "Native Clerk" in Colonial West Africa', *African Affairs*, 82.326 (1983), 65–6.

[5] A. Adu Boahen, *African Perspectives on Colonialism* (Baltimore, MD: Johns Hopkins University Press, 1987), 107; Ruth Watson, '"What Is Our Intelligence, Our School Going and Our Reading of Books Without Getting Money?" Akinpelu Obisesan and His Diary', in *Africa's Hidden Histories: Everyday Literacy and Making the Self*, ed. Karin Barber (Bloomington, IN: Indiana University Press, 2006), 66.

claims on the sanction of 'tradition' (and were backed in doing so by the colonial state). Furthermore, in many cases (and particularly so in the first decades of the century) white-collar workers had to overcome lowly social origins that did not matter much in the colonial economy, but were not so easily ignored in the communities they came from.

During the period of decolonization many white-collar workers had opportunities for accelerated career advancement when their European superiors left as part of Africanization strategies (the replacement of Europeans with Africans in managerial roles), but they also faced suspicion because of their close association with the colonial state or expatriate business. Furthermore, as access to education, and therefore access to clerical positions, had been unequally distributed during the colonial period, white-collar workers could find themselves faced with accusations that they favoured members of their own ethnic group, and with calls for ethnic quotas. Later, during the 1980s, at a time when their salaries had declined considerably in real terms, many found themselves described as being part of bloated and inefficient bureaucracies that would have to be drastically reduced to turn around the economies of former African colonies.

A number of aspects of white-collar work in Africa will be explored in this chapter: a first section will look at employment opportunities and career progression for white-collar workers compared to other workers during the first decades of the twentieth century. Following this, the chapter will consider those who, because of their education and skills, were recruited for employment as white-collar workers with colonial administrations, missions or commercial firms during the colonial period.

The next section will focus on the 1930s, when colonial administrations started to perceive African white-collar workers as a problem, partly because the recession had led to unemployment among educated would-be white-collar workers, and partly because of colonial attitudes towards educated Africans. This will be followed by a discussion of Africanization and other changes that took place following the Second World War and up to the 1970s.

The two sections that follow depart from chronology to explore thematic aspects of white-collar work that are of relevance throughout the century. The first will discuss how white-collar workers were perceived by, and interacted with, other Africans. This includes claims to status and influence in local communities and in a nationalist arena, and the translation by white-collar workers, through consumption and other means, of their achievements in terms that made sense in local African cultural understandings. The second will look at the frequent accusations against white-collar workers as being prone to corruption and abuse of their position in dealings with other Africans.

The subsequent section returns to chronology and explores the changing structures and opportunities for training and career progression, focused largely on the decolonization period and the first decades of independence. The final section relates to the 1970s–1990s, and discusses how white-collar workers coped with the economic crises of postcolonial African states. A brief conclusion will revisit main themes from the chapter, and explore how experiences of recruitment and training, status and consumption, and of insecurity and migration, have changed over the course of the twentieth century.

WHITE-COLLAR WORKERS AND THE 'LABOUR QUESTION'

The history of twentieth-century white-collar work must start in the nineteenth century, as it was at that time that colonial administrations and African and expatriate businesses started to hire white-collar workers. The idea of a 'career ladder' is often associated with white-collar work.[6] It was indeed possible to climb the ranks in the administration for African white-collar workers who had started employment during the nineteenth century. A. W. Thompson, from Cape Coast in Ghana, for instance, started with the colonial administration as an assistant clerk in 1873 and worked his way up to District Commissioner, which position he held from 1889 until his death in 1907.[7] Thompson was one of a number of Africans to make such a career in the British colonial service during the nineteenth century.[8] From the first decade of the twentieth century, however, such positions became the preserve of Europeans. The resulting limit on promotions frustrated African white-collar workers in government employment until the end of colonial rule.

Outside colonial service, a limited number of other opportunities for career progression remained. Many African-owned merchant firms and mines were pushed out of business during the first decades of the twentieth century, but employment with a European private enterprise remained an option, as it 'did not have a colour bar as rigid as the colonial administration' and offered

[6]   Clark Davis, *White-Collar Life and Corporate Cultures in Los Angeles, 1892–1941* (Baltimore, MD: Johns Hopkins University Press, 2000), 9.

[7]   Michel R. Doortmont, *The Pen-Pictures of Modern Africans and African Celebrities by Charles Francis Hutchison: A Collective Biography of Elite Society in the Gold Coast Colony* (Leiden: Brill, 2005), 417.

[8]   *Ibid.*, 27.

better prospects.[9] It was, for instance, possible for an African to join a British company as a storekeeper in 1914, receive a string of promotions, and get appointed to a management position in 1935, carrying out the same duties as a European manager and receiving a commission of a percentage of the net profits of the business.[10]

Another way to avoid getting stuck as a civil servant at a relatively low level was to leave salaried employment. A number of frustrated government clerks opted to pursue a career in the legal profession, and some became very successful.[11] Thomas Hutton-Mills (1865–1931), for instance, initially worked as a clerk in a commercial firm and, after that, in the colonial administration. After getting sacked he worked as a clerk for his uncle, who was a lawyer and newspaper proprietor, before leaving for the UK to study law. Hutton-Mills is an example of a frustrated clerk who became very successful as a lawyer, although it should be noted that his career benefited from having as his father a businessman who belonged to, and was well-connected in, Gold Coast African elite society.[12] Other clerks went into trading or other business ventures such as setting up a printing press or transport business. The Nigerian entrepreneur Adeola Odutola (1902–95), started work at the age of nineteen, working first as a clerk in the Treasury Department, and later as a court clerk. He remained employed as a clerk for twelve years, and during this time he also traded privately in food and textiles. He resigned as a court clerk in 1933 to become a full-time trader. He started industrial production, weaving cloth, during the Second World War. He later set up a plastic foam factory, a tyre plant, a brewery, a cannery and a biscuit factory.[13]

---

[9]   Derrick, 'The "Native Clerk"', 68. On the fate of African merchants, see Anthony
      I. Nwabughuogu, 'From Wealthy Entrepreneurs to Petty Traders: The Decline of
      African Middlemen in Eastern Nigeria, 1900–1950', *Journal of African History*, 23.3
      (1982), 365–79; Raymond E. Dumett, 'African Merchants of the Gold Coast, 1860–
      1905 – Dynamics of Indigenous Entrepreneurship', *Comparative Studies in Society and
      History*, 25.4 (1983), 661–93.

[10] Unilever Archives and Records Management, Port Sunlight, UK (UARM), United
      Africa Company Collection (UAC)/2/20/3/2/1 UAC of Ghana Ltd, General
      Manager's Private Files (1933–1940). This employee's name has been withheld in
      accordance with the author's agreement with Unilever not to reveal the identity of
      individual employees where information about them is not already in the public
      domain.

[11] Derrick, 'The "Native Clerk"', 67.

[12] Doortmont, *Pen-Pictures*, 261.

[13] Tom Forrest, *The Advance of African Capital: The Growth of Nigerian Private Enterprise*
      (Edinburgh: Edinburgh University Press, 1994), 60–4.

The colonial limits to career progression meant that for many junior clerks, white-collar work provided merely a starting point, to be left behind to pursue a subsequent career that offered better opportunities. Nevertheless, clerical work was still sufficiently attractive, and there were enough qualified applicants, for colonial administrations and commercial businesses to be able to recruit the numbers they needed without much difficulty. This was in marked contrast to the difficulties experienced when recruiting manual labour. At the start of the twentieth century, mining companies, European businesses, African farmers, colonial government departments, plantations and others were all looking for a regular supply of efficient, reliable and cheap workers.[14] The inability or unwillingness to offer attractive wages and working conditions meant that European-owned mines and plantations suffered constant labour shortages: the 'labour question'. Colonial officers and European entrepreneurs claimed that their recruitment difficulties stemmed from a scarcity of labour resulting from the 'inherent laziness' and 'unreliability' of the African population, and that until these cultural traits changed, the use of force to recruit and manage labour was not only acceptable, but also in the long-term interest of the African population itself.[15]

This explanation remained widespread through much of the colonial period, despite the observable fact that African farmers and entrepreneurs, as well as those European employers who paid adequate wages and treated their workers well, had no difficulties recruiting labour.[16] Labour in colonial Africa was often migrant, and workers in mines, on railways, on plantations or in towns had to adjust to new circumstances, become part of networks in their places of work, and find ways to maintain relations with their places of origin, fulfilling social obligations there and claiming or achieving social status while absent from home.[17] Most white-collar workers were similarly working

---

[14] See the chapters by Tischler and Brown in this volume.

[15] Jeff Crisp, *The Story of an African Working Class: Ghanaian Miners' Struggles 1870–1980* (London: Zed Books, 1984), 14–17.

[16] Carola Lentz, *Ethnicity and the Making of History in Northern Ghana* (Edinburgh: Edinburgh University Press, 2006), 138–43; Michael Mason, 'Working on the Railway: Forced Labor in Northern Nigeria, 1907–1912', in *African Labor History*, ed. Peter C. W. Gutkind, Robin Cohen and Jean Copans (Beverly Hills, CA: Sage, 1978), 59–61; Gareth Austin, 'Cash Crops and Freedom: Export Agriculture and the Decline of Slavery in Colonial West Africa', *International Review of Social History*, 54.1 (2009), 1–37.

[17] Carolyn A. Brown, *'We Were All Slaves': African Miners, Culture and Resistance at the Enugu Government Colliery* (Portsmouth, NH: Heinemann, 2003); Jens A. Andersson, 'Reinterpreting the Rural-Urban Connection: Migration Practices and Socio-Cultural Dispositions of Buhera Workers in Harare', *Africa*, 71.1 (2001), 82–112;

away from their places of origin and faced similar struggles to adapt to new environments while maintaining links with home. However, their trajectories were frequently more individual and more complex than those of manual labourers, involving travel for education and training, as well as postings and transfers to other regions.[18] For instance, Senegalese government clerks served as far away as French Equatorial Africa, and Ghanaian clerks recruited by Unilever were sent to the Belgian Congo, although usually the postings were closer to home.[19]

During the first decades of the twentieth century, the number of potential white-collar workers was very small compared to the potential number of unskilled labourers, which reflected the very limited educational opportunities available. Educated Africans had a choice of many different employment opportunities with the administration, expatriate firms or missions, and they frequently moved from one to another in an attempt to improve their prospects.[20] African white-collar workers were nevertheless crucial to the functioning of colonial administrations and European businesses in colonial Africa, and remained so for independent African governments and businesses. However, the 'labour question' did not arise in the context of clerical labour, presumably because colonial administrations and expatriate enterprises did not expect to be able to exploit white-collar workers to the same degree as unskilled and semi-skilled workers, and they were thus prepared to offer their clerical workers better working conditions and pay them higher wages. The continued popularity of clerical work as offering at least the starting point for a career in the colonial economy allowed employers to raise the education requirements for entry-level positions by the 1930s without raising wages, even though opportunities for career advancement remained limited until after the Second World War.

Josef Gugler, 'The Son of the Hawk Does Not Remain Abroad: The Urban-Rural Connection in Africa', *African Studies Review*, 45.1 (2002), 21–41. On migrant labour, see the chapter by Pérez Niño in this volume; on transport, see the chapter by Bellucci in this volume.

[18]   Andreas Eckert, *Herrschen und Verwalten. Afrikanische Bürokraten, staatliche Ordnung und Politik in Tanzania, 1920–1970* (Munich: Oldenbourg, 2007), 172.

[19]   Derrick, 'The "Native Clerk"', 66; UARM UAC 2/20/3/6/1 *Gold Coast U.A.C. News*, 3, 3 (February 1952).

[20]   Archive of the Church Missionary Society, Birmingham (CMS) G3 A3 e5 Annual Report Dennis Memorial Grammar School for 1935.

THE COLONIAL PERSPECTIVE: WHITE-COLLAR WORKERS AS A 'PROBLEM'

Colonial administrators began to regard African white-collar workers as a 'problem' during the first half of the 1930s, which was a time of reduced opportunities for African civil servants and white-collar workers. The global economic depression forced colonial administrations to drastically reduce spending. Civil servants were laid off where contracts allowed it, vacancies were left unfilled, and perks such as travelling and housing allowances were reduced. Meanwhile, commercial firms, faced with losses due to the declining price of commodities, reduced their staffing levels and cut the wages of those who remained.[21] Many Africans who completed secondary school during these years found it difficult to find employment, in contrast to earlier years. Another difference from the early years of colonial rule were the higher entry standards that employers demanded. School leavers who had attained qualifications which previously would have been sufficient to find employment as a clerk in government service or with a commercial firm discovered that they fell short in the 1930s.[22] The declining benefits of education went along with a stagnation of remuneration for white-collar jobs, resulting in a decline in purchasing power in real terms for those thus employed.[23]

Western-style educated youth – still a small minority of the population in this period – nevertheless continued to flock to the towns in the hope of finding white-collar work. Young men even worked for expatriate firms without pay as learning clerks, hoping to be put on the payroll after six months if their work was considered good enough.[24] This can at least partly be explained by the general labour surplus at the time, which did not leave them many alternatives.[25] Colonial administrators suspected that those who had been to school had come to believe that farming or manual work was beneath them, perhaps because of the nature of the curriculum in missionary and government schools, or the attitude of those who had taught them. The Nigerian Education Department, for instance, was convinced of the need to

---

[21] Moses E. Ochonu, *Colonial Meltdown: Northern Nigeria in the Great Depression* (Athens, OH: Ohio University Press, 2009), 52; David K. Fieldhouse, *Merchant Capital and Economic Decolonization: The United Africa Company 1929–1987* (Oxford: Clarendon Press, 1994), 97.

[22] UK National Archive, Kew (TNA) CO583/258/30150 B. H. Bourdillon to Viscount Granborn, 19 November 1942.

[23] Nate Plageman, *Highlife Saturday Night: Popular Music and Social Change in Urban Ghana* (Bloomington, IN: Indiana University Press, 2013), 83.

[24] UARM UAC/2/19/3/6/4/1 *UAC Pensioners' Newsletter*, 1, 1 (1982), 10.

[25] Crisp, *The Story of an African Working Class*, 61.

familiarize African youth 'with other methods of earning a livelihood besides that of sitting on an office stool'.[26]

This episode reveals a lot about the place of white-collar workers, including those working as civil servants, in twentieth-century Africa. The Nigerian administration was correct that many Africans in clerical posts with the colonial administration or with commercial firms made status claims on the basis of their position. This was not limited to the colonial period. In the 1970s Paul Kennedy found that, in Ghana,

> those who hold professional, technical and administrative positions (not necessarily at a high level) in the public or foreign sectors of the economy by virtue of their educational attainments normally enjoy a good deal of prestige and security in addition to relatively high financial rewards – the latter accruing through the unofficial income opportunities provided by graft in addition to official salary.[27]

The allegation of corruption as a feature of such a position is one that will be explored below, as there are strong indications that this was a feature of white-collar work that was equally widespread during both colonial and postcolonial periods.[28] Kennedy's observation also suggests that the status claims of white-collar workers were mainly based on the income and job security that this type of employment brought, rather than the actual work itself – 'sitting on an office stool'.

The British colonial administrators' dismissive comments primarily reveal the unease that colonial administrators felt about what they called 'educated natives': while African clerks were absolutely crucial to the functioning of the colonial administration, these same administrations felt threatened by colonial subjects who acted, spoke and dressed like them. Paul Nugent has described this as the colonial contradiction: colonial rule was based on difference and justified with the claim of bringing 'civilization' to 'backward' people, but the success of such a project (which would result in colonized subjects becoming less different) would challenge the basis for colonial domination. As a result, 'those who had bought most completely into the civilising mission ended up being castigated by European officialdom as the very worst kind

---

[26] TNA CO583/205/30150, *Annual Report on the Education Department for the Year 1934* (Lagos, 1935).

[27] Paul T. Kennedy, *Ghanaian Businessmen: From Artisan to Capitalist Entrepreneur in a Dependent Economy* (Munich: Weltforum, 1980), 145.

[28] Dmitri van den Bersselaar and Stephanie Decker, '"No Longer at Ease": Corruption as an Institution in West Africa', *International Journal of Public Administration*, 34.11 (2011), 741–52.

of Africans'.[29] Such unease with Western-educated colonial subjects was equally present in French colonialism – despite its reputation for policies of 'assimilation' – as it was in the British colonialism of 'indirect rule'.[30]

In West and Central Africa bureaucratic hierarchies were split, with Africans at the lower and medium levels, and Europeans at higher levels. Where exactly the career ceiling for African white-collar workers sat was in each case the result of the balancing of, on the one hand, the colonial suspicion of educated Africans and the implicit assumption that Europeans were more competent and trustworthy, against, on the other hand, the higher wages demanded by European white-collar workers, who would have to be recruited in Europe for service in the colonies. In countries where there were resident populations of European descent, such as in southern Africa, African white-collar workers faced competition from locally recruited white workers, who had the advantage of whiteness when bargaining in racialized administrations.[31] Government bureaucracies there had a lower career ceiling for Africans as a result. In some territories in East Africa and parts of South Africa, the existence of an Indian population largely descended from indentured labourers resulted in a three-way split. Colonial administrations tended to award mid-level bureaucratic positions to Indians and were prepared to pay them more than Africans, leading to frustrated career progression and resentment among African white-collar workers in the service of the colonial administration.[32]

WHITE-COLLAR WORKERS AND 'AFRICANIZATION'

Opportunities for career progression increased during the 1940s, when colonial administrations as well as expatriate business firms started to Africanize their managements, aiming to promote or appoint Africans to positions of responsibility. This significant change, which altered the

---

[29] Paul Nugent, *Africa since Independence: A Comparative History* (Basingstoke: Palgrave Macmillan, 2004), 13.

[30] *Ibid.*, 10–19; Prosser Gifford and Timothy C. Weiskel, 'African Education in a Colonial Context: French and British Styles', in *France and Britain in Africa: Imperial Rivalry and Colonial Rule*, ed. Prosser Gifford and Wm. Roger Louis (New Haven, CT: Yale University Press, 1971), 675–7; Jeremy Rich, 'Troubles at the Office: Clerks, State Authority, and Social Conflict in Gabon, 1920-45', *Canadian Journal of African Studies*, 38.1 (2004), 58–87.

[31] William Beinart, *Twentieth-Century South Africa* (Oxford: Oxford University Press, 2011), 180–1.

[32] Eckert, *Herrschen und Verwalten*, 169–70.

individual career expectations of African white-collar workers as well as expectations for the future of African colonies more generally, is usually linked to the rise of African nationalism. Nationalist politicians identified the limit to the career progression of African white-collar workers as symptomatic of colonial domination and agitated against it. The formulation of Africanization policies by businesses and colonial administrations was a response to this. Published statistics show an increase in the number of African managers, while both internal communications and public relations emphasize the opportunities for career advancement.

However, a number of additional factors contributed to the rise of Africans in management positions. In many government departments and expatriate businesses, the number of Africans in positions of responsibility had already started to increase before the rise of nationalist politics. One factor was that during and immediately after the Second World War, there were fewer qualified Europeans available to fill middle-management positions in African colonies. Another factor was the new, developmentalist style of colonialism that emerged out of the Second World War, which, more than pre-war colonial rule, aimed to develop colonial economies and prepare the colonies for self-government and, eventually, independence. This meant the incorporation of educated Africans in regional and local authorities, to the chagrin of the chiefs who had hitherto been privileged by colonial authorities. It also meant the opening up to Africans of posts that had been the preserve of Europeans.

Related to this was the expansion of government and parastatal bureaucracies as a result of funds from the colonial development and welfare programmes of this era, resulting in a rapid expansion of the public sector across Africa during the final decades of colonial rule.[33] These funds also stimulated the expansion of the private sector and attendant opportunities for white-collar employment. A further factor was the rapid expansion of businesses in a number of sectors that relied on relatively large numbers of managers, such as banking and (due to the rise of local mass consumer goods production) marketing and sales. At a time when European managers were relatively scarce, such expansion could only take place if companies were prepared to appoint more Africans as branch managers, account managers and sales managers.[34]

---

[33] Jean-François Bayart, *The State in Africa: The Politics of the Belly* (London: Longman, 1993), 93.

[34] Frederick Cooper, *Africa since 1940: The Past of the Present* (Cambridge: Cambridge University Press, 2002), 38–53; Stephanie Decker, 'Decolonising Barclays Bank DCO? Corporate Africanisation in Nigeria, 1945–69', *Journal of Imperial and Commonwealth History*, 33.3 (2005), 419–40.

The question was, of course, how to find sufficient experienced and qualified Africans to fill all these management posts. During the first half of the twentieth century little staff development had been provided. Even in the expatriate firms where Africans could be promoted to management positions, successful individuals would have gone through a long, slow process of working themselves up through the ranks. Rather than being trained, capable Africans had been 'tried out' in positions of responsibility, and appointed to them permanently if successful. Their availability having been taken for granted throughout the colonial period, only in the run-up to independence did the recruitment and training of African white-collar workers become the focus of discussion among managers in both public and private sectors.

The 1950s and the first half of the 1960s formed a period of opportunities for white-collar workers. Those who had previously gained experience had the prospect of a rapid promotion to a 'European' post with associated perks, while secondary school leavers had a choice of employers and could expect quickly to start earning well. The strong demand for qualified Africans opened white-collar work up for women, whose opportunities had hitherto been limited to a small number of positions as nurses or as sales assistants, which were assumed to be taken up by daughters of 'good families'.[35]

This second period of opportunities for African white-collar workers did not last long. Things had already started to look less optimistic by the mid-1960s, as the channels for promotion flowed more slowly once the majority of 'European' posts had been taken by (relatively young) African appointees. This development was exacerbated by the economic slow-down in many African countries, which meant that expatriate and local businesses had to scale back their initial plans for growth. As a result, many secondary school graduates were again having difficulties finding employment.[36] Those who did find clerical employment straight from secondary school realized that the opportunities for promotion had declined due to a development that occurred independently from the deteriorating business outlook: government departments and companies began to employ university graduates, either from new African universities or from overseas, with the intention of appointing them to management positions following a one- or two-year probation period. Young graduates thus employed were, in their turn,

---

[35] Jonathan Roberts, 'Remembering Korle Bu Hospital: Biomedical Heritage and Colonial Nostalgia in the *Golden Jubilee Souvenir*', *History in Africa*, 38 (2014), 205–6; Bianca Murillo, '"The Modern Shopping Experience": Kingsway Department Store and Consumer Politics in Ghana', *Africa*, 82.3 (2012), 380–2.

[36] Keith Hart, 'The Politics of Unemployment in Ghana', *African Affairs*, 75.301 (1976), 494.

frustrated with the less-qualified people who were taking up more senior positions, and who considered the young graduates a threat to their own jobs. The period of decolonization thus shows a similar pattern of inflation of education requirements, along with declining real wages, as the colonial period did.

STATUS, HABITUS AND INFLUENCE

During the first half of the twentieth century, the stereotype of the African white-collar worker resembled the fictional Mr Johnson from Joyce Cary's novel: an ambitious male dressed in European fashion, claiming social status from his position, and able to influence the lives of others. Many white-collar workers, however, did not fit this description. While there were examples of individuals from well-respected families who opted, at least initially, for a clerical position, this type of employment was not always regarded as conferring status on the individual. Indeed, many of the examples given above involved Africans who came from coastal societies that had had previous, often intensive, contact with European societies. Such contacts included European traders marrying into prominent local African families; resettlement on the coast and the education of formerly enslaved Africans who had been 'recaptured' by anti-slave trade vessels; and the return migration of people of African descent from the Americas as well as, to a lesser degree, from Europe.[37] During the nineteenth century, European-style education was regarded among these groups as essential, and employment in a white-collar job or profession as desirable.

Away from the coast, however, this was not the case until much later. In many instances, the opportunities that investing in cash-crop agriculture for export offered were more appealing than white-collar work, at least initially. Furthermore, there was very limited availability of European-style education beyond the basic level generally provided by Christian missions, and even where education was available, take-up could be low as the benefits were often unclear. These educational constraints meant that relatively few people

---

[37] Margaret Priestley, *West African Trade and Coast Society: A Family Study* (London: Oxford University Press, 1969); Kristin Mann, *Marrying Well: Marriage, Status and Social Change Among the Educated Elite in Colonial Lagos* (Cambridge: Cambridge University Press, 1985); A. Adu Boahen, *Mfantsipim and the Making of Modern Ghana* (Accra: Sankofa Educational Publishers, 1996); Toyin Falola, *Nationalism and African Intellectuals* (Rochester, NY: University of Rochester Press, 2001), 60–84; Alcione M. Amos, 'Afro-Brazilians in Togo: The Case of the Olympio Family, 1882–1945', *Cahiers d'études africaines*, 41.162 (2001), 293–314.

in the interior were in a position to aim for white-collar employment. Those who were frequently hailed from marginalized social backgrounds (slaves or dependants, for instance), for whom the alternative to traditional society that Christian missionaries proposed was more appealing than it was for more successful and socially respected members of traditional society.[38] This was especially the case in the first decades of the colonial period. Thus, the association, in parts of colonial Africa, of white-collar work with people from lower social backgrounds hurt its popularity as a possible career for freeborn males from established families. It also led to tensions when a white-collar worker of low status, dressed in European style, was seen to be inflexible, arrogant or unreasonable in how he carried out his duties.

Most white-collar workers in the colonial economy wore European-style clothing. This way of dressing had been inculcated in the schools that all clerks would have attended. It was also an expectation in expatriate firms, including the wearing of shirts and company ties, along with 'cleanliness and strict personal hygiene'.[39] Colonial administrations were probably less strict, but most clerks nevertheless wore European-style clothing. In 1916 the Nigerian colonial administration even sent out a circular letter to correct the 'prevalent, but entirely erroneous, opinion that African dress is forbidden during office hours'.[40] The colonial administration advocated the use of African dress, ostensibly because it considered it to be 'more comfortable, healthy and economical', but probably to emphasize the distinction between the administration's European and African white-collar workers. Most clerical workers nevertheless continued to wear a shirt and tie to work and were supported in this choice by their immediate European superiors. This reflected the white-collar workers' strategy of claiming social status through consumption: the acquisition of European-style, fashionable, probably imported items of clothing, furniture and books was intended to communicate authority and prestige.[41]

Most white-collar workers, while displaying European-style indicators of wealth and success, were also aiming to achieve the indicators that were

---

[38] Caroline Ifeka-Moller, 'White Power. Social-Structural Factors in Conversion to Christianity. Eastern Nigeria, 1921–1966', *Canadian Journal of African Studies*, 8.1 (1974), 55–72; Wolfgang Gabbert, 'Social and Cultural Conditions of Religious Conversion in Colonial Southwest Tanzania, 1891–1939', *Ethnology*, 40.4 (2001), 291–308.

[39] UARM UAC/2/20/3/6/1, *Gold Coast U.A.C. News*, 5, 9 (1954), 4.

[40] National Archive of Nigeria, Enugu Branch (NAE) CSE3/8/10, circular letter from Bertram Hodges, Lagos, 18 September 1916.

[41] Plageman, *Highlife Saturday Night*, 71; Jeremy Rich, 'Civilized Attire: Refashioning Tastes and Social Status in the Gabon Estuary, c. 1870-1914', *Cultural and Social History*, 2 (2005), 189–213.

common in their societies of origin. They aimed to build one or more houses, to acquire plots of farmland, to marry, to educate their children at the very least to secondary school level, to support family members, and, more generally, to create a legacy.[42] Some white-collar workers were very successful in this regard. One retired Ghanaian manager with an expatriate firm left behind after his death in 1948 three women, at least seven sons and three daughters, nine houses, twenty plots of land, six business ventures, clothing, cuff links, masonic signs and a gold watch presented as a long-service award by his employer. His last will and testament contained detailed instructions on how to pay for the education (in Europe) for several of his sons, as well as for the education of other members of the family.[43]

While many would attempt to convert a position as white-collar worker into higher social status, the outcome would vary from individual to individual, depending among other things on the family background of the person. Those from disadvantaged social backgrounds might have been more successful in towns away from their communities of origin, as there would be fewer people around with knowledge of their backgrounds to challenge their claims. One means for white-collar workers away from home to convert their employment position into social status was through setting up hometown associations, the diverse activities of which could include the funding of educational opportunities and the introduction of modern amenities in the communities of origin, in return for social status or political influence for its leaders.[44] It was quite common for successful white-collar workers to gain recognition in their communities of origin. There are numerous examples of African managers employed by expatriate businesses who were awarded traditional titles.

Before the Second World War colonial administrators did not favour educated migrants claiming political influence in their communities of origin, as this was considered a threat to the position of traditional chiefs and hence to the stability of colonial administration. They refused to work together with

---

[42] Stephan Miescher, 'The Life Histories of Boakye Yiadom (Akasease Kofi of Abetifi, Kwawu): Exploring the Subjectivity and "Voices" of a Teacher-Catechist in Colonial Ghana', in *African Words, African Voices: Critical Practices in Oral History*, ed. Luise White, Stephan Miescher and David William Cohen (Bloomington, IN: Indiana University Press, 2001), 185.

[43] UARM UAC/2/20/3/2/2, UAC of Ghana Ltd, General Manager's Private Files: The Estate of [name withheld], last will and testament.

[44] Rex Honey and Stanley Okafor, eds, *Hometown Associations: Indigenous Knowledge and Development in Nigeria* (London: Intermediate Technology Publications, 1998); Dmitri van den Bersselaar, 'Imagining Home: Migration and the Igbo Village in Colonial Nigeria', *Journal of African History*, 46.1 (2005), 60–1.

the organizations set up by educated migrants until the 1940s, when a change of colonial policy meant that such organizations were henceforward regarded as potential partners for delivering development. Yet already from the beginning of the twentieth century, and in contrast to the expectations of the colonial administrators, leading families in a number of local communities had been selecting white-collar workers as chiefs.[45]

White-collar workers became much more prominent in local – and soon national – politics after the Second World War. Not only were colonial administrations more willing to work with white-collar workers who sought influence in the affairs of their rural communities of origin; in urban areas, town councils began to be elected through universal adult suffrage. Such elections offered opportunities to claim local influence and status, following decades of colonial policies that had attempted to prevent African white-collar workers from becoming part of local administrations (other than as agents on behalf of the colonizers). The newly elected town councils did indeed have many white-collar workers among their members. These developments did not, however, signal the end of the colonial administrators' distrust of white-collar workers. Soon after the inauguration of the elected town councils, colonial administrators began to voice accusations of inefficiency, nepotism and corruption.[46]

The changes in local governance took place against a background of increasing anti-colonial nationalist mobilization. Many leading nationalist politicians, such as the Congolese former postal clerk Patrice Lumumba or the Gabonese former customs agent Léon Mba, were former or current white-collar workers. White-collar workers were also prominent among the supporters of demands for independence. This is not surprising, as white-collar workers often had first-hand experience of racist colonial ideology and were frustrated about the limits placed on their ambitions, particularly (but not uniquely) within the colonial civil service.

Not only did white-collar workers experience discrimination in the colonial system: being literate they also had access to anti-colonial literature and critical political thought. Furthermore, having an intimate understanding of the functioning of bureaucracy, speaking the colonizers' language, and being able to take part in political debate on European terms, it stands to reason that ambitious white-collar workers would regard themselves as the obvious successors to the colonial rulers upon the achievement of

---

[45] Public Records and Archives Administration Department of Ghana (PRAAD)/A ADM/11/1091, Minutes Colonial Secretary, C.E.P., 17 August 1916.

[46] Robert L. Tignor, 'Political Corruption in Nigeria before Independence', *Journal of Modern African Studies*, 31.2 (1993), 185.

independence, even though the illiterate majority of the population did not necessarily agree.[47]

Oppression, Corruption and Perks

It was not just the colonial administrators who had their suspicions about white-collar workers as a category (colonial officers invariably made an exception for individual African clerks whom they trusted and relied on, and with whom they worked closely). Many ordinary Africans had had experiences with clerks that made them deeply distrust white-collar workers. This stemmed in part from the place of clerks in colonial (as well as commercial) hierarchies. As a result of the distribution of educational opportunities, most white-collar workers ended up being stationed outside their communities of origin. Thus, most Africans experienced clerks as outsiders who were associated with the oppressive (colonial) state, and with whom they had to deal to get a licence or permit; or they encountered them as court clerks, or perhaps (in a commercial setting) as sales clerks who refused to give them imported goods on credit. Even if clerks followed procedures to the letter and applied every administrative rule fairly, many ordinary Africans who did not understand the detailed workings of a bureaucracy would have felt frustrated, unfairly treated and perhaps discriminated against by the outsider-clerks.

However, as Adiele Afigbo has shown, white-collar workers were among those groups in colonial society who frequently abused their positions.[48] There are indeed many documented cases of corrupt African clerks who did not apply the rules fairly, who exploited their knowledge of the colonizers' language and bureaucratic systems to manipulate those who did not, who took bribes from the population or who fiddled the accounts. Commercial firms took such cheating very seriously and employed teams of auditors to travel round the various branches to audit departments in turn. Employees who were caught fiddling the accounts were dismissed, as is documented in surviving personnel records, but of course not all fraudulent behaviour was discovered. Also, it was not just those actions that were strictly fraudulent that caused concern among the population. For instance, cases whereby clerks or sales managers gave preferential treatment to some buyers by allowing them to purchase scarce goods that were not made available to

---

[47] Obafemi Awolowo, *Path to Nigerian Freedom* (London: Faber and Faber, 1947), 31–2.

[48] Adiele E. Afigbo, *The Warrant Chiefs: Indirect Rule in Southeastern Nigeria, 1891–1929* (London: Longman, 1972).

other customers were of less concern to the companies as long as the goods were sold at the agreed price. But even the mere suspicion of such behaviour could create great unrest among potential customers.

European senior managers understood that the expectations and demands of the capitalist firm competed with the expectations that their African employees experienced in other aspects of their lives. The management view was that there were situations when African employees had to be 'safe-guarded ... against themselves' – for instance, when an employee was 'being worried by his family in any way that interferes with his job'.[49] In 1944 the general manager of G. B. Ollivant Ltd in Accra informed his staff that '[a]ll Senior Africans must break away from the rotten system of dashes [gifts] from friends because they always want something in return eventually', warning them that he would dismiss 'any Senior African no matter how senior or how long he has been with us' if the person was found to have accepted a gift from anyone.[50]

Colonial administrations, for all their suspicion of educated Africans, appeared less concerned about the possibly corrupt behaviour of their employees. Of course, clerks who were found to have demanded or accepted bribes, or who had stolen supplies, were fined or dismissed, depending on the severity of the offence. However, there were no systematic efforts to uncover fraud, and until after the Second World War there was no sense in the colonial correspondence that corruption in the administration was considered a real or potential problem. Rather, a certain amount of corruption at the local level was accepted as an unavoidable aspect of indirect rule.[51] The result of this was a culture of corruption among colonial white-collar workers, or at the very least a widespread popular expectation that a white-collar worker was probably corrupt or corruptible, which persisted after the transition to independence.

Aside from the benefits that white-collar workers were thought to allocate to themselves through corrupt practices, there were also legitimate perks of white-collar work. In addition to relative job security and stable pay, these could include a transport allowance or the use or purchase of a car, scholarships to help with the education of children, medical treatment and a pension upon retirement. In Ghana, for instance, from 1936 onwards, employees with the colonial administration received a pension upon

---

[49]   UARM UAC/2/10/3/4/2, R. Barrow, confidential circular letter No. 156, Accra, 23 June 1944.

[50]   *Ibid.*

[51]   Van den Bersselaar and Decker, '"No Longer at Ease"', 741–52.

retirement as a reward for loyal service.[52] From as early as 1929, white-collar employees with a commercial firm such as the United Africa Company (UAC) received a lump sum at the time of their retirement, something not available to UAC's blue-collar workers until much later, though the sum could be insufficient to cover the retiree's needs, especially in the case of lower-ranked employees.[53] In some instances, individuals spent their lump sum quickly, leaving them with insufficient resources to live comfortably. In such cases, the company could decide to allocate a monthly or annual allowance, calculated at between one-third and one-quarter of the final salary earned.[54] The company eventually changed its retirement provision into a pension fund that paid out annual benefits, because 'experience ... had shown that some retired employees had been unfortunate in losing the lump sums which were granted to them on retirement, thus leaving them financially insecure, probably for the remainder of their lifetime'.[55] The company did not expand on the circumstances in which retirees had lost their money, but the issue appears connected to a broader concern among managers of European-owned businesses and colonial economic planners about the claims that African extended families could make on the benefits intended to support workers' nuclear families.[56]

CAREERS AND TRAINING

During most of the colonial period, even though white-collar work took place in the context of hierarchical bureaucracies, there was no training on offer to improve skills and prepare staff for new responsibilities, and no established path for career progression.[57] This is perhaps not surprising in the case of the colonial administrations where higher positions were the preserve of Europeans. However, expatriate firms, where Africans could be

---

[52] Michael W. Kpessa, 'The Politics of Retirement Income Security Policy in Ghana: Historical Trajectories and Transformative Capabilities', *African Journal of Political Science and International Relations*, 5.2 (2011), 93.

[53] UARM UAC/1/1/1/12 UAC, Board Loose Minutes and Memoranda: Employee Welfare 1930–32.

[54] UARM UAC/1/1/1/2/1-7 UAC, Board Minutes – this series contains many examples of such allowances being agreed by the London Board of Directors upon recommendation from general managers in Africa.

[55] UARM UAC/2/20/3/6/1, *Gold Coast UAC News*, 3, 8 (1952), 4.

[56] Frederick Cooper, *Decolonization and African Society: The Labor Question in French and British Africa* (Cambridge: Cambridge University Press, 1996), 281.

[57] See the chapter by Pilossof in this volume.

promoted to higher posts, similarly neglected to prepare their employees for new responsibilities and promotions. By the 1930s the UAC at least had a system of performance review, using report forms to be completed for each member of staff. The report forms addressed 'conduct', 'business ability' and 'initiative' but did not include rubrics for potential or training, although comments about future potential were sometimes added under the rubric 'General Manager's remarks'. In one 1934 example, the general manager noted that the member of staff concerned was 'a very capable book-keeper and office man generally', who 'should make a good office manager'.[58] Preparation for a new post was done by trying it out: if it looked as if the staff member was doing well in the new position, he would stay, and if he appeared to be floundering, he would be put back in his previous role.

This haphazard process points to a crucial skill that white-collar workers had to have to be successful: the ability to understand the hierarchy, to identify who mattered and to build relationships with those who could further one's career or provide protection in times of trouble. An example of this was the case of a Ghanaian employee of the UAC who, in 1933, was downgraded from his position as manager to that of clerk, because he had been unable to prevent his staff from stealing merchandise from the company (although this was not explained to him). The employee in question, after acknowledging the downgrade, wrote and explained his predicament in a lengthy letter to a European manager of the company, based in the Manchester office. The latter interceded on behalf of the downgraded employee through the head office in London, whereupon the London office instructed the general manager in Ghana to reinstate the employee in his old position.[59] Clearly, the ability to identify useful and powerful allies in the organization, and the skill to present one's own case in a convincing manner, were crucial for career survival. Although white-collar jobs were generally seen as stable positions with job security, individuals' experiences and opportunities were to a large degree determined by how their performance and personality were assessed by their immediate superiors.

With Africanization in the 1940s, processes for recruitment, staff development and promotion became more formalized. Training courses were developed for government bureaucracy as well as business, initially by adapting training that had been developed for European workers to

---

[58] UARM UAC/2/20/3/2/3, UAC of Ghana Ltd, General Manager's Private Files; Report form 1934.

[59] UARM UAC/2/20/3/2/1, UAC of Ghana Ltd, General Manager's Private Files; Letter M. G. Lewis to Gold Coast Control, 21 January 1933, and associated correspondence.

an African context. Training managers were appointed to work alongside personnel managers to develop the workforce, and specialized staff-training facilities were erected. Some of the courses offered were aimed at developing specific management skills, while others sought to improve the general knowledge of white-collar workers. There was collaboration between businesses and government, with businesses offering places to civil servants on its management courses, and vice-versa. One of the most ambitious initiatives was the Institute of Public Administration, Greenhill, in Ghana (currently known as GIMPA), which was originally set up in 1961 to train public servants, though private businesses soon made use of its facilities for staff training. Business and government also supported, and made use of, the newly established universities. University staff contributed to staff training and offered extra-mural courses at business premises.[60]

Much was made in public announcements and internal communications to staff about the contribution that staff training was making to the development of decolonizing or newly independent African nations. Staff development would benefit not only the individuals concerned and their employers, but the young developing nation as a whole. In newspaper advertisements, the UAC explained that its staff-training programme not only ensured that its customers would receive the highest possible standards of service, but that it also provided 'numerous opportunities' in 'careers for both present and future generations of West Africans'.[61] Real motivations for the development of staff training were more complex, of course. For example, when Barclays bank established its own training centre in Lagos in 1956, this was not so much intended as a contribution to Nigerian development, but more as a response to complaints that the best graduates entered government service due to the better salaries offered and opportunities for further education and training in West Africa as well as abroad.[62] Similarly, the establishment of the UAC's management course in Nigeria in 1958 was a response to the need for management development in the organization, rather than a philanthropic contribution to the nation.

The focus on Africanization and decolonization might imply that the earlier absence of staff-development schemes was an effect of colonial oppression, and that Africa was 'catching up'. This was not the case, however. Even in a leading economy such as Britain, training and development for

[60] Jonathan Frimpong-Ansah, *The Vampire State in Africa: The Political Economy of Decline in Ghana* (London: James Currey, 1991), 78–82; UARM UAC/2/20/3/6/1, *Gold Coast UAC News* 2:11 (1951), 3.

[61] UARM UAC/111/20/1, Guardbook UAC Ltd, Goodwill 1949–1954.

[62] Decker, 'Decolonising Barclays Bank DCO?', 427.

managers only took off after the Second World War, around the same time as similar schemes began to emerge in West Africa.[63] It thus appears that the development of staff training in post-war Africa was less the consequence of decolonization and rather the result of a more general shift in personnel management that was taking place at the time.

In contrast to earlier periods, white-collar workers who started their career in the 1960s would have a clear career trajectory ahead of them, with expectations of regular promotion and support, in theory, through staff-training programmes. Annual report forms for staff had been updated to include rubrics that explored the future potential of the member of staff, and possible training needs to develop this potential. In addition to local staff-development courses, promising employees were sent overseas for training, mainly to Britain, France and the USA, but also to the Netherlands and India. Being selected for training overseas was a good sign, because it not only contributed to personal development but was also an indication that a promotion was coming.

However, the focus on graduate recruitment for white-collar staff with management potential reflected a further decline of the benefits of education. Now that education systems had expanded, and many more Africans completed secondary school, they found that the number of white-collar jobs available had not expanded at the same rate. Furthermore, positions that, in the first decade after the Second World War, had been filled by secondary school leavers now required a university degree. Governments and commercial firms did still hire some secondary school leavers as white-collar workers, but these tended to be clerical posts with less potential for future promotion. This development led to frustration and tensions in many businesses and government departments.[64]

During the colonial period, white-collar work had been the preserve of men, partly as a result of educational opportunities, and partly as a result of the gender prejudices of European managers. Under the new graduate-recruitment management-development schemes, however, women with university degrees could outperform men with secondary school certificates. In the competition between businesses and governments to recruit the best candidates, women thus entered on the graduate-recruitment schemes and had careers as managers, while still remaining a minority compared to men. At the workplace, these young women were confronted with two kinds of frustrated males: the young men who, due to their lack of university degree,

[63] John F. Wilson and Andrew Thomson, *The Making of Modern Management: British Management in Historical Perspective* (Oxford: Oxford University Press, 2006), 161–3.

[64] 'Areas of Friction', *The Pioneer*, 31 July 1967.

had limited prospects for career development; and a cohort of older men who had joined the organization more than a decade earlier, had made a slow career progression, and now found that they were joined, or even managed, by what they regarded as inexperienced females.

WHITE-COLLAR WORK AND ECONOMIC DECLINE

White-collar work offered income and job security, but the salaries paid to white-collar workers tended to lag behind increases in the cost of living at times of rapidly rising inflation. Their incomes were often allowed to decline quite significantly in real terms, because African governments, confronted with budget deficits, tended to postpone salary increases as long as politically possible. In such circumstances, the private sector could also afford to offer only very limited pay rises. At times governments decreed complete wage freezes that the private sector had to comply with, which were later followed by negotiated pay increases that applied to all civil servants, or throughout the economy.[65] This process over time further eroded some of the advantages of white-collar work compared to, for instance, being an independent entrepreneur. For some of those on the lower rungs of the career ladder, the goal was no longer to struggle up to become a white-collar manager, but rather to become an affluent businessman.[66] Many of their role models were traders, transporters, contractors and builders who had been previously employed by the government or expatriate enterprises and had set themselves up in business on the basis of their savings from salaried employment.[67]

Most African economies collapsed at some stage during the 1970s (Ghana, Tanzania), 1980s (Nigeria, Zaire) or 1990s (Cameroon). The resulting hardship was experienced throughout the economy, yet was particularly frustrating for white-collar workers who were used to, and had come to expect, a middle-class lifestyle but who instead saw their spending power decline rapidly, with many products becoming unaffordable.[68] Those who could would take on what in Cameroon was called a PJ: a private job,

---

[65] There are many examples of this in the UAC Board Meetings for the 1960s–1980s, for the company's activities in East as well as West Africa. See the UARM UAC/1/1/1/2/ series.

[66] See the chapter by Berry in this volume.

[67] Adrian Peace, *Choice, Class and Conflict: A Study of Southern Nigerian Factory Workers* (Brighton: Harvester Press, 1979), 49–50.

[68] Jane Guyer, *Marginal Gains: Monetary Transactions in Atlantic Africa* (Chicago: University of Chicago Press, 2004), 85.

which meant using one's own skills and the facilities offered by formal employment to make additional income. Many female and male government office workers tried to add to their income through informal trading. Other coping strategies involved the corruption that clerical workers were already being accused of: clerical workers who processed financial transactions might demand a percentage fee to facilitate payments, while others made a little extra money through the sale to service users of the official forms that had previously been given out free of charge.[69] Those who had already retired from their white-collar jobs with a pension experienced hardship as their pensions lost value.

The economic crisis would also impact on job security, but not always immediately. When profits plunged, private enterprise tried to hold on to those white-collar workers with the most skills and experience for as long as possible, while trying to drastically reduce staffing elsewhere in the business. However, this had to be done carefully for fear of popular or political backlash, and was further complicated by the local-level managers' reluctance to reduce staffing in their own departments. Thus, UAC Nigeria discovered that, during the crisis of the early 1980s in Nigeria, despite a board-level decision to drastically reduce headcount to match plummeting income, staffing instead continued to increase. It was even more difficult for African governments to significantly reduce their staffing, as this would result in social and political unrest. Bureaucracies thus remained very large in relation to the countries' income, though at the same time inadequate – and insufficiently resourced – to efficiently perform the tasks expected of them.

Most African economies have since recovered from the depths of crisis, as have the salaries and prospects of white-collar workers. The status of white-collar work, however, has declined compared with the respect accorded to self-made entrepreneurs (whose actions at times may be of dubious legality), who build houses, acquire plots of land, marry, educate their children and support family members, much as white-collar workers were able to do during the colonial and early postcolonial periods.[70]

---

[69] Margaret Niger-Thomas, 'Excerpts from "Buying Futures": The Upsurge of Female Entrepreneurship: Crossing the Formal/Informal Divide in Southwest Cameroon', in *Readings in Modernity in Africa*, ed. Peter Geschiere, Birgit Meyer and Peter Pels (Bloomington, IN: Indiana University Press, 2008), 46–7.

[70] Basile Ndjio, 'Evolués and Feymen: Old and New Figures of Modernity in Cameroon', in *Readings in Modernity in Africa*, ed. Peter Geschiere, Birgit Meyer and Peter Pels (Bloomington, IN: Indiana University Press, 2008), 205–14.

CONCLUSION

The history of white-collar workers in colonial and postcolonial Africa sees a number of continuities and some changes. The changes include the disappearance of the initial hesitation to engage with white-collar work in certain parts of Africa, given the low social status of many of the early educated males who ended up in clerical employment. Following the Second World War, those who entered clerical employment from a low social background may still have had difficulties convincing those in their communities of origin of their newly elevated social status, but white-collar work itself was no longer associated with low social status and attracted entrants from across the social spectrum. Another change was the opening up of higher management positions after the Second World War. Until then, the possibilities for career progression for white-collar workers had been limited, as in departments under the colonial administration any position of responsibility had been reserved for a European employee. Expatriate businesses had offered more opportunities for career progression, and Africans had been promoted into management positions throughout the colonial period, but nevertheless, here as well, Africans were prevented from reaching top management roles until the period of decolonization.

A further change was the attitude of governments, which during most of the colonial period had displayed a strong dislike of educated Africans and thus of white-collar workers, yet came to regard them as partners in development after the Second World War. A final change was the shift in how white-collar work was gendered. During the colonial period, white-collar work was the preserve of men, but this changed during decolonization, as businesses and government departments were competing for the best-qualified candidates for their management-development schemes. While during the 1960s and 1970s the majority of white-collar workers were still men, they had been joined by an ambitious and successful minority of women.

Continuities include the use that white-collar workers made of their income and access to imported goods to claim status through their consumption of material goods, the building of houses, and agreeing to help family members. Another continuity was the expectation among the population that white-collar workers were probably corrupt, requiring a bribe to do the work they were paid to do anyway, or giving advantages to their friends or family. A further continuity was the tendency for the benefits of education to decline: the requirements for employment continued to increase from very basic education at the beginning of the twentieth century to a university degree by the 1970s. What also declined was the relative financial rewards that white-collar work offered: although pay was rarely reduced in absolute terms, in relative terms the salaries offered to those starting out in white-collar employment gradually declined throughout the century (and at certain times of extreme inflation dramatically so).

The focus on white-collar work in colonial and postcolonial Africa might give the impression that the experiences of African white-collar workers were unique to Africa, or perhaps to colonial society in general. There were indeed a number of very specific aspects that are linked to colonial rule, such as the tendency of colonial administrators to regard white-collar workers as a 'problem' and the tendency for white-collar workers to be outsiders to the communities in which they were stationed. In other aspects, however, the history of white-collar work mirrors developments elsewhere in the world. Particularly relevant in this respect is the issue of the declining benefits of education, which can be observed in many societies. Another, perhaps more unexpected, example is that of the changes in policies regarding recruitment and career development. While locally these changes tended to be associated with decolonization and Africanization, they occurred at the same time as elsewhere and appear to reflect changes in management thinking more generally, rather than a specific response to the challenge of decolonization.

FOURTEEN
Sport, Tourism and Entertainment

SAMUEL ANDREAS ADMASIE

International Institute of Social History in Africa

A general twentieth-century history of labour in entertainment in Africa requires simultaneously a level of detail and a level of abstraction that is difficult to reconcile, especially so in an area of labour so broad. The problem is aggravated by the paucity of literature on African labour history in this area, where references are often scattered and sources are fragmentary. This chapter has been structured around shifting labour relations within three broad fields of entertainment that demonstrate both commonalities and differences: tourism, performing and recording arts, and sport. The discussion will centre on various forms of labour relations and converge on a number of focuses. The selection of the particular kinds of labour relations and the specific places on which to focus the different discussions has been informed by three concerns: the availability of literature, the representation of geographical areas and the magnitude of labour within them. Of course, no such selection can ever be comprehensive, and there will necessarily be gaps. Yet what follows makes it possible to conceive of the contours of the changing conditions of labour within entertainment in twentieth-century Africa.

The taxonomic division of what frequently appears in very fluid and hybrid forms of labour relations poses a real challenge. The taxonomy that has been adopted here is meant to illustrate the shifts between unpaid and paid labour and between self-employment and wage labour.[1] As van der Linden has noted, 'the borderline between "free" wage labour, self-employment and unfree labour is in reality not clear-cut', and 'the intermediate forms between the different categories are fluid rather than

---

[1] See the chapters by Eckert, Berry and Pilossof in this volume.

sharply defined'.[2] For this reason, the categories employed below should not be considered as definitive and uniform, but rather as porous, compound and fluid. As will be made clear, the character of labour relations within these categories was every bit as fluid as that between them.

A final note pertains to the absence of a discussion of relatively 'free' and decidedly unfree labour. The reason for this is pragmatic. The references to unfree entertainment labour in the twentieth century are scarce in the literature. This certainly does not mean to suggest that decidedly unfree and forced labour did not exist within the field. One need only think of the porters employed in early tourist expeditions, for example, to be able to conceive of situations in which such relations prevailed. However, the paucity of references seems to indicate that such relations were never dominant, and given the space available, it is argued that the issue of unfree labour can justifiably be reverted to in other chapters of this volume.

FROM UNPAID TO PAID WORK AND SELF-EMPLOYMENT

Many of the activities that involve providing entertainment to onlookers and listeners were initially considered leisure, and only later came to be considered work. Where this transition took place, the prevalence, type and level of remuneration also underwent changes. Football, for example, was introduced to southern Africa by English colonizers and soldiers in the nineteenth century. By the turn of century the organizational infrastructure in terms of amateur clubs, leagues and association was already quite well developed. The spread of football in South Africa coincided with industrial development and the concomitant urbanization. The industrial workforces were exposed to the promotion of football by employers in the new towns and mining areas. Not all early efforts were successful. Mineworkers at Roan Antelope mine, for example, demanded payment to participate in football games. What the management considered leisure or welfare activities was seen as work by the mineworkers, for which they ought to be paid.[3] In general, however, the introduction of football resonated with the workers, and the game became very popular. It was played informally by youths and children as much as in

---

[2]   M. van der Linden, *Workers of the World: Essays Toward a Global Labor History* (Leiden: Brill, 2008), 17, 22.

[3]   R. Archer and A. Bouillon, *The South African Game: Sport and Racism* (London: Zed Books, 1982).

formal leagues, and it soon became 'the most social game in South Africa, played by the greatest numbers of people over the country and at all levels, for exercise and pleasure'.[4]

Race running had been promoted by colonial institutions and missionary schools in East Africa since the turn of the century.[5] Early running, however, lacked facilities and structures. It was only in the 1920s that associations were established and athletic events formalized. Still, athletes mostly consisted of soldiers, police officers and students. Rewards and remuneration were meagre. In 1933 it was recorded that the winner of a race organized by a tea plantation for its workers was awarded with four gallons of oil.[6] In 1951 a central Kenyan Amateur Athletics Association was formed, and this spelled the beginning of a more concerted national promotion of athletics as well as its incremental professionalization. The most successful Kenyan athletes were identified and given increased levels of training. Participation in international sporting events became increasingly common for top Kenyan athletes, and prizes – even if consisting mostly of commodities rather than cash – came to offer an added incentive.

It is reasonable to assume that similar trends prevailed in other forms of entertainment, such as the performing arts. This, however, was probably not the case in the field of tourism, where labour was typically organized on a somewhat larger scale. Within the tourist sector, the scale and type of operations lent itself to the employment of wage labour at an early stage. This, however, was not always the case. Self-employment was also relatively widespread among those providing services and goods for tourists. The producers of artefacts sold as souvenirs came to constitute a sizeable category of people employed in this manner. In Egypt, tourist artefact manufacture and sale had a history dating back to well before the turn of the twentieth century, but in other parts of Africa tourism and the demand it created were not as developed. As early as the 1910s, woodcarvings were on sale in Nairobi, and by the 1930s souvenirs were being sold around the Victoria Falls.[7] By the middle of the century, the manufacture of culturally inspired products and artefacts had developed to the extent that schools,

[4]   *Ibid.*, 98.

[5]   J. Bale, 'Kenyan Running before the 1968 Mexico Olympics', in *East African Running: Towards a Cross-Disciplinary Perspective*, ed. Y. Pitsiladis, J. Bale, C. Sharp and T. Noakes (London: Routledge, 2007), 11–23.

[6]   *Ibid.*

[7]   A. Roberts, 'African Cross-Currents', in *The Cambridge History of Africa, Volume 7: From 1905 to 1940*, ed. A. Roberts (Cambridge: Cambridge University Press, 1986), 223–65.

cooperatives, craft workshops and networks of entrepreneurs and hawkers dedicated to the production and sale of such artefacts had developed around the continent.[8]

In other forms of entertainment, self-employment was the dominant trend. A famous form of entertainment that predated the twentieth century was provided by the West African *griot* – a poet and musician. In contrast to the communal non-professional musicians widely prevalent in the continent, and the semi-professional farmer/musicians, the *griot* already constituted a professional category at the turn of the century.[9] However, the conditions and forms under which *griots* worked and were remunerated changed during the century. In the early part of the century, the *griot* was usually either employed as a praise-singer in a noble household or worked independently by singing praise for those who could afford it. The patron of the *griot* would reward performances with goods such as metals, textiles and animals. A successful *griot* could also be rewarded with wives or slaves.[10] Such rewards, however, incrementally gave way to payment in cash. A *griot* from Niger could, by the 1960s, make as much US$160 – the equivalent of three months' wages for a skilled worker – by performing at the installation of a chief. In the 1980s a group of *griots* from Niger could take home more than US$1,000 – the equivalent of a skilled worker's yearly wage – from a short tour to Côte d'Ivoire.[11] *Griots* could also supplement their income by teaching aspiring musicians. In some cases, they even opened schools, where students paid to learn for extended periods. Cash, however, remained only one form of payment out of several. A famous *griot* could also be rewarded with attractive treats, such as houses, vehicles, diamonds or aeroplane tickets for tours abroad.

By the last quarter of the century, European or North American tours came to offer lucrative income opportunities. A *griot* touring the United States in the late 1990s was recorded as having received as much as US$80,000.[12] But it could also mean frustration. The *griot*–patron relation was historically considered a personal relation, often stretching over extended periods of time. On tour, however, the *griot* would have to rely on

---

[8]   J. Vansina, 'Arts and Society Since 1935', in *The General History of Africa, Volume 8: Africa since 1935*, ed. A. Mazrui (Paris: United Nations Educational, Scientific and Cultural Organization, 1993), 582–632.

[9]   F. Bebey, *African Music: A People's Art* (New York: Lawrence Hill, 1975).

[10]   T. A. Hale, *Griots and Griottes: Masters of Word and Music* (Bloomington, IN: Indiana University Press, 1998).

[11]   *Ibid.*

[12]   *Ibid.*

one-off transactions that resembled the commercial relation between the hired performer working for a contractual payment and his paying audience, mediated by an organizing promoter.

Musical performers in general became more susceptible to entering into commercialized relationships throughout the century. In 1912 a group of troubadours called Banda-Kat were reported as singing praises to well-dressed, usually European passers-by in the Senegalese city of Saint-Louise, attracting crowds of attendees and expecting money or gifts in return.[13] Similar groups of street musicians pandering to those who could afford it were on view in Brazzaville.[14] From the 1930s onwards, commercial leisure 'spectacles', such as music performances but also theatrical plays and film shows, became increasingly important aspects of urban leisure life throughout the continent. In Brazzaville and Kinshasa, a flurry of dance halls were opened in the 1920s and 1930s, where modern bands performed. Brass bands became popular, too. In the 1930s Brazzaville was home to no less than six such bands, and by 1948 eight *poto-poto* groups composed of 168 members were officially registered.[15] The *highlife* trend offered a comparable example in West Africa, as did the *beni* trend in East Africa. By the 1940s a number of groups were travelling throughout Ghana and Nigeria, and in Kenya, touring musical teachers were paid in cash to instruct local bands.[16]

However, music generally continued to be a non-professional activity, and a recording artist in the 1950s could be remunerated with drinks alone.[17] The *poto-poto* bands in Brazzaville that performed at private parties were rewarded in food and drinks, although a collection of contributions from the audience provided an irregular source of cash income. When performing in bars, a share of the income from the drinks sold could provide a source of such income. Recording fees were also meagre. Paul Kamba, a famous musician in Brazzaville in the 1940s, continued to work as a civil servant in order to make ends meet.[18] Yet this state of things had begun to change. Urbanization, recording and broadcasting technology all contributed to making the musical trade more viable as a profession.

---

[13] K. J. Ngalamulume, 'Leisure in Colonial Saint-Louis (Senegal), 1850–1920', in *Leisure in Urban Africa*, ed. P. T. Zeleza and C. R. Veney (Trenton, NJ: Africa World Press, 2003), 71–84.

[14] P. M. Martin, *Leisure and Society in Colonial Brazzaville* (Cambridge: Cambridge University Press, 1995).

[15] *Ibid.*

[16] Roberts, 'African Cross-Currents'.

[17] Bebey, *African Music*.

[18] Martin, *Leisure and Society in Colonial Brazzaville*.

By the 1960s a number of fully professional bands had emerged in West Africa.[19] In Ghana and Nigeria, the trend of hugely popular 'concert parties' contributed to this trend in the 1960s and 1970s.[20] However, technology in terms of video reproductions of such parties and economic crises contributed to repressing demand for live performances in the 1980s. By the end of the twentieth century, however, Ghana's music industry had not only rebounded but expanded.[21] Much as in most of the rest of the continent, a music industry had by then been created, employing a variety of musical artists ranging from those with world-wide audiences and tour itineraries, to local recording artists, and the dance bar and cover bands entertaining a more limited audience.

In Egypt, commercial entertainment work already had a long tradition by the turn of the twentieth century. One of the most popular and famous form was the performance of female singers/dancers. By the early twentieth century, privately owned cabarets and clubs were the venues in which many dancers plied their trade. Income from dancing alone was generally low, as it had become expected of the dancers that they would entertain clients by drinking with them at their table. Although this did not automatically lead to prostitution, it did encourage a certain overlap.[22] It also contributed to lowering the social status of the work of the performer, and it made the working environment more precarious for the dancers, who risked jealous reactions. Still, it was possible for the most famous dancers to become quite wealthy. It was relatively common for a famous dancer to open her own establishment.

Meanwhile, more respectable forms of female artistry in music and dancing were also thriving. Organized as a troupe around a female master – the *usta* – they would perform at festive occasions and holidays. The *usta* would receive payments from the audience and distribute them among the troupe members. Payments – or tips – to the troupes did not only take monetary form, but items such as cigarettes, coffee beans and sugar were

[19] E. M. Smith, 'Popular Music in West Africa', *African Music*, 3.1 (1962), 11–17.

[20] D. W. Ames, 'Igbo and Hausa Musicians: A Comparative Examination', *Ethnomusicology*, 17.2 (1973), 250–78.

[21] J. Collins, 'A Social History of Ghanian Popular Entertainment since Independence', *Transactions of the Historical Society of Ghana*, New Series, 9 (2005), 17–40.

[22] M. Franken, 'From the Streets to the Stage: The Evolution of Professional Female Dance in Colonial Cairo', in *Leisure in Urban Africa*, ed. P. T. Zeleza and C. R. Veney (Trenton, NJ: Africa World Press 2003), 85–104; K. van Nieuwkerk, *'A Trade like Any Other': Female Singers and Dancers in Egypt* (Austin, TX: University of Texas Press, 1995).

also offered.[23] The prevalence of dancing establishments, however, continued to constitute a thorn in the side of religious and conservative forces, and in 1973 President Anwar Sadat's government moved to establish firmer control over the business. A ban on drinking with or entertaining guests was enforced, and all workers in entertainment establishments were subject to artistic quality control and licensing from the authorities.

With the growing affluence in some parts of society that followed the Sadat government's policy of economic liberalization, demand for commercial entertainment grew in the last decades of the twentieth century. As a result, popular entertainers were increasingly sought after and paid. The mode of payment and the organization of music and dancing troupes also changed in line with increased profitability. While, at the beginning of the century, the performers usually received no wages but shared the income received as tips, by the end of the century most performers worked for a fixed rate with no claim on the tips. As to their form of organization, dancers and musicians were less inclined to belong to a fixed troupe. Instead, they tended to sell their services to the highest bidder and formed temporary troupes.[24]

In sport, self-employment was widespread, especially among elite athletes. Although African women have generally been under-represented in sport,[25] race running has produced a large number of amateur and professional female athletes. The motivations and conditions for female runners seem to have been relatively similar to those of men. A discussion of these, based on a study conducted by Jarvie and Sikes among former runners in Eldoret,[26] therefore illuminates the changing labour conditions and motivations of self-employed, semi-professional and professional East African runners in general.

At the time of the breakthrough of East African runners in the 1960s, most athletes were semi-professional. Although runners were not permitted to receive prize money before the 1980s, this did not mean that material incentives were absent. Successful runners received gifts and could win material prizes that were quite lucrative. Pots, knives, teabags, crates of drinks, sugar, shoes, bedsheets, towels and buckets are examples mentioned. This was to change with the increasing professionalization of athletics. In the 1980s national and international bans on monetary prizes were lifted,

[23] van Nieuwkerk, 'A Trade like Any Other'.

[24] Ibid.

[25] A. Mazrui, 'Africa's Triple Heritage of Play: Reflections on the Gender Gap', in *Sport in Africa: Essays in Social History*, ed. W. J. Baker and J. A. Mangan (New York: Africana, 1987), 217–28.

[26] G. Jarvie and M. Sikes, 'Running as a Resource of Hope? Voices from Eldoret', *Review of African Political Economy*, 39.34 (2012), 629–44.

triggering a sharp rise in the material value of such prizes that combined with increasingly lucrative sponsorship opportunities. By the end of the century, prize money for the winner of a single international race could reach more than US$100,000. A few very successful runners thus came to be extremely wealthy, and an increasing number of prospective runners emerged seeking to emulate the successful ones. While female runners of the 1960s had emphasized non-material motivations in their decision to take up running, money had become the prime stated motivation by the early 2000s. The increasing potential rewards and number of prospective runners also meant that training commenced at an earlier age. As in the past, most successful runners tended to come out of an environment that provided institutional support to pursue running. Frequently, this was pursued as a paid member of a team belonging to the armed forces, the police or the like.

WAGE EMPLOYMENT

As noted above, tourism provided an environment ripe for the mass employment of wage labour. Tourism – a labour-intensive industry – came to provide a profitable and attractive means of exploiting natural and labour endowments.[27] The seeds were planted in the nineteenth century. Expeditions and hunting parties of Europeans became a feature in parts of sub-Saharan Africa. By the early twentieth century, the embryonic forms and patterns of this sector remained much the same. This meant that similar types of labour were required: porters, guides, chefs for the travelling parties, and additional staff at the few lodges and hotels that sprang up. This form of early tourism was mostly confined to southern and eastern Africa. Most of the employees were relatively local to the areas of excursion, but workers were also brought in from farther away. At the Victoria Falls, for instance, a hotel was established in the first years of the twentieth century. The owner of the hotel was European, as was the chef. The barman was American and the waiters were from the Arabian peninsula. For less senior positions, however, labourers were brought in from as far away as Central Africa, but also recruited locally.

Due to the nature of work in the tourist sector, wage employment predominated from the beginning. While labour conditions for Africans were harsh and degrading – including verbal and physical abuse – the wages were

---

[27] W. P. Gamble, *Tourism and Development in Africa* (London: John Murray, 1989); I. Christie, E. Fernandes, H. Messerli and L. Twinging-Ward, *Tourism in Africa: Harnessing Tourism for Growth and Improved Livelihoods* (Washington DC: World Bank, 2013).

perceived to be good. In the case of the employees from the Victoria Falls, the push to take up wage employment in the tourist sector was the result of increasing tax demands combined with land alienation.[28]

In eastern Africa, tourism emerged a few years later than in the south. By the late 1910s, however, safari tourists had begun to trickle mainly into Kenya and its game reserves and parks. Much as in the south, local employment opportunities were confined to the perceived lowliest tasks, such as those of guards, gardeners, porters, cleaners, waiters and entertainers. Moreover, the parties frequently included women who served as paid mistresses of the male leisure travellers.[29] Ownership of tourist facilities, however, was in the hands of the colonial state and resident Europeans. An example of the labour required for a major hunting party at the time is provided by the hunting safari that Theodore Roosevelt undertook in 1909. Accompanying the former US president were 46 Americans, 15 police officers and no less than 246 Kenyan carriers.[30] Although not all parties were of this size, their numbers ensured a steady demand for labourers: between 1910 and 1911, 715 hunting parties were organized.[31]

The type of tourism that developed in eastern Africa was dominated by the safari. This shaped the type of work that was conducted in the sector, as park rangers, porters, drivers and camp attendants catered to the needs of the safari tourists. The growth of tourism was most spectacular in Kenya. It has been estimated that tourism provided employment for over 100,000 and an income on whom 340,000 people were dependent in 1994, as well as further indirect employment.[32] More spectacular estimates are available for 2005, when it was said that tourism was the source of direct employment for 400,000 Kenyans, and the source of indirect employment for 550,000.[33]

In Tanzania, development proceeded at a relatively slower pace than in Kenya. By the 1970s the accommodation sector provided direct employment to several thousand people,[34] and by the early 2000s some 11,000 porters, guides and cooks were employed at Mount Kilimanjaro alone. The

---

[28] J. McGregor, 'The Victoria Falls 1900–1940: Landscape, Tourism and the Geographical Imagination', *Journal of Southern African Studies*, 29.3 (2003), 717–37.

[29] W. Kibicho, *Sex Tourism in Africa: Kenya's Booming Industry* (Farnham: Ashgate, 2009).

[30] *Ibid.*

[31] *Ibid.*

[32] T. G. Ondicho, 'International Tourism in Kenya: Development, Problems and Challenges', *Eastern Africa Social Science Research Review*, 16.2 (2000), 49–69.

[33] Christie et al., *Tourism in Africa*.

[34] W. Elkan, 'The Relation between Tourism and Employment in Kenya and Tanzania', *Journal of Development Studies*, 11.2 (1975), 123–30.

conditions of the labourers at Kilimanjaro provide an illuminating example of labour conditions in African tourism. Although these jobs were generally seasonal, it was calculated that each employee would make between fourteen and seventeen trips per year to the mountain, each lasting for an average of one week. This would generate a yearly income of US$770 for cooks, US$840 for porters and US$1,830 for guides, compared with an estimated average daily salary of US$2 for Tanzanian farm labourers. More than one-third of this income was constituted by tips, while a bit less than two-thirds originated in wages paid by the tour operators. The labour conditions, however, were harsh. Diseases such as altitude sickness, hypothermia and pneumonia were common.[35]

Most jobs in African tourism have been of a menial nature, and remuneration has often been low. Management jobs and skilled labour needs have generally been few. This is because, as Poirer points out, 'tourism creates relatively few managerial and professional posts, and these are often filled from other sectors', even in cases where they are not filled by 'specially recruited expatriates'.[36] Yet within the tourism sector, a layer of better-paid managerial staff has emerged. From the early beginnings, tourist facilities in Kenya were generally owned and managed by Europeans. Ownership patterns, however, changed slightly after independence, when the government came to promote a greater share of Kenyan state and private ownership. Another turn occurred in the 1970s, when large-scale foreign investment was sought. By 1994 it was estimated that about half of Kenyan hotel enterprises were foreign owned.[37] Throughout, however, attempts to expand the Kenyan share of the management staff were promoted, and this led to the creation of a category of locally trained professionals working in the sector. Most importantly, this was the result of the institution and multiplication of schools and training facilities for management and general staff for the sector. The Kenyan Utalii College, for example, trained over 11,000 Kenyans between 1973 and the 1990s.[38]

Still, the preponderance of foreign management staff – connected to the continued high levels of foreign ownership – continues to frustrate the ambitions of Kenyans employed in the sector. Meanwhile, labour conditions in the sector have been characterized by the menial nature of tasks and

---

[35] Christie et al., *Tourism in Africa*.

[36] R. A. Poirer, 'Tourism and Development in Tunisia', *Annals of Tourism Research*, 22.1 (1995), 165.

[37] I. Sindiga, 'Employment and Training in Tourism in Kenya', *Journal of Tourism Studies*, 5.2 (1994), 45–52.

[38] *Ibid.*

low skill requirements, low wages, the subordinate position of Kenyans to foreigners, and the temporary nature of much employment determined by the seasonality of tourist flows.[39] By the late 1980s and the early 1990s, furthermore, a number of factors contributed to a downturn in the profitability of the sector, leading to the laying off of 'thousands of workers in the [Kenyan] tourism and other related sectors'.[40]

At the beginning of the twenty-first century, tourism had come to provide direct employment to 5.3 million people in sub-Saharan Africa alone, according to a World Bank study. When indirect employment was taken into consideration, this figure grew to 12.8 million.[41] As for the gender composition of the workforce, recent figures indicate that women currently constitute somewhere between one-third and one-half of the employees in the hospitality sector in sub-Saharan Africa.[42] This may, of course, not have been the case over the entirety of the last century or over the whole continent. In a study of hotel and tour agency employees in Kenya and Tanzania conducted in the mid-1970s, women comprised less than 7 per cent.[43] Yet it is likely that women have generally constituted a relatively large share of the workforce in the tourist and hospitality sector. Poirer and Enloe explain the relatively high proportion of female employees through two interrelated causal factors: 1) as many of the tasks required in the hospitality sector are similar to household work, they have been construed as 'women's work'; and 2) low wages.[44]

Within the African film industry, meanwhile, wage labour came to coexist with a number of hybrid forms. Production of films began early in the century. Such early films were produced by almost exclusively European

---

[39] Sindiga, 'Employment and Training'; Ondicho, 'International Tourism in Kenya'. Seasonality also has a bearing on the mobility of labour. High seasonality and fluctuations in employment opportunities tend to favour a more local workforce, as locals are more likely to be able to supplement income with other activities during low season.

[40] J. Akama and D. Kemboi, 'The Development of Cultural Tourism in Kenya: A Case Study of the Bomas of Kenya', in *Cultural Tourism in Africa: Strategies for the New Millennium: Proceedings of the ATLAS Africa International Conference, December 2000, Mombasa, Kenya*, ed. J. Akama and P. Sterry (Arnhem: Association for Tourism and Leisure Education, 2002), 137.

[41] Christie et al., *Tourism in Africa*.

[42] *Ibid.*

[43] Elkan, 'The Relation between Tourism and Employment'.

[44] Poirer, 'Tourism and Development in Tunisia', 165; C. Enloe, *Bananas, Beaches and Bases: Making Feminist Sense of International Politics* (Berkeley, CA: University of California Press, 1990).

crews and starred a European cast.[45] With independence, however, African film-making took off. The most vibrant African film industry emerged in Egypt. In 1945 the pioneering Misr Studio was producing forty films a year. With the Nasserite revolution, the film industry was nationalized, and the state continued to churn out films. By the end of the twentieth century, some three thousand Egyptian films had been produced. In Algeria too, the film industry was nationalized at independence. Producers and actors became state employees, picking up a monthly salary regardless of whether or not films were produced. As finance was restricted and censorship imposed, only a trickle of productions came to be released. In francophone West Africa, finance was also a major constraint. Directors and producers had to take on multiple tasks where raising scarce funds from the private and public sectors was a major concern. As a result, film-makers could often only produce a couple of films throughout their careers, with periods of fundraising required in between.[46]

A solution to the problem of the high costs of film production presented itself with the spread of the video cassette player in the 1980s. By this time, structural adjustment programmes and retrenchments had aggravated the situation by contributing to unemployment among film professionals. The opportunity presented by video films was exploited most successfully in Nigeria, and the films that resulted were relatively cheap productions. The films were long, and they were often shot simultaneously with several sequels to enable economies of scale. The prospective film-maker was – much like those discussed above – the organizer of a major endeavour, as he often took on the role of the scriptwriter, caster, director, producer, marketer, wholesaler and/or retailer. As the industry matured, funds were made available through the emergence of a plethora of private investors. A successful film-maker could, by the end of the century, sell a finalized film – or even a promising script – directly to an investor, to market or produce.[47]

The success of the industry also translated into higher incomes for actors and crew members. Most films were originally cast through a system of reciprocal favours, where actors would simply turn up where it was rumoured that a production was taking place. Since the film-maker was expected to find roles for prospective actors, this meant that the plot could not be entirely fixed before production. But most actors were not expecting pay for their

---

[45] R. Armes, *African Filmmaking: North and South of the Sahara* (Edinburgh: Edinburgh University Press, 2006).

[46] *Ibid.*

[47] A. Adesanya, 'From Film to Video', in *Nigerian Video Films*, ed. J. Haynes (Athens, OH: Ohio University Press, 2000), 37–50.

performance. Career promotion and the expectation of reciprocal favours – most importantly the expectation that producing cast and crew would participate in any film production eventually organized by the actor – were often sufficient.[48] Although work continued to be assigned in such a manner, it became increasingly possible for famous directors and actors to request large sums to perform in the 1990s.

Musicians, as has been noted above, have also been employed in hybrid arrangements closely resembling wage labour and as formal wage labourers. Musicians employed in this way have provided a rare example within entertainment of the most typical economic form of workers' collective action – that of withholding labour. This was the case with the Cape Town musicians' strike in 1918, when several hundred unionized musicians employed by the monopolistic African Theatres Trust went on strike in response to a failure to pay wages for the time that the theatres had been forced to close as a result of the influenza epidemic. Other demands that the strikers made were for salary increases in response to wartime inflation and a ban on hiring non-unionized musicians. The strike was supported by solidarity gestures from other workers, and the public were sympathetic to the striking musicians' cause – not least because the musicians wooed the public by staging free concerts and parades on the street. The strike, however, ended after one and a half months with the striking musicians' demands only partly met.[49]

Labour relations in football have showcased the same level of hybridity, although wage labour has here exercised a more prominent position than in more individualist sports. As noted above, football began as either a leisure activity or an unpaid form of work. Football as a profession emerged as a later phenomenon. The first professional South African footballers were white players playing for British clubs in the 1930s. While formal salaries were not available for home-based players, other perks were. By the 1930s attendances and business interest in elite games were booming.[50] Clubs were often relatively large endeavours. In 1959, when the first professional league was created, 5,000 players playing for 256 clubs were registered in the

---

[48] J. Haynes and O. Okome, 'Evolving Popular Media: Nigerian Video Films', in *Nigerian Video Films*, ed. J. Haynes (Athens, OH: Ohio University Press, 2000), 51–88.

[49] A. E. Mantzaris, 'Another Victory for Trade Unionism: The 1918 Cape Town Musicians' Strike', in *Studies in the History of Cape Town*, ed. C. Saunders and H. Phillips, vol. 3 (Cape Town: University of Cape Town, 1980), 114–30.

[50] C. Martinez-Mullen, 'The Influence of Global Sports Culture on South African Football', in *Contemporary Social Issues in Africa: Cases in Gaborone, Kampala and Durban*, ed. M. S. Mapadimeng and S. Khan (Pretoria: Africa Institute of South Africa, 2010), 15–27.

Durban district alone.[51] By this time, however, apartheid policies had begun to seriously undermine non-white football and, as a result, the ability of even elite black players to pursue a career. The fact that a number of black players emigrated in the late 1950s serves to underline this point.[52] While white professional football continued to flourish for a number of years, the increasing international isolation of South Africa hampered its development. After a non-racial national association was formed in the early 1990s, however, the South African league became a televised attractor of talent from across the continent.

In West Africa too, the popularity of the sport and footballing wage labour developed in tandem. After Ghana's independence, Kwame Nkrumah's government came to take an active interest in the sport, offering support, building stadiums and funding the association. As a result, professional Ghanaian footballers could develop their skills under favourable conditions, receiving decent pay for their contributions. The high standard of football infrastructure and of remuneration helped to ensure that Ghanaian football talent remained in the country. When Nkrumah was toppled in 1966, the state came to adopt a neglectful attitude towards the football establishment, and football infrastructure went into decline. As a result of the prior investment in football, a trend that was obvious in much of the rest of the continent came late to Ghana: that of a haemorrhage of talented footballers.

Football labour migration out of Africa began in the colonial era and was intrinsically linked to the colonial relationship. For this reason, migration was almost exclusively directed to the colonial metropolis. In the 1930s, for instance, professional French football clubs recruited a handful of players from North Africa. In the 1950s French clubs established scouting and transfer networks in West Africa, enabling the regular tapping of football talent. Between 1955 and 1960 alone, several dozen players made this transition.[53] Similarly, Portuguese clubs began scouting Lusophone Africa for football talent, and football labour migration from these areas to Portugal almost came to match the West African football migration to France. When the Portuguese club Benfica won the European Cup in 1961, four African players were part of the team. Belgian clubs meanwhile tapped into the talent provided by Congolese football players.

[51] Archer and Bouillon, *The South African Game*.

[52] P. Alegi, 'A Biography of Darius Dhlomo: Transnational Footballer in the Era of Apartheid', in *South Africa and the Global Game: Football, Apartheid and Beyond*, ed. P. Alegi and C. Bolsmann (London: Routledge, 2010), 46–62.

[53] R. Poli, 'Migrations and Trade of African Football Players: Historic, Geographical and Cultural Aspects', *Africa Spectrum*, 41.3 (2006), 393–414.

In the 1960s a counter-trend emerged in a number of concerted attempts by African states and football associations to keep talented players at home. By the 1980s, however, the gap between the resources and facilities available was becoming unbridgeable. As a result of this factor, combined with the deregulation of access to the European football market, the outflow of players increased several-fold. In the mid-1990s an estimated 350 African players were playing in European first or second division teams.[54] By this time, however, increasing exploitation of African football labour migrants by agents and clubs had become a major problem. Several cases were reported of African players who had been made to sign contracts forfeiting the lion's share of future income, and of prospective youthful talents who had been abandoned after failing to secure contracts. As a result, the regulatory framework was tightened to prevent underage players being the subject of transfers. Instead, a number of European clubs came to establish academies on the African continent that would allow them to cultivate young talents in a controlled environment and sign outstanding players when they were over eighteen years of age. In the best academies and those run by the most serious clubs, promising young footballers were offered housing, training facilities, food and education. A plethora of less reputable academies run by agents or local businessmen followed. Here, prospective players could be made to pay, facilities and training staff were often of lower quality, while non-football education was frequently not on offer.

By the end of the century, football labour migration had come to be seen as an entirely viable career path by thousands of young African men, training alone or in the different academies. Meanwhile an ever-increasing number of footballers were active in Europe: in 2002/03 no less than 1,156 African players were playing professional or semi-professional football in the European leagues. To be sure, professional footballers also plied their trade in Africa. In many leagues, however, salaries remained low and infrastructure weak. The average salary of a Ghanaian Premier League player, for instance, was somewhere between US$100 and US$200 a month in the early 2000s.[55] A number of clubs in North and South Africa could offer more competitive salary levels and better training facilities. These, too, however, could not compare favourably with the incomes of top players in Europe or the salaries made available by the moneyed Gulf state clubs that emerged at the close of the century. Meanwhile, the successful football labour migrant had become an

[54] P. Darby, 'Out of Africa: The Exodus of Elite African Football Talent to Europe', *Working USA: The Journal of Labour and Society*, 10 (2007), 443–56.

[55] P. Darby, '"Go Outside": The History, Economics and Geography of Football Labour Migration', *African Historical Review*, 42.1 (2010), 19–41.

increasingly valuable commodity in himself, in that a transfer between clubs could fetch the selling club dozens of millions of US dollars in transfer fees.

CONCLUSION

Labour relations in the fields discussed have been characterized by convergences as well as differences; by continuities as well as changes. In tourism, large parts of the workforce were employed as wage labourers at the beginning of the twentieth century. They have been characterized as being *directly* employed within the sector, and have continued to constitute a major part of the workforce employed in the sector – whether by the state or by private enterprises. Side by side with this part of the workforce, an increasing number of people have found self-employment among the activities that tourism generates. In this manner, millions of Africans have come to work in tourism-related activities, and a relatively large number have been women. Tourism has contributed immensely to the commodification of labour across Africa through constituting a major sector based on wage labour. The nature of the jobs generated in the sector, however, has generally been menial and characterized by low skill requirements. Yet work in the sector has remained an attractive and lucrative option, with levels of remuneration often considerably higher than those available from agricultural work.

In the performing and recording arts too, waged work – a relatively rare feature at the beginning of the century – has become a widespread phenomenon, despite the fact that self-employment probably remains the major form of employment in the sector. One important feature of the evolving conditions of labour in the performing and recording arts in twentieth-century Africa has been the increasing commodification of the products and the work of the artist. This has combined with a slow shift from self-employment to waged forms. State intervention in line with varying political priorities has been another feature in the shaping of conditions of cultural work, much as economic priorities have shaped such interventions in the tourist sector. The advent of the recording arts has hastened a process of bifurcation of work already prevalent in the sphere, with some very lucrative opportunities emerging for the most successful performers and actors, and the majority eking out a living with less lucrative work under less attractive conditions.

Not surprisingly, some of the same dynamics that have driven the evolution of work in other fields of entertainment have also driven the evolution of sport as work. On the one hand, the commodification of sport has led to sporting activities becoming increasingly viewed as a profession. On the other, the conditions under which these activities take place have been shaped by the priorities of the state and international regulatory institutions. In some sports, such as football, this has led to the increasing importance and normalization of wage work, as players are contracted and salaried by clubs. In others, such as race running, wage work – which was important as long as runners derived the majority of their income from clubs and institutions, and as long as prizes were meagre – has given way to increasing self-employment.

PART V

ENTREPRENEURS AND SELF-EMPLOYMENT

FIFTEEN

Capitalists and Labour in Africa

GARETH AUSTIN

Faculty of History, University of Cambridge

A volume focused on workers' problems and experiences would be incomplete without a chapter that approaches the relations between labour and capital by exploring how capitalists sought to manage their relationships with workers, thereby affecting the latter's experiences in the labour market and the workplace. Thus, this chapter discusses the changing nature of 'the labour problem' as understood and reacted to by masters and employers in the twentieth and early twenty-first centuries. In turn, any analysis of capital–labour relations, especially in economies in which much of the population was – and remains, albeit to a steadily diminishing extent – primarily engaged in agriculture, needs to take account of the availability of natural resources, especially cultivable land and economically useful minerals. The argument here focuses upon the uneven and incomplete transition from a general abundance of land in relation to labour at the beginning of the colonial occupation of most of Africa (1879–c. 1900), to the early twenty-first-century situation of increasingly widespread shortages of land and relative abundance of labour in large parts of the continent. It must be said that the notion of this incomplete transition is much more salient south rather than north of the Sahara. It is of particularly little relevance to the most populous country of North Africa, Egypt, where population densities in its arable zone were already relatively high long before the twentieth century. So, while the discussion below is framed in continental terms, the focus will be on sub-Saharan Africa.

'Capitalists' are understood here as owners and managers of capital. The term overlaps with 'entrepreneurs', in the sense of those who bring the factors of production (labour, land and capital) together.[1] But not all

---

[1] See the chapter by Berry in this volume.

entrepreneurs in Africa are capitalists, unless the latter term is overstretched to include family farmers and lone market stallholders, among others. Besides its definition as a role or structural position, entrepreneurship is also often defined as an attitude towards investment: one of taking the long view and willingly accepting risk.[2] Again, not all capitalists in Africa or anywhere else are entrepreneurial in attitude, nor is such an attitude confined to owners of capital, though having capital to invest creates the opportunity to display or develop such an orientation.

It is useful to distinguish three dimensions within which capitalists may try to manage their relationships with workers. The most immediate is the micro level of a master's or employer's contacts with prospective and actual servants or employees. The second is competition and collaboration with fellow capitalists in the labour market, including attempts to restrict or eliminate competition by agreement. The third is the option of approaching third parties to seek their assistance, directly or indirectly, in capitalists' relations with labour, in recruitment or in the workplace. By 1900 the usual third party was the state, in that every part of Africa was at least claimed by one state or another, usually colonial, even if these states were often far from consolidating their authority in the more remote rural areas. Overall, the importance of the state as third party tended to be strengthened during the twentieth century. However, the capacity of the central government to ensure, among other things, the enforcement of employment legislation has, up to the present, been one of the many manifestations of central authority that have been limited in many countries by lack of revenue.[3] This chapter pays particular attention to this third dimension, and specifically to business–state relations in the context of labour.

Within this framework, the main discussion is organized in three parts. The first section identifies the main categories of capitalists in Africa at the beginning of the twentieth century and analyses the labour problem they faced. The second section considers how capitalists responded to the issue of labour availability and cost as it unfolded during what for most African countries was the colonial period, to about 1960. The third section

---

[2] It was essentially in this sense, not in relation to labour or the means of production generally, that Polly Hill defined 'capitalists' in her classic *The Migrant Cocoa-Farmers of Southern Ghana: A Study in Rural Capitalism* (Cambridge: Cambridge University Press, 1963; 2nd edn with preface by G. Austin, Hamburg: LIT, 1997). See also Polly Hill, *Studies in Rural Capitalism in West Africa* (Cambridge: Cambridge University Press, 1970), ch. 2: 'Ghanaian Capitalist Cocoa-Farmers', 21–9.

[3] On the historic challenges of state-building south of the Sahara, see Jeffrey Herbst, *States and Power in Africa: Comparative Lessons in Authority and Control*, rev. edn (Princeton, NJ: Princeton University Press, 2014).

examines the same issue from then, that is, from the episode of widespread decolonization, to the present. This section therefore considers the era of state-led economic development policies in the 1960s–1980s, and then the liberal economic dispensation that has been in place since the 1980s. As we will see, the continuing growth of the population, coupled with a range of other demands for land, is redefining the labour question.

1900: WHO WERE THE CAPITALISTS, AND WHAT WAS THEIR PRINCIPAL LABOUR PROBLEM?

Capitalism as a system of production based on landless workers selling their labour to the owners of land and capital was far from dominant in Africa in 1879, when the European 'scramble' for Africa really got going; nor by 1900, when it was mostly over. On the contrary, despite the substantial minorities of slaves that by then existed in many of the arable-based economies of tropical Africa,[4] the great majority of people had rights of access to land, for cultivation or cattle keeping, usually mediated by households and/or the chief or other head of the local community.[5] Yet capitalists were widespread, varying greatly in social identity and economic size and specialization. African merchant capitalists could be found in most of the continent: anciently established and in some cases very rich in North Africa, but also for centuries in the Swahili-speaking islands and ports along the East Coast,[6] and likewise in the Zambezi valley and over most of West Africa as well as on Saharan and Nile valley trade routes. In all these cases, much of this commercial specialization was self-organized in ethnic and/or religious diasporas, which

---

[4] Gareth Austin, 'Slavery in Africa', in *The Cambridge World History of Slavery, Volume 4: AD 1804 to AD 2016*, ed. David Eltis, Stanley L. Engerman, Seymour Drescher and David Richardson (Cambridge: Cambridge University Press, 2017), 174–96.

[5] John Iliffe, *The Emergence of African Capitalism* (London: Macmillan, 1983), 1–22; Gareth Austin, 'Factor Markets in Nieboer Conditions: Pre-colonial West Africa, c.1500–c.1900', *Continuity and Change*, 24.1 (2009), 23–53; Morten Jerven, 'The Emergence of African Capitalism', in *The Cambridge History of Capitalism, Volume I, The Rise of Capitalism: From Ancient Origins to 1848*, ed. Larry Neal and Jeffrey G. Williamson (Cambridge: Cambridge University Press, 2013), 431–54.

[6] Abdul Sheriff, *Slaves, Spices and Ivory in Zanzibar: The Integration of an East African Commercial Empire into the World Economy, 1770–1873* (London: James Currey, 1987); Edward A. Alpers, *The Indian Ocean in World History* (New York: Oxford University Press, 2014).

have been the subject of many fruitful studies.[7] For reasons that are not entirely clear, female entrepreneurs were particularly prominent in certain parts of what became Nigeria: in trade in the Yoruba-speaking south-west, in textile production and innovation in the mainly Igbo-speaking south-east and in parts of the mainly Hausa-speaking north.[8]

In several parts of the continent, we can identify groups of African capitalists who were not simply (and not always) merchants, but directly controlled production for the market. Plantations using slave labour to produce for markets elsewhere in Africa or beyond were conspicuous on the East Coast,[9] in places along the Senegal and Niger river valleys and in the Sokoto caliphate.[10] The latter, especially the commercial metropolis of Kano, was also a major centre of production and accumulation in the weaving and dyeing industry, and indeed to some extent of technical change and investment which appears to have delivered economies of scale.[11] There were instances where African capitalists established small states of their own:

[7]   Philip D. Curtin, *Cross-Cultural Trade in World History* (New York: Cambridge University Press, 1984); Paul E. Lovejoy, *Salt of the Desert Sun: A History of Salt Production and Trade in the Central Sudan* (Cambridge: Cambridge University Press, 1986); Ralph A. Austen and Dennis D. Cordell, 'Trade, Transportation, and Expanding Economic Networks: Saharan Caravan Commerce in the Era of European Expansion, 1500–1900', in *Black Business and Economic Power*, ed. Alusine Jalloh and Toyin Falola (Rochester, NY: University of Rochester Press, 2002), 80–113; Ghislaine Lydon, *On Trans-Saharan Trails: Islamic Law, Trade Networks, and Cross-Cultural Exchange in Nineteenth-Century Western Africa* (New York: Cambridge University Press, 2009).

[8]   Toyin Falola, 'The Yoruba Caravan System of the Nineteenth Century', *International Journal of African Historical Studies*, 24.1 (1991), 111–32; Colleen E. Kriger, 'Textile Production and Gender in the Sokoto Caliphate', *Journal of African History*, 34.3 (1993), 361–401; Colleen E. Kriger, *Cloth in West African History* (Lanham, MD: AltaMira Press, 2007).

[9]   Frederick Cooper, *Plantation Slavery on the East Coast of Africa* (New Haven, CT: Yale University Press, 1977).

[10]   Paul E. Lovejoy, 'Plantations in the Economy of the Sokoto Caliphate', *Journal of African History*, 19.3 (1978), 341–68; Paul E. Lovejoy, *Jihād in West Africa During the Age of Revolutions* (Athens, OH: Ohio University Press, 2016), 102–32.

[11]   Heinrich Barth, *Travels and Discoveries in North and Central Africa: Being a Journal of an Expedition Undertaken under the Auspices of H.B.M.'s Government, in the Years 1849–1855*, vol. II (1857; repr., Cambridge: Cambridge University Press, 2011), 97–147; Philip J. Shea, 'Economies of Scale and the Indigo Dyeing Industry of Precolonial Kano', *Kano Studies*, 1.2 (1975), 55–61; Philip J. Shea, 'Big is Sometimes Best: The Sokoto Caliphate and Economic Advantages of Size in the Textile Industry', *African Economic History*, 34 (2006), 5–21.

examples include the kingdom of Kong in Côte d'Ivoire, founded by Dioula merchants, and – in more warlord mode – the polity established by the Nyamwezi slave and ivory trader Msiri, around the copper mines of Katanga.

In the late nineteenth century, some Asante capitalists, in exile in British territory, petitioned the British authorities for a colonial annexation of the Asante kingdom, in the hope that British rule would free them to accumulate, especially by abolishing death duties.[12] That particular expectation was fulfilled, but, in general, African entrepreneurs hoping for colonial support would have been alarmed by the British overthrow of Ja Ja (Jubo Jubogha) of Opobo, the former slave who became a merchant and founded his own city-state in what is now south-east Nigeria.[13]

Meanwhile, the later nineteenth century had seen major changes in the involvement of European capitalists in Africa, of which three were perhaps particularly important. Plantation (or estate) agriculture had been established at the Cape since the seventeenth century, resulting – originally through the use of slave labour – in great wealth for some.[14] But this was now joined by mining capital, targeting diamonds and gold in the interior of South Africa. There has been a long-running debate about whether European mining interests sought to bring about the eventual British invasion of the independent Boer republics, starting with the Jameson Raid of 1895–96. An old hypothesis made a direct link with the cost of labour, suggesting that foreign deep-mining firms did not trust the Transvaal republic to supply them with cheap African labour, because they would be in competition with the labour demands of Afrikaner farmers. It is now clear that competition for labour was only one element – but it still appears to have been *an* element

---

[12] Ivor Wilks, 'Dissidence in Asante Politics: Two Tracts from the Late Nineteenth Century', in *African Themes: Northwestern University Studies in Honor of Gwendolen M. Carter*, ed. Ibrahim Abu-Lughod (Evanston, IL: Northwestern University Press, 1975), 47–63; reprinted with some changes in Ivor Wilks, *Forests of Gold: Essays on the Akan and the Kingdom of Asante* (Athens, OH: Ohio University Press, 1993), 169–88. See further Kwame Arhin, 'Some Asante Views of Colonial Rule: As Seen in the Controversy Relating to Death Duties', *Transactions of the Historical Society of Ghana*, 15 (1974), 63–84.

[13] K. Onwuka Dike, *Trade and Politics in the Niger Delta, 1830–1885: An Introduction to the Economic and Political History of Nigeria* (Oxford: Oxford University Press, 1956; 2nd edn, Ibadan: Bookcraft, 2011).

[14] Johan Fourie, 'An Inquiry into the Nature, Causes and Distribution of Wealth in the Cape Colony, 1652–1795', PhD dissertation, Utrecht University, 2012.

– in the origin of the South African War of 1899–1902.[15] Second, French and then increasingly British financial capital had invested heavily in the Suez Canal project and in Egypt generally, leading to the British annexation of 1882.[16] Third, European merchants had traded with West Africa since the fifteenth century, but it was apparently not until the late nineteenth century that, seeking to secure their interests in the palm oil and groundnut trades, such merchants widely petitioned their respective governments – via the chambers of commerce in Liverpool, London, Bordeaux and Hamburg – for annexations of the hinterlands of the coasts to which they (the Portuguese notably excepted) had previously been confined.[17] Whatever the precise causation, they got what they wanted.

To comprehend the actions of capitalists in relation to labour, we first need to consider the principal labour problem that faced all of them – in their very different situations – and about which the foreign capitalists complained loudly to their governments all over early colonial Africa. Supervision and training are perennial concerns of employers, but the great problem facing them at the beginning of the twentieth century was the cost of recruiting and retaining workers.

In 1900 most of Africa south of the Sahara remained, in physical terms, characterized by a relative abundance of land suitable for extensive methods of agriculture, notably long-rotation agriculture and transhumant pastoralism, rather than – in most areas – for such intensive methods as ploughing and permanent cultivation.[18] In arable areas, in the absence of significant economic advantages of scale and with capital also scarce, the conditions tended to make coercion profitable for users of labour.[19] In some cases, such as the

[15] Patrick Harries, 'Capital, State and Labour on the Nineteenth-Century Witwatersrand: A Reassessment', *South African Historical Journal*, 18.1 (1986), 25–45; P. J. Cain and A. G. Hopkins, *British Imperialism, 1688–2000* (London: Longman, 2002), 320–4.

[16] A. G. Hopkins, 'The Victorians and Africa: A Reconsideration of the Occupation of Egypt, 1882', *Journal of African History*, 27.2 (1986), 363–91.

[17] A. G. Hopkins, *An Economic History of West Africa* (London: Longman, 1973), 124–66; Ewout Frankema, Jeffrey Williamson and Pieter Woltjer, 'An Economic Rationale for the West African Scramble? The Commercial Transition and the Commodity Price Boom of 1835–1885', *Journal of Economic History*, 78.1 (2018), 231–67.

[18] Gareth Austin, 'Resources, Techniques and Strategies South of the Sahara: Revising the Factor Endowments Perspective on African Economic Development, 1500–2000', *Economic History Review*, 61.3 (2008), 587–624.

[19] Hopkins, *Economic History of West Africa*; Charles Feinstein, *An Economic History of South Africa: Conquest, Discrimination and Development* (Cambridge: Cambridge University Press, 2005); Austin, 'Factor Markets in Nieboer Conditions'.

Asante kingdom (occupied by the British in 1896), there was no wage rate for regular (as opposed to casual) labour whose acceptance would have been in the interests of both prospective employer and prospective employee.[20] In less extreme cases, a market in regular wage labour was possible, but coercion was usually still profitable as a means by which employers could reduce the cost of labour.[21] An alternative strategy for ruling elites might have been to dispossess commoners of land, obliging them to produce surplus in the form of tribute or rent. In nineteenth-century sub-Saharan Africa, before colonization, most elites lacked the coercive capacity to make such dispossession feasible. In any case, even in the more centralized polities such as Asante, it was politically safer for elites to unite with commoners in exploiting the labour of outsiders, in the form of people who, in their first generation of enslavement, were imported as foreign captives.

This is not to say that wage labour, recruited for periods longer than a day or two of casual work, was absent south of the Sahara. A case where wage labour predominated was the ivory trade from eastern Congo to the coast. Evidently, the wages were high enough to make it worthwhile for Nyamwezi men from western Tanzania to serve as caravan porters, while the employers preferred waged porters to slaves, because the latter were liable to try to escape.[22]

Where pastoralism prevailed, slave labour was generally much less important, as would be predicted from the presence of substantial fixed capital in the form of the cattle.[23] The exception that proves the rule existed where herders used slaves outside pastoralism, as with salt mining in the Sahara. None of this made coercion inevitable: a purely economic explanation for a non-economic phenomenon such as coercion cannot be sufficient. Given the physical, social and political capacity and willingness to coerce, however, the incentive to do so usually came where a market existed for goods, whether for shipping from the coasts or for intra-regional markets, as in the Sokoto caliphate.[24] Note that this analysis does not apply to much of northern Ethiopia, and still less to Egypt. In these cases, a higher ratio of labour to cultivable land, and the advantage of environmental sustainability

---

[20] Gareth Austin, *Labour, Land and Capital in Ghana: From Slavery to Free Labour, 1807–1956* (Rochester, NY: University of Rochester Press, 2005), 155–70, 495–8.

[21] Hopkins, *An Economic History of West Africa*, 23–7.

[22] Stephen J. Rockel, *Carriers of Culture: Labour on the Road in Nineteenth-Century East Africa* (Portsmouth, NH: Heinemann, 2006).

[23] Austin, 'Slavery in Africa'.

[24] Paul E. Lovejoy, *Transformations in Slavery: A History of Slavery in Africa*, 3rd edn (Cambridge: Cambridge University Press, 2012).

of plough agriculture, made it possible for rulers to extract substantial surpluses from free peasants.[25]

The use of coercion to recruit labour had taken various forms on the eve of the European 'Scramble for Africa', all of which continued to exist in 1900 in much of Sub-Saharan Africa, including debt bondage and *corvée*.[26] The biggest change in the nineteenth century had been a widespread proliferation of slaveholding, responding in part to expanded demand for labour in one form or another of extra-subsistence production.[27] From a careful study of admittedly very imperfect French surveys, Martin Klein estimates that, at the beginning of the twentieth century, over 30 per cent of the population of French West Africa were slaves.[28] The slave trades within sub-Saharan Africa, as well as to North Africa and beyond, constituted a labour market, the prices paid responding to fluctuations in supply and demand.[29]

CAPITALISTS' RESPONSES TO THE LABOUR PROBLEM IN THE (MOSTLY) COLONIAL ERA, TO c. 1960

The mere fact of alien rule did not change the economic conditions that made labour coercion profitable: with a physical and institutional abundance of land in relation to labour, workers were comparatively expensive to hire, if affordable at all, whether by established or incoming capitalists. For colonial governments, the option of simply continuing and expanding the widespread use of slave labour was complicated by their own rhetoric: they had committed themselves to abolishing both slave trading and slavery. This political context directly affected firms, too: in 1907 the British chocolate manufacturer Cadbury shifted its main cocoa-buying operation from the Portuguese colony of São Tomé and Principe

---

[25] E.g. Donald Crummey, 'Abyssinian Feudalism', *Past & Present*, 89.1 (1980), 115–38.

[26] See the chapter by Fall and Roberts in this volume.

[27] Austin, 'Slavery in Africa'.

[28] Martin A. Klein, *Slavery and Colonial Rule in French West Africa* (Cambridge: Cambridge University Press, 1998), 252–6.

[29] Paul E. Lovejoy and David Richardson, 'British Abolition and its Impact on Slave Prices Along the Atlantic Coast of Africa, 1783–1850', *Journal of Economic History*, 55.1 (1995), 98–119; Paul E. Lovejoy and David Richardson, 'Competing Markets for Male and Female Slaves: Prices in the Interior of West Africa, 1780–1850', *International Journal of African Historical Studies*, 28.2 (1995), 261–94; Austin, *Labour, Land and Capital*, 122–34, 486–90.

to the Gold Coast (Ghana) in response to reports of continued slavery on plantations in the former.[30]

In this context, several policy responses were available to governments wishing to facilitate the recruitment and retention of workers. One was to ameliorate the problem that abolition caused for masters by postponing it as long as possible. This was precisely the approach taken by most colonial administrations in non-settler colonies, though there were internal arguments and a few exceptions.[31]

The second option was to limit the effects of abolition by legislating to strengthen the contractual position of employers and/or by using administrative coercion to recruit labour for private employers. Thus, Master and Servant ordinances were widely adopted in British colonies, which usually (not in the Gold Coast) made breach of contract a civil offence when perpetrated by the employer, but a criminal offence when committed by the employee. Forced recruitment for private employers was practised in most colonies, though more so in earlier decades of the colonial period than in later ones. The decline was partly thanks to economic changes that reduced the demand for forced recruitment, but also thanks to the efforts of the ILO, through its Forced Labour Convention of 1930.[32] France abstained from voting on the Convention at the time, and Portugal declined to sign it, continuing forced labour until 1962. The *indigenato*, the legal code that subjected Africans to far-reaching control of their work and personal lives, made what the state defined as work compulsory for men in the Portuguese colonies. The system served to supply cheap labour to Portuguese capitalists, while thousands of Mozambican men took what was often the only alternative – registering with the Witwatersrand Native Labour Association (Wenela) to work in the South African mines.[33]

---

[30] Roger Southall, 'Cadbury on the Gold Coast, 1907–38: The Dilemma of a "Model Firm" in a Colonial Economy', PhD dissertation, University of Birmingham, 1975; Catherine Higgs, *Chocolate Islands: Cocoa, Slavery and Colonial Africa* (Athens, OH: Ohio University Press, 2012).

[31] Suzanne Miers and Richard Roberts, eds, *The End of Slavery in Africa* (Madison, WI: University of Wisconsin Press, 1988); Paul E. Lovejoy and Jan S. Hogendorn, *Slow Death for Slavery: The Course of Abolition in Northern Nigeria, 1897–1936* (Cambridge: Cambridge University Press, 1993); Suzanne Miers and Martin A. Klein, eds, *Slavery and Colonial Rule in Africa* (London: Frank Cass, 1999).

[32] Frederick Cooper, *Decolonization and African Society: The Labour Question in French and British Africa* (Cambridge: Cambridge University Press, 1996); see the chapter by Maul, Puddu and Tijani in this volume.

[33] Jeanne Marie Penvenne, *African Workers and Colonial Racism: Mozambican Strategies and Struggles in Lourenço Marques, 1877–1962* (Portsmouth, NH: Heinemann, 1995).

As was mainly the case elsewhere, in French West Africa the private employers who benefited from forced labour were exclusively European. Significantly, it was the young leader of the African commercial farmers in Côte d'Ivoire, Félix Houphouët-Boigny, who, as a member of the post-liberation French assembly in 1945, moved what became known as the 'loi Houphouët-Boigny', which abolished forced labour in the French Empire.[34] This freed migrant labourers from the West African savannah to offer their services to African cocoa and coffee growers without the forcible distraction of compulsory recruitment for European employers. This in turn enabled African growers to compete for labour on equal terms – a move that helped to unleash the rapid growth of export agriculture in late colonial and independent Côte d'Ivoire, during which European planters were quickly almost eliminated by African competition.[35]

The third option was the most drastic: to try to drive Africans out of the produce market and on to the labour market by a combination of land seizures and a ban on Africans finding a back door back into farming for themselves by renting land now owned by Europeans. This was the main strategy of the rulers of settler economies in sub-Saharan Africa in the early twentieth century, epitomized by the 1913 Natives Lands Act in South Africa. Algeria was different in that the alienation of land to European settlers was more gradual and piecemeal than in Southern Rhodesia or in the parts of South Africa colonized in the later nineteenth century.[36]

Finally, the state could make it easier for employers to pay the relatively high free-market wages by investing in transport infrastructure and defending any local monopolies of the most profitable farmland that prospective employers might enjoy.[37] To the extent permitted by the generally low level of state revenues, this was the policy in the so-called 'peasant' colonies, in which most of the land remained under African ownership and control. The epitome was British West Africa, though investment in Ghana and Nigeria in lorry transport (as distinct from the mostly earlier construction of railways) was in large part pioneered by African entrepreneurs.[38] Less conspicuously

[34]   Cooper, *Decolonization and African Society*, 186–9.

[35]   Hopkins, *Economic History of West Africa*, 219.

[36]   Claude Lützelschwab, 'Settler Colonialism in Africa', in *Settler Economies in World History*, ed. Christopher Lloyd, Jacob Metzger and Richard Sutch (Leiden: Brill, 2013), 141–67.

[37]   On the relationship between labour and the state, see the chapter by Britwum and Dakhli in this volume.

[38]   Philip Drummond-Thompson, 'The Rise of Entrepreneurs in Nigerian Motor Transport: A Study in Indigenous Enterprise', *Journal of Transport History*, 14.1 (1993), 46–63.

than the building of transport links, colonial states often (though not always) helped to uphold local monopolies of ownership of land on which export crops could profitably be grown, rather than allowing alienation to immigrants. The result in Ashanti (the heartland of the former Asante kingdom, today part of Ghana) was the preservation of the opportunity for locals blessed with such land to employ migrant workers, rather than being obliged to allow them to rent or buy land.[39]

Lobbying by specific groups of capitalists may have contributed to the adoption of certain of these four policies, but a crucial consideration for colonial administrations was raising revenue, directly or indirectly. The specific configuration of (often rival) capitalist interests also mattered. Consider the repeated refusal of the colonial administration in Nigeria to allow W. H. Lever to establish a huge palm oil plantation – thus maintaining the fourth option, rather than adopting a variation of the second and/ or third, by alienating land to a European company, which might well have gone on to request forcible recruitment of labour. This was a setback for the British (later Anglo-Dutch: Unilever) soap manufacturer, but a victory for the British merchant capitalists whose interests lay in preserving the primacy of African producers, exporting agricultural commodities and buying manufactured imports.[40]

In the context of one or more of these policies, how did capitalists in Africa respond to the combination of a relative abundance of land and the colonial commitment to ending slavery: in other words, to relatively high reservation wages (defined as the minimum wage for which a person would be prepared to sell his or her labour rather than work for himself or herself, or for the family)?

In the conveniently but misleadingly named 'peasant' colonies, African capitalists adapted where they could. A vivid example comes from Agege near Lagos, where J. K. Coker (a Creole and former Lagos merchant who became a passionate disseminator of the 'cocoa gospel')[41] adjusted his labour relations to keep up with successive colonial ordinances, moving from employing slaves to pawns, and then to wage labour. Indeed, according to Babatunde Agiri, the annual wage contract in southern Nigerian agriculture

---

[39] Austin, *Labour, Land and Capital.*

[40] Hopkins, *Economic History of West Africa*, 209–15; Anne Phillips, *The Enigma of Colonialism: British Policy in West Africa* (London: James Currey, 1989), 85–110.

[41] A. G. Hopkins, 'Innovation in a Colonial Context: African Origins of the Nigerian Cocoa-Farming Industry, 1880–1920', in *The Imperial Impact: Studies in the Economic History of Africa and Asia*, ed. Clive Dewey and A. G. Hopkins (London: Athlone Press for University of London, 1978), 83–96, 341–2.

'was developed on the Coker farms'.[42] As early as 1904 Coker was 'employing about 200 unskilled Yoruba labourers annually, with six or seven headmen'.[43] But Coker and his colleagues were fortunate in being able to grow cocoa, the exotic crop that yielded the highest returns to labour of any in the export repertoire of tropical Africa at the time. In Ashanti, where slavery was abolished only in 1908, the growth of hired labour on cocoa farms, in the form of male seasonal migrants from the savannah, took the ratio of labourers to farm owners to 1.89:1 by 1956.[44] In West Africa as a whole, where slave owners were able to make the transition to becoming employers of hired labour, it was because they enjoyed access to land in places with a combination of favourable soil characteristics and low transport costs that was sufficient to enable them to pay wages and still make a profit. Conversely, rural slave owners without such a combination of environmental and political circumstances found themselves unable to recruit from the labour market.[45] In those cases, as Don Ohadike quoted in a south-east Nigerian context, 'when the slaves left, the owners wept'.[46]

When slavery was over, at least for able-bodied males, employers faced high reservation wages. This proposition is confirmed in comparative terms by recent research, notably Ewout Frankema and Marlous van Waijenburg's investigation of real wages in the capitals of the larger British colonies in tropical Africa. They used the 'welfare ratio' technique, where real wages are calculated as multiples of the sum of money needed to sustain two adults and two children at a 'barebones' subsistence level (taking into account the local market prices of the main items in the local diet, clothing, etc.). In this kind of study, the real incomes of most people in pre-industrial economies usually come out not very much above 1.00. By this standard, illustrated in Table 15.1, real wages in Accra and Lagos, both coastal cities with increasingly cocoa-growing hinterlands, were notably high. The table excludes the decades disrupted by the world wars.

[42] Babatunde Agiri, 'The Development of Wage Labour in Agriculture in Southern Yorubaland 1900–1940', *Journal of the Historical Society of Nigeria*, 12.1/2 (1983–84), 102.

[43] *Ibid.*, 98.

[44] Austin, *Labour, Land and Capital*, 319–20, 529.

[45] Gareth Austin, 'Cash Crops and Freedom: Export Agriculture and the Decline of Slavery in Colonial West Africa', *International Review of Social History*, 54.1 (2009), 1–37.

[46] Don C. Ohadike, '"When the Slaves Left, the Owners Wept": Entrepreneurs and Emancipation Among the Igbo People', in *Slavery and Colonial Rule in Africa*, ed. Suzanne Miers and Martin A. Klein (London: Frank Cass, 1999), 189–207.

Table 15.1. Real wages of unskilled workers in the capitals of four British non-settler colonies, 1900–50

Capital	1900s	1920s	1930s	1950s
Dar es Salaam	not available	1.9	1.4	1.6
Kampala	1.2	1.7	1.7	1.7
Lagos	3.3	2.3	3.2	not available
Accra	2.4	2.6	3.4	4.1

Family subsistence basket = 1.00

Source: E. Frankema and M. van Waijenburg, 'Structural Impediments to African Growth? New Evidence from Real Wages in British Africa, 1880–1965', *Journal of Economic History*, 72.4 (2012), 908–10.

It is difficult to overstate the importance of this kind of basic research for a general labour history of Africa. The data come from the colonial annual compilation of statistics, the *Blue Books*, presumably reflecting the wages paid by the Public Works Department and other government bodies. However, it is reasonable to assume that, from the 1920s at least, they are representative of the trends (not necessarily the precise levels) across the countries concerned, wherever the labour market was national and indeed transnational – as it was, for example, in Ghana, Nigeria and Uganda – thanks to tens and eventually hundreds of thousands of migrant labourers.

It was not simply a matter of wages. In the cocoa-growing districts of Ashanti, migrant labourers from the savannah in the north were able to negotiate successively better contracts, with annual wage terms being replaced by a form of managerial sharecropping (at the workers' insistence),[47] and the workers' share then increasing, from time to time, for the rest of the colonial period and beyond.[48] Strikingly, success in the labour market was converted into higher physical living standards, to judge from a Ghana study: children born in years of high cocoa incomes (price × volume) tended to be taller than their predecessors.[49]

[47] Marshallian logic would suggest that sharecropping was an employer's choice, to delegate the risk of price falls. But both written and oral evidence stress the opposite. As it turned out, in Ashanti at least the workers got their sums right for most years. Austin, *Labour, Land and Capital in Ghana*, 412–24, 542–4.

[48] *Ibid.*, 318–20, 401–30, 528–9, 540–5.

[49] Alexander Moradi, Gareth Austin and Jörg Baten, 'Heights and Development in a Cash-Crop Colony: Living Standards in Ghana, 1870–1980', African Economic History Network Working Paper Series, No. 7/2013.

Conversely, in colonies which had broadly similar institutions to Ghana and Nigeria (i.e. 'peasant' colonies) but lacked the soils and/or transport links required for high returns on labour, real wages were much lower: as in Uganda, which was exporting cotton rather than cocoa, and with a much longer rail journey to the port than for cocoa beans in West Africa; or in mainland Tanzania, which lacked a really profitable 'mass' export crop. In these contexts, and still more so in southern Sudan or the West African Sahel, most farmers and traders were probably unable to afford to hire regular wage labour at all.[50]

Across sub-Saharan Africa, black capitalists faced a collective action problem: the very large numbers of employers (most of them small-scale) meant that it was virtually impossible to organize among themselves to restrict competition for labour. Remarkably, between 1904 and 1938 the cocoa producers and brokers of southern Ghana did succeed in combining in successive 'hold-ups' (refusals to sell produce) against a series of cartelistic price-fixing 'pools' organized by the European cocoa-buying companies. The final hold-up, of 1937/38, achieved at least a tactical victory, when the imperial government in London intervened to persuade both sides to call off their respective collective action and appointed a commission of inquiry whose report (though not the eventual outcome) was favourable to the farmers and brokers.[51] Chiefs played a key role in enabling hundreds of thousands of farmers and traders to resist the individual temptation to break the hold-up by selling their own beans.[52] But I know of no similar case of sustained collective action by cash-cropping peasants and small capitalists (employing up to 10–20 labourers) elsewhere in colonial Africa, not even in the comparable cocoa-producing region of south-western Nigeria.

Perhaps focusing on the very difficult as opposed to the impossible, an early voice for African capitalists, Winfried Tete-Ansá of Ghana, who became the founder of the Nigerian indigenous banking movement, also concentrated not on the struggle over labour, but instead on the struggle with foreign monopoly capital. In a book he self-published in New York, he accused 'foreign corporations, mostly European' of 'attempting to

---

[50] See Andreas Eckert, 'Capitalism and Labour in Sub-Saharan Africa', in *Capitalism: The Reemergence of a Historical Concept*, ed. Jürgen Kocka and Marcel van der Linden (London: Bloomsbury Academic, 2016), 165–85.

[51] For an introduction, see John Miles, 'Rural Protest in the Gold Coast: The Cocoa Hold-ups, 1908–1938', in *The Imperial Impact: Studies in the Economic History of Africa and Asia*, ed. Clive Dewey and A. G. Hopkins (London: Athlone Press for University of London, 1978), 152–70, 353–7.

[52] Gareth Austin, 'Chiefs and Capitalists in the Cocoa Hold-ups in South Asante, 1927–1938', *International Journal of African Historical Studies*, 21.1 (1988), 63–95.

monopolize the marketing by creating a vicious barrier between the producers and the consumers abroad through organized systems of banking and trading which practically deny those facilities required in an international exchange of commodities'.[53]

Even in Ghana, the united front of African cocoa capitalists and peasants fighting to improve the terms on which they traded with foreign capitalists – in this case, by striving to keep competition unrestricted – was not matched by any attempt to strengthen the terms on which they contracted with African workers, which would have entailed restricting competition among themselves. There was no Ghanaian cocoa-farmers' equivalent of Wenela to control the flow of migrant labourers into the cocoa-growing forest zone from the savannahs of what are now northern Ghana and Burkina Faso. Indeed, the settler economies were very different.

In South Africa and Southern Rhodesia, and in part in Kenya, the state made land institutionally scarce for Africans, in order to drive them into the labour market. In South Africa, the mine owners took their own measures to reduce competition among themselves, through concentration of ownership and the formation of collective organizations such as the Chamber of Mines and monopsonistic recruitment agencies, respectively for the domestic and foreign labour markets (Wenela was the latter). The combined effect of state and employer action was to ratchet downwards the real wages of black gold miners in South Africa. They remained below their 1890s–1900s levels until after 1970, despite a major increase in labour productivity, with a ratio of white to black miners' wages of more than 11 in 1911 and 1931, for example.[54] Charles Feinstein provided quantitative support for the proposition that the profitability of the gold industry, and therefore also its contribution to government revenue, depended on labour exploitation. Having noted Herbert Frankel's estimate of the net rate of return on capital in South African gold mining as 4.1 per cent during 1897–1932, Feinstein estimated (for two representative years) that a mere doubling of the wages of unskilled black workers would have cut total profits by well over 60 per cent.[55] He concluded 'that for … some five decades from the beginning of mining to devaluation in 1933, the industry as a whole would not have

---

[53] Winfried Tete-Ansá, *Africa at Work* (New York: self-published, 1930), 63.

[54] Merle Lipton, *Capitalism and Apartheid: South Africa, 1910–84* (London: Wildwood House, 1986), 410; Patrick Harries, 'Kinship, Ideology and the Nature of Pre-Colonial Labour Migration: Labour Migration from the Delagoa Bay Hinterland to South Africa, up to 1895', in *Industrialisation and Social Change in South Africa*, ed. Shula Marks and Richard Rathbone (Harlow: Longman, 1982), 142–66.

[55] Feinstein, *Economic History of South Africa*, 109–12.

survived if obliged to pay its black workers even the modest improvement assumed in this exercise'.[56] Crucially, the mine owners' capacity to repress wages depended on state support. It was the state that not only tolerated the firms' collusion in the labour market but deliberately denied most blacks the alternative of obtaining cash by selling their own farm produce. Conversely, the South African state was not prepared to allow mine owners to force down the wages of white workers.

Indeed, greatly as the mining companies benefited from cheap black labour, they ran into a political brick wall when they sought to extend their programme of reducing the cost of labour to the white workers, who enjoyed a monopoly of the better-paid jobs.[57] When the Chamber of Mines decided to open certain jobs to black workers, it provoked a violent reaction from white workers, which went beyond a strike to armed occupation of the surrounding area.[58] Though the government of Jan Smuts suppressed the Rand Revolt of 1922, the white workers got their revenge at the next (mostly white) election in 1924. Smuts was defeated, replaced by a coalition of nationalists and the (white) Labour Party, which proceeded to use mine royalties to embark on a policy of import substitution industrialization, while institutionalizing the colour bar in mining and manufacturing. Still, the mine owners had no need to cry. When the price of gold rocketed upwards with the US and British withdrawal from the gold standard in the early 1930s, they could easily have raised black wages, but they decided not to do so. The contrast between wage repression in the settler economies, above all South Africa, and the strong bargaining position of workers after the end of slavery in West Africa is reflected in the figures for real wages and infant mortality. Real wages began to rise, and infant mortality rates to fall, earlier and more steadily in colonies where the indigenous population retained control over land.[59]

While wage minimization was initially the priority for employers in modern mining, once the industry was established more emphasis tended to be devoted to raising labour productivity. From the late 1920s the Belgian copper-mining companies in Katanga pioneered a trend among mine owners towards labour stabilization, that is, phasing out migrant labour, which

---

56   *Ibid.*, 111.

57   On mining, see the chapter by Brown in this volume.

58   Jeremy Krikler, *White Rising: The 1922 Insurrection and Racial Killings in South Africa* (Manchester: Manchester University Press, 2005).

59   Sue Bowden, Blessing Chiripanhura and Paul Mosley, 'Measuring and Explaining Poverty in Six African Countries: A Long-Period Approach', *Journal of International Development*, 20.8 (2008), 1049–79.

tended to be hired on 'bachelor wages', in favour of long-term employees who were hired on higher, 'family', wages, and who would settle with their families in the mining area and stay long enough to be – from the employers' perspective – worth training.[60] The mines in what is now Zambia eventually followed suit in the 1950s and early 1960s, after a delay partly caused by government anxiety to keep money flowing into rural areas (partly to pay tax), plus opposition from the white miners' unions, who feared the erosion of their monopoly of the higher-paid jobs.[61]

Mining was the one sector of colonial economies in Africa that attracted large overseas investment. Frankel estimated all overseas investment in sub-Saharan Africa, 1870–1936, as averaging only £12.70 per head (in nominal terms). The biggest share was in mining; hence South Africa alone accounted for 42 per cent of the total. The modest scale of private investment in colonial Africa was underlined by Frankel: it constituted little more than half (55.2 per cent) of the unimpressive total.[62] Even allowing for the opposition of some officials in British West Africa to the alienation of land to overseas investors, epitomized by their rejection of W. H. Lever in Nigeria (who, however, found a welcome for his mega-plantation in the Belgian Congo), one fundamental reason why proletarianization was not pursued in colonial Africa was the very limited scale of European (and American) business interest in the non-extractive sectors of African economies.

Still, by 1960, the year of independence for the most populous Belgian, French and British colonies south of the Sahara, the problem that land abundance caused for employers had been ameliorated by a combination of trends. Population had roughly doubled since 1900.[63] More profitable products (such as cocoa beans) and technologies (such as deep mining) had expanded the opportunities for employers to pay wages while remaining profitable. Finally, while the massive appropriation of land from the African populations under pro-settler governments had deliberately stopped short of full proletarianization, it had driven very large proportions of young adult males to offer their services on the market.

[60] Bruce Fetter, *The Creation of Elizabethville, 1910–1940* (Stanford, CA: Hoover Institution Press, 1976), 80–118.

[61] Elena L. Berger, *Labour, Race and Colonial Rule: The Copperbelt from 1924 until Independence* (Oxford: Clarendon Press, 1974).

[62] S. Herbert Frankel, *Capital Investment in Africa: Its Course and Effects* (London: Oxford University Press, 1938), 156–70. Frankel's remains the only comprehensive estimation of foreign investment in colonial sub-Saharan Africa.

[63] Ewout Frankema and Morten Jerven, 'Writing History Backwards and Sideways: Towards a Consensus on African Population, 1850–2010', *Economic History Review*, 67.4 (2014), 907–31.

Full proletarianization was indeed something that all the governments of white-ruled Africa, both the European colonies and the (from 1910) independent settler state of South Africa, sought to avoid. Because they had access to resources of coercion from the imperial metropolis, or had the advantage of major revenues from mining royalties, the governments of the colonial era had a greater possibility than most pre-colonial states of depriving the mass of the population of land-use rights, thereby rendering them dependent on 'free' labour market, as was mainly the case in the European metropoles themselves. But until the 'development' push of the late (post-1945) colonial period, most European administrations in Africa were committed to minimizing expenditure in order to balance their budgets. This militated against extremely unpopular social engineering that would be expensive to administer and might provoke rebellions that would be costly to suppress. Even so, South Africa especially demonstrated the possibility of massive land appropriations. But colonial and white-minority governments wanted black households to retain enough access to land to avoid a wholesale, permanent exodus from country to town (ironically, the one population to experience such proletarianization was the Afrikaners themselves, with many having to sell their farms, especially after widespread loss of assets during the Anglo-Boer War). The consensus among colonial-era policymakers was that the mass of the population was more easily controlled via rural chiefs, and at a 'safe' physical distance from the centre of government. Moreover, the same policy kept a lid on government spending, in accordance with the general doctrine that colonial rule in Africa should be on the cheap. Major Orde Brown, the director of the Tanganyika (mainland Tanzania) labour department, expressed it this way in an overview book, *The African Labourer*, in 1933:

> It seems clear that the retention of the connexion between the worker and the land will in a large measure afford a substitute in Africa for the elaborate provisions required in Europe to meet the needs of the wage-dependent population. As long as the displaced worker can if necessary be re-absorbed into tribal life, provision for unemployment, old age pensions, and similar obligations of modern industrialized society will be largely superfluous; if, however, a considerable class of landless manual workers be created, and European conditions reproduced, the government concerned will sooner or later be compelled to recognize the inevitability of appropriate measures to meet the attendant problems.[64]

The implications for employers of the colonial-era policy of avoiding proletarianization were mixed. In settler economies, where the amount of

---

[64]   G. St John Orde Brown, *The African Labourer* (1933; 2nd edn, London: Frank Cass, 1967), 116.

land retained by most of the population was usually barely enough to support subsistence, the policy reduced the cost of unskilled labour to the companies, as the South African Chamber of Mines recognized in 1944.[65] In 'peasant' colonies, migrant labourers tended to come from households with rather more land, which implied higher reservation wages, thereby adding to the expenses of the African small-scale rural capitalists and (partly) labour-hiring peasants who tended to predominate in export agriculture.[66] The policy of keeping African workers rural-based was clearly inconsistent with any generalized labour stabilization, with its promise of reduced disruption to the family lives of no-longer-migrant workers, and its potential for greater opportunities for training on the job. While there was still no question of colonial regimes seeking to create 'a considerable class of landless manual workers' (in Orde Brown's phrase), by the beginning of the 1950s British and French officials had come to realize that African labourers were not peasants on leave.

As Frederick Cooper has shown, colonial officials increasingly accepted that African urban workers were exactly that, rather than being in the towns as temporary working visitors from rural homes. Officials – and metropolitan politicians – also recognized the corollary, anticipated by Orde Brown, that 'sooner or later' governments would have to spend much more on social welfare. Rather than opting to mobilize the resources to begin paying such bills, however, the two largest colonial empires withdrew: at least, Cooper has argued convincingly, this consideration was a major accelerator of decolonization in British and French Africa.[67]

CAPITALISTS AND LABOUR SINCE INDEPENDENCE (MOSTLY), c. 1960–2015

During the decade or so when most of the European colonies in Africa achieved independence, there were reasons to see relations between capitalists and workers as being in the process of becoming what contemporary Western observers, and some Africans, considered to be 'modern'. Most fundamentally, there had been a general shift from the various forms of coerced labour towards free labour – in prevailing ideology,

---

[65] Quoted in Harold Wolpe, 'Capitalism and Cheap Labour-Power in South Africa: From Segregation to Apartheid', in *The Articulation of Modes of Production*, ed. Harold Wolpe (London: Routledge and Kegan Paul, 1980), 298.

[66] Austin, *Labour, Land and Capital in Ghana*; Bowden, Chiripanhura and Mosley, 'Measuring and Explaining Poverty'.

[67] Cooper, *Decolonization and African Society*, 389–472, 596–625.

in law, and even to a very considerable extent in practice; and the trend was expected to continue. Slavery had been prohibited across the continent, albeit not for the last time in the case of Mauretania. Even the main remaining colonial power, Portugal, renounced forced labour in 1962. When it came to the more indirect ways of controlling labour – coupled with direct controls over workers' movements – apartheid was admittedly at its most entrenched in South Africa, but with that state withdrawing from the Commonwealth in 1961, the regime was beginning its slide towards international isolation.

In other ways, too, the tendency seemed to be towards the kind of labour institutions found in richer capitalist countries. The modest trend towards labour stabilization has already been mentioned. Since the late 1930s, trade unions had become quite widespread, especially among transport and mine workers, with the conditional encouragement (for 'responsible', apolitical unionism) of at least the British administrations. In some countries, their strikes had contributed significantly to the cause of independence from colonial rule. The expansion of state-owned enterprises was also a feature of the 1930s to 1950s in Africa, as in much of the rest of the mid-century world, an important example being the introduction of statutory agricultural marketing boards across tropical Africa: they became a major source of government revenue in economies based on agricultural exports.

Again, while the urban 'informal sector' had grown (though the term had not yet been coined), economists were inclined to believe that it would ultimately be absorbed by the permanent expansion of the formal sector, both private and public.[68] Modern manufacturing was also becoming much more widespread than it had been even in 1950, though only in a very few countries did it account for as much as 10 per cent of output.[69] With population growth having accelerated after 1945, and with the urban population growing faster than the rural, it was reasonable to envisage the hypothetical situation envisaged by Orde Brown as the African future: 'a considerable class of landless manual workers be[ing] created, and European conditions reproduced'.

Yet, around 1960, there was a long way to go. The continental population had been expanding since the end of the 1918 influenza pandemic, but as of 1959, as the United Nations' *Economic Survey of Africa* remarked: 'Although in parts of Africa population density is high, the continent as a whole is still

---

[68]   On the informal sector, see the chapter by Barchiesi in this volume.

[69]   Gareth Austin, Ewout Frankema and Morten Jerven, 'Patterns of Manufacturing Growth in Sub-Saharan Africa: From Colonization to the Present', in *The Spread of Modern Industry to the Poor Periphery since 1870*, ed. Kevin O'Rourke and Jeffrey G. Williamson (Oxford: Oxford University Press, 2017), 345–73.

sparsely populated.'[70] On UN data, only in Egypt and South Africa had the urban population reached about a quarter of the total.[71] And yet the average density per square kilometre of agricultural land remained low: estimated for 1959 as 27 for West Africa, and 21 for southern and eastern Africa.[72] Meanwhile, it was generally thought that any capitalist class was too small to be the economic or political engine of structural transformation: foreign investment being relatively modest, despite some growth since Frankel's estimate, while black business was prosperous but small-scale and confined to agriculture and trade in the 'peasant' colonies, and actively excluded from most business opportunities in the settler economies.

Some of the trends apparent around 1960 continued in the following decades, though often only in part. Labour coercion has certainly not disappeared. To take just the latest example, at the time of revising this chapter there were distressing videos of African men, who had sought to take the sea route to Europe, being auctioned as field slaves in Libya. Where the liberating trend has continued, however, is that most if not all post-independence 'modern forms of slavery' have been outside or against the law, and the overall scale is far less than in the early twentieth century.

Seasonal labour migration is not as central to African economies as it was in the first half of the twentieth century, because it has been overtaken by more permanent rural–urban migration and by large-scale labour migration to Europe and beyond. In the particular case of apartheid South Africa, because of the state's resistance to black people becoming permanent residents in the towns, as well as the white unions' continued reluctance to retreat from their original monopoly of the more skilled jobs, labour stabilization was largely deferred until the 1970s, when technological advances had cumulatively raised the profit advantage of greater mechanization, accompanied by a partial shift towards employing fewer unskilled workers and more who were at least semi-skilled. This transition in the labour force of the mines in South Africa was facilitated by higher gold prices after the United States dollar finally left the gold standard in 1971; it was made more urgent by the reduced availability of foreign migrant labour, as the end of Portuguese colonialism in 1975 contributed to the tightening of what became the 'front line' against the Pretoria regime. However, since

---

[70] United Nations Department of Economic and Social Affairs, *Economic Survey of Africa Since 1950* (New York: United Nations, 1959), 5.

[71] *Ibid.*, 14.

[72] Hans Singer, 'Demographic Factors in Subsaharan Economic Development', in *Economic Transition in Africa*, ed. Melville J. Herskovits and Mitchell Harwitz (London: Routledge and Kegan Paul, 1964), 253–4.

1970 the volume of gold output has been declining, primarily because of exhaustion of ore, leading to lower employment in its production. For the South African mining industry, however, this has been offset by the growth of coal and iron ore production.

Trade unions generally faced severe pressure from the state in the years following independence.[73] The nationalist leaders had welcomed strikes during the struggle against colonial rule but informed the workers very firmly that their place was now at work, rather than protesting. States from Egypt southwards were jealous of autonomous interest groups: this applied to unions, and often to business.

Where the course of capitalist–worker relations in post-1960 Africa has most departed from the expected path of 'modernity' is in the double destabilization of employment. First, far from being absorbed into the formal sector, informal enterprises have proliferated. Certainly, the small, usually under-capitalized enterprises associated with that term have done so, though in recent years states' capacity to register and tax has been extended in many cases, thereby making small enterprises less 'informal' insofar as that means completely uncaptured by the state. Second, the economic liberalism introduced in many parts of the world around the 1980s entailed a shift from regular to casual contracts, and the growth of what has come to be called 'the precariat'. In this respect, it was not that Africa departed from the path of Western development; rather, the West joined Africa and other parts of the former 'Third World' in having labour markets characterized much more by short-term hiring and high turnover of workers than by long-term, stable employment.[74] Let us now consider two possible explanations for the prevalence of informality and, increasingly, precarity: the weakness (or strength) of capitalists in Africa, and the insufficiency of economic growth and structural transformation.

Despite notable traditions of economic nationalism in British West Africa – in the shape of the Gold Coast cocoa hold-ups and the Nigerian indigenous banking movement – in general, business people as an interest group played little direct role in the nationalist movements of the decolonization era in Africa.[75] Not only did this limit their influence in shaping the newly independent states, but many governments in the 1960s and 1970s were

---

[73] See the chapter by Freund in this volume.

[74] For historical perspective, see the concluding reflections of G. Balachandran, 'Making Coolies, (Un)making Workers: "Globalizing" Labour in the Late-19th and Early-20th Centuries', *Journal of Historical Sociology* 24.3 (2011), 289–91.

[75] Chibuike Uche, 'Indigenous Banks in Colonial Nigeria', *International Journal of African Historical Studies*, 43.3 (2010), 467–87.

committed to some form of socialism and were therefore suspicious of capitalists, domestic as well as foreign, or even actively hostile to them as a lobby. The promotion of African capitalism was explicitly not on the agenda of presidents Kwame Nkrumah in Ghana or Julius Nyerere in Tanzania. Nor was it an aim of President Gamal Abdel Nasser of Egypt, who in 1960 nationalized the Banque Msir, which had acted as the main coordinator of large-scale Egyptian private enterprise, including in manufacturing.

In tropical Africa, the relatively fast economic growth of a few countries in the 1960s and even 1970s inspired hopes that they were on course for a breakthrough into capitalist development. A lively debate arose among foreign observers of Kenya, specifically among left-wing scholars, about whether the country was, after all, not a 'neo-colony' (as they had originally believed) but rather an increasingly capitalist economy led by a state determined to fight for the interests of domestic against foreign capitalists.[76] The vanguard of indigenous capitalist accumulation under President Jomo Kenyatta's government came to be the Gema Holding Company, founded in 1973 and named on ethnic lines ('Gikuyu, Embu and Meru Association') but essentially representing 'large-scale Kenyan capital', which enjoyed strong support and personal participation from members of the ruling elite.[77] A striking feature of the scholarly debate, however, was how little it considered labour.

On the other side of the continent, Côte d'Ivoire was outpacing Kenya in economic growth under the rule of the above-mentioned Houphouët-Boigny, a large cocoa farmer who already led the indigenous export farmers of the country before he became its first president. His government could make perhaps the strongest case to be considered as creating conditions for capitalist development. For instance, whereas Nkrumah in neighbouring Ghana extended the state (officially, the ruling-party) monopoly of exporting cocoa beans to a monopsony of buying them directly from the farmers, thus

[76] The debate was started by Colin Leys, 'Capital Accumulation, Class Formation, and Dependency: The Significance of the Kenyan Case', *Socialist Register*, 15 (1977), 241–66; for critical reviews, see Björn Beckman, 'Imperialism and Capitalist Transformation: Critique of a Kenyan Debate', *Review of African Political Economy*, 19 (1980), 48–62, and Gavin Kitching, 'Politics, Method, and Evidence in the "Kenya Debate"', in *Contradictions of Accumulation in Africa: Studies in Economy and State*, ed. Henry Bernstein and Bonnie K. Campbell (Beverly Hills, CA: Sage, 1985), 115–52. Colin Leys, 'Learning from the Kenya Debate', in *Political Development and the New Realism in Sub-Saharan Africa*, ed. David E. Apter and Carl G. Rosberg (Charlottesville, VA: University of Virginia Press, 1994), 220–43, was perhaps the last word.

[77] Nicola Swainson, *The Development of Corporate Capitalism in Kenya 1918–1977* (London: Heinemann, 1980), 206.

excluding indigenous as well as foreign private firms from cocoa marketing, under Houphouët private enterprise continued in the buying of export crops. Most pertinently, Houphouët did his best to ensure that Ivoirian farmers could compete successfully with Ghanaian ones in the labour market. This policy included a promise that labourers coming from the savannah (whether from northern Côte d'Ivoire or from Mali or Burkina Faso) to work in the forest zone for coffee or cocoa growers would be rewarded ultimately with land rights in the forest zone.

Taking these stories forward, neither turned out so well from the perspective of the development of national capitalism. Following Kenyatta's death in 1978, his successor, Daniel Arap Moi, systematically dismantled the patronage system that Kenyatta had built up, closing Gema Holdings in the process. After Houphouët's death in 1993, his promise of land was repudiated, having never been turned into law: a betrayal, as far as the migrant labourers were concerned, which contributed to the outbreak of civil war in 2002.

Overall, in the 1960s and 1970s, over most of Africa, indigenous capitalists had relatively little collective voice, even if some among them were able to negotiate lucrative contracts within economic systems that were becoming increasingly politicized, with the market often displaced by administrative setting of prices. The latter practice applied less in Kenya, the smaller southern African states and perhaps least in the franc zone. It applied most in Guinea, Zaire and in many anglophone countries in tropical Africa, especially after they followed political independence, sooner or later, with a declaration of monetary independence. Foreign capitalists also negotiated lucrative contracts, but they were perhaps particularly reliant on political patrons. Their bargaining position might be strong in small states, less so in larger ones. The great majority of the 80,000-strong Asian community, very important as traders and to some extent as employers, was expelled from Uganda in 1972. In Nigeria, a succession of laws in the 1970s extended Nigerian ownership in foreign companies, including by nationalizing BP Nigeria.[78] It could be argued that this political context made less likely the kind of large, fixed investments that would generate the big factories with relatively stable workforces that were associated with Orde Brown's 'European conditions'.

---

[78] Chibuike Uche, 'British Government, British Businesses, and the Indigenization Exercise in Post-Independence Nigeria', *Business History Review*, 86.4 (2012), 745–71; Ann Genova, 'Nigeria's Nationalization of British Petroleum', *International Journal of African Historical Studies*, 43.1 (2010), 115–36.

In the 1980s the very widespread adoption of 'Structural Adjustment'[79] across the continent meant a major increase in the extent to which labour was allocated by market rather than administrative mechanisms. Small capitalists had played a part in obliging governments to retreat from the policies of state-led development that had become ever more far-reaching since 1939, and especially in the 1960s and 1970s. When governments fixed prices – for foreign currency, imported goods, or in some cases even domestically produced foodstuffs – far below what the commodity would fetch on the market, suppliers tended to bypass official markets, selling instead on parallel markets. This eroded the tax base: one of the reasons that led governments to resort to the International Monetary Fund and the World Bank.[80] But this collective power of small traders and producers, being unorganized, did not generate much day-to-day influence in the running of national economies.

Ironically, Structural Adjustment did not necessarily amplify the political voices of capitalists. It brought in a more radically market-oriented set of institutions than had ever existed before in Africa, including under colonial rule. But, as Dani Rodrik and Arvind Subramanian have pointed out, pro-market and pro-business policies are not the same thing: the former favours competition and new entrants, the latter tames competition to keep incumbents' profits (or economic rents) high. Their example is the timing of the historic Indian transition to fast economic growth. Though often attributed to the economic liberalization of 1991, it actually began a good decade earlier, apparently triggered by a package of concessions to business under Indira Gandhi's last government.[81] To be sure, concessions to business may simply result in unearned income, wastefully used. The point is, this is different from extending market relations as such.

Let us consider the most successful case of Structural Adjustment in Africa, Ghana, where a 40 per cent fall in GDP during the eight years before its

---

[79] Initial capital letters because I treat 'Structural Adjustment' in 1980s Africa as a proper noun, as it refers here to a specific policy regime, distinct from other structural adjustments in history, such as collectivization in the Soviet Union or the Great Leap Forward in China.

[80] Gareth Austin, 'Is Africa too Late for "Late Development"? Gerschenkron South of the Sahara', in *Diverse Development Paths and Structural Transformation in the Escape from Poverty*, ed. Martin Andersson and Tobias Axelsson (Oxford: Oxford University Press, 2016), 222; for an example of such fiscal collapse, see Douglas Rimmer, *Staying Poor: Ghana's Political Economy 1950–1990* (Oxford: Pergamon Press for the World Bank, 1992), 207, 212.

[81] Dani Rodrik and Arvind Subramanian, 'From "Hindu Growth" to Productivity Surge: The Mystery of the Indian Growth Transition', NBER Working Paper No. 10376 (2004).

introduction, which reduced GDP per capita to about its level at the time of independence,[82] was transformed: the fall was immediately replaced by a rise, which was sustained through to the beginning of oil exports in 2011. Yet in all this, no close contacts were established between government and organized business, as distinct from the occasional patrimonial contact between an individual capitalist and contacts in government.[83] To be sure, what Margaret Thatcher called 'management's right to manage' was restored after Structural Adjustment began (in disguise) in May 1983, following the first sixteen months of Jerry Rawlings's 31 December 1981 revolution, when managing boards (including the Ghana Cocoa Marketing Board) were subject to dictation from the Workers' Defence Committees. But capitalists as such never became a significant pressure group under Rawlings, either before or after his conversion from military revolutionary to elected president (before stepping down after his two permitted terms in 2000). Perhaps that is not surprising in this case, because Rawlings's regime was thoroughly left-wing in origin: the fact that its leaders made a pragmatic decision to restore market forces in order to stop the economic slide did not mean that they had to start liking capitalists. It is more surprising that there is not much evidence of strong relationships emerging elsewhere between organized business and the state.[84]

If there is an exception, perhaps it is foreign firms, now including Chinese enterprises, in certain countries. These companies have the capital and technology to convert market opportunity into an employment- and revenue-generating activity, based on fixed investment – to undertake which, however, they expect favourable and predictable political conditions. In Zambia, for instance, Structural Adjustment enabled Chinese copper-mining companies largely to abandon regular contracts in favour of casual terms of employment.[85] More recently, however, a Chinese-government-owned mining company operating in Zambia demonstrated that it had a choice of timescale in its avowed pursuit of profit. When the price of copper fell 80 per cent in the months following the Western financial crisis of 2008, 30 per cent of the copper-mining workforce in Zambia were laid off. But none of the 30 per cent had worked for the Chinese state enterprise. Putting its long-term

[82] Rimmer, *Staying Poor*.

[83] Roger Tangri, 'The Politics of Government-Business Relations in Ghana', *Journal of Modern African Studies*, 30.1 (1992), 97–111; Antoinette Handley, *Business and the State in Africa: Economic Policy-Making in the Neo-Liberal Era* (Cambridge: Cambridge University Press, 2008), 165–206.

[84] For an exploration, see Handley, *Business and the State in Africa*.

[85] Steven C. Nakana, 'Chinese Capital and African Labour in Zambian Mining, 1997–2008', PhD dissertation, Graduate Institute of International and Development Studies, Geneva, 2013.

relationship with the state ahead of current profit, this firm adopted a '"Three Noes" policy: no layoffs, no production reduction, no salary cuts'.[86] Clearly, that is an option rarely available to private companies.

Overall, while individual capitalists, foreign and sometimes domestic, have been able to strike deals with political patrons, capitalists as a class or interest group have not been very strong during the postcolonial era to date, either before or since Structural Adjustment. The risky investment environment that this has entailed, especially but not exclusively before Structural Adjustment, is one of the reasons why there has not been more of the kind of investment that has generated large-scale employment elsewhere. Overall, capitalists have tended to be followers rather than leaders in economic policy in Africa: taking the opportunity to replace regular by casual contracts when economic liberalization permitted them to do so, and (Chinese state enterprises apart) probably not daring to do otherwise.

Let us turn to the insufficiency of economic growth and structural change as a possible approach to explaining the persistence and growth of informal employment, the growth of the precariat even within the formal sector, and the continued existence, in some countries, of forms of labour coercion.

In aggregate, African economies grew faster than their populations between 1960 and 1980. This period of generally slow growth (for most countries, about 1 per cent a year per head) ended earlier in sub-Saharan Africa, with the 1973 oil-price shock, than in North Africa, because of the latter's greater oil exports per head. The first decade after the beginning of Structural Adjustment (1983 to 1986 in most countries) saw income per head actually fall south of the Sahara, though North Africa managed slow growth. From about 1995 to the time of writing, the continent has experienced pretty steady economic growth: for sub-Saharan Africa, probably about 2 per cent per year faster than population growth. This is the most widespread boom the continent has seen, yet structural transformation – based on industrial and agricultural revolutions – has made little progress overall, despite some optimistic qualifications. While manufacturing expanded during the general post-1995 economic expansion, it has only quite recently begun to grow as a share of output. In 2015 manufacturing contributed 15.5 per cent of total value added, compared to 14.8 per cent in 1995.[87]

---

[86] Ching Kwan Lee, 'The Spectre of Global China', *New Left Review*, 89 (2014), 28–65 (p. 38).

[87] United Nations Economic Commission for Africa, *Economic Report on Africa 2018* (Addis Ababa: UNECA, 2018), Fig. 1.17. For historical perspectives, see Austin, 'Is Africa too Late for "Late Development"', 206–35; Austin, Frankema and Jerven, 'Patterns of Manufacturing Growth'.

Again, the inadequacy of formal sector growth has left tens or even hundreds of millions of Africans, over the decades, reliant on the urban informal sector. The latter is a notoriously broad category.[88] It has room for sites of capital accumulation and innovation, as in small-scale manufacturing in particular localities in Ghana, Kenya and Nigeria, during the generally unpromising conditions of the 1970s and 1980s.[89] But it also had plenty of room for new entrants who bring little more than their own labour, patience and ingenuity to the challenge of making a living by doing exactly what large numbers of people are already doing.[90] 'Excessive competition', which drives profit rates too low for accumulation to be possible, has often been observed. Sayre Schatz noted for Nigeria in the 1970s that new entrants were willing to accept a '"wage of management" so low that entry continues long after it would stop in a more-developed economy'.[91] In such contexts, actual wages tend to be very low. In Suame Magazine, the centre of small-scale manufacturing in Kumasi, Ghana, it was reported that masters hired not wage labourers but apprentices who were paid 'chop money' plus training (after which, the apprentice would easily set up in competition with his former master).[92]

Slow average rates of economic growth in the 1960s and 1970s, even before the widespread debacle of the later 1980s and early 1990s – and on average for the 1960–2015 period as a whole – left many localities in which labour productivity was low, often because of the constraints of the physical environment. In the Ader region of Niger, as Benedetta Rossi has shown, the difficulty of obtaining high returns on investments encouraged successive regimes, colonial and postcolonial, themselves short of revenue, to demand that local people work on 'development' projects for little or no

---

[88] See the chapter by Barchiesi in this volume.

[89] Jonathan Dawson, 'Development of Small-scale Industry in Ghana: A Case Study of Kumasi', in *Small-scale Production: Strategies for Industrial Restructuring*, ed. Henk Thomas, Francisco Uribe-Echevarría and Henny Romijn (London: Intermediate Technology Publications, 1991), 173–207; Kenneth King, *Jua Kali Kenya: Change and Development in an Informal Economy, 1970–95* (London: James Currey, 1996), 88–111; Kate Meagher, *Identity Economics: Social Networks and the Informal Economy in Nigeria* (Woodbridge: James Currey, 2010), 56–61.

[90] See the chapter by Pilossof in this volume.

[91] Sayre P. Schatz, *Nigerian Capitalism* (Berkeley, CA: University of California Press, 1977), 114. See also Kwame Ninsin, *The Informal Sector in Ghana's Political Economy* (Accra: Freedom Publications, 1991).

[92] Dawson, 'Development of Small-scale Industry in Ghana'. To 'chop' is to eat.

pay.[93] Poverty at all levels can facilitate the persistence of labour coercion and personal dependence.

South Africa during the last years of apartheid presents a different kind of story, where deficient economic performance contributed to liberating change. As noted above, the mining sector had been built on the underpayment of black labour. Mining in turn provided foundations for the development of manufacturing, which, by 1946, had overtaken agriculture and even mining itself as the biggest contributor to GDP, though most of it was not competitive internationally. But the system of labour repression, which had made the striking growth of industries in the late nineteenth and early twentieth centuries possible, became a brake on the further development of the economy. By the 1970s, on the labour front, South African capitalism became increasingly mired in politically induced costs, as the economy reached the limits of extensive growth (in the sense of growth achieved through more inputs of labour and capital, without significantly raising total factor productivity). To make the transition to intensive growth required an abundant supply of skilled labour, which was exactly what was lacking, thanks to the deliberate paucity of 'Bantu education' as well as the formal colour bar in the workplace. Some progress towards a more efficient allocation of labour was achieved, but at a high cost: as in deals whereby companies bought out white jobs in order to transfer them to much lower-paid black workers, with the bulk of the savings going in higher wages for the whites.[94] Much as South African companies had benefited from the colour bar, it was not surprising that representatives of white-owned businesses opened negotiations with the exiled leadership of the African National Congress, while the party was still banned in South Africa.

The general African economic boom since 1995 has reduced poverty ratios, but only relatively slowly. An obvious reason for the rather low conversion rate of growth into poverty reduction is precisely the prevalence of precarious labour, in the formal as well as the informal sector, though it has been in the latter that employment seems to have risen most.[95]

As we have argued, precarious labour is accompanied in the informal sector by precarious capitalism. This has occurred without wholesale proletarianization: labourers' loss of rights over land. While it is difficult to count precisely, it is clear that the number of hired labourers in Africa, at least

---

[93] Benedetta Rossi, *From Slavery to Aid: Politics, Labour, and Ecology in the Nigerien Sahel, 1800–2000* (New York: Cambridge University Press, 2015).

[94] Francis Wilson, *Labour in the South African Gold Mines 1911–1969* (Cambridge: Cambridge University Press, 1972), 110–19.

[95] See the chapter by Pérez Niño in this volume.

south of the Sahara, was vastly greater by 1960 than it had been in 1900, and is much greater today than it was in 1960.[96] Yet, ironically, the only population group to have experienced large-scale proletarianization was the Afrikaners. A large proportion of them had to sell up because of debt in the early years of the twentieth century, following the war with Britain; whereas the consistent policy of the white-controlled government in South Africa was to sustain the migrant labour system by avoiding the complete proletarianization of the black population. During much of the last half-century, as before, for sub-Saharan Africa as a whole, it has remained unclear whether there is a real cumulative trend towards the dispossession of the majority of the population from the land. The absence of this put a floor under real wages in the 'peasant' colonies,[97] and is presumably partly responsible for the fact that, as late as the end of the twentieth century, wage costs in Ghana were apparently too high to permit the country to be internationally competitive in manufacturing.[98] Actually, real wages in sub-Saharan Africa have been overtaken by those in China, to take the most important example.

But since the land grabs of the early twentieth century in the settler colonies, any downward pressure on wages has been exerted much less by large-scale alienation of land than by population growth: the population of the continent as a whole rose from under 137–151 million in 1900 to 220–240 million in 1950 and to over 800 million by 2000.[99] Over twenty years ago, Sara Berry wrote persuasively of 'exploitation without dispossession'; some years later, Pauline Peters countered that there are limits to the negotiability of land rights, suggesting that, beneath the flux, class formation was actually happening.[100] In the last decade there have been many reports of 'land grabs', or more neutrally of a 'land rush', in many parts of sub-Saharan Africa, with states helping to alienate land to both foreign and domestic capitalists.[101] Reliable figures are hard to find, but taken together with the

[96] As argued for the period up to the mid-1980s by John Sender and Sheila Smith, *The Development of Capitalism in Africa* (London: Methuen, 1986).

[97] Bowden, Chiripanhura and Mosley, 'Measuring and Explaining Poverty'.

[98] Francis Teal, 'Why Can Mauritius Export Manufactures and Ghana Not?', *The World Economy*, 22.7 (1999), 981–93.

[99] Frankema and Jerven, 'Writing History Backwards and Sideways'.

[100] Sara Berry, *No Condition is Permanent: The Social Dynamics of Agrarian Change in Sub-Saharan Africa* (Madison, WI: University of Wisconsin Press, 1993); Pauline E. Peters, 'The Limits of Negotiability: Security, Equity, and Class Formation in Africa's Land Systems', in *Negotiating Property in Africa*, ed. Kristine Juul and Christian Lund (Portsmouth, NH: Heinemann, 2002), 45–66.

[101] Carlos Oya, 'The Land Rush and Classic Agrarian Questions of Capital and Labour: A Systematic Scoping Review of the Socioeconomic Impact of Land Grabs in

increasing pressure of population on land and on soil fertility,[102] it may well be that the major source of poverty in Africa in the mid-twenty-first century will be not the lack of labour power but landlessness. That would, if nothing else, increase the bargaining power of employers.

CONCLUSION

This chapter complements the chapters on workers' experiences by offering a perspective on 'the labour problem' as experienced and reacted to by the biggest category of masters and employers: capitalists. By their nature, it has focused on labour recruited through a market, whether for slaves, wage workers, or (for example) sharecroppers or apprentices. In a single chapter it is impossible to do justice to the heterogeneity of Africa, so the account here is necessarily simplified.

The nature of the labour problem changed fundamentally over the twentieth century. Around 1900 labour was scarce in relation to cultivable land as well as capital, while returns to labour were in most areas severely constrained by the natural environment. In this context, we examined the options available to colonial governments, who faced the contradiction of being committed ideologically to the abolition of slavery in conditions in which the coercion of labour was profitable. We went on to explore the reactions of capitalists to the policies adopted in different kinds of colonies, all of which shared the aim of avoiding the general proletarianization of the African population. At one end of the range were small-scale African cocoa capitalists in the forest zones of British West Africa who took advantage of controlling soils suitable for growing relatively lucrative crops to attract wage-workers, later sharecroppers, from the savannah. At the other extreme was South Africa, where the black population was deprived of rights to most of the land, leaving households no alternative but to export labour, at least that of young men.

Around mid-century, it seemed possible to discern a combination of ways in which the recruitment and management of labour in Africa was moving towards what then seemed to colonialists and some Africans as modernity:

Africa', *Third World Quarterly*, 34.9 (2013), 1532–57.

[102] T. S. Jayne, Jordan Chamberlin and Derek D. Headey, 'Land Pressures, the Evolution of Farming Systems, and Development Strategies in Africa: A Synthesis', *Food Policy*, 48 (2014), 1–17; Gareth Austin, 'Africa and the Anthropocene', in *Economic Development and Environmental History in the Anthropocene: Perspectives on Asia and Africa*, ed. Gareth Austin (London: Bloomsbury Academic, 2017), 95–118.

the widespread replacement of slavery by hired labour, recently joined by the emergence of trade unions, and state enterprises alongside private ones. For some of the mining companies in central and southern Africa, the labour problem was no longer one of recruitment but of productivity: a consideration that motivated some movement towards the stabilization of previously migrant workforces. It was also expected that what would later be called 'the informal sector' would be progressively absorbed by the expansion of the formal sector.

To date, on the whole, the post-independence era has seen, rather, a double destabilization of labour: the proliferation of informal enterprise and, starting with the introduction of radically liberal economic regimes in the 1980s, the strong tendency for regular labour contracts to be replaced by casual ones. The rise of the precariat turned out to be the 'millennial' version of labour-market modernity, not just in Africa but in the West as well.[103] In aggregate, economic growth in Africa has been more widespread and much more sustained since about 1995 than during 1960–95, but so far without industrialization. Meanwhile, the state-led development policies of the early independence years have given way to market-friendly policies, not necessarily accompanied by a strengthening of the political voice of organized capital, as distinct from patrimonial links between individual politicians and business people.

But ultimately, the most striking trend of recent decades is perhaps the continuing growth of population, which now amounts to an increase of at least six times since 1900. The pressure on land has been ratcheted up in the majority of countries and has led in many cases to at least local alienations of land from smallholders. While proletarianization has never been a policy aim, something like it seems to be in progress in a number of countries, with potentially profound implications for relations between workers and capitalists. In the colonial period, as long as labour remained relatively scarce, the bargaining position of capitalists in relation to workers depended crucially on the capacity and willingness of the state to use coercion, directly or indirectly, to force peasant households to sell labour. While the state remains crucial in matters of access to land,[104] the gradual proliferation of labour surpluses in different parts of the continent is implicitly redefining the labour problem.

---

[103] In different words, cf. Eckert, 'Capitalism and Labour in Sub-Saharan Africa', 176–7.

[104] Catherine Boone, *Property and Political Order in Africa: Land Rights and the Structure of Politics* (New York: Cambridge University Press, 2014).

SIXTEEN
Entrepreneurial Labour

SARA S. BERRY

History Department, Johns Hopkins University, Baltimore

Entrepreneurship – defined here as the process of managing, and often launching, an income-generating entity – is often depicted as a combination of personal attributes that enable certain individuals to perceive and act on economic opportunities more quickly and effectively than others do, and economic conditions in which economic opportunities are abundant and widely accessible.[1] The present chapter seeks to shift the focus from innovation and individual ability to entrepreneurship as a form of work – as Austin points out in Chapter 16, most capitalists are entrepreneurs, but not all entrepreneurs are capitalists. In Africa, many who launch and manage productive enterprises operate too close to the margin to accumulate even small amounts of capital.

In sub-Saharan Africa, where small and medium-sized enterprises have greatly outnumbered large ones throughout the twentieth and early twenty-first centuries, proprietors often work alongside their assistants (employees, apprentices, clients, unpaid family members), gathering information about market conditions and methods of production, negotiating prices and delivering goods to market. Entrepreneurs also engage in what might be called 'social work' – creating and managing relationships with a variety of other people (customers, creditors, employees, authorities) to gain access to markets and resources, direct and coordinate processes of production, and keep the enterprise going in good times and bad.[2]

---

[1] People initiate and manage programmes, projects, institutions, etc. in all walks of life – politics, government, education, religion, social movements and more. For purposes of this volume, the present chapter is limited to economic entrepreneurship.

[2] In using this term, I am not referring to the efforts of professional 'social workers' who provide services for people in need, but rather to the work of building and managing relations with other people.

After outlining major shifts in economic and political contexts for entrepreneurial endeavour in Africa since the late nineteenth century, this chapter takes a closer look at entrepreneurial social work, placing it in the literature on entrepreneurship in twentieth-century Africa, then presents a few examples from my own research in Nigeria and Ghana to illustrate variations in entrepreneurial labour that have taken place at different times and locations.[3] Approaching entrepreneurship as a social process rather than a collection of personal attributes, I argue that, while forms of social work vary across space and time, all entrepreneurial endeavour involves managing and sustaining social relations. Like relationships with co-workers, neighbours, etc., family relationships involve ongoing exchanges of material goods, attention and affect.[4]

HISTORICAL OVERVIEW

Throughout the twentieth century, African economies were dominated by small-scale enterprises, many of them run by a single proprietor with the assistance of a few other people. Larger enterprises existed long before the late nineteenth century – plantations on the East African coast and the West African savannahs worked by large numbers of slaves and tribute-paying peasants; also owners of large herds of livestock and merchants who moved goods over long distances, managing far-flung networks of herders, porters and agents. These large enterprises operated alongside many small-scale farmers, traders, artisans and labourers drawn by expanding market

---

[3]   Many aspects of entrepreneurial labour in Ghana and Nigeria are similar to those observed elsewhere in Africa. See, for example, Kenneth King, *Jua kali Kenya: Change and Development in an Informal Economy, 1970–1995* (London/Nairobi/Athens, OH: James Currey/EAEP/Ohio University Press, 1996); Dorothy McCormick, 'African Entrepreneurial Clusters and Industrialization: Theory and Reality', *World Development*, 27.9 (1999), 1531–51; John Akoten and Keijiro Otsuka, 'From Traders to Mini-Manufacturers: The Role of Traders in the Performance of Garment Enterprises in Kenya', *Journal of African Economies*, 16.4 (2007), 564–95.

[4]   Among many others, see Elizabeth Colson, *Marriage and the Family among the Plateau Tonga of Northern Rhodesia* (Manchester: Manchester University Press 1959); John Comaroff, ed., *The Meaning of Marriage Payments* (London: Academic Press, 1980); Barbara Cooper, *Marriage in Maradi: Gender and Culture in a Hausa Society in Niger, 1900–1989* (Portsmouth, NH: Heinemann, 1997); Jean Allman and Victoria Tashjian, *'I Will Not Eat Stone': A Women's History of Colonial Asante* (Portsmouth, NH: Heinemann, 2000); A. F. Robertson, ed., *The Dynamics of Productive Relationships: Sharecropping in Comparative Perspective* (Cambridge: Cambridge University Press, 1987).

opportunities or forced by colonial taxation to seek paid employment or produce for the market.

Rather than consolidating many small-scale enterprises into large ones, motorized transport intensified the commercialization of everyday life.[5] In turn, farmers, traders and even labourers used part of their earnings to buy some of the goods consumed by members of their households, leading to the growth of domestic markets in foodstuffs and other goods that people had previously produced for themselves or done without. To take just one example, thousands of women – many of them wives and daughters of small-scale farmers and artisans – began to earn small amounts of money by preparing and selling cooked food to neighbours too busy or tired to cook for themselves.

The spreading commercialization of daily life worked, in turn, to alter the character of entrepreneurial labour. As increasing numbers of women began to trade or sell cooked food, farmers, traders and others began to replace the labour of their dependants with various forms of hired labour.[6] Supervising and negotiating with workers who requested payment in cash or a share of the output involved new kinds of social arrangements, as employers sought to balance their need for reliable workers against efforts to keep down costs and manage money as well as commodities through seasonal swings in income and consumption and unstable market conditions. Similar shifts occurred in trade, transport, crafts and service industries. Often short of cash and facing many competitors in markets with low barriers to entry, both large- and small-scale entrepreneurs sought to strengthen their control over their businesses by developing and sustaining new kinds of social relationships – with customers, creditors, suppliers and, of course, employees.

THE SOCIAL DIMENSIONS OF ENTREPRENEURIAL LABOUR

Much of the empirical research on entrepreneurship in Africa begins with the premise that entrepreneurs are people endowed with particular attributes and skills that are evoked or inhibited by economic and cultural influences. Entrepreneurs are quick to perceive opportunities, to innovate, show

---

[5] See the chapter by Bellucci in this volume.

[6] See, among others, Robertson, ed., *The Dynamics of Productive Relationships*; Charles van Onselen, *The Seed is Mine: The Life of Kas Maine, a South African Sharecropper, 1894–1985* (New York: Hill and Wang, 1996); Gareth Austin, *Labour, Land and Capital in Ghana: From Slavery to Free Labour in Asante, 1807–1956* (Rochester, NY: University of Rochester Press, 2005).

initiative and take risks, and cope effectively with unforeseen events and setbacks. In her pioneering studies of migrant cocoa farmers in southern Ghana, Polly Hill characterized them as 'capitalists' – able to think and act strategically, accumulate assets and 'take a long view'.[7] Others agreed that African entrepreneurs were active in launching new ventures, but failed to manage their businesses effectively – operating at a loss, neglecting to maintain equipment and consuming rather than reinvesting profits. Citing evidence that few African-owned firms outlived their founders, some attributed this to inexperience, while others blamed Africans' 'faulty concept of business' or 'traditions' that discouraged specialization and constructive supervision of subordinates.[8]

More recently, several authors have challenged this conclusion, pointing to firms that did grow or were successfully transferred to the founders' heirs.[9] Others have argued that low income levels, global market concentration, instability and repressive state policies prevented African entrepreneurs from realizing their potential, and that achieving even 'marginal gains' in chronically depressed and/or volatile markets takes significant managerial resourcefulness and skill.[10]

---

[7] Polly Hill, *Migrant Cocoa Farmers of Southern Ghana: A Study in Rural Capitalism* (Cambridge: Cambridge University Press, 1963); Polly Hill, *The Gold Coast Cocoa Farmer: A Preliminary Survey* (London: Oxford University Press, 1956); Polly Hill, *Studies in Rural Capitalism in West Africa* (Cambridge: Cambridge University Press, 1970).

[8] John R. Harris, 'Nigerian Entrepreneurship in Industry', in *Entrepreneurship and Economic Development*, ed. Peter Kilby (Glencoe, IL: Free Press 1971); A. G. Hopkins, *An Economic History of West Africa* (London: Longman, 1973), 444; Peter Kilby, *Industrialization in an Open Economy: Nigeria, 1946–1966* (Cambridge: Cambridge University Press, 1969); Peter Kilby, ed., *Entrepreneurship and Economic Development* (Glencoe, IL: Free Press 1971). Further examples illustrating variations on all these arguments may also be found in Catherine Coquery-Vidrovitch and Alain Forest, eds, *Actes du colloque entreprises et entrepreneurs d'Afrique, XIXeme et XXeme siècles*, 2 vols (Paris: L'Harmattan, 1983); Anita Spring and Barbara McDade, eds, *African Entrepreneurship: Theory and Reality* (Gainesville, FL: University of Florida Press, 1998); Alusine Jalloh and Toyin Falola, eds, *Black Business and Economic Power* (Rochester, NY: University of Rochester Press, 2002).

[9] Tom Forrest, *The Advance of Capital in Africa: The Growth of Nigerian Private Enterprise* (Edinburgh: Edinburgh University Press, 1994); Monibo Sam and Peter Kilby, 'Nigeria 1961–1991: Closure, Survival and Growth of Small Enterprise', GEMINI Working Paper 54, Bethesda, MD, 1995.

[10] Gracia Clark, *Onions are My Husband: Survival and Accumulation by West African Market Women* (Chicago: University of Chicago Press, 1994); Gracia Clark, *African Market Women: Seven Life Stories from Ghana* (Bloomington, IN: Indiana University Press, 2010); William F. Steel, *Small-scale Employment and Production in Developing Countries:*

Some critics have questioned this entire debate, arguing that culture and economy are interrelated rather than separate aspects of social life. Economic cultures vary, making it difficult or erroneous to rate entrepreneurial success according to a uniform set of market-oriented criteria. Studies of pre-colonial trading diasporas concluded that family and/or home town networks strengthened trading diasporas by facilitating communication and credit transactions over long distances,[11] or served as vehicles of socio-economic transformation.[12] More recently, an intensive two-year survey of farming households in Ghana showed that social status enhances farmers' access to resources, implying that outlays on status-making activities complement rather than detract from entrepreneurial success.[13] Like many analyses of 'social capital', Goldstein and Udry treat it as a separate, measurable variable: those who possess it have an economic advantage over those who do not. In other words, social capital acts *on* rather than *through* economic action.[14]

Unlike much of the literature on social capital, this chapter approaches social networking as an ongoing process, rather than a factor of production or a cultural parameter. In a recent essay, Ayodeji Olukoju presents entrepreneurship in late nineteenth- and early twentieth-century western Nigeria as a process of interaction between the constraints of colonial rule and a culture that valued honour, wealth and generosity. '[B]oth dynamics should be taken together', he argues, 'in any meaningful explanation' of the history of economic and entrepreneurial development in nineteenth- and early twentieth-century western Nigeria.[15] In treating entrepreneurship as

---

Evidence from Ghana (New York: Praeger, 1977); Jane Guyer, *Marginal Gains: Monetary Transactions in Atlantic Africa* (Chicago: University of Chicago Press, 2004); Lillian Trager, *Home Towns: Community, Identity and Development in Nigeria* (Boulder, CO: Lynne Rienner, 2001); King, *Jua kali Kenya*.

[11]   Stephen Baier, *An Economic History of Central Niger* (Oxford: Clarendon Press, 1980); Paul Lovejoy, *Caravans of Kola: The Hausa Kola Trade, 1700–1900* (Zaria: Ahmadu Bello Press, 1980).

[12]   Jonathon Glassman, *Feasts and Riot: Revelry, Rebelliousness and Popular Consciousness on the Swahili Coast, 1856–1888* (Portsmouth, NH/London/Nairobi/Dar es Salaam: Heinemann/James Currey/EAEP/Mkuki na Nyota, 1995).

[13]   Markus Goldstein and Christopher Udry, 'The Profits of Power: Land Rights and Agricultural Investment in Ghana', *Journal of Political Economy*, 6.6 (2002), 981–1022.

[14]   Pierre Bourdieu, 'The Forms of Capital', in *Handbook of Theory and Research for the Sociology of Education*, ed. J. Richardson (New York: Greenwood Press, 1986).

[15]   Ayodeji Olukoju, 'Accumulation and Conspicuous Consumption: The Poverty of Entrepreneurship in Western Nigeria, ca. 1850–1930', in *Africa's Development in Historical Perspective*, ed. Emmanuel Akyeampong et al. (New York: Cambridge University Press, 2014), 208–30.

a product of interaction among several, simultaneous and interdependent social processes, Olukoju's analysis parallels the approach taken in this chapter. Rather than lament the 'poverty' of entrepreneurship, however, I argue that entrepreneurship – together with market conditions, state practices and cultural understandings – figures in the valuation of economic activities and the roles they play in trajectories of economic and social change.

Money and goods spent on rituals such as marriage or children's education build social relationships that influence the growth and sustainability of output and income. Such relationships figure centrally in competitive markets with relatively low barriers to entry that are common across Africa, but it does not follow that they always promote economic progress, any more than that they invariably hold it back. Like the people who participate in them, social networks face contradictory pressures. The more people are threatened by economic instability and decline, the more they need social support. Rather than withdraw from family or other social engagements in hard times, people often seek to expand and diversify them in an effort to keep their options open. That they may not be able to afford to do this does not mean that they wouldn't if they could.[16]

In short, investing in social relationships is not an additive process in which the entrepreneur adds to a stock of 'social capital', but a creative and sometimes contradictory one, that may limit as well as enhance the productive capacity of an enterprise.[17] Entrepreneurial labour is performative as well as productive, working to persuade others of the entrepreneur's capabilities, often in advance of actual gains in production and income. In some cases, entrepreneurs perform success – demonstrating small gains now in order to leverage larger ones later on. Others strengthen relationships by performing commitment – contributing materially or symbolically to individuals or social groups whose support they may need at another time. The point is illustrated vividly by Guyer in her influential book *Marginal Gains*. Describing a day she spent waiting in line at a petrol station during a nationwide oil crisis in Nigeria, Guyer focuses on the performative skills

---

[16]   Kate Meagher, *Identity Economics: Social Networks and the Informal Economy in Nigeria* (Woodbridge: James Currey, 2010). See also Adrian Peace, *Choice, Class and Conflict: A Study of Southern Nigerian Factory Workers* (Atlantic Highlands, NJ: Humanities Press, 1979); Sara Berry, *No Condition is Permanent: The Social Dynamics of Agrarian Change in Sub-Saharan Africa* (Madison, WI: University of Wisconsin Press, 1993); Dzodzi Tsikata, *Living in the Shadow of the Large Dams: Long-term Responses Upstream and Downstream of the Volta River Project* (Leiden: Brill, 2006); Clark, *African Market Women*.

[17]   My emphasis on social process contrasts with Austin's, which explains capitalists' recruitment and management of labour in terms of shifts in aggregate factor proportions. See Austin, *Labour, Land and Capital in Ghana*, ch. 10.

of the proprietress, who managed a long, restive, sometimes unruly queue of drivers and vehicles waiting to fill their tanks with diplomacy and no small degree of social acumen. Playing on recognized differences in status among her customers, she rationed a limited supply of petrol among an overflow crowd of anxious, impatient, uncomfortable people, persuading most that they had been treated appropriately, even if their tanks remained empty at the end of the day.[18]

CASE STUDIES

The following pages present cases drawn from my own work in Nigeria and Ghana to illustrate the arguments outlined above. While the focus is on West Africa, the discussion includes citations of studies that point to similar dynamics at work in other regions. The cases presented here are meant to illustrate the foregoing argument, however, and are in no sense 'representative' of the continent as a whole.

FARMERS[19]

Towards the end of the nineteenth century, farmers in the semi-humid forest zone of West Africa began to clear and occupy previously uncultivated forests to plant cocoa – not to consume themselves, but to sell on the world market. At the time, most people in western Nigeria lived in towns, moving out to farming hamlets to grow food crops during the rainy season, but cocoa drew people farther into the forests and kept them there for longer periods. As commodity prices soared after the end of the Second World War, they were joined by migrants from the savannahs who settled in the forest zone, travelling to their home towns for a few weeks during the dry season to conduct family business and maintain ties with friends and neighbours. Most Nigerian growers were not wealthy: cocoa farms occupied no more than 10–15 acres, although many people had more than one farm. Once matured, however, the trees yielded income for long periods, enabling farmers to increase their consumption of purchased goods and supplement family labour with that of share tenants and hired workers.

[18] Guyer, *Marginal Gains*, 107–10.

[19] Material in this section is drawn from Sara Berry, *Cocoa, Custom and Socioeconomic Change in Rural Western Nigeria* (Oxford: Clarendon Press, 1975); and Sara Berry, *Fathers Work for Their Sons: Accumulation, Mobility, and Class Formation in an Extended Yoruba Community* (Berkeley, CA: University of California Press, 1985).

Cocoa required little in the way of material capital, but it did require working capital, to maintain the farm for a decade or more until the trees reached full bearing age. As Polly Hill argued *à propos* southern Ghana, cocoa farmers had to take a long view – investing labour in a farm for years before it began to yield at all, and finding ways to support themselves and their dependants in the meantime. Most farmers began on a very small scale, relying on their own labour with the assistance of their wives and older children to establish a small plot of cocoa; they then expanded the farm, or started a second one, when the first plot of trees began to bear fruit.[20] To keep a new farm going until it paid for itself, seven to ten years after planting, a farmer had to persuade his dependants that years of unpaid labour would be remunerated, if not directly, then with future gifts, extra household consumption, and future assistance in starting farms or businesses of their own. In other words, cocoa farming was as much a matter of managing relations with other people as of agronomic skill or physical labour.

The social work of establishing and managing cocoa farms took several forms. In Nigeria, most established farmers relied on their relatives to get started, while aspiring farmers typically worked without pay for a father, elder brother, uncle or spouse, in exchange for support while they established their own farms later on.[21] As cocoa cultivation spread, and farmers had

---

[20]   Cocoa farming in Ghana, which led the world in sales of the crop from 1911 to 1977, is the subject of a large body of literature. In addition to Hill, *Migrant Cocoa Farmers of Southern Ghana*, see, among others, Christine Okali, *Cocoa and Kinship in Ghana: The Matrilineal Akan* (London: Kegan Paul, 1983); Kwame Arhin, *The Expansion of Cocoa Production: The Working Conditions of Migrant Cocoa Farmers in the Central and Western Regions*, Institute of African Studies, University of Ghana (Legon: Mimeographed 1986); Allman and Tashjian, *'I Will Not Eat Stone'*; Austin, *Labour, Land and Capital in Ghana*; Stefano Boni, *Clearing the Ghanaian Forest: Theories and Practices of Acquisition, Transfer and Utilization of Farming Titles in the Sefwi-Akan Area* (Legon: Institute of African Studies, 2005); Kojo Amanor, *Land, Labor and Family in Southern Ghana: A Critique of Land Policy under Neo-Liberalism* (Uppsala: Nordiska Afrikainstitutet, 2001); Tsutomu Takane, *The Cocoa Farmers of Southern Ghana: Incentives, Institutions and Change in Rural West Africa* (Chiba: Institute of Developing Economies, Japan External Trade Organization, 2002).

[21]   In both Nigeria and Ghana, the great majority of cocoa farmers were men. Women did plant or acquire farms of their own, but most sources indicate that they used hired labour to plant and maintain them, rather than relying on a pool of dependants. By the 1950s some farmers' widows succeeded in claiming a portion of their deceased husbands' farms, in recognition of the years of unpaid labour they had contributed to establish and maintain them. Okali, *Cocoa and Kinship in Ghana*; Gwendolyn Mikell, 'Filiation, Economic Crisis, and the Status of Women in Rural Ghana', *Canadian Journal of African Studies*, 18.1 (1984), 195–218; Allman and

more cash to spend, demand for hired labour increased, allowing juniors or migrant workers to live on their earnings while they established farms of their own. Many also entered sharecropping arrangements with established cocoa growers, receiving a portion of the crop (or sometimes the farm) that they had helped to produce, and using that to support themselves while they started farms of their own.

All of these arrangements involved continuing effort on the part of the farmer/entrepreneur to motivate workers, supervise daily tasks, negotiate terms of service and exchange, and manage relationships with hired workers, sharecroppers, traders and dependants who helped to keep the enterprise going. Since cocoa grows best on partially cleared old-growth forest land, the spread of cocoa cultivation involved migration throughout the West African forest zone. While geographies of migration and the social composition of host and migrant communities varied from one country to another, over time cocoa farmers had not only to manage their farms, but also to navigate major transformations in the spatial arrangement and temporal rhythms of social life.

In both Nigeria and Ghana, family networks that were crucial to launching and expanding cocoa production were, in turn, both sustained and altered by the spread of the crop. By the time a farmer's first plot had matured, land in the immediate vicinity had all been spoken for, and people had to seek additional land in other locations. It became common for a farmer to settle a wife, son or junior brother (àbúrò) on each of his farms, to manage them on a daily basis, while he travelled from one to another to supervise.[22] Farmers also invested part of their earnings in expanding and endowing their families – taking additional wives, supporting junior brothers and sons in establishing farms of their own, or investing in schooling or apprenticeships for their children.

Cocoa also altered settlement patterns in Ghana as men moved into distant forest areas, accompanied by their wives and children, where they lived and worked for much of the year. As Allman and Tashjian explained in their richly documented study of women and family life in colonial Asante, these new settlement patterns represented a major reorganization of family life. Previously, most married couples did not reside together but remained with their respective families, growing together or apart as their relatives accepted or kept their distance from each other. Descent was reckoned

---

Tashjian, '*I Will Not Eat Stone*'; Berry, *Cocoa, Custom and Socioeconomic Change*; Berry, *Fathers Work for Their Sons*; François Ruf and P. S. Siswoputranto, eds, *Cocoa Cycles: The Economics of Cocoa Supply* (Cambridge: Woodhead Publishing, 1995).

[22] See Berry, *Cocoa, Custom and Socioeconomic Change*; Berry, *Fathers Work for Their Sons*; compare Hill, *Migrant Cocoa Farmers of Southern Ghana*.

matrilineally: children were under the care and authority of their matrilineal uncles rather than their fathers. Cocoa disrupted these practices, rearranging residential patterns into conjugal households, where children worked for and were governed by their fathers rather than their maternal uncles, and weakening the role of extended families in mediating conjugal life.[23]

ARTISANS

To trace the long-term implications of cocoa growing for farmers and their descendants, in 1978–79 I carried out an intensive study of one cocoa-farming village in western Nigeria, collecting information on the whereabouts of farmers' children, and then conducting follow-up studies of the children's occupations.[24] Among farmers' descendants who were employed, the most popular occupations proved to be school teaching and motor repair. The numbers of children attending school increased rapidly in the 1950s and after independence. Education was politically popular: government outlays were constrained during the Biafran war, but rising oil revenues allowed both state and federal governments to increase spending during the 1970s, creating a strong demand for teachers.[25] Flush with oil export earnings, Nigerians also spent liberally on imported motor vehicles. Traffic volumes grew faster than roads could be built and maintained, and vehicles fell apart quickly, creating a booming market for motor mechanics, electricians, panel beaters, vulcanizers and other auto repair specialists. Like other small-scale artisanal and industrial businesses, the motor repair industry ran on apprenticeships. Established mechanics relied almost entirely on the unpaid labour of apprentices, provided in exchange for learning the trade.

---

[23]   Allman and Victoria Tashjian, *'I Will Not Eat Stone'*; Okali, *Cocoa and Kinship in Ghana*. New cropping patterns also altered family and other social arrangements in eastern and southern Africa. See, among others, Berry, *No Condition is Permanent*; Tabitha Kanogo, *Squatters and the Roots of Mau Mau, 1905–1963* (London/Athens, OH: James Currey/Ohio University Press, 1987); Sally Falk Moore, *Social Facts and Fabrications: 'Customary' Law on Kilimanjaro, 1880–1980* (Cambridge: Cambridge University Press, 1986); Pauline Peters, *Dividing the Commons: Politics, Policy and Culture in Botswana* (Charlottesville, VA: University of Virginia Press, 1994); van Onselen, *The Seed is Mine*.

[24]   Berry, *Fathers Work for Their Sons*.

[25]   David Abernethy, *The Political Dilemma of Popular Education: An African Case* (Stanford, CA: Stanford University, 1969); Ben U. Omojimite, 'Education and Economic Growth in Nigeria', *African Research Review*, 4.3a (2010), 90–108.

Apprenticeships were arranged for young men by their fathers or senior male relatives,[26] who negotiated terms of service, paid the fee due to the master mechanic in exchange for feeding, lodging and training the apprentice during his several years of service, and hosted a celebration when the apprentice was 'freed' at the end of his training. (The fee increased if the apprentice stayed only two or three years with the master, rather than the customary four or five years – reflecting the value of the apprentice's labour to the mechanic's business.) Once freed, a young man still had to recruit a regular clientele in order to establish himself as an independent master mechanic, capable of recruiting apprentices of his own. Some of the mechanics I interviewed had drawn clients away from their former master, but this was a sensitive issue which many preferred to avoid. Others began as journeymen, sharing tools, work space and occasionally apprentices with their former masters or other independent mechanics, and taking a few clients of their own until they had enough steady customers to set up their own shops. Over time, the financial advantage of apprentices' unpaid labour turned into a liability, as former apprentices became competitors.

The long-term prospects of a motor repair business hinged crucially on the mechanic's ability to recruit 'regular customers' – defined by one man as 'someone who sends for me when his car breaks down in Ibadan', rather than turn to one of the hundreds of mechanics available on the spot. In a highly competitive market, vehicle owners scrutinized the quality of mechanics' work, taking into account the reliability and comportment of the mechanic as well as his skill. As one customer commented to me, *à propos* a mechanic we both knew well, 'he may not know everything there is to know about Volkswagens, but he is a very respectful young man'. In contrast to cocoa farming, then, the social work of building and sustaining relationships with sponsors, employees, creditors and customers in the motor repair business shifted away from family ties to networks based on a mechanic's reputation for reliability and comportment as well as mechanical skill.[27]

---

[26] At the time I carried out my research, motor repair was an exclusively male occupation. Farmers' daughters were more likely to go into trade, tailoring or school teaching, if they had done well enough in school themselves to qualify. While some fathers contributed to school fees for their daughters, or gave them some money to start trading, most young women received training or school fees from their mothers or grandmothers. Compare Judith Byfield, *The Bluest Hands: A Social and Economic History of Women Dyers in Abeokuta, 1890–1940* (Oxford: James Currey, 2002); Trager, *Home Towns*; Clark, *Onions are My Husband*; Clark, *African Market Women*.

[27] In many ways, the mechanics' shops I visited illustrated Wariboko's contention that African entrepreneurs manage employees (here apprentices) by results, rather than

Family could even become a liability. To attract customers, some mechanics took in partners – usually specialists in some aspect of motor repair, such as electricians or 'panel beaters' (auto body repairmen), whose proximity would expand the range of services available in a single shop. Asked if they took relatives as partners, however, many of my informants demurred. 'If a stranger steals the money in the till', one man explained, 'I can prosecute him.' But if the thief is a relative, the family will object: 'Don't go to the police! He's your brother!'

Cocoa farmers and motor mechanics both invested in social relationships to sustain and advance their enterprises, but mechanics focused less on family ties and more on building relationships with customers, suppliers, apprentices and other mechanics, with whom they shared economic interests. In 1979 the Ifẹ Mechanics Association listed over 1,200 master mechanics and journeymen as members, and it met every other Friday to discuss common concerns and settle disputes. While only a fraction of the members were likely to attend a particular meeting, mechanics throughout the city stayed away from work during the Friday meeting hours, to signal their solidarity with their fellow entrepreneurs. Anyone caught at his shop during that time risked being reported to the Association's officers, fined and forced to apologize in order to reinstate himself as a member in good standing. While the Association was in no position to fix prices in such a competitive market, it clearly played an important role in sharing commercial and technical information and mediating disputes among the members.[28]

'RECOMBINANT PROPERTY': INFRASTRUCTURE, AGRO-INDUSTRY AND TRADITIONAL AUTHORITY[29]

For several weeks in the summers of 2001 and 2002, I lived in a rural town in eastern Asante that was frequently cited as an example of successful development. By the early 2000s the town of Juaben (capital of an ancient Asante polity of the same name) boasted a rural bank, a complex

---

close supervision. Nimi Wariboko, *The Mind of African Strategists: A Study of Kalabari Management Practice* (Madison, NJ: Fairleigh Dickinson University Press, 1997).

[28] Compare Peace, *Choice, Class and Conflict*; King, *Jua kali Kenya*; Stella Silverstein, 'Sociocultural Organization and Locational Strategies of Transportation Entrepreneurs: An Ethnoeconomic History of the Nnewi Igbo of Nigeria', PhD dissertation, Boston University, 1983.

[29] The term 'recombinant property' is borrowed from David Stark, 'Recombinant Property in East European Capitalism', *American Journal of Sociology*, 101 (1996), 993–1027.

of enterprises engaged in cultivating oil palm and processing palm fruit and other oilseeds, and infrastructure that was well above average among rural towns in the region. Driving into Juaben on a well-maintained road flanked by deep, cement-lined gutters, the traveller confronted an imposing two-storey market that dominated the centre of the town. Containing some two dozen one-room shops, the market was built around a paved courtyard, where vendors who could not afford to rent a shop in the market building displayed their wares in kiosks or on wooden tables. On market days, the courtyard was full and vendors spilled out into the surrounding street and alleys, selling their goods from blankets and baskets that they had brought with them for the day. At the time of my research, most of the shops had not yet been rented, and the rooms set aside for toilets and a day care centre stood empty, while the market committee tried to figure out how to recruit and pay staff to maintain them.

The primary instigator of all these projects was the Paramount Chief (Juabenhene), who had been in office since 1971 and showed no signs of slowing down any time soon. A relatively young man at the time of his installation, the chief held a university degree in civil engineering and took office eager to use it to make a name for himself and put Juaben on the map. During the 1970s he launched several infrastructure projects, including public toilets, drainage ditches and a paved road from Juaben to the main highway from Kumasi to Accra that cut miles off the journey to Kumasi.[30] To finance these projects, the chief first summoned the townspeople to perform 'communal (i.e., unpaid) labour',[31] then put them to work digging pits for the toilets or drainage ditches along the road. He then appealed to the government for money and equipment, pointing to the ditches as evidence of grassroots 'self-help' that deserved matching support from the state. While construction was underway, the chief maintained a visible presence,

---

[30] Previously, the chief explained, the only route to Kumasi was an unpaved road that wound through numerous smaller villages and was frequented primarily by slow-moving, wooden-bodied trucks.

[31] No longer enforced by the colonial state, communal labour today is voluntary, and many wonder why people bother to show up. Some do not, of course, but others do as a gesture of civic commitment or good will, much as farmers made small gifts of produce at harvest time to the people who showed them land to farm on, before landholders charged rent for the use of their land. See, for example, Jean-Pierre Chauveau, 'How Does an Institution Evolve? Land, Politics, Intergenerational Relations and the Institution of the *tutorat* amongst Autochthones and Immigrants (Gban Region, Côte d'Ivoire)', in *Land and the Politics of Belonging in West Africa*, ed. Richard Kuba and Carola Lentz (Leiden: Brill, 2006), 213–40.

overseeing the work, joking with the labourers and inviting the press to observe and write about the town's achievements.[32]

As the Ghanaian economy slid further into crisis in the early 1980s, funds and materials for infrastructural investment dried up.[33] Looking for ways to bolster both his personal finances and those of the stool, in 1984 the Juabenhene launched a series of new ventures intended to stimulate the town's economy and his own. With capital supplied by one of Juaben's most successful businessmen (who was also a friend of the chief) and a few other shareholders, Juaben opened a rural bank, which secured enough business to remain viable by serving as paymaster for school teachers and other local civil servants. In the same year, the chief and several members of his family launched Juaben Oil Mills Ltd, a privately owned factory that was intended to process locally grown palm fruit and kernels into commercially profitable oils. Unable to secure enough high-quality fruit on a regular basis to break even, the owners soon abandoned their role as an outlet for local farmers. Refitting the mill with equipment for processing groundnuts and shea nuts, they contracted with Lever Brothers to supply nuts and purchase the oil produced at guaranteed prices negotiated in advance.[34]

While plans for the bank and the privately owned Juaben Oil Mills were underway, the Traditional Council turned its attention to the Juaben Oil Palm Plantation, a state-owned enterprise established in the 1970s when large commercial farms featured prominently in Ghana's development policy.[35] In the new policy environment of structural adjustment, the chiefs saw opportunity in the derelict farm. Mobilizing local farmers to begin rehabilitating the plantation with communal labour, the chief and the Traditional Council then put in a bid to purchase the plantation under the state's new neoliberal policy of divestment. Seventy per cent of the shares were sold to private buyers – Juaben Rural Bank, Juaben Oil Mills, Vanguard Assurance and a few private individuals known to members of the Traditional

---

[32] For further details, see Sara Berry, 'Questions of Ownership: Proprietorship and Control in a Changing Rural Terrain. A Case Study from Ghana', *Africa*, 83.1 (2013), 36–56.

[33] Following years of stagnant or declining export earnings, income and employment, in 1983 a severe Sahelian drought combined with Nigeria's abrupt expulsion of undocumented aliens to send the Ghanaian economy into deep crisis. Imported goods disappeared from shops and markets, and some parts of the country experienced famine. Ernest Aryeetey, Jane Harrigan and Machiko Nissanke, *Economic Reforms in Ghana: The Myth and the Mirage* (Oxford: James Currey, 2000).

[34] Berry, 'Questions of Ownership'.

[35] Piet Konings, *The State and Rural Class Formation in Ghana: A Comparative Analysis* (London: Routledge and Kegan Paul, 1986).

Council – while the remaining 30 per cent were credited to the Traditional Council, in recognition of the Juaben stool's customary authority over the land and the townspeople's advance contributions of 'communal labour' to begin rehabilitating the farm.[36] In effect, customary prerogative had been converted to equity capital.

Just what this meant in terms of ownership and control of the farm was not entirely clear. Legally, the Traditional Council and the shareholders owned the farm, but the chief and Council – who took the lead in rehabilitating the farm in 1984, and acquiring it from the government in 1995 – like to represent it as a 'community' endeavour, undertaken by the Council for the benefit of all Juaben 'citizens', not just for the stool.[37] A sign at the entrance to the farm describes it as 'A Joint Venture of the Juaben Traditional Council' – a phrase that leaves open the question of who is participating jointly with the Council, and on what terms.

In 1997 the Juaben Traditional Council launched what was arguably its most ambitious project to date: the Juaben Oil Palm Outgrowers' Cooperative Scheme (JOPOCS). As Juaben Oil Mills had done with Lever Brothers, local farmers now signed contracts with JOPOCS, planting oil palm on their own land in exchange for seeds, fertilizer and hired labour supplied by JOPOCS on credit, and a promise to purchase fruit harvested from the contracted trees at prices to be negotiated by the farmers and managers of the scheme. Once a farmer had repaid her loan to the scheme, the trees would be hers to cultivate, rent out or sell as she chose.

Well publicized in the media, JOPOCS was billed as a multifaceted experiment in participatory development, social welfare and corporate governance. Community participation in the outgrower scheme was mediated through a complex governing structure consisting of the Juaben Rural Bank, Juaben Oil Mills and the Outgrowers' Cooperative Society. All three members of the 'Tripartite', as it was commonly known, were to be represented on the oversight committee, which set policy and made major managerial decisions for the scheme. Chaired by the managing director of Juaben Oil Mills, in 2002 the oversight committee included the outgrower manager (a professional horticulturalist with twenty years' experience in government service), a member of the Traditional Council and representatives of the participating farmers.

Eager to support a project so in tune with its advocacy of public–private partnerships, the World Bank granted an initial loan of US$700,000. The

---

[36] Ghana Divestiture Implementation Committee, Accra, to Juaben Traditional Council, 24 February 1995, Nana Otuo Siriboe Papers, Juaben.

[37] *Ghanaian Times*, 17 February 1984; *Daily Graphic*, 17 February 1984.

money was quickly exhausted, long before any of the trees had begun to bear. At the time of my fieldwork, the loan remained outstanding, while the Tripartite searched for new sources of credit to cover the farmers' costs, including that of hired labour, until their farms began to yield income. Having failed to persuade the African Development Bank to accept its members as guarantors for the loan, in 2002 the Tripartite was still searching.[38]

The most recent example of the chiefs' entrepreneurial endeavours – the new Juaben market – had been years in the planning. As they had in many of the projects described above, the Juabenhene and the Traditional Council[39] primed the pump by summoning the townspeople to initiate the project with 'communal labour', then invoked their efforts at 'self-help' to raise money from outside sources, including the World Bank, in order to complete the construction.

Rather than invoke 'self-help' and customary prerogative to establish a stake in a *private* enterprise, with the market the Traditional Council used this approach to claim part-ownership of a *public* facility. Appealing to the Ejisu-Juaben District Assembly, the chiefs argued that the stool's gift of the land and the townspeople's contribution of 'communal labour' merited both government support for construction and a share of the rents and market tolls to be collected once the market was in operation. When the District Assembly dragged its feet, the Council once again used communal labour, plus materials purchased from the stool's treasury, to add a second storey to the uncompleted market building, then presented it to the District Assembly as a *fait accompli*. In 2002 the chiefs and the District Assembly were negotiating over how to divide operating expenses and market revenues.

CONCLUSION

In the half century since independence, international economic and political pressures, together with Africans' own struggles to build viable self-governing societies in the wake of colonial rule, have brought technological advances, business opportunities and material prosperity to some, but left a great many people behind. Overstretched during the early years of independence and cut back under structural adjustment, public services are very uneven

---

[38] Berry, 'Questions of Ownership'.

[39] During his long sojourn on the stool, the Juabenhene had encouraged local families to choose educated individuals with professional experience who had lived and worked abroad, as successors to their seats on the Traditional Council. By 2002 the Council was filled with enthusiastic supporters of the chief's development initiatives.

in quality and accessibility, as are private supplies of financial and material capital. Africans' history of investing in 'wealth in people', once widely seen as a source of at least modest upward mobility, is now often cited as a victim of concentrated power and hardening inequalities brought on by capitalist accumulation, unregulated markets and the self-seeking behaviour of political elites. Stretched to the limit to put together meagre livelihoods in precarious and impoverished circumstances, many people are unable to provide for their immediate dependants, let alone additional clients and associates.

As people's resources are strained, their declining capacity to help support others reinforces their need for social networks. While recognizing the severe strains placed on family and community networks by years of economic uncertainty and deprivation, some observers suggest that these pressures transform social relationships, rather than simply breaking them down. Social elders who have exhausted their savings or sold off family land may be unable or unwilling to provide for their descendants, leaving young people at a loose end, angry with their elders or driven to deception, illegal trade or violence to try to get ahead. Within the cocoa-farming economies of southern Ghana and Nigeria, some argue that the division of farms among growers' heirs has had a downward levelling effect, pushing farm sizes towards a smaller average for all.[40]

Yet other studies suggest that changing economic and political pressures are reshaping social networks, rather than destroying them. As more people leave rural areas or West Africa altogether in search of a better life, the flow of remittances sent to support relatives or community projects has increased. Some of this money has been invested in children's education, business ventures, family houses, or ceremonies such as weddings, funerals and naming ceremonies that strengthen social bonds.[41]

Researchers have also observed new kinds of social groupings – three-generation matrilateral households, religious groups, or business and professional associations – whose members often compete with one another

---

[40] Agnes Quisumbing, Jonna Espadilla and Kejiro Otsuka, *Land and Schooling: Transferring Wealth Across Generations* (Baltimore, MD: Johns Hopkins University Press, 2004); Takane, *The Cocoa Farmers of Southern Ghana*.

[41] Valentina Mazzucato, Mirjam Kakbi and Lothar Smith, 'Transnational Migration and the Economy of Funerals: Changing Practices in Ghana', *Development and Change* 37.6 (2006), 1047–72; Mirjam Kabki, Valentina Mazzucato and Ernest Appiah, "*Wo benane a ɛyɛ bebree*": The Economic Impact of Remittances of Netherlands-Based Ghanaian Migrants on Rural Ashanti', *Population, Space and Place*, 10.2 (2004), 85–97; K. S. Twum Baah, J. S. Nabila and A. F. Aryee, *Migration Research Study in Ghana* (Accra: Ghana Statistical Service, 1995).

but also pool resources or assist one another in times of need.[42] To the extent that people form groups among equally needy relatives, or fellow artisans and traders, they may reflect or reinforce inequalities of wealth and opportunity, rather than offsetting them.[43] Helping to navigate the pressures of competition when markets are expanding, entrepreneurial social work is equally important when they decline. Entrepreneurs who survive economic and political turbulence do so, in part, by engaging in the social work of sustaining and/or reinventing their relationships with other people.[44]

[42] Tsikata, *Living in the Shadow of the Large Dams*; Amanor, *Land, Labor and Family in Southern Ghana*; Abdou Maliq Simone, *For the City Yet to Come: Changing African Life in Four Cities* (Durham, NC: Duke University Press, 2004). See the chapter by Nyanchoga in this volume.
[43] Meagher, *Identity Economics*; Tsikata, *Living in the Shadow of the Large Dams*.
[44] See the chapters by Austin and Pilossof in this volume.

SEVENTEEN
Professionals and Executives

RORY PILOSSOF

International Studies Group,
University of the Free State, Bloemfontein

Over the course of the twentieth century there have been radical changes to the working lives and employment opportunities of millions of Africans. This is true of waged labour as well as entrepreneurs, self-employed artisans or what might be deemed professionals. The development and growth of professional occupations, such as lawyers, doctors and nurses, have had major impacts on the social and political history of the continent. At the same time, however, these developments have been highly contested and uneven across the continent, and they open interesting questions about middle-class aspirations and how these connect with wider dynamics.[1]

Professionals – those educated, trained and practising in a specific occupation – have always been a minority in the working and economically active populations in Africa, especially considering that most labour in Africa has historically been found in the agricultural, manufacturing and mining sectors. However, educated and professionally trained Africans have had a significant impact on the political shifts on the continent from the nineteenth century to the present. African doctors, lawyers and academics, in particular, were often key protagonists in opposing colonialism. The educated elite were also foundational members of the nationalist and liberation movements that emerged across the continent and, after that, in the governance and politics of the postcolonial era.

This political dimension of African professionals has been well documented. In Egypt, professionals, students and entrepreneurs joined together to protest against British enforced economic reforms in 1919,

---

[1] On middle-income earners and white-collar workers, see the chapter by van den Bersselaar in this volume.

while in Tunisia and Algeria new professionals confronted the pro-settler stance of the French after 1907.[2] In Ghana, lawyers were crucial in the early elite-led nationalist movement. As for Southern Rhodesia (Zimbabwe), the two most prominent nationalists, Robert Mugabe and Joshua Nkomo, were both teachers who had studied outside the country. In South Africa, Nelson Mandela was a trained and practising lawyer. Doctors and physicians had the education and social advantages that enabled them to be 'accepted in elite circles and be taken seriously as political candidates'.[3] For example, Dr Félix Houphouët-Boigny became the first president of Côte d'Ivoire, and Miltion Margai became the first prime minister of Sierra Leone. In southern Africa, influential figures such as Dr Hastings Kamuzu Banda, Samora Machel and Dr Agostinho Neto were all trained physicians turned politicians.

This chapter, however, focuses more on the issues that affected the working lives of professionals in Africa. Professional labour, and the development of such a class, cannot be understood without an overview of educational trends in Africa, the impact of economic context on employment and the effects of global labour migration (internal and external). This chapter is broken down into three sections. The first is a brief history of education across the continent and how this impacted on the growth of professional classes. The second looks at the growth in the number of African professionals after the Second World War and the conditions of work for these groups. The third focuses on the challenges professionals have faced in Africa and explores processes of migration, brain drain and job security.

The term 'professional' is not without complications. In terms of labour, it implies a level of training and education that grants certificates or degrees that allow the individual to undertake a certain profession, such as doctor, nurse, lawyer, accountant. These systems of training and education, and the certificates issued, are largely based on Eurocentric or Western models of attaining professional status. They conform to a modernist interpretation of labour and progress that creates a dichotomy between 'Western and literate' and 'traditional and illiterate'. This process is most observable with the spread of 'modern medicine' across Africa and the conflict with traditional forms of medicine and healthcare. Iliffe has argued, specifically in relation to health professionals, that more ambiguous definitions of professionalism are needed in order to better trace the contradictions and ambivalences of being a professional in Africa, and elsewhere in the developing world for

---

[2]   J. Whidden, 'Colonialism, Overthrow of: North Africa', in *Encyclopaedia of African History*, ed. K. Shillington, vol. I (London: Fitzroy Dearborn, 2005), 268–70.

[3]   A. Patton Jr, *Physicians, Colonial Racism, and Diaspora in West Africa* (Gainesville, FL: University Press of Florida, 1996), 18.

that matter.[4] The problem with many strict definitions of professionalism is that they ignore other processes of apprenticeship or training that may lead to other livelihoods, which could easily be seen as professional occupations. Some of these are specific to certain parts of Africa, some to the developing world in general. In addition, the spread of mobile technology and Internet access has created 'postmodern' forms of professionals, with a range of skills and specialities, who differ from the traditional 'modern' professionals 'who typically were internal experts or employed by an expert-organisation [or the state]',[5] and hence fall beyond the purview of professional labour discussions. For the purposes of this chapter, the standard models of professional training and employment will remain the focus, but this observation highlights that other realities are possible, as are other constructions of who or what a professional is.

EDUCATION AND GROWTH OF THE PROFESSIONAL CLASSES

The education of colonial subjects in Africa was extremely limited, both in scale and substance. Colonial budgets sought to limit social expenditure in the colonies and extract as much profit as possible. Across the continent, profits were exported to the metropole, while the colonial administrations complained that there was little or no money for social infrastructure. For example, in Northern Rhodesia (Zambia), the copper mines were producing profits in excess of £4 million a year in the 1930s, yet barely 10 per cent of this remained in the colony.[6] The African population did not have one single secondary school, as the authorities claimed that they were too poor to establish and run one.[7] In richer colonies such as Northern Rhodesia, less than one in ten children were in school, while in poorer colonies, such as Nyasaland (Malawi), the proportion, according to Basil Davidson, could be less than one in a hundred.[8] Africa had a handful of elite tertiary institutions and universities. In Morocco, the University of al-Qarawiyyin traces its heritage back to the al-Qarawiyyin mosque and the linked madrasa founded

---

[4]   J. Iliffe, *East African Doctors: A History of the Modern Medical Profession* (Cambridge: Cambridge University Press, 1998), 3–4.

[5]   M. Kakihara and C. Sørensen, '"Post-Modern" Professionals' Work and Mobile Technology', paper presented to the Department of Information Systems, London School of Economics and Political Science, 8 October 2002, 2.

[6]   On mining, see the chapter by Brown in this volume.

[7]   B. Davidson, *Modern Africa: A Social and Political History* (Harlow: Longman, 1994).

[8]   *Ibid.*, 87–8.

by Fatima al-Fihri in 859, but it only became a university in 1965. Fourah Bay College in Sierra Leone, founded as an Anglican missionary school by the Church Missionary Society, began to offer degrees in the 1920s, serving all of the British West African colonies. In Egypt, Cairo University was established in 1908, and the independent American University of Cairo opened in 1919. The University of Algiers was established in 1909. After the Second World War, the now famous universities of Ibadan and Dakar were opened.[9] However, these institutions were very limited in capacity and served very small African elites.

By the 1960s only 43 per cent of children were enrolled in school, while only 3 per cent were enrolled in secondary school and less than 0.2 per cent in universities.[10] Few children went to school, and most stayed too briefly to learn anything useful. These education levels were not enough to create professional classes of Africans who could work alongside colonial administrators and professionals, even if what was being taught to Africans was not itself limiting and curtailed. What Africans were taught in schools indicated what they were meant to achieve by the colonial authorities. The Patriarch of Lisbon, Cardinal Cerejeira, said in 1960 that 'we want to teach the natives to write, to read, and to count, but not to make them learned men'.[11] Similar statements can be found from colonial administrators and district commissioners across Africa, from South Africa to Senegal.

Ultimately, the colonial authorities were wary of creating an educated African elite who, if politicized, would have the capacity to incite the African masses to oppose settler rule. British colonial administrations, in particular, were often vehemently opposed to the creation of an African middle class, educated to be 'civilized' and alienated from their 'tribal' roots, because they feared that such a group would, eventually, threaten white colonial authority and control. As Michael West has commented, 'colonialists were especially fearful that a politicized black elite, its aspirations frustrated by racial barriers, would seek to mobilize the African masses against settler rule'.[12] This policy had huge ramifications on the education of Africans and the development of skilled workers and trained professionals in British colonies. French and Portuguese colonial administrations differed slightly because of the respective 'assimilationist' projects that were in place. The purpose of assimilation

[9] F. Cooper, *Africa since 1940* (Cambridge: Cambridge University Press, 2002), 111.
[10] The World Bank, *Can Africa Claim the 21st Century?* (Washington, DC: World Bank, 2000), 106.
[11] Davidson, *Modern Africa*, 185.
[12] M. West, *The Rise of an African Middle Class: Colonial Zimbabwe 1898–1965* (Bloomington, IN: Indiana University Press, 2002), 13.

was to turn African natives into civilized 'French' or 'Portuguese' men and women by educating them in the language and culture of the colonialists and hence helping them advance from their 'tribal' state to become citizens or equals.[13] A number of African students studied in Portuguese and French universities in Europe, under government scholarships. However, the process of 'assimilation', and the theory or rationale behind it, was contested and faced much resistance from populations, elite or otherwise, in African colonies. The rigid conditions set for assimilation and citizenship meant that it was impossible for most African subjects to become 'civilized' citizens, especially because the imperial powers did not provide the means to educate their colonized subjects.

Development and training was uneven, even in the places where it did happen. In Kenya, Nigeria, Tanzania, Botswana and Nyasaland, local alternatives and opportunities were provided to train and develop nurses and doctors.[14] However, in settler colonies such as South Africa, the opposition 'of a very powerful rival interest group in the form of a white settler medical profession obstructed proposals for blacks even to train in these roles'.[15] The first medical training scheme for Africans was only established in 1937 at Fort Hare, but recruitment was so poor that it was shut down in 1943.[16] By the late 1940s the universities such as Cape Town and Witwatersrand provided for black students, but 'the institutional context for this advance remained that of an overwhelmingly white university'.[17] Soon, the apartheid state developed separate systems of medical training and employment, where doctors and caregivers of particular ethnic groups were made to serve their own people in their own locations. The result was limited training, exposure and opportunities for black doctors, as well as other professionals.

Across the continent, training and education were expensive and prolonged processes. In the case of South African doctors, Digby has observed that, typically:

> [A]n individual would train as a teacher, work for several years and then, having earned some funding for the next career stage, train abroad to become

---

13 M. Lambert, 'From Citizenship to *Négritude*: "Making A Difference" in Elite Ideologies of Colonized Francophone West Africa', *Comparative Studies in Society and History*, 35.2 (1993), 239–62.

14 A. Beck, *Medicine, Tradition and Development in Kenya and Tanzania, 1920–1970* (Waltham, MA: Crossroads Press, 1981).

15 A. Digby, 'Early Black Doctors in South Africa', *Journal of African History*, 46.3 (2005), 433.

16 *Ibid.*, 433.

17 *Ibid.*, 435.

a doctor. Later, the availability of training within South Africa widened the social intake, so that students from black working-class backgrounds entered medicine for the first time. Increasing numbers of medical bursaries became available but this involved official intervention to constrain later profitable careers in private practice by imposing periods of public service.[18]

In settler colonies, discriminatory legislation meant that the salary differentials between black and white doctors were significant. In South Africa in the 1950s, 'Coloured and Indian doctors earned 70–81 per cent, and African doctors 65–76 per cent of their white counterparts, as well as suffering from disadvantageous conditions of service'.[19] As a result, salaried positions became unappealing and other avenues of income, such as private practice, were more popular.

After the first wave of independence, there was a massive drive to expand education delivery across much of the continent. While the universal ideals were never met, the gains made after 1960 were impressive. Primary school enrolment grew from 43 per cent in 1960 to 77 per cent in 1997. Over the same period, secondary school enrolment rose from 3 per cent to 26 per cent, and tertiary enrolment from 0.2 per cent to 3.9 per cent. Education and public services increased, and Africans were given opportunities to enter professions to which access had previously been denied or severely restricted.

There was a massive growth in university teaching and student numbers. The case of Cameroon is illustrative here. In 1960 the University of Yaoundé was established and remained the only university in Cameroon until 1993. The initial student population of 213 in 1961 increased to over 10,000 in 1981 and to almost 45,000 in 1991. The number of teaching staff rose from 21, to 544, to 1,518 at the corresponding dates. According to Tafah Edokat:

> Initially, about 60 per cent of the teaching staff was made up of foreigners, mostly from the Western developed countries. This tendency was maintained up to the mid 1970s when the ratio of Cameroonian staff to the total teaching staff increased steadily until 1993 where almost all the teaching staff were made up of Cameroonians.[20]

By the 1960s 'education had become the surest means for individual upward mobility. For the newly independent African states, it became an unavoidable

---

[18] Ibid., 436.

[19] Ibid., 441.

[20] T. Edokat, 'Effects of Brain Drain on Higher Education in Cameroon', paper presented to the Regional Conference on Brain Drain and Capacity Building in Africa, Addis Ababa, 22–24 February 2000, 2.

instrument for national socio-economic development.'[21] Also, these arenas were important spaces of nation building, national identity construction and history making, highly prized and promoted by the new nationalist leadership. In turn, the numbers of doctors, nurses, engineers and other professional classes also expanded; many trained locally, but many were also offered study assistance and bursaries in the United States, Europe, Russia and other socialist countries. This growth started from dismally low numbers. In 1955 Uganda had 79 Asian, nine African and four European private doctors. At independence in 1961 Tanzania only had 12 African doctors. Kenya had roughly 300 private medical practitioners in 1961, with two-thirds being Asian. With increases in training and education, Kenya, Uganda and Tanzania went from producing twenty certified doctors a year in the 1950s to 200 a year by the 1970s.[22] Law as a profession was vigorously discouraged by the colonial state because of the fear that those trained would become actively involved in opposition politics. Botswana had only one Motswana lawyer in the country at independence in 1966, and the second only qualified in 1975.[23] Zambia had no lawyers when independence was granted in 1964.[24] In 1964 'Zambia had a mere one hundred university graduates, of whom only two were medical doctors and one [was] an engineer; the rest were graduates in the field of education.'[25] In 1959 there were only 23 people with university degrees in Nyasaland.[26] By 1962, in Southern Rhodesia, of an African population of nearly four million, only 18,000 had been to primary school. The number of Africans with college degrees increased from six in 1948 to forty-five in 1954. By the end of the decade, nearly 700 Africans were in higher education institutions, locally and abroad. Even still, in 1965 there were only 30 black medical doctors in the country and even fewer lawyers.[27]

---

[21] N. Assié-Lumumba, *Higher Education in Africa: Crises, Reforms and Transformations* (Dakar: CODESRIA, 2006), 44.

[22] Iliffe, *East African Doctors*, 123, 127.

[23] R. Dale, *Botswana's Search for Autonomy in Southern Africa* (Westport, CT: Greenwood Press, 1995), 66.

[24] N. A. Kahn-Fogel, 'The Troubling Shortage of African Lawyers: Examination of a Continental Crisis Using Zambia as a Case Study', *University of Pennsylvania Journal of International Law*, 33.3 (2012), 723; M. Ndulo, 'Legal Education in Africa in the Era of Globalization and Structural Adjustment', *Penn State International Law Review*, 20.3 (2002), 487.

[25] Ndulo, 'Legal Education in Africa', 489.

[26] S. O. Manteaw, 'Legal Education in Africa: What Type of Lawyer Does Africa Need?', *McGeorge Law Review*, 39 (2008), 914.

[27] West, *The Rise of an African Middle Class*, 66.

In West and North Africa, the numbers of professionals were higher than in southern Africa, but still comparatively low in terms of the total population.[28]

Those who did qualify and practise, however, could be considered the African elite, due to their education, their enhanced earning capacity and the positions of authority they occupied in African social and political settings.[29] In their working lives, nevertheless, they faced a number of challenges after the end of colonial rule. Working conditions in most public settings were hard, as positions were poorly paid, institutions were often understaffed, there was little professional support and infrastructure remained rudimentary. There was a desperate need to increase the numbers of professionals to cater to the new circumstances of independence. However, at the same time, only limited opportunities for promotion existed in many professions, such as law or engineering, as the higher echelons of employment were still managed by expatriates or beneficiaries of previous regimes. Amos Odenyo has observed this in relation to lawyers in Kenya in the 1970s.[30]

Ethnic and racial divisions also inhibited professional development. State patronage often favoured particular ethnic groups after independence, and this resulted in many trained professionals being unable to find employment because of their perceived difference. In Kenya there was a 'Kikuyunization' of the state civil service, while in places such as Zimbabwe and elsewhere a strong tendency prevailed to favour those of the dominant ethnic group. While this affected local populations, it also adversely affected Africans who had moved to other parts of the continent because of poverty, conflict, forced removals, ethnic tensions or changing political realities.[31]

However, one of the biggest dilemmas faced by this new group of professionals was the ambiguity between politics and employment. Massive tensions existed between pursuing a professional career and serving the

[28] Patton, *Physicians, Colonial Racism, and Diaspora in West Africa*; A. Nwauwa, *Imperialism, Academe, and Nationalism: Britain and University Education for Africans, 1986–1960* (London: Frank Cass, 1997).

[29] L. Kuper, *An African Bourgeoisie: Race, Class and Politics in South Africa* (New Haven, CT: Yale University Press, 1965); M. Lukhero, 'The Social Characteristics of an Emergent Elite in Harare', in *The New Elites of Tropical Africa*, ed. C. Lloyd (London: Oxford University Press, 1966), 126–38; C. Kileff, 'Black Suburbanites: An African Elite in Salisbury, Rhodesia', in *Urban Man in Southern Africa*, ed. C. Kileff and C. Wade (Gwelo: Mambo Press, 1975), 81–97.

[30] A. Odenyo, 'An Assessment of the African Brain Drain, with Special Reference to the Kenyan Mid-Career Professionals', *Issue: A Journal of Opinion*, 9.4 (1979), 45.

[31] J. Valenzuela, 'Latin American Professionals in Africa: A New Direction to the Flow of Highly Skilled Personnel', *West African Journal of Sociology and Political Science*, 2.1–2 (1977), 1–21.

needs of the nationalist movements or the independent state. As Digby has noted of black doctors in South Africa, pressures existed 'between professional altruism and entrepreneurialism in pursuing a medical career, as well as that between self-interest and selflessness in attempting to balance the requirements of a medical practice against those involved in political leadership'.[32] Doctors and other professionals often faced questions about what they could do for the country or for processes of liberation. African professionalism involved ambiguity in that, as Iliffe has suggested, it embraced 'specialist knowledge, altruistic service, thirst for power and blatant self-interest', as well as an 'ambivalent symbiosis' with a state heavily involved in professional regulation.[33] Iliffe was able to show just how the symbiotic relationship between doctors and the state existed. During the colonial era, doctors relied on the state for physical and professional protection, as hostile domestic populations often turned their anger and resentment on those Africans who seemed to be complicit with the state. At the same time, the colonial state 'was both their enemy, blocking their aspirations, and their protector against latent hostility of the unsophisticated'.[34] After independence, trained professionals still relied on the regulatory protection of the state, but were also often just as frustrated by those measures that curtailed freedoms and limited opportunities. In addition, there was the added pressure that those who had benefited from training and education should use that education for the good of the nation and other forms of national development, rather than self-interest and personal gain.

Many gave up political careers for professional ones, but often at a personal and social cost. As West has observed:

> Educated blacks, especially the younger university-trained men, became the targets of increasingly sharp criticism, castigated for selfish behavior and an abdication of leadership responsibility. The critics included older members of the elite more firmly grounded in the self-improvement tradition and possessed of a greater sense of mission ... One critic lamented that although there were 'men who have attained a high standard of education ... they have done nothing to uplift their people,' choosing instead 'to content themselves with attaching the initials "B.A." after their signatures only and no more.'[35]

There was also a very uneven spread of new black professionals, who were mostly based in urban areas. Early doctors in South Africa mostly

---

[32] Digby, 'Early Black Doctors', 427.

[33] Iliffe, *East African Doctors*, 3.

[34] *Ibid.*, 91; see also West, *The Rise of an African Middle Class*, 2.

[35] West, *The Rise of an African Middle Class*, 66.

concentrated in Cape Town, Johannesburg and Durban. Indeed, by the 1960s four out of five doctors were urban based, because those with the ability to afford healthcare were in urban areas, and relatively good standards of living could be achieved through private practice.[36] Iliffe has observed similar trends in East Africa.[37] As a result, rural areas were often even more under-represented by African professionals, which negatively impacted on healthcare and service delivery in these areas.

The rapid growth of education systems and opportunities for employment resulted in a dramatic rise in the number of professionals in and from the continent. The new economic and social realities of these educated classes created new dynamics within many African countries, which often manifest as class division.

MIDDLE-CLASS ASPIRATIONS

The massive expansion of secondary and university education in Africa in the 1950s and 1960s produced a substantial class of educated people who craved more knowledge and imagined better working futures for themselves.[38] However, deteriorating political stability, harsh working conditions and limited employment opportunities resulted in trained Africans leaving the continent in large numbers. Many of those who benefited in the 1960s and 1970s were often from modest backgrounds. As the twentieth century progressed and the economic fortunes of nations and the middle classes fell, 'education of sufficient quality to lead to professional opportunities has increasingly become a privilege for children of those already in such a position'.[39] The middle class and the elite entrenched themselves and have been able to educate their children and beneficiaries. The result is a large and growing gap between the haves and the have-nots in many parts of Africa.[40]

This gap is nothing new, but rather a current manifestation of historical fault lines between educated or middle-class Africans and others. Early African intellectuals and activists often talked about acquiring the franchise for 'civilized men', relegating their uneducated or 'uncivilized' compatriots to

---

[36]   Digby, 'Early Black Doctors', 430.

[37]   Iliffe, *East African Doctors*, 111.

[38]   C. Achebe, *The Education of a British-Protected Child: Essays* (London: Knopf, 2009); W. Soyinka, *Aké: The Years of Childhood* (London: Rex Collings, 1981); Ngugi Wa Thiong'o, *Dreams in a Time of War: A Childhood Memoir* (London: Pantheon, 2010).

[39]   Cooper, *Africa since 1940*, 115.

[40]   H. Melber, 'Africa and the Middle Class(es)', *Africa Spectrum*, 48.3 (2013), 111–20.

subjects and not citizens. These tensions were often clouded over during the struggles for national liberation, but, as Cooper has stressed, the ambiguities of liberation and the nature of the independent state were deeply contested, and there were numerous divisions between nationalist, educated elites and other protagonists.[41]

The space between the educated or middle class and the poor and uneducated has been observed recently by Afrobarometer studies. In 2013 an Afrobarometer survey reported that:

> [M]iddle class people displayed a pervasive suspicion that their fellow citizens are incapable of casting a responsible vote. The evidence they put forward repeatedly shows that, as education rises, individuals are more likely to agree that 'only those who are sufficiently well educated should be allowed to choose our leaders' and to disagree that 'all people should be permitted to vote, even if they do not fully understand all the issues in an election'.[42]

Other studies have also suggested that the middle classes are much more apathetic towards voting, especially in authoritarian electoral regimes such as Zimbabwe or Angola.[43]

The 2013 *World Migration Report* by the International Organization for Migration (IOM) indicated that the middle class and aspirants are also those most likely to leave Africa.[44] Increased expectations and domestic failures or limitations often result in such people leaving to look for better alternatives, because reality does not match their aspirations. In addition, in the case of trained professionals, they have the skills and education to find employment in more stable countries. The report shows that African emigration rates to the countries of the Organisation for Economic Co-operation and Development are strongly related to GDP per capita (and household wealth), 'as these migrants are more likely to have the resources to pay for transport to and resettlement expenses in the OECD countries, and are more likely to have the education and other skills required to find jobs there'.[45] The report also shows

---

[41] F. Cooper, 'Possibility and Constraint: African Independence in Historical Perspective', *Journal of African History*, 49.2 (2008), 167–96.

[42] M. Bratton, 'Voting and Democratic Citizenship in Africa: Where Next?', in *Voting and Democratic Citizenship in Africa*, ed. M. Bratton (Boulder, CO: Lynne Rienner, 2013), 281.

[43] K. Croke, G. Grossman, H. Larreguy and J. Marshall, 'Deliberate Disengagement: How Education Decreases Political Participation in Electoral Authoritarian Regimes', Afrobarometer Working Paper 156, 2015.

[44] On labour migration, see the chapter by Pérez Niño in this volume.

[45] C. Mungai, 'Africans Get Richer, But Only So They Can Afford to Move to the West – It's a Very Complicated Story', *Mail and Guardian Africa*, 23 April 2015, https://goo.gl/4M8Ab8 (accessed 10 August 2017).

that high emigration rates from relatively peaceful countries with healthy economic prospects reveal a certain logic. Families who have a member who emigrates are able to hedge their bets and diversify risk by securing a revenue stream that is protected from local political and economic shocks.

However, the scope for middle-class expansion in Africa is still bleak. From 1990 to 2010 the Global South's share of the world's middle-class population grew from 26 to 58 per cent. The United Nations Development Programme (UNDP) estimates that, by 2030, 80 per cent of the world's middle class will be residing in the South.[46] Two-thirds of this growth will be in Asia, one-tenth in Central and South America and a mere 2 per cent in sub-Saharan Africa. This austere outlook for Africa's future reminds us that the current resource boom impacting much of the continent is not generating sustainable growth or conditions favourable to entrenching professionals within the continent.

The aspirations of the educated middle classes not only affected the political fortunes of these groups. Their education gave them the opportunity to explore employment prospects outside Africa. By the 1970s, social, political and economic changes had dampened much of the initial optimism about liberation on the continent. As the economic downturn hit, living standards dropped and political repression increased. Professionals, new and old, responded to these developments largely by leaving. A huge number of professionals took the decision to emigrate in the last quarter of the twentieth century, in what is widely termed the 'brain drain'.

THE BRAIN DRAIN

During the 1970s and 1980s many African countries 'experienced periods of economic and political crises and conflicts leading to an exodus of emigrants out of the continent, mostly professionals'.[47] By 1982, 22 African countries had military rulers. Three years later the continent had experienced 60 military coups. These conflicts often resulted in the repression of human rights and academic freedom. The lack of political protections and safeguards made many professionals question remaining in Africa.[48] Besides

---

[46] United Nations Development Programme, *The Rise of the South: Human Progress in a Diverse World. Human Development Report 2013* (New York: UNDP, 2013), 14.

[47] M. Kiggundu and B. Oni, *An Analysis of the Market for Skilled African Development Management Professionals: Towards Strategies for Skills Retention and Utilization in Sub-Saharan Africa* (African Capacity Building Foundation, 2004), 11.

[48] See the chapter by Scully and Jawad in this volume.

an increasing number of war and conflict zones, economic downturn and mismanagement also impacted on job security and retention. Already poor infrastructures were put under more stress, and the weak institutional capacity meant that working conditions became unmanageable and depressing. Due to failing economic fortunes, a number of African countries began to adopt structural adjustment programmes in the 1970s and 1980s that curtailed public spending. This limited employment opportunities even further, which, in turn, resulted in many skilled professionals seeking work elsewhere in the world.

Such developments came at a time when many parts of Europe and the United States were actively encouraging skilled migrants to immigrate to fill gaps in their own professional development. Nurses and doctors were targeted specifically. As Elizabeth Hull has observed, 'following the worldwide expansion of health services since the 1960s, the employment of internationally trained nurses has been an increasingly important strategy to meet growing demands'.[49] Migration patterns are obviously affected by broader economic and political trends, particularly as healthcare industries became more and more driven by 'market' ideology in the West post-1960.[50]

The result was a massive exodus of a wide range of skilled and trained professionals from the continent. While exact data is hard to come by, some estimates and calculations made by international organizations make depressing reading. According to the IOM and the United Nations Economic Commission for Africa (UNECA), from 1960 to 1975 over 27,000 highly qualified Africans emigrated to the West. This number increased to c. 40,000 from 1975 to 1984, and then leapt to c. 80,000 from 1984 to 1987. The IOM estimated that this represented over 30 per cent of the entire highly skilled African human capital. From 1990 to 2000 roughly 20,000 skilled people left the continent every year.[51]

The World Bank reported that, between 2000 and 2004, over 70,000 qualified African experts and scholars left their homes to work aboard every year, most often in the West (North America, Europe or in the United Nations system). The World Bank also noted that, in 2004, there were more African engineers working in the United States than in the whole of Africa.[52]

---

[49] E. Hull, 'International Migration, "Domestic Struggles" and Status Aspiration among Nurses in South Africa', *Journal of Southern African Studies*, 36.4 (2010), 857.

[50] *Ibid.*, 859.

[51] United Nations Economic Commission for Africa, 'Aide Memoire', Regional Conference on Brain Drain and Capacity Building in Africa, Addis Ababa, Ethiopia, 22–24 February 2000.

[52] Kiggundu and Oni, *An Analysis of the Market*, 15

The figures for doctors are just as shocking. Zambia, at one time, had 1,600 medical doctors. By the early 2000s there were barely 400 in practice.[53] More than 21,000 Nigerian doctors worked in the USA just after the turn of the millennium. Over 60 per cent of Ghanaian doctors who trained in Ghana had left by 2000.[54] In 2000 the South African Corporate Services estimated that the shortage of managerial and technical staff was between 350,000 and 500,000 in South Africa, due both to the poor levels of education and the effects of brain drain dynamics.[55]

These numbers make discouraging reading and have had numerous negative impacts on the countries and institutions that have lost such professionals. Not only has the cost of training often been borne by the host country, but the capacity to continue training has often deteriorated, resulting in more poorly trained graduates. This has affected healthcare training facilities as well as academic spheres. Some have estimated that the loss to Africa can be measured in the billions. South Africa lost US$7 billion in human capital between 1997 and 2002 due to the loss of professionals who emigrated to work abroad. It was also estimated in 2002 that it cost Africa over US$4 billion a year to fill the capacity gaps that exist by hiring external consultants.[56]

In practical terms, such forces have resulted in massive understaffing problems and limited capacity. Stella Anyangwe and Chipayeni Mtonga have outlined the critical shortages of healthcare professionals in Africa:

> In the 1980s, one doctor catered for 10,800 persons in sub-Saharan Africa, compared to 1 for 1,400 in all developing countries combined, and 1 for 300 in industrialized countries. In the same period, one nurse catered for 2,100 persons in Africa, compared to 1 for 1,700 persons in all developing countries combined, and 1 for 170 in industrialized countries. Conversely, sub-Saharan Africa, with about 11% of the world's population bears over 24% of the global disease burden, is home to only 3% of the global health workforce, and spends less than 1% of the world's financial resources on health. In most developing countries, the health workforce is concentrated in the major towns and cities, while rural areas can only boast of about 23% and 38% of the country's doctors and nurses respectively.[57]

---

[53] *Ibid.*

[54] S. Sako, 'Brain Drain and Africa's Development: A Reflection', *African Issues*, 30.1 (2002), 25–30.

[55] Kiggundu and Oni, *An Analysis of the Market*, 15.

[56] Sako, 'Brain Drain and Africa's Development', 25.

[57] S. Anyangwe and C. Mtonga, 'Inequities in the Global Health Workforce: The Greatest Impediment to Health in Sub-Saharan Africa', *International Journal of Environment Research and Public Health*, 4.2 (2007), 93.

As in the late colonial and early independent era, the rural–urban distribution of educated professionals remains an issue of concern. The most common factors influencing the geographical distribution of health workers, which push such professionals out of the rural areas in Africa, include limited opportunities, insecure pay, few incentives to work, poor amenities and few opportunities for promotion. The low salaries of health workers in sub-Saharan Africa mean that professionals often augment their income 'through unauthorized private practice, or resort to predatory behaviour such as extracting under-the-counter payments from patients, or misappropriating drugs or other supplies'. Such opportunities are limited in rural settings. In Tanzania, Dar es Salaam had nearly thirty times as many medical practitioners and specialists as any of the rural districts in 2007.[58] Scheffler et al. forecast in 2009 that, by 2015, thirty-one countries in Africa would 'experience needs-based shortages of doctors, nurses, and midwives, totalling approximately 800,000 health professionals [and that] the additional annual wage bill required to eliminate the shortage [would be] about $2.6 billion'.[59]

It must be noted that the 'brain drain' and movement of trained professionals is not just a South to North phenomenon but also encompasses South to South and regional migration, with the dominant economies on the continent (South Africa and Nigeria, for example) attracting a great deal of these forms of labour. Since Zimbabwe's economic decline started in earnest in the late 1990s, increasing numbers of teachers, nurses and doctors have migrated to South Africa for work.

Yet some have argued that the emigration of professionals has not been totally negative. While many African countries are concerned by the effects of the 'brain drain', any output losses from the migration of skilled workers may be compensated by remittances from those working abroad. In 2010 the African diaspora remitted US$51 billion. In the same year, official development assistance amounted to US$43 billion. The leading African recipients of remittances as a percentage of GDP were Lesotho (26.5 per cent), Cape Verde (13.6 per cent), Morocco (9.7 per cent) and Uganda (8.5 per cent).[60] Zimbabwean emigrants in South Africa remitted almost

[58] *Ibid.*, 95.

[59] R. Scheffler, C. Mahoney, B. Fulton, M. Dal Poz and A. Preker, 'Estimates of Health Care Professional Shortages in Sub-Saharan Africa by 2015', *Health Affairs*, 28.5 (2009), 849–62.

[60] D. Ratha, 'Workers' Remittances: An Important and Stable Source of External Development Finance', in *Global Development Finance: Striving for Stability in Development Finance* (Washington, DC: World Bank, 2003), 159.

ZAR7 billion (US$58 million) in 2012.[61] However, it is questionable whether the returns in remittances can or could make up for the loss in human capital and expertise that the continent has witnessed over the last half-century. Despite a number of measures put in place by organizations such as the IOM and individual countries, the number of emigrants to the West and other parts of the developing and developed world does not seem to be diminishing. In part, this is due to the aspirations and hopes of those who made it into the middle class after the end of colonial rule.

CONCLUSION

Becoming and being a professional, whether a teacher or a nurse or a lawyer, has been a tough and challenging process for many Africans on the continent. Most who tried were denied opportunities before independence through lack of education, lack of funds and other deliberate obstacles placed in their way by the colonial state. Once they were admitted, however, their ambition and position had to negotiate a whole set of problematic relationships with politics, the state and other Africans who were not as fortunate as them. Education and the growth of the professional classes expanded massively with the end of colonialism. However, working conditions remained hard, with low pay for many waged professionals, while independent professionals often struggled to establish businesses, clients and secure income in economically and politically unsettled contexts. In addition, both public and private professionals had to contend with poor infrastructure and the expectations of populations and politicians. Professionals once again found themselves in complex negotiations with the new nationalist and majority-elected governments and had to make hard choices about pursuing a career or serving the country. As the economic fortunes of Africa collapsed in the 1970s and 1980s, large numbers of trained Africans left the continent seeking opportunities in the West and other parts of the globe. While strategies have been put in place to try and attract professionals back to Africa, because of massive shortfalls in the numbers of doctors, nurses, teachers, engineers and the like, there are still debilitating levels of emigration of human capital and skilled professionals from the continent. Working conditions remain tough, due to a range of circumstances, while investment in infrastructure, education and reforms continue to be a low priority.

[61]   S. Truen and S. Chisadza, *The South Africa-SADC Remittance Channel* (Pretoria: DNA Economics, 2012), 52.

The situation remains bleak and, as has been illustrated, the middle classes and those who have professional skills remain ambivalent about staying in Africa. Those of wealthy backgrounds or with education are most likely to leave and emigrate, regionally or internationally. Increased expectations and domestic failures mean that reality does not match their aspirations and, in the case of trained professionals, they have the skills and education to find employment in better-off countries. While the endeavour and aptitude of those who have fought for their education and have moved to make better lives for themselves must be applauded, as Cooper has illustrated there is a huge difference in the make-up of those becoming professionals in Africa today. Education of sufficient quantity and quality to result in professional qualification 'has increasingly become a privilege for children of those already in such a position'.[62] The poor and uneducated have few avenues of escape, an escape that was promised and hoped for as liberation spread across the continent. The bleak economic outlook for the continent, aside from the boom in extraction industries, offers little hope of this situation changing in the twenty-first century.

[62] Cooper, *Africa since 1940*, 115.

PART VI

THE STATE, UNIONS AND WELFARE

EIGHTEEN
Labour and the State

AKUA O. BRITWUM

Department of Labour and Human Resource Studies,
University of Cape Coast

LEYLA DAKHLI

French Centre for National Research,
Marc Bloch Centre, Berlin

The relationship between labour and the state in Africa does not differ greatly from what it is in other parts of the world. It is regulated through institutions and legislation and conditioned by production systems. To be able to trace the history of the changing relations between state and labour, one has to keep in mind not only the diverse capitalist modes of production that are prevalent on the continent, but also the different forms of states, be they colonial or national. The other key factor for the understanding of these labour–state relations are the scales on which they take place. Recent interpretations of the state insist on the fallacy of the view that takes 'the state' as a monolithic entity. The state, in the different places where labour operates, makes itself visible through a large array of institutions, norms and policies, practices and gestures. In the same way, labour cannot be defined simply; it is determined by the structure of the existing economy and the political conditions, as well as by the production system. These systems determine policies, such as migration procedures and access to education and training, which shape the emerging labour arrangements.[1]

The present legislative and institutional architecture regulating labour relations in Africa has its roots in the different production modes that were shaped in particular historical contexts. Although various forms of

---

[1] See the chapters by Pérez Niño and Pilossof in this volume.

pre-capitalist statehoods for organizing production existed in Africa before European contact, the colonial state played a significant role in determining the present forms of work and the kinds of labour that operate in large parts of Africa.[2] The colonial experience is among the major factors of change at the continental scale. Under colonial rule and long after, labour legislation was used as a tool to rein in militancy among the African workforce.

This chapter explores the emergence and operation of state institutions and legislation regulating labour relations in Africa. It starts with the emergence of labour institutions in Africa but does not deal with forced and indentured labour, which is discussed in other chapters of this volume. This chapter outlines the institutional framework that states produced to mediate the relations between labour and capital, and tries to show the diversity as well as the similarities in the experiences that shaped the production modes in different parts of the continent. In addition, it outlines the specific factors dictating the evolution of institutions and legislation set up by the various African states. It focuses specifically on the emergence of labour laws as well as trade unions in Africa and on the interconnectedness between legislation and the various forms of labour. This chapter relies on the existing literature on African labour history as well as on accounts of labour legislation and industrial relations institutions. The authors have attempted to paint a picture of the different situations on the continent, giving significant examples from the different states and regions under discussion. They are conscious of the limits of this appproach.

The history of state and labour relation is examined in four chronological phases. The first section examines the founding legislation, mainly under colonial rule, that shaped the African labour market. It describes the laws that compelled Africans to work and those that dictated where they could find waged employment. These directives included the control of mobility, which was very important in giving shape to the African labour market. The second and third sections account for the development of trade unions on the continent. These sections make a distinction between the colonial period and the post-independence era. The last section looks at the so-called adjustment period, noting the common difficulty for both labour and enacted laws of maintaining resistance to the erosion of working people's rights under neoliberalism.

---

[2]   S. H. Hymer, 'Economic Forms in Pre-Colonial Ghana', *Journal of Economic History*, 30.1 (1970), 33–50; R. Roberts, 'Peculiarities of African Labour and Working-Class History', *Labour/Le Travail*, 8.9 (1982), 317–33.

THE COLONIAL FOUNDATIONS OF LABOUR LEGISLATION IN AFRICA

Some general legislation has had a bearing on the African labour market. As observed by Ahmed, Ahmad and Idris, labour relations are governed by both direct and indirect regulations, including national constitutions, direct labour laws and legislation on the mobility of persons.[3] While industrialized western Europe and North America laid out their labour market institutions in the second half of the nineteenth century, detailing labour codes, trade union operations and equity legislation, developing nations in Africa had to build on a pattern that was largely defined through the lens of the laws and traditions of their colonial overlords.[4] The development of institutions regulating labour and their supporting legislation were largely shaped by the diversity in the political economic contexts of African colonial experiences.[5]

The origins of legislation notwithstanding, there are variations in legislative frameworks across the continent. The literature shows some differences in labour market structures, as well as in their corresponding labour-regulating institutions.[6] The significant variation, according to Wood, arises out of how the colonial legacy impacts the scale and scope of subsequent industrialization and the strength of trade unions that emerge.[7] The colonial experiences can be considered one of the major factors of change at the scale of the continent. The nature of the labour force itself and the subsequent labour market segmentation can also be considered a key factor for these variations.[8] Whatever the emerging forms, the foundations

---

[3]   A. B. Ahmed, A. A. Ahmad and N. M. Idris, 'Emerging Trends in Labour Law and Industrial Relations in Nigeria', *International Journal of Humanities and Social Science*, 4.11 (2014), 29–44.

[4]   G. Betcherman, *Labor Market Institutions: A Review of the Literature* (Washington, DC: World Bank, 2013).

[5]   See, for example, G. Wood, 'Employment Relations in South Africa and Mozambique', in *Research Handbook of Comparative Employment Relations*, ed. M. Barry and A. Wilkinson (Cheltenham: Edward Elgar, 2011), 303–21; C. Phelan, 'West African Trade Unionism Past and Present', in *Trade Unions in West Africa: Historical and Contemporary Perspectives*, ed. C. Phelan (Oxford: Peter Lang, 2011), 1–22; D. Perfect, 'Trade Unionism in The Gambia, 1929–2010', in *Trade Unions in West Africa: Historical and Contemporary Perspectives*, ed. C. Phelan (Oxford: Peter Lang, 2011), 99–128.

[6]   W. Ananaba, *The Trade Union Movement in Africa: Promise and Performance* (New York: St Martin's Press, 1979).

[7]   Wood, 'Employment Relations'.

[8]   A. Drew, 'Bolshevizing Communist Parties: The Algerian and South African Experiences', *International Review of Social History*, 48.2 (2003), 167–202.

of African industrial relations architecture were laid during colonial rule in response to particular needs. The type of European settlement in the colonies and the country of origin of the colonizers were important factors that caused variations in the forms of industrial regimes that emerged. In tracing labour migration in the nineteenth century from Europe across the Atlantic to the rest of the world, Bosma makes a few observations that help to explain the racially segmented labour market in colonial Africa.[9] First, one has to distinguish between 'white settler colonies versus tropical exploitation colonies where white migrants were only sojourners'. His argument is based on what he terms the 'hierarchy of human races [in which] ... black labour was enslaved, Asian labour indentured, whereas the apex was firmly held by the free white well-educated northern European'. This formed the basis not only for dividing colonies between 'the domains of white rule and the domains where whites lived in freedom' but, in addition, it helps to understand the 'ensuing hierarchy of labour, in which white is on top and other labour markets are segmented, but always with Europeans in control'.[10]

Within this general frame, one has to keep in mind differences between the national colonizing regimes. Besides the main Anglophone/Francophone divide, the small-scale Portuguese experience (and the even smaller Belgian and Italian experiences in Angola, Guinea Bissau, Mozambique, the Congo, Burundi, Rwanda as well as Libya and Ethiopia) should be taken into account. The type of colonial settlement, adapted to the different territories and modes of exploitation, also had an impact on the management of the workers. The Algerian, Namibian, South African and Zimbabwean models of settlement colonies, where racial repression was institutionalized to ensure cheap and easily controllable black labour supplies, were specific cases. Local communities in these countries were subjected to long processes of proletarianization through land dispossession.[11]

Going beyond land dispossession, legal instruments were used to grant differential rights to European and African workers in order to divide the workforce. The policy aimed to unite European settlers with preferential citizenship. One form of division was the introduction of racially motivated mobility laws, which resulted in segmenting the colonial labour market by race. White European settlers constituted the privileged labour force with

[9]   U. Bosma, 'Beyond the Atlantic: Connecting Migration and World History in the Age of Imperialism, 1840–1940', *International Review of Social History*, 52.1 (2007), 117.

[10] *Ibid.*, 117–18, 122.

[11] Drew, 'Bolshevizing Communist Parties'; R. Cohen, J. Copans and P. C. W. Gutkind, 'Introduction', in *African Labor History*, ed. P. C. W. Gutkind, R. Cohen and J. Copans (London: Sage, 1978), 7–30.

ease of entry into well-paid ranks and sectors. As a consequence of these policies, Africans and other peoples of colour in South Africa, Algeria, Namibia and Zimbabwe were almost invariably at the lower end of the employment hierarchy. Racially motivated educational systems served to seal this development.[12] For example, the Crémieux decree of 1870 was intended to incorporate non-French whites and the Jewish population of Algeria into a special category of 'European', offering them access to French citizenship, whereas the North African Muslim people in Algeria were ruled by the (in)famous *Code de l'Indigénat* of 1865, which provided an inferior legal status. The Crémieux decree opened new ways of social mobility and new access to jobs to a certain category of the population. The mobility of workers and access to the labour market was also used as a means to create hierarchies among the different populations. In the French colony of Senegal, immigration was facilitated for French workers, foreign white workers (Levantines, for example) or *métis* (from Portuguese Cabo Verde) through a decree issued in 1911.[13] Again, legislation in Algeria facilitated international migration – notably from Africa to the metropolis – while in South Africa, it confined blacks to rural settlements.

Legislation that controlled labour mobility determined where particular categories of workers could find employment. The introduction of pass laws regulating rural and urban movement for blacks in South Africa was, as in the Algerian example, aimed at restricting mobility rights for the local populations, especially the right to live in towns and cities. Such restrictions had implications for choices regarding participation in the labour force. Internal mobility restrictions, for instance, made out-migration to France a better option for Algerians. They were induced to migrate to France, where restrictions were less severe and working conditions better, and where they were able to fill job vacancies created by French workers drafted to fight in the First World War. In response to pressures from large landowners, who were feeling the pinch of the large-scale movement of Algerian labour to France, the Algerian Doumergue decree of 4 August 1926 (followed up by the Sarraut decree on 4 April 1928) were passed, imposing strict new requirements and a stiff fine on out-migrants to France. However, this legislation failed to stop the flow of labour out-migration.[14]

Other measures of labour market segmentation on the basis of race through the use of legislation were applied in Southern Rhodesia and

---

[12] Ananaba, *The Trade Union Movement in Africa*.

[13] I. Der Thiam, 'L'Évolution politique et syndicale du Sénégal colonial de 1840 à 1936', PhD dissertation, Université de Paris I, 1983.

[14] Drew, 'Bolshevizing Communist Parties'; Bosma, 'Beyond the Atlantic'.

Namibia, where the minority European settlers introduced the 'colour bar'.[15] The main focus of the racially motivated labour legislation was to maintain white privilege, even though white workers were also an exploited labour force. Although white workers were a privileged segment of the working class, the divide between white workers and indigenous African workers ended up serving the interests of capital.[16]

The absence of a uniform labour code in French West Africa under colonial rule meant that the European workforce earned wages far in excess of their African counterparts for the same kind of work. This inequality of treatment was abolished by the French government through the enactment of the Labour Code for Overseas Territories in December 1952.[17]

Other instruments applied in colonial Africa can be identified as ways to manage the myriad of competing interests for the supply and control of waged labour before the development of what were accepted as traditional industrial relations instruments. They included, for instance, pass laws, the Native Regulations Ordinance and the compound system.[18] The Bantustan system in South Africa, in which black African workers were considered *Gastarbeiter*, that is, temporary workers from tribal homelands, is an extreme form of this control to ensure an acquiescent labour force adapted to the dictates of colonial capital.[19] Race was the basis not only for the colonial political system but also for the economy. It regulated the availability of labour and helped to lower the costs of non-European labour. Racist mobility laws, differential living spaces and pass systems, in particular that in South Africa, were the tools used to lower the cost of labour, as well as the colour bar in union membership.[20]

The colonial state directed the extent to which rural Africa was allowed to de-peasantize. Tax legislation was used to dislodge subsistence farmers from dependence on the land and force them to escape the countryside in

---

[15]   J. R. Hooker, 'The Role of the Labour Department in the Birth of African Trade Unionism in Northern Rhodesia', *International Review of Social History*, 10.1 (1965), 1–22; Drew, 'Bolshevizing Communist Parties'.

[16]   Drew, 'Bolshevizing Communist Parties'; Hooker, 'The Role of the Labour Department'.

[17]   Ananaba, *The Trade Union Movement in Africa*.

[18]   R. Roberts, 'Peculiarities of African Labour and Working-Class History'; J. Baskin, *Striking Back: A History of COSATU* (Johannesburg/London: Ravan Press/Verso, 1991).

[19]   Baskin, *Striking Back*.

[20]   Roberts, 'Peculiarities of African Labour and Working-Class History'.

search of waged labour that could provide the cash to pay the taxes.[21] It was, however, necessary to preserve subsistence production to support the reproduction of labour. The need for waged labour was paramount; however, pre-capitalist production forms were not always detrimental to colonial interests. Restricted residence in urban settlements allowed the African labour force to maintain its connection with rural communities, deriving direct support during times of unemployment or retirement.[22]

An additional dimension to the environment within which labour legislation was fashioned beyond the traditional labour/capital interface and the state/capital interrelation was added by the internal tensions within the various interest groups among capital. Citing Robert Davies,[23] Roberts distinguishes the various forms of capital as mining, agriculture and manufacturing, as well as national and international capital. Each group, he further explains, sought to control the nation state to advance its particular labour force needs. He refers to the South African railway strike of 1922/23, the response to which marked the transition between the hegemony of mining capital and the rise of national capital.[24] The survival of the colonial state itself as a political entity also imposed particular labour force needs. It called for alliances within the dominant capitalist groups and strict rules to ensure that the needs of private capital did not deprive the colonial administration of workers for the construction of transport infrastructure, for example railways and roads. Roberts cites the example of the Belgian Congo, where mining companies were restricted by law to employing just 25 per cent of the rural working population.[25] This situation has been used to explain the recourse to forced labour in areas with low labour concentrations, such as West Africa.[26] The colonial state was the largest employer in this region.

In other situations, like that in Egypt, where up to 100,000 European workers came to the country in response to the need for construction at the turn of the twentieth century, the employment of the indigenous workforce was soon considered a good way to prevent the organizing of a

[21]   Drew, 'Bolshevizing Communist Parties'; Gutkind, Cohen and Copans, 'Introduction'; Phelan, 'West African Trade Unionism Past and Present'.

[22]   J. Crisp, *The Story of An African Working Class: Ghanaian Miners Struggles, 1870–1980* (London: Zed Books, 1984).

[23]   R. Davies, 'The 1922 Strike on the Rand: White Labor and the Political Economy of South Africa', in *African Labor History*, ed. P. C. W. Gutkind, R. Cohen and J. Copans (London: Sage, 1978), 80–108.

[24]   Roberts, 'Peculiarities of African Labour and Working-Class History', 329.

[25]   *Ibid.*, 321.

[26]   See the chapter by Fall and Roberts in this volume.

European labour force that was increasingly difficult to control. The cases of Alexandria and Cairo at the turn of the century illustrate the paradoxical relationship between a colonial state and European workers who were considered migrants and troublemakers. Avoiding possible 'contamination' of the local workers by the left-wing proletariat from southern Europe (especially from southern Italy) became a crucial preoccupation of the local governors. They tended to identify 'good Arab workers' and considered them more docile at work and in urban society.[27] In the context of Mediterranean port cities, the question of foreignness and localness became a political issue.[28] The same observations can be made in Tunisia, where the majority of the poor European workers were perceived with contempt and fear by the colonial authorities and elites.[29] In this particular case, the large size of the colonial state is insufficient to explain the tensions between state and labour: the local scale of the growing cities as well as the specific Mediterranean geopolitical and strategic context play an important role.

FORMALIZING WORKERS' MOVEMENTS: THE COLONIAL PROJECT

The industrial relations systems constitute the context in which labour organizes its rights, as well as the ideological underpinning that determines labour's place within the national development agenda. The relations between labour and capital are characterized by constant struggle and sometimes by negotiation and compromise. Discerning this relationship within industrial relations literature is informed by a number of positions. Literature on industrial relations is split on the benefit of labour legislation to workers and the overall health of national economies. The liberal schools consider a strong labour front as a disincentive to the growth of capital and, therefore, emphasize structures that give greater room for workers to act as individuals. This position emphasizes the individualization of worker–management relations, which has become a key industrial relations practice around the

---

[27]   A. Turiano, 'Le Consul, le missionnaire et le migrant. Contrôler et encadrer la main-d'œuvre italienne à Alexandrie à la fin du XIXème siècle', in *Étudier en liberté les mondes méditerranéens: mélanges offerts à Robert Ilbert*, ed. L. Dakhli and V. Lemire (Paris: Publications de la Sorbonne, 2016), 337–46.

[28]   A. Gorman, 'Foreign Workers in Egypt 1882–1914: Subaltern or Labour Elite?', in *Subalterns and Social Protest: History from Below in the Middle East and North Africa*, ed. Stephanie Cronin (London: Routledge, 2008), 240–2.

[29]   J. Clancy-Smith, *Mediterraneans: North Africa and Europe in an Age of Immigration, 1800–1900* (Berkeley, CA: University of California Press, 2011).

world since the 1980s.[30] The corporatists see labour and capital as having mutual interests in the preservation of an enterprise, and they call on strong union leadership to cede the rights of the labour movement in return for negotiated gains from capital. The more radical perspective, however, sees an inherent connection between pro-socialist governments with their welfare-oriented ideals and the tendency to enact pro-worker legislation.[31] The difficulty lies in the ways in which this motive is established and in the ability to sustain the relationship over time, as governments' orientations change. In the case of the African continent, as elsewhere, the role of the unions has been a subject of dispute in a number of writings.[32] The main position is that, by their actions, they tend to distort labour markets, producing asymmetries in labour standards, particularly for self-employed workers in the informal economy, and worse of all increasing the price of labour for employers.[33]

Organizing a front to struggle for better working conditions was a long-lasting preoccupation for workers in all of colonial Africa. In the absence of institutions to regulate relations between workers and their employers, African workers used the means available, relying on a core industrial relations ingredient, solidarity, to promote their collective interests. Mass protests were their major weapon, and harsh repression failed to intimidate them. Significant protests that ended in strikes included mineworkers' strikes in 1919 in the Gold Coast,[34] the strike of several thousand coal heavers in Port Saïd as early as April 1882,[35] and the strike of the workers on the Dakar–Niger railway in French West Africa in April 1919, which united both European and African workers, resulting in a total paralysis of the line.[36]

The right to organize in trade unions was granted slowly, and initially only to white workers. Thus, while European workers in African colonies were allowed to form trade unions and bargain collectively, this facility was not available to blacks and non-whites in Algeria, South Africa, Namibia and

---

[30] Betcherman, *Labor Market Institutions*.

[31] On welfare in Africa, see the chapter by Scully and Jawad in this volume.

[32] Ahmed, Ahmad and Idris, 'Emerging Trends in Labour Law'.

[33] K. Panford, *African Labor Relations and Workers' Rights: Assessing the Role of the International Labor Organization* (London: Greenwood Press, 1994). On informal labour, see the chapter by Barchiesi in this volume.

[34] Trades Union Congress (Ghana), *Trade Unions and Industrial Relations in Ghana* (Accra: Ghana Trades Union Congress and Rosa Luxemburg Foundation, 2012).

[35] J. Beinin and Z. Lockman, *Workers on the Nile: Nationalism, Communism, Islam, and the Egyptian Working Class (1882–1954)* (Cairo: The American University in Cairo Press, 1998).

[36] B. Ndour, 'Luttes laborieuses en "situation coloniale": cheminots du Dakar-Niger, 1919–1951', *Historiens et Géographes du Sénégal*, 6 (1991), 43–53.

Northern Rhodesia.[37] Unions in Angola served the interest of whites until the leftist Portuguese military coup in 1974 and the resulting transition to Angolan independence that allowed the exiled unions – the União Nacional dos Trabalhadores Angolanos, the Confederação Nacional dos Trabalhadores de Angola and the Central Sindical Angolana – to operate. Over time, the União Nacional dos Trabalhadores Angolanos, as the industrial wing of the ruling party, gained recognition as the national union centre of Angola. It was suspended in 1977 on suspicion of complicity in an abortive coup to overthrow the government of Agostinho Neto.

Union formation in South Africa was a racial problem, and the first effective unions were mainly composed of white workers. Although not all races were legally barred from setting up unions, black unions were denied access to registration, a condition that prevented them from operating as full-fledged trade unions. According to Ananaba, they could not 'access industrial councils or wage boards'.[38] The Industrial Conciliation Act of 1924 granted the right to bargain with employers to white workers only. The 1973 Amendment to the Bantu Labour Relations Regulation Act of 1953 allowed blacks to be appointed to the Central Bantu Labour Board, but stopped short of recognizing their right to bargain collectively. In Mozambique as well, unions were initially only for white workers. The only advantage for black workers in joining the unions – when they were not denied access – was to benefit from social security.[39]

In settler communities such as South Africa, the labour market was racially segmented with limits on labour and union rights for black workers. Under the apartheid system, however, the need to prevent the radicalization of trade unions obliged the state to grant black workers the right to form and join trade unions. The Wiehahn report of 1979, for example, recommended that the early registration of unions would counter 'polarization', ensure 'a more orderly process of bargaining' and expose African unions 'more directly to South Africa's trade union traditions and the existing institutions, thus inculcating a sense of responsibility to the free market'.[40]

---

[37]   Bosma, 'Beyond the Atlantic'; L. D. Dekker, D. Hemson, J. S. Kane-Berman, J. Lever and L. Schlemmer, 'Case Studies in African Labour Action in South Africa and Namibia (South West Africa)', in *The Development of an African Working Class: Studies in Class Formation and Action*, ed. R. Sandbrook and R. Cohen (London: Longman, 1975), 206–38.

[38]   Ananaba, *The Trade Union Movement in Africa*, 71.

[39]   *Ibid.*

[40]   Baskin, *Striking Back*, 29.

A lot has been said about the pioneering role of the British colonial administration in facilitating the formation of trade unions in British colonies. A considerable amount of attention has been devoted to early experiments in industrial relations under what is presented as colonial British largesse in setting up unions in the Gold Coast and Nigeria. Thus, as workers' protests mounted, the secretary of state for colonial affairs issued Orders in Council for colonial governors to permit workers to organize.[41] The motive, far from being altruistic, has been identified as a strategy to prevent the development of radicalized labour movements in the colonies. Unions, when they developed in Africa, had no option but to duplicate what pertained in their respective colonial metropolis. Legislation was passed to allow trade union to function, while spelling out the remit of their operations. Such legislation included the 1938 Colonial Ordinance in Nigeria that allowed workers limited unionization. In 1941 the Trade Union Ordinance (Cap 91) in Ghana granted waged workers in the Gold Coast permission to form unions for the first time.[42] Zambia followed in 1949 with the Trade Union, Trade Disputes and Industrial Conciliation Ordinances.

In Southern Rhodesia, union existence was only possible after 1960, brought about by the need to develop a legal framework to facilitate the existence of the Southern Rhodesian part of the Railway African Workers' Union, when the railway broke up after Zambian independence. African railway workers were absorbed under the Industrial Conciliation Act of 1959. But the vote valuation incorporated in the Act, which put different values on the votes of union members depending on their levels of skill, immediately subjected the African railway workers to white control. Skills training was only available to whites. As a consequence, irrespective of their numerical strength, the African railway workers were required by legislation to include white workers in their unions. The votes of white workers would count twice as much as those of African workers. African trade unions did not have the right to bargain collectively. Special labour boards were created to take up their pay claims and demands.[43]

In Francophone Africa, real freedom of association was granted to all workers without distinction of race and capacity with the promulgation of the French decree of 7 August 1944, which removed the legal obstacles

[41] P. B. Arthiabah and H. T. Mbiah, *Half a Century of Toil, Trouble and Progress: The History of the Trades Union Congress of Ghana* (Accra: Gold Type Press, 1995); Panford, *African Labor Relations and Workers' Rights*.

[42] Panford, *African Labor Relations and Workers' Rights*.

[43] Ananaba, *The Trade Union Movement in Africa*.

to unionization in the French colonies.[44] In fact, the French could be said to have granted the right to form unions in their African colonies as early as 1884, well ahead of the British.[45] This right was selectively extended to Africans with French citizenship in 1922.[46] After this, the Popular Front government of Léon Blum granted skilled African citizens in the colonies the right to form unions in March 1937. This decision made it possible for forty-two unions to be recognized in Dakar alone by November 1937: they soon formed the Union des Syndicats Africains de la Circonscription de Dakar, recognized in 1938.

While unions in English-speaking West Africa struggled over their relations with the state, in francophone West Africa they had to fight the attempts to reproduce French national unions in the colonies. Thus, until 1957, most unions in francophone West Africa were mere extensions of the three national centres in France. This situation was seen as untenable later on since, as Ananaba observed: 'No matter what the French organizations did, and were prepared to do, to protect and promote their interests, African workers tended to feel that they were nothing more than black men in white men's organizations.'[47] Attempts to break the link saw the formation of a regional body, the Union Générale des Travailleurs d'Afrique Noire, whose membership over time constituted about 80 per cent of organized labour in French West Africa.

Allowing workers in the colony to form unions was the first step in the struggle for recognition in the workplace. Getting employers to recognize unions and accept bargaining with them in the determination of working conditions was a hurdle to be overcome. Thus, in Ghana, employers in the mining industry refused to bargain with the unions until they were forced to do so by order of a British court, which employed the services of a judge as an arbitrator.[48] Collective bargaining brought substantial dividends in the

---

[44]   O. O. Sidibé, 'Political Pluralism and the Trade Union Movement in Mali', in *Trade Unions in West Africa: Historical and Contemporary Perspectives*, ed. C. Phelan (Oxford: Peter Lang, 2011), 179–96.

[45]   J. A. Jones, 'The 1947–1948 Railway Strike in French West Africa', in *Trade Unions in West Africa: Historical and Contemporary Perspectives*, ed. C. Phelan (Oxford: Peter Lang, 2011), 45–68; Sidibé, 'Political Pluralism and the Trade Union Movement in Mali'.

[46]   Sidibé, 'Political Pluralism and the Trade Union Movement in Mali'.

[47]   Ananaba, *The Trade Union Movement in Africa*, 23.

[48]   See K. Adu-Amankwah, *The State, Trade Unions and Democracy in Ghana, 1982 to 1990* (The Hague: Institute of Social Studies, 1990); A. O. Britwum, *The Ghana Trades Union Congress: Sixty Years of Promoting Workers' Rights* (Accra: Ghana Trades Union Congress, 2007); P. Obeng-Fosu, *Industrial Relations in Ghana: The Law and Practice* (Accra: Ghana Universities Press, 2007).

form of increased wages (there was a threefold increase in wages in the Gold Coast over the eighteen-year period from 1939 to 1957).[49]

In francophone Africa, union formation was predicated as in anglophone Africa on colonial interests. A difference, however, was the fact that existing unions in French West Africa formed local counterparts in other colonies. In Burkina Faso, the pluralist tradition in unionism can be considered a direct result of colonial rule.[50] Thus, while union pluralism in anglophone Africa was a development of smaller, in-house unions that lacked a centre, in the francophone context it was the work of existing metropolitan unions setting out to replicate their systems in the colonies. The motive for setting up single unions was, therefore, received with suspicion in the colonies. Laws were used everywhere to control the spread of trade unions. For example, a law of 31 August 1959 put the trade union movement in Burkina Faso (then Upper Volta) into 'voluntary hibernation'.[51]

The observation by Ahmed, Ahmad and Idris that Nigerian labour laws and industrial relations under colonial rule were derived from those prevailing in Britain holds true for a number of African countries.[52] Specific industrial relations instruments included labour departments and statistical and labour registration organs. The functions of these institutions expanded over time from merely recording potential workers and those in employment. These structures formed the basis for the development of industrial relations institutions in colonial Africa.[53] Other formalized labour institutions were the wages boards that supervised working conditions with special emphasis on levels of remuneration.[54]

---

[49] K. Ewusi, *The Distribution of Monetary Incomes in Ghana* (Legon: University of Ghana, 1971).

[50] G. Silga, 'Burkina Faso: The Land of Incorruptible Men', in *Trade Unions and Sustainable Democracy in Africa*, ed. G. Kester and O. O. Sidibé (Aldershot: Ashgate, 1997), 147–71.

[51] *Ibid.*, 151.

[52] Ahmed, Ahmad and Idris, 'Emerging Trends in Labour Law'.

[53] A. O. Britwum, *Labour in African History from the 19th Century to the Present* (Lomé: ITUC-Africa, 2012).

[54] Silga, 'Burkina Faso: The Land of Incorruptible Men'.

POST-INDEPENDENCE AND THE CONSOLIDATION OF INDUSTRIAL RELATIONS IN AFRICA

The focus of industrial relations after independence was to strengthen workers and their movements in the context of building the young states. The close relations between the state and the labour movements was generally the result of the recognition by independent governments of labour's role in the nationalist struggles that had led to self-rule.[55] In general, the workers had shown a greater consciousness of the exploitative relations between the colonial governments and the colonized states. For the workers, their full participation in nationalist struggles meant that independence would bring them greater rights and access to their deserved share of the fruits of their labour. Unions were in many cases not only participants in the anti-colonial struggle but were considered an avant-garde in the achievement of independence. In the case of Tunisia, the Union Générale Tunisienne du Travail (UGTT), part of the National Dialogue Quartet that was awarded the Nobel Peace Prize in 2015, emerged as a 'national symbol' in this period.

The transition from colonial rule to self-rule presented notable differences. Some countries, such as most of the West African ones, had short transition periods, whereas Zimbabwe, South Africa, Mozambique, Angola and Algeria had to contend with long periods of civil war. This had an impact on the nature of the industrial relations regimes that were established to regulate employment relations. For most African countries, the postcolonial nation-building project was located in the transformation from agrarian subsistence production to full industrialization.[56] The incorporation of the national economy into Western capital was maintained, except for some rare flirtations with socialist-inclined economic models from Eastern Europe, such as the Yugoslavian workers' self-management.[57] Some countries became laboratories for new kinds of labour–state relations. Zambia experimented with humanist principles, with the expectation that capitalist enterprises would be transformed into workers' self-managed entities in a system that emphasized human dignity and social justice. The Tanzanian *ujamaa* experiment favoured various forms of worker participation. Egypt formalized workers' participation in the management of enterprises in a way that was more corporatist and paternalistic than socialist.[58] Governments in a

---

[55]   Adu-Amankwah, *The State, Trade Unions and Democracy in Ghana*; G. Kester, *Trade Unions and Workplace Democracy in Africa* (Aldershot: Ashgate, 2007); Ananaba, *The Trade Union Movement in Africa*; Panford, *African Labor Relations and Workers' Rights*.

[56]   Kester, *Trade Unions and Workplace Democracy*.

[57]   Britwum, *Labour in African History*.

[58]   Beinin and Lockman, *Workers on the Nile*.

number of independent African states were the main economic players, and state-owned enterprises dominated the economic landscape. This period is characterized by most observers as a historic collaboration between political and labour leaders in the pursuit of common goals.[59]

There was no question about the connection between national concerns and workers' interests. What has been pointed out is that, beyond state gratitude and a feeling of indebtedness for organized labour's support, there was also the political economic framework that was predicated on the domestic market for success.[60] This was based on import substitution industrialization that required a vibrant local consuming market. A waged labour force was, therefore, important.[61] The notion that organized labour had a developmentalist role to play was largely shared, and consequently it was the state's duty to nurture this role for the common good of its citizens.[62] The ensuing periods, for some nations, were characterized by an industrial relations environment which supported workers' rights and investment in social wages, as well as greater participation of workers in workplace decision making.[63] State–labour relations operated within the corporatist mode. The agreement was that unions would play productionist roles, stimulating productivity and tempering their wage demands in the interest of the national purse.[64] This seemingly mutually supportive relationship between labour and the state was not always voluntary. In some instances, it was extracted with force in what, according to Kester, was termed 'responsible participation' in francophone Africa.[65] This was the environment that industrial relations systems were expected to regulate. It resulted in industrial relations instruments and structures that were labour-friendly and provided high social incomes.

Some examples of labour-friendly legislation were laws that institutionalized sole labour centres in a number of anglophone countries. The Ghanaian Industrial Relations Act No. 56 of 1958, passed one year after independence, was the first of this kind to give legal backing to unions and to strengthen the Ghana Trades Union Congress as the sole labour centre.

[59] Kester, *Trade Unions and Workplace Democracy*.

[60] Panford, *African Labor Relations and Workers' Rights*.

[61] A. O. Britwum, 'Union Democracy and the Challenge of Globalisation to Organised Labour in Ghana', PhD dissertation, Maastricht University, 2010.

[62] Panford, *African Labor Relations and Workers' Rights*; Kester, *Trade Unions and Workplace Democracy*.

[63] Arthiabah and Mbiah, *Half a Century of Toil, Trouble and Progress*; Kester, *Trade Unions and Workplace Democracy*.

[64] Ananaba, *The Trade Union Movement in Africa*.

[65] Kester, *Trade Unions and Workplace Democracy*.

This was amended in 1965 by the Industrial Relations Act No. 299 of 1965.[66] Refusing to recognize unions or allow their formation was a contravention of the law and was enforceable in court.[67] In Kenya, a unified labour centre, the Central Organization of Trade Unions, was established in 1965 through a presidential declaration.[68] The Zambian Congress of Trade Unions was given legal backing to operate as the sole labour federation through the enactment of the first Industrial Relations Act in 1971.[69] In Nigeria, the absence of a single federation produced at one point well over 900 registered unions organizing 800,000 workers. The creation of a strong labour centre in Nigeria was to follow Ghana's example. Legislation to this effect was implemented in 1978 under military rule. The Nigerian Labour Congress was formed when legal backing was given to forty-two affiliates to form a hub.[70] In Zambia, too, an Act of Parliament in 1965 led to the creation of a single union, the federation of the Zambia Congress of Trade Unions. In Congo, the Confédération Syndicale Congolaise, affiliated with the ruling party, resulted from the same need to create a single union. In Botswana, the Trade Union Act 1969 addressed the need to unite organized labour. A referendum conducted by the Labour Department in Botswana led to the creation of the Botswana Federation of Trade Unions in April 1977.[71]

The institutionalization of labour centres through national legislation gave African unions monopoly status over trade union organizing in their respective countries. This meant that these centres became the official voice of organized labour and its representation at international forums such as the International Labour Conference.[72] Other privileges included union registration and certification, a key requirement for authorizing unions to collectively bargain and obtain the right to strike.[73] These industrial relations laws outlined clearly areas such as workers' and employers' rights and the settlement of industrial conflicts. They were significant in terms of the wide sweeping rights they granted the labour confederations. Other advantages beyond monopoly status were the benefits accrued to the workers

---

[66] Panford, *African Labor Relations and Workers' Rights*.

[67] Britwum, *The Ghana Trades Union Congress*; Arthiabah and Mbiah, *Half a Century of Toil, Trouble and Progress*.

[68] Panford, *African Labor Relations and Workers' Rights*.

[69] *Ibid.*

[70] *Ibid.*

[71] Ananaba, *The Trade Union Movement in Africa*.

[72] Panford, *African Labor Relations and Workers' Rights*.

[73] *Ibid.*

by compulsory union membership and the legislatively imposed automatic check-off of union dues.[74]

The main trend among a number of trade unions was their close relationship with the ruling parties or their involvement in politics.[75] Union leaders and management were incorporated into the state apparatus in a number of countries. According to Ananaba, the countries that tried to incorporate trade unions into the ruling party included Ghana, Tanzania and Kenya.[76] Although Ghana took the lead with early incorporation, Kenya's development was slower and Tanzania's took the longest. The basis for union incorporation in the ruling parties across African countries was laid in a resolution adopted by the All-African People's Conference in Accra in December 1958, which urged African workers to 'realize their unity in the interest of the struggle for independence and the affirmation of the African personality'.[77]

In furtherance of the goal of making the Ghana TUC acceptable to lead the efforts to form a continental trade union federation, the colonial Trade Union Ordinance of 1941, which had created the Ghana TUC, was repealed by the Industrial Relations Act (IRA) of 1958. Ghana's first IRA in 1958 was amended because, as captured in the following statement by the Minister of Labour:

> It is a well-considered view that the success of the organization of the All-African Trade Union Federation (AATUF) is dependent largely on the prestige of the Ghana TUC. This means that the TUC has to do everything possible to attract as much following and support throughout Africa, and its organizational machinery built up as a model to be followed by the other TUC movements in Africa. The Ghana TUC must therefore be free from criticism internationally and the new law is aimed at achieving this.[78]

In the Kenyan case, relations between union and party began with a tripartite agreement between the Kenyan Federation of Labour, the government and private employers. They agreed, on the one hand, to create jobs and, on the other hand, not to recognize splinter unions. The Federation of Labour assured its partners of one year free of strikes and was, in turn, guaranteed its hegemony. As a result of the agreement over 32,000 jobs were created. However, some union leaders refused to recognize the deal and formed their own unions under the umbrella of the Kenyan Federation of Progressive

---

[74] *Ibid.*; Ananaba, *The Trade Union Movement in Africa.*

[75] Ananaba, *The Trade Union Movement in Africa.*

[76] *Ibid.*

[77] *Ibid.*, 11.

[78] Quoted in *ibid.*, 12.

Trade Unions. These unions operated without official recognition by the state. The struggle for hegemony and the rivalry between unions and workers resulted in a violent clash. An investigating committee report recommended the creation of a single federation and the disaffiliation from unions external to Kenya. The Central Organization of Trade Unions was formed, and the registrations of the two rival unions were revoked.[79]

Uganda is another example where the relationship between the unions and the ruling party played an important role in shaping trade union law. Efforts to replicate the Tanzanian example in the 1960s led to splinter unions such as the Federation of Uganda Trade Unions, founded in 1964. There were repeated attempts to unify splinter organizations and deeply divided rival unions through law. The Trade Union Act of 1970 dissolved all unions registered under the 1965 Act and made them automatic members of the newly created Uganda Labour Congress. In Ethiopia, as well, legal instruments were developed to facilitate the formation of unions, notably through the 1962 Labour Relations and Public Employment Administration Order. The decree allowed for the registration of trade unions and organs of employers and established a machinery to manage labour disputes. This facilitated the formation of the Confederation of Ethiopian Labour Unions in April 1963, just in time for the May meeting of the African heads of state. However, its existence was again subject to government decree, and in June 1976 it was dissolved by the military administration. Trade union integration can also be observed in Mauritania before 1969 and after 1974. In an effort to gain political control of the direct engagement of the labour centre in national politics, the amended Industrial Relations Act of 1974 offered both sole and joint unionism. It gave recognition to 'any union representing a majority of workers in a given industrial sector'. It further made room for multiple unions to operate in instances where 'two unions represented a sizeable number of workers'.[80]

In Cameroon, Konings noted that the union's bargaining position was strengthened through legislation in 1962, which introduced the check-off system and provided union leaders with space in political decision making.[81] In Egypt under President Nasser, the industrial relations regime was supportive of the workers, and collective bargaining was structured to protect the interests of labour within the public sector by providing social wages.[82]

---

[79] *Ibid.*

[80] *Ibid.*, 69.

[81] P. Konings, 'Assessing the Role of Autonomous Teachers' Trade Unions in Anglophone Cameroon, 1959–1972', *Journal of African History*, 47.3 (2006), 415–36.

[82] B. Beckman and L. M. Sachikonye, 'Labour Regimes and Liberalisation: An Introduction', in *Labour Regimes and Liberalisation: The Restructuring of State-Society*

The legislation was directed at regulating trade unions. At the time of its enacting, the number of unions dropped from the 1956 figure of 1,456 to 65 in 1962. In the same period, the number of unionized workers doubled.[83]

Legislation on trade unions in Algeria in 1969 sought to define a role in the socio-economic development of the nation after the war. In Libya, the political system of absolute monarchy affected trade union organization. Ensuing political rivalry also meant that human subjectivities undermined the operation of the Libyan Labour Code. The Labour Code Amended was adopted in November 1961 to reduce the power of organized labour; it barred public-sector workers from joining trade unions and made it an offence for what were described as workers in 'utility' and 'essential' services to go on strike. A decree issued in 1970 by the military regime of Colonel Muammar al-Ghadhafi set up a single confederation, and introduced closed shop unionism and the check-off system for collecting union dues. External affiliation of this confederation was subject to the approval of the Ministry of Labour.[84]

In Morocco, the labour legislation of 1957 restricted union membership to Moroccans, thereby effectively dissolving the local branches of French national centres.[85] In Sudan, the suspension of the unions' right to exist and strike, imposed by the military regime in 1958, was reversed by a Trade Unions (Amendment) Act in 1960. Union membership was pegged at fifty workers and above, and single-union federations were barred. Later, in February 1972, a new trade union decree permitted only two national confederations and fifty unions to exist. The decree instituted the check-off system and banned strikes.[86] There were also other laws restricting union membership: for example, in Uganda a bill was passed limiting the right of workers in the public sector to join trade unions.

But exceptions existed, too. In Sierra Leone, trade unions took a conscious decision to remain distant from national politics. In the Gambia, there was bitter rivalry between the government and the unions.[87] The government attempted to control unions through legislative restrictions of

---

Relations in Africa, ed. B. Beckman and L. M. Sachikonye (Harare: University of Zimbabwe Publications, 2001), 1–22.

[83] Ananaba, *The Trade Union Movement in Africa*.

[84] *Ibid*.

[85] *Ibid*.

[86] *Ibid*.

[87] Perfect, 'Trade Unionism in The Gambia'.

their ability to strike, by repealing the law that set the period of notice for intended strikes at 21 days and extending the required period to 28 days.[88]

The single union status granted through legislation was in contravention of significant conventions by the International Labour Organization promoting the protection of workers, in particular Conventions No. 87 and No. 98.[89] Panford provides a detailed analysis of the implications of such labour-friendly legislation, passed ostensibly to promote labour unity and avoid union fragmentation along the divisive lines of ethnicity and social status that characterize Africa.[90] These laws received widespread support and, in some instances, were adopted at the instigation of the unions themselves.

In French-speaking West Africa the sub-continental labour organ created in January 1954, Union Générale des Travailleurs d'Afrique Noire (UGTAN) had gained strength and over a period of five years covered 80 per cent of organised labour within the region (Ananaba). The election of UGTAN's President Sékou Touré as president of independent Guinea according to Ananaba (1979) was a source of great anxiety amongst nationalist leaders in the sub-region who had voted against independence. Fearing that Sékou Touré might use the influence UGTAN had over the countries in the region, most governments at independence set out to nationalise the UGTAN. As state-union relations deteriorated further with worsening economic conditions in the countries after independence, elected governments used all means possible to dismember UGTAN and weaken workers front even further.[91] This set in motion attempts by elected governments to control the workers. Trade unions were forcibly repressed, as in Benin under President Kerekou and in Guinea, or they were integrated into the ruling party, as in Mauritania, where this integration was described as 'a political choice'.[92] In Senegal, the response was to encourage union pluralism, with the idea that constitutional provisions supported the creation of multiple political groupings.

Trade unions in the Belgian colonies of the Congo, Burundi and Rwanda copied the French model, whereby African unions were branches of the Belgian trade unions. After gaining the legal right to organize in 1946, African

---

[88] Ananaba, *The Trade Union Movement in Africa*; Perfect, 'Trade Unionism in The Gambia'.

[89] See the chapter by Maul, Puddu and Tijani in this volume.

[90] Panford, *African Labor Relations and Workers' Rights*.

[91] Ananaba, *The Trade Union Movement in Africa*.

[92] *Ibid.* See Imorou's account of unionization among teachers in Benin for more details on the tensions between the unions and the government under Kerekou.
A. C. Imorou, 'Trade Unionism among Teachers in Benin since 1945', in *Trade Unions in West Africa: Historical and Contemporary Perspectives*, ed. C. Phelan (Oxford: Peter Lang, 2011), 129–44.

workers across the three Belgian colonies were united in the Fédération Générale du Travail de Belgique-Congo Belge, Rwanda-Burundi. Civil wars and other forms of instability saw the proliferation of unions until May 1967, when, in response to the political organization instituted by Mobutu Sese Seko's rule, the Congo wing united under the single federation Union Nationale des Travailleurs du Congo. It was renamed 'du Zaire' in 1971 to remain consistent with the change of the country's name.

Though strong viable national federations were created in these countries, this had a cost. The first instance was the loss of the right to freedom of association.[93] Labour laws in anglophone Africa facilitated the unity of trade unions, but they did not always seek the workers' interests. Strikes serve as an important tool for labour to register its protest against unfair conditions and to extract concessions from employers. A number of nation states, realizing the power of strikes, set out measures to control this power. Legislation played a significant role in this effort. For Panford, the right to strike remains an important source of conflict between governments and labour unions in Africa, and it therefore plays a central role in labour legislation.[94] He recounts how, in 1958 in Ghana and 1971 in Zambia, as well as in Nigeria, legislation and 'cumbersome dispute settlement procedures … virtually outlawed workers' industrial actions'.[95] Not only were the laws used to frustrate workers' attempts to strike, they were also applied to restrict union membership. In a number of African countries, public-sector workers were banned from trade union membership. This trend continues even in the twenty-first century, and laws still seek to control the ability of workers to inflict damage on employers for refusing to address their needs.[96]

Industrial relations were mostly corporatist in character and largely dominated by what Beckman and Sachikonye termed 'state-supported monopoly unions'.[97] Organized labour derived its influence from state sponsorship, not from union members – a situation that exposed trade unions to easy dissolution by legislation.[98] This situation made unions vulnerable to the same instruments that were used to grant them influence in the industrial relations systems of a number of African countries.

---

[93] See Panford for a detailed account of how the industrial relations Acts of Ghana, Kenya, Nigeria and Zambia violated ILO Conventions 87 and 96. Panford, *African Labor Relations and Workers' Rights*, 35–68.

[94] *Ibid*, 3.

[95] *Ibid*.

[96] Ahmed, Ahmad and Idris, 'Emerging Trends in Labour Law'.

[97] Beckman and Sachikonye, 'Labour Regimes and Liberalisation'.

[98] Panford, *African Labor Relations and Workers' Rights*.

Ghana is one example. The overthrow of the government led by Kwame Nkrumah and the Convention People's Party in 1966 brought unions into conflict with its replacement, the Progress Party-led government of Kofi Abrefa Busia. The latter dissolved the Ghana TUC under a certificate of urgency with the Industrial Relations (Amendment) Act 1971. It took another decree by the leaders of the military coup, who ousted the Progress Party government in 1971, to restore the Ghana TUC. Another incidence of the use of legislation to dissolve a trade union can be observed in eastern Africa with the Tanganyika National Assembly. In 1964 it passed the National Union of Tanganyika Workers (Establishment) Act, which set up the National Union of Tanganyika Workers to replace the Tanganyika Federation of Labour.[99] In fact, this has been described as the most extreme form of union incorporation into the ruling party, as well as the longest. This occurred despite initial resistance to moves by the government, which eventually saw the arrest of over two hundred union leaders. According to Ananaba, the new law made an organic link with the ruling party mandatory, and the appointment of union leaders was the responsibility of the president. In return, the union was granted automatic check-off and the closed shop.[100]

In Tunisia, the UGTT and other unions had signed a social agreement in January 1977 to 'maintain social peace, enforce growth of production, better the *pouvoir d'achat* and the conditions of life of the workers' for five years. During this same year the economic situation worsened, and inflation rose to such a high level that the government was in crisis. The first general strike of independent Tunisia was called in January 1978. More than one hundred people were killed and many others injured, while a state of emergency was declared in the country. Thirty-three union leaders were imprisoned, among them Habib Achour, the general secretary of the UGTT.[101]

Labour market institutions were formalized and given structure after independence. Dispute management between workers and employers were also structured and corresponding institutions set up to regulate such relations: the National Labour Commission in Ghana,[102] the National Economic Development and Labour Council in South Africa, and the National Industrial Court in Nigeria, set up in 2006 by the National Industrial Court Act.[103]

---

[99] Ananaba, *The Trade Union Movement in Africa*.

[100] *Ibid.*, 34.

[101] D. Le Saout and M. Rollinde, eds, *Émeutes et mouvements sociaux au Maghreb: perspective comparée* (Paris: Karthala, 1999), 112.

[102] Trades Union Congress (Ghana), *Trade Unions and Industrial Relations in Ghana*.

[103] Ahmed, Ahmad and Idris, 'Emerging Trends in Labour Law', 32.

ADJUSTMENT AND THE DEVELOPMENT OF LABOUR LEGISLATION

At the core of efforts to institutionalize labour legislation are rules that cover various components of employment – what Ahmed, Ahmad and Idris term 'employment protection legislation'.[104] Such rules are intended to reduce the tendency to hire employees on a non-permanent basis and, in addition, to hike up the cost of unfair dismissals in order to provide employment security and commit employers to a socially responsible position with regard to their employees. If the post-independence era, especially during the late 1950s and 1960s, was marked by the use of labour relations instruments to enhance the power of workers and their representative organs and to secure higher social wages, then the period from the mid- to late 1980s was characterized by the reversal of such gains using the same tools – labour laws and institutions. Betcherman, reiterating an ILO observation about the impact of the financial crisis on employment protection legislation, notes how the removal of protection, even for permanent workers, had been made easier.[105] Thus, whatever gains had been made by labour in the post-independence era were quickly eroded by the policies of economic restructuring, which attacked the very basis of all forms of employment protection legislation. This trend has continued well into the twenty-first century, given a new impetus by the financial crisis of 2008. Long before the period of adjustment, poor management had undermined wages through inflation, and cuts in public spending had put a number of social protection schemes under severe strain.[106]

Hence the cost of adjustment was high for workers who, according to Beckman and Sachikonye, met deteriorating living conditions with resistance.[107] Some examples include the Senegalese national strike against the 'austerity plan' in 1993 and the massive stay-aways in South Africa in 1993 and 1994 after the introduction of value-added tax. In Zimbabwe, there were protests and national strikes in 1997 and early 1998 against high state-sponsored taxes. Zambian and Nigerian workers adopted several industrial actions to seek relief from the strangling effect of adjustment strategies.[108] The most remarkable were the general strikes organized by the Nigerian

[104] *Ibid.*

[105] Betcherman, *Labor Market Institutions.*

[106] R. Rathbone, 'Businessmen in Politics: Party Struggle in Ghana, 1945–57', *Journal of Development Studies*, 9.3 (2003), 391–403.

[107] Beckman and Sachikonye, 'Labour Regimes and Liberalisation'.

[108] *Ibid.*, 16; Ahmed, Ahmad and Idris, 'Emerging Trends in Labour Law'.

Labour Congress in protest against fuel price hikes.[109] Ghanaian workers, too, went on a general strike during the era of economic recovery.[110] As in Ghana, trade unions in Burkina Faso also faced suppression through the use of legal instruments. The height of tensions between the union and the state was in the early 1980s, when the trade union strongly opposed the military revolution of August 1983.[111]

A number of the protests in Africa centred around changes in labour legislation that sought to reduce the power of trade unions. In Egypt, for example, the new Unified Labour Law of 2003 included provisions restricting the right to strike. The Zambian amendments to the Labour and Industrial Relations Act in 1993 included provisions expunging the closed shop and check-off system, and the Senegalese labour code amendment in 1999 saw significant power given to employers to 'high or fire'.[112] In Ghana, the Labour Act of 2003 reduced the number of workers in the same company who might form a union from five to two, effectively outlawing the closed shop.[113]

Many of the conflicts emerging between the state and the unions during the era of adjustment were struggles over labour legislation and its centrality in the reform process. The struggles were precipitated by amendments and revisions of the labour laws. In most cases, we find within the post-adjustment industrial relations regime an established body of labour law which tended to regulate in great detail the parameters of collective bargaining, union and workers' rights, and the position of national labour confederations and their relations to the government or the ruling party.[114]

Ahmed, Ahmad and Idris, in their overview of the Nigerian situation, explain that workers' instruments for expressing their grievances consisted of strikes and picketing. The response to such actions was mainly the use of legal provisions to contain workers' agitation. In Nigeria, it was the Trade Unions (Amendment) Act of 2005 which 'amended sections 33 and 34 of the principal Act to derecognize Central Labour Organization and retain federation of trade unions. Thus, the NLC has ever since been deemed to exist as a federation of trade unions.'[115]

---

[109] Ahmed, Ahmad and Idris, 'Emerging Trends in Labour Law', 40.

[110] Y. Graham, 'From GTP to Assene: Aspects of Industrial Working Class Struggles in Ghana 1982–1986', in *The State, Development and Politics in Ghana*, ed. E. Hansen and K. A. Ninsin (Dakar: CODESRIA, 1989), 43–72.

[111] Silga, 'Burkina Faso: The Land of Incorruptible Men'.

[112] Beckman and Sachikonye, 'Labour Regimes and Liberalisation'.

[113] Britwum, *The Ghana Trades Union Congress*.

[114] Betcherman, *Labor Market Institutions*.

[115] Ahmed, Ahmad and Idris, 'Emerging Trends in Labour Law', 40.

Many of the labour laws adopted at an early point in the post-independence period presented an explicit commitment to protect workers' interests. For the liberal reformers now in charge, such laws were part of a defunct national-developmentalist social order with excessive statist and welfarist features, considered responsible for the strangulation of the free development of wealth through market forces.

Where labour laws secured union monopoly in the late 1950s and early 1960s, they were used to weaken organized labour in the adjustment years of the 1990s up to the 2000s. Paradoxically, the most important tool to weaken the unions was the promotion of union pluralism. Most post-adjustment laws were couched in an era of the so-called democratizing process, and the attitude towards organized labour was hostile. Laws were therefore enacted to ensure minimal rights of labour.[116] In Zimbabwe, laws were passed in the mid-1990s to reverse the 'one industry, one union' principle. As a consequence of the new approach, the Ghana TUC lost its status as the sole trade union federation in 1996, when the Ghana Federation of Labour successfully gained certification to organize as a labour hub. Thus, this period saw the weakening of unions, especially in francophone countries such as Benin and Mali. They witnessed severe forms of union pluralism during the adjustment years, when legislation was used to encourage pluralism.[117] The period after the financial crisis of 2008, however, brought more challenges for employment protection laws through extensions of temporary contracts.[118] Labour sought refuge in the overthrow of dictatorial military regimes and the restoration of multi-party liberal governance. Labour's hope was that such governance forms could provide the basis for democratizing political and economic structures. Sidibé and Venturi note the inherent contradiction in this assumption.[119]

Adegbidi and Agossou, giving an account of the trade union situation in Benin during the adjustment phase, note how the state power that created the single confederation, the National Union of the Unions of the Workers of Benin (Union Nationale des Syndicats des Travailleurs du Benin), was used to incorporate union leaders into the ruling party.[120] This resulted in distancing

---

[116] Betcherman, *Labor Market Institutions*.

[117] Sidibé, 'Political Pluralism and the Trade Union Movement in Mali'.

[118] Betcherman, *Labor Market Institutions*.

[119] O. O. Sidibé and B. Venturi, 'Trade Unions and the Process of Democratisation', in *Trade Unions and Sustainable Democracy in Africa*, ed. G. Kester and O. O. Sidibé (Aldershot: Ashgate, 1997), 19–45.

[120] F. V. Adegbidi and J. S. Agossou, 'Benin: The Challenge', in *Trade Unions and Sustainable Democracy in Africa*, ed. G. Kester and O. O. Sidibé (Aldershot: Ashgate, 1997), 125–46.

union interests and the focus of attention away from the workers who made up union membership. Here again, the state project was seen as synonymous with union goals. State creation of single confederations has the effect of isolating trade unions from their members and thus creating the need for workers to develop alternative spaces for their struggles. The inability of workers to utilize the centre to protect their employment rights during the imposition of adjustment regimes led to the creation of alternative spaces by workers to defend their interests.[121]

Institutionalizing neoliberal democratic pluralism brought workers a new lease of life as a result of the provisions of freedom of association formally guaranteed in a number of national constitutions in the transition from military to civilian regimes. Such provisions facilitated the erection of plural, liberal democracies in a number of African countries. The spirit of such constitutions gave workers a new space for organizing and legally recognized interest representation. In Benin, the freedom of association written into the new constitution facilitated the erection of a medley of civil society groups operating under the banner of non-governmental organizations. Workers were able to use such spaces to support their actions, such as strikes and sit-ins. But this space was quickly whittled away, once governments had consolidated their rule after elections.

The space created for activism and the multitude of organizational forms emerging as a result spelt misfortune for union unity. Union pluralism was the outcome. Fragmented structures brought into existence new unions, largely fuelled by an environment that compelled workers to utilize non-trade union formations to pursue their interests. Commenting on this development, Adegbidi and Agossou explain:

> [T]rade union pluralism was predictably revealed for what it was: a large number of national centres strongly influenced by the personalities of its leaders and by political and ethnic links ... Furthermore, as if they stood to benefit from division, unions even attempted to form themselves into autonomous centres that were almost identical philosophically and strategically.[122]

The effect, they went on to explain, was 'divisiveness' which prevented 'unity of action' – a state of affairs exploited by the government. The effect was workers' loss of confidence in their unions. Silga notes how, in addition to laws guaranteeing trade union formation and labour codes on collective bargaining, the Burkina Faso constitution established fundamental civil,

---

[121] *Ibid.*

[122] *Ibid.*, 133.

political and trade union rights in the form of freedom of association.[123] Such provisions were inadequate to guarantee the freedom of unions from the debilitating effect of pluralism.

While the tendency has been to use legal instruments to improve the conditions of workers through wage increases and the institution of social wages, in other situations there have been attempts to reduce wages, in particular public-sector wages: a strategy used by governments to save money for national development. Most of these policies have failed, some at the conception stage and others at the stage of implementation. A number of such attempts have brought about the fall of governments. Ananaba gives an account of how such an attempt led to the overthrow of the government of President Maurice Yaméogo in Upper Volta in 1966.[124]

CONCLUSION

Most African countries worked to make their labour laws compliant with international standards. Labour laws in most African countries derive from ILO standards, largely influenced by the need to conform as signatories to its conventions and recommendations. Making this case for Nigeria, Ahmed, Ahmad and Idris note that the labour movement there showed a desire to 'attain international best practice in her labour and industrial relations practice at both individual and collective labour law levels'.[125] In terms of content, the laws cover a number of issues in the interest of workers. They determine, for example, the conditions of the contract of employment, the rights and responsibilities of employers and of their employees, as well as dispute settlement and other forms of employee entitlements, such as leave, rest and remuneration. In some countries, there have been attempts to unify all employment laws (for example in Ghana), while in others (such as Nigeria), there exist several employment-related laws: the Trade Union Act of 2005, the National Industrial Court Act of 2006 and the Employees Compensation Act of 2010. In a number of instances, ILO missions helped to stop abuses of union rights, as in the case of Libya in January 1962, though with difficulty. Unions, at this point, sought to derive maximum benefit from the international standard setting of the ILO. The 1960s saw the highest number of ILO labour standard ratifications. A good example is Ghana, where of the 68 per cent of the ILO Conventions ratified by 2015 had been ratified

---

[123] Silga, 'Burkina Faso: The Land of Incorruptible Men', 166.

[124] Ananaba, *The Trade Union Movement in Africa*, 32.

[125] Ahmed, Ahmad and Idris, 'Emerging Trends in Labour Law', 43.

between 1957, when the country gained independence, and 1966, when the labour-friendly government of the CPP was overthrown.[126]

This chapter has examined the conditions under which labour, labour institutions and legislative frameworks developed in Africa and has described the nature of state–labour relations that determined their form. It has highlighted the way in which state–labour relations played a key role in the form and nature of labour regulatory organs and legislation. The concern has been the extent to which labour was ready to yield to the dictates of the state, as it transitioned from its original colonial form to an independent system that was supposed to serve the interest of its citizens. State transition has spanned democratic nationalist governments, which later often turned into single-party or military dictatorships. The resulting hostile environment meant that the interests of labour were subsumed among other concerns, and, in a number of cases, legislation was used to control workers in Africa. In all this, irrespective of the political forces holding power over the state, labour's interests were subsumed under those of capital. Two phases that had brought hope to labour were the post-independence period and the struggle in the 1990s to institute multi-party democracy. However, labour-friendly legislation and institutions set up to advance the interests of labour were short-lived. Labour's ability to defend its rights and expand the space for impacting labour institutions and legislation rest on union power and influence. The question is how unions develop this power and gain access to decision-making sites to influence policy and advance change.

The role of the state in determining the shape of industrial relations is predicated on a number of factors. These include the shape of the capitalist mode of production needed to extract surplus value within the colony. As a result, the nature and content of legal instruments for regulating how work is supervised, and consultative structures and procedures for embarking on industrial action and handling grievances, vary across nations. So does the basis for rewarding labour productivity and the legislation and institutions set up to regulate relations and ensure compliance to laws. The regulatory regime within nation states has gone through significant alterations. Most of the gains made by working people to secure their interests have been largely the result of struggle. The ILO now provides the framework for setting standards and supervising their application. Adherence, however, where workers' interests are concerned, still requires the policing of a vigilant and robust labour movement.

---

[126] Trades Union Congress (Ghana), *Trade Unions and Industrial Relations in Ghana.*

NINETEEN
Trade Unions

BILL FREUND

University of KwaZulu-Natal, Durban

This chapter will consider three phases in the history of African trade unions. The first is the organizational antecedents of trade unions. The second is unions structured along the lines of the formations in industrial societies. Unions began largely through the activities of expatriate or racial minorities, such as Greeks in Egypt, Indians in Kenya or white immigrants in South Africa. However, the native workforce learned from this model and became interested in this form of social force. In the conjuncture of the years just after the Second World War, large, territory-wide, union-led strikes exploded in many colonies (Nigeria, the Gold Coast, Tanganyika, the Rhodesias, French West Africa), not to speak of South Africa. Unions were inevitably linked to burgeoning nationalist movements.[1]

After independence, the militancy of unions worked against the ambitions of new governments, which no longer favoured insurgency and were hostile to an autonomous modern civil society. Typically, unions were reorganized as bureaucratic structures responsible to the state, leaders were bought off or persecuted and growing economic problems undermined initial attempts by the state to reward wage workers. However, despite this, the struggle for union independence often continued under the surface and tended to become more effective with time.

---

[1] For older but not unrelated views, see Bill Freund, *The African Worker* (Cambridge: Cambridge University Press, 1988), ch. 5. There is considerable detailed material in this volume, notably on South Africa, Ghana and Kenya, based on the literature then available, which I have not repeated here. My one obvious mistake was my less than optimistic conclusion based on my failure to anticipate the democratization movement that would take off. I have tried to concentrate on mending that here and on highlighting more recent scholarship.

In fact, this relatively quiescent phase was succeeded by a third phase, linked to grassroots movements calling for political democracy and the end to dictatorships or one-party rule in many countries. Trade unionism was critical in bringing about the end of apartheid in South Africa. This new phase has continued all the way to the Arab Spring in very recent years. Trade unions continue to throw up politically significant leaders and now function as a salient part of civil society. However, their importance in the success of democracy movements does not mean that they succeed, or know how to succeed, in turning such movements into government policy to the advantage of organized workers.

CONTEXTUALIZING AFRICAN TRADE UNIONS

In very different kinds of work situations where there is a sharp divide between workers and management, workers will organize, withhold their labour as a bargaining tool and turn into a collective force in particular situations in more or less every part of the world. This is inherent in the labour process and the contradictions that flow from that process. The vast African continent has as much as anywhere been the site of such situations. Some early examples that have been well described would include the coal heavers' strike on the Suez Canal in 1882,[2] the 1897 rolling strike in Lagos, Nigeria, that began in the Public Works Department,[3] the contemporary strike of Duala slaves in German Cameroon against planting cocoa trees,[4] numerous early strikes in the Witwatersrand gold mines and elsewhere in South Africa documented recently by Peter Limb[5] and the 1913 indentured sugar cane workers' strike in Natal, South Africa, associated with M. K. Gandhi.[6]

---

[2] Joel Beinin and Zachary Lockman, *Workers on the Nile: Nationalism, Communism, Islam and the Egyptian Working Class 1882–1954* (London/Princeton, NJ: I.B.Tauris/ Princeton University Press, 1988).

[3] A. G. Hopkins, 'The Lagos Strike of 1897: An Exploration in Nigerian Labour History', *Past and Present*, 35.1 (1966), 133–55.

[4] Andreas Eckert, 'Slavery in Colonial Cameroon 1880s–1930s', in *Slavery and Colonial Rule in Africa*, ed. Suzanne Miers and Martin Klein (London: Frank Cass, 1999), 133–48.

[5] Peter Limb, *The ANC's Early Years: Nation, Class and Place in South Africa before 1940* (Pretoria: University of South Africa Press, 2010), ch. 3.

[6] Maureen Swan, *Gandhi: The South African Experience* (Johannesburg: Ravan Press, 1985).

However, interesting as protests of this kind are in the history of labour, trade union organization represents a further development. Trade unions arose in Europe essentially in the nineteenth century in the rising capitalist milieu. They stylized opposition to management not merely in the form of strikes which could be licit under specific juridical conditions but also in the form of collective bargaining procedures that could lead to agreements that covered whole industries. Such agreements covered not merely wages but many other facets of the life of labour: rules about seniority and promotion, about hiring and about dismissal. The unions could also come together in a federation with a management structure of its own. When this system operated plausibly, it was considered to be the cornerstone of industrial democracy as opposed to a despotic regime of labour control in which workers' rights were purely arbitrary or perhaps customary. For workers, the union as a legal institution promised a powerful protective resource against the arbitrary commands of management.

However, the rules that unions engaged to honour in agreement barred spontaneous and destructive work stoppages, sabotage and the like, and could become a barrier to workers' aspirations as they saw things. This is more comprehensible because management views of trade unions were themselves ambiguous and varied over time. Management might choose to honour signed and sealed agreements, but inevitably the existence of limits over their control of labour at work was resented, particularly when the tide of change in technological applications or the economic conjuncture, those features that power competition in capitalism, flowed strongly. Often the politics of trade union members was deeply resented as well. The expression of grievances of workers can reflect wider tensions about class within society, and workers and their leaders can respond to those tensions by organizing labour or socialist parties or becoming an influential lobbying force within a political party.

However, bosses generally have also understood the need in normal circumstances for a kind of useful and predictable order in the workplace on which they could count in order to do business. A strong effective order based on a deal with a trade union could resolve tensions and chaotic conditions in the workplace. Consequently, especially as capitalism became more organized on national foundations, management was not necessarily hostile to unions, which they found useful in dealing with the actual innumerable problems that arose on the factory floor and in other workplaces. Negotiating with unions might be a powerful control weapon if it was not possible to disregard the interests of workers altogether.

In addition, while the state may simply be in the hands of people eager to do the bidding of capitalists, in general it has a wider and more complex field of action, and it needs to consider the role of workers as legitimate citizens whose rights demand recognition. Politicians may be beholden to organized labour, or to some fraction of organized labour, for getting into power. As a result, union politics are not necessarily straightforward. Unions may do deals with unlikely bedfellows and they may come into conflict with political regimes usually thought to be their dear friends. They can be awkward allies.

Finally, it is important to perceive the union as a field involving individuals. For the intelligent, determined and ambitious, the trade union is sometimes the route to success and power, if they are also politically very skilled. These individuals are at the heart and soul of union militancy at key moments. In the nationalist era, some striking African examples of men at the highest level of political activity here would include Sekou Touré, long-time president of Guinea and union radical; the Sierra Leonean president Siaka Stevens; Hamani Diori, first president of Niger; and Tom Mboya of Kenya. If we look for more contemporary figures, they are still with us: Frederick Chiluba, the miners' leader who became president of Zambia; Morgan Tsvangarai, the leader of the Movement for Democratic Change (MDC) who failed to become president of Zimbabwe; Cyril Ramaphosa, president of South Africa today who rose to fame as a miners' leader just like Chiluba; or the irrepressible Adams Oshiomhole, presently governor of Bendel State in Nigeria. Individuals of this calibre tended to come, not from the ranks of the unskilled and illiterate, but from the ranks of white-collar workers, elite in educational terms and usually government employees in one or another department. They exemplify the potential of unions to offer such individuals their chance for leadership and power. These are outsize figures, sometimes heroes and sometimes villains, performing on a stage with complex roles that alter over time. Their activities also are critical for understanding particularly the political aspect of trade unions. And that aspect is inevitably what engages the social scientists, apart from narrow specialists in law and industrial relations.

PIONEER DAYS: THE TRANSFER OF THE TRADE UNION IDEA TO THE AFRICAN CONTINENT

In many parts of the world, including in North and, to a lesser extent, West Africa, what we can loosely call guilds are vastly more ancient in derivation than trade unions. Guilds, however, had a somewhat different character that involved control over trade standards, the admission of self-employed artisans (whom they represented primarily) to a trade, and often linked with merchants, whose need for trust and security they could benefit. Trade unions defined by skill in Europe did genuinely have an important historic link to guilds in their origins and some of their culture, but they also marked a distinct break with the guild form of organization. The emergence of trade unions in Africa is quite a separate story.

In the years after Gandhi's departure, Natal Indians organized urban-based unions as their participation in cane field agriculture diminished. The two best-known figures associated with these were the Revd Bernard Sigamoney and Albert Christopher. Christopher had been active in the 1913 strike, while Sigamoney learned considerably about unions from white radicals in South Africa. These unions, none of which obtained legal recognition for long, were designed in good part to create job opportunities for the ex-indentured Indians in the wake of white prejudice and exclusionism.[7] Simultaneously, Indian workers, notably on the railways and also with an indentured past, organized unions that also achieved very limited gains in Kenya.[8] Labour was structured severely on racial lines in interwar Kenya, but the potential for African workers to learn from the talk and activities of Indians was there.

European artisans and skilled workers were far more significant in this respect than Indians, if one takes the whole of Africa. And in colonial situations, they generally had the rights of citizens, so their ability to create and sustain unions, often with a motivation to keep together a bounded working class, was much greater. In Alexandria, Greek cigarette makers were the pioneers of trade unionism before the end of the nineteenth century; the exclusion of Egyptians and the creation of a bounded Greek working class was inherent in their activities.[9] At the same time, citizens of France had the same right to form trade unions in Algeria as in France.[10] This included a very limited number of Algerians who qualified as voting citizens. Small numbers of skilled French workers, for instance on the railways, established trade union rights, even in French West Africa where they numbered only in the hundreds, to which they held on effectively until independence.[11]

[7]   Bill Freund, *Insiders and Outsiders: The Indian Working Class of Durban 1910–90* (London/Portsmouth, NH/Pietermaritzburg: James Currey/Heinemann/University of Natal Press, 1996).

[8]   Makhan Singh, *History of Kenya's Trade Union Movement to 1952* (Nairobi: East African Publishing House, 1969), ch. 6.

[9]   Beinin and Lockman, *Workers on the Nile*.

[10]   François Weiss, *Doctrine et action syndicales en Algérie* (Paris: Ed. Cujas, 1970).

[11]   In West Africa, African artisans seem to have been the pioneer trade unionists, although it is not clear how they accessed the model. Ibrahim Abdullah, 'Rethinking African Labour and Working-Class History: The Artisan Origins of the Sierra Leonean Working Class', *Social History*, 23.1 (1998), 80–96.

The most important phenomenon of this genre existed – and to some extent, its historical heirs are still of some importance – in South Africa. Jon Lewis traced the origin of craft unionism in the Cape to the 1840s. By the 1880s, engineering workers and builders had established branches of existing British unions both in the Cape and the much newer colony of Natal.[12] Craft unions in the Cape also attracted workers from the group of people deemed to be Coloured, neither colonizing whites nor subject Africans. Lewis is one of many authors who capture the delicate and complex business of melding organization and race on paper. Too much exclusion leads to the possibility of employers colluding in the formation of a competitive union that may agree to lower wage rates; this has been critical to trade unions shifting on racial policy in trying to steer between the practical needs of workers, their prejudices and the changing dictates of state policy.

However, in the gold mines, the most dramatic example of capitalist investment on the African continent, things had to be different. White workers included thousands of miners, originally immigrants from Britain but, especially after the first massive failed strike in 1907, increasingly Afrikaner men off the farms, who had some sense of how to survive in a mineshaft, but no certifiable skills.[13] Africans could learn these skills on the job, too, with time. In early decades the pay was good, but men died in horrific numbers of accidents in the mines and of lung diseases from the dust. For the organized miners of the Witwatersrand, racial exclusion from key positions in the labour force was an absolute desideratum. Miners' organizations called four strikes starting in 1907, charged up at the threat of dilution to their trade as they saw it. All were epic events for the whole population of the new city of Johannesburg, and they culminated in the so-called Rand Revolt in March 1922 as the industry appeared to demand restructuring. The revolt spread to other workers and called forth the spectre of a kind of white soviet in South Africa. This insurrection ended in severe repression and a death toll that included judicial execution.[14] There was no question on the part of management of getting rid of white labour in the mines, but there was also an absolute rejection of the idea associated with the Labour Party politician Frederick Creswell of running mines purely on the

---

[12] Jon Lewis, *Industrial and Trade Union Organisation in South Africa 1924–55: The Rise and Fall of South Africa's Trade and Labour Council* (Cambridge: Cambridge University Press, 1984).

[13] This structural weakness was captured in Frederick Johnstone's classic *Class, Race and Gold* (London: Routledge and Kegan Paul, 1976).

[14] Jeremy Krikler, *The Rand Revolt: The 1922 Insurrection and Racial Killing in South Africa* (Johannesburg: Jonathan Ball, 2005).

basis of white labour. This was an unstable phase of trade union history, and probably two outcomes need to be stressed.

The first was incorporation. The Labour Party in South Africa to which Creswell belonged formed a junior partnership in the Pact government of 1924–33 and again joined the government of General Smuts during the Second World War by co-optation. In this context, the Industrial Conciliation Act of 1924 paved the way for the formation of the South African Trades and Labour Council (SAT&LC) to find traction, and for a system of procedures to govern labour relationships within the citizenry. This form of trade unionism was a significant link in the chain of institutional structures that created a solid basis as a foundation for racialized labour citizenship in South Africa.[15] Plenty of whites remained working in deep-level gold mines, but they either possessed definable skills or were relegated to supervising black labour.

It should be noted that the union culture tended for long to be dominated by British immigrants and their sons. Afrikaners infused their own intense nationalism into their politically related organizations more generally and were not necessarily comfortable, especially in the mines and on the railways, with the pragmatic elements of the SAT&LC and its compromises on race in some situations. They rather looked towards politicians to create a *chasse gardée* for themselves. The white mineworkers, for instance, never organized a strong union until the 1970s. This part of the story is hardly irrelevant to what follows: the struggle to incorporate and the complex consequences would play themselves out in black Africa in later generations in comparable ways.

The second aspect of the story is that individual white unionists came to understand, just as the Indian radical Makhan Singh in Kenya did, that a genuine trade union drive that would bring about substantial change for workers and a voice in building society depended on transcending racial lines. In French North Africa, the post-First World War emergence of the Confédération Générale des Travailleurs (CGT) under strong communist influence certainly allowed for far-seeing individuals to encourage the construction of new unions in Algeria, Tunisia and Morocco. This is a story that has been well told for South Africa with much detail. The Industrial Workers of Africa tried to inculcate trade unionist and socialist ideas in

---

[15] Robert H. Davies, *Capital, State and White Labour 1900–1960: A Historical Materialist Analysis of Class Formation and Class Relations* (Brighton: Harvester Press, 1979); David Yudelman, *The Emergence of Modern South Africa: State, Capital and the Incorporation of Organized Labour on the South African Goldfields 1902–1939* (Cape Town/Westport, CT: David Philip/Greenwood Press, 1983).

Johannesburg during the First World War.[16] The key figure was Brian Bunting, an educated English immigrant and future Communist Party militant. Another such figure was the Scotsman J. T. Bain.[17] However, black workers, with their myriad reasons to revolt, were also capable of opening their ears and eyes and learning to imitate the whites without traceable contacts, as witnessed by the strike of 70,000 black mineworkers at its peak in the harsh conditions of February 1920, about which little is known.[18]

In South Africa, we can see two further lines of development in the 1920s that have deservedly attracted more attention. Post-First World War agitation by the fledgling Communist Party was accompanied by efforts to organize black workers, barred from any legal recognition. Simultaneously, the Industrial and Commercial Workers' Union (ICU) arose out of a dockworkers' strike in Cape Town in 1919. The key outside agitator here was an educated Malawian, Clements Kadalie, who ultimately settled in South Africa.[19] The ICU eventually organized many tens of thousands of black Africans during the 1920s (mostly in parts of the countryside where capitalist labour relations were increasingly taking hold more directly), many of whom really did not grasp the conditions of a plausible trade union. This was despite the efforts of William Ballinger, a British trade unionist recruited by Kadalie to try to create a union recognizable to British working men in this stony soil. The ICU was really, according to Helen Bradford, a black protest movement rather than a recognizable trade union.[20]

The final trend worth noting in this period was the organizing work of Solly Sachs, a man who experienced phases in the Communist Party. Sachs organized the women in the Garment Workers' Union, Afrikaners who were increasingly threatened with undercutting in Johannesburg by women of

---

[16]   Frederick Johnstone, 'The IWA on the Rand: Socialist Organising among Black Workers on the Rand 1917–18', in *Labour, Townships and Protest*, ed. Belinda Bozzoli (Johannesburg: Ravan Press, 1979), 248–72.

[17]   Jonathan Hyslop, *The Notorious Syndicalist: J. T. Bain, a Scottish Rebel in Colonial South Africa* (Johannesburg: Jacana, 2004).

[18]   Philip Bonner, 'The 1920 Black Mineworkers' Strike: A Preliminary Account', in *Labour, Townships and Protest*, ed. Belinda Bozzoli (Johannesburg: Ravan Press, 1979), 273–97.

[19]   However, Kadalie in turn derived some of his ideas from a British immigrant named Arthur F. Batty, who understood union organization well.

[20]   Helen Bradford, '"A Taste of Freedom": Capitalist Development and Response to the ICU in the Transvaal Countryside', in *Town and Countryside in the Transvaal*, ed. Belinda Bozzoli (Johannesburg: Ravan Press, 1983), 128–50; Philip Bonner, 'The Decline and Fall of the ICU: A Case of Self-Destruction?', in *Essays in Southern African Labour History*, ed. Eddie Webster (Johannesburg: Ravan Press, 1978), 114–20.

colour, Indians and Coloureds. He therefore struggled to organize the whole labour force and encouraged the hatching of an unrecognized equivalent 'parallel' African union in the communist fold.[21] These South African events, and notably the Sachs story, resonate with how interwar unionism developed in other parts of Africa whereby white or Indian cores started to reach out to African affiliates and begin a process of incorporation, ultimately uncontrollable, that led to the wider inculcation of union ideas. For instance, in Libya, a former Fascist of populist inclinations turned communist named Cibelli began, after the Allied liberation of this territory in the Second World War, to organize Arab workers.[22] In 1936 the astonishing victory of a Popular Front government in France that was friendly to unions and hostile to formal racial barriers (in great contrast to its predecessors) provided a turn-around for two years that proved ultimately to be an important platform for organizational gains after the war. In Algeria, the CGT began deliberately to organize Muslim workers after 1936 along somewhat paternalistic lines. As in Libya, it was the Fascist defeat that led quickly to the emergence of a more substantial union movement in Tunisia, at first under the wing of the CGT.[23]

By this time Egyptian unionism had already advanced, if in a stuttering way. Even before the First World War, in sectors in the modern economy, railway workers, tramway operators, gasworks and electrical plant workers began to organize unions, some of which involved themselves in the nationalist agitation of 1919. A big step occurred when the Wafd Party came to power in 1924–30. Wafd was prepared to tolerate and even encourage trade union formation. It needed the support of workers but, by contrast to nationalists in independent Africa several decades later, Egypt was not fully self-governing, and the Cairo regime lacked the ability to control the workers. Moreover, the British became willing to set up a system of negotiations with workers that would deflect inflammatory actions. Dependence on nationalist fervour or the state administration pushed the General Federation of Labour Unions in the Nile Valley towards dependence on relatively well-off patrons. Indeed, with the nationalists under wraps and Wafd back on the streets in the 1930s, it was rather a committed member of the royal family, Abbas Halim, who served as generous patron to much of whatever union militancy existed.[24]

[21] Iris Berger, *Threads of Solidarity 1900–80* (Bloomington, IN/Cape Town: Indiana University Press/James Currey, 1982).

[22] John Norman, *Labor and Politics in Libya and Arab Africa* (New York: Bookman, 1965).

[23] Eqbal Ahmad, 'Trade Unionism in the Maghreb', in *State and Society in Independent North Africa*, ed. Leon Carl Brown (Washington, DC: Middle East Institute, 1966), 146–91.

[24] Beinin and Lockman, *Workers on the Nile*.

By contrast to these ambivalent and complex stories, even under the apparently democratic rule of the first republic, the Portuguese government was not prepared to tolerate strike action at all by the União Ferroviário in 1925/1926, when an individual dispute blossomed into a long strike that was mercilessly crushed. The union, actually quite long-standing, was destroyed, workers at best retired and at worst sent into exile, and a completely new authoritarian work order restored. This in fact heralded the end of republican democracy in Mozambique and Portugal itself.[25]

THE HEROIC AGE: AFRICAN NATIONALISM AND AFRICAN TRADE UNIONISM, 1935–60

The years identified in the subtitle of this section represent a phase in which strikes and trade union activity often took centre stage in the course of African political and social development. A number of the great strikes, with varying levels of union organization involved, have themselves received very considerable scholarly attention, especially in countries where union activity was virtually new. These include the rail strike in the Rhodesias in 1945 under the auspices of a new union,[26] the strikes at the copper mines in Northern Rhodesia of 1935 and 1940,[27] the Mombasa dock strikes of 1939 and 1947,[28] the strike on the railway system of French West Africa in 1947–48,[29] the

[25] Jeanne Penvenne, *African Workers and Colonial Racism: Mozambican Strategies and Struggles in Lourenço Marques 1877–1962* (Portsmouth, NH: Heinemann, 1992), 86–7.

[26] Jon Lunn, *Capital and Labour on the Rhodesian Railway System, 1888–1947* (Basingstoke: Palgrave Macmillan, 1997); Ian Phimister, *An Economic and Social History of Zimbabwe 1890-1948: Capital Accumulation and Class Struggle* (London: Longman, 1988); Kenneth Vickery, 'The Rhodesian Railways African Strike of 1945, Part I: A Narrative Account', *Journal of Southern African Studies*, 24.3 (1998), 545–60; Kenneth Vickery, 'The Rhodesian Railways African Strike of 1945, Part II: Cause, Consequence, Significance', *Journal of Southern African Studies*, 25.1 (1999), 49–72.

[27] L. J. Butler, *Copper Empire: Mining and the Colonial State in Northern Rhodesia c.1930–1964* (Basingstoke: Palgrave Macmillan, 2007).

[28] Frederick Cooper, *On the African Waterfront: Urban Disorder and the Transformation of Work in Colonial Mombasa* (New Haven, CT: Yale University Press, 1987).

[29] Frederick Cooper, 'The Dialectics of Decolonization: Nationalism and Labor Movements in Postwar French Africa', in *Tensions of Empire: Colonial Cultures in a Bourgeois World*, ed. Frederick Cooper and Ann Stoler (Berkeley, CA: University of California Press, 1997), 406–36; Frederick Cooper, *Decolonization and African Society: The Labour Question in French and British Africa* (Cambridge: Cambridge University Press, 1996); James Jones, *Industrial Labor in the Colonial World: Workers of the Chemin de Fer Dakar-Niger 1881–1963* (Portsmouth, NH: Heinemann, 2002).

Nigerian general strike of 1945,[30] the 1948 Enugu Colliery shooting[31] and the 1947 general miners' strike in the Gold Coast[32] which spread to other sectors. In Egypt, too, workers in the big new textile mill at Shubra-al-Khayma north of Cairo went on strike in 1946 in a major event, but the strike was broken. Without a political reform context, while unions could legally register with the state after 1942, labour activity was far more restrained.[33] The Congress of Non-European Trade Unions in South Africa flourished for a time, notably during the war years, but the epic gold miners' strike under the nominal leadership of the Communist Party trying to form a union was extinguished, also in 1946, signalling a period of decline for many years.[34] The dominant party of General Smuts came around to favouring the legal registration of black unions, although this had not yet been enacted when he went down to electoral defeat in 1948, but the exclusion of black public-sector workers, above all those in the critical gold mines, from trade union activity was always part of the deal.

The continental strike wave of the mid-1940s both represented a dramatic change itself but also contributed to the beginning of the end of European colonial systems. The place for narratives of strike history lies elsewhere; here some general themes will be gathered together. The modern economies of African colonies were very substantially affected by the Great Depression which drastically cut the demand for industrial raw materials. From about 1935, however, there was a notable revival in mining and secondary industry that went together with the growing wave of rearmament in Europe. Poorly paid African workers (almost always male) now had an unprecedented opportunity to make their potential strength known. This demand especially for mineral products and the concomitant pressure on transport systems bore up into the 1950s.

Although there was obviously a difference between colonies, it cannot be said that an African working class was replacing the world of cultivators and pastoralists in general. However, the very heart of these economies did rely on African labour to make offices function, run the transport services,

---

[30] Toyin Falola, *Colonialism and Violence in Nigeria* (Bloomington, IN: Indiana University Press, 2009).

[31] Carolyn A. Brown, *'We Were All Slaves': African Miners, Culture and Resistance at the Enugu Government Colliery* (Portsmouth, NH: Heinemann, 2003).

[32] Jeff Crisp, *The Story of an African Working Class: Ghanaian Miners' Struggles 1870–1960* (London: Zed Books, 1984).

[33] Beinin and Lockman, *Workers on the Nile*.

[34] Dunbar Moodie (with V. Ndatshe), *Going for Gold: Men, Mines and Migration* (Berkeley, CA: University of California Press, 1994).

particularly the railways but also the telegraph and post offices, and to dig gold, copper and other minerals. Thus, the workers' bargaining position was surprisingly strong, especially in the hands of agile and determined leadership.

As to the mass of workers, a historian must note their sense of crude, racialized, colonial work culture, and their hopes at the start of change towards the conventions of collective bargaining. Thus, Ken Vickery writes that 'at its heart, the 1945 Rhodesia Railways African strike was not so much about human grievances as it was a desperate assertion of basic human dignity'.[35] Jasper Savanhu, an early union leader in Southern Rhodesia, declared that the strike 'had proved that Africans had been born …The days when a white man could exploit us at will are gone and gone forever.'[36] Carolyn Brown points to the persistence into the late 1940s of employed 'hammock boys' in the Enugu coal mines, who physically carried white supervisory staff into work each day; these humiliating distinctions were deeply resented.[37] A key factor in the great French West African rail strike was the demand for the end of distinctions between white and black employees.

The common feature of this period is the intervention of forces outside the labour workforce, which set in place the systems of industrial relations that have taken root since that time in Africa, with obvious variations in individual cases. Colonial governments were alarmed at the potential, sometimes activated, for anarchic and destructive labour revolts. From 1935 a British Conservative government underwent the shock of labour unrest in various parts of the empire, often outside Africa. For instance, in 1938 a big cane workers' strike affected the sugar island of Mauritius. Thereafter, labour organization and indeed a Labour Party (Africa's most successful) were allowed to take off. With the war over, the British economy was in poor shape and depended heavily on colonial exports and the defence of the pound zone. Officials worked hard to create predictable labour systems with acceptable conditions and hierarchies and rising levels of productivity, and that meant recognizing trade unions.[38]

Particularly during the period of Labour Party rule in Britain (1945–51), this involved sending to Africa experienced trade unionists who would teach their African counterparts the right way to go about structuring an organization and working towards a rational bargaining system. Of key economic importance was surely the Copperbelt, where the 1935 and 1940 strikes had found organization in *beni* dance societies and the Watchtower

[35] Vickery, 'The Rhodesian Railways African Strike of 1945, Part II', 63.

[36] Lunn, *Capital and Labour*, 139.

[37] Brown, *'We Were All Slaves'*, 291.

[38] See the chapter by Scully and Jawad in this volume.

movement derived from the Jehovah's Witnesses rather than even nascent unions.[39] In 1947 William Comrie was sent from the British Trades Union Congress to help create a non-political, bargaining-oriented union for African miners, capable of effective negotiating capacity. The African Mine Workers' Union was created in 1949, and the Trades Union Congress of Northern Rhodesia two years later.[40] In Southern Rhodesia, African trade unionism took root particularly in the growing rail and industrial centre of Bulawayo. Charles Mzingeli, leader of the Southern Rhodesian branch of the ICU, established an important friendship with a Labour Party politician, Gladys Maasdorp, who offered help to build African trade unionism. While Mzingeli could point out the injustices of African life in the country on the right occasion, he actually was an archetypal early figure who did not much take up national politics.[41]

An important aspect of colonial intervention into the shaping of trade unions in Africa was the impress of Cold War ideology. Communist links via the CGT in the French colonies were very significant in the extent to which unions began to be able to function effectively. It was the West that broke off from the World Federation of Trade Unions (WFTU) to form the International Confederation of Free Trade Unions (ICFTU) in 1949, and it was a feather in the cap to get the increasingly important trade union movement in Tunisia to sign up early on. As a rather naïve American observer of Libya noted with a wink, 'more than a few of the future political leaders of the nation are destined to emerge from the Libyan labor movement'.[42] Cold War politics strongly invested international trade unionism and played a corrupting role in Africa, where individuals who took the right trips to the right conferences were supported and others effectively blackballed. This also removed them from the approbation or otherwise of the rank and file. Indeed, skilful manoeuvres between West and East could allow a leader considerable autonomy and headway.

The reform era, which permitted trade unions to organize, wage strikes and earn respectability and clout, also opened the door to a rapidly emergent African nationalism, which moved quickly in key countries to force the

---

[39] Until 1946 white unions had not got really organized either in the copper mines.

[40] Miles Larmer, *Mineworkers in Zambia: Labour and Political Change in Post-Colonial Africa* (London: I.B.Tauris, 2007), 33; see also, for Sierra Leone, Ibrahim Abdullah, 'The Colonial State and Wage Labor in Colonial Sierra Leone 1945–1960: Attempts at Remaking the Working Class', *International Labor and Working-Class History*, 52 (1997), 87–105.

[41] Timothy Scarnecchia, *The Urban Roots of Democracy and Political Violence* (Rochester, NY: University of Rochester Press, 2008).

[42] Norman, *Labor and Politics in Libya and Arab Africa*, 54.

pace of political reform into a process of rapid devolution, partly affected by the declining economic weight of the African resource economies. The relationship of trade unionism to nationalism, a major subject in the literature, became extremely important in this context. African nationalists, albeit confronting different regimes in political outlook, were able to leverage timid colonial initiatives, intended in a gradualist spirit, into major political concessions that could speed up the drive to independence that would proceed at a far faster pace than anticipated. Moreover, they could fasten on the ability of strikers to cripple seriously the economic life of colonies, at a time when the halting post-war recovery of France and Britain depended on them to some degree. In the Gold Coast, the mine and rail strikes of 1947–48 paved the way for a rapid political advance. The Burns reform of 1946 had already opened the door towards self-government, but a radical movement then undermined the idea of a merely slow transfer of power to a small, largely coastal elite of professionals and businessmen. Kwame Nkrumah was the man who would break away from the original political party of this indigenous elite and enthuse a much wider public. In Nigeria, independence would not come before 1960, with many issues to be settled outside the sphere of labour, but Carolyn Brown has noted that the Iva Valley massacre of striking coal miners near Enugu in 1949 initiated a wave of sabotage and violence in eastern Nigerian cities and that 'most Nigerians cite the Iva Valley Massacre as a primary event ending British colonialism in Nigeria'.[43] Brown underscores the importance of mining in African labour politics, since union recognition and devolution were cornerstones of a new kind of political order.[44]

However, in many, probably most, cases, the path was more crooked, and there were important variations. In the French colonies, a complication was the role of the CGT and its links to the French Communist Party as the Cold War deepened. The Parti Communiste Français in France accepted the idea of a French Union and discouraged or opposed nationalist movements aimed at independence. Thus, until the final collapse of French rule in 1962, it opposed Algerian independence, and Algerian trade unionism played little role in the midst of a brutal ongoing armed struggle.[45] By contrast, in Tunisia the main body of the trade union movement left the pro-communist WFTU for the ICFTU in 1951, of which it became a steadfast and important

---

[43] Brown, *'We Were All Slaves'*, 283.

[44] See the chapter by Brown in this volume.

[45] Weiss, *Doctrine et action syndicales.*

member.[46] A dockers' strike sustained by an affiliate of the Union Générale Tunisienne du Travail (UGTT) sealed a crucial alliance between the union movement and the Neo-Destour Party, which Habib Bourguiba would lead to independence.

Near the other end of the African continent, the Southern Rhodesian government was anything but eager for a peaceful road to majority rule. From the late 1950s, after some rather quiescent years, the nationalist movement leapt ahead, although it was fraught with divisions and the thrusting ambitions of new actors. In this context, the most senior trade unionists, such as Mzingeli and his effective successor Reuben Jamela, were effectively bypassed and marginalized.[47] Here, the historical course was more like that in Algeria than Tunisia; after the Unilateral Declaration of Independence (UDI) in 1965, the nationalist movements were illegal and turned to armed struggle. Although certainly trade unionists sometimes got involved and were imprisoned and tortured, the movement as a whole, retaining links to the ICFTU – which did support African nationalism purged of any Red elements[48] – was rather weak and played little political role in the UDI years. In Kenya, by contrast, officials balked at dealing with radicals but gradually came to terms with trade unionism. In Tom Mboya – a leader who was respected in the West but was no stooge and able to assist in trade union development under some real condition of autonomy – a key figure was found with no equivalent at the time in Southern Rhodesia. Here, the British remained in charge and accepted in time the march towards independence under majority rule.

On the Copperbelt, the situation was somewhere in between.[49] The legal union movement, the African Mineworkers' Union (AMWU), also found a substantial but politically moderate leader in Lawrence Katilungu. Katilungu at first accepted the creation of a Central African Federation of the Rhodesias and Nyasaland in 1953 but, as Northern Rhodesian black nationalism took off, the union came into increasing tension with it, foreshadowing the important historic opposition between left nationalism and union organization in this economically important hub. Still, the union

[46] Willard Beling, *Modernization and African Labor: A Tunisian Case Study* (New York: Praeger, 1965).

[47] Scarnecchia, *The Urban Roots*.

[48] Brian Raftopoulos and Ian Phimister, *Keep on Knocking: A History of the Labour Movement in Zimbabwe 1900–1997* (Harare: Baobab, 1997).

[49] Ian Henderson, 'Wage-Workers and Political Protest in Colonial Africa: The Case of the Copperbelt', *African Affairs*, 72.288 (1973), 288–99; Larmer, *Mineworkers in Zambia*.

was prepared to join a United Trade Union Congress which itself in 1961 affiliated with the United National Independence Party (UNIP), led by Kenneth Kaunda; the latter would take Northern Rhodesia out of federation with Southern Rhodesia and create the republic of Zambia in 1964. Here, the point was not the good will of UNIP but the fact that the AMWU had been able steadily to improve the prospects and wages of black miners, and with them of the mining towns. At the same time, these miners jostled with the large minority of white workers, who continued to earn far more in a racially defined workplace, so they acquired a deep commitment to nationalism.[50] This is perhaps a key general comment to make as well: the ordinary worker, whether in Dakar or Bulawayo, was moved by nationalist rhetoric and did not understand trade unionism in this era as something apart from politics, de-racialization and an end to colonial rule. Katilungu was sidelined and driven from office in 1960, sharing the fate of his less politically driven colleagues south of the Zambesi. Where colonial rule continued without plans for change, notably in the Portuguese colonies, repression of worker movements inevitably continued.

AWKWARD CUSTOMERS

Towards the end of his study of labour and colonialism in post-war Africa, Cooper points to the *Schadenfreude* apparent in comments from British and French colonial officials witnessing the end of the road and thinking about their African successors having to deal with these awkward customers, the trade unions. Would they have more success in this department? In fact, the story is a complex one, and the phases shift such that it is really impossible to come up with a concrete answer for the fifty plus countries of the continent as governments come and go.

   The new governments' views on labour were changeable, and at times one aspect dominated over others. On the one hand, the labour movements represented an important and impressive power base that leaders were most reluctant to see pass to a legal or illegal opposition. Moreover, it continued to be the case that unionized workers for either multinationals or the government itself were in strategically very crucial positions to make publicity, dominate the capital or prevent strategic installations from working, so their influence in a strike was surprisingly large. On the other hand, most African countries soon ceased to be democracies and presidencies resented sharing

---

[50] As a parallel figure, the Federation premier was a white trade unionist from Northern Rhodesia, Roy Welensky.

power. If there were to be unions, they needed to be structured logically and hierarchically, with recognizable leaders under the watchful eye of those in power in the state. In some cases, unions were made the repository of a limited carapace of social welfare reforms.[51] Development, according to the theories of well-disposed economists such as Simon Kuznets and W. Arthur Lewis, depended on competitiveness, and competitiveness meant keeping the wages, especially of low-skilled workers, down, at least in the short term. Key nationalist figures such as Senegalese President Léopold Sédar Senghor took this to heart. Lewis himself was for a time a key figure in the policy entourage of the *Osagyefo*, Kwame Nkrumah.

However, in some countries the state proved unable to exert very tight controls. In Senegal, and despite Senghor, unions were closely linked to particular political parties. The Confédération Nationale des Travailleurs du Sénégal (CNTS) was aligned with the ruling party, but eventually it acquired more autonomy. Rival federations emerged, and Alfred Inis Ndiaye sees this drive to autonomy as a central theme of union history. In 2000 the CNTS finally abandoned the party link as it was swept from power.[52] The Nigerian Labour Congress (NLC) – which had enjoyed considerable autonomy once reorganized by the post-Biafra War military regime – despite the state's intentions, continued a relatively autonomous existence until it was suppressed for a time, first after a general strike in 1988 and then by the kleptocratic dictator Sani Abacha between 1994 and his fortuitous death three years later. The NLC had been formed from a multitude of smaller unions forced to create a federation and was later also obliged to abjure links with any particular political party during the phases of civilian rule in Nigeria. By the time of the revival from the Abacha years, the unions organized two million Nigerian workers.[53]

Unions were especially significant in North Africa given the relative complexity of the economy despite the repressive examples of Libya

[51] See the chapter by Scully and Jawad in this volume.

[52] Alfred Inis Ndiaye, 'Autonomy or Political Affiliation? Senegalese Trade Unions in the Face of Economic and Political Reforms', in *Trade Unions and Party Politics: Labour Movements in Africa*, ed. Bjørn Beckman, Sakhela Buhlungu and Lloyd Sachikonye (Cape Town: HSRC Press, 2010), 23–38.

[53] Gunilla Andrae and Bjørn Beckman, *Union Power in the Nigerian Textile Industry: Labour Regime and Adjustmen* (Uppsala: Nordiska Afrikainstitutet, 1998). They argue convincingly for a union and labour history separated conceptually from the usual political narratives.

and Algeria.[54] In Egypt, the Nasser military government at first ruthlessly repressed an important strike in Kafr el Dawar in 1952. However, Nasser found the union movement important to encourage, empowered it while inserting state controls, and allowed it to expand, creating the General Federation of Egyptian Trade Unions, intended to replace numerous patrimonial unions, while pursuing ambitious plans to advance the industrial development of the country. This was hardly a hands-off labour regime, but in its socialist phase in the 1960s there is no doubt that workers were able to achieve higher living standards; the working class grew substantially and received unprecedented acknowledgement as a force in society. The aura of this lingers until today. An important wing of the trade unions as of recent years still thinks in terms of the Nasserist tradition.[55] As Posusney points out, frequent attempts at liberalizing the economy at the expense of workers – already on the part of Nasser's successor Sadat, and then of Mubarak after Sadat's assassination – met with stolid resistance and were often compromised or withdrawn.[56] Union leaders won lustre, saving jobs in pursuing defensive strategies while incurring state patronage.

A striking feature of North African trade unionism has been the important role of highly skilled, professional workers. This is one reason why the UGTT, after a period of strife, was able to adjust to a changing economy in Tunisia. Indeed, whatever its limitations, Beinin has described the Tunisian union confederation as notoriously the 'strongest labor federation in the Middle East in the 1950s and 1960s'.[57] Tunisia, by comparison with Egypt, reads like the story of a good marriage with bad interludes. The excellent initial relations between the Bourguiba regime and the union movement, a powerful component in his support network, went through different phases, as economic conditions altered, affecting employment opportunities, and in response to government frustration at overly contentious internal union democracy. Despite a paper organization based around logic and order, in reality Tunisian unions formed a lively

---

[54] To be fair, however, the union movement in exile during the Algerian war for independence turned to workers' self-government models *à la yougoslave*, and these had some purchase and significance under the rule of the Front de Libération Nationale (FLN).

[55] Beinin and Lockman, *Workers on the Nile*; Marsha Pripstein Posusney, *Labor and the State in Egypt: Workers, Unions and Economic Restructuring* (New York: Columbia University Press, 1997).

[56] See also Joel Beinin, *Workers and Peasants in the Modern Middle East* (Cambridge: Cambridge University Press, 2001).

[57] *Ibid.*, 137.

political debating society under the surface, and frequently unionists challenged federation and government policies.[58]

Episodes of repression were followed by renewed linkages under Bourguiba and later Ben Ali.[59] Owen reports that both Tunisia and Egypt represented models taken up throughout the entire Arab world in terms of the incorporation of labour.[60] Morocco was another story again. Here, there were several union federations, and unions operated more freely, but as pressure groups linked usually to political parties, with more and less influential periods depending on the balance of the day. Here, too, the politics of state–union relations could be byzantine. Relatively good labour legislation was matched by poor implementation and surveillance.[61]

Independent Ghana's cocoa economy, on which the state depended, was in trouble by 1960, and the new industries that the Nkrumah government set up were unprofitable. The result was collision: unlike Nasser and Bourguiba, Nkrumah was unable to offer workers much, and the offer with time was steadily reduced. Consequently, the radical state and the unions fell out, for all the fine plans aimed at a developmental trajectory. An iconic moment was the large-scale failed transport strike of 1961, as economic conditions were deteriorating fast, centred in the port and railway twin cities of Sekondi and Takoradi. The railway workers' leader, Pobey Biney, militant nationalist, scourge of colonial officialdom and anti-communist socialist, was reduced by 1961 to working as a security officer.[62] After the overthrow of Nkrumah, the new Ghanaian rulers let the trade union movement, not that they much liked it, go its own way organizationally as times became harder. At various stages, workers experienced a phase of pro-union government under General Ignatius Acheampong (1972–78), who courted them, and then fairly harsh

---

[58] Delphine Cavallo, 'Trade Unions in Tunisia', in *Political Participation in the Middle East*, ed. Ellen Lust-Okar and Saloua Zerhouni (Boulder, CO: Lynne Rienner, 2008), 75–94.

[59] Ahmad, 'Trade Unionism in the Maghreb'.

[60] Roger Owen, *State, Power and Politics in the Making of the Modern Middle East*, 3rd edn (London: Routledge, 2004), 204–5.

[61] M. Laetitia Cairoli, *Girls of the Factory: A Year with the Garment Workers of Morocco* (Gainesville, FL: University Press of Florida, 2011). In Morocco, there has also been an oscillation between phases of patronage leading to episodes of repression as unions became seen as threatening, while a juridically liberal regime encouraged unions to affiliate with various political parties.

[62] Richard Jeffries, 'Populist Tendencies in the Ghanaian Trade Union Movement', in *The Development of an African Working Class: Studies in Class Formation and Action*, ed. Richard Sandbrook and Robin Cohen (London: Longman, 1975), 261–80.

conflict with Jerry Rawlings, when he imposed a neoliberal settlement on the country not long after his 1981 coup.

Nigeria is a society shot through with patronage structures, and the unions have certainly fallen victim to them both before and after the NLC was born. Thus, Paul Lubeck reported on a textile union in Kano where 'the union deteriorated into a management-sanctioned extortion agency, forced workers, especially recent rural origin migrants, to pay initiation fees and monthly dues … when interviewed, almost all workers denounced the union as useless, corrupt and exploitive'.[63] In a contemporary study of the tobacco factory in Zaria, Dorothy Remy described the union as ineffectual and the labour structure as dominated by an 'ethnically-based patronage system'.[64] Yet the Nigerian union movement has hardly been moribund. It went on an impressive general strike in 1964, and Andrae and Beckman stress that large, industrially structured factories also generated not merely union activity, but a labour regime shot through with the participation of relatively democratic union power by contrast to the patrimonial social ties reported by Lubeck and Remy in smaller plants.[65] General strikes followed by commissions advocating large salary increases (Adebo, 1970/71, Udoji 1975/76) were massively popular events that particularly improved the life chances of civil servants. The unions led general strikes in 1981 and 1988,[66] and they structured a major range of protest actions over 2008–09. They were in the vanguard of organizing resistance to increases to the low domestic petrol price, a historic public benefit which did not suit liberal economic strategies. The strength of the union movement has partly lain in the private sector; between the Sahara and the Limpopo, Nigeria had the strongest industrial economy outside of state control by a long way, but it has been badly affected, often devastated, by Chinese imports.[67]

For another consideration of a relationship that was not merely a contentious marriage but one that ultimately fell apart, one could turn back

---

[63]   Paul Lubeck, 'Unions, Workers and Consciousness in Kano, Nigeria: A View from Below', in *The Development of an African Working Class: Studies in Class Formation and Action*, ed. Richard Sandbrook and Robin Cohen (London: Longman, 1975), 139–60.

[64]   Dorothy Remy, 'Economic Security and Industrial Unionism: A Nigerian Case Study', in *The Development of an African Working Class: Studies in Class Formation and Action*, ed. Richard Sandbrook and Robin Cohen (London: Longman, 1975), 161–77.

[65]   Andrae and Beckman, *Union Power in the Nigerian Textile Industry*.

[66]   *Ibid.*

[67]   Sha Dung Pam, 'Street and Boardroom Politics: The Nigerian Labor Movement, the State and the Struggle for Democracy', in *Organising for Democracy: Nigerian and Comparative Experiences*, ed. Bjørn Beckman and Y. Z. Ya'u (Stockholm and Kano: PODSU, ACKDRAT and CRD, 2012), 32–41.

to Zambia and the copper miners whose product fell precipitately in value, turning to shreds national development planning based on newly nationalized copper. Even before that, the copper miners, and indeed the Copperbelt region and the important Bemba ethnic group who were strongest there, had offered a challenge to President Kenneth Kaunda. In 1971 Simon Kapwepwe, a Copperbelt politician, tried to establish a rival political party to UNIP but was nipped in the bud by the proclamation of the one-party state. The stifling of union influence in Lusaka created a seed of alienation that started to blossom as the economy faltered and Kapwewe began to be remembered as a forerunner of justifiable dissent.[68] A decade later, it was clear that this had begun a restless yearning for union independence and a loss of faith that the state could ever be a real workers' state, even though the conflict between them was not overt until late in the 1980s. As in Ghana, while it is not that the unionists were not infused with nationalism, especially vis-à-vis expatriate whites, it was a different shade of nationalism than the form politicians such as Kaunda were trying to consolidate.[69]

TRADE UNIONS AND STRUGGLES FOR DEMOCRACY IN AFRICA, 1990–2015

A new approach to trade unions and politics in Africa has surfaced, linking trade union activity and militancy to political struggles against authoritarian regimes. This approach is influenced by the idea of civil society as a force for good. This is not a question of Gramscian civil society, where the idea was to infuse and transform civil society with revolutionary ideas. It fits rather the broader, essentially liberal, picture of a society of free institutions and forces operating as interest groups. Labour in this perspective is something less than a voice speaking for all of society. Nonetheless, this new democracy literature is very respectful of the positive influence that organized workers are able to bear on society.[70]

There are therefore elements here which easily refer back to the post-Second World War heyday of union emergence. Unions have continued to occupy strategically pivotal positions in their relevant sectors; in addition,

---

[68] Miles Larmer, 'Enemies Within: Opposition to the Zambian One-Party State, 1972–1980', in *One Zambia, Many Histories: Towards a History of Post-colonial Zambia*, ed. Jan-Bart Gewald, Marja Hinfelaar and Giacomo Macola (Leiden: Brill, 2008), 98–126.

[69] Larmer, *Mineworkers in Zambia*.

[70] Jon Kraus, ed., *Trade Unions and the Coming of Democracy in Africa* (Basingstoke: Palgrave Macmillan, 2007).

they can focus popular anger, as was done in a number of massive protests in Nigeria over petrol price rises, and galvanize a much bigger public. Kraus has surprised us with a list of countries where trade union protest has been very important in regime change: Mali, Niger, Congo and even the Central African Republic – countries virtually lacking in industrial production.[71] However, he also mentions a major strike wave in Algeria in 1987–88, and here we have exactly the situation that would recur in quite a few other places: a strong state with historically Leftist credentials that at one time offered workers a sense of centrality in the development process and benefits within that process that were tangible. In Algeria as elsewhere, the changes in world capitalism from the later 1970s onwards made this increasingly untenable. Such governments went in for structural adjustment, partly under compulsion from aid donors. Cuts in the very large, previously secure workforces in infrastructural and industrial operations, which were not profitable and were now vulnerable to privatization, squeezed the life out of the political compacts typical of the 1960s in country after country.

In Algeria, the big strike wave led to the union movement moving away from an institutional alliance with the state on a subordinate basis to a freer situation, as existed in Nigeria or Kenya already and was simultaneously manifesting itself in Senegal. In Ghana, the Trades Union Congress chafed under the military rule of Jerry Rawlings and led protests, especially as the regime adopted a democratic dispensation and was eventually replaced.[72]

When the Tigray People's Liberation Front (TPLF) succeeded in ousting the Mengistu regime in Ethiopia in 1991, this group of revolutionaries with a strong socialist formation allowed a long-repressed union movement to reform, but in so doing it replicated the conflicts typical of a generation before elsewhere, and the unions were shut down, with their leaders exiled. The state, again classically, created a new federation under tighter control. This has not worked out well despite the state's impressive development project. Unions disliked the restructured federal policy of Meles Zenawi still in place, and one may well wonder if union incorporation as a state strategy will not be abandoned in time.[73]

A far better-known situation, given its historical importance, was the one in Zambia. UNIP's rule weakened steadily in the 1980s, and the government was forced to rescind efforts to raise prices and, in the mines, to reduce services; as it became more threadbare, the state's once substantial services

[71] *Ibid.*, 2.

[72] Rita Abrahamsen, *Disciplining Democracy: Development Discourse and Good Governance in Africa* (London: Zed Books, 2000).

[73] John Markakis, *Ethiopia: The Last Two Frontiers* (Woodbridge: James Currey, 2011).

diminished in value.[74] Kaunda was in such a weak position that he was forced to concede a return to multi-party elections in 1990 after twenty years. The man of the hour, and his best-known and most formidable opponent, was the miners' leader Frederick Chiluba, who became the front-runner of a new political party that won the national election of 1991. Obviously, trade unionists at first expected that Chiluba would do everything he could to shore up a deteriorating living situation. Instead he famously asked the mineworkers to 'die a little'. The Zambian economy, given the hostile prescriptions of aid donors, was in terrible shape. Ever tighter austerity was called for, and, at the end of the decade, the mines were returned to private ownership as were other national economic institutions. Chiluba became a very rich man, belying his former reputation for probity, in this hard-nosed environment. The Chiluba Labour Code outlawed sympathy strikes, opened the door to contract work and limited collective bargaining across the industry. Through the first decade of democracy, the lives of miners became harder, and step by step the union movement lost members and traction and began to separate itself from the state. This would push by degrees towards a separation from party politics entirely.[75]

The Zambian narrative, however, enables us to underscore an important point. African workers have not necessarily turned against dictatorships; they have turned against dictatorships imposing structural adjustment and hitting at their material interests. This in turn may well make them see the leader of the day as the enemy who must be toppled. However, in general, democracy has not of itself brought better conditions economically or, more crucially, a change in priorities. Nonetheless, workers are apt to settle for autonomy, organizational rights and the ability to take on the state or employers on particular issues, especially concerning dismissals or a loss of valued benefits.[76]

South of the Zambesi, an interesting history also unfolded. When the Lancaster House settlement brought an end to the guerrilla war and allowed a universal suffrage election which brought the ZANU-PF government of Robert Mugabe to power in 1980, there was an outpouring of worker activity and even some factory takeovers where the union movement had shown little militancy for many years. The new government responded with severe repression, workers' leaders being imprisoned and tortured. It then proceeded along lines now very well-established in Africa to create a Zimbabwe Confederation of Trade Unions, rationalized and closely watched, just as noted for Ethiopia. Certainly, there was hope that a dynamic

---

[74] Larmer, *Mineworkers in Zambia*.

[75] *Ibid*.

[76] See the chapters by Austin, Berry, Pilossof and Britwum and Dakhli in this volume.

economic policy would be accompanied by the state expediting improved labour conditions; this was borne out to a limited extent in the next few years. However, with the end of Zimbabwe's status as a Front Line state, pressure from the West to rationalize, reduce government budgets and tear down protectionist barriers intensified; Zimbabwean-instituted structural adjustment – ESAP – failed to improve the core economy. As organized workers saw their wages fall in value, they rallied behind a trade union movement now infused with vitality, led by Morgan Tsvangarai; conflict and strikes intensified. In 1999 Tsvangarai, at first uninterested in party politics, accepted the leadership of the Movement for Democratic Change (MDC) to challenge the long-time president, Robert Mugabe.[77]

The MDC was no labour party; indeed, Tsvangarai was no socialist. Strongly supported by foreign-funded NGOs, leaning on the grievances of ethnic siNdebele speakers and with the assistance also of the remaining white community where no love was lost for Mugabe, it never produced any clear strategy aimed at workers, and, when finally in 2008 it entered the government as a junior partner, it cannot be said to have done anything concrete to sustain the unions. Indeed, it can be argued that the movement fell into the arms of what would normally have been the workers' antagonists. Obviously, the union members, who by the late 1990s were already becoming the victims of state-directed violence and persecution, favoured an opening up of the political system and the widening of Zimbabwean democracy, but they were hardly stalwart supporters of neoliberal policy; the relationship with the MDC weakened. In the end, Mugabe remained in power despite the poor economic condition of the country, which greatly reduced the number of the regularly employed. It was the recharged unions that failed to create a telling new kind of politics.[78]

The complex relationship of trade unionism, democracy and the state is at least as central to an assessment of what has gone on yet further south beyond the Limpopo.[79] During the 1950s the Trade and Labour Council

[77] Raftopoulos and Phimister, *Keep on Knocking*; Lovemore Matombo and Lloyd Sachikonye, 'The Labour Movement and Democratisation in Zimbabwe', in *Trade Unions and Party Politics: Labour Movements in Africa*, ed. Bjørn Beckman, Sakhela Buhlungu and Lloyd Sachikonye (Cape Town: HSRC Press, 2010), 109–30.

[78] Paris Yeros, 'The Rise and Fall of Trade Unionism in Zimbabwe, Part I: 1990–1995', *Review of African Political Economy*, 40.136 (2013), 219–32; Paris Yeros, 'The Rise and Fall of Trade Unionism in Zimbabwe, Part II: 1995–2000', *Review of African Political Economy*, 40.137 (2013), 394–409.

[79] William [Bill] Freund, 'Organized Labor in the Republic of South Africa: History and Democratic Transition', in *Trade Unions and the Coming of Democracy in Africa*, ed. Jon Kraus (Basingstoke: Palgrave Macmillan, 2007), 199–227.

dissolved, and a sharp divide existed between the successor Trade Union Congress (which also shed the most right-wing member organizations) and the South African Congress of Trade Unions (SACTU), overwhelmingly black in membership. SACTU was strongly influenced by the illegal Communist Party and turned its attention in time to the armed struggle adopted primarily by the African National Congress (ANC). By the mid-1960s, while not actually defunct, it hardly existed except among a few bureaucrats in exile.

However, from the start of the next decade, a new wave of strikes and labour resistance was set in motion, at first in prosperous times, and devoted young activists helped to forge new unions that liked to describe themselves as non-racial and independent. This was an extraordinary movement that developed a strong tradition of democratic leadership through its shop stewards, the culture of report-backs and a discourse about radical social change.[80] The state, responding partly to a general new spirit of resistance as the economy went into much lower gear, and partly to stifle disorder in the workplaces, set in motion, via the Wiehahn Commission, steps that would start to legalize these unions in 1979 and permit their registration, at first a matter of deep contention.

The success of the new unionism was spectacular; bigger and bigger strikes, whether legal or not, took place, and the ANC, despite its attachment to SACTU, began to realize the importance of the movement. The biggest general strike of all in 1992 would bring four million workers out on the streets, a decisive political moment. In 1985 the Congress of South African Trade Unions (COSATU) was born and soon affiliated itself to the liberation movement. COSATU restructured the differently constituted unions into large bodies that gradually and inevitably, especially after the negotiations that led to the end of the apartheid era, became bureaucratized and distant from ordinary workers.

In the early period of ANC government, trade unions were empowered by favourable legislation. With their write-off membership fees, provident and investment funds and shop stewards respectably paid by management, they were by African standards organizations with real financial clout. Trade union leaders were taken up into cabinet positions, top posts in the party and parliament, as indeed continues to be the case, and the government defines itself as the core of a Triple Alliance with the Communist Party

[80] Jeremy Baskin, *Striking Back: A History of COSATU* (Johannesburg: Ravan Press, 1991); Steven Friedman, *Building Tomorrow Today: African Workers in Trade Unions 1970–1984* (Johannesburg: Ravan Press, 1987); Gay Seidman, *Manufacturing Militance: Workers' Movements in Brazil and South Africa, 1970–1985* (Berkeley, CA: University of California Press, 1994).

and COSATU. However, initially ambitious ideas whereby the unions would help mould social policies of real substance never came about.[81] The secretary general of COSATU, Jay Naidoo, was quickly removed from his super-cabinet post aimed at realizing the union-backed Reconstruction and Development Programme. The National Economic Development and Labour Council, which was initially proposed as a powerful consultative corporatist institution, never acquired teeth. The second ANC president, Thabo Mbeki, was business-oriented and had a poor relationship with COSATU. The unionists co-opted by the government showed little interest in holding to those ideals in any case.

The union movement, looked at more profoundly, also came up against serious structural issues.[82] It was unable to save jobs where restructuring took place or to prevent a massive infusion of contracts that replaced permanent workforces in many sectors. It could not organize domestic workers, security workers or agricultural workers beyond very small numbers. Eckert underscores the limits to registered wage labour in African economies, true even in South Africa.[83]

COSATU came to depend more and more on state employees, such as nurses and teachers, as its core members. From 2012 the important National Union of Mineworkers started to lose members to new upstart militants with little ideological coherence; the discontent of platinum miners at conditions which had been part of a negotiated bargain led to a situation where more than thirty miners were killed by police during a strike at Marikana.[84] Tensions with the other strong private-sector union, the National Union of Metalworkers of South Africa (NUMSA), also came to the boil. In 2014–15 NUMSA broke away, the general secretary of COSATU was removed and the question of a new independent trade unionism advanced. What brings this story in line with events further north is the gradual disaggregation of

[81] Bill Freund, 'Swimming Against the Tide: The Macro-Economic Research Group in the South African Transition 1991–94', *Review of African Political Economy*, 40.138 (2013), 519–36.

[82] Sakhela Buhlungu, 'Union Party Alliances in the Era of Market Regulation: The Case of South Africa', *Journal of Southern African Studies*, 31.4 (2005), 701–17; Franco Barchiesi, *Precarious Liberation: Workers, the State, and Contested Social Citizenship in Postapartheid South Africa* (Albany, NY: SUNY Press, 2011); Eddie Webster and Karl von Holdt, eds, *Beyond the Apartheid Workplace: Studies in Transition* (Pietermaritzburg: University of KwaZulu-Natal Press, 2005).

[83] See the chapter by Eckert in this volume.

[84] Peter Alexander, *Marikana: A View from the Mountain and a Case to Answer* (Johannesburg: Jacana, 2013); Judith Hayem, 'Marikana: répression étatique d'une mobilisation ouvrière indépendante', *Politique Africaine*, 133.1 (2014), 111–30.

the state–union alliance and the thinking behind it, although, at the time of writing, this process is still far from complete.

At the other end of the African continent, the Arab Spring in 2011 had some of the same impact as the liberation movement in South Africa. Trade unions and their political involvement were very important. In 2006 a massive strike broke out at the giant Misr Spinning and Weaving Company, which dominated the economy of the small city of al-Mahalla al-Kubra. The strike, which concerned withheld bonuses (and involved a considerable number of women), was a complete success, and the state, which owned the plant, gave in. The Nasserist labour system was by this time in decay. Workers constantly had to be anxious about the growth of privatization, which could cost jobs, and about heavily bureaucratized structures, which offered little space for protests or solidarity but brilliant careers in government for a few cooperative figures. Only the paternalist waving of the finger from the top often saved the day on issues affecting jobs, but so as to stifle autonomy or resistance from below.

Now the ice had broken. For the next five years the environment changed substantially. Nests of dissidents and activists in the Egyptian Trade Union Federation (ETUF) came alive. At the same time, withdrawal from the ETUF from about 2009 onwards became commonplace, and independent unions, hundreds and hundreds, often organizing highly educated professional workers, began to form. This created a space in which criticism of President Hosni Mubarak could gather force. The 2011 explosion that led to his overthrow therefore had much to do with the revival of Egyptian trade unionism, but it did not involve coherent union organization or politics that could take command of the resistance to the state, particularly in the giant, economically complex cities of Alexandria and Cairo.

The bracing new politics flowed in and out of labour contexts. Still more complicated was the situation as political organization formed, but without an alternative that spoke clearly to workers who were taken up in these new currents. Masses of people turned to the venerable Muslim Brotherhood Party, the Wafd's old rivals, which captured the presidency in democratic elections. The new president, Mohammed Mursi, turned to old ETUF bureaucrats as his allies. These had no programme for labour beyond minor concessions, and trade unionists were divided between those whose hostility to Mursi was such as to push them, with many supporters of the old regime, into the arms of General Abdel-Fattah al-Sisi, who seized power in 2013, and those who continued to stress belief in political democracy first and foremost. A prominent unionist in time-honoured fashion was named al-Sisi's minister of labour. Up against an entrenched system enmeshed with military power in the economy and a formidable establishment embedded in the Egyptian state, the labour movement relished its new-found freedom but did not really find a structural form to bring significant institutional change to bear.[85]

Tunisia was the first site of the Arab Spring. Under Bourgiba's successor Ben Ali, who first used and then turned against the unions, the movement tended to break away and become genuinely far more independent while hosting a rich array of political ideas and traditions never entirely abandoned. Here, too, the Arab Spring revolt, in putting paid to Ben Ali, had an important labour component. The phosphate miners of Gafsa struck at the start of the crisis and the regime disintegrated when the UGTT called a general strike in Tunisia. However, the unions, which established from this point a reasonable understanding with employers, stayed politically neutral as Tunisians voted to establish a somewhat shaky coalition government.

CONCLUSION

This discussion has hopefully indicated that the union movement in Africa has undergone an evolution that can now be traced briefly. With organizational ideas brought in through settler communities in colonial times and encouragement from colonial reform regimes that felt the need for a less despotic order in work contexts, trade unions emerged in Africa and acquired membership and leadership in the African population. The late colonial context was such as to promote a mix of ideas that married nationalism, the striving for independence and hostility to racial privilege with more traditional trade union demands.

While the picture is not uniform, independence then brought about a radically altered situation whereby the state, typically the biggest employer of labour, tried to create a different balance, reorganizing federations, co-opting militant leaders and serving as patrons to a working class that could benefit from legislation that stabilized jobs and conditions. The results here were variable and depended increasingly on the economic situation. Structured and regulated wage labour in Africa has always existed in the midst of a sea of precarious, casual, intermittent and unprotected labour defining the actual lives of workers and their dependants.[86] This became far more apparent in the deteriorating situation that characterized the final quarter of the twentieth century. Where economic decline was engaged by fierce structural adjustment interventions, workers were alienated from the nationalist state. They turned

---

[85] Anne Alexander and Mostafa Bassiouny, *Bread, Freedom, Social Justice: Workers in the Egyptian Revolution* (London: Zed Books, 2014).

[86] See the chapter by Barchiesi in this volume.

against it and, where they could, worked towards making unions more independent.

The call for political democracy played another siren song. It is possible to say that workers who struggled to build up trade unions bought into the dream of national independence under a party run by indigenous Africans at one time, and at another they bought into the dream of democracy. Neither trajectory has, however, been more than ambiguously or temporarily successful in making a better life for most union members. Today, organized workers in Africa can look back on a rich history with many lessons; they take up the cudgels for their interests willingly and effectively very often but, lacking a more wide-reaching agenda, the arrival of a democratic dispensation has by no means necessarily brought material rewards. Whether they will search for a new answer remains to be seen.

TWENTY
Social Welfare

BEN SCULLY

Department of Sociology,
University of the Witwatersrand, Johannesburg

RANA JAWAD

Department of Social and Policy Sciences,
University of Bath

In the last decades of the nineteenth and first decades of the twentieth century, widespread wage labour emerged across the African continent for the first time. The continent's population and economy remained, as it would throughout the twentieth century, largely rural and agrarian. Forced labour, driven by both colonial states and private employers, also remained widespread. However, the growing importance of capitalist mining and agriculture, along with the increasing development of roads, railways and other infrastructure by colonial states, produced a market for wage labour in locations across the continent on an unprecedented scale.

In this same period, European intellectuals were in the midst of a fervent debate on the 'social question'. The rapid transformation that nineteenth-century capitalist expansion had initiated called for a reconsideration of welfare, well-being and the very structure of social life. This debate might have seemed distant from the African context at the time. The emerging groups of urban wage workers on the continent were assumed by colonial states to be temporary sojourners from their natural and permanent homes in the countryside. The welfare and social reproduction of African workers were seen as the domain of the rural and traditional. However, as capitalism and colonialism continued to disrupt and dislocate extant forms of social life, this assumption was increasingly exposed as fiction. Already by the 1930s the question of social welfare had been brought to the centre of colonial administrators' attention through burgeoning nationalist and labour movements across the continent. Since the period of late colonial reforms, through the developmentalism of the post-independence era, and into the more recent focus on poverty reduction, social welfare has remained a central focus of African political debates and policy initiatives.

Social welfare in Africa has had both political and economic dimensions. Waves of contention, advancing demands for independence and democracy, have repeatedly reshaped the relationship between states and citizens. The state provision of welfare first emerged from the colonial authorities, who hoped that improving standards of living would quell growing demands for political transformation. For post-independence states, welfare provided by the government and by private employers was a tool for securing the support of workers, who were among the most organized, and in some cases oppositional, constituencies in the political landscape of many new countries. In the 1980s economic crisis and neoliberal ideologies led to declining welfare provisions and the generalized erosion of living standards. This set off a new protest wave which produced democratic openings in countries across the continent. In the years since, social welfare has become an important tool for political parties to mobilize electoral constituencies, and workers have played varying roles in shaping these developments.

At the same time, questions of welfare have been intertwined with debates about development. Leaders from across the political spectrum have often viewed welfare spending as a distraction from the pressing task of economic growth. However, a contrasting view, running from the colonial era to the present, has held that improved welfare is a necessary precursor to sustained economic expansion. While these positions are shaped by ongoing political debates, they cannot be described as simply reflecting opposing ideological positions. For example, neoliberal international finance institutions (IFIs) were leading critics of welfare expenditure in the late 1970s and early 1980s, claiming that it put pressure on the fiscus and constrained more productive spending. In the contemporary period, the same organizations have become vocal proponents of the developmental role of social protection.

Because wage workers constituted a minority of the overall population in large parts of the continent throughout much of the twentieth century, it is necessary to think of social welfare in a broad sense, including but extending beyond the workplace and state policy. Land has remained a central pillar of welfare, even for many wage workers. Non-state and non-market systems of support, ranging from informal family networks to more organized mutual aid societies, have long been important to workers' well-being, especially in the face of emergencies. However, this broader understanding of welfare should not suggest that the state is absent. In the last few decades Africa has become a site of significant innovation and expansion of state welfare provision, even as welfare states of many wealthy countries elsewhere in the world are being undermined.

This chapter discusses social welfare in relation to workers in Africa from the early twentieth century to the present. This history is divided into three periods: the colonial era (1900–60), the post-independence period (1960–80) and the neoliberal era (1980–present). These periods are, of course, rough approximations which do not accurately describe major turning points in each country. Many countries underwent significant political transformations, such as transitions from democracy to authoritarian rule, during the post-independence era. Some countries, especially in southern Africa, only overcame minority rule at the beginning of the neoliberal era. And in many countries, major new policies have been introduced since the 1990s, especially with regard to social welfare, which represent a significant departure from the neoliberal policy recommendations that prevailed in the 1980s. However, despite such variations, the periodization below provides a general framework for thinking about the changing relationship between work and welfare on the continent.

THE COLONIAL PERIOD AND THE DEVELOPMENT OF 'WELFARE', 1900–60

EARLY TWENTIETH CENTURY, 1900–1930S

In the early twentieth century, in many parts of the continent, demand for labour from capitalist and colonial state enterprises exceeded the supply of people willing to work for wages. In some places, the development of capitalist sectors, especially mining, provided new market opportunities for African agricultural producers which were more attractive than wage work for many rural dwellers.[1] Elsewhere, the very low wages provided by the emerging capitalist sector made wage work more of an occasional strategy to meet cash needs than a viable economic alternative to agricultural or other own-account production.[2] This labour shortage was a central focus of colonial labour policy. In many areas, especially in the French and Belgian colonies, various forms of forced labour persisted well into the twentieth

---

[1]   Giovanni Arrighi, 'Labour Supplies in Historical Perspective: A Study of the Proletarianization of the African Peasantry in Rhodesia', *The Journal of Development Studies*, 6.3 (1970), 197–234; Colin Bundy, *The Rise and Fall of the South African Peasantry* (London: James Currey, 1988).

[2]   A. G. Hopkins, 'The Lagos Strike of 1897: An Exploration in Nigerian Labour History', *Past & Present*, 35.1 (1966), 133–55.

century. In some instances, forced labour was direct, relying on the coercive power of the colonial state and/or 'traditional' authorities.[3] In other instances, the coercion of labour was indirect, through what could be thought of as anti-social policy. While social policy often aims to provide security to those who are unable to participate in wage labour (e.g., the elderly, the infirm and the unemployed), the anti-social policy of colonial states aimed to reduce the security of independent peasants in order to compel them to seek wage employment. This was accomplished through a variety of means, including taxes, the restriction of land ownership and the subsidization of white capitalist farmers, which compromised black farmers' ability to compete.[4]

While the state put a great deal of effort into creating a reliable labour supply, whether through direct or indirect coercion, there was much less concern about developing skills and supporting the welfare of wage workers. Where efforts were made to protect workers, they tended to be limited to prohibiting egregious forms of violence and life-threatening conditions of work. In Kenya, for example, in 1920, the government followed a series of laws aimed at compelling Africans into wage labour with an amendment to the Masters and Servants Ordinance that 'attempt[ed] to make this coercion physically humane'.[5] The new amendment created a Principal Labour Inspector of the colony, who had authority to prosecute offences and who could 'inspect workplaces and ask to see all employees, housing, food, water and medical equipment'.[6]

In the first part of the century, state provision of social protection for workers rarely went beyond this type of literal protection from physical violence and preventable death in the workplace. African wage workers were employed almost exclusively in low-skill and low-paying jobs. Furthermore, there was a contradiction between the colonial demand for a labour supply and the widespread view of colonial officials that Africans were not suited to permanent, urbanized wage work. As such, colonial states gave minimal attention to their development or protection as wage workers. There was slightly more attention to protection in the sphere of small-scale agriculture. One important institution in French Colonial Africa were the *sociétés de prévoyance*. The first such *sociétés* were established in Algeria in 1894 to maintain communal granaries which would protect against food shortages

---

[3]   See the chapter by Fall and Roberts in this volume.

[4]   Arrighi, 'Labour Supplies in Historical Perspective'; Bundy, *Rise and Fall of the South African Peasantry*; Hopkins, 'The Lagos Strike of 1897'.

[5]   Anthony Clayton and Donald C. Savage, *Government and Labour in Kenya, 1895–1963* (London: Frank Cass, 1974), 110.

[6]   *Ibid.*, 111.

in times of crop failure.[7] In 1910 the Algerian model was implemented in French West Africa, and, in the subsequent decades, they spread throughout the French African colonies. The *sociétés* had significant autonomy at the local level, and so their structures and activities varied, but, on the whole, they were funded by membership fees (which were voluntary in Algeria, but compulsory for all adult males throughout West Africa), paid in cash or in kind. The funds raised were used to maintain grain supplies (or cash to purchase food in times of shortage) as well as a source of credit for various agricultural improvement projects.[8]

Beyond this type of social protection, much of what may be thought of as broader forms of social policy, such as public health and education, had historically been dominated by religious organizations, whether Christian missionaries or Islamic schools, rather than the state. The health and education facilities that existed were primarily for the benefit of European colonialists, rather than Africans, and services that were accessible to Africans tended to target specific 'vulnerable' groups, such as the disabled or orphans. There was, in the first half of the twentieth century, increasing cooperation between the state and missionaries, especially with regard to education.[9] The French colonial government in particular attempted increasingly to assert control over schooling in this period, setting out requirements for new schools to register and teach a government-approved curriculum. However, the number of schools remained limited, and policy required their enrolment to correspond to the 'estimate of job availability for graduating students'.[10]

The effects of the general lack of social protection can be seen in the social welfare indicators that are available for the period. While there are few reliable statistics, Tarik Yousef uses the example of Egypt to illustrate the low levels of well-being: 'the neglect of human services allowed periodic epidemics and malnutrition to keep mortality rates high until the late 1940s'.[11] Education levels were also well below those of other developing regions,

[7] G. Mann and J. I. Guyer, 'Imposing a Guide on the *Indigène*: The Fifty Year Experience of the *Sociétés de Prévoyance* in French West and Equatorial Africa', in *Credit, Currencies and Culture: African Financial Institutions in Historical Perspective*, ed. E. Stiansen and J. I. Guyer (Uppsala: Nordiska Afrikainstitutet, 1999), 125.

[8] *Ibid.*

[9] P. Kallaway, 'Education, Health and Social Welfare in the Late Colonial Context: The International Missionary Council and Educational Transition in the Interwar Years with Specific Reference to Colonial Africa', *History of Education*, 38.2 (2009), 217–46.

[10] B. W. White, 'Talk about School: Education and the Colonial Project in French and British Africa (1860–1960)', *Comparative Education*, 32.1 (1996), 11–12.

[11] Tarik M. Yousef, 'Development, Growth and Policy Reform in the Middle East and North Africa since 1950', *Journal of Economic Perspectives*, 18.3 (2004), 91.

with adult illiteracy estimated at 85 per cent in 1939 and only 23 per cent of children aged 5–19 enrolled in school.[12]

Despite the relative lack of state social policy for African wage workers, the continued spread of both capitalist employment and colonial political control in this period laid the groundwork for the eventual emergence of social welfare as a political issue in colonial Africa. Policies aimed at generating a labour supply, such as forced labour and restrictions on access to land, were leading to unintended consequences for colonial states. In some areas, particularly in southern Africa, the decline of rural incomes was already undermining the ability of rural households to gain a livelihood and to support the reproduction of migrant wage workers.[13] As Charles van Onselen has argued, some of the earliest expressions of a 'worker consciousness' among African wage workers were the widespread desertions that plagued colonial and capitalist enterprises, such as the mines of Rhodesia that were his focus.[14] However, more formal and collective action was also emerging in urban and industrial locations across the continent.[15]

Much of this early black workers' protest was met with repression and piecemeal attempts at pacification. It took an organized and militant wave of protest from white workers to first prompt an African state to treat (a section of) workers' welfare as a state concern. The recruitment of foreign white workers had been undertaken in part as a solution to the labour shortage that prevailed in the aftermath of the discovery of diamonds and gold in southern Africa. However, already by the turn of the century, multi-racial poverty and unemployment were emerging in the urban mining centres in the region. In the 1890s city leaders in Johannesburg established the first public works programme and relief fund for poor Afrikaners.[16] In 1908, also in Johannesburg, a group of white workers organized around the identity of 'the unemployed', demanding support from the state. In response to these workers' protests, the city established a public works programme to absorb

[12] *Ibid.*

[13] Harold Wolpe, 'Capitalism and Cheap Labour-Power in South Africa: From Segregation to Apartheid', *Economy and Society*, 1.4 (1972), 425–56.

[14] Charles van Onselen, 'Worker Consciousness in Black Miners: Southern Rhodesia, 1900–1920', *Journal of African History*, 14.2 (1973), 237–55.

[15] Hopkins, 'The Lagos Strike of 1897'; van Onselen, 'Worker Consciousness in Black Miners'; Clayton and Savage, *Government and Labour in Kenya*, 44–5.

[16] John Iliffe, *The African Poor: A History* (Cambridge: Cambridge University Press, 1987), 118.

the labour of urban unemployed whites.[17] In 1913, and more dramatically in 1922, white workers rose up in violent rebellions that shook the foundations of the South African state. These protests, especially in 1922, were explicitly racist and cannot be said to have improved the conditions or welfare of the non-white majority of workers. However, they are important as they led to the first instance of a colonial or settler state recognizing an obligation to provide social protection to workers on a large scale, albeit on a racially exclusive basis. In the aftermath of the 1922 'Rand rebellion', the South African government introduced some welfare programmes, including a pension system, which would eventually be transformed by subsequent waves of black workers' protests into the contemporary, non-racial South African system of social grants.

The fact that a racially exclusive pension programme stands as the main state social welfare achievement of early twentieth-century workers' struggles is evidence of the degree to which colonial officials avoided engaging with the social question in this period. As Robin Kendrick argued, up until the Second World War 'the colonists easily and often mistook the smooth working and expansion of colonial enterprises to be the *sine qua non* of improving economic and social welfare'.[18] It was only once scattered cases of labour protest turned into a wave of worker-driven contestation, and especially once these workers' demands were linked with political demands, that colonial states made a concerted effort to broadly improve the welfare of Africans. Throughout the last decades of colonial rule, welfare policy emerged as a tool by which the colonial state attempted to build legitimacy for the continuation of the colonial project.

THE LATE COLONIAL PERIOD, 1930S–1950S

Labour unrest in the global South spiked in the period immediately after the First World War and remained at relatively high levels through the global depression of the 1930s.[19] The growing ranks of wage workers in the colonies were quickly becoming a significant political force. By the end of

---

[17] Charles van Onselen, *Studies in the Social and Economic History of Witwatersrand, 1886–1914. Vol. 1: New Babylon. Vol. 2: New Nineveh* (Johannesburg/London: Ravan Press/Longman, 1982).

[18] Robin Kendrick, 'Survey of Industrial Relations in Cameroon', in *Industrial Relations in Africa*, ed. U. Damachi, H. D. Seibel and L. Trachtman (London: Macmillan, 1979), 101.

[19] Beverly J. Silver, *Forces of Labor: Workers' Movements and Globalization since 1870* (Cambridge: Cambridge University Press, 2003), 128.

the 1930s, British colonial authorities viewed the wave of labour protest as a crisis. As Frederick Cooper argues, while the unrest in the British West Indies captured the most attention, labour protest throughout Africa in this period 'showed that the problem was empire-wide'.[20] In 1940 the British parliament passed the Colonial Welfare and Development Act, which was intended to signal a major shift in the approach to the social question in the colonies. Development would no longer be assumed to be the natural outcome of the 'smooth working and expansion of colonial enterprises'. Instead, the colonial state would make the improvement of well-being its explicit focus. As Cooper summarized the debates around the Act, '"social services" became a watchword, the sign that something *new* was being done ... Spending money merely to improve the standard of living of colonial peoples was new.'[21]

The pairing of 'Welfare' and 'Development' in the title of the Act is significant. The two words represent contrasting approaches to the social question in the colonies (and Africa in particular), which have continued to be debated up until the present. As Cooper shows, the title of the bill reflected a disagreement within the British political establishment about the proper way to respond to the demands that the protest wave of the 1930s had raised. For some sections of the political elite, the idea of development was more palatable than welfare. 'Development' suggested economic growth and could be reconciled with the extension of wage labour and capitalist social relations in the colonies. 'Welfare' implied more of a departure from existing colonial activities. It suggested spending 'merely to improve the standard of living'. The Colonial Office, which was the driving force of the 'welfare' vision, supported the concept by arguing that, far from being an extraneous luxury, welfare was a necessary component of the development agenda. Cooper quotes a colonial official who argued that it was '"impossible to draw any logical dividing line" between economic and social services in that "certain social services were in themselves economic development, i.e. they were necessary for the mise en valeur of the Colonies"'.[22] This debate – between those who view welfare as a means to economic development and those who see growth as a precursor to improved welfare – would continue to be contested long after the colonial system had been overturned.

In the end, real-world examples of the 'new' approach to the colonies did not match the rhetoric of the 'welfarists'. Bill Freund concludes that '[o]ften far less innovative than the ideologues claimed, the kind of development

[20]   Frederick Cooper, *Decolonization and African Society: The Labor Question in French and British Africa* (Cambridge: Cambridge University Press, 1996), 58.

[21]   *Ibid.*, 69.

[22]   *Ibid.*, 71.

that did occur [in this period] stood more in line with the older forms of colonial exploitation, for instance in the emphasis on road and harbour construction'.[23] The Colonial Welfare and Development Act was, however, a significant moment in the emergence of the 'development project',[24] which would come to define economic and social policy in the mid-twentieth century, even after independence.

It was not only the British who were rethinking the social question in Africa during this period. From 1955 the Belgian colonial government in the Congo required all companies employing more than twenty workers to publish codes governing various aspects of working conditions. In 1956 the colony set up the first pension scheme on the continent, which would cover all 'permanent' wage workers (i.e. excluding day labourers and informal workers).[25] The French also shifted towards developmentalist policies in this period, establishing, in 1946, an empire-wide social and economic development fund (FIDES). However, for French colonialism, development was secondary to the concept of citizenship as a tool for rescuing the legitimacy of the colonial project. After the Second World War, the French colonies were reconceptualized as constituents within a French Union. The ideological commitment to equality across this Union raised a number of questions about the rights, including rights to social welfare, of the populations of the Union outside France, who had been transformed from the legal category of *indigènes* into citizens.

Even in the decade before the establishment of the French Union, French colonial officials took steps towards universalizing certain forms of labour law and social protection across the empire. In 1936, when the French National Assembly passed a series of labour laws establishing a forty-hour work week, paid holidays and collective bargaining, the Popular Front government immediately began a process of applying these reforms to workers in the colonies, an effort that faced resistance from colonial businesses and conservative politicians, who saw such reforms as too costly and inappropriate for the African workforce.[26] The Popular Front government fell before most aspects of the French labour legislation had been implemented in the colonies, but some more modest forms of social protection were provided to African workers in this period. In 1936 the same

---

[23]   Bill Freund, *The African Worker* (Cambridge: Cambridge University Press, 1988), 15.

[24]   Philip McMichael, *Development and Social Change: A Global Perspective*, 5th edn (Los Angeles: Sage, 2011).

[25]   Joseph Nicaise, 'Belgian Congo and Ruanda-Urundi 1955–1956', *Civilisations*, 6.4 (1956), 663–69.

[26]   Cooper, *Decolonization and African Society*, 92.

workmen's compensation regulations that applied in France were introduced to French African colonies. In addition, Africans who worked for the French colonial administration were entitled to the social benefits associated with their level of employment, although Cooper notes that the concentration of Africans in lower ranks of the civil service effectively created racial discrimination in benefit levels.[27] However, it is noteworthy that, in French West Africa, even in the late 1940s 'state-owned or partially state-owned enterprises employed approximately one-third of wage-earners',[28] so policies for publicly employed workers played a major role in shaping working conditions for wage workers as a whole. French commitment to universalism became a tool that African workers and politicians used against the colonial authorities to demand increased access to various forms of social protection.

Colonial businesses and some colonial officials continued to argue well into the mid-twentieth century that the vast majority of Africans were not permanent workers in the European sense, and therefore should not be subject to regulations intended for wage workers. However, this line of argument was undermined by the increasingly frequent and militant strikes of the 1940s. The Dakar General Strike of 1946 saw both public- and private-sector wage workers demanding equal treatment regardless of race, including social benefits such as family allowances.[29] The debate about the appropriateness of 'French' social protections for African workers continued throughout the late 1940s, as the French government worked to enact general labour legislation, a *Code du Travail*, which would regulate work across French Africa. The final *Code*, passed in 1952, granted family allowances, paid holidays and an array of other protections to a wide range of workers.

In Portuguese colonies, the pattern was somewhat similar to that in French Africa. Early social protection schemes were for the sole benefit of Portuguese colonial officials, although the small numbers of urbanized, 'assimilated' Africans could participate. Forced labour, especially the forced cultivation of cotton, was the primary focus of the state's labour policy towards Africans. It was not until 1954 that the first occupational health and safety standards which applied to Africans were introduced.

The limited protection provided directly through state social policy was not the only, and perhaps not even the primary, source of social welfare for African workers in the colonial period. Large public and private employers cultivated paternalistic relationships with their workers, often providing a

[27]   *Ibid.*, 103.

[28]   Jean Meynaud and Anisse Salah-Bey, *Trade Unionism in Africa: A Study of its Growth and Orientation* (London: Methuen, 1967), 30.

[29]   Cooper, *Decolonization and African Society*, 282.

wide array of benefits beyond wages, including housing, healthcare, education, training and insurance schemes. The public railway of colonial Kenya, for example, maintained a range of social services that outstripped those provided by the government itself. In the 1940s it was the colony's largest employer, with more than 20,000 African employees in Kenya and Uganda.[30] All employees were provided with housing, mostly in company-owned housing estates. The company set up food shops in Mombasa which provided subsidized food to its employees during the wartime food shortages. It ran two schools to train employees in disciplines relating to the industry. It even sponsored public radio stations in townships 'for both entertainment and education'.[31]

In some places, employers created entire cities, complete with non-work related social services. The state phosphate mining company of Morocco established the town of Khouribga 'from scratch' in the 1920s.[32] By 1952 it had become the third largest centre of wage work in the country, and workers enjoyed employer-provided 'housing, education and basic infrastructure such as water and electricity … [as well as] particular social benefits … that could not be matched by other employers'.[33] These company welfare provisions often followed a similar historical trajectory as the state welfare described above. For example, in the first few decades of mining in the Zambian Copperbelt in the early twentieth century, the social provisions from employers amounted to little more than small plots for workers to grow vegetables. The lack of services reflected the assumption that miners were temporary migrants from their rural homes, rather than permanent workers.[34] However, by the 1950s the Copperbelt mines provided workers with subsidized housing, 'good schools and health facilities, and offered various skills-training programmes, including adult literacy'.[35] In addition, 'for recreation, mine employees had the option of sports clubs, libraries, theatres, cinemas and ballroom dancing facilities, which were also open to their families'.[36]

[30] Clayton and Savage, *Government and Labour in Kenya*, 300.

[31] *Ibid.*, 299.

[32] Koenraad Bogaert, 'The Revolt of Small Towns: The Meaning of Morocco's History and the Geography of Social Protests', *Review of African Political Economy*, 42.143 (2015), 134.

[33] *Ibid.*

[34] Patience Mususa, 'Mining, Welfare and Urbanisation: The Wavering Urban Character of Zambia's Copperbelt', *Journal of Contemporary African Studies*, 30.4 (2012), 571–87. One exception is the Union Minière du Haut-Katanga, a Belgian mining company in the Congo, which provided workers' compensation from 1928. Iliffe, *The African Poor*, 208.

[35] Mususa, 'Mining, Welfare and Urbanisation', 575.

[36] *Ibid.*

WELFARE BEYOND THE STATE AND THE WORKPLACE

An understanding of workers' access to welfare cannot focus only on forms of protection provided by employers and/or the state. Even under advanced capitalism, significant aspects of social reproduction take place beyond the reach of wage work and state policy. In rural and agrarian economies such as those found throughout Africa for most of the twentieth century, non-wage and non-state support has been central for a large proportion of workers.

Indigenous forms of social protection remain an understudied phenomenon, and especially the pre-colonial history of indigenous practices and institutions. There is, unquestionably, a long history of various forms of social support across the continent. Almsgiving and charity were long a part of Islamic, Christian (in Ethiopia) and various African religious traditions. John Iliffe argues that the Yoruba tradition of charitable giving even influenced British authorities to increase charitable acts in turn-of-the-century colonial Nigeria.[37] These historical forms of charity were generally personalized and oriented towards the sick, disabled, elderly, landless poor or others who were unable to provide for themselves through agricultural or other work. However, there were other 'institutionalised, culturally mandated practices' which acted as social security for rural agricultural producers, including 'livestock sharing, communal grain storage, cooperative harvesting, and a variety of other community-based supports', many of which persisted throughout the colonial period, and in some cases up to the present.[38]

As wage work and the urban economy expanded in the first half of the twentieth century, new forms of urban associational life emerged, much of which served to provide protection against specifically urban and wage work-associated risks, such as unemployment, inability to work because of sickness or injury, robbery or legal troubles. One of the most prominent forms in twentieth-century African associations has been the Rotating Savings and Credit Association (ROSCA). One of the early anthropological studies of urban associations, by Kenneth Little in 1953, described ROSCAs in Accra, Ghana, which, unlike linguistic or hometown associations, were open to any members and provided various forms of insurance as well as benefits for childbirth or the death of a member. Many Accra societies of the 1950s even extended various forms of charity to non-members, for example by giving

---

[37] *Ibid.*, 197.

[38] Leila Patel, Edwell Kaseke and James Midgley, 'Indigenous Welfare and Community-Based Social Development: Lessons from African Innovations', *Journal of Community Practice*, 20.1/2 (2012), 12–31.

gifts at hospitals or prisons.[39] Little also described occupational associations which provided similar benefits to ROSCAs but brought together members of a specific profession, such as market traders, tailors or taxi drivers. In addition to various forms of insurance, occupational associations often regulated various aspects of the work, for example by setting standard rates to prevent undercutting.[40] ROSCAs were not limited to urban areas, and they date back to long before widespread wage work; however, they took on new forms in both urban and rural settings in early to mid-twentieth-century Africa. As Bridget O'Laughlin has pointed out in the case of rural Mozambique, the various forms of mutual aid that are often called 'traditional' social protection by contemporary commentators are actual historical products of the expansion of wage work and labour migration.[41]

The changing forms of 'traditional' mutual aid can be taken as an indication that the growing provision of social benefits from states and employers was insufficient to meet the new dislocations caused by the expansion of colonialism and capitalist wage relations. By the late colonial period this inadequacy had become a political issue and fed into growing movements for independence across the continent. Yet even after independence was won, the concept of 'development' which colonial states' reform projects had introduced, as well as the paternalistic employment relationships that colonial enterprises had established, would continue to influence economic and social life in Africa.

THE 1960S TO THE 1980S: THE POST-INDEPENDENCE PERIOD

A WORKPLACE-CENTRED WELFARE SYSTEM EMERGES

The years between the Second World War and the 1970s were a high point for the strength and influence of labour movements in both the global North and many parts of the South, including Africa. After more than a decade of dislocation caused by war and economic depression, political configurations were being reorganized across the world, often on terms

---

[39] Kenneth Little, 'Some Traditionally Based Forms of Mutual Aid in West African Urbanization', *Ethnology*, 1.2 (1962), 198.

[40] *Ibid.*, 201.

[41] Bridget O'Laughlin, 'Rural Social Security and the Limits of "Associativismo" in Southern Mozambique', paper presented at the Conference on 'Poverty Dynamics and Patterns of Economic Accumulation in Mozambique' (*Dinâmicas da pobreza e padrões de acumulação económica em Moçambique*), Maputo, 22–23 April 2009, 15, https://goo.gl/S52748 (accessed 20 March 2016).

relatively more friendly to labour. In the North, this took the form of the expansion of the welfare state, driven in part by the demands of unions for a social democratic compromise between capital and labour. African trade unions also increased their influence in this period, and they also made calls for expanded state provision of social welfare. However, for African workers, social policy, and indeed most other issues, were always subsumed within the broader programme of seeking political transformation. Sakhela Buhlungu has argued that the emergence of trade unionism under colonialism has produced among African workers a lasting orientation towards what he calls a 'politics of national liberation, as opposed to the social democratic politics their Northern counterparts often engage in'.[42]

This orientation is important for understanding the development of social policy in the decades after independence. Unions played a major role in the wave of decolonization that swept across the continent in the 1950s and 1960s. They also became key players in post-independence politics in many states.[43] However, their political programmes were shaped by the lingering influence of colonial power relations, both in the political realm and in the workplace. Across the continent, one of the central demands of unions after independence was the elimination of racial disparities in the labour market. For workers, calls for the 'Africanization' of higher-status jobs in both the public and private sectors, as well as attacks on racial pay disparities, were a natural continuation of the struggle for national liberation. In this context, there was no coordinated political voice calling for the expansion of social welfare. As such, social protection remained, in a certain sense, a 'depoliticized' issue in the decades after independence.

Without pressure from unions, the political leadership of new African states rarely framed welfare expansion as a political priority. If the expansion of the welfare state in the North was an attempt to secure peace and stability among the poor and working classes, the analogous African project was 'national development'. Some leaders were reflective about the relationship between welfare and development. Julius Nyerere's essay 'Freedom and Development' contains passages that echo the 'welfarist' views advanced by the British Colonial Office during debates over 'development' policies a generation earlier:

---

[42] Sakhela Buhlungu, 'Trade Unions and the Politics of National Liberation in Africa: An Appraisal', in *Trade Unions and Party Politics: Labour Movements in Africa*, ed. B. Beckman, S. Buhlungu and L. Sachikonye (Cape Town: HSRC Press, 2010), 200.

[43] *Ibid.*; Ben Scully, 'From the Shop-Floor to the Kitchen Table: The Shifting Centre of Precarious Workers' Politics in South Africa', *Review of African Political Economy*, 43.148 (2016), 295–311.

Roads, buildings, the increases of crop output, and other things of this nature, are not development: they are tools of development ... An expansion of the cotton, coffee, or sisal crop is only development if these things can be sold, and the money used for things which improve the health, comfort, and understanding of the people.[44]

However, this sort of reflexivity was often swamped by the pressing need for rapid economic growth. Kwame Nkrumah of Ghana famously argued that 'what other countries have taken three hundred years or more to achieve', the new countries would have to 'accomplish in a generation'.[45] This urgency tended to push policy towards a narrower conceptualization of development, primarily centred on industrialization. All other efforts, including the provision of social protection, took a back seat in the drive for development. Workers were seen as key to this development drive, as industrialization and expansion of the 'modern' sectors were to be the main drivers of growth. And while states relied heavily on 'sticks' to discipline workers into the development project, there was a role for some welfarist 'carrots' as well.

As a result of this development orientation of policy, a significant proportion of welfare issues remained within the realm of wage work. The paternalistic employment relations that had prevailed in the late colonial period were maintained after independence. Employers continued to provide services that extended far beyond the wage to their employees. When new forms of social protection were introduced, the workplace was often the central institution that determined access to new benefits. The various pension laws and provident funds that were set up across the continent in the wake of independence followed this model.[46] For example, Uganda passed a Social Security Act in 1967, five years after gaining independence. The act established a compulsory savings scheme for workers in the formal sector. Registered employers were required to withhold 5 per cent of the employees' wages and add an additional 10 per cent as the employer's contribution for the Social Security fund.[47]

---

[44] Julius K. Nyerere, 'Freedom and Development' (Dar es Salaam: Government Printer, 1973), 1–2.

[45] Kwame Nkrumah, *Ghana: The Autobiography of Kwame Nkrumah* (New York: International Publishers, 1957).

[46] Clive Bailey and John Turner, 'Social Security in Africa: A Brief Review', *Journal of Aging & Social Policy*, 14.1 (2002), 105–14.

[47] Stephen O. A. Ouma, 'The Role of Social Protection in the Socioeconomic Development of Uganda', *Journal of Social Development in Africa*, 10.2 (1995), 5–12; Brian Nicol, 'Industrial Relations in Uganda', in *Industrial Relations in Africa*, ed. U. Damachi, H. D. Seibel and L. Trachtman (London: Macmillan, 1979), 301.

In other cases, workplace-centred social protection arose out of direct negotiation between employers and workers rather than through state policy. For example, the Mineworkers Union of Zambia negotiated, in 1974, the establishment of a retirement scheme with the mining companies operating in the country.[48] The scheme was funded entirely by the employers and paid a lump sum upon retirement, based on the employee's length of employment and salary at the time of retirement.[49] In addition to employers, African states often turned to the unions themselves to provide various forms of social services. For example, the initial post-independence labour code in Mali gave unions scope to establish everything from pension funds and mutual aid societies to experimental farming stations and education schemes for their members.[50] In Tanzania, the Labour Department prepared a model constitution for unions which was 'adopted by most unions word-for-word'.[51] The document included clauses in which unions undertook to provide insurance against sickness, injury or unemployment, as well as retirement allowances.[52] In Ghana, the state aligned Trades Union Congress (TUC) expanded its social services to include 'clinics, vocational schools, literacy classes, consumer cooperatives and credit unions'.[53]

Given the fraught relationships that developed between many post-independence governments and their trade union allies,[54] political leaders were probably hopeful that unions would give their attention to providing social protection and other services for their members rather than engaging with government and private employers over issues such as wages and Africanization. Richard Sandbrook suggested that this was the case in Kenya where, '[a]t the same time that the government ... restricted the unions' bargaining powers and advocated productionism, it ... also encouraged

[48] Cherry Gertzel, 'Industrial Relations in Zambia to 1975', in *Industrial Relations in Africa*, ed. U. Damachi, H. D. Seibel and L. Trachtman (London: Macmillan, 1979), 328.

[49] James Ferguson, *Expectations of Modernity: Myths and Meanings of Urban Life on the Zambian Copperbelt* (Berkeley, CA: University of California Press, 1999), 124.

[50] William H. Friedland, 'Labor's Role in Emerging African Socialist States', in *The Role of Labor in African Nation-Building*, ed. W. Beling (London: Praeger, 1968), 29.

[51] *Ibid.*

[52] *Ibid.*

[53] Yvonne Asamoah and D. N. A. Nortey, 'Ghana', in *Social Welfare in Africa*, ed. J. Dixon (New York: Croom Helm, 1987), 27.

[54] Buhlungu, 'Trade Unions and the Politics of National Liberation'; Ben Scully, 'Lessons from the Political Strategies of Post-Independence African Trade Unions', in *COSATU in Crisis: The Fragmentation of an African Trade Union Federation*, ed. V. Satgar and R. Southall (Sandton, South Africa: KMM Review, 2015), 35–53.

unions to undertake new social welfare functions'.[55] Such efforts by governments might have played a part in steering union demands away from welfare issues and towards questions of autonomy and political voice.

But it must be noted that the politicization of African trade unionism, and the orientation towards a 'politics of national liberation' rather than a 'social democratic politics', was not driven only by politically ambitious union leadership. Workers as a whole were often sceptical of the association between wage work and social welfare. Robin Cohen argued in his 1974 study of labour in Nigeria that trade unions play a 'limited role … in the social experience of individual workers … Tribal unions, improvement organizations, or religious bodies, all provide social outlets for their members, and trade unions are generally relegated to their purely economic function.'[56] Cohen quotes the economist T. M. Yesufu, who argues that the broad social and economic support offered by

> tribal organization[s], or 'improvement' union[s] in the town … explains the seeming paradox that whereas the worker will not regularly subscribe to the funds of a trade union (apparently because he is too poor) he does pay regular subscriptions to the fund of his tribal 'union'; and the contributions here are usually higher than those required by the trade union …[57]

James Ferguson provides another example of the scepticism of workers towards workplace-based welfare in his account of Zambian mineworkers' rejection of ostensibly pro-worker reforms to the pension scheme. In the mid-1980s the Mineworkers Union of Zambia negotiated a new retirement scheme to replace the initial system established in the 1970s (mentioned above). In the earlier system, the employers covered the entire cost. With regard to the new scheme:

> [It] was supposed to provide workers with a more secure retirement. But it required a mandatory contribution by the workers of 5 percent of their monthly salary. For this reason, the scheme had been fiercely unpopular with the financially pressed workers, who had eventually (in 1985) broken with the union leadership and walked out of the scheme en masse (some 47,485 miners left the scheme, leaving only about 7,800 participating).[58]

These examples point towards a possible explanation for the relatively depoliticized nature of social welfare in the post-independence period.

[55] Richard Sandbrook, *Proletarians and African Capitalism: The Kenyan Case, 1960–1972* (Cambridge: Cambridge University Press, 1975), 175.

[56] Robin Cohen, *Labour and Politics in Nigeria* (London: Heinemann, 1974), 132.

[57] Yesufu quoted in *ibid.*, 132–3.

[58] Ferguson, *Expectations of Modernity*, 124.

African states focused primarily on industrially oriented development, and allowed welfare regimes to expand along the employment-centred model that had been established in the colonial era. The workplace remained a key site for accessing a wide range of social benefits, including housing, healthcare, education and training, various forms of insurance, and some form of old age security. African workers did not vigorously engage with state welfare policy as a political issue, as they saw social and economic connections beyond the workplace as more important to their long-term security. A large proportion of the African working-age population remained outside formal wage work. Furthermore, as Deborah Kasente notes, even in the contemporary period, 'the small percentage of people able to benefit from formal social security [in Africa] includes an even smaller number of women, thus making formal social security almost irrelevant to the majority of African women'.[59] The result of these factors was the emergence of the types of 'highly segmented welfare regime[s]' that Thandika Mkandawire has identified as typical of Southern welfare generally.[60]

Between the 1950s and the 1970s North African states pursued and implemented various social reform policies.[61] These had a strong interventionist-redistributive character and included some of the following policies:

1. nationalisation of foreign assets and large domestic enterprises such as the Suez Canal in Egypt;

2. land reform;

3. mass education and, in some cases, such as Tunisia, secularization of state institutions and the education system;

4. the support of low-income groups through direct financial transfers by the state and large programmes of state-provided education, housing, healthcare and food subsidies;

5. the emergence of centralized, hierarchical and tightly controlled trade unions, professional associations and ruling-party governments, in which political contestation was discouraged and, as the years rolled on, directly repressed.

---

[59] Deborah Kasente, 'Gender and Social Security Reform in Africa', *International Social Security Review*, 53.3 (2000), 27.

[60] Thandika Mkandawire, 'Social Policy and the Challenges of the Post-Adjustment Era', in *Getting Development Right: Structural Transformation, Inclusion, and Sustainability in the Post-Crisis Era*, ed. E. Paus (New York: Palgrave Macmillan, 2013), 63.

[61] Yousef, 'Development, Growth and Policy Reform'.

Post-independence laws and constitutions reflected a new discourse of radical populism in which the state directly controlled the workings of the private sector. New conceptions of citizenship were emerging which supported the image of a strong state as an agent of public welfare. New rights to political action were emerging in tandem with new forms of political and social mobilization such as trade unionism, political parties and professional associations.

For example, in Tunisia, a powerful trade union movement, the UGTT, developed close links with the leading nationalist political party, the Neo-Destour, which negotiated Tunisia's independence from France. Egyptian nationalists also viewed organized labour as an extension of the nationalist movement. Thus, the colonial construction of state institutions throughout North Africa during moments of nationalist mobilization was critical for the later emergence of interventionist-redistributive social contracts across the region. Statist orientations, mass politics and anti-colonial struggles often led to the strong involvement of the military in politics, as came to be the case in several of the countries under study.

Thus, well into the 1980s, the North African region experienced immense social transformations, due to the further key influence of the unprecedented oil wealth that affected the entire North African context. Oil- and gas-producing countries were able to develop welfare systems of state-provided social transfers. These were used to establish and fund state social services such as guaranteed government employment for graduates; new labour legislation (favouring workers in large public enterprises) such as health insurance, retirement pay and maternity pay; free education; free hospital care; and basic consumer subsidies, the most important of which were food and housing. Urbanization and economic development were accompanied by significant attainments in education and enhanced female labour participation. Labour-exporting countries such as Egypt reaped the benefits from the foreign remittances. At the height of the oil boom in the early 1980s, around 3.5 million Arab migrants were employed in the Persian Gulf states. Loans, grants and other forms of assistance from oil-producing states to non-oil-producing countries strengthened government revenues and helped to sustain distributive commitments.

With state legitimization as an important objective while resources were scarce, North African countries have suffered high levels of underdevelopment. Disparities between rural and urban areas have been particularly prominent in this region with, for example, rural migrants accounting for almost 60 per cent of residents in Morocco's major urban centres in the 2000s. In Libya, uneven development curbed political opposition, while in Tunisia and Morocco it has been more a result of having to prioritize in the face of difficult economic circumstances.

BROADER FORMS OF STATE WELFARE

Despite the wage-worker bias in welfare regimes, African states did expand access to certain forms of basic social spending in the years immediately after independence. Perhaps the most remarkable gains were made in the area of education. The new independent states of Africa inherited education systems that were underdeveloped and highly segmented. At the time of independence, school enrolment levels were low and often concentrated in and around urban areas. For example, in Ghana, just after independence, enrolments in 'parts of' the south 'reached 60 per cent, while in the North, they drop to an average of a little over 10 per cent'.[62] Similar differentials were found in immediate post-independence Côte d'Ivoire.[63]

The expansion of educational access was a priority of most governments, and the successes achieved are impressive. Mkandawire notes that the post-independence period in Africa witnessed 'some of the most dramatic changes in school enrolment ratios in human history'.[64] A 1977 report by the United Nations Educational, Scientific and Cultural Organization (UNESCO) estimated that total enrolment in Africa more than doubled between 1960 and 1970, from 21 million to 54 million.[65] Eighty per cent of enrolment in 1975 was at the primary level, reflecting the focus on expanding mass basic education.[66] However, secondary and tertiary education also received considerable resources. Enrolment at these levels increased at more than 10 per cent per year from 1960 to 1975, albeit from very low bases.[67]

Educational expansion in this period primarily focused on young people. However, the historical legacy of insufficient colonial education meant that new countries also inherited generations of adults who had not had access to formal schooling. A number of African countries embarked on mass

---

[62] Remi P. Clignet and Philip J. Foster, 'French and British Colonial Education in Africa', *Comparative Education Review*, 8.2 (1964), 195.

[63] *Ibid.*

[64] Thandika Mkandawire, 'Shifting Commitments and National Cohesion in African Countries', in *Common Security and Civil Society in Africa*, ed. L. Wohlgemuth et al. (Uppsala: Nordiska Afrikainstititutet, 1999), 24.

[65] Christopher Colclough, 'The Impact of Primary Schooling on Economic Development: A Review of the Evidence', *World Development*, 10.3 (1982), 167–85.

[66] *Ibid.*

[67] *Ibid.*

adult literacy campaigns, many of them funded by the United Nations Development Programme (UNDP) and UNESCO's Experimental World Adult Literacy Programme. Tanzania's adult education programme was the most successful in Africa and among the most successful in the world. Between 1971 and 1975 about 1.4 million adults passed the national literacy examination, thereby increasing the literacy rate from 33 per cent to 61 per cent in the space of four years.[68]

In some countries, educational attainment was incentivized with guaranteed employment in the public sector for graduates. The longest running of these guarantees was in Egypt, where graduates of universities as well as technical and vocational schools were entitled to employment from the mid-1960s until the late 1980s.[69] Similar guarantees were in place in the decades after independence in Somalia, the Central African Republic and Benin.[70]

These forms of welfare expenditure were not driven directly by the demands of workers or any narrow political constituency. But as with welfare expenditure everywhere, they retained a political component. They constituted one arm of new governments' efforts at 'nation building'.[71] They created expectations on the part of citizens for a basic level of social services. Perhaps most importantly, the provision of basic services was carried out by a growing number of public-sector workers, such as teachers and nurses. In many countries, these workers would come to be central actors in the labour movement. When fiscal pressures and shifting ideological winds forced the curtailment of such basic spending in the 1970s and 1980s, the political importance of such programmes became clear, and the public-sector workers who were directly affected often played an important role in calling for both political and economic reforms.

The mutual aid organizations and other forms of 'informal' welfare described above for the colonial era continued to play an important role in the post-independence period. As with the colonial era, they can be read, in part, as a sign of the inadequacy of 'formal' forms of security that emerged in the period. Despite being widespread, the fragmented and often loosely institutionalized nature of many mutual aid organizations meant that

---

[68] Jeff Unsicker, 'Tanzania's Literacy Campaign in Historical-Structural Perspective', in *National Literacy Campaigns: Historical and Comparative Perspectives*, ed. R. F. Arnove and H. J. Graff (New York: Springer Science & Business Media, 1987). 220.

[69] Ragui Assaad, 'The Effects of Public Sector Hiring and Compensation Policies on the Egyptian Labor Market', *The World Bank Economic Review*, 11.1 (1997), 86–7.

[70] Derek Robinson, *Civil Service Pay in Africa* (Geneva: ILO, 1990), 61.

[71] Mkandawire, 'Shifting Commitments and National Cohesion in African Countries'.

post-independence policymakers could not use existing forms of support as a basis to build new state institutions of social welfare. As such, and as in the colonial period, the practice of mutual aid remained beyond the reach of the state.

THE CRISIS AND THE EMERGENCE OF NEW FORMS OF WELFARE: 1980S TO THE PRESENT

ECONOMIC CRISIS AND LABOUR CASUALIZATION IN THE 1980S

The 1950s to mid-1970s had been a period of sustained economic growth for countries across the global South, including many newly independent African states. This growth had facilitated an expansion of social spending, both by employers and by states. However, by the late 1970s and increasingly in the 1980s, two shifts took place which undermined the post-independence social welfare regimes of many countries. First, the global post-Second World War economic expansion came to an end with the economic crisis of the 1970s. The crisis was first felt primarily in wealthy countries of the global North, as increased competition from newly industrialized countries of the South cut into corporate profitability. However, by the late 1970s aggressive monetary policy on the part of the United States and the growing influence of neoliberal ideology put pressures on African states which led to a widespread economic slowdown.[72] Declining economic performance led to declining state revenues, and, 'by the mid-1980s, within the new ideological disposition towards stabilization and structural adjustment, social policy was associated with the fiscal crisis of the state, and thus treated as one more source of economic instability and inflation'.[73]

At the same time as the economic crisis, precarious employment relations began to be incorporated into formal enterprises across the continent. Of course, precarious work itself was not new in Africa.[74] However, this period did see an erosion of formalized and paternalistic employment relations in private companies, and later within the public sector. In part, this reorganization of work was driven by the rise of neoliberal ideologies, which emphasized 'flexibility'. However, as Andries Bezuidenhout and Sakhela Buhlungu argue in the case of the dissolution of mineworker housing compounds in South Africa, some trends towards informalization were a

[72] Arrighi, 'Labour Supplies in Historical Perspective'.

[73] Mkandawire, 'Shifting Commitments and National Cohesion in African Countries'.

[74] Ronaldo Munck, 'Globalisation, Labour and Development: A View from the South', *Transformation: Critical Perspectives on Southern Africa*, 72.1 (2010), 205–24.

response to organized workers' ability to co-opt formalized systems designed for the control of workers.[75]

The dual effect of these two developments was to erode both the state-provided and workplace-based forms of welfare that had been expanded in the years since independence. Yousef characterizes the period of the 1980s to the 1990s as a new phase in the history of post-independence social protection in North Africa.[76] The immediate post-independence period had seen rapid urbanization and economic growth, proactive state-led social reforms and nation building. By the 1960s–1970s a process of liberalization and opening up to the global economy had begun, while still maintaining healthy levels of public social expenditure with burgeoning state bureaucracies. It was in the 1980s–1990s that cracks in the economy began to appear and many regimes began to revert to repressive, security-focused tactics in the face of rising social discontent and deprivation. Various explanations for the economic downturn in the MENA (Middle East and North Africa) have been put forward such as weak economic bases, the 'curse' of abundant natural reserves of oil and gas, ineffective political systems, war and civil conflict and even culture and religion.[77]

This welfare roll-back was not limited to North Africa, and it pushed the weight of the economic crisis into the private spaces of Africa's poor and working classes. Given the contradiction of workplace-centred welfare regimes in economies dominated by agrarian production and/or informal employment, household and land-based sources of livelihood were essential for providing an informal social protection floor. An example is provided by Bruce Frayne's research on residents of Windhoek, Namibia, which found that a majority of these urban households relied on food transfers from rural relatives, and of those who received such transfers a significant majority considered them 'very important' or 'critical to [the household members'] survival'.[78]

However, the structural adjustment programmes that were forced on to many African countries undermined the security of rural livelihoods at exactly the moment they were becoming an important source of last-resort social protection. At the behest of IFIs, crop subsidies were scrapped,

[75] Andries Bezuidenhout and Sakhela Buhlungu, 'From Compounded to Fragmented Labour: Mineworkers and the Demise of Compounds in South Africa', *Antipode*, 43.2 (2011), 237–63.

[76] Yousef, 'Development, Growth and Policy Reform'.

[77] *Ibid.*, 92.

[78] Bruce Frayne, 'Migration and the Changing Social Economy of Windhoek, Namibia', *Development Southern Africa*, 24.1 (2007), 98–9.

state-run marketing boards were phased out and farming parastatals were privatized.[79] Similarly, other social services were marketized, with school fees and fee-based health clinics replacing the state-subsidized versions of these institutions that had been established in the post-independence years.[80] These trends reduced the social security role that rural households could play, but they also exacerbated the growing precarity of the wage labour market, as rural households sought informal wage labour and self-employment opportunities to meet their increasing cash requirements.[81]

Such insecurity was not limited to rural areas. Urban households in areas where wage work was becoming informal, or even disappearing altogether, were often sites of increasing conflict and social divisions just as their role as centres of security was becoming more significant.[82] As the level and reliability of wages declined, women's unpaid household labour often stood in as the social protection of last resort. But such dependence on women exacerbated existing gender inequalities in access to security. As Kasente notes, women 'play a key role of providers of traditional [informal] social security even though they themselves are not guaranteed protection under the same system'.[83]

By the mid-1980s urban African spaces were witnessing intense conflict in response to the declining standard of living that followed the erosion of social protection and the informalization of work. The unrest of the 1980s could be considered the first sustained collective action that was explicitly related to issues of welfare. That is not to say that these protests advanced a coherent demand around social policy. As their common characterization as 'riots'[84] indicated, they tended to be driven by unorganized sections of the urban poor. However, they were a direct response to the diminishing well-being precipitated by the withdrawal of both state- and employer-provided social security.

Despite, or perhaps because of, the informalization of wage work, trade unions also grew increasingly militant in this period. By the late 1980s and early 1990s workers had become leaders of the growing popular resistance

---

[79]   Deborah Fahy Bryceson, 'The Scramble in Africa: Reorienting Rural Livelihoods', *World Development*, 30.5 (2002), 728.

[80]   *Ibid.*, 729.

[81]   *Ibid.*, 730

[82]   Sarah Mosoetsa, *Eating from One Pot: The Dynamics of Survival in Poor South African Households* (Johannesburg: Wits University Press, 2011).

[83]   Kasente, 'Gender and Social Security Reform in Africa', 36.

[84]   For example, John Walton and David Seddon, *Free Markets and Food Riots: The Politics of Global Adjustment* (Oxford: Blackwell, 1994).

to austerity policies in a number of African countries. The study by Jon Kraus and his colleagues of this wave of democratization demonstrated the 'seminal role' played by unions.[85] Unions still did not advance clear demands for increased social welfare, but their protests did lay the groundwork for a major expansion of social protection in the period from 1990 to the present. Kraus's study helps illuminate why welfare re-entered the policy space despite not being an explicit demand of the unions.

In the cases that Kraus's book covers, 'major strikes and protests tended to originate in workers' consciousness of falling wages and living conditions'.[86] Governments were under external pressure to implement structural reforms, and some might have also have seen neoliberal ideology as an opportunity to undermine organized political opposition such as trade unions.[87] Whatever the reason, states responded to union activism with repression, which 'compelled union leaders' to shift attention from economic issues and to 'demand forcefully their own political liberties, such as the right to oppose and protest ... [and a] renewal of democratic institutions'.[88] These political demands allowed unions to successfully reach out to broader constituencies and social movements, including 'student, teacher, legal, and religious groups'.[89] In the end, protests that had begun in workers' resistance to their flagging economic positions turned into broad-based social demands for democratization and political openness.

WELFARE AND DEMOCRATIC POLITICS AFTER 1990

This wave of protest led to various levels of political change, ranging from near-revolutionary transformations (e.g. South Africa and Namibia) to significant reforms (e.g. Senegal and Ghana) to renewed space for political debates but with no clear sustained outcomes (e.g. Nigeria and Zimbabwe). In many countries, this contestation had demonstrated the fragility of the post-independence social order. It showed that the promise of development and the expansion of basic services had been pillars of the 'state-building' project in the 1950s to the 1970s, since their removal had precipitated such a widespread crisis of legitimacy. The post-1990 expansion of democracy

[85] Jon Kraus, ed., *Trade Unions and the Coming of Democracy in Africa* (New York: Palgrave Macmillan, 2007).

[86] *Ibid.*, 268.

[87] Raewyn Connell and Nour Dados, 'Where in the World Does Neoliberalism Come From?', *Theory and Society*, 43.2 (2014), 117–38.

[88] Kraus, ed., *Trade Unions and the Coming of Democracy*, 268.

[89] *Ibid.*

did not lead to a complete rejection of neoliberal ideology. The casualization of labour and the marketization of economic life would continue in various forms up until the present. But the 1990s did seem to be a turning point for many states in their approach to the question of social welfare. From this period onwards there was a steadily expanding number of state programmes that provided new social entitlements, in many cases on a more generalized basis than the workplace-centred regimes of the earlier period.

As Figure 20.1 shows, the expansion of welfare programmes in Africa in this period was part of a larger trend among countries across the global South.[90] From the early 1990s to the mid-1990s there was an unprecedented growth in state provision of social protection. The synchronicity of this growth across continents suggests that global economic forces exerted a common influence on local policy developments. There is a common view that the expansion of welfare can be largely explained by its increasing support within global donor organizations and non-governmental organizations. To be sure, there has been a 'dominance of international actors in designing, financing, and even delivering social protection in Africa'.[91] Yet a comparison across African countries reveals that a range of local political and historical factors shaped the varying forms that new welfare provisions took.

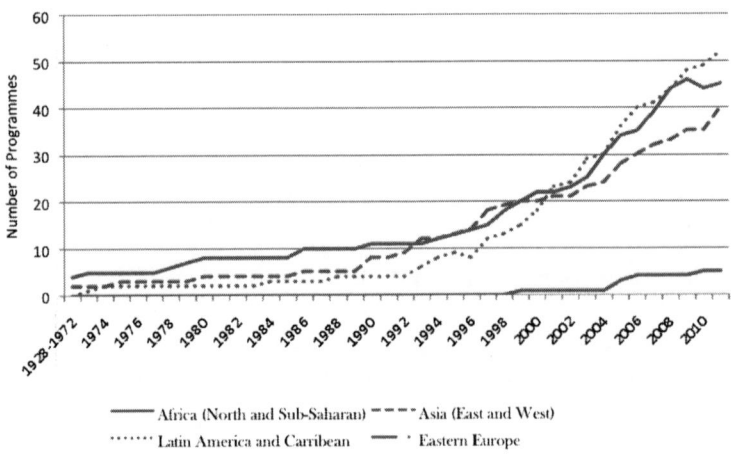

Figure 20.1. Active flagship social assistance programmes in middle- and low-income countries, by region and year

[90] Kevan Harris and Ben Scully, 'A Hidden Counter-movement? Precarity, Politics, and Social Protection before and beyond the Neoliberal Era', *Theory and Society*, 44.5 (2015), 415–44.

[91] Stephen Devereux and Philip White, 'Social Protection in Africa: Evidence, Politics and Rights', *Poverty & Public Policy*, 2.3 (2010), 53–77.

South Africa provides one of the more dramatic examples of the relationship between political transformation and the extension of social protection. The South African old-age pension had been established for whites in the 1920s and extended to non-whites at reduced levels in the 1940s and 1950s.[92] By the 1970s the apartheid government had already begun to reduce the racial disparities in pension expenditures by increasing the amounts given to blacks while decreasing the payment levels of whites. The reform was an attempt to combat rising militancy among black workers and broader social movements. By routing pension payments through the 'homeland' governments, the white regime hoped to establish some legitimacy for these bastions of the apartheid project.[93] Also in the 1970s the government began to increase the portion of education spending going to non-white beneficiaries.[94]

By 1993, on the eve of democratic elections that would bring the African National Congress (ANC) to power, racial inequalities in social spending had already been significantly reduced. Overall, the share of social spending going to non-whites increased from 45 per cent in 1975 to 82 per cent in 1993.[95] In the post-apartheid era, the ANC did modestly increase the share of non-interest government spending,[96] but due to its commitment to fiscal restraint, it was extremely reluctant to introduce significant new entitlement programmes. ANC officials were more likely to speak of welfare in terms of dependency and laziness rather than as a right or a developmental tool.[97] The only major new welfare programme in the post-apartheid period, the child support grant, required significant social pressure, especially from the trade union federation COSATU, in order to secure its implementation.[98]

For Sam Hickey, South Africa and Namibia, which also implemented a broadly accessible old-age pension, are unique in Africa for having 'a particular form of what might be termed a political contract between

---

[92] Servaas van der Berg, 'South African Social Security under Apartheid and Beyond', *Development Southern Africa*, 14.4 (1997), 481–503.

[93] *Ibid.*

[94] Servaas van der Berg, 'The Transition from Apartheid: Social Spending Shifts Preceded Political Reform', *Economic History of Developing Regions*, 29.2 (2014), 238.

[95] *Ibid.*, 237.

[96] *Ibid.*, 239

[97] Franco Barchiesi, *Precarious Liberation: Workers, the State, and Contested Social Citizenship in Postapartheid South Africa* (Albany, NY: State University of New York Press, 2011).

[98] Scully, 'Lessons from the Political Strategies of Post-Independence African Trade Unions'.

states and citizens'[99] which shapes welfare expenditure. But even in his scepticism of such a contract elsewhere on the continent, Hickey recognizes the importance of the relationship between social spending and politics. He cites the example of Uganda, where a number of scholars have noted that the re-establishment of democratic elections in 1996 after a series of dictatorships played an important role in reforms of state provision of healthcare and education. In the first post-dictatorship elections in 1996, President Yoweri Museveni's party made the abolition of fees for primary school a part of its election manifesto, despite the fact that Museveni had repeatedly expressed scepticism of similar proposals prior to 1996.[100] Universal primary education (UPE) became a major campaign issue, and after his victory 'it was widely perceived that President Museveni's strong performance in the election was in part attributable to his UPE manifesto commitment'.[101] In the next presidential election, in 2001, an opposition candidate ran on a platform calling for reform of social services, which, according to Kajula et al.,[102] prompted President Museveni, in the midst of the campaign, to abruptly announce the scrapping of controversial user fees at state health facilities, which had been first implemented as part of neoliberal reforms in 1993.

The case of the National Health Insurance Scheme (NHIS) in Ghana provides an example of the complex role that workers have played in this post-1990 welfare expansion. Ghana was another country where multi-party democracy was reinstated in the early 1990s. The ruling party won the first two elections, in 1992 and 1996, but faced growing opposition in the later election from the New Patriotic Party (NPP), whose manifesto promised the implementation of an NHIS that would provide comprehensive health insurance for all citizens.[103] The NPP won a large majority in the 2000

---

[99] Sam Hickey, 'Conceptualising the Politics of Social Protection in Africa', in *Social Protection for the Poor and Poorest*, ed. A. Barrientos and D. Hulme (London: Palgrave Macmillan, 2008), 258.

[100] David Stasavage, 'The Role of Democracy in Uganda's Move to Universal Primary Education', *The Journal of Modern African Studies*, 43.1 (2005), 58–9.

[101] *Ibid.*, 70.

[102] Peter Waalwo Kajula, Francis Kintu, John Barugahare and Stella Neema, 'Political Analysis of Rapid Change in Uganda's Health Financing Policy and Consequences on Service Delivery for Malaria Control', *The International Journal of Health Planning and Management*, 19.S1 (2004), S133–53.

[103] Hassan Wahab, 'Universal Health Care Coverage: Assessing the Implementation of Ghana's NHIS Law', in *Intellectual Agent, Mediator and Interlocutor: A. B. Assensoh and African Politics in Transition*, ed. T. Falola and E. M. Mbah (Newcastle upon Tyne: Cambridge Scholars Publishing, 2014), 190.

election and introduced the NHIS bill in 2001. The main union federation, the TUC, joined the International Monetary Fund in vehemently opposing the new health insurance, since it would be financed in part by reallocating 2.5 per cent of workers' contributions from the existing pension scheme. The bill was eventually passed over the unions' and the political opposition's objections, which was viewed by the TUC as a significant political defeat for the workers.[104]

These cases show that the trend of declining state welfare provisions, which marked the late 1970s and 1980s, has been reversed in the post-democratization period of the 1990s to the present. While the circumstances of welfare expansion differ in each case, there seems to be a general trend of newly democratizing states using welfare policy as a tool for gaining legitimacy and political support. However, the contrast between the unions' supportive role in South Africa, their relative absence in Uganda, and their resistance to new social expenditure in Ghana shows that organized wage-workers have played a mixed role in this welfare expansion. One reason for this complexity is that the other major trend of the 1980s discussed above, the informalization of work, has not been arrested or reversed on a large scale anywhere on the continent. It is possible that informal workers could be, or could become, a political block pushing states towards increased provision of welfare, as Agarwala has argued is the case in contemporary India.[105] There are signs of this in South Africa, where the decline of formal wage work has shifted workers' politics away from shopfloor issues and towards broader livelihood issues.[106] However, the exact political role of precarious workers in the politics of welfare remains an open question.

CONCLUSION

The expansion of state-provided welfare in Africa over the past twenty years has captured the attention of both scholars and policymakers. This chapter has attempted to show that these recent forms of social protection are part of a longer historical lineage of welfare on the continent. At various times

---

[104] Emmanuel Akwetey and David Dorkenoo, 'Disengagement from Party Politics: Achievements and Challenges for the Ghana Trades Union Congress', in *Trade Unions and Party Politics: Labour Movements in Africa*, ed. B. Beckman and S. Buhlungu (Cape Town: HSRC Press, 2010), 56.

[105] Rina Agarwala, *Informal Labor, Formal Politics, and Dignified Discontent in India* (New York: Cambridge University Press, 2013).

[106] Scully, 'From the Shop-Floor to the Kitchen Table'.

both state and private actors have been providers of protection, which has taken both formal and informal forms. And at every turn, the provision of welfare has been both critiqued and celebrated, often in terms that would sound familiar to those who follow contemporary debates.

Two key lines of disagreement on questions of social protection have been the political and economic justifications for, and effects of, welfare provision. From the late colonial states, through to the early independent nations, and into the present period of renewed democratic contestation, welfare has been used as a tool to gain legitimacy by political leaders. This political use of social protection makes Africa rather unexceptional in comparison to other regions, where it has long been argued that social welfare serves to 'regulate the poor', as Francis Fox Piven and Richard Cloward's classic formulation in 1971 put it.[107] And yet, in Africa, the strategic use of welfare has often been the subject of sharp criticism. Formal, urban workers with access to workplace-based welfare provisions have always been a minority of the labour force. As a result, such welfare spending has often been critiqued as benefiting a 'labour aristocracy' at the expense of the poor majority, despite the widely acknowledged social and material connections that often exist between more secure formal workers and the poor and unemployed. (Jeremy Seekings's description of some African welfare regimes as 'workerist' is a contemporary example of this critique.)[108]

It is the economic rationale for welfare that has most often led to broader, generalizable forms of social protection. When social spending has been framed as a developmental, rather than a political, necessity it has often taken more egalitarian forms. The expansion of access to public education in the post-independence period, as well as various forms of subsidies for rural agricultural producers, would be the clearest examples of this. Of course, separating developmental objectives from political strategies is ultimately impossible. The developmental imperative of the post-independence era was itself seen as necessary for producing political legitimacy. A further problem is that there is rarely a clear political constituency making demands for broad social development. Instead, this sort of social policy tends to be driven by ideological assumptions that development depends on improved welfare. Yet without an organized political base for such developmental spending, such

[107] Frances Fox Piven and Richard Cloward, *Regulating the Poor: The Functions of Public Welfare*, 2nd edn (New York: Vintage, 1993).

[108] Jeremy Seekings, 'Welfare Regimes and Redistribution in the South', in *Divide and Deal: The Politics of Distribution in Democracies*, ed. I. Shapiro, P. A. Swenson and D. Donno (New York: New York University Press, 2008), 19–42.

programmes are easier to abandon when economic conditions deteriorate or ideological positions change.

While it is always dangerous to argue for the novelty of the present, there is reason to believe that the developmental and political justifications for welfare are coming closer together than they have in previous periods. The 'deagrarianization'[109] of the countryside and the informalization of urban wage work means that a growing proportion of the labour force are facing common experiences of precarity. While high levels of inequality remain in many countries, it is becoming less plausible to characterize large sections of formal workers as privileged. The nexus between democratic politics and welfare expansion across the continent over the past twenty years shows the extent to which the neoliberal era has produced a broad political constituency which supports the provision of basic forms of social protection. At the same time, development theory has begun to point towards the importance of expanding the well-being and education of the population as a precursor to, rather than an outcome of, economic growth. This has led to calls for what Peter Evans has termed the '21st century developmental state',[110] which should depart from the twentieth-century developmental state's exclusive orientation towards industrialization and economic growth. As Evans has put it, under earlier development models, 'it was possible to imagine that "growth policy" could be separated from "social policy" or "welfare policy" ... The 21st century developmental state cannot afford such myopia.'[111]

---

[109] Deborah Fahy Bryceson, 'Deagrarianization and Rural Employment in sub-Saharan Africa: A Sectoral Perspective', *World Development*, 24.1 (1996), 97–111.

[110] Peter Evans, 'Constructing the 21st Century Developmental State: Potentialities and Pitfalls', in *Constructing a Democratic Developmental State in South Africa: Potentials and Challenges*, ed. O. Edigheji (Cape Town: HSRC Press, 2010), 37–58.

[111] *Ibid.*, 50.

TWENTY-ONE
Mutualism and Cooperative Work

SAMUEL A. NYANCHOGA

Department of History,
The Catholic University of Eastern Africa, Nairobi

This chapter discusses the salient aspects of mutualistic associations and cooperative labour in Africa in the twentieth century. The introduction covers the conceptualizations of mutualistic associations and cooperative labour in Africa. They are discussed under the theory of African communalism and neoliberalism, highlighting the contending issues. Given the regional variations and contexts, the study of mutualistic association and cooperative labour takes cognizance of their similarities and differences in North, East, West and Southern Africa. The focus is on the factors for their growth, scope, performance and the challenges they faced. The role of state and/or governments in either promoting mutualism or cooperative labour or in the demutualization of African societies is investigated.

Mutualism is an alternative means of economic organization, namely common ownership of the means of production, where workers share in its profitability. In social mutualism, employees share in the management of public services. It is the process of bringing together cooperative and voluntary associations to achieve the desired objectives.[1] According to the labour theory of value, labour or a service must be paid for commensurately. In the context of utopian socialist theory, Robert Owen outlined the selfish principle in humans, called the competition principle, for the gratification of their wants and propensities as embedded in neoliberalism.[2] Conversely, the cooperative principle promotes acts of benevolence and reciprocity.

---

[1] W. Outhwaite, ed., *The Blackwell Dictionary of Modern Social Thought*, 2nd edn (Oxford: Blackwell, 2006).

[2] Robert Owen, *A New View of Society and Other Writings* (1813), ed. G. Claeys (London: Penguin, 1991).

Neoliberalism promotes an economy based on competition, leading to inequality and unstable societies. This is what led to the establishment of cooperatives in England in the mid-nineteenth century, when liberalism undermined the social foundations of society and promoted inequality and unstable business.[3]

The concept of mutualistic associations and cooperative labour principles was ingrained in African societies even before colonialism. These principles were modelled on kinship and neighbourhood groups formed to perform certain tasks. They allowed the pooling of resources and the sharing of proceeds. These traditional cooperative principles were adopted in the building of homesteads, the breaking of land, planting, herding, harvesting and hunting. The cooperative spirit or the notion of self-help and mutualistic association was widespread. In Arab North Africa, traditional and informal types of self-help and mutual help societies referred to as *Jam'iyyat*, or *Al taawaniya* for formal cooperatives, were popular. Many of them were seen as a combination of 'self-help' and 'charitable' activities, as well as providing social services and assisting poor families.[4] In East African societies, mutualistic association principles were located in institutions known as *ngwatia* among the Agikuyu and as *mwethiya* among the Kamba. In Ethiopia, the concept of *idir* defines mutualistic associations and cooperative labour principles. In West Africa, the *tontines* in Cameroon are based on mutualistic principles. The underlying philosophies of such institutions as *ubuntu*, *harambee* and *ujamaa* grew out of traditional African principles of socialism or the extended family. African communalism, in essence, projected the spirit of mutualism and cooperative effort.

Colonialism did little to develop traditional cooperative labour principles and discouraged the participation of Africans in cooperative endeavours in order to redirect labour to the colonial capitalist economy. Colonialism contributed to the demutualization of a large spectrum of African society and the destruction of African cooperative principles. These principles and the corresponding associational life existed outside the mainstream of colonial life. Focusing on welfare issues, they later became the focal point of African agitation against exploitative colonial labour regimes. Where these principles were encouraged by the colonial establishment, it was for the purpose of articulating the proceeds of pre-capitalist economies into embryonic colonial capitalism.

[3]   *Ibid.*

[4]   C. Wickham, *The Muslim Brotherhood: Evolution of an Islamist Movement* (Princeton, NJ: Princeton University Press, 2013).

Colonialism encouraged cooperative labour principles among white settlers. It was not until the depression of the 1930s and the post-Second World War era – following open agitation from Africans and the realization by the colonial state of the viability of the African economy – that the colonial state encouraged mutualistic associations and cooperative labour principles among Africans. The model of African cooperative principles differed from one colonial power to another.

The post-independence era witnessed the increased pace of cooperative labour efforts and mutualistic associations as an important mobilizer of the economy. This grew out of the realization that the capacity of the African states was inadequate to mobilize important resources for the development of African economies. Cooperative labour principles were largely influenced by colonial traditions and the postcolonial state. Despite the centrality of mutualistic associations and cooperative labour principles, the sector has faced many challenges including inefficiency, financial mismanagement and lack of cooperative education, among others. There is also the external influence of liberalized economies and globalization that continues to shape the environment in which mutualistic associations and cooperative labour movements operate.

AFRICAN MUTUALITY, ASSOCIATIONAL LIFE AND COOPERATIVE LABOUR EFFORTS ON THE EVE OF COLONIALISM

Cohen et al. regard African mutuality, associational and cooperative labour efforts as having evolved around hunting, gathering, subsistence farming, pastoralism, trade, weaving and mining.[5] Kin groups, age groups and lineage groups formed the organizational core of African mutualistic and labour activities. According to Kirunda, these institutions influenced interactions, and conferred on their members specific duties, obligations, privileges and responsibilities.[6] More crucial, economic activities, appropriation and redistribution of wealth were largely influenced by these principles of mutuality and cooperative networks.

The ideology of African mutuality was based on symbiotic and egalitarian values between the individual and the community. According to John Mbiti,

---

[5]   R. Cohen, J. Copans and P. C. W. Gutkind, 'Introduction: African Labor and Colonial Capitalism', in *African Labor History*, ed. P. C. W. Gutkind, R. Cohen and J. Copans (London: Sage, 1978), 7–30.

[6]   M. K. Kirunda, *Environmental Challenges in Sub-Saharan Africa: Possible Solutions* (Boca Raton, FL: Dissertation.com, 2008).

central to our understanding of the African drive towards mutualism and interdependence between the community and the individual is the saying: 'I am because we are; and since we are, therefore I am.'[7] According to Mbiti, in traditional life, individual self-realization and actualization is in the corporate entity: 'The community creates or produces the individual; the individual depends on the corporate group.' Mbiti argues that African society was founded on egalitarianism, harmony and interdependence.[8] Similarly, in the words of the South African philosopher Augustine Shutte, 'a person is a person through persons'.[9] This Xhosa proverb resonates in many African cultures and explains the interdependence of people for development and self-fulfilment. In the words of Nyasani, the individual in the traditional context has little latitude for self-determination outside the context of the community or the family.[10] Senghor argues that the lack of private ownership of the land or other means of production was the core of communalism,[11] while Nyerere states that the idea of mutualism implied consensus through dialogue whereby people 'talk until they agree'.[12] This also explains the African concept of democracy in action.

Beller introduces the life of a person (*muntu*) as related to that of the community (*ubumwe* in kinyarwanda).[13] *Ubumwe* is the oneness of life, and life comes to *muntu* (the person) through *ubumwe* (oneness); hence the relationship between the individual and the community is one of functional dialogue as the individual assumes his or her functions for the well-being of the community. This view is complemented by the observations of Martin that African traditional society was founded on reciprocal relations that discouraged individualism as a basic unit and the focus of attention in

---

[7]   John S. Mbiti, *African Religions and Philosophy* (Nairobi/London: East African Educational Publishers/Heinemann, 1969).

[8]   *Ibid.*

[9]   Quoted in Kirunda, *Environmental Challenges in Sub-Saharan Africa.*

[10]   J. M. Nyasani, *The African Psyche* (Nairobi: University of Nairobi and Theological Printing Press, 1997), referred to and quoted extensively in James E. Lassiter, 'African Culture and Personality: Bad Social Science, Effective Social Activism, or a Call to Reinvent Ethnology?', *African Studies Quarterly*, 3.1 (2000), 1–21, https://goo.gl/fMJLPr (accessed 2 June 2015).

[11]   Leopold Senghor, *Liberté 1: négritude et humanisme* (Paris: Éditions du Seuil, 1964).

[12]   Julius K. Nyerere, 'One-Party Government', in *African Intellectual Heritage: A Book of Sources*, ed. M. K. Asante and A. A. Abarry (Philadelphia, PA: Temple University Press, 1996), 555–8.

[13]   Remy Beller, *Life, Person and Community in Africa: A Way towards Inculturation with the Spirituality of the Focolare* (Nairobi: Pauline Publications Africa, 2001).

industrial societies.[14] Rodney, in his observation of labour in African societies, points out that labour recruitment and activities revolved around family units. Societies conducted joint farming, fishing and hunting activities for the mutual benefit of all.[15] In societies such as that of the Bemba (Zambia) and in Dahomey, suitors provided some of labour's rewards to the parents of the bride. As shown by Shenton, and in reference to the Sokoto caliphate in the nineteenth century, household labour activities embraced both the nuclear family and the extended kin as joint production and consumption units in order to fulfil the social obligations of integrating clients into the household.[16]

The concept of mutuality and cooperative labour effort is also well elaborated in the work of Ochieng'.[17] He observes that East African societies in the pre-colonial era displayed self-help principles whereby members of kin or neighbourhood came together to perform certain tasks in rotation. Among the Agikuyu of Kenya, the self-help principle was known as *ngwatio*, *mwenthiya* among the Akamba, *kwat* and *saga* among the Luo, *risaga* and *egesangio* among the Abagusii and *kokwet* among the Kalenjin. In a similar context, Ehret introduces an interesting aspect of mutualism among the Fula and Takrur communities of West Africa along the Senegal River.[18] The Fula centred their economy on cattle herding, while the Takrur were cultivators. The Takrur allowed the Fula to graze their livestock in fields already harvested or left fallow, and the Fula provided limited labour services to the cultivators. In return, the Takrur benefited from cattle manure left behind by the animals, which increased the crop yields. Similar mutualistic activities are also cited by Shivji in reference to the nineteenth-century exchange of surplus goods among communities in Tanganyika.[19] The Nyamwezi and Pare iron smelters produced iron implements, such as hoes, that they supplied to the Chagga cultivators and Masaai herders, in return receiving grain and livestock. This traditional exchange economy was not based on profit but on equalization due to differences in production, as communities disposed of perishable surpluses and others gained access

[14] N. Martin, *African Vitalogy: A Step Forward in African Thinking* (Nairobi: Pauline Publications Africa, 1999), 52.

[15] Walter Rodney, *How Europe Underdeveloped Africa* (Nairobi: East African Educational Publishers, 1972).

[16] Robert W. Shenton, *The Development of Capitalism in Northern Nigeria* (London: James Currey, 1986), 49.

[17] W. R. Ochieng', ed., *Themes in Kenyan History* (Nairobi: Heinemann Kenya, 1990).

[18] Christopher Ehret, *The Civilizations of Africa: A History to 1800* (Oxford: James Currey, 2002).

[19] Issa G. Shivji, *Law, State and the Working Class in Tanzania* (Dar es Salaam: Tanzania Publishing House, 1986), 1.

to capital goods to increase production. Gichure introduces the ethics of work and collective ownership of land in an African setting, when people worked together on communally owned land and shared proceeds according to need.[20] Her view of African societies is that resources existed for community use, and they were not to be accumulated by the individual. Gichure's notion resonates with the ideas of Léopold Sédar Senghor on the mutualistic philosophy of the traditional African society based on dialogue and reciprocity that existed between the community and the individual.[21]

The philosophy of *ubuntuism* describes the African values of humanness, caring and compassion. as well as mutual support and cooperation. This philosophy was replicated throughout African societies, for example among the Xhosa and the Shona. It is a principle of caring for each other and acknowledging the rights and responsibilities of every member of society to promote the well-being of the society and the individual.[22]

In the Arab world, informal associations such as *Jam'iyyat* and cooperative types such as *Al taawaniya* underlined mutualism and cooperative labour efforts that focused on the provision of societal needs and welfarism and generally acted as safety nets for the community.[23] This economic philosophy was similar to stock associateship among the pastoral communities. Stock associateship is a relationship of mutual assistance, whereby stock associates maintained reciprocal stock rights. One might seek stock in time of need and give stock when others were in need.[24] Stock might be needed from stock associates at times of marriage, compensation, during feasts and important ritual functions. Stock would be depleted following epidemics, failure of pasture or drought. In order to rebuild stock, one would seek help or a loan from one's stock associates.[25] *Iquip* and *idir* are informal institutions among the Ethiopians to provide substantial rotating funds for members in order to improve their lives and living conditions. These institutions are informal, bottom-up and widely practised.[26]

[20]   C. W. Gichure, *Ethics for Africa Today: An Introduction to Business Ethics* (Nairobi: Pauline Publications Africa, 2008).

[21]   Senghor, *Liberté 1: négritude et humanisme*.

[22]   T. A. Chimuka, 'Ethics Among the Shona', *Zambezia: The Journal of Humanities of the University of Zimbabwe*, 28.1 (2001), 23–37.

[23]   Wickham, *The Muslim Brotherhood*.

[24]   P. H. Gulliver, *The Family Herds: A Study of Two Pastoral Tribes in East Africa, the Jie and Turkana* (London: Routledge and Kegan Paul, 1955), 196.

[25]   R. C. Soper, ed., *Socio-Cultural Profile of Turkana District* (Nairobi: Uzima Press, 1985), 101.

[26]   Ayele Bekerie, 'Iquib and Idir: Socio-Economic Traditions of the Ethiopians', PhD dissertation, Africana Studies and Research Center, Cornell University, 2003; see also https://goo.gl/xK2M19 (accessed 29 March 2015).

CRITIQUE OF AFRICAN MUTUALISM AND COOPERATIVE LABOUR

African communalism has been criticized as an idealization of traditional life in the African community. Vincent G. Simiyu describes African mutualism as a mere 'democratic myth', contradicting scholars such as Fortes and Evans-Pritchard by depicting some African political systems as having been highly authoritarian and not functioning for the well-being of the community.[27] In reference to the old kingdom of Congo, Simiyu argues that it exhibited several trajectories of exploitation of human labour as hunters of ivory, and the enslavement of others in the trans-Atlantic slave trade.

In practice, the existence of tributary activities, the lineage mode of production, contributed to the extraction and expropriation of surplus labour value from others. The existence of class-like social institutions and evidence of slave labour in pre-colonial modes of production contributed to the exploitation of others. Involuntary human servitude, such as chattel slavery, existed in Islamic North Africa and in countries such as Mauritania and Sudan. Debt bondage or peonage which involved the use of people as collateral against debt also existed in many African societies. Meillassoux, in his analysis of pre-colonial modes of production among the Curo of Ivory Coast, pointed out that older men and women exploited the younger generation through labour control, marriage and bridewealth.[28] These facts show that pre-colonial African societies were not always founded on principles of fairness.

DEMUTUALIZATION OF AFRICAN SOCIETIES AND COOPERATIVE PRINCIPLES IN THE COLONIAL ERA

The articulation of the colonial capitalist economy into a communal African set-up led to the distortion or destruction of traditional African mutualistic institutions through legal frameworks, land alienation, taxation and the proletarianization of African labour. With reference to the articulation of the modes of production theory as set out by Rey and Arrighi, African mutualistic associations and cooperative labour principles were not articulated into the emerging colonial capitalist economy, because they were

---

[27] Vincent G. Simiyu, 'The Democratic Myth in African Traditional Societies', in *Democratic Theory and Practice in Africa*, ed. W. O. Oyugi and A. Gitonga (Nairobi: Heinemann, 1987), 49–70; M. Fortes and E. E. Evans-Pritchard, *African Political Systems* (London: Oxford University Press, 1970).

[28] Claude Meillassoux, 'From Reproduction to Production: A Marxist Approach to Economic Anthropology', *Economy and Society*, 1.1 (1974), 93–105.

perceived to be working contrary to the motivations of colonial capitalism.[29] Where African mutualistic principles persisted, they existed outside the mainstream of colonial life, focusing on welfare issues, and later became the focal point of African agitation against exploitative colonial labour regimes. However, Meillassoux has a different perception with regard to French colonialism in West Africa, where colonial capitalism did not necessarily replace the previous economies but transformed them, creating a unified economic system.[30]

The process of integrating the pre-colonial African economy into the capitalist economy was a conscious effort by the colonial state.[31] This process led to a gradual transformation of African societies. There was also the destruction of indigenous modes of production through outright colonial wars of pacification, diversion of domestic labour into the colonial economy, punitive taxation, land alienation and seizure of livestock. Consequently, the substructure as well as the superstructure upon which African mutualism and cooperative principles were built was destroyed or distorted by the colonial capitalist economy. There was also the subordination of the institutions upon which African mutualism was based.[32] The net effect was the creation of a proletarianized African population and the phenomenon of forcing a migrant African population into a settler economy and an urban setting.[33] In this context, Gillian and Suzanne Cronjé postulate that the colonial state in Namibia created the Bantustans as labour reservoirs for the colonial economy.[34] This perception corresponds well with the observation of Ochieng' and Maxon with regard to colonial Kenya, where African reserves were created not necessarily to sustain African household needs but as labour

---

[29]   P. P. Rey and G. Arrighi, 'Articulation of Modes of Production', in *Marxist Theories of Imperialism: A Critical Survey*, ed. A. Brewer (London: Routledge and Kegan Paul, 1980), 183–206.

[30]   Meillassoux, 'From Reproduction to Production'; John Lamphear, *The Scattering Time: Turkana Responses to Colonial Rule* (Oxford: Clarendon Press, 1992).

[31]   R. M. A. van Zwanenberg, *Colonial Capitalism and Labour in Kenya, 1919–1939* (Nairobi: East African Literature Bureau, 1975), 76–103; B. Warren, *Imperialism: Pioneer of Capitalism* (London: New Left Books, 1980), 126; Bruce Berman and John Lonsdale, *Unhappy Valley: Conflict in Kenya and Africa. Book One: State and Class* (London: James Currey, 1992), 140.

[32]   P. C. Salzman, ed., *When Nomads Settle: Processes of Sedentarisation as Adaptation and Response* (New York: Praeger, 1980); Lamphear, *The Scattering Time*.

[33]   See the chapter by Pérez Niño in this volume.

[34]   Gillian Cronjé and Suzanne Cronjé, *The Workers of Namibia* (London: International Defence and Aid Fund, 1979), 30.

reservoirs for the settler colonial economy.[35] The net effect of this process was the fundamental distortion of the pre-colonial African economy and its mutualistic principles. However, Sharon Stichter introduces an interesting observation that the proletarianization of the African peasantry was never fully realized, because Africans constantly moved from a communal mode of production to a capitalist mode and vice versa, and the phenomenon of migrant workers resulted simply in migration from the rural to the urban/colonial economy and back. What Stichter's observation clearly demonstrates is that labour migration altered the social relations and networks of African societies.[36] This corresponds well again with Lazreg's observation of French colonialism in Algeria and Morocco, which eroded the community values of communalism and solidarity and hence created a sense of loss for individuals.[37] Additionally, the forms of cooperation that existed in pre-colonial Africa did not have the capacity to expand and organically grow into large-scale, trans-ethnic cooperative movements.[38]

MUTUALISM AND COOPERATIVE PRINCIPLES IN THE COLONIAL ERA

The colonial environment contributed to the emergence of dual mutualistic and cooperative principles in colonial Africa. African mutualism remained within the informal setting to provide a form of insurance network for an African population uprooted from the traditional setting as they moved into urban areas. The cooperative movement became a tool for the mobilization of resources for colonial settlers. The cooperative spirit that emerged out of the realm of solidarity and social networks that characterized pre-colonial African societies such as the *Idir* (Ethiopia), *Tontines* (Cameroon) and *Stokvels* (South Africa) were distorted, disrupted and sometimes destroyed through the operations of colonial capitalism.[39] Putting these assertions aside, it is

---

[35] W. R. Ochieng' and R. M. Maxon, *An Economic History of Kenya* (Nairobi: East African Educational Publishers, 1992), 172; A. Clayton and D. C. Savage, *Government and Labour in Kenya, 1895–1963* (London: Frank Cass, 1974).

[36] Sharon Stichter, *Migrant Labourers* (Cambridge: Cambridge University Press, 1985); Sharon Stichter, 'Women and the Labor Force in Kenya, 1895–1964', *Rural Africana*, 29 (1975–76), 45–67.

[37] M. Lazreg, 'The Reproduction of Colonial Ideology: The Case of the Kabyle Berbers', *Arab Studies Quarterly*, 5.4 (1993), 380–95.

[38] P. Develtere, 'Cooperative Development in Africa up to the 1990s', in *Cooperating out of Poverty: The Renaissance of the African Cooperative Movement*, ed. P. Develtere, I. Pollet and F. Wanyama (Geneva: ILO, 2008), 1–37.

[39] *Ibid.*

important to understand how cooperative activities were greatly conditioned by the social, political and economic milieu of the colonial environment.

First, the cooperative movement was tied to the dependency path in the sense that they were both involved with the export of raw materials. The cooperatives organized the farmers in the production of coffee, cocoa, bananas, cotton or other export crops. They also focused on primary productive activities and were defined by economic objectives. In the view of dependency theorists such as Immanuel Wallerstein, the exchange between the core and the periphery takes place on unequal terms, where the periphery is consigned to be the producer of raw materials for the benefit of the core.[40] The cooperative activities should be seen as mobilization strategies or tools to meet the raw material demands of the core, and they were hence entangled in the dependency web.

The cooperatives were also dominated by the colonial settlers. In colonial Africa, the cooperative movement was largely restricted to the European settlers. It was an attempt to protect European settler farmers, traders and miners. In Kenya, the Kenya Farmers Association was founded in 1923 by white settler farmers for the purpose of marketing their produce.[41] Even after independence in 1963, the colonial settlers were still in charge of the association until 1971. In Zambia, as elsewhere in anglophone Africa, the first cooperative movement was formed in 1914 by European settler farmers to market their agricultural produce. This was because Africans were not recognized as farmers until after the Second World War. According to the Farmers Licensing Ordinance Number 30 of 1946, a farmer was defined as any person other than an African or any company or body of persons where the controlling interest was not held by Africans. This background continued to present obstacles to the formation of cooperatives by Africans. In Northern Rhodesia, even after independence in 1964, the Northern Rhodesia Farmers' Union was essentially a union for the European commercial farmers until 1966, when it was abolished. From this perspective, colonialism did little to develop cooperative labour principles and discouraged the participation of Africans in cooperative endeavours in order to redirect labour to the colonial capitalist economy.

While colonialism encouraged cooperative labour principles among white settlers, it was not until the depression of the 1930s and in the post-Second World War era – following open agitation from Africans and upon

[40]　Immanuel Wallerstein, *The Modern World-System: Capitalist Agriculture and the Origins of the European World-Economy in the Sixteenth Century* (New York: Academic Press, 1974).

[41]　E. Huxley, *No Easy Way: A History of the Kenya Farmers' Association and Unga Limited* (Nairobi: East African Standard, 1958).

the realization by the colonial state of the viability of the African economy – that the colonial state encouraged cooperative labour principles among Africans. African cooperatives emerging out of the colonial environment were radicalized as they attempted to respond to the challenges of racism and harsh economic realities. In British colonial East Africa, the cooperative movements were racially divided in their membership, with Asians, Africans, Arabs and Europeans forming separate movements.[42]

Cooperative labour principles were modelled along the traditions of the colonial masters. In British colonies, the cooperative environment was more unified and built around the processing and marketing of agricultural products such as tea, coffee, pyrethrum, cocoa beans and sisal. The cooperative movement seemed to be well established at the grassroots to mobilize the peasantry and the white settlers for the production of much-needed agricultural products for the industries abroad. They also operated vertically and horizontally and were well integrated at the grassroots. In the French colonies, the cooperative movement was based on common bonds, traditions and objectives, while in the Portuguese colonies such as Angola, Mozambique and São Tomé and Principe, the cooperatives were influenced by the production traditions of the rural population and entrepreneurs. Finally, some of the countries that did not experience intense colonization, such as Ethiopia, Liberia and Sierra Leone, developed homegrown cooperative traditions.[43]

In the Belgian colonies such as Congo, Rwanda and Burundi, the colonial state allowed dual cooperative societies to mobilize resources and development for the colonized population.[44] The cooperatives were involved in a wide variety of activities, such as dairy and construction, and local industries, such as pottery, oil pressing and tanning. These cooperatives ran parallel to the European-based business associations. The Portuguese colonies of Angola, Cape Verde, Guinea-Bissau, Mozambique and São Tomé and Principe restricted cooperative activities among Africans, while big businesses were allowed to set up cooperatives and associations to deal with the export and marketing of crops such as coffee, cotton and bananas.[45]

---

[42] Ochieng' and Maxon, *An Economic History of Kenya*, 358.

[43] J. Schwettmann, 'Capacity Building for Africa's Cooperative and Social Economic Organisations. A Contribution to the Expert Group Meeting "Cooperatives in Development: Beyond 2012", Ulaanbaatar, Mongolia, 3–6 May 2011, https://goo.gl/eSvnMs (accessed 3 March 2015); P. Develtere, I. Pollet and F. Wanyama, eds, *Cooperating out of Poverty: The Renaissance of the African Cooperative Movement* (Geneva: ILO, 2008).

[44] Develtere et al., eds, *Cooperating out of Poverty*.

[45] *Ibid.*

With regard to the trade union movement in British and French colonies in Africa, Africans were not allowed to form trade unions until the 1930s. In British colonies, the enactment of the 1937 Trade Unions' Ordinance stipulated the conditions under which Africans could organize themselves into trade unions. It was followed by a proliferation of trade union activities, starting with the East African Standard Union, the East African Standard Staff Union and the Labor Trade Union of East Africa. Others were the Asian Railway Trade Union in Kenya, the Nairobi Taxmen Union, the General Maskini (Poor People's) Union, the Transport and Allied Workers' Union, the Domestic and Hotel Workers' Union, the Quarry Workers' Union, the Night Watchmen Workers' Union, the East African Federation of Building Construction Workers' Union and the Tailors' Union. This was followed by the formation of the Kenya Federation of Registered Trade Unions in 1950. In Uganda, the colonial administration prohibited the formation of trade unions until 1952, when trade unions such as the Basoga African Motor Drivers' Union, the Railway Asian Union and the Uganda Posts and Telegraph African Welfare Union were formed. In French West Africa, such as in Senegal, the trade union movement dates back to 1938, when the first professional trade unions were created.[46] It is evident from the foregoing analysis that the colonial regimes did create the climate for the African labour force to become unionized.

Finally, when African labour unions were allowed, they became the driving force of the anti-colonial liberation struggle, as some later transformed into political parties that captured power at independence. With the emerging resistance against colonial rule, African trade unions quickly took a decisive part in the national liberation struggle. The South African trade union federation, COSATU (Congress of South African Trade Unions), which was founded in 1985, became the rallying point against the apartheid regime.

THE POSTCOLONIAL ERA AND THE IDEOLOGIZATION OF MUTUALISTIC PRINCIPLES IN AFRICA'S DEVELOPMENT PROCESS

The post-independence era witnessed an increased pace of cooperative labour efforts and activities by mutualistic associations as an important mobilizer of the economy. This grew out of the realization that the capacity of the African states was insufficient to mobilize important resources for the

---

[46] H. R. Schillinger, 'Trade Unions in Africa: Weak but Feared', Global Trade Union Program, International Development Cooperation, Occasional Paper, March 2005, https://goo.gl/ZiM8c5 (accessed 3 March 2015)

management and development of African economies. Cooperative labour principles were largely influenced by colonial traditions and the postcolonial state. Despite the centrality of mutualistic associations and cooperative labour principles, the sector faced many challenges, ranging from inefficiency to financial mismanagement and lack of cooperative education, among other factors. There was also the external influence of liberalized economies and of globalization, which continues to shape the environment in which mutualistic associations and cooperative labour movements operate.

The struggle for independence, decolonization politics and the creation of the postcolonial state in Africa necessitated a search for a new philosophy of development. In order to provide a radical shift, albeit temporary, from colonial development approaches, a new political philosophy of development founded on African mutualistic principles became increasingly relevant. Scholars such as Ekanem capture the role of African philosophy and culture in Africa's development discourse, resulting from the embracing of principles of equality and mutual social responsibility.[47] African countries declared adherence to African socialism. This was called humanism in Zambia, the Common Man's Charter in Uganda, *ujamaa* in Tanzania, *authenticité* in Zaire, *ubuntuism* in South Africa, *harambeeism* and *nyayoism* in Kenya and *négritude* in Senegal. African socialism, in summary, was an attempt to incorporate fairness, justice and equality in the development process. In reality, the political elites capitalized on these principles to perpetuate corruption, inequality and exploitation. A few examples are described below.

UJAMAAISM IN TANZANIA

In the Arusha Declaration of 1967, Julius Nyerere and the Tanzania African National Union defined African socialism in terms that affirmed the difference between Western socialism and the social doctrines of African societies. *Ujamaa*, or socialism made in Tanzania, meant sharing and the absence of exploitation. *Ujamaa*, therefore, allowed for the equal distributive ethos to be practised in society to prevent the detrimental accumulation of resources by individuals.[48] *Ujamaaism* emphasized self-reliance and the traditions of communalism and cooperation.[49] It brought together all the major means of production and exchange in the nation under the control of

---

[47] S. A. Ekanem, 'African Philosophy of Development: Contemporary Perspectives', *SOPHIA: An African Journal of Philosophy*, 9.1 (2006), 85–90.

[48] Martin, *African Vitalogy*.

[49] Chambi Chachage and Annar Cassam, *Africa's Liberation: The Legacy of Nyerere* (Kampala: Fountain Publishers, 2010).

the people.[50] It discouraged foreign aid and private investment, because these had the potential to entrench exploitation.[51]

Tanzania's model of development was based on the village life of mutual assistance, in which rural Tanzanians worked together for the community and to produce a surplus. The village became the focal point of contact with government officials for the dissemination of modern technology and agricultural production. The government also invested in human resources through education and in the health sector in order to improve the quality of life.[52] *Ujamaa* villages were supposed to integrate social equality into economic activities.

Ujamaaism had its shortcomings because of the politicized nationalization of foreign assets and investments, which was counterproductive.[53] Tanzania's education system, which was one of the pillars of *ujamaaism*, remained undeveloped and uncompetitive. This was partly because of its orientation towards socialist attitudes and its lack of innovation and investment.[54] The agricultural sector, the foundation of *ujamaa*, failed because productivity fell by about 50 per cent compared to what was achieved on independent farms.[55] The villagization programme, which was another important pillar of development, was affected by challenges of illiteracy, a poor capital base, lack of technology and cultural resistance.[56] The use of force to implement the programme demonstrated the shift towards an authoritarian regime in Tanzania, masked behind the *Ujamaa* principle of participation.[57]

[50] B. Ibhawoh and J. I. Dibua, 'Deconstructing Ujamaa: The Legacy of Julius Nyerere in the Quest for Social and Economic Development', *African Journal of Political Science*, 8.1 (2003), 59–83.

[51] Samuel S. Mushi, *Development and Democratisation in Tanzania* (Kampala: Fountain Publishers, 2001).

[52] P. Kaiser, 'Structural Adjustment and the Fragile Nation: The Demise of Social Unity in Tanzania', *Journal of Modern African Studies*, 34.2 (1996), 229.

[53] Mushi, *Development and Democratisation in Tanzania*.

[54] *Ibid.*

[55] Priya Lal, 'Militants, Mothers, and the National Family: *Ujamaa*, Gender and Rural Development in Postcolonial Tanzania', *Journal of African History*, 51.1 (2010), 1–20.

[56] Leander Schneider, 'Freedom and Unfreedom in Rural Development: Julius Nyerere, *Ujamaa Vijijini*, and Villagization', *Canadian Journal of African Studies*, 38.2 (2004), 344–92.

[57] Chachage and Cassam, *Africa's Liberation*; Dharam Ghai, Eddy Lee, Justin Maeda and Samir Radwan, eds, *Overcoming Rural Underdevelopment, Proceedings of a Workshop on Alternative Agrarian Systems and Rural Development. Arusha, Tanzania, 4–14 April 1979* (Geneva: ILO, 1979).

GHANA'S CONSCIENCISM

Martin describes Kwame Nkrumah's new consciousness as being focused on African values of identity, humanism and communitarianism.[58] According to Nkrumah, consciencism established the link between humanism and egalitarianism. It was a philosophy used to fight capitalism and colonialism and to ensure the well-being of Africans. Nkrumah's consciencism seems to have borrowed from Marxist and Leninist revolutionary ideas. As a philosophy and ideology for decolonization and development, using African revolutionary ideas, consciencism failed to capture the attention of the masses. Again, Nkrumah's ideas were far removed from the lives of ordinary people and appeared too philosophical and abstract. Nkrumah's attempt to engender the unity of the African continent using the philosophical ideals of consciencism appeared premature, as the continent was still reeling from its transition out of colonialism.

ZAMBIA'S HUMANISM

Kenneth Kaunda conceptualized humanism as the embodiment of the African personality. Humanism entails taking care of both the individual and community interests or needs. Kaunda tried to build a model society based on humanism in which the dignity and well-being of the individual and society alike were upheld. Humanism discouraged individualism and promoted collectivism and communitarianism values.[59] Kaunda's humanism also emphasized societal cohesion. Humanism was a fight against individualism that placed the community at the centre, promoting the common good as well as the life of the individual. These humanistic principles were hampered by two factors: Zambia's educational policies and infrastructure were poorly developed and ill prepared to provide the ideological legitimation for humanism; and its economy was largely in the hands of various multinational corporations that controlled enormous resources such as minerals. Such an economic structure was unlikely to implement humanistic principles. The economic slump of the 1970s and increased poverty defeated the objective of humanism.[60]

[58] Martin, *African Vitalogy*.

[59] *Ibid.*

[60] *Encyclopædia Britannica*, 'Kaunda, Kenneth', https://goo.gl/AVfBjd (accessed 9 April 2015).

UBUNTUISM IN SOUTH AFRICA

The philosophy of *ubuntuism* sustained many African communities in southern Africa. Many African societies had variants of *ubuntuism*, or humanness, with an emphasis on respecting and valuing the dignity of the human being irrespective of her or his social and economic status.[61] *Ubuntuism* considers the community not as an aggregate of competing individuals but as a composite and reciprocal organ that meets the needs of both the individual and the community. The words of a Xhosa community saying summarize the philosophy of *ubuntuism*: 'Your pain is my pain, my wealth is your wealth and your salvation my salvation.' Nelson Mandela's conceptualization of *ubuntuism* captures the generosity and benevolence of the human person. In reference to the apartheid system in South Africa, Mandela argued that it imprisoned both the oppressor and the oppressed, and the only liberation was to set both of them free through reconciliation and love. *Ubuntuism*, in Mandela's view, was the political philosophy that led to the dismantling of apartheid and the reconstruction of post-apartheid South Africa.[62] But many observers agree that the political reconciliation in South Africa has not been accompanied by economic equity and justice. The emerging phenomenon of the South African urban poor and xenophobic attacks against immigrants and foreign workers is a manifestation of the internal contradictions between ideology, welfarism and the inability of the state to cater for the needs of its people.[63]

HARAMBEEISM AND NYAYOISM IN KENYA

The ideology of *harambeeism*, meaning pulling together, and *nyayoism*, following the footsteps of our predecessors, became the political and economic principles for development under the Kenyatta and Moi regimes in Kenya. *Harambee* became the tool for mobilizing resources for the construction of community schools, roads, bridges, hospitals and the raising of funds for the education of the needy. *Nyayoism* also propagated peace, love and unity. The ideology of *harambeeism* and *nyayoism* have been criticized for exploiting the peasantry and the poor. The political elites and civil servants have been accused for using the ideology to perpetuate exploitation and corruption.[64]

---

[61] Munyaradzi Felix Murove, ed., *African Ethics: An Anthology of Comparative and Applied Ethics* (Pietermaritzburg: University of KwaZulu-Natal Press, 2009), 63.

[62] *Ibid.*

[63] See the chapters by Britwum and Dakhli, Scully and Jawad in this volume.

[64] Ali A. Mazrui, ed., *General History of Africa. VIII: Africa since 1935* (London: UNESCO/James Currey, 1993).

Harambee is a traditional approach to resource mobilization. The word has also been adopted as a political slogan to symbolize unity and solidarity, and therefore aimed to encourage citizens to support either financially or in kind the undertaking of a certain call, task or project for the benefit of the community or the nation. The spirit of *harambee* as a traditional principle existed in all indigenous Kenyan communities, where self-help or cooperative work groups existed and were organized for the common good. Chieni notes that each of the Kenyan societies had self-help or cooperative work groups, by which groups of women on the one hand and men on the other organized common work parties to cultivate or build houses for each other, clear bushes and harvest, among other activities.[65]

The philosophy of *harambee* has been used by the independence governments for national and community self-help events. Akong'a elaborates that the term *harambee* is used in the discussion of economic and social developments in Kenya in the same way that similar concepts are employed in many other developing countries all over the world – for example, *ujamaa* in Tanzania and humanism in Zambia. *Harambee* has been used as a synonym for fundraising and contributions of materials and labour for the common good.[66] On Kenyan independence in 1963, *Harambee* was given a boost when President Kenyatta declared that the development and the destiny of the country was now in the hands of indigenous people, and that the aspirations of the nation were to be pursued through indigenous approaches, citing *harambee* as key to success. In the early years of independence, Kenyans responded positively to the call of *harambee* and contributed to the building of roads, dams, water pipelines, dispensaries and schools. Local communities raised money and started schools and even hired teachers.[67]

The report of the Ad-Hoc Committee on Legislation on *harambee* of 2014 indicates that, despite the multiple benefits of *harambee*, the fundraising activities evolved from a decent and selfless institution into one driven by corruption and fraud; it encouraged laziness and lack of transparency and accountability. The *harambee* spirit contributed to the government's abdication of its responsibilities to provide adequate social services and support.

[65] S. N. Chieni, *The Harambee Movement in Kenya: The Role Played by Kenyans and the Government in the Provision of Education and Other Social Services* (Eldoret: Moi University Press, 2001).

[66] J. Akong'a, 'Culture in Development', in *Kenya: An Official Handbook*, ed. S. A. Idha (Nairobi: Ministry of Information and Broadcasting, 1989).

[67] B. A. Ogot and W. R. Ochieng', eds, *Decolonization and Independence in Kenya, 1940–93* (London/Nairobi: James Currey/East African Educational Press, 1995).

According to an analysis by Transparency International Kenya, *harambee* funds raised between 2000 and 2002 amounted to a total of 1.53 billion Kenyan shillings. The report indicated the prevalence of 'increased monetization, forced contributions and corrupt use of resources'.[68] Many critics also observed that the movement did little to reduce inequality in development and the provision of social amenities. The Kenyan political elites also exploited the movement to perpetuate patronage among the people. With Kenya's ethnic problems, politicians capitalized on the movement to buy loyalty from the masses or even to obtain political favours from them. It was not uncommon to witness an increase in *harambee* activities during election periods, as politicians conducted *harambee* drives in pursuit of votes.[69] Despite this criticism, the *harambee* movement remained one of the successful self-help efforts in independent Kenya. It became the national rallying point for resource mobilization for development among the social classes.

Nyayoism became a national motto during Daniel arap Moi's presidency from 1978 to 2002. It symbolized peace and living together in love and unity. Moi argued that there were three important forces that drove development: the use of force; the use of a single political party (i.e. the Kenya African National Union) as the mobilization tool; and the philosophy of *nyayo*. He demanded undivided loyalty and commitment from the Kenyan people. He spearheaded *nyayo* projects such as the building of schools, the planting of trees, and the construction of roads and hospitals. But as in the case of the *harambee* spirit, the Moi regime has been criticized for having been authoritarian and repressive in curtailing people's liberties. The movement was also riddled with corruption, in contrast to the spirit of *nyayoism* as professed by Moi.[70]

FAITH-BASED ORGANIZATIONS

Faith-based organizations include churches, synagogues, mosques, temples and other religious-based organizations that are founded, supported and incorporated by religious congregations.[71] These play an important role

---

[68]   Republic of Kenya (The Senate), 'Report of the Ad Hoc Committee on Legislation on Harambee (Voluntary Contribution)', May 2014, 12.

[69]   Ogot and Ochieng', eds, *Decolonization and Independence in Kenya*.

[70]   S. A. Nyanchoga, F. M. Muchoki, P. K. Wanyonyi and S. W. Mwangi, *Constitutionalism and Democratisation in Kenya, 1945–2007* (Nairobi: The Catholic University of Eastern Africa Press, 2008).

[71]   Elizabeth Ferris, 'Faith-Based and Secular Humanitarian Organizations', *International Review of the Red Cross*, 87.858 (2005), 311–25.

in social welfare and social development, and they respond to a variety of humanitarian issues that are not limited to wars, epidemics, economic crises and the social needs of individuals and communities. In South Africa, faith-based organizations such as the Dutch Reformed Churches, the social development branch of the Anglican Church and the Salvation Army contribute to efforts aimed at the alleviation of poverty and the fight against HIV and AIDS. Islamic organizations such as the Al-Imdaad Foundation, Gift of Givers, Islamic Relief and the Muslim Refugee Association based in South Africa have programmes in support of needy orphans and widows, water purification, primary healthcare, food supplies, educational assistance and counselling for drug rehabilitation, HIV and AIDS. The Muslim Refugee Association of South Africa also provides employment services, language courses in Arabic and English, computer skills and instruction in tailoring and dressmaking.[72]

In North Africa, there are several Islamic faith-based organizations, such as the Muslim Brotherhood, that are transnational and operate in Egypt, Algeria, Libya, Mauritania, Somalia, Sudan and Tunisia. This organization provides literacy programmes, and assists its members in setting up small business enterprises and hospitals. The Muslim Society also operates in Algeria, Tunisia and Morocco, while the Islamic Salvation Front is based in Algeria, An-Nahada is active in Tunisia, and Justice and Charity in Morocco. The Ahmadiya Muslim Community, which is more widespread in Muslim North Africa, also supports the education of Muslim converts.[73] Charity (*zakat*) is said to be a duty for all Muslims. Compulsory *zakat* is 2.5 per cent of one's total savings per annum. Charitable endowments (*waqafs*) are obligatory and underpin Islamic faith-based organizations.[74]

Several observations have been made with regard to the claims, accountability and transparency of faith-based organizations. The conduct of their leaders, their sources of funding, the money available to them and its use have brought controversy in the public realm. The faith-based organizations tend to use aid to further their religious objectives, such as seeking converts, through their humanitarian assistance. Critics argue that public funds should not be used to support conversions, which are a private matter. Some of the theological stances of faith-based organizations are openly opposed to the use

---

[73] J. P. Entelis, ed., *Islam, Democracy and the State in North Africa* (Bloomington, IN: Indiana University Press, 1997).

[74] G. Clarke, 'Agents of Transformation? Donors, Faith-Based Organisations and International Development', *Third World Quarterly*, 28.1 (2007), 77–96.

of contraceptives and discriminatory against homosexuals, and yet they are using public funds to project such partisan policies.[75]

Despite the criticisms of faith-based organizations, they have exhibited mutualistic and cooperative effort by helping vulnerable members of their congregation to pay rent, medical expenses and school fees; providing food rations and clothing and subsidizing burial expenses; enabling the provision of clean water by digging wells; and funding orphanage homes, farming training, vocational skills, education, nutritional support and free medical camps.[76] Among faith-based institutions with mutualistic networks are Christ is the Answer Ministry in Kenya, the Catholic Church networks in Kenya, and the Seventh Day Adventist and Christian charities of Africa based in Uganda. The Salvation Army churches also provide hunger relief, housing assistance, homeless services, Christmas celebration assistance and after-school programmes for children and families through their established networks in Africa. They also support a variety of adult programmes such as substance abuse rehabilitation, prison ministries and care for the elderly. The Catholic Relief Services' agricultural programmes help farmers rebuild their farms after natural disasters or civil unrest, as well as funding water and sanitation programmes and micro-finance programmes that give poor households access to community-based financial services where they can save and borrow money at low interest rates.[77] These are just some of the examples that demonstrate mutual and cooperative activities in Africa.

WOMEN'S SELF-HELP GROUPS

Women's self-help groups are mutual aid or support groups that help women to chart their own path out of poverty and disenfranchisement and to become agents of development in a patriarchal culture. They mobilize resources and promote empowerment, ownership, control and management. Many groups also form financial saving cooperatives that give loans to members to enable them to invest in flour mills and shops or operate a revolving grant scheme for personal loans. Others conduct micro-savings

---

[75] *Ibid.*

[76] M. Chaves, *Religious Congregations and Welfare Reform: Who Will Take Advantage of Charitable Choice?* (Washington, DC: Aspen Institute, 1998).

[77] Population Research Institute, *Investigation of Catholic Relief Services – Kenya*, http://www.lepantoinstitute.org/wp-content/uploads/2015/02/Final-report.pdf (accessed 30 June 2017); see also the Seventh Day Adventist Relief Services, https://www.adventist.org/en/service/humanitarian-work (accessed 30 June 2017).

scheme, including so-called 'merry-go-rounds', group revolving funds whereby members make monthly contributions into a fund that is then awarded to one member through a ballot for personal investment. There also exist income-generating projects such as market stalls, the sewing of clothing and the raising of poultry, as well as mutual support schemes to solve common problems such as accessing safe drinking water and medical care. There is also a table banking concept, in which women pool their resources, bank them and later invest them in buying plots or buildings, among other viable investment opportunities.[78]

Through these activities, women have managed to increase their access to resources in the form of credit, loans and capital. Women have also managed to increase their savings, backed up by group support, and have accumulated social capital. In countries such as Uganda, several women's self-help groups – such as Katojo Women's Development Association, Ruti and Katyzo – promote financial inclusion, enabling women to engage in meaningful economic opportunities. Ghana also has active women's self-help groups. In metropolitan Kumasi, there are several women's self-help groups: the Christian Mothers Association, the Federation of Muslim Associations, SDA Women Fellowship, the Help to Help Traders Association, the Progressive Hairdressers and Beauticians Association, the Ghana Association of Women Entrepreneurs, the Single Parent Association and the Disabled Women Fellowship.[79] In North Africa, in Kerdassa, Egypt, there exist well-established women's self-groups with links to financial institutions and cooperative networks that assist women to obtain sewing machines and set up small handicraft businesses. Women also operate revolving credit associations for weddings, feasts and funerals. These self-help groups have low-income members, operate at the grassroots level and lack access to information.[80] There are challenges associated with women's self-help groups that may include tension in the household, domestic violence and stigmatizing as women try to cultivate financial and political independence. Illiteracy also

[78] P. S. Amaza, P. V. Kwagbe and A. A. Amos, 'Analysis of Women's Participation in Agricultural Cooperatives: Case Study of Borno State, Nigeria', *Annals of Borno*, 15/16 (1999), 187–96.

[79] V. A. Blay, 'Empowerment of Women Through Participation in Women Self-Help Groups in Kumasi Metropolis', MSc thesis, Kwame Nkrumah University of Science and Technology, Kumasi, Ghana, 2011.

[80] P. D. Lynch and H. Fahmy, *Craftswomen in Kerdassa Egypt: Household Production and Reproduction* (Geneva: ILO, 1984).

prevents the movement of women into well-paid jobs in the formal sector and into the political limelight.[81]

Women's self-help groups are also focal points for creating social networks as members help each other by pooling resources, setting up mutual self-support systems, and empowering each other through support in education, health and shelter. Drawing on some examples from Kenya, women of different ethnic backgrounds and from diverse geographical regions have organized themselves on the basis of ascriptive criteria such as age, class or territorial units.[82] Groups such as *Amasaga* or *Ebisangio* among the Abagusii, *Bulala* or *Buhasio* among the Luhya, *Saga* among the Luo, *Ngwatio* among the Agikuyu and *Mwenthya* among the Akamba are some of the mutualistic networks established to alleviate periodic labour shortages and hardships during planting, weeding and harvesting season, mostly in agricultural societies.[83] Mutualistic networks for the pooling of labour enable members to work their land on a rotational basis. In addition, they help in the organization of informal groups to provide assistance with agricultural work as well as funerals and childbirth support networks. In this way, each individual group member benefits a system of mutual reciprocity, with members steered towards the alleviation of common problems and the attainment of desired objectives.

Such groups are often small and based on ethnic, clan and familial affiliations. However, some women's self-help groups are more formal with a wider membership; for instance, the *Maendeleo Ya Wanawake* Organization (Organization for the Development of Women) formed in 1952 in Kenya. Its focus is mainly on women in rural areas and it aims to strengthen women's participation in rural community projects. It has rapidly grown into a national organization focusing not only on economic but political mobilization of women into party politics. Other organizations such as the Forum of African Women Educationists help with funds to facilitate efforts to increase female participation in technical and educational areas.[84]

The emergence and proliferation of self-help groups in Africa is a significant development as they spread into the economic, political and social

---

[81]   Lucy Johnson, 'Community Development through Women's Self-Help Groups, Mbarara Uganda', MSc thesis, Cambridge University, 2015, https://goo.gl/1ePwdK (accessed 4 January 2015).

[82]   I. P. K. Nyataya, 'Women Self Help Groups Enhancing Women's Development Processes in Kenya', *International Journal of Research in Sociology and Anthropology*, 2.2 (2016), 18–25.

[83]   Ochieng', ed., *Themes in Kenyan History*.

[84]   History Maendeleo ya Wanawake Kenya Projects, http://mywokenya.org/index. php/projects (accessed 30 June 2017).

spheres of society. The women's self-help groups have become a mainstay in promoting agricultural production, small-scale business enterprises and other income-generating activities.

THE ENVIRONMENT FOR COOPERATIVES

Africa has more than seventy million cooperative members.[85] African governments took control of the affairs of cooperatives in promotion, control and guidance activities.[86] In the agricultural sector, cooperatives became the sole agents for processing and marketing export crops such as coffee, cotton and pyrethrum. These organizations were mandated by the state to buy produce from farmers and process it for export; they also acted as agents for the state marketing boards.[87] Consequently, cooperatives ceased to be voluntary in character, and hence failed to promote solidarity and participation among the people. In Kenya, for example, the government amended the 1997 Co-operative Societies Act to re-enforce state regulation of the cooperative movement through the office of the Commissioner for Cooperative Development to monitor the organization, registration, operation, advancement and dissolution of the cooperative sector.[88]

The foregoing overview has shown that state-controlled cooperative development resulted in negative consequences for the cooperative movement. Cooperative policy and legislation that gave the state power to strictly supervise these organizations led to interference in their governance and management, with the result that cooperatives ended up being politicized, corrupted and mismanaged. The implication is that state control over the cooperative movement is not conducive to cooperative development in Africa.

Cooperative activities in North Africa focus on water, which has an impact on agricultural production, food security and livelihoods. Transboundary water resources often lead to competition and conflict in the region. Many North African countries, such as Egypt, Libya, Algeria and

---

85   Schwettmann, 'Capacity Building for Africa's Cooperative and Social Economic Organisations'.

86   Develtere, 'Cooperative Development in Africa'.

87   H. H. Muenkner and A. Shah, *Creating a Favourable Climate and Conditions for Cooperative Development in Africa* (Geneva: ILO, 1993).

88   F. O. Wanyama, 'Surviving Liberalization: The Cooperative Movement in Kenya', CoopAFRICA Working Paper No. 10, International Labour Organization, Dar es Salaam, 2009.

Tunisia, depend on external sources of water or trans-boundary water sources.[89] Cooperative efforts in trans-boundary water management improve stewardship, increase productivity, reduce costs and enhance security and relationships. For example, in Tunisia, there are about 2,500 cooperative associations for water use and water conservation.[90] In Egypt, water-use organizations along the Nile assist in regulating water use and managing conflict.[91]

Apart from water cooperative activities, there are also dairy cooperative chains in countries such as Tunisia, Algeria and Morocco that include, among others, the Centrale des Produits Laitiers Souani, Le Bon Lait, COPAG and Colait Extralait. These cooperative activities include milk-collecting centres and the processing and marketing of dairy products. But the dairy cooperatives are highly fragmented and face a number of financial and technical challenges. The introduction of structural adjustment programmes in the 1980s and the liberalization of the dairy industry brought competition from global companies such as Nestlé, leading to stiff competition for the dairy market and affecting grassroots cooperative efforts.[92]

INTERNATIONAL DIMENSION

International donors, such as the Nordic cooperative movements and the American and Canadian credit union movements, funded African cooperatives through the governments of their respective countries. More importantly, however, African governments became the instruments for channelling grants to the cooperatives and hence took advantage in this dispensing of patronage.[93]

[89] United Nations Educational, Scientific and Cultural Organization (UNESCO), *World Water Development Report 4: Managing Water Under Uncertainty and Risk*, vol. 1 (Paris: UNESCO, 2012), 210, https://goo.gl/qdUfi2 (accessed 4 March 2015).

[90] The World Bank, *Tunisia – Water Sector Investment Loan, Report No. PID8415* (Washington, DC: World Bank, 2000).

[91] D. Arafa, L. El-Fattal and H. Laamrani, 'Gender and Water Demand Management in the Middle East and North Africa', Canadian International Development Agency (IDRC/CRDI), 2007, https://goo.gl/Zgx2JK (accessed 10 March 2016).

[92] Mohamed Taher Sraïri, Mohammed Tahar Benyoucef and Khemais Kraiem, 'The Dairy Chains in North Africa (Algeria, Morocco and Tunisia): From Self Sufficiency Options to Food Dependency?', *Springer Plus*, 2.216 (2013), https://goo.gl/11qHWY (accessed 2 February 2015)

[93] A. Braverman et al., 'Promoting Rural Cooperatives in Developing Countries: The Case of Sub-Saharan Africa', World Bank Discussion Papers, No. WDP 121 (Washington, DC: World Bank, 1991).

Donor support worked contrary to the interests of cooperative members, and states used this avenue to control cooperative activities to the disadvantage of the members. Instead of funding cooperative movements directly, the donors channelled their funds through the state, and the state took this opportunity to further entrench state control over the cooperative movement. Some of the cases in point include the Oromia cooperatives in Ethiopia and the Kenya National Federation of Cooperatives.[94]

TOP-DOWN APPROACH

The state patronage of cooperative movements meant that movements were not organically emerging from the grassroots. This contributed to a lack of local ownership that led to increased cases of corruption, mismanagement, inefficiency and embezzlement of funds. In Kenya, for instance, many of the giant cooperatives began to collapse due to state patronage. These included the Kenya National Trading Cooperation, Kenya Cooperative Creameries, the Kenya Pyrethrum Cooperative and the Kenya Farmers Association.

LIBERALIZATION

The era of structural adjustment programmes in Africa from the 1980s also targeted the cooperative movements, which, in the eyes of the donors, were seen to be inefficient, corrupt and lacking proper leadership and supervision. The liberalization of the economies in Africa contributed to changes in cooperative development in Africa. Due to liberalization, many governments in Africa withdrew their support services for cooperatives, such as auditing, supervision, management and training. Without proper contingency plans to replace these support services, the cooperative movement began to decline, leaving many members without a coordinated grassroots organization for resource mobilization and development. This created numerous problems for the movement. Cases of corruption, gross mismanagement by officials, theft of cooperative resources, split of viable cooperatives into unviable units, failure to hold elections, favouritism in hiring and dismissal of staff, endless litigation, unauthorized cooperative investments and illegal payments to management committees contributed to the collapse of many cooperative movements across the continent.[95]

---

[94] Wanyama, 'Surviving Liberalization', 9–10.

[95] *Ibid.*

The liberalization of the market attracted new actors in economic sectors where cooperatives had previously enjoyed a monopoly status. The market now comprised many sellers and buyers, who were guided not by ownership but by efficiency, competitive pricing and transparency. The cooperatives had, therefore, to compete with other players in buying and selling agricultural produce if they were to remain in business. Ultimately, many of the cooperative movements were unable to survive in such a competitive environment. Coupled with the lack of financial resources to provide services to their members, many of the cooperatives closed down. The pyrethrum sector in Kenya is one such example. Originally, it had a membership of 200,000, but it declined to only 20,000 because of the inability of the Pyrethrum Board of Kenya to pay members for the product.[96]

REALIGNMENT OF COOPERATIVES

Initially, the cooperatives were regarded as extensions of the government rather than membership organizations. This resulted in inefficiencies and the withdrawal of effective participation by the members. On the other hand, liberalization of the economies in Africa contributed to economic hardship. Coupled with the inability of the state to provide effective services, people began to fall back on their own solidarity to rejoin or form new cooperatives to solve their socio-economic problems. The result was the emergence of vibrant cooperatives, especially savings and cooperative movements popularly known as SACCOs (Savings and Credit Scheme Organizations) to provide much-needed funds for individual and community development.

For example, Kenya has almost 7,000 registered SACCOs, with a membership of about seven million, while Tanzania has about 4,780 registered SACCOs, with 800,000 members. Ghana is another country with a strong membership in its cooperative movements.[97] The SACCOs in Kenya have rapidly grown to be the largest in Africa, accounting for 63 per cent of the continent's savings, loan and assets. The SACCOs operate in a range of activities, from housing to education and transport. They provide self-generated capital, without any dependence on outside funding to cover

[96] *The Daily Nation*, Nairobi, 12 February 2012.

[97] P. O. Alila and P. O. Obado, 'Co-operative Credit: The Kenyan SACCOS in a Historical and Development Perspective', Working Paper No. 474, Institute for Development Studies, University of Nairobi, 1990; Kembo M. Bwana and Joshua Mwakujonga, 'Issues in SACCOS Development in Kenya and Tanzania: The Historical and Development Perspectives', *Developing Country Studies*, 3.5 (2013), 114–21.

operating costs and loan services. Members normally have common ties which they share. For example, employment-based SACCOs are united through their employment contracts. Besides employment, the employees are pushed by self-help motives to be members of the SACCOs. Members pursue the goal of improving their economic and social situation through joint actions. The SACCOs are begun on the self-help philosophy to provide self-generated capital as well as to create a social network that is beneficial to their members.[98]

Most of the SACCOs in Kenya and Tanzania are in urban areas and formed by salary and wage earners who have common bonds, and whose employers are willing to implement the check-off system from members' monthly contributions and loan repayments. The SACCOs found in rural areas are community based and depend on agricultural activities.

THE POLITICAL CULTURE

The African cooperative movement up to the 1990s operated in a non-democratic environment. This was a severe constraint for the development of cooperatives. In Zambia, for instance, the cooperatives operated under a legal framework that allowed the government to control them. The Cooperative Act of 1989 allowed the government to appoint agents and fix prices of produce for cooperatives. The cooperatives were also compelled to provide annual reports to the government. But democratization in Zambia made it possible for the cooperative movement to gain self-reliance and independence. The cooperative movement started to show remarkable improvements due to the liberalization of politics and the economy. In Kenya, the political culture of authoritarianism in the 1980s led to the collapse of many cooperatives in the dairy industry and the pyrethrum, tea and coffee sectors. Another good example of political interference was in Uganda from 1971 to 1985, when Idi Amin declared an economic war on the country's Asian population. The departure of Asians and other expatriates from Uganda that followed, together with the flight into exile of the country's professionals, worsened the situation. Bureaucrats invaded the cooperatives, leading to mismanagement, corruption and embezzlement. The economic war also affected prices of controlled crops such as cotton and coffee, sectors in which the cooperatives were dominant players. As prices

---

[98] C. Kabuga and P. K. Batarinyebwa, eds, *Cooperatives: Past, Present and Future* (Kampala: Uganda Cooperative Alliance, 1995).

dropped, the production of raw materials fell, affecting the cooperative movement.[99]

THE SOCIAL CULTURE

Cooperatives are based on the values of self-help, self-responsibility, democracy, equality, equity and solidarity. Traditional systems of cooperation, mutuality, reciprocity and solidarity exist in all African societies and have remained to the present, especially in rural areas and in the informal economy.[100] These traditions have adapted to modern times and have been used to form mutual self-help groups that are often locally rooted, confined to a village or a neighbourhood. The groups and associations are mostly small in membership, and membership is based on a common bond derived from ethnic origin, social class, professional background, or a combination of two or more of these characteristics. Social capital and social control are of paramount importance, since these groups may handle large amounts of cash without any collateral or security. The groups are often temporary or periodic in nature and emerge when need arises; moreover, they seldom build secondary bodies such as unions and federations.[101]

These traditional African self-help groups share many of the values and principles of modern cooperatives. The implication is that there already exists a social base that is conducive to the development of cooperatives in Africa. The challenge is to nurture this social culture in the wake of the neoliberal wave with its individualistic tendencies.

CONCLUSION

For mutualistic and cooperative principles of labour to be effective in Africa it is important to focus on the following. For cooperative and mutualistic associations to be actively involved in African development, active leadership and citizen participation is of paramount importance. Leaders must excel in good governance and in social and political representation of their members. Leaders require business skills, political acumen, managerial competence and

---

[99] P. Mutibwa, *Uganda since Independence: A Story of Unfulfilled Hopes* (Kampala: Africa World Press, 2010); A. R. Kyamulesire, *A History of the Uganda Cooperative Movement, 1913–1988* (Kampala: Uganda Cooperative Alliance, 1988).

[100] See the chapters by Tischler and Barchiesi in this volume.

[101] Schwettmann, 'Capacity Building for Africa's Cooperative and Social Economic Organisations'.

financial and accounting skills. They also require legal knowledge in order to fully comprehend the environment in which the movements operate.

Since Africa has about seventy million members in cooperative movements, and in the absence of strict government control, it is important that members implement checks and balances and make their leaders accountable. Members require financial and economic literacy to be able to understand the operations of cooperative movements. Cooperative and mutualistic associations deal with members who constantly interact with the environment as either producers or consumers. The cooperative movement may be a good avenue for educating members about solid management and waste disposal in both urban and rural settings, about soil erosion controls, and about drought-resistant crops. Countries that have adopted these models include Ethiopia, Somalia, the Democratic Republic of Congo and Egypt.

Since the cooperative movement and the mutualistic movement are important pillars of African development, it is crucial to invest in capacity building. Although many countries in Africa, such as Uganda, Kenya, Lesotho, Swaziland, Kenya, Ghana, Nigeria and Cameroon, have established cooperative colleges, the tendency is to train civil servants and cooperative members, leaders and employees.[102] It is important to implant mutualistic and cooperative studies in the tertiary educational institutions. The movement is founded on the principles of autonomy and voluntary cooperation for the mutual social, economic and cultural benefit of its members. It is essential that governments in Africa adhere to the fundamentals of the movement. In many parts of Africa, the movement operates in a climate of authoritarianism that stifles its performance.

The history of mutualism and cooperative development in Africa has shown that some of the key challenges have been excessive state control; the sudden withdrawal of state regulation without an alternative regulatory mechanism; the lack of effective membership participation in cooperatives; the authoritarian political culture under which mutualism and cooperative movements operated; and political patronage. The fragile financial base of cooperatives affects their services to members. These challenges constrain their efforts, and the democratic reforms that are taking place in many African countries ought to be nurtured to facilitate a better political environment for cooperative and mutualistic development.

---

[102] L. Shaw, 'Cooperative Education in East and Southern Africa', (Draft) CoopAfrica Working Paper, Dar Es Salaam, ILO, 2010.

PART VII
CONCLUSIONS

TWENTY-TWO

The 'Labour Question' in Africa and the World

FREDERICK COOPER

Department of History, New York University

This collection of essays is both the fruit of and a contribution to a recent rebirth of interest in the history of labour in Africa. Labour has never ceased to be an important part of social and economic life in Africa, but serious research on the topic has wavered. With some notable exceptions – especially among specialists on southern Africa – historians had lost interest by the late 1980s. The trend was not unique to Africa; indeed, it was part of a crisis in Marxist scholarship and social history and sociology more generally. Scholars are as fashion conscious as anybody, and they often follow trends – be it the 'cultural turn', the 'linguistic turn' or the 'imperial turn'. Interest in labour's past has long been associated with an interest in labour's future – with projects of social reform and social revolution. The collapse of the communist alternative to capitalist hegemony had much to do with the disaffection at century's end of leftist scholars from political economy. Much of the energy of progressive scholars that had once gone into such subjects went in other directions.[1]

The struggle to liberate South Africa from apartheid and the hopes vested in the post-1994 future kept the subject alive in that part of Africa. More generally, the International Institute of Social History and journals such as *International Labor and Working-Class History* and *Movement Social* tried to keep labour and social history alive. In the last decade or so, labour history has revived, but with different emphases. The Centre for the Study of Labour and Life Course in Global History at Humboldt University in

---

[1] The pattern held for francophone as well as anglophone scholarship. Jean Copans, 'Pourquoi travail et travailleurs africains ne sont plus à la mode en 2014 dans les sciences sociales. Retour sur l'actualité d'une problématique du XXe siècle', *Politique Africaine*, 133 (2014), 25–44.

Berlin has since 2009 brought together scholars with an interest in the subject for regular conferences, summer academies for advanced graduate students and post-doctoral fellowship years. Perhaps the revival of this domain of scholarship has something to do with the cyclical nature of scholarly fashions – as new trends prove themselves no more able than older approaches to provide a convincing way of looking at the world. Perhaps the moments of citizen mobilization in certain African countries have encouraged renewed attention to popular mobilizations of different sorts. And perhaps growing concern with the extremes of inequality that global capitalism has produced – within and among states – has fostered a desire to understand the changing mechanisms through which exploitation takes place and the movements of people, capital and ideas that link the labour question in different parts of the world.[2]

A CHANGING THEORETICAL LANDSCAPE

As this volume clearly demonstrates, an outstanding feature of the 2010s version of labour history – compared with that of the 1970s or 1980s – is the variety of forms of labour that come under scrutiny. The woman doing household labour, the entrepreneur trying to start a small business, the civil servant doing the work of government, the soldier and the policeman, the man or woman compelled to build a local road, the young man eking out a living with occasional work in a city, the smuggler – all of these figure in the pages of this book. They were not particularly visible in the version of labour history of previous decades. If we are to gain some insight into the possibilities and limits of our own time perspective, we might look briefly at the perspectives of the earlier heyday of labour history.[3]

First, the 1970s was a time when scholars of Africa were anxious to prove that, in any domain, 'Africans can do it too'. They could do industrial work and organize trade unions and strikes, just as they could govern themselves and excel at commerce, export agriculture and other economic activities.

---

[2]   For other broad discussions of African labour history, see the collections of articles edited by Stefano Bellucci and Bill Freund in *Africa*, 87.1 (2017), 27–119; and by Franco Barchiesi and Stefano Bellucci in *International Labor and Working-Class History*, 86 (2014), 4–158; see also Frederick Cooper, 'African Labor History', in *Global Labour History: A State of the Art*, ed. Jan Lucassen (Bern: Peter Lang, 2006), 91–116. For an Africanist's perspective on a wider context, see Andreas Eckert, ed., *Global Histories of Work* (Berlin: De Gruyter, 2016).

[3]   For an excellent summary of the state of labour history as of the mid-1980s, see Bill Freund, *The African Worker* (Cambridge: Cambridge University Press, 1988).

Second was a linear conception of history. There was a strong narrative drive from the 1970s into the 1980s: Africans entered wage labour, they became proletarians, they became conscious of themselves as a class, and they engaged in union organizing and strikes. They challenged colonial governments, and the narrative of worker organization sometimes overlapped with the narrative of nationalist movements conquering the state. This phase of African labour history was much influenced by one of the most important texts of British labour history, published in 1963: E. P. Thompson's *Making of the English Working Class*. Books appeared with titles such as 'the development of an African working class', 'the making of an African working class' – telling references to Thompson's title, if not to the more ambiguous content of his book.[4]

Third was a deterministic view of history, whether this took the form of world systems theory that consigned Africa to the periphery by virtue of the fact that it was in the periphery, or variants on Marxism that postulated that, in the last instance, Africa's place in the world was defined by the articulation of modes of production, by which capital's costs were subsidized by the continued viability of African modes of reproduction.[5]

Fourth, increasingly evident from the late 1970s through the 1990s was an obligatory miserabilism. The task of the historian was to reveal how bad things were, and the observer of contemporary society was – not without some reason – showing by the 1980s that, as the proletarianization thesis was collapsing, things were getting even worse. In some quarters, the miserability thesis was reversed in the early 2000s: 'Africa rising' became a new cry, a response to improving export markets and higher GNP growth in some countries. The notion of 'Africa rising' was just as linear a conception of change as the immiseration notions of previous years, assuming that

---

[4]   Richard Sandbrook and Robin Cohen, eds, *The Development of an African Working Class* (London: Longman, 1975); Jeff Crisp, *The Making of an African Working Class: Ghanaian Miners' Struggles 1870–1980* (London: Zed Books, 1984); Paul Lubeck, *Islam and Urban Labor in Northern Nigeria: The Making of a Muslim Working Class* (Cambridge: Cambridge University Press, 1986); John Higginson, *A Working Class in the Making: Belgian Colonial Labor Policy, Private Enterprise, and the African Mineworkers, 1907–1951* (Madison, WI: University of Wisconsin Press, 1989). For a perspective on Thompson's influence published shortly after his death, see Frederick Cooper, 'Work, Class, and Empire: An African Historian's Retrospective on E. P. Thompson', *Social History*, 20.2 (1995), 235–41.

[5]   Key texts include Immanuel Wallerstein, *The Modern World System*, 4 vols (New York: Academic Press, 1974), and Claude Meillassoux, *Femmes, greniers et capitaux* (Paris: Maspero, 1975).

short-term trends would persist.[6] Nevertheless, the images we see in the press of Africans risking their lives in small boats to enter a European job market in which they will be vulnerable to exploitation makes it clear that misery, if not miserabilism, is still with us.

Perceptions have changed. That Africans can do it too is taken for granted, at least by anyone who could possibly be convinced. Events have proven the proletarianization thesis wrong. The African working class did not continue to grow in numbers. Unionization was subject to reversal, too, this time as a political process, when the first generation of African rulers were quicker than the last generation of European ones, in British and French Africa anyway, to suppress or co-opt trade unions. Determinist arguments proved unable to predict the past any better than the future.[7] Misery and progress have a relationship more uneven and more complex than either a miserabilism thesis or an Africa rising scenario.

Scholars have flailed around to find alternative concepts: informal labour was one, even though social relations of work could be quite highly structured. 'Precarity' is a more recent arrival, even though the basis of capitalism ever since its inception has been the precarity of people without property. This is a point made in this volume by Barchiesi. Both concepts are responses to the apparent reversal of the apparent trend towards 'proletarianization': instead of a continued movement towards wage labour and struggles to assure its stabilization and protection, capital came to demand that its social costs be minimized and its flexibility maximized, even if this meant a less stable relationship of capitalists and workers.

The question – raised in these pages – is whether proletarianization and informalization can be seen as a sequence or whether we need better tools to understand the relationship of different forms of work that overlap in time. Can we explain the interplay of these tendencies under the rubric of 'the logic of capitalism', 'globalization' or 'flexibilization', or have the actions of workers, however limited their power, shaped the unfolding of work regimes?

The proletarianization thesis, fashionable as it was in the 1970s or early 1980s, did not actually get a free pass. Some of the criticisms represented theoretical conflicts among Marxist scholars, along the lines of the contention between British social historians, such as E. P. Thompson and Eric Hobsbawm, and French theoretical Marxists such as Louis Althusser and Claude Meillassoux. The South African literature was particularly

---

[6]   'Africa Rising', *The Economist*, 3 December 2011.

[7]   Frederick Cooper, Allen Isaacman, Florencia Mallon, William Roseberry and Steve Stern, *Confronting Historical Paradigms: Peasants, Labor, and the Capitalist World System in Africa and Latin America* (Madison, WI: University of Wisconsin Press, 1993).

rich in this regard, for it represented the best case for a thorough capitalist transformation of the economy, but was full of complexities. The specifically racial construction of the labour regime seemed to entail 'super-exploitation' – the harnessing of racial distinction to divide the working class and the sloughing off on to the deliberately truncated remnants of pre-capitalist societies in rural South Africa the costs of reproducing the labour force. At the same time, historians uncovered evidence of Africans finding niches within the system where they could keep subordination to wage labour at arm's length, where they could organize themselves in ways not visible to authorities.[8] Meanwhile, the very racialization of the social and political structure allowed whites to claim higher wages and monopolize skills, so that some sectors of capital faced high costs while others prospered. The clash of alternative modes of organizing labour lay not in the hindsight of historians, but in the politics of different periods of South African history, in the 1920s, 1940s, 1970s most acutely, but indeed throughout the twentieth century. The history of work and capital in South Africa turns out to be a history of struggle more than the unfolding of a certain kind of logic.

The rest of Africa offers lessons too: look at the vast quantity of labour power that went unharnessed, that was not producing very much of the surplus value that was the life blood of capitalists.[9] Complaints that Africans were lazy and unproductive or that they needed 'development' were signs that the captains of capitalism did not think that 'colonial capitalism' was an altogether functional system for maximizing profits. Such a structure provided opportunities for evasion or desertion as well as pressures to work for low wages, and the argument that the balance was just right for capital could only be tautological.

---

[8] See the epic text in which Charles van Onselen uses a biography to reveal the partial success of some Africans in avoiding total subordination to capitalism and white domination: *The Seed is Mine: The Life of Kas Maine, A South African Sharecropper, 1894–1985* (New York: Hill and Wang, 1996). Particularly influential in the 1980s and 1990s was the pioneering work of Stanley Trapido and his students (of whom van Onselen was one), for example, 'South Africa in a Comparative Study of Industrialization', *Journal of Development Studies*, 7.3 (1971), 309–20. The work of Philip Bonner has been particularly important over a long span of years, for example, *Holding Their Ground: Class, Locality, and Culture in 19th and 20th Century South Africa* (Johannesburg: Witwatersrand University Press, 1989).

[9] Gareth Austin, 'Capitalism and the Colonies', in *Cambridge History of Capitalism, Volume 2: The Spread of Capitalism: From 1848 to the Present*, ed. Larry Neal and Jeffrey Williamson (Cambridge: Cambridge University Press, 2014), 301–47; Frederick Cooper, 'From Enslavement to Precarity? The Labour Question in African History', in *The Political Economy of Everyday Life in Africa: Beyond the Margins*, ed. Wale Adebanwi (Woodbridge: James Currey, 2017), 135–56.

The miserabilist approach ran into the problem of Africans who did quite well for themselves. Some of them, that is. The story isn't new. The extent of economic extraction from slave labour before the European colonization of the continent – and the variety of other forms of commanding resources – became increasingly evident once historians got over the need to portray an angelic Africa as a foil to a diabolical Europe. Africa in this sense looked like other parts of the world. The challenge is to write a history with multiple dimensions to it: to see how African elites used external connections for their own gain or saw their power over their subalterns undermined, how young men and women used new possibilities to sell their labour to escape patriarchal authority, perhaps to become trapped in relations with European or indigenous employers that were even more confining.

There were other gains to be had by moving beyond the proletarianization narrative. Not least was overcoming the primacy that narrative had given to males. Having to think about gender shed a new light on labour history, not just to think more about women but to think about men and above all to think about relationships, in production, reproduction and commerce.[10]

AFRICA IN A HISTORY OF CAPITALISM

The challenge is to confront such complexities without losing the moral force of a critical engagement with the history of capitalism and colonialism in Africa. E. P. Thompson long ago remarked that British workers struggled *not to be a class* – not to be reduced to labour power and nothing more – before they struggled *as a class*. Such a perspective encourages us to think of class as a variable, not an inevitability, not the be all and end all of social analysis. The multiple forms of associational life need to be examined, and how they articulate with relations of production becomes a question, not a trajectory following its own logic. In this light, asking about the networks that Africans formed in moving between original communities and places of work, about labour cooperatives, and about self-help associations of workers becomes

---

[10]   Lisa A. Lindsay and Stephan F. Miescher, eds, *Men and Masculinities in Modern Africa* (Portsmouth, NH: Heinemann, 2003). It is important to acknowledge contributions to the study of gender and labour going back to the 1980s and 1990s, for example Iris Berger, *Threads of Solidarity: Women in South African Industry 1900–1980* (Bloomington, IN: Indiana University Press, 1992); Karen Tranberg Hansen, *Distant Companions: Servants and Employers in Zambia, 1900–1985* (Ithaca, NY: Cornell University Press, 1989); Claire Robertson, *Sharing the Same Bowl? A Socioeconomic History of Women and Class in Accra, Ghana* (Bloomington, IN: Indiana University Press, 1984).

an integral part of labour history.[11] So too, from a different point of view, are the policies of the 1940s for the 'stabilization' – as both French and British officials called it – of labour. They can be seen as a colonial attempt to imagine a working class, separated from what was seen as truly African life, the moulding of a subset of the African population into a cultureless embodiment of the modernization ideal.[12]

The flip side of this was the imagination of Africans who didn't fit, and colonial and later African governments directed much effort to define certain social categories as deviant, criminal and dangerous.[13] There is a fine line between labour that is useful to capital – and often cheap – and labour that is dangerous and defined as criminal. In some circumstances, governments were (and are) content to preside over the operation of entrepreneurs and networks that organize exchange in their own ways, hidden from licensing and taxation regulations, whether it be the sale of cheap commodities on city streets or drug trafficking or prostitution. In other cases, they see such activities as producing the wrong kind of society, one that cannot be disciplined.[14]

The defining of class categories and the provision of social services are not linear processes; a grid of control can unravel, at the level of the state and at the level of the family. Defining categories is very much connected to questions of political economy, global as well as local. The economic crisis of the 1980s and the imposition of structural adjustment devastated social services and urban employment. By undermining life chances and social cohesion, these 'reforms' helped to create a body of alienated young men, possible recruits to gangs or for the armies assembled by warlords in the regional civil wars that affected some African countries in the 1990s and 2000s.

If the worker can be defined by the state in different ways – and in different political economic contexts – workers also imagine themselves in different ways. In this volume, Brown and Glasman and Moyd point to the

---

[11] See the chapters by Pérez Niño, Nyanchoga and Scully and Jawad in this volume.

[12] See the chapters by Eckert, Barchiesi, Brown and Pilossof in this volume. See also Frederick Cooper, *Decolonization and African Society: The Labor Question in French and British Africa* (Cambridge: Cambridge University Press, 1996).

[13] See the chapter by Fourchard in this volume.

[14] A pioneering study along these lines is Luise White, *The Comforts of Home: Prostitution in Colonial Nairobi* (Chicago: University of Chicago Press, 1990). She shows that, in the early colonial period, British officials in Nairobi did little to interfere with African women who provided sexual and other services to migrant men, sometimes acquiring the ownership of houses. But in the late 1930s they decided that these women were reproducing the wrong kind of society and cracked down not only on prostitution but on the autonomy of the neighbourhood.

different constructions of masculinity. A wage labour job could be a way out of the authority of one's father, but deprivation – loss of access to land without alternative employment – can prevent a young man from achieving adulthood, a factor cited as a cause of the rallying of ex-squatters and other marginalized men to the Mau Mau rebellion, but more often an incitement to desperate measures to get resources, from joining criminal gangs to a risky boat trip to the Canaries or Sicily. The decline of regularized (often masculinized) employment and women's position in irregular employment changed relations between the sexes.[15] What Bryceson describes as the 'juggling act' that women perform in paid and non-paid work reflects the intertwining of different gender regimes and exacerbates the difficulty women face in establishing their own career paths.

GREY AREAS AND SHARP DISTINCTIONS: COERCION AND LABOUR

As Fall and Roberts make clear, the forced labour question remains of great concern to scholars, and it is a political issue today. It is part of a very long story that has to do both with the often ugly particularity of power and with the ambiguity of categories. In recent scholarship, the line between free and coerced labour has begun to blur, mainly as 'free' labour begins to look less free.[16] The employer–worker relationship, even in 'liberal' Great Britain, was nested in layers of state regulation, juridical enforcement and outright coercion – vagrancy laws, masters and servants legislation, the poor laws. These methods were transported to Africa, as were other methods to extract work from people who had alternatives and might not be willing to sell their labour power, at least for the wages offered. In many cases – but not in Portuguese Africa – overt coercion was phased out as enough Africans were caught up in a cash-demanding world to supply labour, but pressures could still be brought and they escalated during the Second World War and in

---

[15] Aili Mari Tripp, *Changing the Rules: The Politics of Liberalization and the Urban Informal Economy in Tanzania* (Berkeley, CA: University of California Press, 1997).

[16] The work of Alessandro Stanziani has been particularly important in this regard: 'Labour Institutions in a Global Perspective, from the Seventeenth to the Twentieth Century', *International Review of Social History*, 54.3 (2009), 351–58; and *Bondage: Labor and Rights in Eurasia from the Sixteenth to the Early Twentieth Centuries* (New York: Berghahn Books, 2014).

forced resettlements during the Mau Mau and Algerian wars.[17] Independent African governments had their own ways of pressuring people into work for allegedly collective (i.e. state) purposes.[18]

But if free and coerced labour were not dichotomous, the representation of labour in such terms was crucial to the ideological justification of capitalism. The anti-slavery movement, however diverse the motivations of its leading actors, had the effect of defining an ethically defensible form of labour neatly distinguished from slavery. In such a political structure, working-class movements could still make claims, but the domain of claim making was defined by the acceptance of the wage relationship itself. Some decades after Britain and later France had renounced slavery in their own colonies, the continued practice of slavery in parts of Africa became a justification for colonization. European powers went through ideological contortions to claim both the anti-slavery agenda and the use of coerced labour in the various forms delineated by Fall and Roberts. By clearly marking 'slavery' and eventually 'forced labour' (or 'child labour'), colonial powers, independent African states and the elites of some African societies could distance themselves from a large grey area of constrained choice about when and for whom to work. This was, of course, a variant on the 'normal' constraints of wage labour systems, but it was at times an embarrassing one. It leaves us with a question: how should we interpret the cocoa farm that employs children compelled by their parents to work on the harvest or the continued pressures on people of slave descent in some Sahelian societies to serve the people who had enslaved their ancestors? Is there a danger of treating 'twentieth-century slavery' as an exotically African practice that we can all agree to condemn or can it be seen in the context of a history of Euro-African connections that provide the conditions in which such exploitation is possible?[19]

---

[17] On Portuguese Africa, see Eric Allina, *Slavery by Any Other Name: African Life under Company Rule in Colonial Mozambique* (Charlottesville, VA: University of Virginia Press, 2012).

[18] 'Development' and the provision of benefits to local communities could become a rationale for coercive labour recruitment in both the late colonial and postcolonial periods. See Benedetta Rossi, 'What "Development" Work Does', in *Developmentalism, Labor, and the Slow Death of Slavery in Twentieth-Century Africa*, ed. Benedetta Rossi and Franco Barchiesi, special issue of *International Labor and Working-Class History*, 92 (2017), 7–23.

[19] Benedetta Rossi, *From Slavery to Aid: Politics, Labour, and Ecology in the Nigerian Sahel, 1800–2000* (Cambridge: Cambridge University Press, 2015).

MAKING WORKERS

So how does one conceptualize the on-the-ground relations of production that have shaped and reshaped work in Africa? Much of this book is occupied with this issue, in its agricultural dimension,[20] in the trajectory of wage labour,[21] in regard to industry,[22] and the specific forms of work that one finds in mining,[23] administrative labour,[24] entertainment,[25] in relation to capitalists and entrepreneurs,[26] and in the sense of connections and changes across the continent.[27] One Marxist concept that has been underutilized in African studies is primitive (sometimes translated as original) accumulation. The first twenty-five chapters of *Capital* portrayed a powerful systemic logic, built on the assumption that labour was fully commoditized. In chapter 26, Marx argued that these assumptions had, notably in the case of Great Britain, been met by the forceful removal of most cultivators from the land and the legal and administrative structure that enforced this social, political and coercive process. How this came to be could not be explained on the basis of capital logic. Primitive accumulation was thus a contingent process, located at the intersection of different historical trends, including the relationship of crown and aristocracy in Britain, the changing legal framework in which landlords and different categories of tenants operated, the slave trade and plantation agriculture in the West Indies, and inter-imperial rivalries that shaped the capacity of the state and financial institutions to reinforce each other. All these points have been the subject of scholarly investigation and questioning ever since.

It is better to focus on multiple patterns of accumulation, the English among them, than to assume one model from which others deviate.[28] One can focus on specific processes in Africa by which people acquired productive resources and excluded others from them – land, productive trees,

---

[20] See the chapter by Tischler in this volume.

[21] See the chapter by Eckert in this volume.

[22] See the chapter by Neveling in this volume.

[23] See the chapter by Brown in this volume.

[24] See the chapter by van den Bersselaar in this volume.

[25] See the chapter by Samuel Andreas Admasie in this volume.

[26] See the chapters by Berry and Austin in this volume.

[27] See the chapters by Barchiesi and Pérez Niño in this volume.

[28] A related criticism was made some years ago of the work of German historians who took the British case as the norm and explained the particularities of German history as a deviation from it. David Blackbourn and Geoff Eley, *The Peculiarities of German History: Bourgeois Society and Politics in Nineteenth-century Germany* (Oxford: Oxford University Press, 1984).

nodal points on trade routes. The concept encourages us to ask exactly what resources were commanded, by whom, on what basis, and who was excluded from them, on what basis, and with what effects.[29] These are empirical questions and will give rise to diverse answers.

In South Africa, the alienation of land went further than elsewhere in Africa, complicated by the racialized nature of the process and the fiction that Africans maintained the integrity of pre-capitalist societies. Elsewhere, there were specific regions where such alienation took place and more where differential access to land and other resources took forms more complicated than a dichotomy of 'land alienation' and 'communal land tenure'. The classic case here is that of West African cocoa producers, where the people with a prior claim to land, migrants who planted the cocoa trees, and kinsmen, clients, labour tenants and other workers who did the labour mark a system of relations that brought about innovation and relative prosperity without corresponding to the alleged norms of freehold property. Cocoa producers, like slave traders and the users of slave labour, were engaged in commodity production. We can take a broad view of commodity production, but the exact form that it takes – and the overlap of different forms – matters a great deal.

In some instances, Africans were able to straddle the individual life cycle or the family unit between wage labour and agriculture. In recent decades, governing elites and foreign investors have been buying up land, not necessarily using it productively, but leaving many people without either the security that access to land through kinship and community had once provided or any realistic possibility of supporting themselves through wage labour.[30] It has taken a while, but scholars such as Carola Lentz, Sara Berry and Catherine Boone have looked from different angles at the complexities of landed property and its relationship to production.[31]

Their work makes clear that a variety of social relations of production coexisted in time and over space. It makes sense to analyse them not in relation to the individual worker at any point in time, but to the worker over the life course, and each life course in relation to kinship groups, networks, patron–client relations and so on. This complexity, this overlapping of social

---

[29] Particularly important in this regard is the work of Sara Berry, *No Condition is Permanent: The Social Dynamics of Agrarian Change in Sub-Saharan Africa* (Madison, WI: University of Wisconsin Press, 1993). See also Austin's chapter in this volume.

[30] See the chapter by Tischler in this volume.

[31] Carola Lentz, *Land, Mobility, and Belonging in West Africa* (Bloomington, IN: Indiana University Press, 2013); Berry, *No Condition is Permanent*; Catherine Boone, *Property and Political Order in Africa: Land Rights and the Structure of Politics* (Cambridge: Cambridge University Press, 2014).

forms over the life course and over different kinds of social connections, was both a protection and, over time, a constraint.

What I am arguing here is that, by turning a model of capitalist development into a set of questions, one can develop a set of perspectives that take us away from singular stories of the ever-extending reach of proletarianization. The stories are about time – life cycle and growth spurts more than linear time – and they are about space, but lumpy space, uneven space, not the infinitely connected space that the word 'globalization' implies.

LIFE CYCLES AND GROWTH SPURTS: CHANGE OVER TIME

Instead of asking why Africa has experienced 'slow growth' over a long period of time compared to other parts of the world, Morten Jerven points out that Africa has experienced 'growth spurts'.[32] African producers responded quite vigorously to incentives in certain conjunctures and produced rapid growth, for example in the cash-crop revolution of the late nineteenth and early twentieth centuries, the post-Second World War commodities boom (extending into the early 1970s), and one might add – with a grain of salt – the period of 2000–2014 or so, when African growth rates were high. These spurts produced dramatic changes in social relations – some highlighted in this volume – but not a sustained pattern of structural transformation. The chapters in this volume do not directly explain the overall pattern, but there are some hints here and elsewhere. Africa in the nineteenth century had zones of relatively dense population and concentrated political power (kingdoms such as Asante or the Sokoto caliphate) but also zones that were less populated. The combination of relatively strong kinship groups and places to flee from an oppressor or exploiter constrained elites' chances of gaining exclusive control of the means of production.

Colonization occurred at a time when European powers had particular technological advantages – the machine gun, the telegraph and the steam engine – that enabled rapid conquest but not systematic administration. Some areas – near coasts or railway lines – experienced a growth spurt. This – and the chance of being colonized by powers distinguished politically and linguistically from each other – added to the fragmentation of the continent.

[32] Morten Jerven, 'African Growth Recurring: An Economic History Perspective on African Growth Episodes, 1690–2010', *Economic History of Developing Regions*, 25.2 (2010), 127–54.

The chapters of this book make clear the multiple trajectories of different parts of Africa and the unevenness of the impact of new means of transportation, new possibilities for agricultural and mineral exports, and new possibilities for geographic mobility. Trade routes within Africa had long favoured specific (if changing) commodities, often of relatively high value and ecological specialization. The colonial pattern of railway construction produced a narrowly focused drainage network, as well as roads, often of poor quality, that fed the network while providing minimal intra-African connections. The differentials between regions served by an effective means of communication and those that were not were stark, given the slowness and high cost of alternative forms of transport. Such structures could respond effectively to specific demands and take advantage of the low cost – but uneven supply – of labour from regions without the export outlet. Colonial policy did not necessarily encourage entrepreneurship outside of certain limits; indeed, it protected European monopolies. The match-up of European and African political and economic trajectories is consistent with the unevenness – temporal and spatial – in Jerven's conception of the importance and limitation of growth spurts.

But the post-Second World War conjuncture revealed the limits of the pattern in the eyes of colonial rulers, especially in Britain and France, both of which acutely needed Africa's raw materials and the foreign exchange they could earn to recover from a war that had badly weakened them. They also needed legitimacy in the face of challenges from African political and social movements. That both – and other powers too – saw 'development' as a state initiative in the interest of empire reflected the fact that the logic of capital was not sufficient to do the job. There was a great deal of labour power in Africa that was going untapped, and it could be useful to bring out a great quantity of commodities; officials fantasized about 'mountains' of minerals. Such considerations lay behind the closely interrelated policies of the 1940s – economic development and labour stabilization. Whether the specific policies were effective has been a matter of debate, but they did create for a time the situation in quite a few African territories of growing workforces with better wages and benefits than before.[33] If the results fell short of the economic revolution its boosters had promised, they did in these instances produce enough growth to finance a large expansion of education,[34] a vast expansion of transportation networks,[35] and a segment of the workforce with reasonable job security and career prospects. It added to the fragmentation

[33] See the chapters by Eckert, Barchiesi, Brown and Neveling in this volume.

[34] See the chapter by Pilossof in this volume.

[35] See the chapter by Bellucci in this volume.

of Africa, for the impact was quite uneven. And instead of taming conflict, it exacerbated it. Wage workers were in a better position to make claims, but the stakes of conflict with white settlers and with people of different regional and ethnic origins rose. These conflicts were part of the cost-benefit calculation that French and British officials undertook in the late 1950s.[36]

Decolonization suited international capital rather well. It could use or write off different states. Foreign aid could be provided, but as donors saw fit. A market-centred view of the world – of the individual actor making choices in a field of alternatives – was compatible with a view of individual states acting autonomously in relation to each other. In the 1940s and 1950s international discourse was changing not only in turning the possibility of African self-government from inconceivable to an international norm, but in redefining the labour question. The International Labour Organization was one of several international bodies rethinking the labour question on a global scale, and not in an entirely consistent manner. Up to the time of the Second World War, the ILO's interest in Africa focused above all on the forced labour question (plus contract labour and migrancy) rather than the complex social dimensions of labour and labour–capital conflict that received so much attention with regard to Europe and North America. This pattern changed in the 1940s. As Maul, Puddu and Tijani point out, the ILO's position by the late 1940s was premised on the notion that Africans could become 'universal workers', whose conditions of work and life could be regulated and protected in the same manner as those of workers anywhere in the world. But it soon ran into the particularity of conditions in Africa: the poverty of African countries led international experts to emphasize the need for the 'development' of the entire economy, and independent African states' sensitivity to any intrusion on their newly acquired sovereignty made the imposition of universal standards a touchy subject. ILO policies have gone through several transformations since the 1950s, but the most recent incarnation is revealing: the Decent Work Agenda. Its name makes clear that in much of the world, and especially Africa, the conditions of work are not decent.

The labour question in Africa was never self-contained – not in the era of the slave trade, not in the era of independent states. Migration had long been fostered by the spatial fragmentation of Africa, and in the 1950s – with European economies flourishing – African migrants could seek in Europe some of the possibilities they had sought in African cities (and, in the French

---

[36] I developed this argument at length in *Decolonization and African Society*. Several of the chapters in this volume present evidence consistent with this analysis.

case, they could do so as citizens).[37] Elites in African territories coming into self-government could for a time capture for their own benefit much of the tax revenue that the post-war economy generated and still provide something for their citizens – schools, roads and clinics most prominently. Even if we keep in mind the political conflicts and efforts by elites to demobilize citizens who had struggled against colonial rule, the gains in education, declining infant mortality and extended life spans in the first decade or two of independence should not be overlooked.

But what many proclaimed to be the policy goal of an independent government – building a national economy – was much more elusive. For the most part, African economies remained 'extroverted' and exposed to changes in the world economy.[38] The possibilities for African states – and notably for their rulers – were conditioned by the extremes of inequality in the world they faced: in economic power, in resources, in education, in positions within international organizations. In such a situation, with weak levers of power over the varied forms of production within national territory, it was not irrational for governing elites to make the most of what they had: control of the interface between the territorially bounded national economy and the rest of the world. That often meant co-opting or discouraging possible opposition to political control, and that, in turn, meant keeping both organized labour and national capitalists in check.[39] Labour organizations encountered both a carrot and a stick in hitching their own demands to state-centred development, exposing them to co-optation and repression. In some cases, labour unions eventually became a force for political reform – although their political allies (Chiluba in Zambia) did not necessarily stay with them. Freund, and Scully and Jawad both conclude that it is hard to find that organized labour either consistently promoted or consistently benefited from the promotion of social democracy.

When the world economy went into recession in the 1970s, the most vulnerable parts of it suffered the most durable reversal. Demand for African products fell, and restrictions were imposed on Africans (and others) who wanted to enter European labour markets. The weak finances of African states made them targets for international financial institutions concerned

---

[37] The pioneering research of François Manchuelle emphasized the initiative of migrants in shaping patterns of movement: *Willing Migrants: Soninke Labor Diasporas, 1848–1960* (Athens, OH: Ohio University Press, 1997).

[38] Jean-François Bayart, 'Africa in the World: A History of Extroversion', *African Affairs*, 99.395 (1999), 217–26.

[39] Britwum and Dakhli chart the ups and downs of state–labour relations and conclude that, overall, 'labour's interests have been subsumed under those of capital'.

above all with the financial situation – balancing budgets and assuring the repayment of loans on the backs of Africans who needed social services. The effects of structural adjustment on different domains of African labour are well documented in this book. Why were the effects of the world recession more durable in Africa than in other parts of the world? While this book does not address the question at that level of generalization, part of the answer is undoubtedly in the effects of structural adjustment itself: undermining education, healthcare and infrastructure, reversing the fragile and uneven gains of the development era. Part of the answer lies in the economic and social situation that made African states turn to the international financial organizations in the first place. If the effects of the recession were widely felt (complicated in some cases by oil production and in others by civil war), the recovery has been highly uneven, with expanded employment in large-scale mining in some areas, wildcat, often violent, episodes of extractive production in others, a few instances (Uganda, Ghana, South Africa) of expanded social protections, and more generally a focus on the kinds of labour described, for better or worse, as 'informal' or 'precarious'.[40] Austin points out that capitalist classes in Africa did not necessarily get stronger during and after structural adjustment. All this has accentuated the fragmentation of African societies, and politics has at times taken the form of episodes of collective action by the urban poor and disenfranchised youth. For many, the quest for betterment is individual: finding a patron with state connections, working for a warlord or wildcat mine operator, trying one's luck in petty commerce in a city or a peri-urban settlement, or getting on an overloaded fishing boat headed for southern Europe.

CONFRONTING CAPITAL, FIGHTING PRECARITY

In the early phase of writing African labour history, the story of struggle was relatively straightforward. Workers become conscious of themselves; they formed unions; they went on strike; they came to see imperialism as well as capitalism as the basis of exploitation and they joined with nationalist movements to challenge their oppressors. The story, most observers recognized, did not end in triumph, for African labour movements were often repressed or their leaders co-opted by postcolonial regimes. There were flashes of labour mobilization afterwards – the big transport strikes

---

[40] See the chapter by Pérez Niño in this volume, where the author cites statistics to the effect that 93 per cent of the new jobs created in Africa in the 1990s were in the informal sector.

in Ghana in 1961, the strong role of the labour movement in the May 1968 movement in Senegal, and the participation of organized labour in some of the democracy movements in the 1990s.[41] The South African case followed a different chronology, for the great strike wave began in Durban in 1973 and continued in the form of 'social movement unionism' – movements that located the situation of wage workers within a wider structure of oppression that required an attack on the entire apartheid system.[42] The South African case, too, has an ambiguous endpoint, since the government led by the African National Congress has in its own way privileged capitalists over workers, and some leaders of the struggle, Cyril Ramaphosa most notoriously, have gone over to the other side. But the main trade union federation, the Congress of South African Trade Unions, has maintained a certain autonomy from its ANC ally, and strikes and demonstrations for social justice erupt with greater frequency and less repression than in other parts of Africa.

This volume does not contain a systematic exploration of the range of social movements that confronted capital. To some extent, the politics of contention are integrated into discussions of different forms of labour (mines and transport most prominently), but the issue is dealt with most explicitly in Freund's chapter on trade unions. He describes the 'heroic age' as 1935–60, a periodization that says a lot about what happened in the postcolonial era.

The question this leaves us with is how to articulate the history of strike movements – whether organized by unions or otherwise – with a wider range of protest movements embracing people whose positions relative to wage labour are quite varied, such as boycotts of buses and beer halls by women in apartheid South Africa, consumer boycotts, student protests, demonstrations against high food prices and shortages, land seizures, and urban demonstrations of the unemployed or marginally employed, not to mention attacks on 'foreign' workers.[43] Moreover, the study of labour militance in Africa should follow Africans abroad – to protests of the *sans papiers* in France for instance – and should explore connections between organizations

---

[41] In addition to Freund's chapter, see Omar Gueye, *Mai 1968 au Sénégal: Senghor face aux étudiants et au mouvement syndical* (Paris: Karthala, 2017).

[42] Gay W. Seidman, *Manufacturing Militance: Workers' Movements in Brazil and South Africa 1970–85* (Berkeley, CA: University of California Press, 1994).

[43] For an example of new research on the wide range of protest actions, see Johanna Siméant, *Contester au Mali: formes de la mobilisation et de la critique à Bamako* (Paris: Karthala, 2014). On the relationship of the economic conjuncture, precarious work and labour militance, see also Alexander Beresford and Hannah Cross, 'The Politics of Globalized Labour in Africa', *Critical African Studies* 7.1 (2015), 1–6, and the articles that follow in this issue.

in Africa and organizations rooted elsewhere, including a variety of NGOs and human rights organizations, as well as trade union internationals and the ILO. At the same time, we need to avoid the fantasy that in a highly connected world, a global 'multitude' will arise to challenge global capitalism on its own spatial level. Neither a resolutely 'national' focus nor insistence on the 'global' captures the actual connections that social movements form or their limitations.

The study of workers' agency should not be limited to collective action. As individuals, workers and the children of workers may try to alter their situation by migration, by learning a trade or acquiring education, by calling on kinship ties and by finding a patron. Unequal relationship are still relationships.

AFRICAN LABOUR IN THE TWENTY-FIRST CENTURY

Africa's recovery from recession at the beginning of a new century, some economists argue, was driven by increased demand for its raw materials from China and to a lesser extent South and South-East Asian economies that have been the dynamic force in manufacturing around the world. There has been some expansion in light industry in parts of Africa, and the new technology of the mobile phone – because it allows communication to be divided into small units rather than demanding a country-wide infrastructure and expensive subscriptions – has had a significant economic impact. But we are no closer in 2019 than in 1957 to the dream of self-sustaining economic growth that provides opportunity and security to Africa's working population.

Looked at another way, the entry into the world economy of the labour power coming from China's population of over one billion – kept out of these circuits by Maoist communism – has changed the labour question worldwide. Given the mobility of capital – and particularly of the financial industry – the entry of China into world markets has been an opportunity as well as a challenge, but on the world scene, Africa has become more marginal as a source of labour power. The contention, however mythic, that workers in China are putting European or American workers out of jobs has made the actually visible 'immigrants' into Europe and North America a target for xenophobic politics. Some observers contend that, in Africa as well as the industrial world, the need for unskilled or semi-skilled labour power has so much diminished that the idea of a full employment economy is no longer feasible and, alongside struggling to get people into decent jobs, policymakers should plan for a future in which employment – in wage labour, farming or artisanal production – should no longer be seen as the basis for both subsistence and respect. Something like a basic income grant to all families

– not such a remote possibility in South Africa at least – could be a first step towards confronting this situation.

Yet the way this question is posed is problematic. In South Africa, where capitalism is the most developed in Africa, capital as currently constituted – and the state as currently funded – cannot employ the entire population of working age.[44] But if South Africa were to provide running water, sewage systems, electricity and high-quality education to its entire population, there would be lots of jobs to be had, even more so in other parts of Africa. The problem is not the inherent nature of the job–people ratio, but a political issue. If more of the world's resources went into the supply of public goods to people who lack them, the labour question would look quite different.

The basic problem is, and has long been, that capital is mobile, raw materials and manufactured goods are readily transportable, while workers move with considerable disruption to their social existence, and states are not mobile at all. Profits can be made globally; social costs are borne nationally.

Two centuries ago, people in parts of Africa were forced onto boats to be taken to places where plantation owners of European origin wanted their labour. Now, Africans pay traffickers to put them onto boats, to take them to work for Europeans, risking their lives at sea and putting themselves in a precarious position should their odyssey succeed. Within the African continent, even larger movements of people take place, in response to loss of land, ecological catastrophe, wars, banditry, and also because of the ambition to find a better life. Africans have both responded to and resisted the demands and impositions they have faced, and the consequences of the encounters have therefore been varied and volatile. Forty years ago, as African labour history was coming into its own, the outlines of a narrative seemed to be emerging. Instead, the direction of change became less clear, and the past – not just the future – has had to be reimagined.

The studies in the *General Labour History of Africa* have taken on this task, and they illustrate the variety of experiences that make up the history of labour, of possibilities that opened and closed, of exploitation imposed and resisted. Taken together, they suggest that the future, like much of the past, will be a time of individual and collective struggle in a world whose most basic characteristic is unevenness and inequality.

---

[44] For an intelligent but not entirely convincing take on this issue, see James Ferguson, *Give a Man a Fish: Reflections on the New Politics of Distribution* (Durham, NC: Duke University Press, 2015).

SELECT BIBLIOGRAPHY

Abdullah, I., '"Bush Path to Destruction": The Origin and Character of the Revolutionary United Front/Sierra Leone', *Journal of Modern African Studies*, 36.2 (1998), 203–35.

Abdullah, I., 'The Colonial State and Wage Labor in Colonial Sierra Leone 1945–1960: Attempts at Remaking the Working Class', *International Labor and Working-Class History*, 52 (1997) 87–105.

Abdullah, I., '"I Am a Rebel": Youth Culture and Violence in Sierra Leone', in *Makers and Breakers: Children and Youth in Postcolonial Africa*, ed. F. de Boeck and A. Honwana (Oxford: James Currey, 2005), 172–87.

Abdullah, I., 'Rethinking African Labour and Working-Class History: The Artisan Origins of the Sierra Leonean Working Class', *Social History*, 23.1 (1998), 80–96.

Abdullah, I., and I. Rashid, 'Juvenile Combatants: Child Soldiers in the Sierra Leone Civil War', in *Between Democracy and Terror: The Sierra Leone Civil War*, ed. I. Abdullah (Dakar: CODESRIA, 2004).

Abel, G. J., and N. Sander, 'Quantifying Global International Migration Flows', *Science*, 343.6178 (2014), 1520–2.

Abernethy, D., *The Political Dilemma of Popular Education: An African Case* (Stanford, CA: Stanford University Press, 1969).

Abrahamsen, R., *Disciplining Democracy: Development Discourse and Good Governance in Africa* (London: Zed Books, 2000).

Abul-Magd, Z., *Imagined Empires: A History of Revolt in Egypt* (Berkeley, CA: University of California Press, 2013).

Acemoglu, D., S. Johnson and J. A. Robinson, 'The Colonial Origins of Comparative Development: An Empirical Investigation', *American Economic Review*, 91.5 (2001), 1369–401.

Achebe, C., *The Education of a British-Protected Child: Essays* (London: Knopf, 2009).

Adams, R. H., *International Migration, Remittances, and the Brain Drain: A Study of 24 Labor-Exporting Countries*, Policy Research Paper 3069 (Washington, DC: World Bank, Poverty Reduction and Economic Management Network, 2003).

Adegbidi, F. V., and J. S. Agossou, 'Benin: The Challenge', in *Trade Unions and Sustainable Democracy in Africa*, ed. G. Kester and O. O. Sidibé (Aldershot: Ashgate, 1997), 125–46.

Adepoju, A., *Migration in Sub-Saharan Africa* (Uppsala: Nordiska Afrikainstitutet, 2008).

Aderinto, S., *When Sex Threatened the State: Illicit Sexuality, Nationalism, and Politics in Colonial Nigeria, 1900–1958* (Urbana, IL: University of Illinois Press, 2015).

Adesanya, A., 'From Film to Video', in *Nigerian Video Films*, ed. J. Haynes (Athens, OH: Ohio University Press, 2000), 37–50.

Adler, G., 'Shop Floors and Rugby Fields: The Social Basis of Auto Worker Solidarity in South Africa', *International Labor and Working-Class History*, 51 (1997), 96–128.

Adu-Amankwah, K., *The State, Trade Unions and Democracy in Ghana, 1982 to 1990* (The Hague: Institute of Social Studies, 1990)

Afigbo, A. E., *The Warrant Chiefs: Indirect Rule in Southeastern Nigeria, 1891–1929* (London: Longman, 1972).

Agarwala, R., *Informal Labor, Formal Politics, and Dignified Discontent in India* (New York: Cambridge University Press, 2013).

Agier, M., J. Copans and A. Morice, eds, *Classes d'ouvrières d'Afrique Noire* (Paris: Karthala, 1987).

Agiri, B., 'The Development of Wage Labour in Agriculture in Southern Yorubaland 1900–1940', *Journal of the Historical Society of Nigeria*, 12.1/2 (1983–84), 95–107.

Ahmad, E., 'Trade Unionism in the Maghreb', in *State and Society in Independent North Africa*, ed. L. C. Brown (Washington, DC: Middle East Institute, 1966), 146–91.

Ahmed, A. B., A. A. Ahmad and N. M. Idris, 'Emerging Trends in Labour Law and Industrial Relations in Nigeria', *International Journal of Humanities and Social Science*, 4.11 (2014), 29–44.

Akama, J., and D. Kemboi, 'The Development of Cultural Tourism in Kenya: A Case Study of the Bomas of Kenya', in *Cultural Tourism in Africa: Strategies for the New Millennium: Proceedings of the ATLAS Africa International Conference, December 2000, Mombasa, Kenya*, ed. J. Akama and P. Sterry (Arnhem: Association for Tourism and Leisure Education, 2002), 137–54.

Akong'a, J., 'Culture in Development', in *Kenya: An Official Handbook*, ed. S. A. Idha (Nairobi: Ministry of Information and Broadcasting, 1989).

Akoten, J., and K. Otsuka, 'From Traders to Mini-Manufacturers: The Role of Traders in the Performance of Garment Enterprises in Kenya', *Journal of African Economies*, 16.4 (2007), 564–95.

Akurang-Parry, K. O., '"The Loads Are Heavier than Usual": Forced Labor by Women and Children in the Central Province, Gold Coast (Colonial Ghana), ca. 1900–1940', *African Economic History*, 30 (2002), 31–51.

Akwetey, E., and D. Dorkenoo, 'Disengagement from Party Politics: Achievements and Challenges for the Ghana Trades Union Congress', in *Trade Unions and Party Politics: Labour Movements in Africa*, ed. B. Beckman and S. Buhlungu (Cape Town: Human Sciences Research Council Press, 2010), 39–57.

Akyeampong, E., 'Diaspora and Drug Trafficking in West Africa: A Case Study of Ghana', *African Affairs*, 104.410 (2005), 429–47.

Alcock, A. E., *History of the International Labour Organisation* (London: Macmillan, 1970).

Alegi, P., 'A Biography of Darius Dhlomo: Transnational Footballer in the Era of Apartheid', in *South Africa and the Global Game: Football, Apartheid and Beyond*, ed. P. Alegi and C. Bolsmann (London: Routledge, 2010), 46–62.

Alexander, A., and M. Bassiouny, *Bread, Freedom, Social Justice: Workers in the Egyptian Revolution* (London: Zed Books, 2014).

Alexander, C., 'State, Labor and the New Global Economy in Tunisia', in *North Africa: Development and Reform in a Changing Global Economy*, ed. D. Vandewalle (Basingstoke: Palgrave Macmillan, 1996), 177–202.

Alexander, P., *Workers, War and the Origins of Apartheid: Labour and Politics in South Africa, 1939–1948* (Oxford: James Currey, 2000).

Alexander, P., and R. Halpern, eds, *Racializing Class, Classifying Race: Labour and Difference in Britain, the USA and Africa* (Basingstoke: Palgrave Macmillan, 2000).

Alexander, P., T. Lekgowa, B. Mmope, L. Sinwell and B. Xezwi, *Marikana: A View from the Mountain and a Case to Answer* (Johannesburg: Jacana, 2012).

Alila, P. O., and P. O. Obado, *Co-operative Credit: The Kenyan SACCOS in a Historical and Development Perspective*, Working Paper No. 474 (Nairobi: Institute for Development Studies, University of Nairobi, 1990).

Allen, J., A. Campbell, E. Hobsbawm and J. McIlroy, eds, *Histories of Labour: National and International Perspectives* (Pontypool: Merlin Press, 2010).

Allen, R. B., *European Slave Trading in the Indian Ocean, 1500–1850* (Athens, OH: Ohio University Press, 2014).

Allina, E., *Slavery by Any Other Name: African Life under Company Rule in Colonial Mozambique* (Charlottesville, VA: University of Virginia Press, 2012).

Allman, J., 'Rounding up Spinsters: Gender Chaos and Unmarried Women in Colonial Asante', *The Journal of African History*, 37.2 (1996), 195–214.

Allman, J., and V. Tashjian, *'I Will Not Eat Stone': A Woman's History of Colonial Asante* (Oxford: James Currey, 2000).

Alpers, E. A., *The Indian Ocean in World History* (New York: Oxford University Press, 2014).

Amanor, K., *Land, Labor and Family in Southern Ghana: A Critique of Land Policy under Neo-Liberalism* (Uppsala: Nordiska Afrikainstitutet, 2001).

Amaza, P. S., P. V. Kwagbe and A. A. Amos, 'Analysis of Women's Participation in Agricultural Cooperatives: Case Study of Borno State, Nigeria', *Annals of Borno*, 15/16 (1999), 187–96.

Ames, D. W., 'Igbo and Hausa Musicians: A Comparative Examination', *Ethnomusicology*, 17.2 (1973), 250–78.

Amin, S., *Modern Migrations in Western Africa: Studies Presented and Discussed at the Eleventh International African Seminar, Dakar* (Oxford: Oxford University Press, 1974).

Amin, S., 'The Politics of International Migration in Post-Colonial Africa', in *The Cambridge Survey of World Migration*, ed. R. Cohen (Cambridge: Cambridge University Press, 1995), 166–71.

Amos, A. M. 'Afro-Brazilians in Togo: The Case of the Olympio Family, 1882–1945', *Cahiers d'études africaines*, 41.162 (2001), 293–314.

Amrith, S., and G. Sluga, 'New Histories of the United Nations', *Journal of World History*, 19.3 (2008), 251–74.

Ananaba, W., *The Trade Union Movement in Africa: Promise and Performance* (New York: St Martin's Press, 1979).

Anderson, D., 'Kenya 1895–1939: Registration and Rough Justice', in *Masters, Servants, and Magistrates in Britain and the Empire, 1562–1955*, ed. D. Hay and P. Craven (Chapel Hill, NC: University of North Carolina Press, 2004), 498–528.

Anderson, D., 'Massacre at Ribo Post: Expansion and Expediency on the Colonial Frontier in East Africa', *International Journal of African Historical Studies*, 37.1 (2004), 33–54.

Anderson, D., and D. Killingray, eds, *Policing and Decolonisation: Politics, Nationalism and the Police, 1917–1965* (Manchester: Manchester University Press, 1992).

Andersson, J. A., 'Reinterpreting the Rural–Urban Connection: Migration Practices and Socio-Cultural Dispositions of Buhera Workers in Harare', *Africa*, 71.1 (2001), 82–112.

Andræ, G., and B. Beckman, 'Textile Unions and Industrial Crisis in Nigeria: Labour Structure, Organization and Strategies', in *Workers in Third-World Industrialization*, ed. I. Brandell (New York: St Martin's Press, 1991), 143–75.

Andræ, G., and B. Beckman, *Union Power in the Nigerian Textile Industry: Labour Regime and Adjustmen* (Uppsala/Somerset, NJ/Kano: Nordiska Afrikainstitutet/Transaction/CRD, 1998).

Anker, R., M. Buvinic and N. H. Youssef, *Women's Roles and Population Trends in the Third World* (London: Croom Helm, 1982).

Anti-Slavery International, *The Cocoa Industry in West Africa: A History of Exploitation* (London: Anti-Slavery International, 2004).

Anyangwe, S., and C. Mtonga, 'Inequities in the Global Health African Capacity Building Foundation Workforce: The Greatest Impediment to Health in Sub-Saharan Africa', *International Journal of Environment Research and Public Health*, 4.2 (2007), 93–100.

Arafa, D., L. El-Fattal and H. Laamrani, 'Gender and Water Demand Management in the Middle East and North Africa', Canadian International Development Agency (IDRC/CRDI), 2007.

Archer R., and A. Bouillon, *The South African Game: Sport and Racism* (London: Zed Books, 1982).

Argenti, N., *The Intestines of the State: Youth, Violence and Belated Histories in the Cameroon Grassfields* (Chicago: University of Chicago Press, 2007).

Arhin, K., *The Expansion of Cocoa Production: The Working Conditions of Migrant Cocoa Farmers in the Central and Western Regions, Institute of African Studies, University of Ghana* (Legon, mimeographed, 1986).

Arhin, K., 'Some Asante Views of Colonial Rule: As Seen in the Controversy Relating to Death Duties', *Transactions of the Historical Society of Ghana*, 15 (1974), 63–84.

Armes, R., *African Filmmaking: North and South of the Sahara* (Edinburgh: Edinburgh University Press, 2006).

Arrighi, G., 'Labour Supplies in Historical Perspective: A Study on Proletarianization of the African Peasantry in Rhodesia', in *Essays on the Political Economy of Africa*, ed. G. Arrighi and J. S. Saul (New York: Monthly Review Press, 1973), 180–234.

Arrighi, G., 'Labour Supplies in Historical Perspective: A Study of the Proletarianization of the African Peasantry in Rhodesia', *The Journal of Development Studies*, 6.3 (1970), 197–234.

Arsel, M., and A. Dasgupta, 'Critique, Rediscovery and Revival in Development Studies', *Development and Change*, 46.4 (2015), 644–65.

Arthiabah P. B., and H. T. Mbiah, *Half a Century of Toil, Trouble and Progress: The History of the Trades Union Congress of Ghana* (Accra: Gold Type Press, 1995).

Arthur, J. A., 'Labor Migration Patterns in West Africa', *African Studies Review*, 34.3 (1991), 65–87.

Aryeetey, E., and R. Kanbur, 'Ghana at Sixty: Learning from a Developing African Nation's Past', in *The Economy of Ghana Sixty Years after Independence*, ed. E. Aryeetey and R. Kanbur (Oxford: Oxford University Press, 2017), 3–15.

Aryeetey, E., J. Harrigan and M. Nissanke, *Economic Reforms in Ghana: The Myth and the Mirage* (Oxford: James Currey, 2000).

Asamoah, Y., and D. N. A. Nortey, 'Ghana', in *Social Welfare in Africa*, ed. J. Dixon (New York: Croom Helm, 1987), 22–68.

Assaad, R., 'The Effects of Public Sector Hiring and Compensation Policies on the Egyptian Labor Market', *The World Bank Economic Review*, 11.1 (1997), 85–118.

Assié-Lumumba, N., *Higher Education in Africa: Crises, Reforms and Transformations* (Dakar: CODESRIA, 2006).

Atkins, K. E. '"Kaffir Time": Preindustrial Temporal Concepts and Labour Discipline in Nineteenth-Century Colonial Natal', *The Journal of African History*, 29.2 (1988), 229–44.

Atkins, K. E., *The Moon is Dead! Give Us Our Money! The Cultural Origins of an African Work Ethic, Natal, South Africa, 1843–1900* (Portsmouth, NH: Heinemann, 1993).

Atkinson, D., *Going for Broke: The Fate of Farmworkers in Arid South Africa* (Cape Town: HSRC Press, 2007).

Atmore, A. E., 'Africa on the Eve of Partition', in *Cambridge History of Africa, 6: From 1870 to 1905*, ed. R. Oliver and G. N. Sanderson (Cambridge: Cambridge University Press, 1985), 10–95.

Austen, R. A., 'Africa and Globalization: Colonialism, Decolonization and the Postcolonial Malaise', *Journal of Global History*, 1.3 (2006), 403–8.

Austen, R. A., and D. D. Cordell, 'Trade, Transportation, and Expanding Economic Networks: Saharan Caravan Commerce in the Era of European Expansion, 1500–1900', in *Black Business and Economic Power*, ed. A. Jalloh and T. Falola (Rochester, NY: University of Rochester Press, 2002), 80–113.

Austin, G., 'Africa and the Anthropocene', in *Economic Development and Environmental History in the Anthropocene: Perspectives on Asia and Africa*, ed. G. Austin (London: Bloomsbury Academic, 2017), 95–118.

Austin, G., 'Capitalism and the Colonies', in *Cambridge History of Capitalism*, vol. 2, ed. L. Neal and J. G. Williamson (Cambridge: Cambridge University Press, 2014), 301–47.

Austin, G., 'Cash Crops and Freedom: Export Agriculture and the Decline of Slavery in Colonial West Africa', *International Review of Social History*, 54.1 (2009), 1–37.

Austin, G., 'Chiefs and Capitalists in the Cocoa Hold-ups in South Asante, 1927–1938', *International Journal of African Historical Studies*, 21.1 (1988), 63–95.

Austin, G., 'The Emergence of Capitalist Relations in South Asante Cocoa-Farming, c. 1916–33', *The Journal of African History*, 28.2 (1987), 259–79.

Austin, G., 'Factor Markets in Nieboer Conditions: Pre-colonial West Africa, c.1500–c.1900', *Continuity and Change*, 24.1 (2009), 23–53.

Austin, G., 'Introduction', in P. Hill, *Migrant Cocoa-farmers of Southern Ghana: A Study in Rural Capitalism* (Oxford: James Currey, 1997), ix–xxviii.

Austin, G., 'Is Africa too Late for "Late Development"? Gerschenkron South of the Sahara', in *Diverse Development Paths and Structural Transformation in the Escape from Poverty*, ed. M. Andersson and T. Axelsson (Oxford: Oxford University Press, 2016), 206–35.

Austin, G., *Labour, Land and Capital in Ghana: From Slavery to Free Labour in Asante, 1807–1956* (Rochester, NY: University of Rochester Press, 2005).

Austin, G., 'Resources, Techniques and Strategies South of the Sahara: Revising the Factor Endowments Perspective on African Economic Development, 1500–2000', *Economic History Review*, 61.3 (2008), 587–624.

Austin, G., 'Slavery in Africa', in *The Cambridge World History of Slavery, Volume 4: AD 1804 to AD 2016*, ed. D. Eltis, L. S. Engerman, S. Drescher and D. Richardson (Cambridge: Cambridge University Press, 2017), 174–96.

Austin, G., 'Vent for Surplus or Productivity Breakthrough? The Ghanaian Cocoa Take-off, c. 1890–1936', *Economic History Review*, 67.4 (2004), 1035–64.

Austin, G., E. Frankema and M. Jerven, 'Patterns of Manufacturing Growth in Sub-Saharan Africa: From Colonization to the Present', in *The Spread of Modern Industry to the Poor Periphery since 1870*, ed. K. O'Rourke and J. G. Williamson (Oxford: Oxford University Press, 2017), 345–73.

Awolowo, O., *Path to Nigerian Freedom* (London: Faber and Faber, 1947).

Baccaro, L., and V. Mele, 'Pathology of Path Dependency? The ILO and the Challenge of New Governance', *ILR Review*, 65.2 (2012), 195–224.

Baier, S., *An Economic History of Central Niger* (Oxford: Clarendon Press, 1980).

Bailey, C., and J. Turner, 'Social Security in Africa: A Brief Review', *Journal of Aging & Social Policy*, 14.1 (2002), 105–14.

Bakewell, O., 'Keeping Them in Their Place: The Ambivalent Relationship Between Development and Migration in Africa', *Third World Quarterly* 29.7 (2008), 1341–58.

Bakewell, O., 'Migration and Development in Sub-Saharan Africa', in *Migration in the Global Political Economy*, ed. N. Phillips (Boulder, CO: Lynne Rienner, 2011).

Bakewell, O., and H. de Haas, 'African Migrations: Continuities, Discontinuities and Recent Transformations' in *African Alternatives*, ed. P. Chabal, U. Engel and L. de Haan (Leiden: Brill, 2007), 95–118.

Balachandran, G., 'Making Coolies, (Un)making Workers: "Globalizing" Labour in the Late-19th and Early-20th Centuries', *Journal of Historical Sociology*, 24.3 (2011), 266–96.

Baldwin, P., *The Politics of Social Solidarity: Class Bases of the European Welfare State 1875–1975* (Cambridge: Cambridge University Press, 1990).

Baldwin-Edwards, M., 'Between a Rock and a Hard Place: North Africa as a Region of Emigration, Immigration and Transit Migration', *Review of African Political Economy*, 33.108 (2006), 311–24.

Bale, J., 'Kenyan Running before the 1968 Mexico Olympics', in *East African Running: Towards a Cross-Disciplinary Perspective*, ed. Y. Pitsiladis, J. Bale, C. Sharp and T. Noakes (London: Routledge, 2007), 11–23.

Ball, J., '"I Escaped in a Coffin": Remembering Angolan Forced Labor from the 1940s', *Cadernos de Estudos Africanos – Memórias Coloniais*, 9/10 (2006), 61–75.

Banaji, J., 'The Fictions of Free Labour: Contract, Coercion, and So-Called Unfree Labour', *Historical Materialism*, 11.3 (2003), 69–95.

Bangasser, P. E., 'The ILO and the Informal Sector: An Institutional History', Employment Paper, 9 (Geneva: ILO, 2000).

Bangura, Y., 'The Recession and Workers' Struggles in the Vehicle Assembly Plants: Steyr-Nigeria', *Review of African Political Economy*, 39 (1987), 4–22.

Barchiesi, F., 'Casual Labor and Informal Economy', in *Sociology of Work: An Encyclopedia*, vol. I, ed. V. Smith (Thousand Oaks, CA: Sage, 2013), 74–8.

Barchiesi, F., 'How Far from Africa's Shore? A Response to Marcel van der Linden's Map for Global Labor History', *International Labor and Working-Class History*, 82 (2012), 77–84.

Barchiesi, F., *Precarious Liberation: Workers, the State, and Contested Social Citizenship in Postapartheid South Africa* (Albany, NY: SUNY Press, 2011).

Barchiesi, F., 'Wage Labor and Social Citizenship in the Making of Post-Apartheid South Africa', *Journal of Asian and African Studies*, 42.1 (2007), 39–72.

Barchiesi, F., and S. Bellucci, eds, 'African Labor Histories', *International Labor and Working-Class History*, special issue, 86 (2014), 4–158.

Barnes, T., 'The Fight for Control of African Women's Mobility in Colonial Zimbabwe, 1900–1939', *Signs*, 17.3 (1992), 586–608.

Barnes, T., *'We Women Worked so Hard': Gender, Urbanisation and Social Reproduction in Colonial Harare, Zimbabwe, 1930–1956* (Oxford: James Currey, 1999).

Barrientos, A., *Social Assistance in Developing Countries Database* (Manchester: Brooks World Poverty Institute, University of Manchester, 2013).

Barrientos, S., and A. Kritzinger, 'Squaring the Circle: Global Production and the Informalization of Work in South African Fruit Exports', *Journal of International Development*, 16.1 (2004), 81–92.

Barth, H., *Travels and Discoveries in North and Central Africa: Being a Journal of an Expedition Undertaken under the Auspices of H.B.M.'s Government, in the Years 1849–1855*, vol. II (1857; repr., Cambridge: Cambridge University Press, 2011).

Baskin, J., *Striking Back: A History of COSATU* (Johannesburg/London: Ravan Press/Verso, 1991).

Bassett, T. J., *The Peasant Cotton Revolution in West Africa: Côte d'Ivoire, 1880–1995* (Cambridge: Cambridge University Press, 2001).

Bayart, J.-F., 'Africa in the World: A History of Extroversion', *African Affairs*, 99.395 (1999), 217–26.

Bayart, J.-F., *The State in Africa: The Politics of the Belly* (London: Longman, 1993).

Bayart, J.-F., B. Hibou and S. Ellis, *La Criminalisation de l'État en Afrique* (Paris: Karthala, 1996).

Beauchemin, C., and P. Bocquier, 'Migration and Urbanisation in Francophone West Africa: An Overview of Recent Empirical Evidence', *Urban Studies*, 41.11 (2004), 2245–72.

Bebey, F., *African Music: A People's Art* (New York: Lawrence Hill, 1975).

Beck, A., *Medicine, Tradition and Development in Kenya and Tanzania, 1920–1970* (Waltham, MA: Crossroads Press, 1981).

Beck, K., 'Roadside Comforts: Truck Stops on the Forty Days Road in Western Sudan', *Africa*, 83.3 (2013), 426–45.

Beckman, B., 'Imperialism and Capitalist Transformation: Critique of a Kenyan Debate', *Review of African Political Economy*, 19 (1980), 48–62.

Beckman, B., and L. M. Sachikonye, 'Labour Regimes and Liberalisation: An Introduction', in *Labour Regimes and Liberalisation: The Restructuring of State-Society Relations in Africa*, ed. B. Beckman and L. M. Sachikonye (Harare: University of Zimbabwe Publications, 2001), 1–22.

Beinart, W., 'A Century of Migrancy from Mpondoland', *African Studies*, 7.33 (2014), 387–409.

Beinart, W., *Twentieth-Century South Africa* (Oxford: Oxford University Press, 2011).

Beinart, W., and C. Bundy, *Hidden Struggles in Rural South Africa: Politics and Popular Movements in the Transkei and Eastern Cape, 1890–1930* (London: James Currey, 1987).

Beinin, J., 'Egyptian Workers and January 25th: A Social Movement in Historical Context', *Social Research*, 79.2 (2012), 323–48.

Beinin, J., *Workers and Peasants in the Modern Middle East* (Cambridge: Cambridge University Press, 2001).

Beinin, J., and Z. Lockman, *Workers on the Nile; Nationalism, Communism, Islam and the Egyptian Working Class 1882–1954* (London/Princeton, NJ: I.B.Tauris/Princeton University Press, 1988).

Bekerie, A., 'Iquib and Idir: Socio-Economic Traditions of the Ethiopians', PhD dissertation, Africana Studies and Research Center, Cornell University, 2003.

Beling, W. A., *Modernization and African Labor: A Tunisian Case Study* (New York: Praeger, 1965).

Beling, W. A., and M. F. Lofchie, *The Role of Labor in African Nation Building* (New York: Praeger, 1968).

Beller, R., *Life, Person and Community in Africa: A Way towards Inculturation with the Spirituality of the Focolare* (Nairobi: Pauline Publications Africa, 2001).

Bellucci, S., 'The 1974 Ethiopian Revolution at 40: Social, Economic, and Political Legacies', *Northeast Africa Studies*, 16.1 (2016), 1–13.

Bellucci, S., 'Colonial Ideology Versus Labour Reality: A History of the Recruitment of Italian Workers to the Colony of Eritrea, 1890s–1940s', *Labor History*, 55.3 (2014), 294–308.

Bellucci, S., 'Crisis of Capitalism, Crisis of Labour', *International Review of Social History*, 60 (2015), 97–109.

Bellucci, S., 'Italian Transnational Fluxes of Labour and the Changing of Labour Relations in the Horn of Africa, 1935-1939', *Workers of the World*, 1.3 (2013), 158–74.

Bellucci, S., 'Storia del lavoro: un futuro globale?', *Contemporanea: rivista di storia dell'800 e del '900*, 16.1 (2013), 159–67.

Bellucci, S., 'Wage Labour and Capitalism: A Comparative and Historical Analysis of Eritrea and Kenya', *Labor History*, 58.2 (2017), 145–69.

Bellucci, S., L. R. Corrêa, J. G. Deutsch and C. Joshi, 'Labour in Transport: Histories from the Global South (Africa, Asia, and Latin America), c.1750 to 1950', *International Review of Social History*, special issue, 59.22 (2014).

Bellucci, S., and B. Freund, eds, 'Work across Africa', *Africa*, 87.1 (2017), 27–119.

Bellucci, S., and M. Zaccaria, 'Engine of Change: A Social History of the Car-Mechanics Sector in the Horn of Africa', in *Transforming Innovations in Africa: Explorative Studies on Appropriation in African Societies*, ed. J.-B. Gewald, A. Leliveld and I. Peša (Leiden: Brill, 2012), 238–56.

Bellucci, S., and M. Zaccaria, 'Wage Labor and Mobility in Colonial Eritrea, 1880s to 1920s', *International Labor and Working-Class History*, 86 (2014), 89–106.

Benaría, L., ed., *Women and Development: The Sexual Division of Labor in Rural Societies* (New York: Praeger, 1982).

Bennafla, K., *Le Commerce frontalier en Afrique centrale: acteurs, espaces, pratiques* (Paris: Karthala, 2002).

Bennoune, M., 'Socio-Economic Changes in Rural Algeria: 1830–1954', *Peasant Studies Newsletter*, 11.2 (1973), 14–15.

Benson, W., 'A People's Peace in the Colonies', *International Labour Review*, 47.2 (1943), 141–68.

Benveniste, C., *La boucle du cacao, Côte d'Ivoire: étude régionale des circuits de transport* (Paris: Travaux et documents de l'OSTROM, 1974).

Beresford, A., and H. Cross, 'The Politics of Globalized Labour in Africa', *Critical African Studies* 7.1 (2015), 1–6.

Berg, E., 'The Backward-Sloping Labor Supply Function in Dual Economies: The Africa Case', *The Quarterly Journal of Economics*, 75.3 (1961), 468–91.

Berg, J., and S. Cazes, 'The Doing Business Indicators: Measurement Issues and Political Implications', Economic and Labour Market Paper, 6 (Geneva: ILO, 2007).

Berger, E. L., *Labour, Race, and Colonial Rule: The Copperbelt from 1924 to Independence* (Oxford: Oxford University Press, 1974).

Berger, I., *Threads of Solidarity: Women in the South African Industry, 1900–1980* (Bloomington, IN/London: Indiana University Press/James Currey, 1992).

Berger, I., 'Women in East and Southern Africa', in *Women in Sub-Saharan Africa: Restoring Women to History*, ed. I. Berger and F. White (Bloomington, IN: Indiana University Press, 1999).

Berman, B., 'Bureaucracy and Incumbent Violence: Colonial Administration and the Origins of the "Mau Mau" Emergency', in *Unhappy Valley: Conflict in Kenya and Africa*, vol. 2, ed. B. J. Berman and J. M. Lonsdale (Oxford: James Currey, 1992), 227–64.

Berman, B., *Control and Crisis in Colonial Kenya: The Dialectic of Domination* (Oxford: James Currey, 1990).

Berman, B., and J. Lonsdale, 'Crises of Accumulation, Coercion and the Colonial State: The Development of the Labor Control System in Kenya, 1919–1929', *Canadian Journal of African Studies*, 14.1 (1980), 55–81.

Berman, B., and J. Lonsdale, eds, *Unhappy Valley: Conflict in Kenya and Africa*, 2 vols (London: James Currey, 1992).

Bernal, V., 'Colonial Moral Economy and the Discipline of Development: The Gezira Scheme and "Modern" Sudan', *Cultural Anthropology*, 12.4 (1977), 447–79.

Bernal, V., 'Cotton and Colonial Order in Sudan: A Social History with Emphasis on the Gezira Scheme', in *Cotton, Colonialism, and Social History in Sub-Saharan Africa*, ed. A. Isaacman and R. Roberts (Portsmouth, NH: Heinemann, 1995), 96–118.

Bernards, N., 'Actors and Entanglements in Global Governance: The ILO in Sub-Saharan Africa', PhD dissertation, McMaster University, Hamilton, Ontario, 2016.

Bernards, N., 'The Global Governance of Informal Economies: The International Labour Organization in East Africa', *Third World Quarterly*, 38.8 (2017), 1831–46.

Bernards, N., 'The International Labour Organization and the Ambivalent Politics of Financial Inclusion in West Africa', *New Political Economy*, 21.6 (2016), 606–20.

Bernstein, H., 'Considering Africa's Agrarian Questions', *Historical Materialism*, 12.4 (2004), 115–44.

Berque, J., *French North Africa: The Maghrib between Two World Wars*, trans. Jean Stewart (London: Faber and Faber, 1962).

Berridge, W. J., '"What the Men Are Crying out for Is Leadership": The Khartoum Police Strike of 1951 and the Battle for Administrative Control', *Journal of Imperial and Commonwealth History*, 39 (2011), 121–42.

Berry, S., *Cocoa, Custom and Socioeconomic Change in Rural Western Nigeria* (Oxford: Clarendon Press, 1975).

Berry, S., *Fathers Work for Their Sons: Accumulation, Mobility, and Class Formation in an Extended Yorùbá Community* (Berkeley, CA: University of California Press, 1984).

Berry, S., 'From Peasants to Artisans: Motor Mechanics in a Nigerian Town', in *Actes du colloque entreprises et entrepreneurs d'Afrique, XIXeme et XXeme siècles*, 2 vols, ed. C. Coquery-Vidrovitch and A. Forest (Paris: L'Harmattan, 1983), 421–50.

Berry, S., *No Condition is Permanent: The Social Dynamics of Agrarian Change in Sub-Saharan Africa* (Madison, WI: University of Wisconsin Press, 1993).

Berry, S., 'Questions of Ownership: Proprietorship and Control in a Changing Rural Terrain. A Case Study from Ghana', *Africa*, 83.1 (2013), 36–56.

Betcherman, G., *Labor Market Institutions: A Review of the Literature* (Washington, DC: World Bank, 2013).

Betts, R. F., *France and Decolonisation, 1900–1960* (Basingstoke: Palgrave Macmillan, 1991).

Bezuidenhout, A., and S. Buhlungu, 'From Compounded to Fragmented Labour: Mineworkers and the Demise of Compounds in South Africa', *Antipode*, 43.2 (2011), 237–63.

Bhattachariya, S., *The Labouring Poor and their Notion of Poverty: Late 19th and Early 20th Century Bengal* (Noida: Giri National Labour Institute, 1998).

Bierschenk, T., and J.-P. O. de Sardan, *States at Work: Dynamics of African Bureaucracies* (Leiden: Brill, 2013).

Bitsch, M.-T., and G. Bossuat, eds, *L'Europe unie et l'Afrique: de l'idée d'Eurafrique à la convention de Lomé I* (Brussels: Bruylant, 2005).

Black, R., L. M. Hilker and C. Pooley, 'Migration and Pro-Poor Policy in East Africa', Working Paper C7, Development Research Centre on Migration, Globalisation and Poverty, University of Sussex, 2004.

Blackbourn, D., and G. Eley, *The Peculiarities of German History: Bourgeois Society and Politics in Nineteenth-century Germany* (Oxford: Oxford University Press, 1984).

Blaug, M., 'Employment and Unemployment in Ethiopia', *International Labour Review*, 110.2 (1974), 117–43.

Blay, V. A., 'Empowerment of Women Through Participation in Women Self-Help Groups in Kumasi Metropolis', MSc thesis, Kwame Nkrumah University of Science and Technology, Kumasi, Ghana, 2011.

Boahen, A. A., *African Perspectives on Colonialism* (Baltimore, MD: Johns Hopkins University Press, 1987).

Boahen, A. A., *Mfantsipim and the Making of Modern Ghana* (Accra: Sankofa Educational Publishers, 1996).

Bogaert, K., 'The Revolt of Small Towns: The Meaning of Morocco's History and the Geography of Social Protests', *Review of African Political Economy*, 42.143 (2015), 124–40.

Bolten, C. E., 'Sobel Rumors and Tribal Truths: Narrative and Politics in Sierra Leone, 1994', *Comparative Studies in Society and History*, 56.1 (2014), 187–214.

Bongaarts, J., O. Frank and R. Lesthaeghe, 'The Proximate Determinants of Fertility in Sub-Saharan Africa', *Population and Development Review*, 10.3 (1984), 511–37.

Boni, S., *Clearing the Ghanaian Forest: Theories and Practices of Acquisition, Transfer and Utilization of Farming Titles in the Sefwi-Akan Area* (Legon: Institute of African Studies, 2005).

Bonner, P., 'The 1920 Black Mineworkers' Strike: A Preliminary Account', in *Labour, Townships and Protest*, ed. B. Bozzoli (Johannesburg: Ravan Press, 1979), 273–97.

Bonner, P., 'The Decline and Fall of the ICU: A Case of Self-Destruction?', in *Essays in Southern African Labour History*, ed. E. Webster (Johannesburg: Ravan Press, 1978), 114–20.

Bonner, P., '"Desirable or Undesirable Basotho Women?" Liquor, Prostitution and the Migration of Basotho Women to the Rand, 1920–1945', in *Women and Gender in Southern Africa to 1945*, ed. C. Walker (Cape Town/London: David Philip/James Currey, 1990), 221–50.

Bonner, P., *Holding Their Ground: Class, Locality, and Culture in 19th and 20th Century South Africa* (Johannesburg: Witwatersrand University Press, 1989).

Bonnet, M., 'Child Labor in Africa', *International Labour Review*, 132.3 (1993), 371–89.

Bonnet, M., 'Child Labor in Postcolonial Africa', in *The World of Child Labor: An Historical and Regional Survey*, ed. H. D. Hindman (Armonk, NY: M. E. Sharpe, 2009), 169–72.

Boone, C., *Property and Political Order in Africa: Land Rights and the Structure of Politics* (Cambridge: Cambridge University Press, 2014).

Borowiec, A., *Modern Tunisia: A Democratic Apprenticeship* (Westport, CT: Praeger, 1998).

Boserup, E., *Woman's Role in Economic Development* (London: Earthscan, 1970).

Bosma, U., 'Beyond the Atlantic: Connecting Migration and World History in the Age of Imperialism, 1840– 1940', *International Review of Social History*, 52.1 (2007), 117–23.

Bosma, U., and R. Knight, 'Global Factory and Local Field: Convergence and Divergence in the International Cane-Sugar Industry, 1850–1940', *International Review of Social History*, 49.1 (2004), 1–25.

Bourdieu, P., 'The Forms of Capital', in *Handbook of Theory and Research for the Sociology of Education*, ed. J. Richardson (New York: Greenwood Press, 1986).

Bovill, E. W., *The Golden Trade of the Moors: West African Kingdoms in the Fourteenth Century* (Princeton, NJ: Markus Wiener, 1995).

Bowden, S., and P. Mosley, 'Politics, Public Expenditure and the Evolution of Poverty in Africa 1920–2009', *Working Paper, Sheffield Economic Research Paper Series*, 2 (2012).

Bowden, S., B. Chiripanhura and P. Mosley, 'Measuring and Explaining Poverty in Six African Countries: A Long-Period Approach', *Journal of International Development*, 20.8 (2008), 1049–79.

Bowen, W., *Colonial Trade Unions* (London: Fabian Society, 1954).

Boyden, J., 'Childhood and the Policy Makers: A Comparative Perspective on the Globalization of Childhood', in *Constructing and Reconstructing Childhood: Contemporary Issues in the Sociological Study of Childhood*, ed. A. James and A. Prout (London: Falmer Press, 1990), 190–229.

Bozzoli, B., *The Political Nature of a Ruling Class: Capital and Ideology in South Africa, 1890–1933* (London: Routledge and Kegan Paul, 1981).

Bozzoli, B. (with M. Nkotsoe), *Women of Phokeng: Consciousness, Life Strategy, and Migrancy in South Africa, 1900–1983* (London: James Currey, 1991).

Bradford H., '"A Taste of Freedom": Capitalist Development and Response to the ICU in the Transvaal Countryside', in *Town and Countryside in the Transvaal*, ed. B. Bozzoli (Johannesburg: Ravan Press, 1983), 128–50.

Brass, T., and M. van der Linden, eds, *Free and Unfree Labour: The Debate Continues* (Berne: Peter Lang, 1997).

Bratton, M., 'Voting and Democratic Citizenship in Africa: Where Next?', in *Voting and Democratic Citizenship in Africa*, ed. M. Bratton (Boulder, CO: Lynne Rienner, 2013), 277-88.

Braverman, A., J. L. Guasch, M. Huppi and L. Pohlmeier, 'Promoting Rural Cooperatives in Developing Countries: The Case of Sub-Saharan Africa', Discussion Paper 121 (Washington, DC: World Bank, 1991).

Breman, J., 'A Bogus Concept', *New Left Review*, 84 (2013), 130–8.

Breman, J., *Footloose Labour: Working in India's Informal Economy* (Cambridge: Cambridge University Press, 1996).

Breman, J., and M. van der Linden, 'Informalizing the Economy: The Return of the Social Question at a Global Level', *Development and Change*, 45.5 (2014), 920–40.

Bridge, G., and T. Frederiksen, '"Order out of Chaos": Resources, Hazards and the Production of a Tin-Mining Economy in Northern Nigeria in the Early Twentieth Century', *Environment and History*, 18.3 (2012), 367–94.

Bright, R. K., *Chinese Labour in South Africa, 1902–10: Race, Violence, and Global Spectacle* (Basingstoke: Palgrave Macmillan, 2013).

Britwum, A. O., *The Ghana Trades Union Congress: Sixty Years of Promoting Workers' Rights* (Accra: Ghana Trades Union Congress, 2007).

Britwum, A. O., *Labour in African History from the 19th Century to the Present* (Lomé: ITUC-Africa, 2012).

Britwum, A. O., 'Union Democracy and the Challenge of Globalisation to Organised Labour in Ghana', PhD dissertation, Maastricht University, 2010.

Brower, B., *A Desert Named Peace: The Violence of France's Empire in the Algerian Sahara, 1844–1902* (New York: Columbia University Press, 2009).

Brown, C. A., 'African Labor in the Making of World War II', in *Africa and World War II*, ed. J. Byfield, C. A. Brown, T. Parsons and A. Sikainga (New York: Cambridge University Press, 2015), 43–67.

Brown, C. A., 'Testing the Boundaries of Marginality: Twentieth-Century Slavery and Emancipation Struggles in Nkanu, Northern Igboland, 1920–29', *The Journal of African History*, 37.1 (1996), 51–80.

Brown, C. A., *'We Were All Slaves': African Miners, Culture, and Resistance at the Enugu Government Colliery* (Portsmouth, NH: Heinemann, 2003).

Brown, C.A., and M. van der Linden, 'Shifting Boundaries between Free and Unfree Labor', *International Labor and Working-Class History*, special issue, 78.1 (2010), 4–11.

Brown, N., *Peasant Politics in Modern Egypt: The Struggle against the State* (New Haven, CT: Yale University Press, 1990).

Bryceson, D. F., 'Africa at Work: Transforming Occupational Identity and Morality', in *How Africa Works: Occupational Change, Identity and Morality*, ed. D. Bryceson (Bourton: Practical Action Publishing, 2010), 3–26.

Bryceson, D. F., 'African Rural Labour, Income Diversification and Livelihood Approaches: A Long-Term Development Perspective', *Review of African Political Economy*, 26.80 (1999), 171–89.

Bryceson, D. F., 'African Women Hoe Cultivators: Speculative Origins and Current Enigmas', in *Women Wielding the Hoe: Lessons from Rural Africa for Feminist Theory and Development Practice*, ed. D. F. Bryceson (Oxford: Berg Publishers, 1995), 3–22.

Bryceson, D. F., 'De-agrarianisation: Blessing or Blight?', in *Farewell to Farms: De-Agrarianisation and Employment in Africa*, ed. D. F. Bryceson and V. Jamal (Aldershot: Ashgate, 1997), 237–56.

Bryceson, D. F., 'Deagrarianization and Rural Employment in Sub-Saharan Africa: A Sectoral Perspective', *World Development*, 24.1 (1996), 97–111.

Bryceson, D. F., 'Easing Women's Working Day in Sub-Saharan Africa', *Development Policy Review*, 12.1 (1994), 59–68.

Bryceson, D. F., 'The Scramble in Africa: Reorienting Rural Livelihoods', *World Development*, 30.5 (2002), 725–39.

Bryceson, D. F., 'Sub-Saharan Africa's Vanishing Peasantries and the Specter of a Global Food Crisis', *Monthly Review*, 61.3 (2009), 4–62.

Bryceson, D. F., 'Swahili Creolization: The Case of Dar es Salaam', in *The Creolization Reader: Studies in Mixed Identities and Cultures*, ed. R. Cohen and P. Toninato (London: Routledge, 2010), 364–75.

Bryceson, D. F., 'Who Cares? Family and Lineage Coherence and Caring Capacity during Rural Malawi's AIDS Crisis', in *Family, Ties and Care: Family Transformation in a Plural Modernity*, ed. H. Bertram and N. Ehlert (Opladen: Barbara Budrich, 2012), 503–20.

Bryceson, D. F., 'Wishful Thinking: Theory and Practice of Western Donor Efforts to Raise Women's Status in Rural Africa', in *Women Wielding the Hoe: Lessons from Rural Africa for Feminist Theory and Development Practice*, ed. D. F. Bryceson (Oxford: Berg Publishers, 1995), 201–22.

Bryceson, D. F., 'Youth in Tanzania's Urbanizing Mining Settlements: Prospecting a Mineralized Future', in *African Youth and the Persistence of Marginalization: Employment, Politics, and Prospects for Change*, ed. D. Resnick and J. Thurlow (London: Routledge, 2015), 85–108.

Bryceson, D. F., ed., *Women Wielding the Hoe: Lessons from Rural Africa for Feminist Theory and Development Practice* (Oxford: Berg Publishers, 1995).

Bryceson, D. F., and J. Fonseca. 'Risking Death for Survival: Peasant Responses to Famine and HIV/AIDS in Malawi', *World Development*, 34.9 (2006), 1654–66.

Bryceson, D. F., and J. B. Jønsson, 'Mineralizing Africa and Artisanal Mining's Democratizing Influence', in *Mining and Social Transformation in Africa: Mineralizing and Democratizing Trends in Artisanal Production*, ed. D. F. Bryceson, E. Fisher, J. B. Jønsson and R. Mwaipopo (London: Routledge, 2014), 1–22.

Bryceson, D. F., J. B. Jønsson, E. Fisher and R. Mwaipopo, eds, *Mining and Social Transformation in Africa: Tracing Mineralizing and Democratizing Trends in Artisanal Production* (London: Routledge, 2014).

Bryceson, D. F., J. B. Jønsson and H. Verbrugge, 'Prostitution or Partnership? Wifestyles in Tanzanian Artisanal Gold-Mining Settlements', *Journal of Modern African Studies*, 51.1 (2013), 33–56.

Bryceson, D. F., and U. Vuorela, 'Outside the Domestic Labor Debate: Towards a Theory of Modes of Human Reproduction', *Review of Radical Political Economy*, 16.2/3 (1984), 137–66.

Buelens, F., and D. Cassimon, 'The Industrialization of the Belgian Congo', in *Colonial Exploitation and Economic Development: The Belgian Congo and the Netherlands Indies Compared*, ed. E. Frankema and F. Buelens (London: Routledge, 2013), 229–50.

Buell, R. L., *The Native Problem in Africa*, 2 vols (New York: Macmillan, 1928).

Buhlungu, S., 'Trade Unions and the Politics of National Liberation in Africa: An Appraisal', in *Trade Unions and Party Politics: Labour Movements in Africa*, ed. B. Beckman, S. Buhlungu and L. Sachikonye (Cape Town: HSRC Press, 2010), 191–206.

Buhlungu, S., 'Union Party Alliances in the Era of Market Regulation: The Case of South Africa', *Journal of Southern African Studies*, 31.4 (2005), 701–17.

Bujra, J., *Serving Class: Masculinity and the Feminisation of Domestic Service in Tanzania* (Edinburgh: Edinburgh University Press, 2000).

Bukh, J., *The Village Woman in Ghana* (Uppsala: Scandinavian Institute of African Studies, 1979).

Bundy, C., *The Rise and Fall of the South African Peasantry* (London: Heinemann Educational, 1979).

Burawoy, M., *The Politics of Production: Factory Regimes Under Capitalism and Socialism* (London: Pluto Press, 1985).

Burke, R., *Decolonization and the Evolution of International Human Rights* (Philadelphia, PA: University of Pennsylvania Press, 2010).

Burton, A., *African Underclass: Urbanization, Crime and Colonial Order in Dar es Salaam, 1919–1961* (Athens, OH: Ohio University Press, 2005).

Burton, A., 'Raw Youth, School-Leavers and the Emergence of Structural Unemployment in Late-Colonial Tanganyika', *The Journal of African History*, 47.3 (2006), 363–87.

Burton, A., and H. Charton-Bigot, eds, *Generations Past: Youth in East African History* (Athens, OH: Ohio University Press, 2010).

Butler, L. J., *Copper Empire: Mining and the Colonial State in Northern Rhodesia c.1930–1964* (Basingstoke: Palgrave Macmillan, 2007).

Bwana, K. M., and J. Mwakujonga, 'Issues in SACCOS Development in Kenya and Tanzania: The Historical and Development Perspectives', *Developing Country Studies*, 3.5 (2013), 114–21.

Byfield, J., *The Bluest Hands: A Social and Economic History of Women Dyers in Abeokuta, 1890–1940* (Oxford: James Currey, 2002).

Cain, P. J., and A. G. Hopkins, *British Imperialism, 1688–2000* (London: Longman, 2002).

Cairoli, M. L., *Girls of the Factory: A Year with the Garment Workers of Morocco* (Gainesville, FL: University Press of Florida, 2011).

Campbell, G., *An Economic History of Imperial Madagascar, 1750–1895: The Rise and Fall of an Island Empire* (Cambridge: Cambridge University Press, 2008).

Campbell, G., ed., *Abolition and its Aftermath in Indian Ocean Africa and Asia* (New York: Routledge, 2007).

Canning, D., S. Raja and A. S. Yazbeck, *Africa's Demographic Transition: Dividend or Disaster?* (Washington, DC: World Bank, 2015).

Caplan, P., '"Children are Our Wealth and We Want Them": A Difficult Pregnancy on Northern Mafia Island, Tanzania', in *Women Wielding the Hoe: Lessons from Rural Africa for Feminist Theory and Development Practice*, ed. D. Bryceson (Oxford: Berg Publishers, 1995), 131–49.

Carew, A., 'Conflict within the ICFTU: Anti-Colonialism and Anti-Communism in the 1950', *International Review of Social History*, 41.2 (1996), 147–81.

Carney J., and M. Watts. 'Disciplining Women: Rice, Mechanization and the Evolution of Mandinka Gender Relations', *Signs*, 16.4 (1991), 651–81.

Carrier, N., and G. Klantschnig, *Africa and the War on Drugs* (London: Zed Books, 2002).

Castel, R., *Les métamorphoses de la question sociale: chronique du salariat* (Paris: Gallimard, 1999).

Cavallo, D., 'Trade Unions in Tunisia', in *Political Participation in the Middle East*, ed. E. Lust-Okar and S. Zerhouni (Boulder, CO: Lynne Rienner, 2008), 75–94.

Celasun, M., *State-owned Enterprises in the Middle East and North Africa: Privatization, Performance and Reform* (London: Routledge, 2001).

Cervero, R., and A. Golub, 'Informal Transport: A Global Perspective', *Transport Policy*, 14 (2007), 445–57.

Chachage, C., and A. Cassam, *Africa's Liberation: The Legacy of Nyerere* (Kampala: Fountain Publishers, 2010).

Chalfin, B., *Neoliberal Frontiers: An Ethnography of West Africa* (Chicago: University of Chicago Press, 2010).

Charmes, J., 'A Review of Empirical Evidence on Time Use in Africa from UN-Sponsored Surveys', in *Gender, Time Use, and Poverty in Sub-Saharan Africa*, World Bank Working Paper No. 73, ed. C. M. Blackden and Q. Wodon (Washington, DC: World Bank, 2006), 39–72.

Chassé, D. S., *Die Erfindung des Bruttosozialprodukts: Globale Ungleichheit in der Wissensgeschichte der Ökonomie* (Göttingen: Vandenhoeck and Ruprecht, 2013).

Chauveau, J.-P., 'How Does an Institution Evolve? Land, Politics, Intergenerational Relations and the Institution of the *Tutorat* between Autochthons and Migrant Farmers in the Gban Region (Côte d'Ivoire)', in *Land and the Politics of Belonging in West Africa*, ed. R. Kuba and C. Lentz (Leiden: Brill, 2006), 213–40.

Chauveau, J.-P., and P. Richards, 'West African Insurgencies in Agrarian Perspective: Côte d'Ivoire and Sierra Leone Compared', *Journal of Agrarian Change*, 8.4 (2008), 515–52.

Chaza, G. A., *Bhurakuwacha: The Story of a Black Policeman in Rhodesia* (Harare: College Press, 1998).

Chhachi, A., 'Introduction: The Labour Question in Contemporary Capitalism', *Development and Change*, 45.5 (2014), 895–919.

Chieni, S. N., *The Harambee Movement in Kenya: The Role Played by Kenyans and the Government in the Provision of Education and Other Social Services* (Eldoret: Moi University Press, 2001).

Chimuka, T. A., 'Ethics Among the Shona', *Zambezia: The Journal of Humanities of the University of Zimbabwe*, 28.1 (2001), 23–37.

Chirwa, W., 'Child and Youth Labour on the Nyasaland Plantations, 1890–1953', *Journal of Southern African Studies*, 19.4 (1993), 662–80.

Chojnacki, S., and G. Reisch, 'Perspectives on War: Collecting, Comparing and Disaggregating Data on Violent Conflicts', *Sicherheit und Frieden*, 26.4 (2008), 233–45.

Christie, I., E. Fernandes, H. Messerli and L. Twinging-Ward, *Tourism in Africa: Harnessing Tourism for Growth and Improved Livelihoods* (Washington, DC: World Bank, 2013).

Clancy-Smith, J., *Mediterraneans: North Africa and Europe in an Age of Immigration, 1800–1900* (Berkeley, CA: University of California Press, 2011).

Clapham, C., *African Guerrillas* (Bloomington, IN: Indiana University Press, 1989).

Clarence-Smith, W. G., *Colonial Industrialisation, 1840s–1960s*, paper presented at the Global Economic History Network (GEHN) Conference 2, Irvine, CA, 15–17 January 2004, LSE Research Online, https://goo.gl/5Urssy (accessed 17 June 2016).

Clark, G., *African Market Women: Seven Life Stories from Ghana* (Bloomington, IN: Indiana University Press, 2010).

Clarke, G., 'Agents of Transformation? Donors, Faith-Based Organisations and International Development', *Third World Quarterly*, 28.1 (2007), 77–96.

Clark, G., 'Gender and Profiteering: Ghana's Market Women as Devoted Mothers and "Human Vampire Bats"', in *'Wicked' Women and the Reconfiguration of Gender in Africa*, ed. D. L. Hodgson and S. A. McCurdy (Portsmouth, NH: Heinemann, 2001), 293–311.

Clark, G., 'Money, Sex and Cooking: Manipulation of the Paid/Unpaid Boundary by Asante Market Women', in *The Social Economy of Consumption*, ed. H. Rutz and B. Orlov (Washington, DC: University Press of America, 1989), 323–48.

Clark, G., *Onions are My Husband: Survival and Accumulation by West African Market Women* (Chicago: University of Chicago Press, 1997).

Clayton, A., *Histoire de l'armée française en Afrique: 1830–1962* (Paris: Albin Michel, 1994).

Clayton, A., and D. Killingray, *Khaki and Blue: Military and Police in British Colonial Africa* (Athens, OH: Ohio University Press, 1989).

Clayton, A., and D. C. Savage, *Government and Labour in Kenya, 1895–1963* (London: Frank Cass, 1975).

Clegg, I., *Workers' Self-Management in Algeria* (Harmondsworth: Penguin, 1971).

Clement, J.-F., and J. Paul, 'Trade Unions and Moroccan Politics', *Middle East Research Information Project (MERIP) Reports*, 127 (1984), 19–24.

Cleveland, T., *Diamonds in the Rough: Corporate Paternalism and African Professionalism on the Mines of Colonial Angola, 1917–1975* (Athens, OH: Ohio University Press, 2015).

Clignet, R. P., and P. J. Foster, 'French and British Colonial Education in Africa', *Comparative Education Review*, 8.2 (1964), 191–8.

Cloutier, L., *Income Differentials and Gender Inequality: Wives Earning More than Husbands in Dar es Salaam, Tanzania* (Dar es Salaam: Mkuki na Nyota, 2006).

Cock, J., *Maids and Madams: A Study in the Politics of Exploitation* (Johannesburg: Ravan Press, 1980).

Cohen, R., *Contested Domains: Debates in International Labour Studies* (London: Zed Books, 1991).

Cohen, R., *Labour and Politics in Nigeria, 1945–71* (London: Heinemann, 1974).

Cohen, R., 'Resistance and Hidden Forms of Consciousness among African Workers', *Review of African Political Economy*, 19 (1980), 8–22.

Colclough, C., 'The Impact of Primary Schooling on Economic Development: A Review of the Evidence', *World Development*, 10.3 (1982), 167–85.

Collier, P., *Bottom Billion: Why the Poorest Countries are Failing and What Can Be Done About It* (Oxford: Oxford University Press, 2000).

Collier, P., *Wars, Guns and Votes: Democracy in Dangerous Places* (New York: Harper Collins, 2009).

Collins, J., 'A Social History of Ghanian Popular Entertainment since Independence', *Transactions of the Historical Society of Ghana*, New Series, 9 (2005), 17–40.

Colson, E., *Marriage and the Family among the Plateau Tonga of Northern Rhodesia* (Manchester: Manchester University Press, 1959).

Comaroff, J., and J. Comaroff, 'Home-Made Hegemony: Modernity, Domesticity, and Colonialism in South Africa', in *African Encounters with Domesticity*, ed. K. T. Hansen (New Brunswick, NJ: Rutgers University Press, 1992), 37–74.

Comaroff, J., ed., *The Meaning of Marriage Payments* (London: Academic Press, 1980).

Connah, G., *African Civilizations: An Archaeological Perspective*, 4th edn (Cambridge: Cambridge University Press, 2007).

Connell, R., and N. Dados, 'Where in the World Does Neoliberalism Come From?', *Theory and Society*, 43.2 (2014), 117–38.

Connell, R. W., *Masculinities* (Cambridge: Polity Press, 1995).

Conrad, S., *What is Global History?* (Princeton, NJ: Princeton University Press, 2016).

Cook, A., *Akin to Slavery: Prison Labour in South Africa* (London: International Defence and Aid Fund, 1982).

Cooper, B., *Marriage in Maradi: Gender and Culture in a Hausa Society in Niger, 1900–1989* (Portsmouth, NH: Heinemann, 1997).

Cooper, B., 'Reflections on Slavery, Seclusion and Female Labour in the Maradi Region in the 19th and 20th Centuries', *The Journal of African History*, 35.1 (1994), 156–65.

Cooper, F., 'Africa and the World Economy', *African Studies Review*, 24.2/3 (1981), 1–86.

Cooper, F., *Africa since 1940: The Past of the Present*. 2nd ed. (Cambridge: Cambridge University Press, 2019).

Cooper, F., 'African Labor History', in *Global Labour History: A State of the Art*, ed. J. Lucassen (Berne: Peter Lang, 2006), 91–116.

Cooper, F., 'Back to Work: Categories, Boundaries and Connections in the Study of Labour', in *Racializing Class, Classifying Race: Labour and Difference in Britain, the USA, and Africa*, ed. P. Alexander and R. Halpern (London: Macmillan, 2000), 213–35.

Cooper, F., *Citizenship between Empire and Nation: Remaking France and French Africa, 1945–1960* (Princeton, NJ: Princeton University Press, 2014).

Cooper, F., *Colonialism in Question: Theory, Knowledge, History* (Berkeley, CA: University of California Press, 2005).

Cooper, F., 'Colonizing Time: Work Rhythms and Labor Conflict in Colonial Mombasa', in *Colonialism and Culture*, ed. N. B. Dirks (Ann Arbor, MI: University of Michigan Press, 1992), 209–46.

Cooper, F., 'Conditions Analogous to Slavery: Imperialism and Free Labor Ideology in Africa', in *Beyond Slavery: Explorations of Race, Labor, and Citizenship in Postemancipation Societies*, ed. F. Cooper, T. C. Holt and R. J. Scott (Chapel Hill, NC: University of North Carolina Press, 2000), 107–49.

Cooper, F., *Decolonization and African Societies: The Labor Question in French and British Africa* (Cambridge: Cambridge University Press, 1996).

Cooper, F., 'The Dialectics of Decolonization: Nationalism and Labor Movements in Postwar French Africa', in *Tensions of Empire: Colonial Cultures in a Bourgeois World*, ed. F. Cooper and A. Stoler (Berkeley, CA: University of California Press, 1997), 406–36.

Cooper, F., 'From Enslavement to Precarity? The Labour Question in African History', in *The Political Economy of Everyday Life in Africa: Beyond the Margins*, ed. W. Adebanwi (Woodbridge: James Currey, 2017), 135–56.

Cooper, F., *From Slaves to Squatters: Plantation Labor and Agriculture in Zanzibar and Coastal Kenya, 1890–1925* (New Haven, CT: Yale University Press, 1980).

Cooper, F., *On the African Waterfront: Urban Disorder and the Transformation of Work in Colonial Mombasa* (New Haven, CT: Yale University Press, 1987).

Cooper, F., '"Our Strike": Equality, Anticolonial Politics and the 1947–48 Railway Strike in French West Africa', *The Journal of African History*, 37.1 (1996), 81–118.

Cooper, F., 'Peasants, Capitalists, and Historians', *Journal of Southern African Studies*, 7.2 (1981), 284–314.

Cooper, F., *Plantation Slavery on the East Coast of Africa* (New Haven, CT: Yale University Press, 1977)

Cooper, F., 'Possibility and Constraint: African Independence in Historical Perspective', *The Journal of African History*, 49.2 (2008), 167–96.

Cooper, F., 'Urban Space, Industrial Time, and Wage Labor in Africa', in *Struggle for the City: Migrant Labor, Capital, and the State in Urban Africa*, ed. F. Cooper (Beverly Hills, CA: Sage, 1983), 7–51.

Cooper, F., 'Work, Class, and Empire: An African Historian's Retrospective on E.P. Thompson', *Social History*, 20.2 (1995), 235–41.

Cooper, F., ed., *Struggle for the City: Migrant Labor, Capital and the State in Urban Africa* (Beverly Hills, CA: Sage, 1983).

Cooper, F., A. Isaacman, F. Mallon, W. Roseberry and S. Stern, *Confronting Historical Paradigms: Peasants, Labor, and the Capitalist World System in Africa and Latin America* (Madison, WI: University of Wisconsin Press, 1993).

Cooper, F., T. C. Holt and R. J. Scott, eds, *Beyond Slavery: Explorations of Race, Labor, and Citizenship in Postemancipation Societies* (Chapel Hill, NC: University of North Carolina Press, 2000).

Copans, J., 'Pourquoi travail et travailleurs africains ne sont plus à la mode en 2014 dans les sciences sociales. Retour sur l'actualité d'une problématique du XXe siècle', *Politique Africaine*, 133 (2014), 25–44.

Coquery-Vidrovitch, C., *Africa: Endurance and Change South of the Sahara*, trans. D. Maisel (Berkeley, CA: University of California Press, 1988).

Coquery-Vidrovitch, C., and A. Forest, eds, *Actes du colloque entreprises et entrepreneurs d'Afrique, XIXeme et XXeme siècles*, 2 vols (Paris: L'Harmattan, 1983).

Cordell, D. D., J. W. Gregory and V. Piché, *Hoe and Wage: A Social History of a Circular Migration System in West Africa* (Boulder, CO: Westview Press, 1996).

Cramer, C., C. Oya and J. Sender, 'Lifting the Blinkers: A New View of Power, Diversity and Poverty in Mozambican Rural Labour Markets', *Journal of Modern African Studies*, 46.3 (2008), 361–92.

Crichlow, M., 'Under the Shadows of Capital', in *Informalization: Process and Structure*, ed. F. Tabak and M. Crichlow (Baltimore, MD: Johns Hopkins University Press, 2000), 166–86.

Crisafulli, P., and A. Redmond, *Rwanda, Inc. How a Devastated Nation Became an Economic Model for the Developing World* (London: Macmillan, 2012).

Crisp, J., *The Story of an African Working Class: Ghanaian Miners Struggles, 1870–1980* (London: Zed Books, 1984).

Croke, K., G. Grossman, H. Larreguy and J. Marshall, 'Deliberate Disengagement: How Education Decreases Political Participation in Electoral Authoritarian Regimes', Afrobarometer Working Paper 156, 2015.

Cronjé, G., and S. Cronjé, 'The Workers of Namibia', International Defence and Aid Fund for Southern Africa, London, 1979.

Cross, H., *Migrants, Borders and Global Capitalism: West African Labour Mobility and EU Borders* (Abingdon: Routledge, 2013).

Croucher, R., and J. McIlroy, 'Mauritius 1938: The Origins of a Milestone in Colonial Trade Union Legislation', *Labor History*, 54.3 (2013), 223–39.

Crummey, D., 'Abyssinian Feudalism', *Past and Present*, 89.1 (1980), 115–38.

Crush, J., and C. Ambler, eds, *Liquor and Labor in Southern Africa* (Athens, OH: Ohio University Press, 1992).

Crush, J. S., A. Jeeves and D. Yudelman, *South Africa's Labor Empire: A History of Black Migrancy to the Gold Mines* (Boulder, CO: Westview Press, 1991).

Crush, J., T. Ulicki, T. Tseane and E. Jansen van Veuren, 'Undermining Labour: The Rise of Sub-Contracting in South African Gold Mines', *Journal of Southern African Studies*, 27.1 (2001), 5–31.

Cummings, R. J., 'A Note on the History of Caravan Porters in East Africa', *Kenya Historical Review*, 1.2 (1973), 109–38.

Curtin, P. D., *Cross-Cultural Trade in World History* (New York: Cambridge University Press, 1984).

Cuvelier, J., 'Men, Mines and Masculinities: The Lives and Practices of Artisanal Miners in Lwambo (Katanga Province, DR Congo)', PhD dissertation, University of Leuven, 2011.

Dale, R., *Botswana's Search for Autonomy in Southern Africa* (Westport, CT: Greenwood Press, 1995).

Damachi, U. G., H. D. Seibel and L. Trachtman, eds, *Industrial Relations in Africa* (New York: St Martin's Press, 1979).

Darby, P., '"Go Outside": The History, Economics and Geography of Football Labour Migration', *African Historical Review*, 42.1 (2010), 19–41.

Darby, P., 'Out of Africa: The Exodus of Elite African Football Talent to Europe', *Working USA: The Journal of Labour and Society*, 10 (2007), 443–56.

Daughton, J. P., 'Behind the Imperial Curtain: International Humanitarian Efforts and the Critique of French Colonialism in the Interwar Years', *French Historical Studies*, 34.3 (2011), 503–28.

Daughton, J. P., 'ILO Expertise and Colonial Violence in the Interwar Years', in *Globalizing Social Rights. The International Labour Organization and Beyond*, ed. S. Kott and J. Droux (Basingstoke and Geneva: Palgrave Macmillan and ILO, 2013), 85–97.

David, P., *Les navétanes: histoire des migrants saisonniers de l'arachide en Sénégambie des origines à nos jours* (Dakar: Nouvelles Éditions Africaines, 1980).

Davidson, B., *Modern Africa: A Social and Political History* (Harlow: Longman, 1994).

Davies, R., 'The 1922 Strike on the Rand: White Labor and the Political Economy of South Africa', in *African Labor History*, ed. P. C. W. Gutkind, R. Cohen and J. Copans (London: Sage, 1978), 80–108.

Davies, R., *Capital, State and White Labour 1900–1960: A Historical Materialist Analysis of Class Formation and Class Relations* (Brighton/New York: Harvester Press/Humanities Press, 1979).

Davis, C., *White-Collar Life and Corporate Cultures in Los Angeles, 1892–1941* (Baltimore, MD: Johns Hopkins University Press, 2000).

Dawson, J., 'Development of Small-scale Industry in Ghana: A Case Study of Kumasi', in *Small-Scale Production: Strategies for Industrial Restructuring*, ed. H. Thomas, F. Uribe-Echevarría and H. Romijn (London: Intermediate Technology Publications, 1991), 173–207.

De Lange, A., 'Child Labour in Burkina Faso', in *The World of Child Labor: An Historical and Regional Survey*, ed. H. D. Hindman (Armonk, NY: M. E. Sharpe, 2009), 202–5.

De Lange, A., 'Trafficking for Labor Exploitation in West and Central Africa', in *The World of Child Labor: An Historical and Regional Survey*, ed. H. D. Hindman (Armonk, NY: M. E. Sharpe, 2009), 194–8.

De Miras, C., 'De l'accumulation de capital dans le secteur informel', *Cahiers des sciences humaines*, 23.1 (1987), 49–74.

De Vries, D., *Diamonds and War: State, Capital and Labour in British-Ruled Palestine* (New York: Berghahn Books, 2010).

De Waal, A., *Evil Days: Thirty Years of War and Famine in Ethiopia* (New York: Human Rights Watch, 1991).

Debos, M., 'Living by the Gun in Chad: Armed Violence as a Practical Occupation', *Journal of Modern African Studies*, 49.3 (2011), 409–28.

Decker, S., 'Decolonising Barclays Bank DCO? Corporate Africanisation in Nigeria, 1945–69', *Journal of Imperial and Commonwealth History*, 33.3 (2005), 419–40.

Declich, F., 'Italian Weddings and Memory of Trauma: Colonial Domestic Policy in Southern Somalia, 1910–41', in *Marriage by Force? Contestation over Consent and Coercion in Africa*, ed. A. Bunting, B. N. Lawrance and R. L. Roberts (Athens, OH: University of Ohio Press, 2016), 109–34.

Deeb, M., 'Bank Misr and the Emergence of the Local Bourgeoisie in Egypt', *Middle Eastern Studies*, 12.3 (1976), 69–86.

Dekker, L. D., D. Hemson, J. S. Kane-Berman, J. Lever and L. Schlemmer, 'Case Studies in African Labour Action in South Africa and Namibia (South West Africa)', in *The Development of an African Working Class: Studies in Class Formation and Action*, ed. R. Sandbrook and R. Cohen (London: Longman, 1975), 206–38.

Delius, P., and L. Phillips, 'Introduction', in *A Long Way Home: Migrant Worker Worlds, 1800–2014*, ed. P. Delius, L. Phillips and F. Rankin-Smith (Johannesburg: Wits University Press, 2014), 1–16.

Denov, M., *Child Soldiers: Sierra Leone's Revolutionary United Front* (Cambridge: Cambridge University Press, 2010).

Der Thiam, I., 'L'Évolution politique et syndicale du Sénégal colonial de 1840 à 1936', PhD dissertation, Université de Paris I, 1983.

Derrick, J., 'The "Native Clerk" in Colonial West Africa', *African Affairs*, 82.326 (1983), 61–74.

Deutsch, J.-G., *Emancipation without Abolition in German East Africa c.1884–1914* (Oxford: James Currey, 2006).

Develtere, P., 'Cooperative Development in Africa up to the 1990s', in *Cooperating out of Poverty: The Renaissance of the African Cooperative Movement*, ed. P. Develtere, I. Pollet and F. Wanyama (Geneva: ILO, 2008), 1–37.

Develtere, P., I. Pollet and F. Wanyama, eds, *Cooperating out of Poverty: The Renaissance of the African Cooperative Movement* (Geneva: ILO, 2008).

Devereux, S., and F. Lund, 'Democratising Social Welfare in Africa', in *The Political Economy of Africa*, ed. V. Padayachee (London: Routledge, 2010), 152–71.

Devereux, S., and P. White. 'Social Protection in Africa: Evidence, Politics and Rights', *Poverty & Public Policy*, 2.3 (2010), 53–77.

Devey, R., C. Skinner and I. Valodia, 'Definitions, Data and the Informal Economy in South Africa: A Critical Analysis', in *The Development Decade? Economic and Social Change in South Africa, 1994–2004*, ed. V. Padayachee (Pretoria: HSRC Press, 2006), 302–23.

Di Ruggiero, E., J. E. Cohen and D. C. Cole, 'The Politics of Agenda Setting at the Global Level: Key Informant Interviews Regarding the International Labour Organization Decent Work Agenda', *Globalization and Health*, 10.56 (2014), https://globalizationandhealth.biomedcentral.com/articles/10.1186/1744-8603-10-56.

Diallo, Y., 'Children's Work, Child Domestic Labor, and Child Trafficking in Côte d'Ivoire', in *The World of Child Labor: An Historical and Regional Survey*, ed. H. D. Hindman (Armonk, NY: M. E. Sharpe, 2009), 207–11.

Dickerman, C., 'City Women and the Colonial Regime: Usumbura, 1939–1962', *African Urban Studies*, 18 (1984), 33–48.

Digby, A., 'Early Black Doctors in South Africa', *The Journal of African History*, 46.3 (2005), 427–54.

Dike, K. O., *Trade and Politics in the Niger Delta, 1830–1885: An Introduction to the Economic and Political History of Nigeria* (Oxford: Clarendon Press, 1956).

Dinkelman, T., and V. Ranchhod, 'Evidence on the Impact of Minimum Wage Laws in an Informal Sector: Domestic Workers in South Africa', *Journal of Development Economics*, 99.1 (2012), 27–45.

Diphoorn, T. D., *Twilight Policing: Private Security and Violence in Urban South Africa* (Berkeley, CA: University of California Press, 2015).

Dixon-Mueller, R., 'Women's Work in Third World Agriculture', Women, Work and Development Series, 9 (Geneva: ILO, 1985).

Dodge, C. P., and M. Raundalen, *Reaching Children in War: Sudan, Uganda and Mozambique* (Bergen: Sigma, 1991)

Dodille, N., *Introduction aux discours coloniaux* (Paris: PUP, 2011).

Dolan, C. S., 'Benevolent Intent? The Development Encounter in Kenya's Horticulture Industry', *Journal of Asian and African Studies*, 40.6 (2005), 411–37.

Domar, E. D., 'The Causes of Slavery or Serfdom: A Hypothesis', *Journal of Economic History*, 30.1 (1970), 18–32.

Don, P., *Gang Town* (Cape Town: Tafelberg, 2016).

Doortmont. M. R., *The Pen-Pictures of Modern Africans and African Celebrities by Charles Francis Hutchison: A Collective Biography of Elite Society in the Gold Coast Colony* (Leiden: Brill, 2005).

Dottridge, M., 'The Role of Nongovernmental Organizations', in *The World of Child Labor: An Historical and Regional Survey*, ed. H. D. Hindman (Armonk, NY: M. E. Sharpe, 2009), 143–8.

Drew, A., *Between Empire and Revolution: A Life of Sidney Bunting 1873–1936* (London/Pretoria: Pickering & Chatto/UNISA Press, 2007).

Drew, A., 'Bolshevizing Communist Parties: The Algerian and South African Experiences', *International Review of Social History*, 48.2 (2003), 167–202.

Drummond-Thompson, P., 'The Rise of Entrepreneurs in Nigerian Motor Transport: A Study in Indigenous Enterprise', *Journal of Transport History*, 14.1 (1993), 46–63.

Dubbeld, B., 'Breaking the Buffalo: The Transformation of Stevedoring Work in Durban Between 1970 and 1990', *International Review of Social History*, special issue, 48.11 (2003), 97–122.

Dumett, R. E., 'Africa's Strategic Minerals during the Second World War', *The Journal of African History*, 26.4 (1985), 381–408.

Dumett, R. E., 'African Merchants of the Gold Coast, 1860–1905 – Dynamics of Indigenous Entrepreneurship', *Comparative Studies in Society and History*, 25.4 (1983), 661–93.

Dumett, R., *El Dorado in West Africa: The Gold-Mining Frontier, African Labor, and Colonial Capitalism in the Gold Coast, 1875–1900* (Athens, OH: Ohio University Press, 1998).

Ebeid, D. M., 'Manufacturing Stability: Everyday Politics of Work in an Industrial Steel Town in Helwan, Egypt', PhD dissertation, London School of Economics and Political Science, 2012.

Echenberg, M., *Colonial Conscripts: The Tirailleurs Sénégalais in French West Africa, 1857–1960* (Portsmouth, NH: Heinemann, 1991).

Echenberg, M., '"Morts pour la France": The African Soldier in France during the Second World War', *The Journal of African History*, 26.4 (1985), 363–80.

Echenberg, M., and J. Filipovich, 'African Military Labour and the Building of the *Office du Niger* Installations, 1925–1950', *The Journal of African History*, 27.3 (1986), 533–51.

Eckert, A., 'African Rural Entrepreneurs and Labor in the Cameroon Littoral', *The Journal of African History*, 40.1 (1999), 109–26.

Eckert, A., 'Capitalism and Labor in Sub-Saharan Africa', in *Capitalism: The Reemergence of a Historical Concept*, ed. J. Kocka and M. van der Linden (London: Bloomsbury, 2016), 165–85.

Eckert, A., 'Comparing Coffee Production in Cameroon and Tanganyika, c. 1900 to 1960s: Land, Labor, and Politics', in *The Global Coffee Economy in Africa, Asia, and Latin America, 1500–1989*, ed. W. G. Clarence-Smith and S. Topik (Cambridge: Cambridge University Press, 2003), 286–311.

Eckert, A., 'Exportschlager Wohlfahrtsstaat? Europäische Sozialstaatlichkeit und Kolonialismus in Afrika nach dem Zweiten Weltkrieg', *Geschichte und Gesellschaft*, 32.4 (2006), 467–88.

Eckert, A., *Herrschen und Verwalten. Afrikanische Bürokraten, staatliche Ordnung und Politik in Tanzania, 1920–1970* (Munich: Oldenbourg, 2007).

Eckert, A., 'Regulating the Social: Social Security, Social Welfare and the State in Late Colonial Tanzania', *The Journal of African History*, 45.3 (2004), 467–89.

Eckert, A., 'Slavery in Colonial Cameroon 1880s–1930s', in *Slavery and Colonial Rule in Africa*, ed. S. Miers and M. Klein (London: Frank Cass, 1999), 133–48.

Eckert, A., ed., *Global Histories of Work* (Berlin: De Gruyter, 2016).

Eckert, A., and M. van der Linden, 'New Perspectives on Workers and the History of Work: Global Labor History', in *Global History, Globally: Research and Practice around the World*, ed. S. Beckert and D. Sachsenmaier (London: Bloomsbury, 2018), 145–61.

Ehret, C., *The Civilizations of Africa: A History to 1800* (Oxford: James Currey, 2002).

Eisenstadt, S. N., 'Studies of Modernization and Sociological Theory', *History and Theory*, 13.3 (1974), 225–52.

Ekanem, S. A., 'African Philosophy of Development: Contemporary Perspectives', *SOPHIA: An African Journal of Philosophy*, 9.1 (2006), 85–90.

Ekejiuba, F. I., 'Down to Fundamentals: Women-Centred Hearth-Holds in Rural West Africa', in *Women Wielding the Hoe: Lessons from Rural Africa for Feminist Theory and Development Practice*, ed. D. F. Bryceson (Oxford: Berg Publishers, 1995), 47–61.

Elkan, W., *Migrants and Proletarians: Urban Labour in the Economic Development of Uganda* (Oxford: Oxford University Press, 1960).

Elkan, W., 'The Relation between Tourism and Employment in Kenya and Tanzania', *Journal of Development Studies*, 1.2 (1975), 123–30.

Ellis, G., 'Land Tenancy Reform in Ethiopia: A Retrospective Analysis', *Economic Development and Cultural Change*, 28.3 (1980), 523–45.

Ellis, S., *This Present Darkness: A History of Nigerian Organized Crime* (London: Hurst, 2016).

Elyachar, J., *Markets of Dispossession: NGOs, Economic Development, and the State in Cairo* (Durham, NC: Duke University Press, 2005).

Engerman, D. C., and C. R. Unger, 'Introduction: Towards a Global History of Modernization', *Diplomatic History*, 33.3 (2009), 375–85.

Enloe, C., *Bananas, Beaches and Bases: Making Feminist Sense of International Politics* (Berkeley, CA: University of California Press, 1990).

Entelis, J. P., ed., *Islam, Democracy and the State in North Africa* (Bloomington, IN: Indiana University Press, 1997).

Ernst, K., *Tradition and Progress in the African Village: Noncapitalist Transformation of Rural Communities in Mali* (New York: St Martin's Press, 1976).

Evans, P., 'Constructing the 21st Century Developmental State: Potentialities and Pitfalls', in *Constructing a Democratic Developmental State in South Africa: Potentials and Challenges*, ed. O. Edigheji (Cape Town: HSRC Press, 2010), 37–58.

Ewusi, K., *The Distribution of Monetary Incomes in Ghana* (Legon: University of Ghana, 1971).

Eyzaguirre, P., 'Plantation Economies and Societies', in *New Encyclopedia of Africa*, ed. J. Middelton and J. Miller (New York: Charles Scribner's Sons, 2008), 151–5.

Fall, B., *Social History in French West Africa: Forced Labour, Labour Market, Women and Politics* (Amsterdam: SEPHIS, 2002).

Fall, B., *Le travail au Sénégal au XXe siècle* (Paris: Karthala, 2011).

Fall, B., *Le travail forcé en Afrique-Occidentale française, 1900–1946* (Paris: Karthala, 1993).

Falola, T., *Colonialism and Violence in Nigeria* (Bloomington, IN: Indiana University Press, 2009).

Falola, T., *Nationalism and African Intellectuals* (Rochester, NY: University of Rochester Press, 2001).

Falola, T., 'The Yoruba Caravan System of the Nineteenth Century', *International Journal of African Historical Studies*, 24.1 (1991), 111–32.

Faye, O., and I. Thioub, 'Les marginaux et l'État à Dakar', *Le mouvement social*, 204 (2003), 93–108.

Feichtinger, M., and S. Malinowski., '"Eine Millionen Algerier lernen im 20. Jahrhundert zu leben". Umsiedlungslager und Zwangsmodernisierung im Algerienkrieg 1954–1962', *Journal of Modern European History*, 8.1 (2012), 107–35.

Feierman, S., *Peasant Intellectuals: Anthropology and History in Tanzania* (Madison, WI: University of Wisconsin Press,1990).

Feinstein, C. H., *An Economic History of South Africa: Conquest, Discrimination and Development* (Cambridge: Cambridge University Press, 2005).

Ferguson, J., *Expectations of Modernity: Myths and Meanings of Urban Life on the Zambian Copperbelt* (Berkeley, CA: University of California Press, 1999).

Ferguson, J., *Give a Man a Fish: Reflections on the New Politics of Distribution* (Durham, NC: Duke University Press, 2015).

Ferguson, J., *Global Shadows: Africa in the Neoliberal World Order* (Durham, NC: Duke University Press, 2006).

Ferguson, J., 'Mobile Workers, Modernist Narratives: A Critique of the Historiography of Transition in the Zambian Copperbelt (Part One)', *Journal of Southern African Studies*, 16.3 (1990), 385–412.

Fernandez, B., 'Cheap and Disposable? The Impact of the Global Economic Crisis on the Migration of Ethiopian Women', *Migration Review*, 24.2 (2010), 297–322.

Fernyhough, T. D., *Serfs, Slaves and Shifta: Modes of Production and Resistance in Pre-Revolutionary Ethiopia* (Addis Ababa: Shama Books, 2010).

Ferris, E., 'Faith-Based and Secular Humanitarian Organizations', *International Review of the Red Cross*, 87.858 (2005), 311–25.

Fetter, B., *The Creation of Elizabethville, 1910–1940* (Stanford, CA: Hoover Institution Press, 1976).

Fetter, B., 'The Luluabourg Revolt of Elisabethville', *International Journal of African Historical Studies*, 2.2 (1969), 137–47.

Fieldhouse, D. K., *Merchant Capital and Economic Decolonization: The United Africa Company 1929–1987* (Oxford: Clarendon Press, 1994).

Filipovich, J., 'Destined to Fail: Forced Settlement at the Office du Niger, 1926–45', *The Journal of African History*, 42.2 (2001), 239–60.

Fischer, G., 'Revisiting Abandoned Ground: Tanzanian Trade Unions' Engagement with Informal Workers', *Labor Studies Journal*, 38.2 (2013), 139–60.

Fischer, G., 'Syndicats et décolonisation', *Présence Africaine*, 34/35 (1960/61), 17–60.

Folliet, J., *Le travail forcé aux colonies* (Paris: Éditions du Cerf, 1934).

Food and Agriculture Organization, *Statistical Yearbook 2014, Africa* (Accra: Food and Agriculture Organization of the United Nations. Regional Office for Africa, 2014).

Food and Agriculture Organization, 'Report of the Exploratory Employment Policy Mission Organized by the International Labour Organization and Financed by the United Nations Development Program, Employment and Unemployment in Ethiopia' (Geneva, 1974).

Forclaz, A. R., 'A New Target for International Social Reform: The International Labour Organization and Working and Living Conditions in Agriculture in the Inter-War Years', *Contemporary European History*, 20.3 (2011), 307–29.

Forrest, K., 'Rustenburg's Fractured Recruitment Regime: Who Benefits?', *African Studies*, 73.2 (2014), 149–68.

Forrest, T., *The Advance of African Capital: The Growth of Nigerian Private Enterprise* (Edinburgh: Edinburgh University Press, 1994).

Fortes, M., and E. E. Evans-Pritchard, *African Political Systems* (London: Oxford University Press, 1970).

Fourchard, L., '"Enfants en danger" et "enfants dangereux": expertises et différenciation raciale en Afrique du Sud, 1937–1976', *Politix*, 99.3 (2012), 175–98.

Fourchard, L., 'Lagos and the Invention of Juvenile Delinquency in Nigeria', *The Journal of African History*, 47.1 (2006), 115–37.

Fourchard, L., 'The Limits of Penal Reform: Punishing Children and Young Offenders in South Africa and Nigeria (1930s to 1960s)', *Journal of Southern African Studies*, 37.3 (2011), 517–34.

Fourchard L., *Trier, exclure et policer. Vies urbaines en Afrique du Sud et au Nigeria* (Paris: Presses de Sciences Po, 2018).

Fourchard, L., and S. Bekker, eds, *Governing Cities in Africa: Politics and Policies* (Pretoria: HSRC Press, 2013).

Fourie, J., 'An Inquiry into the Nature, Causes and Distribution of Wealth in the Cape Colony, 1652–1795', PhD dissertation, Utrecht University, 2012.

Frank, D., 'The County of Coal', *Labour/Le Travail*, 21 (1988), 233–48.

Frankel, S. H., *Capital Investment in Africa* (London: Oxford University Press, 1938).

Frankema, E., 'Colonial Taxation and Government Spending in British Africa, 1880–1940: Maximizing Revenue or Minimizing Effort?', *Explorations in Economic History*, 48.1 (2011), 136–49.

Frankema, E., and M. Jerven, 'Writing History Backwards and Sideways: Towards a Consensus on African Population, 1850–2010', *Economic History Review*, 67.4 (2014), 907–31.

Frankema, E., and M. van Waijenburg, 'Structural Impediments to African Growth? New Evidence from Real Wages in British Africa, 1880–1965', *Journal of Economic History*, 72.4 (2012), 895–926.

Frankema, E., J. Williamson and P. Woltjer, 'An Economic Rationale for the West African Scramble? The Commercial Transition and the Commodity Price Boom of 1835–1885', *Journal of Economic History*, 78.1 (2018), 231–67.

Franken, M., 'From the Streets to the Stage: The Evolution of Professional Female Dance in Colonial Cairo', in *Leisure in Urban Africa*, ed. P. T. Zeleza and C. R. Veney (Trenton, NJ: Africa World Press, 2003), 85–104.

Fraser, A., and M. Larmer, eds, *Zambia, Mining, and Neoliberalism: Boom and Bust on the Globalized Copperbelt* (New York: Palgrave Macmillan, 2010).

Fraser, D., and T. Notteboom, 'Port Development in Sub-Saharan Africa: Competitive Forces, Port Reform, and Investment Challenges', in *Dynamic Shipping and Port Development in the Globalized Economy, Vol. 1: Applying Theory to Practice in Maritime Logistics*, ed. P. Tae-Woo Lee and K. Cullinane (Basingstoke: Palgrave Macmillan, 2016), 53–78.

Frayne, B., 'Migration and the Changing Social Economy of Windhoek, Namibia', *Development Southern Africa*, 24.1 (2007), 91–108.

Fremigacci, J., État, économie et société coloniale à Madagascar: de la fin du XIXe siècle aux années 1940 (Paris: Karthala, 2014).

Freund, B., *The African Worker* (Cambridge: Cambridge University Press, 1988).

Freund, B., *Capital and Labour in the Nigerian Tin Mines* (Atlantic Highlands, NJ: Academic Press, 1980).

Freund, B., *Insiders and Outsiders; The Indian Working Class of Durban 1910–90* (Oxford: James Currey, 1995).

Freund, B., 'Labor and Labor History in Africa: A Review of the Literature', *African Studies Review*, 27.2 (1984), 1–58.

Freund, B., 'Labour Studies and Labour History in South Africa: Perspectives from the Apartheid Era and After', *International Review of Social History*, 58.3 (2013), 493–519.

Freund, B., 'Organized Labor in the Republic of South Africa: History and Democratic Transition', in *Trade Unions and the Coming of Democracy in Africa*, ed. J. Kraus (Basingstoke: Palgrave Macmillan, 2007), 199–227.

Freund, B., 'Swimming Against the Tide: The Macro-Economic Research Group in the South African Transition 1991–94', *Review of African Political Economy*, 40.138 (2013), 519–36.

Friedland, W. H., 'Labor's Role in Emerging African Socialist States', in *The Role of Labor in African Nation-Building*, ed. W. Beling (London: Praeger, 1968), 20–40.

Friedman, S., *Building Tomorrow Today: African Workers in Trade Unions 1970–1984* (Johannesburg: Ravan Press, 1987).

Frimpong-Ansah, J., *The Vampire State in Africa: The Political Economy of Decline in Ghana* (London: James Currey, 1991).

Furley, O., 'Child Soldiers in Africa', in *Conflict in Africa*, ed. O. Furley (London: I.B.Tauris, 1995).

Gaanderse, M., and K. Valasek, eds, 'Le secteur de la sécurité et le genre en Afrique de l'Ouest. Une étude de la police, de la défense, de la justice et des services pénitentiaires dans les pays de la CEDEAO', Centre de Genève pour le Contrôle des Forces Armées, Geneva, 2011.

Gabbert, W., 'Social and Cultural Conditions of Religious Conversion in Colonial Southwest Tanzania, 1891–1939', *Ethnology*, 40.4 (2001), 291–308.

Gaitskell, D., 'Housewives, Maids or Mothers: Some Contradictions of Domesticity for Christian Women in Johannesburg, 1903–39', *Journal of Africa History*, 24.2 (1983), 241–56.

Gamble, W. P., *Tourism and Development in Africa* (London: John Murray, 1989).

Gebeyehu, T., 'Land Tenure, Land Reform and the *Qalad* System in Ethiopia, 1941–1974', *Journal of Asian and African Studies*, 46.6 (2011), 567–77.

Genova, A., 'Nigeria's Nationalization of British Petroleum', *International Journal of African Historical Studies*, 43.1 (2010), 115–36.

George, A., 'Within Salvation: Girl Hawkers and the Colonial State in Development Era Lagos', *Journal of Social History*, 44.3 (2011), 837–59.

George, A., *Making Modern Girls: A History of Girlhood, Labor, and Social Development in Colonial Lagos* (Athens, OH: Ohio University Press, 2014).

Gertzel, C., 'Industrial Relations in Zambia to 1975', in *Industrial Relations in Africa*, ed. U. Damachi, H. D. Seibel and L. Trachtman (London: Macmillan, 1979), 307–59.

Geschiere, P., and S. Jackson, 'Autochthony and the Crisis of Democratization, Decentralization, and the Politics of Belonging', *African Studies Review*, 49.2 (2006), 1–8.

Gewald, J.-B., *Forged in the Great War: People, Transport, and Labour, the Establishment of Colonial Rule in Zambia, 1890–1920* (Leiden: African Studies Centre, 2015).

Ghai, D., E. Lee, J. Maeda and S. Radwan, eds, *Overcoming Rural Underdevelopment, Proceedings of a Workshop on Alternative Agrarian Systems and Rural Development. Arusha, Tanzania, 4–14 April 1979* (Geneva: ILO, 1979).

Gibbon, P., D. Benoit and S. Barral, 'Lineages of Paternalism: An Introduction', *Journal of Agrarian Change*, 14.2 (2014), 65–189.

Gibbon, P., and L. Riisgaard, 'A New System of Labour Management in African Large-Scale Agriculture?', *Journal of Agrarian Change*, 14.1 (2014), 94–128.

Gibbs, T., 'Becoming a "Big Man" in Neo-Liberal South Africa: Migrant Masculinities in the Minibus-Taxi Industry', *African Affairs*, 113.452 (2014), 431–48.

Gichure, C. W., *Ethics for Africa Today: An Introduction to Business Ethics* (Nairobi: Pauline Publications Africa, 2008).

Gide, A., *Voyage au Congo* (Paris: Gallimard, 1927).

Gifford, P., and T. C. Weiskel, 'African Education in a Colonial Context: French and British Styles', in *France and Britain in Africa: Imperial Rivalry and Colonial Rule*, ed. P. Gifford and W. R. Louis (New Haven, CT: Yale University Press, 1971), 663–711.

Gladwin, C., 'Introduction', in *Structural Adjustment and African Women Farmers*, ed. C. Gladwin (Gainesville, FL: University of Florida Press, 1991), 1–22.

Glaser, C., *Bo-Tsotsi: The Youth Gangs of Soweto, 1935–1976* (Oxford: James Currey, 2000).

Glasman, J., *Les corps habillés au Togo: genèse coloniale des métiers de police* (Paris: Karthala, 2015).

Glassman, J., *Feasts and Riot: Revelry, Rebelliousness and Popular Consciousness on the Swahili Coast, 1856–1888* (Portsmouth, NH/London/Nairobi/Dar es Salaam: Heinemann/James Currey/EAEP/Mkuki na Nyota, 1995).

Glasman, J., 'Unruly Agents: Police Reform, Bureaucratization, and Policemen's Agency in Interwar Togo', *The Journal of African History*, 55 (2014), 79–100.

Godard, X., *Les transports et la ville en Afrique au sud du Sahara: le temps de la débrouille et du désordre inventif* (Paris: Karthala, 2002).

Goldberg, E., 'Peasants in Revolt: Egypt 1919', *International Journal of Middle East Studies*, 24.2 (1992), 265–80.

Goldberg, E., *Tinker, Tailor and Textile Worker: Class and Politics in Egypt, 1930–1952* (Berkeley, CA: University of California Press, 1986).

Goldberg, E., *Trade, Reputation, and Child Labor in Twentieth-Century Egypt* (New York: Palgrave Macmillan, 2004).

Goldschmidt-Clermont, L., *Economic Evaluations of Unpaid Household Work: Africa, Asia, Latin America and Oceania* (Geneva: ILO, 1987).

Goldstein, M., and C. Udry, 'The Profits of Power: Land Rights and Agricultural Investment in Ghana', *Journal of Political Economy*, 6.6 (2002), 981–1022.

Goodhew, D., 'Working-Class Respectability: The Example of the Western Areas of Johannesburg, 1930–55', *The Journal of African History*, 41.2 (2000), 241–66.

Goodridge, R., 'Plantations and Labor, Colonial', in *Encyclopedia of African History*, ed. K. Shillington, vol. 3 (London: Fitzroy Dearborn, 2005), 1201–2.

Gorman, A., 'Foreign Workers in Egypt 1882–1914: Subaltern or Labour Elite?', in *Subalterns and Social Protest: History from Below in the Middle East and North Africa*, ed. S. Cronin (London: Routledge, 2008), 240–2.

Gorz, A., *Reclaiming Work: Beyond the Wage-Based Society* (Cambridge: Polity Press, 1999).

Gotlub, S. S., 'Entrepôt Trade and Smuggling in West Africa: Benin, Togo and Nigeria', *The World Economy*, 35.9 (2012), 1139–61.

Gould, W. T. S., 'Regional Labour Migration Systems in East Africa: Continuity and Change', in *The Cambridge Survey of World Migration*, ed. R. Cohen (Cambridge: Cambridge University Press 1995), 183–9.

Graham, Y., 'From GTP to Assene: Aspects of Industrial Working Class Struggles in Ghana 1982–1986', in *The State, Development and Politics in Ghana*, ed. E. Hansen and K. A. Ninsin (Dakar: CODESRIA, 1989), 43–72.

Grant, K. A., *A Civilised Savagery: Britain and the New Slaveries in Africa, 1884–1926* (New York: Routledge, 2005).

Gregoire, E., 'Les perspectives d'accumulation dans la petite industrie de transformation: l'exemple de la menuiserie métallique à Maradi (Niger)', *Cahiers d'études africaines*, 81–83 (1981), 221–35.

Grier, B., 'Child Labor in Colonial Africa', in *The World of Child Labor: An Historical and Regional Survey*, ed. H. D. Hindman (Armonk, NY: M. E. Sharpe, 2009), 173–7.

Grier, B., *Invisible Hands: Child Labor and the State in Colonial Zimbabwe* (Portsmouth, NH: Heinemann, 2005).

Grier, B., 'Invisible Hands: The Political Economy of Child Labour in Colonial Zimbabwe, 1890–1930', *Journal of Southern African Studies*, 20.1 (1994), 27–52.

Grundlingh, A. M., *War and Society. Participation and Remembrance: South African Black and Coloured Troops in the First World War, 1914–1918* (Stellenbosch: Sun Press, 2014).

Gueye, O., *Mai 1968 au Sénégal: Senghor face aux étudiants et au mouvement syndical* (Paris: Karthala, 2017).

Gugler, J., 'The Son of the Hawk Does Not Remain Abroad: The Urban–Rural Connection in Africa', *African Studies Review*, 45.1 (2002), 21–41.

Guichaoua, Y., 'Non-Protected Labour in One West African Capital: Characteristics of Jobs and Occupational Mobility in Abidjan, Côte d'Ivoire', Queen Elizabeth House Working Papers, 132, Department of International Development, University of Oxford, 2006.

Gulliver, P. H., *The Family Herds: A Study of Two Pastoral Tribes in East Africa, the Jie and Turkana* (London: Routledge and Kegan Paul, 1955).

Gutkind, P. C. W., 'The Canoemen of the Gold Coast (Ghana): A Survey and an Exploration in Precolonial African Labour History', Cahiers d'études africaines, 29.115 (1989), 339–76.

Gutkind, P. C. W., R. Cohen and J. Copans, eds, *African Labor History* (London: Sage, 1978).

Guy, J., 'The Destruction and Reconstruction of Zulu Society', in *Industrialisation and Social Change in South Africa: African Class Formation, Culture and Consciousness 1870–1930*, ed. S. Marks and R. Rathbone (New York: Longman, 1982), 167–94.

Guy, J., and M. Thabane, 'The Ma-Rashea: A Participant's Perspective', in *Class, Community and Conflict: South African Perspectives*, ed. B. Bozzoli (Johannesburg: Ravan Press, 1987), 436–56.

Guyer, J., *Marginal Gains: Monetary Transactions in Atlantic Africa* (Chicago: University of Chicago Press, 2004).

Guyer, J., 'Women's Farming and Present Ethnography: Perspective on a Nigerian Restudy', in *Women Wielding the Hoe: Lessons from Rural Africa for Feminist Theory and Development Practice*, ed. D. F. Bryceson (Oxford: Berg Publishers, 1995), 25–46.

Gwassa, G. C. K., and J. Iliffe, eds, *Records of the Maji Maji Rising* (Nairobi: East African Publishing House, 1967).

Gwawa, N. N., '"Money as a Source of Tension": An Analysis of Low Income Households in Durban', in *Changing Gender Relations in Southern Africa: Issues of Urban Life*, ed. A. Larsson, M. Mapetla and A. Schylter (Oxford: African Books Collective 1998), 33–55.

Hailey, M. W., *An African Survey* (London: Oxford University Press, 1938).

Hale, T. A., *Griots and Griottes: Masters of Word and Music* (Bloomington, IN: Indiana University Press, 1998).

Hall, C., *Civilizing Subjects: Metropole and Colony in the English Imagination 1830–1867* (Chicago: University of Chicago Press, 2002).

Hamilton, C., B. K. Mbenga and R. Ross, eds, *The Cambridge History of South Africa*, vol. 1 (New York: Cambridge University Press, 2009).

Handley, A., *Business and the State in Africa: Economic Policy-Making in the Neo-Liberal Era* (Cambridge: Cambridge University Press, 2008).

Hansen, K. T., 'Body Politics: Sexuality, Gender and Domestic Service in Zambia', *Journal of Women's History*, 2.1 (1990), 120–42.

Hansen, K. T., *Distant Companions: Servants and Employers in Zambia, 1900–1985* (Ithaca, NY: Cornell University Press, 1989).

Hansen, K. T., 'Gender and Housing: The Case of Domestic Service in Lusaka, Zambia', *Africa*, 62.2 (1992), 24–65.

Hansen, K. T., and M. Vaa, eds, *Reconsidering Informality: Perspectives from Urban Africa* (Uppsala: Nordic Africa Institute, 2004).

Hargreaves, J. D., 'Toward the Transfer of Power in British West Africa', in *The Transfer of Power in Africa: Decolonization 1940–1960*, ed. P. Gifford and W. R. Louis (New Haven, CT: Yale University Press, 1982), 117–40.

Harma, R. F., 'Child Labor in Nigeria', in *The World of Child Labor: An Historical and Regional Survey*, ed. H. D. Hindman (Armonk, NY: M. E. Sharpe, 2009), 225–9.

Harries, P., 'Capital, State and Labour on the Nineteenth-Century Witwatersrand: A Reassessment', *South African Historical Journal*, 18.1 (1986), 25–45.

Harries, P., 'Kinship, Ideology and the Nature of Pre-colonial Labour Migration: Labour Migration from the Delagoa Bay Hinterland to South Africa, up to 1895', in *Industrialisation and Social Change in South Africa*, ed. S. Marks and R. Rathbone (Harlow: Longman, 1982), 142–66.

Harries, P., *Work Culture, and Identity: Migrant Laborers in Mozambique and South Africa, c.1860–1910* (Portsmouth, NH: Heinemann, 1994).

Harries-Jones, P., *Freedom and Labour: Mobilization and Political Control on the Zambian Copperbelt* (Oxford: Blackwell, 1975).

Harris, J. R., 'Nigerian Entrepreneurship in Industry', in *Entrepreneurship and Economic Development*, ed. P. Kilby (Glencoe, IL: Free Press, 1971).

Harris, K., and B. Scully, 'A Hidden Counter-movement? Precarity, Politics, and Social Protection before and beyond the Neoliberal Era', *Theory and Society*, 44.5 (2015), 415–44.

Hart, G. P., *Disabling Globalization: Places of Power in Post-Apartheid South Africa* (Berkeley, CA: University of California Press, 2002).

Hart, J., *Ghana on the Go: African Mobility in the Age of Motor Transportation* (Bloomington, IN: Indiana University Press, 2016).

Hart, K., 'Informal Income Opportunities and Urban Employment in Ghana', *Journal of Modern African Studies*, 11.1 (1973), 61–89.

Hart, K., 'On the Informal Economy: The Political History of an Ethnographic Concept', Centre Emile Bernheim, Working Paper 09/042, Brussels, Solvay School of Economics and Management, 2009.

Hart, K., 'The Politics of Unemployment in Ghana', *African Affairs*, 75.301 (1976), 488–97.

Harvey, D., *The New Imperialism* (Oxford: Oxford University Press, 2003).

Hauf, F., 'The Paradoxes of Decent Work in Context: A Cultural Political Economy Perspective', *Global Labour Journal*, 6.2 (2015), 138–55.

Hayem, J., 'Marikana: répression étatique d'une mobilisation ouvrière indépendante', *Politique Africaine*, 133.1 (2014), 111–30.

Haynes, J., and O. Okome, 'Evolving Popular Media: Nigerian Video Films', in *Nigerian Video Films*, ed. J. Haynes (Athens, OH: Ohio University Press, 2000), 51–88.

Heap, S., '"Their Days are Spent in Gambling and Loafing, Pimping for Prostitutes, and Picking Pockets": Male Juvenile Delinquents on Lagos Island, 1920s–1960s', *Journal of Family History*, 35.1 (2010), 48–70.

Henderson, I., 'Early African Leadership: The Copperbelt Disturbances of 1935 and 1940', *Journal of Southern African Studies*, 2 (1975), 83–97.

Henderson, I., 'Wage-Earners and Political Protest in Colonial Africa: The Case of the Copperbelt', *African Affairs*, 72.288 (1973), 288–99.

Hendricks, F., 'Peasants', in *Encyclopedia of Twentieth-Century African History*, ed. P. T. Zeleza (London: Routledge, 2003), 428–34.

Henley, P., *The Architecture of the Real: Jean Rouch and the Craft of Ethnographic Cinema* (Chicago: University of Chicago Press, 2009).

Hepner, T. R., and S. Tecle, 'New Refugees, Development-Forced Displacement, and Transnational Governance in Eritrea and Exile', *Urban Anthropology and Studies of Cultural Systems and World Economic Development*, 42.3/4 (2013), 377–410.

Herbert, E., *Iron, Gender and Power: Rituals of Transformation in African Societies* (Bloomington, IN: Indiana University Press, 1993).

Herbst, J., *States and Power in Africa: Comparative Lessons in Authority and Control* (Princeton, NJ: Princeton University Press, 2014).

Hibou, B., 'Work Discipline, Discipline in Tunisia: Complex and Ambiguous Relations', *African Identities*, 7.3 (2009), 327–52.

Hickey, S., 'Conceptualising the Politics of Social Protection in Africa', in *Social Protection for the Poor and Poorest*, ed. A. Barrientos and D. Hulme (London: Palgrave Macmillan, 2008), 247–63.

Hidalgo-Weber, O., 'Social and Political Networks and the Creation of the ILO: The Role of British Actors', in *Globalizing Social Rights: The International Labour Organization and Beyond*, ed. S. Kott and J. Droux (Basingstoke: Palgrave Macmillan, 2013), 17–31.

Higginson, J., *A Working Class in the Making: Belgian Colonial Labor Policy, Private Enterprise, and the African Mineworker, 1907–1951* (Madison, WI: University of Wisconsin Press, 1989).

Higgs, C., *Chocolate Islands: Cocoa, Slavery, and Colonial Africa* (Athens, OH: Ohio University Press, 2012).

Hill, P., *The Gold Coast Cocoa Farmer: A Preliminary Survey* (London: Oxford University Press, 1956).

Hill, P., *The Migrant Cocoa-Farmers of Southern Ghana: A Study in Rural Capitalism* (Cambridge: Cambridge University Press, 1963).

Hill, P., *Population, Prosperity, and Poverty: Rural Kano, 1900 and 1970* (Cambridge: Cambridge University Press, 1977).

Hill, P., *Studies in Rural Capitalism in West Africa* (Cambridge: Cambridge University Press, 1970).

Hindman, H. D., 'Worst Forms of Child Labor', in *The World of Child Labor: An Historical and Regional Survey*, ed. H. D. Hindman (Armonk, NY: M. E. Sharpe, 2009), 78–81.

Hindman, H. D., ed., *The World of Child Labor: An Historical and Regional Survey* (Armonk, NY: M. E. Sharpe, 2009).

Hindson, D., *Pass Controls and the Urban African Proletariat* (Johannesburg: Ravan Press, 1987).

Hirson, B., and Y. Hirson, *History of the Left in South Africa: Writings of Baruch Hirson* (London: I.B.Tauris, 2005).

Hochschild, A., *King Leopold's Ghost: A Story of Greed, Terror, and Heroism in Colonial Africa* (New York: Houghton Mifflin: 1998).

Hodges, G., *The Carrier Corps: Military Labor in the East African Campaign, 1914–1918* (Westport, CT: Greenwood Publishing, 1986).

Hoffman, D., 'The City as Barracks: Freetown, Monrovia, and the Organization of Violence in Postcolonial African Cities', *Cultural Anthropology*, 22.3 (2007), 400–28.

Hoffman, D., 'Violence, Just in Time: War and Work in Contemporary West Africa', *Cultural Anthropology*, 26.1 (2011), 34–57.

Holt, T. C., 'The Essence of the Contract: The Articulation of Race, Gender, and Political Economy in British Emancipation Policy, 1838–1866', in *Beyond Slavery: Explorations of Race, Labor, and Citizenship in Postemancipation Societies*, ed. F. Cooper, T. C. Holt and R. J. Scott (Chapel Hill, NC: University of North Carolina Press, 2000), 33–60.

Honey, R., and S. Okafor, eds, *Hometown Associations: Indigenous Knowledge and Development in Nigeria* (London: Intermediate Technology Publications, 1998).

Honwana, A., *Child Soldiers in Africa* (Philadelphia, PA: University of Pennsylvania Press, 2006).

Hooker, J. R., 'The Role of the Labour Department in the Birth of African Trade Unionism in Northern Rhodesia', *International Review of Social History*, 10.1 (1965), 1–22.

Hopkins, A. G., *An Economic History of West Africa* (London: Longman, 1973).

Hopkins, A. G., 'Innovation in a Colonial Context: African Origins of the Nigerian Cocoa-Farming Industry, 1880–1920', in *The Imperial Impact*, ed. C. Dewey and A. G. Hopkins (London: Athlone Press, 1978), 83–96.

Hopkins, A. G., 'The Lagos Strike of 1897: An Exploration in Nigerian Labour History', *Past & Present*, 35.1 (1966), 133–55.

Hopkins, A. G., 'The Lagos Strike of 1897: An Exploration in Nigerian Labor History', in *Peasants and Proletarians: The Struggles of Third World Workers*, ed. R. Cohen, P. C. W. Gutkind and P. Brazier (New York: Monthly Review Press, 1979), 87–106.

Hopkins, A. G., 'The Victorians and Africa: A Reconsideration of the Occupation of Egypt, 1882', *The Journal of African History*, 27.2 (1986), 363–91.

Huggins, M. K., M. Haritos-Fatouras and P. G. Zimbardo, *Violence Workers: Police Torturers and Murderers Reconstruct Brazilian Atrocities* (Berkeley, CA: University of California Press, 2002).

Hughes, A., and R. Cohen, 'An Emerging Nigerian Working Class: The Lagos Experience, 1897–1939', in *African Labour History*, ed. P. C. W. Gutkind, R. Cohen and J. Copans (London: Sage, 1978), 31–55.

Hughes, S., and N. Haworth, 'Decent Work and Poverty Reduction Strategies', *Relations industrielles/Industrial Relations*, 66.1 (2011), 34–53.

Hugon P., 'Le développement des petites activités à Antananarivo. L'exemple d'un processus involutif', *Revue Canadienne des Etudes Africaines*, 16.2 (1982), 293–312.

Hull, E., 'International Migration, "Domestic Struggles" and Status Aspiration among Nurses in South Africa', *Journal of Southern African Studies*, 36.4 (2010), 851–67.

Human Rights Watch, 'Bottom of the Ladder. Exploitation and Abuse of Girl Domestic Workers in Guinea', *HRW Report*, 19, 8 2007, https://www.hrw.org/reports/2007/guinea0607/.

Human Rights Watch, 'Easy Prey: Child Soldiers in Liberia' (New York: Human Rights Watch, 1994).

Hunt, N. R., 'Domesticity and Colonialism in Belgian Africa: Usumbura's Foyer Social, 1946–1960', *Signs*, 15.3 (1990), 447–74.

Huxley, E., *No Easy Way: A History of the Kenya Farmers' Association and Unga Limited* (Nairobi: East African Standard, 1958).

Hymer, S. H., 'Economic Forms in Pre-Colonial Ghana', *Journal of Economic History*, 30.1 (1970), 33–50.

Hynd, S., '"To Be Taken as a Wife Is a Form of Death": The Social, Military, and Humanitarian Dynamics of Forced Marriage and Girl Soldiers in African Conflicts, c. 1990–2010', in *Marriage by Force? Contestation over Consent and Coercion in Africa*, ed. A. Bunting, B. N. Lawrance and R. L. Roberts (Athens, OH: University of Ohio Press, 2016), 290–310.

Hyslop, J., *The Notorious Syndicalist: J.T. Bain, a Scottish Rebel in Colonial South Africa* (Johannesburg: Jacana, 2004).

Ibhawoh, B., and J. I. Dibua, 'Deconstructing Ujamaa: The Legacy of Julius Nyerere in the Quest for Social and Economic Development', *African Journal of Political Science*, 8.1 (2003), 59–83.

Ifeka-Moller, C., 'White Power. Social-Structural Factors in Conversion to Christianity. Eastern Nigeria, 1921–1966', *Canadian Journal of African Studies*, 8.1 (1974), 55–72.

Igué, J., and B. G. Soulé, *L'État entrepôt au Bénin: commerce informel ou solution à la crise?* (Paris: Karthala, 1992).

Ihonvbere, J., 'Organized Labor and the Struggle for Democracy in Nigeria', *African Studies Review*, 40.1 (1997), 77–110.

Iliffe, J., *The African Poor: A History* (Cambridge: Cambridge University Press, 1987).

Iliffe, J., *Africans: The History of a Continent* (Cambridge: Cambridge University Press, 2007).

Iliffe, J., *The Emergence of African Capitalism* (Minneapolis, MN: University of Minnesota Press, 1983).

Iliffe, J., *East African Doctors: A History of the Modern Medical Profession* (Cambridge: Cambridge University Press, 1998).

Iliffe, J., *Honour in African History* (Cambridge: Cambridge University Press, 2005).

Iliffe, J., *A Modern History of Tanganyika* (Cambridge: Cambridge University Press, 1979).

Imorou, A. C., 'Trade Unionism among Teachers in Benin since 1945', in *Trade Unions in West Africa: Historical and Contemporary Perspectives*, ed. C. Phelan (Oxford: Peter Lang, 2011), 129–44.

Ingle, M., 'An Historical Overview of Problems Associated with the Formalization of the South African Minibus Taxi Industry', *New Contree: A Journal of Historical and Human Sciences for Southern Africa*, 57 (2009), 71–87.

International Labour Office, *African Labour Survey*, Geneva, 1958.

International Labour Office, *The Decent Work Agenda in Africa: 2007–2015, Eleventh African Regional Meeting, Report of the Director-General*, Addis Ababa, 2017.

International Labour Office, *Efficient Growth, Employment and Decent Work in Africa: Time for a New Vision*, Geneva, 2011.

International Labour Office, *Employment, Incomes and Equality: A Strategy for Increasing Productive Employment in Kenya*, Geneva, 1972.

International Labour Office, *The Informal Economy in Africa: Promoting Transition to Formality: Challenges and Strategies*, Geneva, 2009.

International Labour Office, 'An Overview of Domestic Work in Africa', Briefing Note No. 1, Geneva, 2013.

International Labour Office, 'Political Transformation, Structural Adjustment and Industrial Relations in Africa: English-speaking Countries', Proceedings of, and Documents Submitted to, a Symposium (Arusha, 1–4 February 1993), Labour Management Relations Series No. 78, Geneva, 1994.

International Labour Office, 'Resolution Concerning Decent Work and the Informal Economy', Report of the Committee on the Informal Economy, Geneva, 2002.

International Labour Office, 'Social Policy in Dependent Territories', Geneva, 1944.

International Labour Office, 'Unleashing Rural Development through Productive Employment and Decent Work: Building on 40 Years of ILO Work in Rural Areas', Committee on Employment and Social Policy, Governing Body, 310th Session (GB.310/ESP/1), Geneva, 2011.

International Labour Office, *World Employment 1995 – The ILO Report*, Geneva, 1995.

International Labour Office and World Health Organization, *The Social Protection Floor*, Geneva, 2009.

International Labour Office, 'Employment, Incomes and Equity: A Strategy for Increasing Productive Employment in Kenya', Geneva, 1972.

International Labour Office, *A Global Alliance against Forced Labour: Report of the Director-General*, International Labour Conference, 93rd Session, Geneva, 2005.

International Labour Office, *Global Estimate of Forced Labour: Results and Methodology*, Geneva, 2012.

International Labour Office, *Reflections on Reform Strategies for Social Protection in English-Speaking African Countries*, Geneva, 2000.

International Labour Office, *Regional Brief for Africa. 2017. Global Estimates of Modern Slavery and Child Labour*, Geneva, 2017.

International Labour Office, *Safety and Health in Opencast Mines. An ILO Code of Practice*, Geneva, 1991.

International Labour Office, *Strengthening Action to End Forced Labour*, Report IV (1), International Labour Conference, 103rd Session, Geneva, 2014.

International Labour Office, *World Report on Child Labour 2015: Paving the Way to Decent Work for Young People*, Geneva, 2015.

International Organization for Migration, *World Migration Report*, Geneva, 2013.

Isaacman, A., *Cotton is the Mother of Poverty: Peasants, Work, and Rural Struggle in Colonial Mozambique, 1938–1961* (London: James Currey, 1996).

Isaacman, A., and R. Roberts, eds, *Cotton, Colonialism, and Social History in Sub-Saharan Africa* (Portsmouth, NH/London: Heinemann/James Currey, 1995).

Jackson, L. A., '"When in the White Man's Town": Zimbabwean Women Remember *Chibeura*', in *Women in African Colonial Histories*, ed. J. Allman, S. Geiger and N. Musisi (Bloomington, IN: Indiana University Press, 2002), 191–218,

Jacobson, H. K., 'The USSR and ILO', *International Organization*, 14.3 (1960), 402–28.

Jalloh, A., and T. Falola, eds, *Black Business and Economic Power* (Rochester, NY: University of Rochester Press, 2002).

James, S., and M. Dalla Costa, *Power of Women and the Subversion of the Community* (Bristol: Falling Water Press, 1972).

Jarvie, G., and M. Sikes, 'Running as a Resource of Hope? Voices from Eldoret', *Review of African Political Economy*, 39.34 (2012), 629–44.

Jayne, T. S., J. Chamberlin and D. D. Headey, 'Land Pressures, the Evolution of Farming Systems, and Development Strategies in Africa: A Synthesis', *Food Policy*, 48 (2014), 1–17.

Jeeves, A. H., *Migrant Labour in South Africa's Mining Economy: The Struggle for the Gold Mines' Labour Supply, 1890–1920* (Montreal: McGill-Queen's University Press, 1985).

Jeffries, R., 'Populist Tendencies in the Ghanaian Trade Union Movement', in *The Development of an African Working Class: Studies in Class Formation and Action*, ed. R. Sandbrook and R. Cohen (London: Longman, 1975), 261–80.

Jensen, S., *Gangs, Politics and Dignity in Cape Town* (Oxford: James Currey, 2008).

Jerven, M., 'African Growth Recurring: An Economic History Perspective on African Growth Episodes, 1690–2010', *Economic History of Developing Regions*, 25.2 (2010), 127–54.

Jerven, M., 'The Emergence of African Capitalism', in *The Cambridge History of Capitalism*, vol. 1, ed. L. Neal and J. G. Williamson (Cambridge: Cambridge University Press, 2013), 431–54.

Johnson, L., 'Community Development through Women's Self-Help Groups, Mbarara Uganda', MSc thesis, Cambridge University, 2015.

Johnson-Odim, C., 'Women and Gender in the History of Sub-Saharan Africa', in *Women's History in Global Perspective*, ed. B. G. Smith, 3 vols (Urbana, IL: University of Illinois Press, 2005), 9–67.

Johnston, G. A., *The International Labour Organisation: Its Work for Social and Economic Progress* (London: Europa, 1970).

Johnstone, F., *Class, Race and Gold: A Study of Class Relations and Racial Discrimination in South Africa* (London: Routledge and Kegan Paul, 1976).

Johnstone, F., 'The IWA on the Rand: Socialist Organising Among Black Workers on the Rand 1917–1918', in *Labour, Townships and Protest*, ed. B. Bozzoli (Johannesburg: Ravan Press, 1979), 248–72.

Jones, J. A., 'The 1947–1948 Railway Strike in French West Africa', in *Trade Unions in West Africa: Historical and Contemporary Perspectives*, ed. C. Phelan (Oxford: Peter Lang, 2011), 45–68.

Jones, J. A., *Industrial Labor in the Colonial World: Workers of the Chemin de Fer Dakar-Niger 1881–1963* (Portsmouth, NH: Heinemann, 2002).

Jordan, J. D., 'Public Transport in Harare', *Zambezia: A Journal of Social Studies in Southern and Central Africa*, 11.2 (1983), 127–38.

Joseph, R. A., 'Settlers, Strikers and Sans-Travail. The Douala Riots of 1945', *The Journal of African History*, 15.4 (1974), 669–87.

Kaberry, P. M., *Women of the Grassfields: A Study of the Economic Position of Women in Bamenda, British Cameroons* (London: HMSO, 1952).

Kaberuka, W., *The Political Economy of Uganda, 1890–1979: A Case Study of Colonialism and Underdevelopment* (New York: Vantage Press, 1990).

Kabki, M., V. Mazzucato and E. Appiah, ' "*Wo benane a εyε bebree*": The Economic Impact of Remittances of Netherlands-based Ghanaian Migrants on Rural Ashanti', *Population, Space and Place*, 10.2 (2004), 85–97.

Kabreab, G., 'Forced Labour in Eritrea', *Journal of Modern African Studies*, 47.1 (2006), 41–72.

Kabuga, C., and P. K. Batarinyebwa, eds, *Cooperatives: Past, Present and Future* (Kampala: Uganda Cooperative Alliance, 1995).

Kahn-Fogel, N. A., 'The Troubling Shortage of African Lawyers: Examination of a Continental Crisis Using Zambia as a Case Study', *University of Pennsylvania Journal of International Law*, 33.3 (2012), 719–89.

Kaiser, P., 'Structural Adjustment and the Fragile Nation: The Demise of Social Unity in Tanzania', *Journal of Modern African Studies*, 34.2 (1996), 227–37.

Kajula, P. W., F. Kintu, J. Barugahare and S. Neema, 'Political Analysis of Rapid Change in Uganda's Health Financing Policy and Consequences on Service Delivery for Malaria Control', *The International Journal of Health Planning and Management*, 19.1 (2004), 133–53.

Kallaway P., 'Education, Health and Social Welfare in the Late Colonial Context: The International Missionary Council and Educational Transition in the Interwar Years with Specific Reference to Colonial Africa', *History of Education*, 38.2 (2009), 217–46.

Kanogo, T., *Squatters and the Roots of Mau Mau, 1905–63* (Nairobi/London: East African Publishers/James Currey, 1987).

Kapferer, B., *Strategy and Transaction in an African Factory: African Workers and Indian Management in a Zambian Town* (Manchester: Manchester University Press, 1972).

Kasente, D., 'Gender and Social Security Reform in Africa', *International Social Security Review*, 53.3 (2000), 27–41.

Kay, G. B., and S. Hymer, *The Political Economy of Colonialism in Ghana: A Collection of Documents and Statistics, 1900–1960* (London: Cambridge University Press, 1972).

Keegan, T., *Facing the Storm. Portraits of Black Lives in Rural South Africa* (London: Zed Books, 1988).

Keese, A., 'The Constraints of Late Colonial Reform Policy: Forced Labour Scandals in the Portuguese Congo (Angola) and the Limits of Reform under Authoritarian Colonial Rule, 1955–61', *Portuguese Studies*, 28.2 (2012), 186–200.

Keese, A., 'Searching for the Reluctant Hands: Obsession, Ambivalence and the Practice of Organising Involuntary Labour in Colonial Cuanza-Sul and Malange Districts, Angola, 1926–1945', *Journal of Imperial and Commonwealth History*, 41.2 (2013), 238–58.

Keese, A., 'Slow Abolition within the Colonial Mind: British and French Debates about "Vagrancy", "African Laziness", and Forced Labour in West Central and South Central Africa, 1945–1965', *International Review of Social History*, 59.3 (2014), 377–407.

Kendrick, R., 'Survey of Industrial Relations in Cameroon', in *Industrial Relations in Africa*, ed. U. Damachi, H. D. Seibel and L. Trachtman (London: Macmillan, 1979).

Kennedy, P. T., *Ghanaian Businessmen: From Artisan to Capitalist Entrepreneur in a Dependent Economy* (Munich: Weltforum, 1980).

Kenny, B., 'From Insurrectionary Worker to Contingent Citizen: Restructuring Labor Markets and Repositioning East Rand (South Africa) Retail Sector Workers', *City and Society*, 15.1 (2003), 31–57.

Kester, G., *Trade Unions and Workplace Democracy in Africa* (Aldershot: Ashgate, 2007).

Khayesi, M., 'Matatu Workers in Nairobi, Thika and Ruiru: Career Patterns and Conditions of Work', in *Negotiating Social Space: East African Microenterprises*, ed. P. O. Alila and P. O. Pedersen (Trenton, NJ: Africa World Press, 2001), 69–96.

Khosa, M. M., 'Accumulation and Labour Relations in the Taxi Industry', *Transformation: Critical Perspectives on Southern Africa*, 24 (1994), 55–71.

Kibicho, W., *Sex Tourism in Africa: Kenya's Booming Industry* (Farnham: Ashgate, 2009).

Kielland, A., and M. Tovo, *Children at Work: Child Labor Practices in Africa* (Boulder, CO: Lynne Reiner, 2006).

Kiggundu, M., and B. Oni, *An Analysis of the Market for Skilled African Development Management Professionals: Towards Strategies for Skills Retention and Utilization in Sub-Saharan Africa* (Harare: African Capacity Building Foundation, 2004).

Kilby, P., *Industrialization in an Open Economy: Nigeria, 1946–1966* (Cambridge: Cambridge University Press, 1969).

Kilby, P., 'Manufacturing in Colonial Africa', in *Colonialism in Africa 1870–1960*, ed. L. H. Gann and P. Duignan (London: Cambridge University Press), 470–522.

Kilby, P., ed., *Entrepreneurship and Economic Development* (Glencoe, IL: Free Press, 1971).

Kileff, C., 'Black Suburbanites: An African Elite in Salisbury, Rhodesia', in *Urban Man in Southern Africa*, ed. C. Kileff and C. Wade (Gwelo: Mambo Press, 1975), 81–97.

Killingray, D., *Fighting for Britain: African Soldiers in the Second World War* (Woodbridge: James Currey, 2010).

Killingray, D., 'Labour Exploitation for Military Campaigns in British Colonial Africa 1870–1945', *Journal of Contemporary History*, 24.3 (1989), 483–501.

Killingray, D., 'The Mutiny of the West African Regiment in the Gold Coast, 1901', *International Journal of African Historical Studies*, 16.3 (1983), 441–54.

Killingray, D., and D. M. Anderson, eds, *Policing and Decolonisation: Politics, Nationalism and the Police, 1917–1965* (Manchester: Manchester University Press, 1992).

Killingray, D., and D. Omissi, eds, *Guardians of Empire: The Armed Forces of The Colonial Powers c. 1700–1964* (Manchester: Manchester University Press, 1999).

King, K., *Jua Kali Kenya: Change and Development in an Informal Economy, 1970–95* (London: James Currey, 1996).

Kinnes, I., 'From Urban Street Gangs to Criminal Empires: The Changing Face of Gangs in the Western Cape', Monograph 48 (Pretoria: Institute for Security Studies, 2000).

Kinyanjui, M. N., *Women and the Informal Economy in Urban Africa: From the Margins to the Centre* (London: Zed Books, 2014).

Kirunda, M. K., *Environmental Challenges in Sub-Saharan Africa: Possible Solutions* (Boca Raton, FL: Dissertation.com, 2008).

Kitching, G., 'Politics, Method, and Evidence in the "Kenya Debate"', in *Contradictions of Accumulation in Africa: Studies in Economy and State*, ed. H. Bernstein and B. K. Campbell (Beverly Hills, CA: Sage, 1985), 115–52.

Kitching, G., *Class and Economic Change in Kenya: The Making of an African Petite Bourgeoisie, 1905–1970* (New Haven, CT: Yale University Press, 1980).

Klein, M. A., *Slavery and Colonial Rule in French West Africa* (New York: Cambridge University. Press, 1998).

Klein, M. A., ed., *Peasants in Africa. Historical and Contemporary Perspectives* (Beverly Hills, CA: Sage, 1980).

Kocka, J., *White Collar Workers in America 1890–1940: A Social-Political History in International Perspective* (London: Sage, 1980).

Kocka, J., 'Work as a Problem in European History', in *Work in a Modern Society: The German Historical Experience in Comparative Perspective*, ed. J. Kocka (Oxford: Berghahn Books, 2010), 1–16.

Konings, P., 'Assessing the Role of Autonomous Teachers' Trade Unions in Anglophone Cameroon, 1959–1972', *The Journal of African History*, 47.3 (2006), 415–36.

Konings, P., 'Organised Labour and Neo-Liberal Economic and Political Reforms in West and Central Africa', *Journal of Contemporary African Studies*, 21.3 (2003), 447–71.

Konings, P., 'Solving Transportation Problems in African Cities: Innovative Responses by the Youth in Douala', *Africa Today*, 53.1 (2006/07), 35–50.

Konings, P., *The State and Rural Class Formation in Ghana: A Comparative Analysis* (London: Routledge and Kegan Paul, 1986).

Koponen, J., *Development for Exploitation: German Colonial Policies in Mainland Tanzania, 1884–1914* (Hamburg: LIT, 1994).

Kott, S., and J. Droux, *Globalizing Social Rights: The International Labour Organization and Beyond* (Basingstoke and Geneva: Palgrave Macmillan and ILO, 2013).

Kpessa, M., and D. Béland, 'Transnational Actors and the Politics of Pension Reform in Sub-Saharan Africa', *Review of International Political Economy*, 19.2 (2011), 267–91.

Kpessa, M. W., 'The Politics of Retirement Income Security Policy in Ghana: Historical Trajectories and Transformative Capabilities', *African Journal of Political Science and International Relations*, 5.2 (2011), 92–102.

Kraus, J., ed., *Trade Unions and the Coming of Democracy in Africa* (Basingstoke: Palgrave Macmillan, 2007).

Kriger, C. E., *Cloth in West African History* (Lanham, MD: AltaMira Press, 2007).

Kriger, C. E., 'Textile Production and Gender in the Sokoto Caliphate', *The Journal of African History*, 34.3 (1993), 361–401.

Krikler, J., *The Rand Revolt: The 1922 Insurrection and Racial Killing in South Africa* (Johannesburg: Jonathan Ball, 2005).

Krikler, J., *White Rising: The 1922 Insurrection and Racial Killing in South Africa* (Manchester: Manchester University Press, 2005).

Kuba, R., and C. Lentz, eds, *Land and the Politics of Belonging in West Africa* (Leiden: Brill, 2006).

Kuper, L., *An African Bourgeoisie: Race, Class and Politics in South Africa* (New Haven, CT: Yale University Press, 1965).

Kyamulesire, A. R., *A History of the Uganda Cooperative Movement, 1913–1988* (Kampala: Uganda Cooperative Alliance, 1988).

Kynoch, G., *We Are Fighting the World: A History of the Marashea Gangs in South Africa, 1947–1999* (Athens, OH: University of Ohio Press, 2005).

Lal, P., 'African Socialism and the Limits of Global Familyhood: Tanzania and the New International Economic Order in Sub-Saharan Africa', *Humanity: An International Journal of Human Rights, Humanitarianism, and Development*, 6.1 (2015), 17–31.

Lal, P., 'Militants, Mothers, and the National Family: *Ujamaa*, Gender and Rural Development in Postcolonial Tanzania', *The Journal of African History*, 51.1 (2010), 1–20.

Lambert, M., 'From Citizenship to *Négritude*: Making a Difference in Elite Ideologies of Colonized Francophone West Africa', *Comparative Studies in Society and History*, 35.2 (1993), 239–62.

Lambert, R., 'Political Unionism and Working Class Hegemony: Perspectives on the South African Congress of Trade Unions, 1955–1965', *Labour, Capital and Society*, 18.2 (1985), 244–77.

Lamphear, J., *The Scattering Time: Turkana Responses to Colonial Rule* (Oxford: Clarendon Press, 1992).

Larmer, M., 'Enemies Within: Opposition to the Zambian One-Party State, 1972–1980', in *One Zambia, Many Histories: Towards a History of Post-colonial Zambia*, ed. J.-B. Gewald, M. Hinfelaar and G. Macola (Leiden: Brill, 2008), 98–126.

Larmer, M., *Mineworkers in Zambia: Labour and Political Change in Post-Colonial Africa* (London: I.B.Tauris, 2007).

Larmer, M., 'Permanent Precarity: Capital and Labour in the Central African Copperbelt', *Labour History*, 58.2 (2017), 170–84.

Larsson, A., M. Mapetla and A. Schlyter, eds, *Changing Gender Relations in Southern Africa: Issues of Urban Life* (Oxford: African Books Collective, 1998).

Lassiter, J. E., 'African Culture and Personality: Bad Social Science, Effective Social Activism, or a Call to Reinvent Ethnology?', *African Studies Quarterly*, 3.1 (2000), 1–21.

Law, R., S. Schwarz and S. Strickrodt, eds, *Commercial Agriculture, the Slave Trade and Slavery in Atlantic Africa* (Woodbridge: James Currey, 2013).

Lawler, N. E., *Soldiers of Misfortune: Ivoirien Tirailleurs of World War II* (Athens, OH: Ohio University Press 1992).

Lawrance, B. N., E. L. Osborn and R. L. Roberts, eds, *Intermediaries, Interpreters, and Clerks: African Employees in the Making of Colonial Africa* (Madison, WI: University of Wisconsin Press, 2006).

Laye, C., *African Child: Memoirs of a West African Childhood* (London: Fontana, 1959).

Lazreg, M., 'The Reproduction of Colonial Ideology: The Case of the Kabyle Berbers', *Arab Studies Quarterly*, 5.4 (1993), 380–95.

Le Saout, D., and M. Rollinde, eds, *Émeutes et mouvements sociaux au Maghreb: perspective comparée* (Paris: Karthala, 1999).

Lee, C. K., 'Raw Encounters: Chinese Managers, African Workers and the Politics of Casualization in Africa's Chinese Enclaves', *The China Quarterly*, 199 (2009), 647–66.

Lee, C. K., 'The Spectre of Global China', *New Left Review*, 89 (2014), 28–65.

Legassick, M., and F. de Clercq, 'Capitalism and Migrant Labour in Southern Africa: The Origins and Nature of the System', in *International Labour Migration: Historical Perspectives*, ed. S. Marks and P. Richardson (London: Temple Smith, 1984).

Lemarchand, R., *The Dynamics of Violence in Central Africa* (Philadelphia, PA: University of Pennsylvania Press, 2009).

Lennihan, L. D., 'Rights in Men and Rights in Land: Slavery, Wage Labor, and Smallholder Agriculture in Northern Nigeria', *Slavery and Abolition*, 3.2 (1982), 111–39.

Lentz, C., *Ethnicity and the Making of History in Northern Ghana* (Edinburgh: Edinburgh University Press, 2006).

Lentz, C., *Land, Mobility, and Belonging in West Africa* (Bloomington, IN: Indiana University Press, 2013).

Levine, S., 'In the Shadow of the Vine: Child Labour in Post–Apartheid South Africa', PhD dissertation, Temple University, 2000.

Levinson, J. I., 'A Missed Opportunity: World Bank's World Development Report 1995: Workers in an Integrating World', International Labor Rights Fund, 1995.

Lewis, J., *Industrial and Trade Union Organisation in South Africa 1924–55: The Rise and Fall of South Africa's Trade and Labour Council* (Cambridge: Cambridge University Press, 1984).

Lewis, J. D., 'Promoting Growth and Employment in South Africa', *South African Journal of Economics*, 70.4 (2002), 725–76.

Lewis, W. A., 'Economic Development with Unlimited Supplies of Labour', *The Manchester School of Economic and Social Studies*, 22.2 (1954), 139–91.

Lewis, W. A., *Labour in the West Indies: The Birth of a Workers' Movement* (London: New Beacon Books, 1977).

Leys, C., 'African Economic Development in Theory and Practice', *Daedalus*, 11.2 (1982), 99–124.

Leys, C., 'Capital Accumulation, Class Formation, and Dependency: The Significance of the Kenyan Case', *Socialist Register*, 15 (1977), 241–66.

Leys, C., 'Learning from the Kenya Debate', in *Political Development and the New Realism in Sub-Saharan Africa*, ed. D. E. Apter and C. G. Rosberg (Charlottesville, VA: University of Virginia Press, 1994), 220–43.

Leys, C., *The Rise and Fall of Development Theory* (London: James Currey, 1996).

Liauzu, C., 'The History of Labor and the Workers' Movement in North Africa', in *The Social History of Labor in the Middle East*, ed. E. J. Goldberg (Boulder, CO: Westview Press, 1996), 163–92.

Lichtenstein, A., 'Making Apartheid Work: African Trade Unions and the 1953 Native Labour (Settlement of Disputes) Act in South Africa', *The Journal of African History*, 46.2 (2005), 293–314.

Lie, J. H. S., *Developmentality: An Ethnography of the World Bank–Uganda Partnership* (Oxford: Berghahn Books, 2015).

Lieten, G. K., 'Child Labor Unions in Africa', in *The World of Child Labor: An Historical and Regional Survey*, ed. H. D. Hindman (Armonk, NY: M. E. Sharpe, 2009), 191–3.

Lieten, G. K., 'International Labor Organization (ILO) and the International Program for the Elimination of Child Labor (IPEC)', in *The World of Child Labor: An Historical and Regional Survey*, ed. H. D. Hindman (Armonk, NY: M. E. Sharpe, 2009), 139–42.

Limb, P., *The ANC's Early Years: Nation, Class and Place in South Africa Before 1940* (Pretoria: University of South Africa Press, 2010).

Lin, J. Y., 'From Flying Geese to Leading Dragons: New Opportunities and Strategies for Structural Transformation in Developing Countries', *Global Policy*, 3.4 (2012), 397–409.

Lindsay, L. A., 'Domesticity and Difference: Male Breadwinners, Working Women and Colonial Citizenship in the 1945 Nigerian General Strike', *American Historical Review*, 104.3 (1999), 783–812.

Lindsay, L. A., *Working with Gender: Wage Labor and Social Change in Southwestern Nigeria* (Portsmouth, NH: Heinemann, 2003).

Lindsay, L. A., and S. F. Miescher, eds, *Men and Masculinities in Modern Africa* (Portsmouth, NH: Heinemann, 2003).

Lipton, M., *Capitalism and Apartheid: South Africa, 1910–84* (London: Wildwood House, 1986).

Little, K., 'Some Traditionally Based Forms of Mutual Aid in West African Urbanization', *Ethnology*, 1.2 (1962), 197–211.

Little, P. D., *Somalia: Economy without State* (Oxford/Bloomington, IN: James Currey/Indiana University Press, 2005).

Little, P. D., and M. Watts, eds, *Living under Contract: Contract Farming and Agrarian Transformation in Sub-Saharan Africa* (Madison, WI: University of Wisconsin Press, 1994).

Livingston, G., S. Schonberger and S. Delaney, *Sub-Saharan Africa: The State of Smallholders in Agriculture* (Rome: International Fund for Agricultural Development, 2011).

Locatelli, F., '"Oziosi, Vagabondi e Pregiudicati": Labor, Law, and Crime in Colonial Asmara, 1890–1941', *International Journal of African Historical Studies*, 40.2 (2007), 225–50.

Lockman, Z., 'Reflections on Labor and Working-Class History in the Middle East and North Africa', in *Global Labour History: A State of the Art*, ed. J. Lucassen (Berne: Peter Lang, 2006), 117–46.

Londres, A., *Terre d'ébène (la traite des noirs)* (Paris: A. Michel, 1929).

Longhurst, R., 'Rural Development Planning and the Sexual Division of Labour: A Case Study of a Moslem Hausa Village in Northern Nigeria', in *Rural Development and Women in Africa* (Geneva: ILO, 1984), 117–22.

Lopes, C. M., '"Hug me, hold me tight!" The Evolution of Passenger Transport in Luanda and Huambo (Angola), 1975–2000', in *The Speed of Change: Motor Vehicles and People in Africa, 1890–2000*, ed. J.-B. Gewald, S. Luning and K. van Walraven (Leiden: Brill, 2009), 107–26.

Lourenço-Lindell, I., 'Introduction: The Changing Politics of Informality. Collective Organizing, Alliances and Scales of Engagement', in *Africa's Informal Workers: Collective Agency, Alliances and Transnational Organizing in Urban Africa*, ed. I. Lourenço-Lindell (London: Zed Books, 2010), 1–30.

Lourenço-Lindell, I., *Walking the Tight Rope: Informal Livelihoods and Social Networks in a West African City* (Stockholm: Almqvist and Wiksell International, 2002).

Lovejoy, P. E., 'Big Is Sometimes Best: The Sokoto Caliphate and Economic Advantages of Size in the Textile Industry', *African Economic History*, 34 (2006), 5–21.

Lovejoy, P. E., *Caravans of Kola: The Hausa Kola Trade, 1700–1900* (Zaria: Ahmadu Bello Press, 1980).

Lovejoy, P. E., *Jihād in West Africa During the Age of Revolutions* (Athens, OH: Ohio University Press, 2016).

Lovejoy, P. E., 'Plantations in the Economy of the Sokoto Caliphate', *The Journal of African History*, 19.3 (1978), 341–68.

Lovejoy, P. E., *Salt of the Desert Sun: A History of Salt Production and Trade in the Central Sudan* (Cambridge: Cambridge University Press, 1986).

Lovejoy, P. E., *Transformations in Slavery: A History of Slavery in Africa*, 3rd edn (Cambridge: Cambridge University Press, 2012).

Lovejoy, P. E., and T. Falola, eds, *Pawnship, Slavery, and Colonialism in Africa* (Trenton, NJ: Africa World Press, 2003).

Lovejoy, P. E., and J. S. Hogendorn, *Slow Death for Slavery: The Course of Abolition in Northern Nigeria, 1897–1936* (Cambridge: Cambridge University Press, 1993).

Lovejoy, P. E., and M. A. Klein, eds, *Slavery and Colonial Rule in Africa* (London: Frank Cass, 1999).

Lovejoy, P. E., and D. Richardson, 'British Abolition and its Impact on Slave Prices Along the Atlantic Coast of Africa, 1783–1850', *Journal of Economic History* 55.1 (1995), 98–119.

Lovejoy, P. E., and D. Richardson, 'Competing Markets for Male and Female Slaves: Prices in the Interior of West Africa, 1780–1850', *International Journal of African Historical Studies*, 28.2 (1995), 261–94.

Lubeck, P. M., *Islam and Urban Labor in Northern Nigeria: The Making of a Muslim Working Class* (Cambridge: Cambridge University Press, 1986).

Lubeck, P. M., 'Islamic Protest Under Semi-Industrial Capitalism: 'Yan Tatsine Explained', *International Journal of African Historical Studies*, 55.4 (1985), 369–89.

Lubeck, P. M., 'Unions, Workers and Consciousness in Kano, Nigeria: A View from Below', in *The Development of an African Working Class: Studies in Class Formation and Action*, ed. R. Sandbrook and R. Cohen (London: Longman, 1975), 139–60.

Lucassen, J., ed., *Global Labour History: A State of the Art* (Berne: Peter Lang, 2006).

Lüdtke, A., 'Soldiering and Working: Almost the Same? Reviewing Practices in Industry and the Military in Twentieth-Century Contexts', in *Work in a Modern Society: The German Historical Experience in Comparative Perspective*, ed. J. Kocka (Oxford: Berghahn Books, 2010), 109–30.

Lugalla, J. L. P., 'The Informal Urban Transport System in Tanzania: The "Dalla-Dalla" Buses of Dar-es-Salaam', *Internationales Afrika-Forum*, 26.4 (1990), 353–60.

Luiz, J. M., 'A Review of Social Welfare in Sub□Saharan Africa: From the Colonial Legacy to the Millennium Development Goals', *Economic Papers*, 31.1 (2013), 110–21.

Lukhero, M., 'The Social Characteristics of an Emergent Elite in Harare', in *The New Elites of Tropical Africa*, ed. C. Lloyd (London: Oxford University Press, 1966), 126–38.

Lumenga-Neso, K., 'La question du chemin de fer Matadi-Kinshasa au 19e siècle', *Zaïre-Afrique*, 18.126 (1978), 343–63.

Lunn, J., *Capital and Labour on the Rhodesian Railway System, 1888–1947* (Basingstoke: Palgrave Macmillan, 1997).

Lunn, J., *Memoirs of the Maelstrom: A Senegalese Oral History* (Portsmouth, NH: Heinemann, 1999).

Lunn, J., '"Les Races Guerrières": Racial Preconceptions in the French Military about West African Soldiers during the First World War', *Journal of Contemporary History*, 334.4 (1999), 517–36.

Lützelschwab, C., 'Settler Colonialism in Africa', in *Settler Economies in World History*, ed. C. Lloyd, J. Metzer and R. Sutch (Leiden: Brill, 2013), 141–67.

Lydon, G., *On Trans-Saharan Trails: Islamic Law, Trade Networks, and Cross-Cultural Exchange in Nineteenth-Century Western Africa* (New York: Cambridge University Press, 2009).

Lynch, P. D., and H. Fahmy, *Craftswomen in Kerdassa Egypt: Household Production and Reproduction* (Geneva: ILO, 1984).

M'Baye, B., 'Marcus Garvey and African Francophone Political Leaders of the Early Twentieth Century: Prince Kojo Touvalou Houénou Reconsidered', *Journal of Pan African Studies*, 1.5 (2006), 2–19.

M'Bemba-Ndoumba, G., *Transports urbains publics et privés au Congo: enjeux et pratiques sociales* (Paris: L'Harmattan, 2010)

MacGaffey, J., *Entrepreneurs and Parasites: The Struggle for Indigenous Capitalism in Zaire* (Cambridge: Cambridge University Press, 1987).

Machel, G., *The Impact of War on Children* (Cape Town: David Philips, 2001).

MacMaster, N., 'Labour Migration in French North Africa', in *The Cambridge Survey of World Migration*, ed. R. Cohen (Cambridge: Cambridge University Press, 1995), 190–5.

Macmillan, H., 'More Thoughts on the Historiography of Transition on the Zambian Copperbelt', *Journal of Southern African Studies*, 22.2 (1996), 309–12.

Maddox, G., *Sub-Saharan Africa: An Environmental History* (Santa Barbara, CA: ABC-CLIO, 2006).

Mager, A., 'The First Decade of "European Beer" in Apartheid South Africa: The State, the Brewers and the Drinking Public, 1962–1972', *The Journal of African History*, 40.3 (1999), 367–88.

Maghraoui, D., 'The *goumiers* in the Second World War: History and Colonial Representation', *Journal of North African Studies*, 19.4 (2014), 571–86.

Maher, V., 'Work, Consumption and Authority within the Household: A Moroccan Case', in *Of Marriage and the Market*, ed. K. Young, C. Wolkowitz and R. McCullagh (London: CSE Books, 1981), 69–87.

Makana, N., 'Metropolitan Concern, Colonial State Policy and the Embargo on Cultivation of Coffee by Africans in Colonial Kenya: The Example of Ofbungoma District, 1930–1960', *History in Africa*, 36 (2009), 315–29.

Mamdani, M., *Citizen and Subject: Contemporary Africa and the Legacy of Late Colonialism* (Princeton, NJ: Princeton University Press, 1996).

Mamdani, M., *When Victims Become Killers: Colonialism, Nativism, and the Genocide in Rwanda* (Princeton, NJ: Princeton University Press, 2001).

Manchuelle, F., *Willing Migrants: Soninke Labor Diasporas, 1848–1960* (Athens, OH: Ohio University Press, 1997).

Mandala, E., *Work and Control in a Peasant Economy: A History of the Lower Tchiri Valley in Malawi, 1859–1960* (Madison, WI: University of Wisconsin Press, 1990).

Mandambwe, J. E. A. (with Mario Kolk), *Can You Tell Me Why I Went to War? A Story of a Young King's African Rifle, Reverend Father John E. A. Mandambwe* (Zomba: Kachere Books, 2008).

Mann, G., *Native Sons: West African Veterans and France in the Twentieth Century* (Durham, NC: Duke University Press, 2006).

Mann, G., 'What was the Indigénat? The Empire of Law in French West Africa', *The Journal of African History*, 50.3 (2009), 331–53.

Mann, G., and J. I. Guyer, 'Imposing a Guide on the *Indigène*: The Fifty Year Experience of the *Sociétés de Prévoyance* in French West and Equatorial Africa', in *Credit, Currencies and Culture: African Financial Institutions in Historical Perspective*, ed. E. Stiansen and J. I. Guyer (Uppsala: Nordiska Afrikainstitutet, 1999), 124–51.

Mann, K., *Marrying Well: Marriage, Status and Social Change Among the Educated Elite in Colonial Lagos* (Cambridge: Cambridge University Press, 1985).

Mann, L., 'Africa's Turn to Industrialize?' *Review of African Political Economy* (ROAPE blog), https://goo.gl/RCn3Uj.

Manning, P., *Slavery and African Life: Occidental, Oriental, and African Slave Trades* (Cambridge: Cambridge University Press, 1990).

Manteaw, S. O., 'Legal Education in Africa: What Type of Lawyer Does Africa Need?', *McGeorge Law Review*, 39 (2008), 903–76.

Mantzaris, A. E., 'Another Victory for Trade Unionism: The 1918 Cape Town Musicians' Strike', in *Studies in the History of Cape Town*, ed. C. Saunders and H. Phillips, vol. 3 (Cape Town: University of Cape Town, 1980), 114–30.

Marchand, T. H. J., *The Masons of Djenné* (Bloomington, IN: Indiana University Press, 2009).

Mare, W. S., *African Trade Unions* (London: Longmans Green, 1949).

Marfaing, L., and M. Sow, *Les opérateurs économiques au Senegal: entre le formel et l'informel, 1930–1996* (Paris: Karthala, 1999).

Markakis, J., *Ethiopia: The Last Two Frontiers* (Woodbridge: James Currey, 2011).

Martin, N., *African Vitalogy: A Step Forward in African Thinking* (Nairobi: Pauline Publications Africa, 1999).

Martin, P. M., *Leisure and Society in Colonial Brazzaville* (Cambridge: Cambridge University Press, 1995).

Martinez-Mullen, C., 'The Influence of Global Sports Culture on South African Football', in *Contemporary Social Issues in Africa: Cases in Gaborone, Kampala and Durban*, ed. M. S. Mapadimeng and S. Khan (Pretoria: Africa Institute of South Africa, 2010), 15–27.

Martino, E., 'Panya: Economies of Deception and the Discontinuities of Indentured Labour Recruitment and the Slave Trade, Nigeria and Fernando Pó, 1890s–1940s', *African Economic History*, 44 (2016), 91–129.

Martin-Prével, A., and F. Mousseau, *New Name, Same Game: World Bank's Enabling the Business of Agriculture* (Oakland, CA: The Oakland Institute, 2014).

Marx, A. W., 'South African Black Trade Unions as an Emerging Working-class Movement', *The Journal of Modern African Studies*, 27.3 (1989), 383–400.

Marx, K., *Capital: A Critique of Political Economy* (1867) (Harmondsworth: Penguin, 1976).

Marx, K., *Grundrisse: Foundations of the Critique of Political Economy* (1857–61) (New York: Vintage Books, 1973).

Mason, M., 'Working on the Railway: Forced Labor in Northern Nigeria, 1907–1912', in *African Labor History*, ed. P. C. W. Gutkind, R. Cohen and J. Copans (Beverly Hills, CA: Sage, 1978), 56–79.

Matombo, L., and L. Sachikonye, 'The Labour Movement and Democratisation in Zimbabwe', in *Trade Unions and Party Politics: Labour Movements in Africa*, ed. B. Beckman, S. Buhlungu and L. Sachikonye (Cape Town: HSRC Press, 2010), 109–30.

Matthews, J. K., 'Reluctant Allies: Nigerian Responses to Military Recruitment 1914–1918', in *Africa and the First World War*, ed. M. E. Page (London: Palgrave Macmillan, 1987), 95–114.

Maul, D. R., *Human Rights, Development and Decolonization: The International Labour Organization, 1940–70* (Basingstoke and Geneva: Palgrave Macmillan and ILO, 2012).

Maul, D. R., 'The ILO, Asia and the Beginnings of Technical Assistance', in *The ILO from Geneva to the Pacific Rim: West Meets East*, ed. J. M. Jensen and N. Lichtenstein (Basingstoke and Geneva: Palgrave Macmillan and ILO, 2015), 110–33.

Maul, D. R., 'The International Labour Organization and the Struggle Against Forced Labour from 1919 to the Present', *Labour History*, 48.4 (2007), 477–500.

Maul, D. R., 'International Organizations and Globalization of Human Rights', in *Human Rights in the Twentieth Century: A Critical History*, ed. S.-L. Hoffmann (New York: Cambridge University Press, 2011), 301–20.

Mazrui, A. A., 'Africa's Triple Heritage of Play: Reflections on the Gender Gap', in *Sport in Africa: Essays in Social History*, ed. W. J. Baker and J. A. Mangan (New York: Africana, 1987), 217–28.

Mazrui, A. A., ed., *General History of Africa, VIII: Africa since 1935* (London: UNESCO/James Currey, 1993).

Mazzitelli, A., 'Transnational Organized Crime in West Africa: The Additional Challenge', *International Affairs*, 83.6 (2007), 1075–95.

Mazzucato, V., M. Kakbi and L. Smith, 'Transnational Migration and the Economy of Funerals: Changing Practices in Ghana', *Development and Change*, 37.6 (2006), 1047–72.

Mbilinyi, M., 'Agribusiness and Casual Labor in Tanzania', *African Economic History*, 15 (1986), 107–41.

Mbilinyi, M., 'Resistance in "Customary" Marriage: Tanzania's Runaway Wives', in *Forced Labour and Migration: Patterns of Movement within Africa*, ed. A. Zegeye and S. Ishemo (London: Hans Zell, 1989), 211–54.

Mbilinyi, M., 'Sweet and Sour: Women Working for Wages on Tanzania's Sugar Estates', in *How Africa Works: Occupational Change, Identity and Morality*, ed. D. F. Bryceson (Bourton: Practical Action Publishing, 2010), 165–84.

Mbiti, J. S., *African Religions and Philosophy* (Nairobi/London: East African Educational Publishers/Heinemann, 1969).

Mbũgua Wa Mũngai, *Nairobi's Matatu Men: Portrait of a Subculture* (Nairobi: Twaweza Communications, 2013).

McCann, J., *People of the Plow: An Agricultural History of Ethiopia, 1800–1990* (Madison, WI: University of Wisconsin Press, 1995).

McClintock, A., *Imperial Leather: Race, Gender and Sexuality in the Colonial Contest* (Abingdon: Routledge, 2013).

McCormick, D., 'African Entrepreneurial Clusters and Industrialization: Theory and Reality', *World Development*, 27.9 (1999), 1531–51.

McDougall, E. A., 'Salts of the Western Sahara: Myths, Mysteries and Historical Significance', *International Journal of African Historical Studies*, 23.2 (1990), 231–57.

McGregor, J., 'The Victoria Falls 1900–1940: Landscape, Tourism and the Geographical Imagination', *Journal of Southern African Studies*, 29.3 (2003), 717–37.

McIntyre, W. D., *British Decolonization, 1946–1997: When, Why and How Did the British Empire Fall?* (Basingstoke: Palgrave Macmillan, 1998).

McKittrick, M., 'Forsaking Their Fathers? Colonialism, Christianity and Coming of Age in Ovamboland, Northern Namibia', in *Men and Masculinities in Modern Africa*, ed. L. A. Lindsay and S. F. Miescher (Portsmouth, NH: Heinemann, 2003), 33–51.

McMichael, P., *Development and Social Change: A Global Perspective*, 5th edn (Los Angeles: Sage, 2011).

McNaughton, P. R., *The Mande Blacksmiths: Knowledge, Power, and Art in West Africa* (Bloomington, IN: Indiana University Press, 1993).

McPherson, A., and Y. Wehrli, eds, *Beyond Geopolitics: New Histories of Latin America at the League of Nations* (Albuquerque, NM: University of New Mexico Press, 2015).

Meagher, K., 'Crisis: Informalization and the Urban Informal Sector in Sub-Saharan Africa', *Development and Change*, 26.2 (1995), 259–84.

Meagher, K., *Identity Economics: Social Networks and the Informal Economy in Nigeria* (Woodbridge: James Currey, 2010).

Meagher, K., 'The Scramble for Africans: Demography, Globalization and Africa's Informal Labor Markets', *Journal of Development Studies*, 52 (2016), 483–97.

Meddeb, H., 'L'ambivalence de la «course à "el khobza"»: obéir et se révolter en Tunisie', *Politique Africaine*, 121.1 (2011), 35–51.

Meillassoux, C., *Femmes, greniers et capitaux* (Paris: Maspero, 1975).

Meillassoux. C., 'From Reproduction to Production: A Marxist Approach to Economic Anthropology', *Economy and Society*, 1.1 (1974), 93–105.

Meillassoux, C., *Maidens, Meal and Money: Capitalism and the Domestic Community* (Cambridge: Cambridge University Press, 1981).

Melber, H., 'Africa and the Middle Class(es)', *Africa Spectrum*, 48.3 (2013), 111–20.

Mercer, C., 'Middle-Class Construction: Domestic Architecture, Aesthetics and Anxieties in Tanzania', *Journal of Modern African Studies*, 52.2 (2014), 227–50.

Mercier, R., *Le travail obligatoire dans les colonies africaines* (Paris: Larose, 1933).

Meynaud, J., and A. Salah-Bey, *Trade Unionism in Africa: A Study of Its Growth and Orientation* (London: Methuen, 1967).

Michel, M., *Les Africains et la Grande Guerre: l'appel à l'Afrique (1914–1918)* (Paris: Karthala, 2014).

Miers, S., *Slavery in the Twentieth Century: The Evolution of a Global Problem* (Walnut Creek, CA: Altamira Press, 2003).

Miers, S., and M. A. Klein, eds, *Slavery and Colonial Rule in Africa* (London: Frank Cass, 1999).

Miers, S., and R. L. Roberts, eds, *The End of Slavery in Africa* (Madison, WI: University of Wisconsin Press, 1988).

Miescher, S., 'The Life Histories of Boakye Yiadom (Akasease Kofi of Abetifi, Kwawu): Exploring the Subjectivity and "Voices" of a Teacher-Catechist in Colonial Ghana', in *African Words, African Voices: Critical Practices in Oral History*, ed. L. White, S. Miescher and D. W. Cohen (Bloomington, IN: Indiana University Press, 2001), 162–93.

Mikell, G., 'Filiation, Economic Crisis, and the Status of Women in Rural Ghana', *Canadian Journal of African Studies*, 18.1 (1984), 195–218.

Miles, J., 'Rural Protest in the Gold Coast: The Cocoa Hold-ups, 1908–1938', in *The Imperial Impact: Studies in the Economic History of Africa and Asia*, ed. C. Dewey and A. G. Hopkins (London: Athlone Press, 1978), 152–70.

Millar, F., 'The Condemnation to Hard Labour in the Roman Empire, from the Julio-Claudians to Constantine', *Papers of the British School at Rome*, 52 (1984), 124–47.

Miracle, M., and B. Fetter, 'Backward-Sloping Labor-Supply Functions and African Economic Behavior', *Economic Development and Change*, 18.2 (1970), 240–51.

Mkandawire, T., 'Shifting Commitments and National Cohesion in African Countries', in *Common Security and Civil Society in Africa*, ed. L. Wohlgemuth, S. Gibson, S. Klasen and E. Rothshild (Uppsala: Nordiska Afrikainstitutet, 1999), 15–41.

Mkandawire, T., 'Social Policy and the Challenges of the Post-Adjustment Era', in *Getting Development Right: Structural Transformation, Inclusion, and Sustainability in the Post-Crisis Era*, ed. E. Paus (New York: Palgrave Macmillan, 2013), 61–82.

Mkandawire, T., 'The Terrible Toll of Post-Colonial "Rebel Movements" in Africa: Towards an Explanation of the Violence against the Peasantry', *Journal of Modern African Studies*, 40.2 (2002), 181–215.

Mlambo, A. S., and E. S. Pangeti, 'Introduction', in *Zimbabwe: A History of Manufacturing, 1890–1995*, ed. A. S. Mlambo, E. S. Pangeti and I. R. Phimister (Harare: University of Zimbabwe Publications, 2000), 1–8.

Moodie, T. D. (with V. Ndatshe), *Going for Gold: Men, Mines and Migration* (Berkeley, CA: University of California Press, 1994).

Moore, S. F., *Social Facts and Fabrications: 'Customary' Law on Kilimanjaro, 1880–1980* (Cambridge: Cambridge University Press, 1986).

Moradi, A., G. Austin and J. Baten, 'Heights and Development in a Cash-Crop Colony: Living Standards in Ghana, 1870–1980', African Economic History Network Working Paper Series, 7, 2013, https://bit.ly/2PtTGDu.

Morice, A., 'Ceux qui travaillent gratuitement: un salaire confisqué', in *Classes ouvrières d'Afrique noire*, ed. M. Agier, J. Copans and A. Morice (Paris: Karthala, 1987), 45–76.

Morice, A,. 'Les vélos de Kaolack', *Cahiers d'études africaines*, 81–83 (1981), 197–210.

Morris, M. L., 'Constructing a Social Safety Net in Africa: An Institutionalist Analysis of Colonial Rule and State Social Policies in Ghana and Côte d'Ivoire', *Studies in Comparative International Development*, 37.3 (2002), 64–90.

Morris, M. L. 'The Development of Capitalism in South African Agriculture: Class Struggle in the Countryside', *Economy and Society*, 5.3 (1976), 292–343.

Morrison, H., 'Child Labor in Egypt', in *The World of Child Labor: An Historical and Regional Survey*, ed. H. D. Hindman (Armonk, NY: M. E. Sharpe, 2009), 713–15.

Morrison, H., 'History of Child Labor in Algeria', in *The World of Child Labor: An Historical and Regional Survey*, ed. H. D. Hindman (Armonk, NY: M. E. Sharpe, 2009), 688–9.

Mosoetsa, S., *Eating from One Pot: The Dynamics of Survival in Poor South African Households* (Johannesburg: Wits University Press, 2011).

Mosse, D., 'Colonial and Contemporary Ideologies of "Community Management": The Case of Tank Irrigation Development in South India', *Modern Asian Studies*, 33.2 (1999), 303–38.

Moussaoui, F. N., 'Le Trabedo ou la mondialisation par la marge', *Politique Africaine*, 137.1 (2015), 117–28.

Mouton, P., *Social Security in Africa* (Geneva: ILO, 1975).

Moyd, M., 'Making the Household, Making the State: Colonial Military Communities and Labor in German East Africa', *International Labor and Working-Class History*, 80.1 (2011), 53–76.

Moyd, M., *Violent Intermediaries: African Soldiers, Conquest, and Everyday Colonialism in German East Africa* (Athens, OH: Ohio University Press, 2014).

Moyd, M., '"We Don't Want to Die for Nothing": Askari at War in German East Africa, 1914–1918', in *Race, Empire, and First World War Writing*, ed. S. Das (Cambridge: Cambridge University Press, 2011), 90–107.

Muenkner, H. H., and A. Shah, *Creating a Favourable Climate and Conditions for Cooperative Development in Africa* (Geneva: ILO, 1993).

Mukonoweshuro, E. G., *Colonialism, Class Formation, and Underdevelopment in Sierra Leone* (Lanham, MD: University Press of America, 1993).

Munachonga, M., 'Income Allocation and Marriage Options in Zambia', in *A Home Divided: Women and Income in the Third World*, ed. D. Dwyer and J. Bruce (Stanford, CA: Stanford University Press), 173–94.

Munck, R., 'Globalisation, Labour and Development: A View from the South', *Transformation: Critical Perspectives on Southern Africa*, 72.1 (2010), 205–24.

Murillo, B., '"The Modern Shopping Experience": Kingsway Department Store and Consumer Politics in Ghana', *Africa*, 82.3 (2012), 368–92.

Murove, M. F., ed., *African Ethics: An Anthology of Comparative and Applied Ethics* (Pietermaritzburg: University of KwaZulu-Natal Press, 2009).

Murphy, C. N., and E. Augelli, 'International Institutions, Decolonization, and Development', *International Political Science Review*, 14.1 (1993), 71–85.

Murray, B. K., 'Wits as an "Open" University 1939–1959: Black Admissions to the University of the Witwatersrand', *Journal of Southern African Studies*, 16.4 (1990), 649–76.

Murray, C., *Families Divided? The Impact of Migrant Labour in Lesotho* (Cambridge: Cambridge University Press, 1981).

Murray, C., 'South Africa's Troubled Royalty: Traditional Leaders after Democracy', Law and Policy Paper 23, Australian National University, 2004.

Murray, M., 'Factories in the Fields: Capitalist Farming in the Bethal District, 1910–1950', in *White Farms, Black Labor: The State and Agrarian Change in Southern Africa, 1910–50*, ed. A. Jeeves and J. S. Crush (Portsmouth, NH/ Pietermaritzburg/Oxford: Heinemann/University of Natal Press/James Currey, 1997), 75–92.

Muschalek, M., 'Violence as Usual: Everyday Police Work and the Colonial State in German Southwest Africa', in *Rethinking the Colonial State*, ed. S. Rud and S. Ivarsson (Bingley: Emerald Publishing, 2017), 129–50.

Museveni, Y., *Sowing the Mustard Seed: The Struggle for Freedom and Democracy in Uganda* (London: Macmillan Education, 1997).

Mushi, S. S., *Development and Democratisation in Tanzania* (Kampala: Fountain Publishers, 2001).

Mustapha, A. R., and G. Williams, 'Agrarian Change', in *Encyclopedia of Twentieth-Century African History*, ed. P. T. Zeleza (London: Routledge, 2003), 18–24.

Mususa, P., 'Mining, Welfare and Urbanisation: The Wavering Urban Character of Zambia's Copperbelt', *Journal of Contemporary African Studies*, 30.4 (2012), 571–87.

Mutibwa, P., *Uganda since Independence: A Story of Unfulfilled Hopes* (Kampala: Africa World Press, 2010).

Nakana, S. C., 'Chinese Capital and African Labour in Zambian Mining, 1997–2008', PhD dissertation, Graduate Institute of International and Development Studies, Geneva, 2013.

Nasson, B., *Springboks on the Somme: South Africa in the Great War 1914–1918* (Johannesburg and New York: Penguin, 2007).

Natchkova, N., and C. Schoeni, 'The ILO, Feminists and Expert Networks: The Challenges of Protective Policy (1919–1934)', in *Globalizing Social Rights: The International Labour Organization and Beyond*, ed. S. Kott and J. Droux (Basingstoke and Geneva: Palgrave Macmillan and ILO, 2013), 49–64.

Naylor, P. C., *North Africa: A History from Antiquity to the Present* (Austin, TX: University of Texas Press, 2009).

Ndiaye, A. I., 'Autonomy or Political Affiliation? Senegalese Trade Unions in the Face of Economic and Political Reforms', in *Trade Unions and Party Politics: Labour Movements in Africa*, ed. B. Beckman, S. Buhlungu and L. Sachikonye (Cape Town: HSRC Press, 2010), 23–38.

Ndjio, B., 'Evolués and Feymen. Old and New Figures of Modernity in Cameroon', in *Readings in Modernity in Africa*, ed. P. Geschiere, B. Meyer and P. Pels (Bloomington, IN: Indiana University Press, 2008), 205–14.

Ndour, B., 'Luttes laborieuses en "situation coloniale": cheminots du Dakar-Niger, 1919–1951', *Historiens et Géographes du Sénégal*, 6 (1991), 43–53.

Ndulo, M., 'Legal Education in Africa in the Era of Globalization and Structural Adjustment', *Penn State International Law Review*, 20.3 (2002), 487–503.

Neal, L., and J. Williamson, eds, *The Cambridge History of Capitalism, Volume I, The Rise of Capitalism: From Ancient Origins to 1848* (Cambridge: Cambridge University Press, 2013).

Neitzel, S., and H. Welzer, *Soldaten – On Fighting, Killing, and Dying: The Secret Second World War Tapes of German POWs* (London: Simon and Schuster, 2012).

Neocosmos, M., *The Agrarian Question in Southern Africa and 'Accumulation from Below': Economics and Politics in the Struggle for Democracy* (Uppsala: Nordiska Africainstitutet, 1993).

Neveling, P., 'Export Processing Zones, Special Economic Zones and the Long March of Capitalist Development Policies during the Cold War', in *Decolonization and the Cold War: Negotiating Independence*, ed. L. James and E. Leake (London: Bloomsbury, 2015), 63–84.

Neveling, P., 'Manifestationen der Globalisierung. Kapital, Staat und Arbeit in Mauritius, 1825–2005', PhD dissertation, Martin Luther University, Halle/Saale, 2012.

Nevinson, H. W., *A New Slavery* (London: Harper, 1906).

Newitt, M. D. D., *A History of Mozambique* (Bloomington, IN: Indiana University Press, 1995).

Ngalamulume, K. J., 'Leisure in Colonial Saint-Louis (Senegal), 1850–1920', in *Leisure in Urban Africa*, ed. P. T. Zeleza and C. R. Veney (Trenton, NJ: Africa World Press, 2003), 71–84.

Ngugi Wa Thiong'o, *Dreams in a Time of War: A Childhood Memoir* (London, Pantheon, 2010).

Niane, D. T., *Sundiata: An Epic of Old Mali*, rev. edn (Harlow: Pearson Longman, 2007).

Nicaise, J., 'Belgian Congo and Ruanda-Urundi 1955–1956', *Civilisations*, 6.4 (1956), 663–9.

Nicol, B., 'Industrial Relations in Uganda', in *Industrial Relations in Africa*, ed. U. G. Damachi, H. D. Seibel and L. Trachtman (New York: St Martin's Press, 1979), 273–306.

Nieboer, H. J., *Slavery as an Industrial System* (The Hague: Martinus Nijhoff, 1900).

Niger-Thomas, M., 'Excerpts from "Buying Futures". The Upsurge of Female Entrepreneurship: Crossing the Formal/Informal Divide in Southwest Cameroon', in *Readings in Modernity in Africa*, ed. P. Geschiere, B. Meyer and P. Pels (Bloomington, IN: Indiana University Press, 2008), 42–8.

Ninsin, K., *The Informal Sector in Ghana's Political Economy* (Accra: Freedom Publications, 1991).

Njung, G. N., 'West Africa', in *1914–1918 Online: International Encyclopedia of the First World War*, ed. U. Daniel, P. Gatrell, O. Janz, H. Jones, J. D. Keene, A. Kramer and B. Nasson (Freie Universität Berlin, 2014), DOI: 10.15463/ie1418.10462.

Nkrumah, K., *Ghana: The Autobiography of Kwame Nkrumah* (New York: International Publishers, 1957).

Norman, J., *Labor and Politics in Libya and Arab Africa* (New York: Bookman, 1965).

Norsky, K. K., *The Influence of the International Labour Organization on Principles of Social Policy in Non-Metropolitan Territories* (Oxford: Oxford University Press, 1951).

North-Coombes, M. D., *Studies in the Political Economy of Mauritius* (Mauritius: Mahatma Gandhi Institute, 2000).

Northrup, D., *Indentured Labor in the Age of Imperialism, 1834–1922* (New York: Cambridge University Press, 1995).

Northrup, D., 'Overseas Movements of Slaves and Indentured Workers', in *The Cambridge World History of Slavery, 4: AD 1804–AD 2016*, ed. D. Eltis, S. L. Engerman, S. Drescher and D. Richardson (Cambridge: Cambridge University Press, 2017), 20–48.

Northrup, D., *Trade Without Rulers: Pre-Colonial Economic Development in South-Eastern Nigeria* (Oxford: Clarendon Press, 1978).

Nugent, P., *Africa since Independence: A Comparative History* (Basingstoke: Palgrave Macmillan, 2004).

Nugent, P., and A. I. Asiwaju, *African Boundaries: Barriers, Conduits and Opportunities* (London: Pinter, 1996).

Nuttall, T. A., '"Do Not Accept Kaffir Standards": Trade Unions and Strikes among African Workers in Durban during the Second World War', *South African Historical Journal*, 29.1 (1993), 153–76.

Nwabughuogu, A. I., 'From Wealthy Entrepreneurs to Petty Traders: The Decline of African Middlemen in Eastern Nigeria, 1900–1950', *The Journal of African History*, 23.3 (1982), 365–79.

Nwauwa, A., *Imperialism, Academe, and Nationalism: Britain and University Education for Africans, 1986–1960* (London: Frank Cass, 1997).

Nyamnjoh, F. B., 'Madams and Maids in Southern Africa: Coping with Uncertainties and the Art of Mutual Zombification', *Afrika Spectrum*, 40.2 (2005), 181–96.

Nyanchoga, S. A., F. M. Muchoki, P. K. Wanyonyi and S. W. Mwangi, *Constitutionalism and Democratisation in Kenya, 1945–2007* (Nairobi: Catholic University of Eastern Africa Press, 2008).

Nyasani, J. M., *The African Psyche* (Nairobi: University of Nairobi and Theological Printing Press, 1997).

Nyberg-Sorensen, N., N. van Hear and P. Engberg-Pedersen, *The Migration–Development Nexus: Evidence and Policy Options* (Geneva: International Organization for Migration, 2002).

Nyerere, J. K., *Freedom and Development* (Dar es Salaam: Government Printer, 1973).

Nyerere, J. K., 'One-Party Government', in *African Intellectual Heritage: A Book of Sources*, ed. M. Kete Asante and A. A. Abarry (Philadelphia, PA: Temple University Press, 1996), 555–8.

Oakley, A., *Housewife* (London: Allen Lane, 1974).

Obbo, C., 'What Women Can Do: AIDS Crisis Management in Uganda', in *Women Wielding the Hoe: Lessons from Rural Africa for Feminist Theory and Development Practice*, ed. D. F. Bryceson (Oxford: Berg Publishers, 1995), 165–78.

Obeng-Fosu, P., *Industrial Relations in Ghana: The Law and Practice* (Accra: Ghana Universities Press, 2007).

Oberst, T., 'Transport Workers, Strikes and the "Imperial Response": Africa and the Post World War II Conjuncture', *African Studies Review*, 31.1 (1988), 117–34.

Ochieng', W. R., and R. M. Maxon, *An Economic History of Kenya* (Nairobi: East African Educational Publishers, 1992).

Ochieng', W. R., ed., *Themes in Kenyan History* (Nairobi: Heinemann Kenya, 1990).

Ochiltree, I. D., '"A Just and Self-Respecting System"? Black Independence, Sharecropping, and Paternalistic Relations in the American South and South Africa', *Agricultural History*, 72.2 (1998), 352–80.

Ochonu, M. E., *Colonial Meltdown: Northern Nigeria in the Great Depression* (Athens, OH: Ohio University Press, 2009).

Ocobock, P., 'Earning an Age: Migration and Maturity in Colonial Kenya, 1895–1952', *African Economic History*, 44 (2016), 44–72.

Odenyo, A., 'An Assessment of the African Brain Drain, with Special Reference to the Kenyan Mid-Career Professionals', *Issue: A Journal of Opinion*, 9.4 (1979), 45–8.

Odukoya, A. O., 'Child Labor in Nigeria: Historical Perspective', in *The World of Child Labor: An Historical and Regional Survey*, ed. H. D. Hindman (Armonk, NY: M. E. Sharpe, 2009), 231–5.

Ogot, B. A., and W. R. Ochieng', eds, *Decolonization and Independence in Kenya, 1940–93* (London/Nairobi: James Currey/East African Educational Press, 1995).

Ohadike, D. C., '"When the Slaves Left, the Owners Wept": Entrepreneurs and Emancipation among the Igbo People', in *Slavery and Colonial Rule in Africa*, ed. S. Miers and M. A. Klein (London: Frank Cass, 1999), 189–207.

Okali, C., *Cocoa and Kinship in Ghana: The Matrilineal Akan* (London: Kegan Paul, 1983).

Okia, O., *Communal Labor in Colonial Kenya: The Legitimization of Coercion, 1912–1930* (Basingstoke: Palgrave Macmillan, 2012).

O'Laughlin, B., 'Land, Labour and the Production of Affliction in Rural Southern Africa', *Journal of Agrarian Change*, 13.1 (2013), 175–96.

O'Laughlin, B., 'Missing Men? The Debate over Rural Poverty and Women-Headed Households in Southern Africa', *Journal of Peasant Studies*, 25.2 (1998), 1–48.

O'Laughlin, B., 'Proletarianisation, Agency and Changing Rural Livelihoods: Forced Labour and Resistance in Colonial Mozambique', *Journal of Southern African Studies*, 28.3 (2002), 511–30.

Olukoju, A., 'Accumulation and Conspicuous Consumption: The Poverty of Entrepreneurship in Western Nigeria, ca.1850–1930', in *Africa's Development in Historical Perspective*, ed. E. Akyeampong, R. H. Bates, N. Nunn and J. Robinson (New York: Cambridge University Press, 2014), 208–30.

Olukoju, A., 'The Travails of Migrant and Wage Labour in the Lagos Metropolitan Area in the Inter-War Years', *Labour History Review*, 61.1 (1996), 49–70.

Omojimite, B. U., 'Education and Economic Growth in Nigeria', *African Research Review*, 4.3a (2010), 90–108.

Ondicho, T. G., 'International Tourism in Kenya: Development, Problems and Challenges', *Eastern Africa Social Science Research Review*, 16.2 (2000), 49–69.

Orde Brown, G. St.-J., *The African Labourer* (1933) (2nd edn, London: Frank Cass, 1967).

Organisation for Economic Co-operation and Development, *Informal Employment and Promoting the Transition to a Salaried Economy*, OECD Employment Outlook, Paris, 2004.

Orr, C. A., 'Trade Unionism in Colonial Africa', *Journal of Modern African Studies*, 4.1 (1966), 65–81.

Orvis, S., 'The Kenyan Agrarian Debate: A Reappraisal', *African Studies Review*, 36.3 (1993), 23–48.

Osborn, E. L., 'Casting Aluminium Cooking Pots: Labour, Migration and Artisan Production in West Africa's Informal Sector, 1945–2005', *African Identities*, 7.3 (2009), 373–86.

Osborn, E. L., 'Work and Migration', in *The Oxford Handbook of Modern African History*, ed. J. Parker and R. Reid (Oxford: Oxford University Press, 2013), 188–207.

Ouma, S. O. A., 'The Role of Social Protection in the Socioeconomic Development of Uganda', *Journal of Social Development in Africa*, 10.2 (1995), 5–12.

Outhwaite, W., ed., *The Blackwell Dictionary of Modern Social Thought*, 2nd edn (Oxford: Blackwell, 2006).

Overton, J., 'The Origins of the Kikuyu Land Problem: Land Alienation and Land Use in Kiambu, Kenya, 1895–1920', *African Studies Review*, 31.2 (1988), 109–26.

Owen, R., *State, Power and Politics in the Making of the Modern Middle East*, 3rd edn (London: Routledge, 2004).

Oya, C., 'Contract Farming in Sub-Saharan Africa: A Survey of Approaches, Debates and Issues', *Journal of Agrarian Change*, 12.1 (2012), 1–33.

Oya, C., 'The Empirical Investigation of Rural Class Formation: Methodological Issues in a Study of Large- and Mid-Scale Farmers in Senegal', *Historical Materialism*, 12.4 (2004), 289–326.

Oya, C., 'The Land Rush and Classic Agrarian Questions of Capital and Labour: A Systematic Scoping Review of the Socioeconomic Impact of Land Grabs in Africa', *Third World Quarterly*, 34.9 (2013), 1532–57.

Oya, C., 'Rural Inequality, Wage Employment and Labour Market Formation in Africa: Historical and Micro-Level Evidence', ILO Working Paper 97, Geneva, 2010.

Oya, C., 'Stories of Rural Accumulation in Africa: Trajectories and Transitions among Rural Capitalists in Senegal', *Journal of Agrarian Change*, 7.4 (2007), 453–93.

Oyemakinde, W., 'The Nigerian General Strike of 1945', *Journal of the Historical Society of Nigeria*, 7.4 (1975), 693–710.

Oyugi, W. O., and A. Gitonga, eds, *Democratic Theory and Practice in Africa* (Nairobi: Heinemann, 1987).

Page, M. E., *The Chiwaya War: Malawians in the First World War* (Boulder, CO: Westview Press, 2000).

Pallaver, K., 'Labor Relations and Population Developments in Tanzania: Sources, Shifts, and Continuities from 1800 to 2000', *History in Africa*, 41 (2014), 307–35.

Palmer, R. H., and N. Parsons, eds, *The Roots of Rural Poverty in Central and Southern Africa* (Berkeley, CA: University of California Press, 1979).

Panford, K., *African Labour Relations and Workers' Rights: Assessing the Role of the International Labour Organization* (London: Greenwood Press, 1994).

Panzac, D., 'The Population of Egypt in the Nineteenth Century', *Asian and African Studies*, 21.1 (1987), 11–32.

Parpart, J. L., '"Wicked Women" and "Respectable Ladies": Reconfiguring Gender on the Zambian Copperbelt, 1936–1964', in *'Wicked' Women and the Reconfiguration of Gender in Africa*, ed. D. L. Hodgson and S. A. McCurdy (Portsmouth, NH: Heinemann, 2001), 274–92.

Parsons, T. H., *The 1964 Army Mutinies and the Making of Modern East Africa* (Westport, CT: Praeger, 2003).

Parsons, T. H., *The African Rank-and-File: Social Implications of Colonial Military Service in the King's African Rifles, 1902–1964* (Portsmouth, NH: Heinemann, 1999).

Parsons, T. H., '"Wakamba Warriors are Soldiers of the Queen": The Evolution of the Kamba as a Martial Race, 1890–1970', *Ethnohistory*, 46.4 (1999), 671–701.

Patel, L., E. Kaseke and J. Midgley, 'Indigenous Welfare and Community-Based Social Development: Lessons from African Innovations', *Journal of Community Practice*, 20.1/2 (2012), 12–31.

Patton, A., *Physicians, Colonial Racism, and Diaspora in West Africa* (Gainesville, FL: University Press of Florida, 1996).

Peace, A. J., *Choice, Class, and Conflict: A Study of Southern Nigerian Factory Workers* (Atlantic Highlands, NJ: Humanities Press, 1979).

Pearce, T. O., O. O. Kujore and V. A. Agboh-Bankole, 'Generating an Income in the Urban Environment: The Experience of Street Food Vendors in Ile-Ife, Nigeria', *Africa*, 58.4 (1988), 385–400.

Pedersen, S., *The Guardians: The League of Nations and the Crisis of Empire* (New York: Oxford University Press, 2015).

Peil, M., *The Ghanaian Factory Worker: Industrial Man in Africa* (London: Cambridge University Press, 1972).

Penvenne, J. M., *African Workers and Colonial Racism: Mozambican Strategies and Struggles in Lourenço Marques, 1877–1962* (Portsmouth, NH: Heinemann, 1995).

Perfect, D., 'Trade Unionism in The Gambia, 1929–2010', in *Trade Unions in West Africa: Historical and Contemporary Perspectives*, ed. C. Phelan (Oxford: Peter Lang, 2011), 99–128.

Perrings, C., *Black Mineworkers in Central Africa: Industrial Strategies and the Evolution of an African Proletariat in the Copperbelt 1911–41* (Portsmouth, NH: Heinemann, 1979).

Peters, P., *Dividing the Commons: Politics, Policy and Culture in Botswana* (Charlottesville, VA: University of Virginia Press, 1994).

Peters, P. E., 'The Limits of Negotiability: Security, Equity, and Class Formation in Africa's Land Systems', in *Negotiating Property in Africa*, ed. K. Juul and C. Lund (Portsmouth, NH: Heinemann, 2002), 45–66.

Peterson, K., *Speculative Markets: Drug Circuits and Derivative Life in Nigeria* (Durham, NC: Duke University Press, 2014).

Phelan, C., 'Trade Unions, Democratic Waves, and Structural Adjustment: The Case of Francophone West Africa', *Labor History*, 52.4 (2011), 461–81.

Phelan, C., 'West African Trade Unionism Past and Present', in *Trade Unions in West Africa: Historical and Contemporary Perspectives*, ed. C. Phelan (Oxford: Peter Lang, 2011), 1–22.

Phillips, A., *The Enigma of Colonialism: British Policy in West Africa* (London: James Currey, 1989).

Phimister, I., *An Economic and Social History of Zimbabwe 1890–1948: Capital Accumulation and Class Struggle* (London: Longman, 1988).

Phimister, I., 'From Preference towards Protection: Manufacturing in Southern Rhodesia, 1940–1965', in *Zimbabwe: A History of Manufacturing, 1890–1995*, ed. A. S. Mlambo, E. S. Pangeti and I. R. Phimister (Mount Pleasant, Harare: University of Zimbabwe Publications, 2000), 31–50.

Phimister, I., *Wangi Kolia: Coal, Capital and Labour in Colonial Zimbabwe 1894–1954* (Harare: Baobab Books, 1994).

Phimister, I., and R. Pilosoff, 'Wage Labor in Historical Perspective: A Study of the De-proletarianization of the African Working Class in Zimbabwe, 1960–2010', in *Wage Labour and Capital in Africa: A Historical Perspective*, ed. S. Bellucci, *Labor History*, special issue, 58.2 (2017), 215–27.

Pietilä, T., 'Drinking Mothers Feeding Children: Market Women and Gender Politics in Kilimanjaro, Tanzania', in *Alcohol in Africa: Mixing Business, Pleasure, and Politics*, ed. D. F. Bryceson (Portsmouth, NH: Heinemann), 197–212.

Pilossof, R., 'Labor Relations in Zimbabwe from 1900 to 2000: Sources, Interpretations, and Understandings', *History in Africa*, 41 (2014), 337–62.

Piven, F. F., and R. Cloward, *Regulating the Poor: The Functions of Public Welfare*, 2nd edn (New York: Vintage, 1993).

Plageman, N., *Highlife Saturday Night: Popular Music and Social Change in Urban Ghana* (Bloomington, IN: Indiana University Press, 2013).

Plata-Stenger, V., '"To Raise Awareness of Difficulties and to Assert Their Opinion": The International Labour Office and the Regionalization of International Cooperation in the 1930s', in *Beyond Geopolitics: New Histories of Latin America at the League of Nations*, ed. A. McPherson and Y. Wehrli (Albuquerque, NM: University of New Mexico Press, 2015), 97–114.

Poirer, R. A., 'Tourism and Development in Tunisia', *Annals of Tourism Research*, 22.1 (1995), 157–71.

Poli, R., 'Migrations and Trade of African Football Players: Historic, Geographical and Cultural Aspects', *Africa Spectrum*, 41.3 (2006), 393–414.

Portes, A., 'The Informal Sector: Definition, Controversy, and Relation to National Development', *Review*, 7.1 (1983), 151–74.

Posel, D., 'Have Migration Patterns in Post-Apartheid South Africa Changed?', *Journal of Interdisciplinary Economics*, 15.3–4 (2004), 277–92.

Posel, D., *The Making of Apartheid, 1948–1961: Conflict and Compromise* (Oxford: Clarendon Press, 1997).

Post, K., *Arise Ye Starvelings: The Jamaican Labour Rebellion of 1938 and its Aftermath* (The Hague: M. Nijhoff, 1978).

Posusney, M. P., *Labor and the State in Egypt: Workers, Unions and Economic Restructuring* (New York: Columbia University Press, 1997).

Pottier, J., 'Defunct Labour Reserve? Mambwe Villages in the Post-Migration Economy', *Africa*, 53.2 (1983), 2–23.

Potts, D., *Circular Migration in Zimbabwe and Contemporary Sub-Saharan Africa* (Woodbridge: James Currey, 2010).

Prashad, V., *The Darker Nations: A People's History of the Third World* (New York: The New Press, 2007).

Priestley, M., *West African Trade and Coast Society: A Family Study* (London: Oxford University Press, 1969).

Prunier, G., *Africa's World War: Congo, the Rwandan Genocide, and the Making of a Continental Catastrophe* (Oxford: Oxford University Press, 2009).

Quisumbing, A., J. Espadilla and K. Otsuka, *Land and Schooling: Transferring Wealth Across Generations* (Baltimore, MD: Johns Hopkins University Press, 2004).

Raftopoulos, B., and I. Phimister, *Keep on Knocking: A History of the Labour Movement in Zimbabwe 1900–1997* (Harare: Baobab, 1997).

Ranger, T. O., 'Growing from the Roots: Reflections on Peasant Research in Central and Southern Africa', *Journal of Southern African Studies*, 5.1 (1978), 101–7.

Ranger, T. O., *Peasant Consciousness and Guerilla War in Zimbabwe: A Comparative Study* (Berkeley, CA: University of California Press, 1985).

Ratha, D., 'Workers' Remittances: An Important and Stable Source of External Development Finance', in *Global Development Finance: Striving for Stability in Development Finance* (Washington, DC: World Bank, 2003), 157–75.

Rathbone, R., 'Businessmen in Politics: Party Struggle in Ghana, 1945–57', *Journal of Development Studies*, 9.3 (2003), 391–403.

Reardon, T., 'African Agriculture: Productivity and Sustainability Issues', in *International Agricultural Development*, ed. C. Eicher and J. Staatz, 3rd edn (Baltimore, MD: Johns Hopkins University Press, 1998), 444–57.

Reinalda, B., *Routledge History of International Organizations: From 1815 to the Present Day* (London: Routledge, 2009).

Remy, D., 'Economic Security and Industrial Unionism: A Nigerian Case Study', in *The Development of an African Working Class: Studies in Class Formation and Action*, ed. R. Sandbrook and R. Cohen (London: Longman, 1975), 161–77.

Reno, W., *Warlord Politics and African States* (Boulder, CO: Lynne Rienner, 1998).

Rey, P. P., and G. Arrighi, 'Articulation of Modes of Production', in *Marxist Theories of Imperialism: A Critical Survey*, ed. A. Brewer (London: Routledge and Kegan Paul, 1980), 183–206.

Reynolds, P., *Dance Civet Cat: Child Labour in the Zambezi Valley* (Athens, OH: Ohio University Press, 1991).

Rich, J., 'Civilized Attire: Refashioning Tastes and Social Status in the Gabon Estuary, c. 1870-1914', *Cultural and Social History*, 2 (2005), 189–213.

Rich, J., 'Troubles at the Office: Clerks, State Authority, and Social Conflict in Gabon, 1920–45', *Canadian Journal of African Studies*, 38.1 (2004), 58–87.

Rich, J., *A Workman is Worthy of His Meat: Food and Colonialism in the Gabon Estuary* (Lincoln, NE: University of Nebraska Press, 2007).

Richards, A., *Land, Labour and Diet in Northern Rhodesia* (Oxford: Oxford University Press/International African Institute, 1939).

Richards, A. I., F. Sturrock, and J. Fortt, eds, *Subsistence to Commercial Farming in Present-Day Buganda: An Economic and Anthropological Survey* (Cambridge: Cambridge University Press, 1973).

Richards, P., 'New Barbarism in Africa?', in *Fighting for the Rain Forest: War, Youth and Resources in Sierra Leone*, ed. P. Richards (Oxford: James Currey, 1996), xiii–xxxv.

Richards, P., ed., *No Peace, No War: An Anthropology of Contemporary Armed Conflicts* (Athens, OH: Ohio University Press, 2005).

Richards, Y., *Maida Springer: Pan-Africanist and International Labor Leader* (Pittsburgh, PA: University of Pittsburgh Press, 2000).

Richardson, P., 'The Recruiting of Chinese Indentured Labour for the South African Gold-Mines, 1903–1908', *The Journal of African History*, 18.1 (1977), 85–108.

Rimmer, D., *Staying Poor: Ghana's Political Economy 1950–1990* (Oxford: Pergamon Press for the World Bank, 1992).

Rispel, L., and H. Schneider, 'Professionalization of South African Nursing: Who Benefits?', *International Journal of Health Services*, 21.1 (1991), 109–26.

Rizzo, M., 'Informalisation and the End of Trade Unionism as We Knew It? Dissenting Remarks from a Tanzanian Case Study', *Review of African Political Economy*, 40.136 (2013), 290–308.

Rizzo, M., '"Life Is War": Informal Transport Workers and Neoliberalism in Tanzania 1998–2009', *Development and Change*, 42.5 (2011), 1179–206.

Rizzo, M., 'Rural Wage Employment in Rwanda and Ethiopia: A Review of the Current Policy Neglect and a Framework to Begin Addressing It', Working Paper No. 103 (Geneva: ILO, 2011).

Rizzo, M., 'What Was Left of the Groundnut Scheme? Development Disaster and Labour Market in Southern Tanganyika 1946–1952', *Journal of Agrarian Change*, 6.2 (2006), 205–38.

Robert, P., and L. Mucchielli, *Crime et sécurité: l'état des savoirs* (Paris: La Découverte, 2002).

Roberts, A., 'African Cross-Currents', in *The Cambridge History of Africa, 7: From 1905 to 1940*, ed. A. Roberts (Cambridge: Cambridge University Press, 1986), 223–65.

Roberts, J., 'Remembering Korle Bu Hospital: Biomedical Heritage and Colonial Nostalgia in the *Golden Jubilee Souvenir*', *History in Africa*, 38 (2014), 193–226.

Roberts, M. L., *Civilization without Sexes: Reconstructing Gender in Postwar France, 1917–1927* (Chicago: University of Chicago Press, 1994).

Roberts, R., 'Peculiarities of African Labour and Working-Class History', *Labour/ Le Travail*, 8.9 (1982), 317–33.

Robertson, A. F., ed., *The Dynamics of Productive Relationships: Sharecropping in Comparative Perspective* (Cambridge: Cambridge University Press, 1987).

Robertson, C. C., 'Invisible Workers: African Women and the Problem of the Self-Employed in Labour History', *Journal of Asian and African Studies*, 23.1–2 (1988), 180–200.

Robertson, C. C., *Sharing the Same Bowl? A Socioeconomic History of Women and Class in Accra, Ghana* (Bloomington, IN: Indiana University Press, 1984).

Robertson, C. C., *Trouble Showed the Way: Women, Men, and Trade in the Nairobi Area, 1890–1990* (Bloomington, IN: Indiana University Press, 1997).

Robertson, C., and M. Klein, eds, *Women and Slavery in Africa* (Madison, WI: University of Wisconsin Press, 1983).

Robinson, D., *Civil Service Pay in Africa* (Geneva: ILO, 1990).

Rockel, S., 'New Labor History in Sub-Saharan Africa: Colonial Enslavement and Forced Labor', *International Labor and Working Class History*, 86.2 (2014), 159–72.

Rockel, S., *Carriers of Culture: Labor on the Road in Nineteenth-Century East Africa* (Portsmouth, NH: Heinemann, 2006).

Rodet, M., 'Forced Labor, Resistance, and Masculinities in Kayes, French Sudan, 1919–1946', *International Labor and Working Class History*, 86 (2014), 107–23.

Rodgers, G., 'India, the ILO and the Quest for Social Justice', *Economic and Political Weekly*, 46.10 (2011), 45–52.

Rodney, W., *How Europe Underdeveloped Africa* (Nairobi: East African Educational Publishers, 1972).

Rodríguez-Piñero, L., *Indigenous Peoples, Postcolonialism, and International Law: The ILO Regime (1919–1989)* (Oxford: Oxford University Press, 2005).

Rodrik, D., and A. Subramanian, 'From "Hindu Growth" to Productivity Surge: The Mystery of the Indian Growth Transition', NBER Working Paper No. 10376, 2004.

Roemer, M., 'Economic Development in Africa: Performance since Independence, and a Strategy for the Future', *Daedalus*, 111.2 (1982), 125–48.

Rogers, B., *The Domestication of Women: Discrimination in Developing Societies* (London: Taylor and Francis, 1981).

Rogerson, C. M., 'Feeding the Common People of Johannesburg, 1930–1962', *Journal of Historical Geography*, 12.1 (1986), 56–73.

Rogerson, C. M., 'Globalization or Informalization? African Urban Economies in the 1990s', in *The Urban Challenge in Africa: Growth and Management of its Large Cities*, ed. C. Rakodi (Tokyo: United Nations University Press, 1997), 337–62.

Rogerson, C. M., and D. M. Hart, 'The Survival of the "Informal Sector": The Shebeens of Black Johannesburg', *GeoJournal*, 12.2 (1986), 153–66.

Roitman, J., *Fiscal Disobedience: An Anthropology of Economic Regulation in Central Africa* (Princeton, NJ: Princeton University Press, 2004).

Roitman, J., 'The Politics of Informal Markets in Sub-Saharan Africa', *Journal of Modern African Studies*, 28.4 (1990), 671–94.

Rosen, D. M., *Child Soldiers: A Reference Handbook* (Santa Barbara, CA: ABC-CLIO, 2012).

Ross, E. A., *Report on Employment of Native Labor in Portuguese Africa* (New York: Abbott Press, 1925).

Ross, R., 'The Origins of Capitalist Agriculture in the Cape Colony: A Survey', in *Putting a Plough to the Ground: Accumulation and Dispossession in Rural South Africa 1850–1930*, ed. W. Beinart, P. Delius and S. Trapido (Johannesburg: Ravan Press, 1986), 56–100.

Ross, R., A. K. Mager and B. Nasson, eds, *The Cambridge History of South Africa*, vol. 2 (New York: Cambridge University Press, 2011).

Rossi, B., *From Slavery to Aid: Politics, Labour, and Ecology in the Nigerian Sahel, 1800–2000* (Cambridge: Cambridge University Press, 2015).

Rossi, B., 'Migration and Emancipation in West Africa's Labour History: The Missing Links', *Slavery & Abolition*, 35.1 (2014), 23–46.

Rossi, B., 'What "Development" Work Does', in *Developmentalism, Labor, and the Slow Death of Slavery in Twentieth-Century Africa*, ed. B. Rossi and F. Barchiesi, *International Labor and Working-Class History*, special issue, 92 (2017), 7–23.

Rostow, W. W., *The Stages of Economic Growth: A Non-Communist Manifesto* (Cambridge: Cambridge University Press, 1990).

Routh, S., and V. Borghi, eds, *Workers and the Global Informal Economy: Interdisciplinary Perspectives* (New York: Routledge, 2016).

Ruf, F., and P. S. Siswoputranto, eds, *Cocoa Cycles: The Economics of Cocoa Supply* (Cambridge: Woodhead Publishing, 1995).

Rutherford, B., and L. Addison, 'Zimbabwean Farm Workers in Northern South Africa', *Review of African Political Economy*, 114 (2007), 619–35.

Ryder, G., 'The International Labour Organization: The Next 100 Years', *Journal of Industrial Relations*, 57.5 (2015), 748–57.

Sabea, H., 'Mastering the Landscape? Sisal Plantations, Land, and Labor in Tanga Region, 1893–1980s', *International Journal of African Historical Studies*, 41.3 (2008), 411–32.

Sabea, H., 'Reviving the Dead: Entangled Histories in the Privatisation of the Tanzanian Sisal Industry', *Africa: Journal of the International African Institute*, 71.2 (2001), 286–313.

Safa, H. I., *The Myth of the Male Breadwinner: Women and Industrialization in the Caribbean* (Boulder, CO: Westview Press, 1995).

Saibou, I., *Les Coupeurs de route: histoire du banditisme rural et transfrontalier dans le bassin du Lac Tchad* (Paris: Karthala, 2010).

Saith, A., 'Reflections: Louis Emmerij', *Development and Change*, 36.6 (2005), 1163–76.

Sako, S., 'Brain Drain and Africa's Development: A Reflection', *African Issues*, 30.1 (2002), 25–30.

Salau, M. B., *The West African Slave Plantation: A Case Study* (New York: Palgrave Macmillan, 2011).

Salole, G., 'Not Seeing the Wood for the Trees: Searching for Indigenous Non-Government Organisations in the Forest of Voluntary Self Help Associations', *Journal of Social Development in Africa*, 6.1 (1991), 5–17.

Salzman, P. C., ed., *When Nomads Settle: Processes of Sedentarization as Adaptation and Response* (New York: Praeger, 1980).

Sam, M., and P. Kilby, 'Nigeria 1961–1991: Closure, Survival and Growth of Small Enterprise', GEMINI Working Paper 54, Bethesda, MD, 1995.

Sandbrook, R., 'The Political Potential of African Urban Workers', *Canadian Journal of African Studies*, 11.3 (1977), 411–33.

Sandbrook, R., *Proletarians and African Capitalism: The Kenyan Case, 1960–1972* (Cambridge: Cambridge University Press, 1975).

Sandbrook, R., and R. Cohen, eds, *The Development of an African Working Class: Studies in Class Formation and Action* (London: Longman, 1975).

Santos, O., *Reply to the Accusation Addressed to the League of Nations by Mr. Edward A. Ross, Against the Portuguese in Angola* (Lisboa: Tipografia inglesa, 1930).

Scarnecchia, T., *The Urban Roots of Democracy and Political Violence* (Rochester, NY: University of Rochester Press, 2008).

Schatz, S. P., *Nigerian Capitalism* (Berkeley, CA: University of California Press, 1977).

Scheck, R., *Hitler's African Victims: The German Army Massacres of Black French Soldiers in 1940* (Cambridge: Cambridge University Press, 2006).

Scheffler, R., C. Mahoney, B. Fulton, M. Dal Poz and A. Preker, 'Estimates of Health Care Professional Shortages in Sub-Saharan Africa by 2015', *Health Affairs*, 28.5 (2009), 849–62.

Scheld, S., 'The "China Challenge": The Global Dimensions of Activism and the Informal Economy in Dakar', in *Africa's Informal Workers: Collective Agency, Alliances and Transnational Organizing in Urban Africa*, ed. I. Lourenço-Lindell (London: Zed Books, 2010), 153–68.

Schillinger, H. R., 'Trade Unions in Africa: Weak but Feared', Global Trade Union Program, International Development Cooperation, Occasional Paper, March 2005.

Schler, L., L. Bethlehem, and G. Sabar, 'Rethinking Labour in Africa, Past and Present', *African Identities*, special issue, 7.3 (2009).

Schmidt, J. D., 'Flexicurity, Casualization and Informalization of Global Labour Markets', in *Globalization and the Third World*, ed. B. N. Gosh and H. M. Guven (London: Palgrave Macmillan, 2006), 129–47.

Schneider, L., 'Freedom and Unfreedom in Rural Development: Julius Nyerere, *Ujamaa Vijijini*, and Villagization', *Canadian Journal of African Studies*, 38.2 (2004), 344–92.

Schneider, L., *Government of Development: Peasants and Politicians in Postcolonial Tanzania* (Bloomington, IN: Indiana University Press, 2014).

Schulze, R., 'Colonization and Resistance', in *Peasants and Politics in the Modern Middle East*, ed. F. Kazemi and J. Waterbury (Miami, FL: Florida International University Press, 1991), 171–202.

Scully, B., 'From the Shop-Floor to the Kitchen Table: The Shifting Centre of Precarious Workers' Politics in South Africa', *Review of African Political Economy*, 43.148 (2016), 295–311.

Scully, B., 'Lessons from the Political Strategies of Post-Independence African Trade Unions', in *COSATU in Crisis: The Fragmentation of an African Trade Union Federation*, ed. V. Satgar and R. Southall (Sandton: KMM Review, 2015), 35–53.

Seekings, J., 'British Colonial Policy, Local Politics and the Origins of the Mauritian Welfare State, 1936–50', *The Journal of African History*, 52.2 (2011), 157–77.

Seekings, J., 'The ILO and Welfare Reform in South Africa, Latin America and the Caribbean, 1919–1950', in *ILO Histories: Essays on the International Labour Organization and Its Impact on the World During the Twentieth Century*, ed. J. van Daele, M. Rodríguez García, G. van Goethem and M. van der Linden (Bern: Peter Lang, 2010), 145–72.

Seekings, J., 'Welfare Regimes and Redistribution in the South', in *Divide and Deal: The Politics of Distribution in Democracies*, ed. I. Shapiro, P. A. Swenson and D. Donno (New York: New York University Press, 2008), 19–42.

Seidman, G. W., 'From Trade Union to Working-Class Mobilization: The Politicization of South Africa's Non-Racial Labor Unions', in *Breaking the Links: Development Theory and Practice in Southern Africa*, ed. R. E. Mazur (Trenton, NJ: Africa World Press, 1990), 223–55.

Seidman, G. W., *Manufacturing Militance: Workers' Movements in Brazil and South Africa, 1970–1985* (Berkeley, CA: University of California Press, 1994).

Sender, J., and S. Smith, *The Development of Capitalism in Africa* (London: Methuen, 1986).

Sene, I., 'Colonisation française et main-d'oeuvre carcérale au Sénégal: de l'emploi des détenus des camps pénaux sur les chantiers des travaux routiers (1927–1940)', *French Colonial History*, 5 (2004), 153–71.

Senghor, L., *Liberté 1: négritude et humanisme* (Paris: Éditions du Seuil, 1964).

Sha, D. P., 'Street and Boardroom Politics: The Nigerian Labor Movement, the State and the Struggle for Democracy', in *Organising for Democracy: Nigerian and Comparative Experiences*, ed. B. Beckman and Y. Z. Ya'u (Stockholm and Kano: PODSU, ACKDRAT and CRD, 2012), 32–41.

Shaw, L., 'Cooperative Education in East and Southern Africa', (Draft) CoopAfrica Working Paper, Dar es Salaam: ILO, 2010.

Shaw, M., 'West African Criminal Networks in South and Southern Africa', *African Affairs*, 101.404 (2002), 291–316.

Shea, P. J., 'Economies of Scale and the Indigo Dyeing Industry of Precolonial Kano', *Kano Studies*, 1.2 (1975), 55–61.

Shenton, R. W., *The Development of Capitalism in Northern Nigeria* (London: James Currey, 1986).

Shepler, S., *Childhood Deployed: Remaking Child Soldiers in Sierra Leone* (New York: New York University Press, 2014).

Sheriff, A., *Slaves, Spices and Ivory in Zanzibar: The Integration of an East African Commercial Empire into the World Economy, 1770–1873* (London: James Currey, 1987).

Shitundu, J. M., *A Study on Labour Migration Data and Statistics in East Africa* (Geneva: ILO, 2006).

Shivji, I. G., *Law, State and the Working Class in Tanzania* (Dar es Salaam: Tanzania Publishing House, 1986).

Sidibé, O. O., 'Political Pluralism and the Trade Union Movement in Mali', in *Trade Unions in West Africa: Historical and Contemporary Perspectives*, ed. C. Phelan (Oxford: Peter Lang, 2011), 179–96.

Sidibé, O. O., and B. Venturi, 'Trade Unions and the Process of Democratisation', in *Trade Unions and Sustainable Democracy in Africa*, ed. G. Kester and O. O. Sidibé (Aldershot: Ashgate, 1997), 19–45.

Sikainga, A. A., *Slaves into Workers: Emancipation and Labor in Colonial Sudan* (Austin, TX: University of Texas Press, 1996).

Silga, G., 'Burkina Faso: The Land of Incorruptible Men', in *Trade Unions and Sustainable Democracy in Africa*, ed. G. Kester and O. O. Sidibé (Aldershot: Ashgate, 1997), 147–71.

Silver, B. J., *Forces of Labor: Workers' Movements and Globalization since 1870* (Cambridge: Cambridge University Press, 2003).

Silverstein, S., 'Sociocultural Organization and Locational Strategies of Transportation Entrepreneurs: An Ethnoeconomic History of the Nnewi Igbo of Nigeria', PhD dissertation, Boston University, 1983.

Siméant, J., *Contester au Mali: formes de la mobilisation et de la critique à Bamako* (Paris: Karthala, 2014).

Simelane, H. S., 'Landlords, the State, and Child Labor in Colonial Swaziland, 1914–1947', *International Journal of African Historical Studies*, 31.3 (1998), 571–93.

Simiyu, V. G., 'The Democratic Myth in African Traditional Societies', in *Democratic Theory and Practice in Africa*, ed. W. O. Oyugi and A. Gitonga (Nairobi: Heinemann, 1987), 49–70.

Simone, A., *For the City Yet to Come: Changing African Life in Four Cities* (Durham, NC: Duke University Press, 2004).

Sindiga, I., 'Employment and Training in Tourism in Kenya', *Journal of Tourism Studies*, 5.2 (1994), 45–52.

Singer, H. W., 'Demographic Factors in Subsaharan Economic Development', in *Economic Transition in Africa*, ed. M. J. Herskovits and M. Harwitz (London: Routledge and Kegan Paul, 1964), 241–61.

Singerman, D., *Avenues of Participation: Family, Politics, and Networks in Urban Quarters of Cairo* (Princeton, NJ: Princeton University Press, 1995).

Singh, M., *History of Kenya's Trade Union Movement to 1952* (Nairobi: East African Publishing House, 1969).

Smith, E. M., 'Popular Music in West Africa', *African Music*, 3.1 (1962), 11–17.

Smyth, R., 'The British Colonial Film Unit and Sub-Saharan Africa, 1939–1945', *Historical Journal of Film, Radio and Television*, 8.3 (1988), 285–98.

Soper, R. C., ed., *Socio-Cultural Profile of Turkana District* (Nairobi: Uzima Press 1985).

Southall, R., 'Cadbury on the Gold Coast, 1907–38: The Dilemma of a "Model Firm" in a Colonial Economy', PhD dissertation, University of Birmingham, 1975.

Soyinka, W., *Aké: The Years of Childhood* (London: Rex Collings, 1981).

Sparks, D. L., and S. T. Barnett, 'The Informal Sector in Sub-Saharan Africa: Out of the Shadows to Foster Sustainable Employment and Equity?', *International Business & Economics Research Journal*, 9.5 (2010), 1–11.

Spittler, G. H., *Die Welt der Kamelhirten und Ziegenhirtinnen von Timia* (Cologne: Köppe, 1998).

Spring, A., and B. McDade, eds, *African Entrepreneurship: Theory and Reality* (Gainesville, FL: University of Florida Press, 1998).

Sraïri, M. T., M. T. Benyoucef and K. Kraiem, 'The Dairy Chains in North Africa (Algeria, Morocco and Tunisia): From Self Sufficiency Options to Food Dependency?', *Springer Plus*, 2, 216 (2013), https://link.springer.com/article/10.1186/2193-1801-2-162.

Standing, G., 'The ILO: An Agency for Globalization?', *Development and Change*, 29.3 (2008), 355–84.

Standing, G., 'The International Labour Organization', *New Political Economy*, 15.2 (2010), 307–18.

Standing, G., *The Precariat: The New Dangerous Class* (London: Bloomsbury, 2011).

Standing, G., J. Sender and J. Weeks, *Restructuring the Labour Market: The South African Challenge. An ILO Country Review* (Geneva: ILO, 1996).

Stanziani, A., 'Labour Institutions in a Global Perspective, from the Seventeenth to the Twentieth Century', *International Review of Social History*, 54.3 (2009), 351–8.

Stanziani, A., *Bondage: Labor and Rights in Eurasia from the Sixteenth to the Early Twentieth Centuries* (New York: Berghahn Books, 2014).

Stanziani, A., *Sailors, Slaves, and Immigrants: Bondage in the Indian Ocean World, 1750–1914* (New York: Palgrave Macmillan, 2014).

Stapleton, T. J., *African Police and Soldiers in Colonial Zimbabwe, 1923–80* (Rochester, NY: University of Rochester Press, 2011).

Stapleton, T. J., *A Military History of Africa*, 3 vols (Westport, CT: Praeger Security International, 2013).

Stark, D., 'Recombinant Property in East European Capitalism', *American Journal of Sociology*, 101 (1996), 993–1027.

Stasavage, D., 'The Role of Democracy in Uganda's Move to Universal Primary Education', *The Journal of Modern African Studies*, 43.1 (2005), 53–73.

Steel, W. F., *Small-Scale Employment and Production in Developing Countries: Evidence from Ghana* (New York: Praeger, 1977).

Stein, H., *Beyond the World Bank Agenda: An Institutional Approach to Development* (Chicago: University of Chicago Press, 2008).

Steinberg, J., 'Policing, State Power and the Transition from Apartheid to Democracy: A New Perspective', *African Affairs*, 113.451 (2014), 173–91.

Steinberg, J., *Thin Blue: The Unwritten Rules of Policing South Africa* (Johannesburg: Jonathan Ball, 2008).

Steinfeld, R. J., *Coercion, Contract and Free Labor in the Nineteenth Century* (Cambridge: Cambridge University Press, 2001).

Steinfeld, R. J., *The Invention of Free Labour: The Employment Relation in English and American Law and Culture, 1350–1870* (Chapel Hill, NC: University of North Carolina Press, 1991).

Stengers, J., 'The Congo Free State and the Belgian Congo before 1914', in *Colonialism in Africa, 1870–1960, vol. 1*, ed. L. H. Gann and P. Duignan (Cambridge: Cambridge University Press, 1969), 261–92.

Stevens, S. P., *What Life Has Taught Me* (London: Kensal Press, 1984).

Stichter, S., *Migrant Labourers* (Cambridge: Cambridge University Press, 1985).

Stichter, S., 'Women and the Labor Force in Kenya, 1895–1964', *Rural Africana*, 29 (1975/76), 45–67.

Sundiata, I. K., *Black Scandal: America and the Liberian Labor Crisis, 1929–1936* (Philadelphia, PA: Institute for the Study of Human Issues, 1980).

Sundkler, B. G. M., *Bantu Prophets in South Africa* (1948), 2nd edn (Oxford: Oxford University Press, 1961).

Sunseri, T., *Vilimani: Labor Migration and Rural Change in Early Colonial Tanzania, 1884–1915* (Portsmouth, NH: Heinemann, 2002).

Surtees, R., *Child Trafficking in Sierra Leone* (New York: UNICEF, 2005).

Sutton, I., 'Labour and Commercial Agriculture in Ghana in the Late Nineteenth and Early Twentieth Centuries', *The Journal of African History*, 24.4 (1983), 461–83.

Swainson, N., *The Development of Corporate Capitalism in Kenya 1918–1977* (London: Heinemann, 1980).

Swan, M., *Gandhi: The South African Experience* (Johannesburg: Ravan Press, 1985).

Swindell, K., 'People on the Move in West Africa: From Pre-Colonial Polities to Post-Independence States', in *The Cambridge Survey of World Migration*, ed. R. Cohen (Cambridge: Cambridge University Press 1995), 196–202.

Swindell, K., 'The Struggle for Transport Labor in Northern Nigeria, 1900–1912: A Conflict of Interests', *African Economic History*, 20 (1992), 137–59.

Taithe, B., *The Killer Trail: A Colonial Scandal in the Heart of Africa* (Oxford: Oxford University Press, 2011).

Takane, T., *The Cocoa Farmers of Southern Ghana: Incentives, Institutions and Change in Rural West Africa* (Chiba: Institute of Developing Economies, Japan External Trade Organization, 2002).

Tangri, R., 'The Politics of Government–Business Relations in Ghana', *Journal of Modern African Studies*, 30.1 (1992), 97–111.

Taraud, C., *La prostitution coloniale: Algérie, Maroc, Tunisie (1830–1962)* (Paris: Éditions Payot & Rivages, 2003).

Teal, F., 'Why Can Mauritius Export Manufactures and Ghana Not?', *The World Economy*, 22.7 (1999), 981–93.

Tete-Ansá, W., *Africa at Work* (New York: self-published, 1930).

Themnér, A., ed., *Warlord Democrats in Africa: Ex-military Leaders and Electoral Politics* (London: Zed Books, 2017).

Thomas, K., *The Oxford Book of Work* (New York: Oxford University Press, 1999).

Thorsen, D., *Child Domestic Workers: Evidence from West and Central Africa* (Dakar: UNICEF, 2012).

Tignor, R. L., 'Political Corruption in Nigeria Before Independence', *Journal of Modern African Studies*, 31.2 (1993), 175–202.

Tijani, H. I., 'Building "Sound" Industrial Relations in Nigeria: The British and Organised Labour, 1940s to 1960', *Lagos Historical Review*, 11 (2011), 21–36.

Tijani, H. I., 'McCarthyism in Colonial Nigeria: The Ban on the Employment of Communists', in *The Foundations of Nigeria: Essays in Honor of Toyin Falola*, ed. A. Oyebade (Trenton, NJ: Africa World Press, 2003), 647–68.

Tijani, H. I., *Union Education in Nigeria: Labor, Empire, and Decolonization since 1945* (Basingstoke: Palgrave Macmillan, 2012).

Tinker, H., *A New System of Slavery: The Export of Indian Labour Overseas, 1830–1920* (London: Oxford University Press, 1974).

Titeca, K., 'Les Opec boys en Ouganda, trafiquants de pétrole et acteurs politiques', *Politique Africaine*, 103.3 (2006), 143–59.

Titeca, K., 'Tycoons and Contraband: Informal Cross-border Trade in West Nile, North-western Uganda', *Journal of Eastern African Studies*, 6.1 (2012), 47–63.

Titeca, K., and T. de Herdt, 'Regulation, Cross-border Trade and Practical Norms in West Nile, North-Western Uganda', *Africa*, 80.4 (2010), 573–94.

Todaro, M. P., 'A Model of Labor Migration and Urban Unemployment in Less Developed Countries', *American Economic Review*, 59.1 (1969), 138–48.

Toledano, E. R., 'Social and Economic Change in the "Long Nineteenth Century"', in *The Cambridge History of Egypt, Vol. 2: Modern Egypt, From 1517 to the End of the 20th Century*, ed. M. W. Daly (Cambridge: Cambridge University Press, 1998), 252–84.

Topalov, C., *Naissance du chômeur* (Paris: Belin, 1984).

Tosh, J., 'Imperial Masculinity and the Flight from Domesticity in Britain, 1880–1914', in *Gender and Colonialism*, ed. T. P. Foley, L. Pilkington, S. Ryder and E. Tilley (Galway: Galway University Press, 1995), 72– 85.

Tosh, J., 'Masculinities in an Industrializing Society: Britain, 1800–1914', *Journal of British Studies*, 44.2 (2005), 330–42.

Toth, J., 'Pride, Purdah, or Paychecks: What Maintains the Gender Division of Labor in Rural Egypt?', *International Journal of Middle East Studies*, 23.2 (1991), 213–36.

Toulabor, C., *Le Togo sous Eyadéma* (Paris: Karthala, 1986).

Trager, L., *Home Towns: Community, Identity and Development in Nigeria* (Boulder, CO: Lynne Rienner, 2001).

Trapido, S., 'Landlord and Tenant in a Colonial Economy: The Transvaal, 1880–1910', *Journal of Southern African Studies*, 5.1 (1978), 26–58.

Trapido, S., 'South Africa in a Comparative Study of Industrialization', *Journal of Development Studies*, 7.3 (1971), 309–20.

Tripp, A. M., *Changing the Rules: The Politics of Liberalization and the Urban Informal Economy in Tanzania* (Berkeley, CA: University of California Press, 1997).

Tripp, A. M., 'Defending the Right to Subsist: The State vs. the Urban Informal Economy in Tanzania', WIDER Working Paper 59, World Institute for Development Economics Research, United Nations University, 1989, 28–31.

Truen, S., and S. Chisadza, *The South Africa-SADC Remittance Channel* (Pretoria: DNA Economics, 2012).

Tsikata, D., *Living in the Shadow of the Large Dams: Long-Term Responses Upstream and Downstream of the Volta River Project* (Leiden: Brill, 2006).

Tucker, J., 'Women in the Middle East and North Africa: The Nineteenth and Twentieth Centuries', in *Women in the Middle East and North Africa: Restoring Women to History*, ed. G. Nashat and J. Tucker (Bloomington, IN: Indiana University Press, 1998), 73–131.

Turiano, A., 'Le Consul, le missionnaire et le migrant: contrôler et encadrer la main-d'œuvre italienne à Alexandrie à la fin du XIXème siècle', in *Étudier en liberté les mondes méditerranéens: mélanges offerts à Robert Ilbert*, ed. L. Dakhli and V. Lemire (Paris: Publications de la Sorbonne, 2016), 337–46.

Turrell, R., *Capital and Labour on the Kimberley Diamond Fields, 1871–1890* (Cambridge: Cambridge University Press, 1987).

Twum Baah, K. S., J. S. Nabila and A. F. Aryee, *Migration Research Study in Ghana* (Accra: Ghana Statistical Service, 1995).

Uche, C., 'British Government, British Businesses, and the Indigenization Exercise in Post-Independence Nigeria', *Business History Review*, 86.4 (2012), 745–71.

Uche, C., 'Indigenous Banks in Colonial Nigeria', *International Journal of African Historical Studies*, 43.3 (2010), 467–87.

Ukpabi, S. C., 'Military Recruitment and Social Mobility in Nineteenth Century British West Africa', *Journal of African Studies*, 2.1 (1975), 87–107.

United Nations Development Programme, 'If Africa Builds Nests, Will the Birds Come? Comparative Study of Special Economic Zones in Africa and China', Working Paper Series No. 6, 2015.

United Nations Development Programme, 'The Rise of the South: Human Progress in a Diverse World. Human Development Report 2013', New York, 2013.

United Nations Economic and Social Council, 'Africa Review Report on Transport', E/ECA/CFSSD/6/6, Addis Ababa, 29 September 2009.

United Nations Economic Commission for Africa, 'Africa Mining Vision', http://www.africaminingvision.org.

United Nations Economic Commission for Africa, 'Aide Memoire', Regional Conference on Brain Drain and Capacity Building in Africa, Addis Ababa, Ethiopia, 22–24 February 2000.

United Nations Economic Commission for Africa, 'Economic Report on Africa 2018', UNECA, Addis Ababa, 2018.

United Nations Economic Commission for Africa, 'Minerals and Africa's Development: International Study Group Report on Africa's Mineral Regimes', Economic Commission for Africa, Addis Ababa, 2011.

United Nations Educational, Scientific and Cultural Organization, 'World Water Development Report 4: Managing Water Under Uncertainty and Risk', volume 1, Paris, 2012.

United Nations High Commissioner for Human Rights, 'Report of the Mapping Project Documenting Serious Violations of International Human Rights Law and International Humanitarian Law Committed within the Territory of Central African Republic between January 2003 and December 2015', Geneva, May 2017.

United Nations, 'The Millennium Development Goals Report 2014', New York, 2014.

United Nations, Department of Economic and Social Affairs, Population Division, 'World Population Prospects: The 2012 Revision', volume 1, New York, 2013.

Unsicker, J., 'Tanzania's Literacy Campaign in Historical-Structural Perspective', in *National Literacy Campaigns: Historical and Comparative Perspectives*, ed. R. F. Arnove and H. J. Graff (New York: Springer Science & Business Media, 1987), 219–44.

Vail, L., and L. White, 'Forms of Resistance: Songs and Perceptions of Power in Colonial Mozambique', *American Historical Review*, 88.4 (1983), 883–919.

Valenzuela, J., 'Latin American Professionals in Africa: A New Direction to the Flow of Highly Skilled Personnel', *West African Journal of Sociology and Political Science*, 2.1–2 (1977), 1–21.

Van Beusekom, M., 'Disjunctures in Theory and Practice: Making Sense of Change in Agricultural Development at the Office du Niger, 1920–60', *The Journal of African History*, 41.1 (2000), 79–99.

Van Beusekom, M., *Negotiating Development: African Farmers and Colonial Experts at the Office du Niger, 1920–1960* (Portsmouth, NH: Heinemann, 2002).

Van Daele, J., 'The International Labour Organization in Past and Present Research', *International Review of Social History*, 53.3 (2008), 485–511.

Van Daele, J., M. Rodríguez García, G. van Goethem and M. van der Linden, eds, *ILO Histories: Essays on the International Labour Organization and Its Impact on the World During the Twentieth Century* (Bern: Peter Lang, 2010).

Van den Bersselaar, D., 'Imagining Home: Migration and the Igbo Village in Colonial Nigeria', *The Journal of African History*, 46.1 (2005), 51–73.

Van den Bersselaar, D., 'Old Timers Who Still Keep Going: Retirement in Ghana', *Österreichische Zeitschrift für Geschichtswissenschaften*, 22.3 (2011), 136–52.

Van den Bersselaar, D., 'Somebody Must Necessarily Go to Bring this Drink: Gin Smugglers, Chiefs and the State in Colonial Ghana', *Cultural and Social History*, 11.2 (2014), 243–61.

Van den Bersselaar, D., and S. Decker, '"No Longer at Ease": Corruption as an Institution in West Africa', *International Journal of Public Administration*, 34.11 (2011), 741–52.

Van der Berg, S., 'South African Social Security under Apartheid and Beyond', *Development Southern Africa*, 14.4 (1997), 481–503.

Van der Berg, S., 'The Transition from Apartheid: Social Spending Shifts Preceded Political Reform', *Economic History of Developing Regions*, 29.2 (2014), 234–44.

Van der Horst, S. T., *African Workers in Town: A Study of Labour in Cape Town* (Cape Town: Oxford University Press, 1964).

Van der Linden, M., 'The "Globalization" of Labor and Working-Class History and its Consequences', *International Labor and Working-Class History*, 65 (2004), 136–56.

Van der Linden, M., 'Labour History beyond Borders', in *Histories of Labour: National and International Perspectives*, ed. J. Allen, A. Campbell and J. McIlroy (Pontypool: Merlin Press, 2010), 353–83.

Van der Linden, M., *Workers of the World: Essays toward a Global Labour History* (Leiden: Brill, 2008).

Van der Waag, I., *A Military History of Modern South Africa* (Johannesburg: Jonathan Ball, 2015).

Van Kessel, I., and B. Oomen, '"One Chief, One Vote": The Revival of Traditional Authorities in Post-Apartheid South Africa', *African Affairs*, 96 (1997), 561–85.

Van Nieuwkerk, K., *'A Trade like Any Other': Female Singers and Dancers in Egypt* (Austin, TX: University of Texas Press, 1995).

Van Onselen, C., *Chibaro: African Mine Labour in Southern Rhodesia 1900–1933* (London: Pluto Press, 1976).

Van Onselen, C., *New Babylon, New Nineveh: Everyday Life on the Witwatersrand, 1886–1914* (Johannesburg: Jonathan Ball, 1982; 2nd edn, 2001).

Van Onselen, C., 'Race and Class in the South African Countryside: Cultural Osmosis and Social Relations in the Sharecropping Economy of the South-Western Transvaal, 1900–1950', *American Historical Review*, 95.1 (1990), 99–123.

Van Onselen, C., *The Seed is Mine: The Life of Kas Maine, a South African Sharecropper, 1894–1985* (Oxford: James Currey, 1997).

Van Onselen, C., 'The Social and Economic Underpinning of Paternalism and Violence on the Maize Farms of the South Western Transvaal, 1900–50', *Journal of Historical Sociology*, 5.2 (1992), 127–60.

Van Onselen, C., *Studies in the Social and Economic History of Witwatersrand, 1886–1914* (Johannesburg: Ravan Press, 1982).

Van Onselen, C., 'Worker Consciousness in Black Miners: Southern Rhodesia, 1900–1920', *The Journal of African History*, 14.2 (1973), 237–55.

Van Schendel, W. 'Stretching Labour Historiography: Pointers from South Asia', *International Review of Social History*, 51.14 (2006), 229–61

Van Walraven, K., 'Vehicle of Sedition: the Role of Transport Workers in Sawaba's Rebellion in Niger, 1954–1966', in *The Speed of Change: Motor Vehicles and People in Africa, 1890–2000*, ed. J.-B. Gewald, S. Luning and K. van Walraven (Leiden: Brill, 2009), 75–103.

Van Zwanenberg, R. M. A., *Colonial Capitalism and Labour in Kenya, 1919–1939* (Nairobi: East African Literature Bureau, 1975).

Vansina, J., 'Arts and Society since 1935', in *General History of Africa, VIII: Africa since 1935*, ed. A. A. Mazrui (London: UNESCO/James Currey, 1993), 582–632.

Vaughan, M., 'Exploitation and Neglect: Rural Producers and the State in Malawi and Zambia', in *History of Central Africa: The Contemporary Years since 1960*, ed. D. Birmingham and P. Martin (London: Longman, 1998), 167–202.

Vega Ruiz, M. L., and D. Martinez, 'Fundamental Principles and Rights at Work: Value, Viability, Incidence, and Importance as Elements for Economic Progress and Social Justice', Working Paper No. 9, International Labour Organization, Geneva, 2002.

Veltmeyer, H., 'The World Bank on "Agriculture for Development": A Failure of Imagination or the Power of Ideology?', *Journal of Peasant Studies*, 36.2 (2009), 393–410.

Vickery, K. P., 'The Rhodesia Railways African Strike of 1945, Part I: A Narrative Account', *Journal of Southern African Studies*, 24.3 (1998), 545–60.

Vickery, K. P., 'The Rhodesia Railways African Strike of 1945, Part II: Cause, Consequence, Significance', *Journal of Southern African Studies*, 25.1 (1999), 49–71.

Viti, F., 'Colonialismo e liberazione degli schiavi nel Baule (Costa d'Avorio)', *Africa: rivista trimestrale di studi e documentazione*, 61.1 (2006), 30–65.

Vos, J., '"Without the Slave Trade, No Recruitment": From Slave Trading to "Migrant Recruitment" in the Lower Congo, 1830–90', in *Trafficking in Slavery's Wake: Law and the Experience of Women and Children in Africa*, ed. N. Lawrance and R. L. Roberts (Athens, OH: Ohio University Press, 2012), 45–64.

Vos, J., 'Work in Times of Slavery, Colonialism, and Civil War: Labor Relations in Angola from 1800 to 2000', *History in Africa*, 41 (2014), 363–85.

Wa Githinji, M., and G. Mersha, 'Untying the Gordian Knot: The Question of Land Reform in Ethiopia', in *Land, Poverty and Livelihoods in an Era of Globalization. Perspectives from Developing and Transition Countries*, ed. A. H. Akram-Lodhi, S. M. Borras Jr and C. Kay (London: Routledge, 2007), 310–43.

Wahab, H., 'Universal Health Care Coverage: Assessing the Implementation of Ghana's NHIS Law', in *Intellectual Agent, Mediator and Interlocutor: A. B. Assensoh and African Politics in Transition*, ed. T. Falola and E. M. Mbah (Newcastle upon Tyne: Cambridge Scholars Publishing, 2014).

Walker, E., 'Peasant Production, Colonial: Cash Crops and Transport', in *Encyclopedia of African History*, ed. K. Shillington, vol. 3 (London: Fitzroy Dearborn, 2005), 1188–90.

Wallerstein, I., *The Modern World System*, 4 vols (New York: Academic Press, 1974).

Wallerstein, I., *The Politics of the World Economy: The States, the Movements, and the Civilizations* (Cambridge: Cambridge University Press, 1984).

Walton, J., and D. Seddon, *Free Markets and Food Riots: The Politics of Global Adjustment* (Oxford: Blackwell, 1994).

Wanyama, F. O., 'Surviving Liberalization: The Cooperative Movement in Kenya', CoopAFRICA Working Paper,10, International Labour Organization, Dar es Salaam, 2009.

Wariboko, N., *The Mind of African Strategists: A Study of Kalabari Management Practice* (Madison, WI: Fairleigh Dickenson University Press, 1997).

Warmington, W. A., *A West African Trade Union: A Case Study of the Cameroons Development Corporation Workers' Union and its Relations with the Employers* (Oxford: Oxford University Press, 1960).

Warren, B., *Imperialism: Pioneer of Capitalism* (London: New Left Books, 1980).

Waterman, P., 'Division and Unity among Nigerian Workers: Lagos Port Unionism, 1940s–1960s', Institute for Social Studies, The Hague, 1982.

Watson, R., '"What Is Our Intelligence, Our School Going and Our Reading of Books Without Getting Money?" Akinpelu Obisesan and His Diary', in *Africa's Hidden Histories: Everyday Literacy and Making the Self*, ed. K. Barber (Bloomington, IN: Indiana University Press, 2006), 52–77.

Webster, D., 'Development Advisors in a Time of Cold War and Decolonization: The United Nations Technical Assistance Administration, 1950–1959', *Journal of Global History*, 6.2 (2011), 249–72.

Webster, D., 'From Peasant to Proletarian: The Development/Underdevelopment Debate in South Africa', *Africa Perspective*, 13 (1980) 1–15.

Webster, E., and K. von Holdt, eds, *Beyond the Apartheid Workplace: Studies in Transition* (Pietermaritzburg: University of KwaZulu-Natal Press, 2005).

Weeks, K., *The Problem with Work: Feminism, Marxism, Antiwork Politics, and Postwork Imaginaries* (Durham, NC: Duke University Press, 2011).

Weiler, P., 'Forming Responsible Trade Unions: The Colonial Office, Colonial Labor and the Trades Union Congress', *Radical History Review*, 28–30 (1984), 367–92.

Weiss, B., 'Contentious Futures: Past and Present', in *Producing African Futures: Ritual and Reproduction in a Neoliberal Age*, ed. B. Weiss (Leiden: Brill, 2004), 1–20.

Weiss, F., *Doctrine et action syndicales en Algérie* (Paris: Éditions Cujas, 1970).

West, M., *The Rise of an African Middle Class: Colonial Zimbabwe 1898–1965* (Bloomington, IN: Indiana University Press, 2002).

Weyland, K., 'External Pressures and International Norms in Latin American Pension Reform', Kellogg Institute for International Studies, Working Paper No. 323, 2006.

Whidden, J., 'Colonialism, Overthrow of: North Africa', in *Encyclopaedia of African History*, 3 vols, ed. K. Shillington (London: Fitzroy Dearborn, 2005), vol. 1, 268–70.

White, B., 'Social Science Views on Working Children', in *The World of Child Labor: An Historical and Regional Survey*, ed. H. D. Hindman (Armonk, NY: M. E. Sharpe, 2009), 10–17.

White, B. W., 'Talk about School: Education and the Colonial Project in French and British Africa (1860–1960)', *Comparative Education*, 32.1 (1996), 9–25.

White, L., 'Cars Out of Place: Vampires, Technology, and Labor in East and Central Africa', in *Tensions of Empire: Colonial Cultures in a Bourgeois World*, ed. F. Cooper and A. L. Stoler (Berkeley, CA: University of California Press, 1997), 436–60.

White, L., *The Comforts of Home: Prostitution in Colonial Nairobi* (Chicago: University of Chicago Press, 1990).

White, L., 'Matrimony and Rebellion: Masculinity in Mau Mau', in *Men and Masculinities in Modern Africa*, ed. L. A. Lindsay and S. F. Miescher (Portsmouth, NH: Heinemann, 2003), 177–91.

Whitehead, A., '"I'm Hungry Mum": The Politics of Domestic Budgeting', in *Of Marriage and the Market*, ed. K. Young, C. Wolkowitz and R. McCullagh (London: CSE Books, 1981), 88–111.

Whitehead, A., 'Rural Women and Food Production in Sub-Saharan Africa', in *Political Economy of Hunger, Volume 1: Entitlement and Well-Being*, ed. J. Drèze and A. Sen (Oxford: Clarendon Press, 1991), 425–73.

Wickham, C., *The Muslim Brotherhood: Evolution of an Islamist Movement* (Princeton, NJ: Princeton University Press, 2013).

Wilks, I., 'Dissidence in Asante Politics: Two Tracts from the Late Nineteenth Century', in *African Themes: Northwestern University Studies in Honor of Gwendolen M. Carter*, ed. I. Abu-Lughod (Evanston, IL: Northwestern University Press, 1975), 47–63.

Wilks, I., *Forests of Gold: Essays on the Akan and the Kingdom of Asante* (Athens, OH: Ohio University Press, 1993), 169–88.

Williams, R. W., 'Trade Unions in Africa', *African Affairs*, 54.217 (1955), 267–79.

Willis, J., '"Men on the Spot": Labor, and the Colonial State in British East Africa: The Mombasa Water Supply, 1911–1917', *International Journal of African Historical Studies*, 28.1 (1995), 25–48.

Willis, J., *Potent Brews: A Social History of Alcohol in East Africa, 1850–1999* (Oxford: James Currey, 2002).

Wilson, F., *Labour in the South African Gold Mines 1911–1969* (Cambridge: Cambridge University Press, 1972).

Wilson, J. F., and A. Thomson, *The Making of Modern Management: British Management in Historical Perspective* (Oxford: Oxford University Press, 2006).

Wilson, M., *For Men and Elders: Change in the Relations of Generations and of Men and Women among the Nyakyusa-Ngonde People 1875–1971* (Boston, MA: Beacon Press, 1977).

Woden, Q., and K. Beegle, 'Labor Shortages Despite Underemployment? Seasonality in Time Use in Malawi', in *Gender, Time Use, and Poverty in Sub-Saharan Africa*, World Bank Working Paper No. 73 (Washington, DC: World Bank, 2006), 97–116.

Wolpe, H., 'Capitalism and Cheap Labour-Power in South Africa: From Segregation to Apartheid', *Economy and Society*, 1.4 (1972), 425–56.

Wood, G., 'Employment Relations in South Africa and Mozambique', in *Research Handbook of Comparative Employment Relations*, ed. M. Barry and A. Wilkinson (Cheltenham: Edward Elgar, 2011), 303–21.

Worger, W. H., *South Africa's City of Diamonds: Mine Workers and Monopoly Capitalism in Kimberley 1867–1895* (New Haven, CT: Yale University Press, 1987).

Worger, W. H., N. L. Clark and E. A. Alpers, *Africa and the West: A Documentary History, 2: From Colonialism to Independence, 1875 to the Present* (New York: Oxford University Press, 2010).

World Bank, 'Africa's Pulse: An Analysis of Issues Shaping Africa's Economic Future', 7, Washington, DC, April 2013.

World Bank, 'Can Africa Claim the 21st Century', Washington, DC, 2000.

World Bank, 'Doing Business 2011: Making a Difference for Entrepreneurs', International Bank for Reconstruction and Development, Washington, DC, 2010.

World Bank, 'Doing Business', Employing Workers Consultative Group, Final Report, Washington, DC, 25 April 2011.

World Bank, 'Doing Business: Changes to the Methodology, 2005–2017', http://www.doingbusiness.org/Methodology/Changes-to-the-Methodology.

World Bank, 'Tunisia: Water Sector Investment Loan', Report PID8415, Washington, DC, 2000.

World Bank, *World Development Report 1995: Workers in an Integrating World* (New York: Oxford University Press, 1995).

World Bank, 'World Development Report 2008: Agriculture for Development', The International Bank for Reconstruction and Development/World Bank, Washington, DC, 2007.

Wright, M., *Strategies of Slaves and Women: Life Stories from East/Central Africa* (London: James Currey, 1993).

Wyse, A. J. G., 'The 1919 strike and Anti-Syrian Riots: A Krio Plot?', *Journal of the Historical Society of Sierra Leone*, 3.1/2 (1979), 1–14.

Yeros, P., 'The Rise and Fall of Trade Unionism in Zimbabwe, Part I: 1990–1995', *Review of African Political Economy*, 40.136 (2013), 219–232.

Yeros, P., 'The Rise and Fall of Trade Unionism in Zimbabwe, Part II: 1995–2000', *Review of African Political Economy*, 40.137 (2013), 394–409.

Yoshikuni, T., *African Urban Experiences in Colonial Zimbabwe: A Social History of Harare before 1925* (Harare: Weaver Press, 2007).

Young, C., *The African Colonial State in Comparative Perspective* (New Haven, CT: Yale University Press, 1994).

Yousef, T. M., 'Development, Growth and Policy Reform in the Middle East and North Africa since 1950', *Journal of Economic Perspectives*, 18.3 (2004), 91–115.

Yudelman, D., *The Emergence of Modern South Africa: State, Capital and the Incorporation of Organized Labour on the South African Goldfields 1902–1939* (Cape Town: David Philip, 1983).

Zeleza, P. T., 'Plantation Agriculture', in *Encyclopedia of Twentieth-Century African History*, ed. P. T. Zeleza (London: Routledge, 2003), 434–7.

Zeleza, P. T., *A Modern Economic History of Africa, 1: The Nineteenth Century* (Dakar: CODESRIA, 1993).

Zerari, H., 'Femmes du Maroc entre hier et aujourd'hui: Quels changements?', *Recherches Internationales*, 77.3 (2006), 65–80.

Zimmerman, A., *Alabama in Africa: Booker T. Washington, the German Empire, and the Globalization of the New South* (Princeton, NJ: Princeton University Press, 2012).

Zimmerman, A., 'German Alabama in Africa: The Tuskegee Expedition to German Togo and the Transnational Origins of West African Cotton Growers', *American Historical Review*, 110.5 (2005), 1362–98.

Zimmerman, S., 'Mesdames Tirailleurs and Indirect Clients: West African Women and the French Colonial Army, 1908–1918', *International Journal of African Historical Studies*, 44.2 (2011), 299–322.

Zimmermann, B., *La constitution du chômage en Allemagne: entre profession et territoire* (Paris: Éditions de la MSH, 2000).

Zimmermann, B., C. Didry and P. Wagner, eds, *Le travail et la nation: histoire croisée de la France et de l'Allemagne* (Paris: Éditions de la MSH, 1999).

Zimmermann, S., '"Special Circumstances" in Geneva: The ILO and the World of Non-Metropolitan Labour in the Interwar Years', in *ILO Histories: Essays on the International Labour Organization*, ed. J. van Daele, M. Rodriguez García, G. van Goethem and M. van der Linden (Bern: Peter Lang Academic, 2010), 221–50.

Ziskind, D., 'Forced Labor in the Law of Nations', *Comparative Labor Law*, 3 (1979–80), 253–83.

Zürcher, E.-J., ed., *Fighting for a Living: A Comparative History of Military Labour 1500–2000* (Amsterdam: Amsterdam University Press, 2013).

INDEX

Page numbers in *italics* refer to figures and maps; page numbers in **bold** refer to tables.